CAMBRIDGE STUDIES IN CRIMINOLOGY, VOLUME XXVII

Editor: Sir Leon Radzinowicz

PRINCIPLES OF SENTENCING

D0162400

THE HEINEMANN LIBRARY OF CRIMINOLOGY
AND PENAL REFORM

CAMBRIDGE STUDIES IN CRIMINOLOGY

PRINCIPLES OF SENTENCING

*The Sentencing Policy of the
Court of Appeal Criminal Division*

Second Edition

by

D. A. Thomas

*Lecturer in Criminology,
University of Cambridge
Fellow of Trinity Hall*

HEINEMANN

LONDON

Heinemann Educational Books Ltd
22 Bedford Square, London WC1B 3HH

LONDON EDINBURGH MELBOURNE AUCKLAND
HONGKONG SINGAPORE KUALALUMPUR NEWDELHI
IBADAN LUSAKA NAIROBI JOHANNESBURG
EXETER(NH) KINGSTON PORTOFSPAIN

First edition first published 1970
Reprinted 1973
Second edition first published 1979

British Library C. I. P. Data

Thomas, David Arthur, Born 1938
Principles of Sentencing — 2nd Ed.
(Cambridge Studies in Criminology; Vol. 27)
1. Sentences (Criminal Procedure) — England
I. Title   II. Series
345′. 42′ 077   KD8406
Cased   ISBN 0 435 82881 9
Paperback   ISBN 0 435 82882 7

Publisher's note: This series is continuous with the Cambridge
Studies in Criminology, Volumes I to XIX, published by
Macmillan & Co., London

Printed and bound in Great Britain by
Richard Clay (The Chaucer Press) Ltd
Bungay, Suffolk

Contents

Foreword

by

Sir Leon Radzinowicz

Mr. Thomas hardly needs introduction as the author of a book on sentencing principles. He has made this his subject for many years and has left his mark in a series of articles and case summaries in the Criminal Law Review and other journals.

I had long hoped that he would find time to marshal all his resources and prepare a systematic study. This volume embodies the second edition of such an analysis.

It is important to recognize at the outset what the book is not. It does not pretend to draw much upon criminological research or to explore sentencing in the context of wider social and philosophical issues.

What it offers is a detailed analysis of the practices of the Court of Appeal, a clear guide to the principles and considerations which shape the thinking of its judges, but which have not hitherto been easily accessible either to lawyers or the public.

The book will provide an important point of departure for those involved in the discussion of sentencing matters at conferences for judges, recorders and magistrates. It will be of value to those, like probation officers, who help them in their difficult task. It will certainly have a wide appeal to legal practitioners. It will also find a place in the required reading for courses in criminal law and criminology, especially now that they are becoming increasingly concerned with the administration of criminal justice. And it will provide an essential foundation for criminologists seeking to interpret these processes from a broader sociological point of view. It fills a gap which must have been noticeable for many years.

I have been particularly pleased to be associated with this enterprise, and that for two reasons. I was consulted about the form of the book and should like to put on record my appreciation of a happy collaboration with an author as tolerant and liberal-minded as Mr. Thomas. Secondly, Mr. Thomas has long been associated with the Institute, first as a visiting lecturer and now as a lecturer and a senior member of its staff. I am delighted that the second edition of this book is now appearing in our Series.

Cambridge
September 1978

Preface

This edition follows the organisation of the first, although the whole of the text has been re-written with the exception of the very first and last sentences. A new chapter dealing with fines and financial orders has been added. The illustrative cases are taken from the period from January 1970 to December 1977; earlier cases are cited only where they appear to have a continuing significance or illustrate changes over a period of time. (The first edition may have some continuing use as a source of reference to earlier decisions, particularly in relation to offences such as bigamy which are now rarely encountered.) Reported cases are cited in the normal way; unreported cases are cited by the date of the judgment and the Court of Appeal register number.

Both editions of the book were made possible by an index of more than ten thousand judgments, compiled between 1962 and 1977. The necessary financial support was provided by a modest annual grant by the Home Office Research Unit; the termination of this grant in March 1977 raises questions over future editions.

The text of the second edition, like much of that of the first, was written in the United States. I am indebted to the Dean and Faculty of the School of Criminal Justice of the State University of New York at Albany, whose invitation to be the Robert A. Pinkerton Visiting Professor for the academic year 1976–77, together with the generous support of the Robert A. Pinkerton Foundation, provided a period sufficiently free from other distractions to allow me to complete the work in a reasonable span of time. I owe a deep debt of gratitude to Miss Isobel Gawler, who has devoted many hours of her free time, over a period of more than six years, to assisting with the maintenance of the index of decisions which is the basis of the book. The skill and patience with which she has performed this task greatly facilitated the selection of cases for inclusion in the text. The greater part of the manuscript was typed at S.U.N.Y., Albany, by Mrs Harriet Spector, who coped most efficiently with my handwriting and English spelling. Miss Margaret Guy of the Institute of Criminology kindly volunteered to type those chapters which I re-drafted, together with the tables and index, in addition to helping with proof reading. My wife, Margaret, and elder daughter, Karen, helped to keep an enormous mass of transcripts in order while I was working on the manuscript, and I was assisted in a variety of ways by my graduate assistant at Albany, Mitch Chamblin. Over a period of many years I have enjoyed the co-operation of Messrs. Cherer and Co., shorthand writers to the Court, and in particular the late Mr R. E. Stutchfield, who on many occasions tracked down an elusive judgment at my request; I have also known that I could rely on the Registrar of Criminal Appeals, Master D. R. Thompson, and his staff whenever the need for their assistance arose. The favourable reception of the first edition by the legal profession, and the generous comments of many members of the judiciary, have provided encouragement to persevere. I thank them all.

D. A. Thomas,
Institute of Criminology,
Cambridge.
October 1978

Table of Statutes

Table of Cases

TABLE OF CASES

PART I

1

The Framework of Sentencing Policy

The Criminal Division of the Court of Appeal[1] occupies a central position in the development and administration of penal policy in England and Wales. Modern sentencing legislation, with few exceptions, confers extensive discretion on the sentencing judge, both in the range of punitive sentences which may be imposed and in the choice of alternative dispositions. Criminal statutes generally authorize terms of imprisonment far longer than are normally imposed in practice, and Parliament, in creating an increasing variety of non-custodial sentences, has generally been content to establish relatively broad conditions of eligibility without requiring sentencers to use particular measures in any specified class of case. With the exception of a few general indications of legislative preferences in the choice of sentences,[2] statutes do not seek to influence the details of sentencing practice. The shaping of sentencing policy is entrusted substantially to the judiciary, and within the judicial hierarchy the authoritative determination of principle and policy is the responsibility of the Court of Appeal (Criminal Division), which has appellate jurisdiction (with minor exceptions) over all sentences passed in the Crown Court.[3]

From its earliest days, the predecessors of the Court of Appeal

[1] The Criminal Division of the Court Appeal was created as a result of the merger of the Court of Criminal Appeal with the Court of Appeal by the Criminal Appeal Act 1966. The legislation governing the powers and procedures of the Court, originally enacted in the Criminal Appeal Act 1907, was consolidated in the Criminal Appeal Act 1968. Throughout this book the term 'the Court' is used capitalized to refer to the Court of Appeal (Criminal Division) or, in relation to the small number of earlier cases which are cited, the Court of Criminal Appeal.

[2] For a review of legislative provisions designed to control the exercise of judicial discretion, see D. A. Thomas, *The Control of Discretion in the Administration of Criminal Justice*, in R. G. Hood (ed.), *Crime, Criminology and Public Policy*, (Heinemann Educational Books, London, 1975).

[3] The Crown Court, established by the Courts Act 1971 to replace the courts of assize and quarter session and certain other courts, has exclusive jurisdiction in the trial of indictments. For the division of criminal business between the Crown Court and magistrates' courts, see Criminal Law Act 1977 part III.

3

(Criminal Division) recognized that 'while . . . no invariable tariff can ever be fixed', the task of the Court was by 'the revision of sentences . . . to harmonize the views of those who pass them, and so ensure that varying punishments are not awarded for the same amount of guiltiness'.[1] In more recent years the Court has referred to 'the well-known duty of this Division to lay down principles and guidelines to assist sentencers of all grades in the application of the discretion which the imposition of sentence requires'.[2] In the performance of this duty the Court has, over a period of seventy years, evolved a sophisticated body of principle which it is the object of this book to describe. The precise jurisprudential nature of this body of principle is uncertain. The Court appears to have taken the view that a principle governing the exercise of a sentencing discretion cannot give rise to a question of law capable of being certified as a question of law of general public importance,[3] although the House of Lords has recognized the existence of a particular sentencing principle as a basis for the interpretation of a statute,[4] and a decision on a question which lay within the scope of judicial sentencing discretion has been reversed by statute.[5] The Court itself has treated its own previous decisions on matters of general sentencing principle as authoritative precedents,[6] and on at least three occasions in recent years has sat as a full court of five judges to overrule earlier decisions which, while articulating a discretionary principle, did not raise any question of law in the narrow sense.[7] The fact that by so doing the Court has treated previous decisions on questions of sentencing principle with the same respect as previous decisions on substantive or procedural law, which can also be overruled only by a full court of five judges, suggests that the Court takes the view that while its decisions on the proper exercise of sentencing discretion do not create law, they are intended to be binding on and followed by judges of the Crown Court and, where they are applicable, magistrates exercising summary jurisdiction.

The scope of the principles developed by the Court is to some extent limited by the procedure of criminal appeal. Only the offender may initiate an appeal against sentence, and is not likely to do so

---

1 *Woodman* (1909) 2 Cr. App. R. 67.

2 *Newsome* (1970) 54 Cr. App. R. 485 at 490.

3 *Ashdown* (1973) 58 Cr. App. R. 339.

4 See *D.P.P. v. Ottewell* (1968) 52 Cr. App. R. 679 at 684.

5 See Criminal Justice Act 1967 s. 58, reversing the effect of *Singh* (1965) 49 Cr. App. R. 184, and recognizing that the decision created a 'rule of practice'.

6 See, for instance, the treatment in the later cases of the proposition stated in *Gooding* (1955) 39 Cr. App. R. 187 (discussed at p. 266 below); and the analysis of earlier decisions in *Genese* (1976) 63 Cr. App. R. 152. Many similar examples could be given.

7 See *Amos* (1960) 45 Cr. App. R. 42; *Newsome* (1970) 54 Cr. App. R. 485; *Jackson* (1973) 58 Cr. App. R. 405.

unless he is dissatisfied with the sentence he has received and believes that there is some chance of a more favourable outcome.[1] Unlike other jurisdictions of the Commonwealth, particularly Canada and several Australian states, England does not allow the prosecution to appeal aganst a sentence on the ground that it fails to reflect the public interest,[2] and the provision for a declaratory appeal by the Crown introduced in 1972 does not extend to sentence.[3] Although, as many of the cases cited in the following chapters will demonstrate, the Court is by no means exclusively concerned with serious crime, its opportunities for refining the principles governing sentences for minor offences are limited, and it has less chance to deal with distinctions between non-custodial measures such as probation and discharge[4] than with the principles affecting the length of sentences of imprisonment. For the same reason the inference of principles from the Court's decisions must be approached with caution, as the decision to uphold a sentence of imprisonment does not necessarily mean that the sentence was correct, but merely that it was not excessive. For this reason wherever possible cases in which the Court has varied a sentence are treated as the best evidence of the Court's view of the proper approach to the class of case concerned; where several sentences of differing lengths are upheld in comparable cases, it seems logical to assume that the longest of the sentences is the closest approximation to the appropriate sentence, assuming all other factors are equal.

While in certain contexts the Court articulates a principle, or series of principles, in a systematic manner, it is frequently necessary to identify the operative principles from the examination of a considerable number of cases, none of which specifically identifies the relevant criteria, but which, when viewed collectively, clearly conform substantially to a pattern which can be described. This is particularly true of what is conventionally known as 'the tariff', the principles governing the lengths of sentences of imprisonment. In describing the substance of the tariff, an attempt has been made to cite a selection of cases which represent the normal pattern of decision; occasional decisions which appear to depart from the usual principles are also mentioned. In relation to the less common offences, the cases cited

---

[1] For an instance of unusual optimism, see *Wehner* (1977) 65 Cr. App. R. 1.
[2] For a discussion of the arguments in greater detail, see Thomas, *Increasing Sentences on Appeal—a Re-examination*, [1972] Crim. L. R. 288.
[3] Criminal Justice Act 1972 s. 36.
[4] These orders do not constitute 'sentences' for the purpose of appeal and may not be challenged unless they have been imposed on contravention of the relevant statutory provisions; an appeal on the merits against a probation order is impossible (see below, p. 391). Principles governing their use may be gathered from cases where the Court substitutes one or other of them on appeal against another form of sentence.

represent a greater proportion of those decided by the Court within the period with which the book is concerned.[1]

The text of this edition is based almost entirely on cases decided between 1 January 1970 and 31 December 1977. Earlier cases are cited only where they appear to have a continuing relevance, as in the case of decisions on the interpretation of relevant statutes, or where the decision illustrates a change in sentencing practice over a period of time. The book does not purport to offer an empirical account of the sentencing practices of the Crown Court, but rather to state the principles by which the sentencer[2] in the Crown Court should be guided. The evaluation of these principles in social, ideological or penological terms is left to the reader.

The Evolution of the Judicial Role in Sentencing

The legislative framework of the sentencing process began to assume its modern form in the middle years of the nineteenth century. The common law allowed the sentencing judge no discretion in cases of felony other than that of reprieving the capitally convicted offender with a recommendation to royal clemency on condition of being transported to one of the colonies, although judges were authorized by an increasing number of statutes enacted during the eighteenth century to impose sentences of transportation, usually for fixed periods. It was not until the major reforms enacted between 1827 and 1840 had substantially diminished the scope of capital punishment, and had substituted terms of transportation fixed by the sentencing judge in the exercise of a statutory discretion, that judges began to perform a sentencing function resembling in any way their modern role in the sentencing process. Transportation gave way in turn to penal servitude in the 1850s, and the Consolidation Acts of 1861 established a statutory foundation for sentencing which remained intact, through partial reconsolidations, until the beginning of the revision of the substantive criminal law in the late 1960s. The origins of current judicial attitudes to sentencing can be traced to the last forty years of the nineteenth century, a period during which the lack of a forum for the articulation of principles in the shape of an appellate tribunal did not prevent the discussion of sentencing issues in other ways. The first comprehensive treatise on sentencing from the judicial viewpoint was published in 1877,[3] and the periodical

[1] In particular, it is believed that every decision of the Court on incest, within the period with which the book is concerned, is cited.

[2] The term 'the sentencer' is used throughout the book to refer, without distinction, to all kinds of judges sitting in the Crown Court.

[3] E. W. Cox, *The Principles of Punishment as applied in the Administration of the Criminal Law by Judges and Magistrates* (London, *The Law Times*), 1877.

literature of the time reflects a considerable interest in all aspects of the subject. The judge of the late nineteenth century had in some respects a simpler task than his twentieth-century counterpart. The law provided few alternatives to custody (in the shape of imprisonment and penal servitude) and the judge's task was primarily to measure the punishment according to the gravity of the offence—or, as one author explained it, to mitigate the severity of the statutory penalty provided for the offence.[1] This period saw the growth, through processes of informal consultations, of a series of conventions regulating the relationship between particular crimes and sentences.[2] By 1885 James Fitzjames Stephen could speak, with detailed illustrations, of the 'customary scale of punishments' for the offences most commonly encountered in practice;[3] this customary scale was formally but privately stated in an agreed memorandum of the judges of the Queen's Bench Division in 1901.[4] Early decisions of the Court of Criminal Appeal suggest that the Court began its task with the assumption that there already existed a body of principle, which it was the Court's duty to articulate and expand.[5]

Almost simultaneously with the introduction of appellate review of sentence in 1907 there began a process of diversification of the objectives of sentencing. Legislation was enacted to confer on the courts power to deal with the offender as an individual, as opposed to following the punitive approach implicit in the nineteenth-century legislation. The Probation of Offenders Act 1907 empowered sentencers to make probation orders against offenders in all cases except those for which the sentence was fixed by law. The probation order, which could be made only if the offender consented to its requirements, was imposed in lieu of any sentence on the charge concerned, and no penalty was fixed in advance to take effect in the event of breach of the order. The following year the Prevention of Crime Act 1908 introduced two new custodial measures, borstal detention for young adult offenders (originally between 16 and 23) and preventive detention for habitual offenders. These new measures constituted the first substantial legislative recognition of the arrival of individualization of sentences and confronted the newly established Court of Criminal Appeal with wholly new problems of sentencing policy, which are frequently reflected in its early decisions. Subsequent

[1] Cox, *ibid.*, p. 18.
[2] For an account of the development of conventions in sentencing during this period. See D. A. Thomas, *Constraints on Judgment* Cambridge, Institute of Criminology 1978.
[3] J. F. Stephen, 'Variations in the Punishment of Crime', *Nineteenth Century*, 17 (1885), p. 755.
[4] See R. M. Jackson, *Enforcing the Law*, Macmillan, London, 1967 p. 250.
[5] See e.g. *Nuttall* (1908) 1 Cr. App. R. 180.

legislation extended the range of choices open to the sentencer; the Criminal Justice Act 1948 reshaped the existing provisions governing special measures and added several more, including the custodial sentence of corrective training, an unrestricted power to fine in cases of felony, a new power to combine probation with psychiatric treatment and a new system of short-term detention for offenders between 14 and 21. Two major statutes of the 1960s made the position more complex, increasing the number of non-custodial methods of disposal open to the courts by the addition of the power to suspend sentences of imprisonment in certain cases; subsequently in 1972 the power to order offenders to perform community service was added, among others.

The Primary Decision

The effect of this legislative structure is to create two distinct systems of sentencing, reflecting different penal objectives and governed by different principles. The sentencer is presented with a choice: he may impose, usually in the name of general deterrence, a sentence intended to reflect the offender's culpability, or he may seek to influence his future behaviour by subjecting him to an appropriate measure of supervision, treatment or preventive confinement. In some instances both objects may be pursued simultaneously and find expression in the same sentence, but more frequently this is not possible. Achievement of the broader objectives of a punitive sentence may require the sentencer to adopt an approach which is not likely to assist the offender towards conformity with the law in the future, and indeed may positively damage such prospects of future conformity as exist already, while a measure designed to assist the offender to regulate his behaviour in the future may appear to diminish the gravity of the offence and weaken the deterrent effect of the law on potential offenders. Faced with that conflict the sentencer must decide which objective should prevail in the particular case; having made this primary decision between what is conventionally, if inelegantly, known as a tariff sentence and a sentence based on the needs of the offender as an individual, the sentencer must apply the appropriate body of principle to determine the precise form of the sentence or measure he will adopt. The principles applicable to tariff sentences differ from those which govern the selection of in-dividualized measures; the detailed criteria which affect the final choice of sentence depend on the primary decision, as do the significance of particular factors in the case and the relevance of various items of information about the circumstances of the offence or the background of the offender. It follows that a sentence which would be considered inappropriate as an application of tariff principles may be considered entirely correct if it is seen as an individualized measure based on the court's assessment of the needs of the offender as an individual, and the converse is equally true.

A number of cases illustrate these propositions. In *Newbury and Jones*[1] two boys, one aged 14 and the other 15, were convicted of manslaughter. It was alleged that they had pushed part of a concrete paving slab over the parapet of a railway bridge as a train was passing underneath, causing the death of the guard. The trial judge ordered both boys to be detained for a period not exceeding five years, under a statutory provision applying to offenders under 17 guilty of grave crimes.[2] On appeal, the Court endorsed the trial judge's choice of general deterrence as the primary objective in the case of the boy who had actually pushed the stone over the parapet. 'Cases have occurred in the past few years of harm being done to persons travelling on trains through stones being dropped or thrown from bridges . . . something has clearly got to be done by the courts to make it clear . . . that youngsters who behave in this way must expect to lose their liberty.' It followed that the boy concerned 'did require punishment'. However, for a boy of his age, notwithstanding the gravity of the offence, 'five years' detention is very severe punishment indeed', and the Court reduced the sentence to one of three years' detention, observing that 'borstal training was inadequate to show the Court's disapproval of such dangerous conduct'. In the case of the second appellant, who was slightly the younger of the two, had not personally pushed the stone over the parapet and had admitted his complicity in the offence from the start, the Court decided that 'training rather than punishment' was the appropriate objective; in consequence of this view, the sentence of five years' detention was varied to borstal training.

As this case indicates, the application of tariff principles requires the sentencer to find the sentence which most accurately reflects the offender's culpability, a process which involves relating the gravity of the offence to the established pattern of sentences for offences of that kind, and then making allowance for such mitigating factors as may be present which tend to reduce the offender's culpability. Both aspects of the process are explored in detail in later chapters. Selection of an individualized measure does not turn on the gravity of the offence, but requires an assessment of the probable future behaviour of the offender and his likely response to various penal measures. Often, as in the case cited, the individualized measure will involve less interference with the freedom of the offender than the

---

[1] (1975) 62 Cr. App. R. 291.
[2] Children and Young Persons Act 1933 s. 53(2), discussed in detail below, p. 285.

tariff sentence which might have been passed for his offence, but this is by no means always the case. The individualized measure may subject the offender to a far greater degree of control and intervention than the alternative tariff sentence. In *Rose*[1] a youth of 17 pleaded guilty to the manslaughter of a woman of 82 and to indecent assault on the same victim. It was alleged that he had gone to the victim's house with intent to steal money which he believed to be there; in the course of searching for it he knocked the victim down, causing injuries from which she subsequently died. The appellant admitted indecently assaulting the victim during the episode. Although the plea of guilty to manslaughter rather than murder was accepted on the basis that the appellant did not intend a sufficient degree of harm to make him guilty of murder, rather than on the ground of diminished responsibility, there was evidence before the trial court that he was suffering from a personality defect which 'unless it is eradicated, in later life is going to make this young man a menace'; however, it did not amount to a disorder for which treatment in a hospital could be ordered. The trial judge imposed a sentence of eighteen years' imprisonment. The Court regretted that this course had been taken; the appropriate solution would have been to select the indefinite sentence of life imprisonment, which would have authorized his detention until 'he was no longer a danger to the public'. This course would have been 'both in the public interest and in mercy to this young man'. (Life imprisonment, as is shown later, is treated by the Court as an individualized measure, justified primarily by the potential dangerousness of the offender, rather than by the gravity of his immediate offence.) The trial judge had however imposed a fixed term of imprisonment which was subject to the basic tariff principle of proportionality between offence and sentence, and considered in the light of the criteria appropriate to the tariff rather than those governing individualized measures, the sentence was too long. 'Once the judge had decided to pass a determinate sentence this Court has to consider whether in all the circumstances the sentence was of appropriate length, and it has come to the conclusion that it was not.' Allowing for the fact that the offence was a grave example of manslaughter, arising from robbery and accompanied by sexual assault, nevertheless 'the quality of the acts he did . . . did not attract a sentence of eighteen years' imprisonment'. The sentence was reduced to ten years.[2]

A third case illustrating the application of different criteria

---

[1] 20.12.73, 2281/B/73, [1974] Crim. L. R. 266.
[2] The Court has no power to impose on appeal a sentence which could be considered more severe than the sentence passed in the court below (see p. 397 below).

according to the nature of the primary decision is *Winnett*.[1] A man of 50 appealed against a sentence of three years' imprisonment for possessing a firearm with intent to endanger life. The evidence was that he had pointed a gun at his mother and fired a number of shots in her presence; it was accepted that the offence was committed under the combined effects of depression arising from long-standing illness, alcohol and domestic stress. The Court endorsed the trial judge's view that the normal choice in such cases would be a tariff sentence—'undoubtedly offences of this kind in the ordinary course of events call for a custodial sentence because they are grave offences meriting punishment'—and declined to reduce the sentence to a shorter term, as to do so might result in the gravity of the offence being diminished in the view of the public—'the public would be surprised . . . to think that a sentence of that level is appropriate for a man who has behaved in this way'. However, the complex of unusual personal circumstances leading up to the offence justified the Court in abandoning the original objective of general deterrence and taking the 'bold course' of varying the sentence to probation, which the Court believed to be 'in the best interests of this man and the public'.

As these cases illustrate, the application to the same case of the different criteria indicated by the choice between a tariff sentence and an individualized measure may result in a major difference in the outcome of the case, although viewed in terms of the degree of intervention in the offender's life, the balance will vary between the two according to the nature of the case. In one case the choice of an individualized measure may mean that a probation order is preferred to a substantial fixed term of imprisonment; in another, it may result in the offender being subject to an indefinite period of confinement, whether under a sentence of life imprisonment or a hospital order coupled with an indefinite restriction order, instead of receiving a term of imprisonment whose upper limit is clearly defined. Equally important conflicts may arise in the application of the secondary principles, whether those of the tariff or those relevant to the choice between individualized measures. Given that the tariff is the appropriate approach, calculating the gravity of the offence and assessing the significance of mitigating factors may leave considerable room for judgment; and the selection of the appropriate individualized measure, where there is no question of a tariff sentence, may present the sentencer with starkly different alternatives, as is illustrated by *Griffith*.[2] A man of 48 with no previous convictions pleaded guilty to manslaughter of a woman by reason of diminished responsibility. It

[1] 15.4.75, 220/A/75.
[2] 1.5.75, 3537/C/74. For similar variations from life imprisonment to probation, see *McBride* 9.11.73, 3573/C/73; *Ainsworth* 6.4.77, 221/A/77.

was alleged that he had struck a prostitute with a brick after an argument over payment; the blow itself was not fatal but the victim died as a result of inhaling blood while unconscious. The appellant was described as a man of limited intelligence whose ability to maintain self-control in the face of severe provocation was substantially diminished, although he had no history of violent behaviour. A second medical view was that his condition was not susceptible to nor in need of treatment and that he was unlikely to be a danger in the future. The trial judge sentenced the appellant to life imprisonment, using the sentence as an individualized measure to provide indefinite preventive confinement for a potentially dangerous offender. The Court endorsed the trial judge's view that the case called for an individualized measure but took a different view both of the dangerousness of the appellant and of the best way of safeguarding against repetition. The sentence was varied to a probation order requiring as a condition submission to psychiatric supervision. The converse occurred in *Lishman*,[1] where the appellant was placed on probation following his conviction for arson of a barn. He subsequently committed a further offence of arson, for which he was sentenced to three years' imprisonment, and was brought before the court which had made the original probation order to be sentenced for the earlier offence. Taking the view that his treatment on probation had been ineffective and that the only alternative was an indefinite period of confinement, the sentencer imposed a sentence of life imprisonment, which was upheld by the Court.

The choice between a tariff sentence and an individualized measure usually involves a choice between different forms of sentence, which are normally identified with one or the other set of principles. The tariff sentence will usually take the form of a fixed term of imprisonment or a fine, while certain kinds of sentence or order—probation, hospital order, life imprisonment—are invariably used as individualized measures not subject to tariff principles. Some forms of sentence, notably borstal training, may be used interchangeably as individualized measures or as tariff sentences:[2] the propriety of such a sentence in a given case must be judged according to the principles derived from the primary decision. Borstal training may be an appropriate sentence in a particular case if it is intended as a measure of individualized training, but not if it is intended as a tariff sentence: in another case the converse may equally be true. The Court has held on many occasions that where borstal training is imposed as an individualized measure intended to provide the offender with the social or vocational training which appears to be necessary in view of

[1] 8.7.71, 543/B/71, [1971] Crim. L. R. 548.
[2] For a detailed account of the principles governing borstal training, see p. 260 below.

his record and behaviour generally, the sentence may be imposed, even though it will subject him to a period of custody longer than would be considered appropriate in the form of a fixed term of imprisonment for the offence for which he is sentenced. In *Graham*[1] a teenage girl appealed against a sentence of borstal training imposed following a conviction for soliciting for prostitution, an offence punishable with a maximum term of three months' imprisonment (the minimum period of detention under a sentence of borstal training is six months). In view of her behaviour in recent years, which included absconding from a local authority home to which she had been committed under a care order, and several other incidents of soliciting, the Court upheld the sentence as being in her own best interest, supported by favourable reports of her response to the sentence. In this instance borstal training was clearly imposed and upheld as an individualized measure, despite the relative triviality of the offence for which it was imposed, which would clearly not have supported a sentence of imprisonment of equivalent length. Where, as a result of statutory restrictions on the availability of imprisonment for young adult offenders,[2] the sentencer uses borstal training as a tariff sentence different criteria apply, and the sentence will be upheld only if it can be considered proportionate to the offence. In *Oates and Kaye*[3] two youths of 18 and 19 respectively, each with a minor record of previous court appearances, appealed against sentences of borstal training imposed for assault occasioning actual bodily harm. The offence, which arose from a dispute in a public house, involved butting and punching but no serious injury was caused. The trial judge had imposed the sentences as a deterrent to similar 'loutish behaviour' in the future. The Court endorsed his judgement that an immediate custodial sentence was appropriate but borstal training was in the circumstances 'too heavy a punishment', although six months' detention or six months' imprisonment would have been justified. The sentence was varied to a short term of imprisonment.

The dual status of borstal training (and to some extent of detention in a detention centre) arises as a result of the enactment in the Criminal Justice Act 1961 of restrictions on the power to imprison young adult offenders. Prior to this legislation the sentence was treated exclusively as an individualized training measure inappropriate to express punitive intentions and a sentence of borstal training would, at that time, be varied to imprisonment where the Court considered general deterrence to be the dominant concern, even

[1] 17.6.75, 927/B/75.
[2] Criminal Justice Act 1961 s. 3, discussed in detail at p. 276 below.
[3] 13.10.75, 2673/A/75.

though the effect of the variation would be to reduce the period during which the appellant was subject to confinement.[1] Other recent legislation affecting sentencing has had the effect of confusing in some instances the clear distinctions between the principles governing the tariff and those affecting individualized measures.

The Tariff

It has been argued that a tariff sentence will be imposed when the sentencer wishes to emphasize to the public the gravity of the offence, while an individualized measure will be chosen where the object is to influence the future behaviour of the offender. Frequently these objectives are in sharp conflict, usually where an offender whose prospects of future conformity to the law are favourable is to be sentenced for an offence which the sentencer considers a serious threat to society—a common example of this dilemma is the case of a young man of good character and great promise convicted of importing or dealing in controlled drugs.[2] In cases such as these the fundamental penal strategy of the Court may be identified and the respective roles of the two elements of the sentencing system defined.

The tariff represents a complex of penal theories—general deterrence, denunciation, occasionally expiation—often coinciding in the same decisions, although occasionally clearly isolable. The overriding principle of proportionality between offence and sentence applies whatever motivating theory supports the sentence. Many examples can be found of the Court justifying a tariff sentence by reference to general deterrence in the narrow sense of inhibiting possible imitators by fear of similar penal consequences. Commonly this justification will be found where long sentences are passed for grave crimes such as robbery,[3] but it is also used to explain shorter sentences imposed for crimes which are less serious but nevertheless in the Court's view significant. In *Kennedy*[4] the Court upheld a sentence of six months' imprisonment on a man of good character who admitted making three false tax returns involving a total loss to the Revenue of £176, stating that 'this kind of offence is very prevalent . . . it is an offence which requires a deterrent penalty from

[1] See *Bull* (1957) 41 Cr. App. R. 133.

[2] See, for example, *Fetters* 18.12.75, 4818/R/75, (youth, 19, three years' imprisonment for importing substantial quantity of cannabis; case 'a dreadful tragedy' and 'a young man may possibly have ruined his life at the age of 19', but sentence upheld 'to make it plain to all people who deal with this sort of traffic . . . that deterrent sentences of several years will inevitably be passed').

[3] See, for example, *McAleny and Griffiths* 5.12.75, 965/B/75, (ten years for robbery for two men, no significant previous convictions; upheld; 'those who commit offences of this type are playing for big stakes, and when they are convicted they must expect severe sentences').

[4] 2.9.75, 3354/B/75.

the very fact that it is . . . not easily detectable'. Similar reasoning was used to justify a sentence of twenty-eight days' imprisonment imposed on a dock worker convicted of handling £3 worth of tinned meat which had been stolen from a cargo being unloaded.[1]

In other cases a tariff sentence may be justified by reference to the concept of denunciation—the theory that if the law fails to impose a sentence of substantial severity for a particular class of offence, the gravity with which it is viewed by society will diminish and increasing tolerance lead to more frequent occurrence. In *Pottinger*[2] the appellant, described as 'a high-ranking civil servant of outstanding ability', appealed against sentences totalling five years for offences of corruption. It was alleged that over a period of several years he had received substantial considerations from an architect who was engaged on various government projects. Replying to the argument that a deterrent sentence was not necessary, as there was little probability that others would follow his example, the Court stated that 'although we accept that a deterrent sentence is not called for, one which marks the public condemnation of misconduct so grave . . . is unavoidable', but reduced the sentence to four years as an act of mercy.

The choice of a tariff sentence in cases like these results from a positive determination by the Court that the gravity of the offence and its likely consequences require to be emphasized, notwithstanding that the effect of the sentence on the offender's future behaviour will not be beneficial. A tariff sentence will normally be upheld, without regard to the problems and needs of the offender, for a wide range of offences, in some cases with a degree of consistency which suggests the existence of a firm policy. Examples of such offences are rape, robbery, wounding with intent to do grievous bodily harm, dealing with controlled drugs, perjury and related offences, arson and blackmail. The lengths of sentence upheld in such cases vary according to the particular circumstances—a detailed examination of the relevant criteria is made in chapters 2 and 3. In other cases a tariff sentence is held to be necessitated not so much by the intrinsic nature of the offence as by the relationship of the offender to the victim. An offence which constitutes a breach of trust or an abuse of privilege will frequently attract a tariff sentence, even though in the absence of this relationship the offence might not be considered particularly serious. Dishonesty[3] or abuse of power[4] by a public servant in the

[1] *Bogle* 3.6.75, 2334/R/75, [1975] Crim. L. R. 726.
[2] 10.7.74, 876/R/74, [1974] Crim. L. R. 675.
[3] See *Deery* 9.6.75, 2848/A/74 (council highway superintendent convicted of conspiracy to defraud council and corruption; two years upheld: 'every public servant knows that if he behaves corruptly, this is what is likely to happen').
[4] See *Lewis* 18.8.75, 791/C/75, [1976] Crim. L. R. 144 (police officer, 45, assaulting

course of his duties, abuse of his clients' confidence by a professional man[1] or indecency with children committed by a person in whose care they have been placed[2] will normally attract a tariff sentence, despite the good character of the offender, the disastrous personal consequences of the conviction and the low probability that he will commit similar offences in the future. Occasionally the prevalence of a specific kind of offence at a particular time or place will be held to justify a tariff sentence where otherwise an individualized measure would be considered appropriate.[3]

Whether the need for a tariff sentence is indicated by the inherent nature of the offence or by the aggravating effect of the offender's status, the primary decision in all of these cases represents a view that the social importance of marking the gravity of the offence outweighs the possibility of influencing the future behaviour of the offender by training, treatment or supervision. Frequently a tariff sentence is the result not of a positive choice but rather of a process of elimination of alternatives. Faced with an offender whose offences are not of such a nature as to make the choice of a tariff sentence obvious, but whose previous history and attitudes suggest that there is little chance of a positive response to whatever individualized measures are available, the sentencer may find himself driven to impose a tariff sentence as a last resort in a case which he would prefer to deal with in a different way. In *Hamer*[4] a woman of 54 with 'a most appalling record' appealed against sentences of four years' imprisonment for a variety of offences committed during the currency of a probation order, which had been made in turn for offences committed while she was on parole from the most recent of many sentences of imprisonment. The Court was 'reluctant to send an accused person back into prison again and again' but accepted that it

---

possible witness in course of informal questioning, causing broken nose and bruising; two years upheld: 'we appreciate the tragedy . . . the public interest has to be served'). Where a police officer commits offences which are wholly unrelated to his duties and do not involve any abuse of authority or position, his position should be ignored in assessing the appropriate sentence. See *Watkins* 23.1.76, 5199/B/75 (senior police officer obtaining loans from finance company by deception, offences 'had nothing to do with his office. They were entirely part of his private life'; wrong to pass deterrent sentence ignoring mitigation; nine months' immediate imprisonment varied to nine months suspended).

[1] See *Bartlett* 11.12.75, 2683/A/75 (stockbroker, 65, misappropriating clients' funds in excess of £30,000; four years upheld).

[2] See *Reeve* 21.4.75, 4644/A/74 (housemaster at children's home, 19, indecent assault on boy in care; three years' upheld: 'obviously if one had only the future of this young man to consider' probation might be appropriate 'but we have to consider the other side'.

[3] See *Farrell* 15.12.75, 1410/A/75, [1976] Crim. L. R. 318 (bomb hoax, in 'times of public anxiety . . . people who commit bomb hoaxes must expect to go to prison'; two years excessive on facts—reduced to twelve months).

[4] 6.5.75, 316/B/75.

was 'hopeless again to put this woman on probation'. Stating that a substantial term of imprisonment was in the circumstances 'an almost inevitable sentence', the Court reduced the sentence to three years to 'give her some help and encouragement'. Similarly in *Cullup*[1] a man of 38 with a substantial record was sentenced to a total of five years' imprisonment for various offences of fraud and deception committed while subject to a probation order made on an earlier appeal and for the offences for which the probation order had been made. The Court was invited to make a further probation order but found it impossible to do so, as the appellant had broken the terms of the previous order immediately after it had been made and the psychiatric opinion on which the earlier variation of sentence had been based was no longer maintained. While accepting that there was no alternative to a term of imprisonment, the Court considered the sentences were, taken as a whole, too long and reduced them to three years. As these cases show, sentences of imprisonment which are imposed following the elimination of individualized alternatives are governed by the same principles as other tariff sentences where calculation of the length of sentence is concerned; the overriding principle of proportionality applies in both cases.

Individualization

It has been argued that, except in those cases where a tariff sentence is forced on the sentencer by the unsuitability of any of the available individualized measures, the choice of a tariff sentence is made by reference to the nature of the offence. Cases in which the primary decision is likely to be in favour of an individualized measure can be identified by the characteristics of the offender. While individualized measures are used in a wide range of cases where the claims of the tariff are not strong and there is reason to suppose that an individualized measure will provide the treatment, guidance or supervision needed to enable the offender to make the necessary adjustments to social demands, four types of offenders are normally considered particularly suitable for individualized measures. These are young offenders (predominantly those under 21), offenders in need of psychiatric treatment, recidivists who appear to have reached a critical point in their life and persistent recidivists who are in danger of becoming completely institutionalized as a result of repeated sentences of imprisonment. Offenders in these categories will normally be dealt with by individualized measures unless their offences are so grave that the case for a tariff sentence is overwhelming or their

[1] 2.5.75, 4534/C/74.

previous reactions to such measures indicate that such an approach would be fruitless.

THE YOUNG OFFENDER

'In the case of a young offender there can hardly ever be any conflict between the public interest and that of the offender. The public have no greater interest than that he should become a good citizen. The difficult task of the Court is to determine what treatment gives the best chance of realizing that objective'.[1] This statement from a judgment delivered in 1963 still represents the general policy of the Court towards the young adult offender and the small number of young persons and children who come before it.[2] The policy is subject to exceptions where the offence concerned is either extremely serious or is thought to require a particular emphasis on deterrence, but the most typical appeal by an offender under 21 centres on the question whether borstal training, probation or some other individualized measure is most likely to contribute to law-abiding behaviour in the future. In a typical case[3] a youth of 19 had been sentenced to borstal training for loitering with intent to steal purses, the offence being committed during the currency of a probation order imposed for theft. The Court was told that the appellant had an unfortunate home background, a weak educational record and a poor employment history. He had been found guilty on several occasions, twice of offences similar to the one for which he was now before the Court. The Court received psychiatric and social inquiry reports and a further report from the borstal institution. The psychiatric report suggested that probation, possibly with some psychiatric assistance, would be the best disposal: the social inquiry report (prepared by the probation officer under whose supervision the appellant had previously been placed) was pessimistic about further use of probation, as his response to the earlier order had been 'perfunctory'. The report from the institution was more optimistic: the appellant was spending part of his working week on remedial education and during the rest of his time appeared to display steady working habits. Observing that 'this is one of the cases where it is clear that a . . . period of borstal training will be in tho best interests of the appellant himself', the Court upheld the sentence. Often, as in this case, the individualized measure will involve a longer period of custody and supervision than would follow if the offender were sentenced on a tariff basis to a term of

---

[1] *Smith* 15.11.63, 1510/63, [1964] Crim. L. R. 70.
[2] The term 'young adult offender' refers to offenders between 17 and 21. Offenders between 14 and 17 are described as 'young persons' and those under 14 as 'children'.
[3] *Barton* 6.2.75, 4251/C/74.

imprisonment. In another case[1] a young man of 20 was sentenced to borstal training for theft and going equipped for burglary, having been caught in possession of a stolen brace while apparently engaged in the preliminary stages of a burglary. The appellant's co-defendant, who was the older of the two, had been sentenced to six months' imprisonment, and the appellant complained that his own sentence was disparate to his co-defendant's. The Court accepted that the co-defendant would spend a shorter period in custody, but observed that 'the disparity in sentence . . . is only a very minor matter when compared with the objectives that a sentence should serve'. In the light of the appellant's record and the information in the social inquiry and borstal reports, the Court considered that borstal training was 'in the true interest of this young man, as it is in the true interest of society' and upheld the sentence.

In many cases the Court will take the view that probation or some other non-custodial measure offers the best hope for the appellant's future. In *Mills*[2] a youth of 19, with seven previous court appearances which had culminated in a sentence of borstal training, appealed against a second sentence of borstal training imposed for being carried in a vehicle taken without authority. The Court heard that since his release from the earlier sentence the appellant had found and maintained regular employment with an employer who was anxious to have him back, and planned to marry as soon as possible. The present offence could be considered 'an isolated lapse' and the Court considered that 'he had earned a chance to put his past behind him', although there was a need for 'some independent and outside support'. The sentence was varied to probation. In *Finney*[3] a 17-year-old girl whose record made 'most unhappy reading' was sentenced to borstal training for offences of handling stolen property and attempting to obtain by deception. She had previously experienced borstal training and had earlier institutional experience under a care order. Her behaviour during these periods had been unruly and disruptive and it was considered unlikely that she would respond to a further period of borstal training. The Court was advised that the regime at a particular probation hostel might be such as to engage her co-operation and help her to mature into 'a law-abiding and decent member of society'. While fully aware that there was 'a high likelihood of further offences occurring' and that the chances of success were 'slender', the Court varied the sentence to a probation order requiring as a condition residence at the hostel.

These cases, not in any way unusual decisions and typical of very

[1] *McKnight* 18.8.75, 2539/C/75.
[2] 13.1.75, 4234/C/74.
[3] 16.6.75, 1506/B/75.

many others, are described to illustrate the general approach of the Court to the use of individualized measures for young offenders. The law and practice governing the use of borstal training and probation are discussed in chapters 6 and 5 respectively. It should be added that where the nature of the offence is such that the demands of the tariff claim priority over those of the future of the individual offender, the relative youth of the offender is normally a substantial mitigating factor in his favour. Where a young offender receives a sentence of imprisonment, it is normally for a shorter term than would be imposed on an older man for the same offence. The relevance of youth as a mitigating factor in relation to tariff sentences is discussed in chapter 4.

THE INTERMEDIATE RECIDIVIST

The term 'intermediate recidivist' is used to describe an offender in his twenties or early thirties who has acquired a substantial history of convictions and findings of guilt as a juvenile, has undergone various individualized measures such as probation and borstal training, and is now steadily adding terms of imprisonment to his record. Faced with the prospect of his developing into an institutionalized habitual offender, the Court will frequently seek to interrupt the sequence by the use of probation or whatever other measure may offer some reasonable chance of success. Many examples can be given. In *White*[1] a man of 26 was sentenced to five years' imprisonment for a series of burglaries. The appellant had made many court appearances and had experienced two probation orders in the past, in addition to a variety of other sentences. The Court, stating that it 'could not possibly disagree' with the sentence of five years' imprisonment, nevertheless decided that the availability of a place in an adult probation hostel justified the Court in giving him 'one final chance to rehabilitate himself'. The sentence was varied to probation. In *Brooks*[2] a man with twenty-two previous convictions was sentenced to a total of twelve months' imprisonment for various offences of dishonesty. Impressed by evidence that the appellant had established a stable home and obtained a job with good prospects, the Court decided that although the sentence was neither wrong in principle nor excessive, it could give the appellant 'his last opportunity . . . impelled to a merciful conclusion by the very blackness of his record'. The sentence was varied so as to allow his immediate release. More typically the Court will substitute for the sentence of imprisonment an in-dividualized measure making substantial demands on the appellant,

[1] 5.5.75, 173/C/175.
[2] 2.10.75, 3317/B/75.

such as a probation order, possibly conditioned to require residence,[1] psychiatric treatment[2] or attendance at a day training centre,[3] or a suspended sentence, often accompanied by a supervision order. In *Hull*[4] a man of 31 with 'a long record of offences of nearly every kind imaginable' appealed against sentences totalling twenty-one months for wounding his wife and other offences for which he had earlier been subjected to probation and a suspended sentence respectively. It was said that after his last release from prison the appellant made 'for the first time in his life a determined attempt to keep out of trouble', and the latest offence was the result of domestic difficulties which had now been resolved. The Court, 'while not criticizing . . . the sentence appealed against', varied it to a total of nine months' imprisonment suspended for two years, in conjunction with a suspended-sentence supervision order.

As these cases indicate, the use of individualized measures for offenders of this kind is not automatic. The Court normally requires some reason to believe that taking this approach at the particular time is likely to prove successful. Factors which are often influential include evidence that the appellant has made a determined, if not wholly successful, attempt to avoid committing further offences since his last release from custody,[5] or that he has established new relationships which may have a stabilizing effect on his behaviour.[6] The fact that the most recent offence constitutes a breach of

---

[1] As in *White* 5.5.75, 173/C/175, above.

[2] See *Butterly* 11.2.75, 4227/C/74 (man, 32, 'really long and bad record'; eighteen months for burglary varied to probation with condition requiring submission to treatment for alcoholism, Court taking chance as otherwise 'the probabilities are that he will be in and out of prison for the rest of his life').

[3] See *Farmer* 16.6.75, 4097/A/74, [1975] Crim. L. R. 594 (man, 28, sixteen previous convictions, previous sentences including detention, borstal training, imprisonment, suspended imprisonment, probation, 'methods of dealing with him that have been tried in the past have proved entirely ineffective'; three years for various offences varied to probation with condition requiring attendance at day training centre).

[4] 18.12.75, 3347/B/75.

[5] See *Cross* 1.7.75, 1192/A/75, [1975] Crim. L. R. 591 (man, 34, 'very bad criminal record'; eighteen months for stealing metal varied to probation: 'his usual pattern . . . has been to be released from one sentence and to commit another offence within a matter of two or three months and be back in custody . . . this time he survived for something like eighteen months, and there is some evidence that the pattern of behaviour has been changed'); see also *McCafferty* 24.7.75, 1741/A/75 (man, 37, 'long list of convictions', thirty months for theft and taking vehicles; sentence not wrong in principle but reduced and suspended as appellant 'made a most determined effort to mend his ways' after last release).

[6] See *Tadman* 4.6.74, 4866/A/73 (man, 26, fourteen previous convictions, borstal training, probation, various terms of imprisonment; three years for handling and theft, although not wrong in principle, reduced and suspended, as appellant had 'formed an apparently genuine attachment for a young woman . . . it does appear that this young man has made . . . genuine efforts to change his way of life'); see also *Adams* 17.10.74, 1950/A/74 (man, 26, ten previous convictions, borstal training, periods of imprisonment and conditional discharge, opportunity to live and work under guidance of prison visitor known over period of years; fifteen months varied to probation).

probation or is committed during the currency of a suspended sentence is not necessarily fatal, if it appears that the appellant has made some effort to respond to the use of these measures.[1] Where the appellant has recently disregarded such an initiative by a sentencer, or has failed to take advantage of a similar opportunity (such as release on parole under licence) he is unlikely to be considered a candidate for individualized treatment unless a particularly strong case can be made. In *Neighbour*[2] the appellant was sentenced to five years' imprisonment for burglary and other offences committed within a few months of his release from a long sentence and while subject to parole licence; the sentence from which the appellant had been released had itself been imposed for offences committed while on probation. Observing that 'it is really impossible to give a man who was given the great chance of probation after such a bad record, and who was unable to complete his probation, any further chance of reforming himself', the Court upheld the sentence.

THE INADEQUATE RECIDIVIST

The term 'inadequate recidivist' is used to describe an offender, middle-aged or older, who has over a long period of years committed numerous offences, not in themselves in the first rank of seriousness, and has served many terms of imprisonment as well as experiencing an extensive selection of other penal measures. Faced with such an offender, the Court will usually grasp any chance of breaking the cycle of offence and sentence, even if the chances of success are obviously limited. In one typical case[3] a man of 48 who had served thirteen terms of imprisonment, including a sentence of eight years' preventive detention, appealed against a sentence of five years' imprisonment imposed for fifty offences of theft and obtaining by deception, all committed while unlawfully at large from an earlier sentence of five years. While it was 'quite impossible to say that the sentence . . . was wrong in principle', the Court took the view that 'it may be that he has reached the time when he might just be persuaded to change his ways'. Given the availability of a place in a probation hostel and the possibility of employment, the Court varied the sentence to a probation order requiring residence at the hostel.

---

[1] For instance, *Hull* 18.12.75, 3347/B/75 (above, p. 21); *Cross* 1.7.75, 1192/A/75, [1975] Crim. L. R. 591 (above, p. 21).

[2] 3.11.75, 2240/C/75; see also *Sibley* 17.1.75, 3680/C/74 (seven years for burglary by man, 34, many previous convictions, last five years almost continuously in prison; impossible to give him 'a young old lag's chance', as offences previously committed while appellant on pre-release hostel scheme, but sentence 'too much for these offences, even having regard to this man's record'; reduced to five years).

[3] *Maron* 10.3.75, 3788/A/74.

Similarly in *Sanders*[1] a woman of 55, who had spent a total of fifteen years in prison and substantial periods on probation, was sentenced to four years' imprisonment for twenty-two offences of forgery and obtaining small sums by means of forged pension books and other documents. The offences were committed within a short period of her release from a sentence of six years for a large number of similar offences. The Court was persuaded that 'the present occasion presents what will probably be the last possible opportunity to give this lady a chance of spending the remaining years of her life otherwise than in an institution', and as there was a home with members of her family to which she could go, the Court decided to 'take a chance . . . however improbable it may be that the lady will respond to the way in which one hopes'. The sentence was varied to probation.

These cases are typical of very many others. In so far as there is a difference, apart from age, which justifies distinguishing between 'intermediate recidivists' and 'inadequate recidivists', it is that the Court may be more willing to take a risk with the older offender and is more tolerant of the failure of such initiatives in the past. As in the case of the intermediate recidivist there must be some prospect of success, however remote. Where recent experience suggests that further experimentation with non-custodial measures will be fruitless, this course will not be taken. In *Rose*[2] a man of 53 appealed against sentences totalling five years' imprisonment for a series of frauds on elderly householders. The appellant, who had made thirty-two previous appearances for offences of dishonesty and had received sentences of imprisonment totalling twenty years, committed the offences while subject to a suspended sentence imposed a few months earlier for similar offences. For this reason the Court declined to vary the sentence, 'having regard to the opportunity that he had . . . and the fact that he continually repeats the same sort of fraudulent conduct'.

OFFENDERS IN NEED OF PSYCHIATRIC TREATMENT

The law provides a variety of special disposals for offenders who are considered to be in need of psychiatric treatment. Under the Mental Health Act 1959 a sentencer may in appropriate cases make a hospital order authorizing the detention of the offender as an involuntary

[1] 18.12.75, 4506/B/75.
[2] 1.5.75, 4797/B/74. See also *Percival* 28.4.75, 23/B/75 (man, 58, numerous previous convictions and sentences of imprisonment, various frauds committed while subject to suspended sentence with supervision; four years upheld: 'the offences from which he had the opportunity of making good . . . are so exactly similar to those which he has since committed' that custodial sentence inevitable).

patient in a mental hospital, and other statutory provisions[1] allow a probation order to include a requirement that the probationer submit to psychiatric treatment. Additionally, the Court has come to use the sentence of life imprisonment, prescribed as the maximum sentence for a considerable number of offences (where its use is not, as in the case of murder, mandatory), as an indeterminate sentence providing indefinite preventive confinement for offenders who are potentially dangerous as a result of mental disturbance or instability. The law and practice governing the use of these measures is described in detail in chapter 7. Within the framework of sentences of imprisonment, administrative arrangements can be made for an offender to receive psychiatric treatment, either by allocation to a special prison designed to provide for such prisoners or by transfer to a mental hospital by the Home Secretary. These arrangements are not within the control of the sentencer and are not further described.[2]

In the general policy of the Court towards the offender who is in need of psychiatric treatment, individualization is the dominant theme and the considerations which underlly the tariff are virtually excluded. Treatability has replaced culpability as the effective criterion; in the majority of cases concerning offenders needing psychiatric treatment, the important questions are the practicability of treatment in various settings and the extent to which the risk of grave offences in the future justifies prolonged confinement. Abandoning the tariff in this context may well mean that the offender is subjected to a period of constraint for longer than would be considered justified by the immediate offence. In *Ashdown*[3] the Court upheld a sentence of life imprisonment on a 'very dangerous' man of 21 said to be suffering from an untreatable psychopathic disorder accompanied by uncontrollable sexual drives, accepting that the appellant might possibly spend the rest of his life in prison and that the fixed-term sentence which would have been justified on the facts of the offence would have been five years. More typically the Court is concerned with the choice between a hospital order, in some cases coupled with an order restricting discharge, and a probation order requiring submission to psychiatric treatment. In *Bond*[4] a man of 48 was sentenced to five years' imprisonment for blackmail—'in the ordinary way . . . one of the most vicious crimes in the calendar'. However the offence was 'wholly out of character' and medical evidence showed that the appellant was suffering from an acute anxiety neurosis. For this reason the Court decided that it was not a

[1] Powers of Criminal Courts Act 1973 s. 3.
[2] For a detailed account, see Report of the Committee on the Treatment of Mentally Abnormal Offenders (1975), Cmnd. 6244, chs. 3–5.
[3] 1.11.73, 3001/C/72, [1974] Crim. L. R. 130, discussed in detail at p. 00 below.
[4] 27.2.75, 4770/B/74.

case for 'the ordinary type of punishment which would be visited upon the ordinary type of offence of this nature' and varied the sentence to a probation order requiring as a condition that the appellant undergo psychiatric treatment as an in-patient at a specified hospital. As this case demonstrates, the demands of general deterrence rarely outweigh those of treatment, where a clear case for treatment can be established in terms of psychiatric need.

In one context tariff principles are generally applied to cases concerning mentally unstable offenders. It has been shown that a tariff sentence may be imposed in default of a more constructive alternative, rather than as the first choice of the sentencer, where no available individualized measure is appropriate. One frequent example is the case of the offender suffering from some untreatable personality disorder, who repeatedly commits minor offences. Where such an offender can be dealt with by a specific psychiatric measure that course will be taken,[1] but where such a disposal is not possible, and the gravity of the offender's conduct, actual or threatened, does not justify a sentence of life imprisonment, the sentencer has no alternative to a tariff sentence. Such a sentence is governed by the overriding principle of proportionality between offence and sentence and a disproportionate sentence will not normally be upheld, whether imposed to afford an opportunity of treatment in prison or to achieve temporary prevention. The relevant cases are discussed in chapter 2.

OTHER CASES

The four categories of offenders discussed above are those for whom an individualized approach is most commonly used and for whom a tariff sentence will normally be upheld only after a careful consideration of the claims of the offender to be treated in terms of his needs as an individual. In other cases, where the nature of the offence is not such that a tariff sentence is clearly indicated without regard to the future of the individual, the Court will approach the primary decision without any presumption either way, endeavouring to balance the competing claims of each approach to sentencing in the context of the particular case.

[1] As in *Eaton*, 31.7.75, 3182/R/75, [1976] Crim. L. R. 390.

Part II

THE TARIFF

The following three chapters describe the process by which the length of a sentence of imprisonment is determined once the sentencer has decided that the case requires such a sentence. Chapter 2 deals with the general principles of the tariff; chapter 3, which is intended primarily for reference, describes in detail the relationships between particular offences in their various forms and the conventional corresponding sentences; chapter 4 examines the mitigating factors which are most frequently influential in securing a reduction in what would otherwise be the appropriate sentence. It is important to emphasize that chapter 3 is not intended to provide, in itself, a comprehensive description of the Court's sentencing practice in relation to the offences discussed. The chapter should be read in conjunction with chapter 2 and subject to chapter 4.

2

The Principles of the Tariff

The use in the context of sentencing of the term 'tariff', although at least a century old,[1] is unfortunate. The expression suggests a process of relating penalties to offences by the application of an inflexible scale and without consideration of the circumstances of the individual offender. Neither implication is true of the complex body of principle which has evolved to guide the sentencer in calculating the length of a sentence of imprisonment. The principles of the tariff constitute a framework by reference to which the sentencer can determine what factors in a particular case are relevant to his decision and what weight should be attached to each of them. Properly used, they offer a basis for maintaining consistency in the sentencing of different offenders, while observing relevant distinctions, making appropriate allowances for individual factors and preserving adequate scope for the exercise of judicial discretion.

Whatever motive has led the sentencer to decide to impose a tariff sentence, whether he seeks to mark the gravity of the offence as a deterrent or has reached the conclusion that no alternative means of dealing with the offender is feasible, the object in determining the length of the sentence is to reflect the culpability of the offender. The process consists of three stages, which may be called 'defining the range within the scale', 'fixing the ceiling' and 'allowing for mitigation'. The overriding principle is that the sentence must not be more severe than is justified by the gravity of the offence for which it is imposed, whatever other considerations might suggest a longer term.

Defining the Range within the Scale

Innovation in crime, although by no means unknown,[2] is relatively

---

[1] The term is used by Lush J. in his reply to the Home Secretary's circular on the adequacy of punishment for brutal assaults, dated 16 November 1876. Arguing that the power to order flogging, which he wished to see extended to various offences of violence, should not be conferred on Recorders, he observes that they 'have not the opportunity, as we have, of consulting with each other, and forming a conventional tariff'. See *Reports to the Secretary of State for the Home Department on the State of the Law Relating to Brutal Assaults* (1875) C. 1138, p. 8.

[2] See *Harris* 12.11.73, 1994/C/73, where the appellant was alleged to have applied

rare. The overwhelming majority of offences which come before criminal courts arise from factual situations which conform to a recurring pattern and which can be categorized by reference to particular elements. This recurring pattern of common factual situations provides a basis for a corresponding pattern of sentences, which can be adjusted to accord with the detailed variations of particular cases. The conventional relationships between frequently encountered factual situations and corresponding levels of sentence constitute the foundations of the tariff. The conventions have developed over a substantial period of time, and in some cases can be traced to a period in the late nineteenth century before the Court of Criminal Appeal was established;[1] the emergence as a regular occurrence of a kind of offence previously encountered only at rare intervals may force the Court to expedite the process and establish a tariff for the various forms the new offence may take.[2]

The maximum penalty fixed by statute plays a limited part in the process of defining the scale of sentences applicable to the various forms in which a particular offence may be encountered.[3] Until relatively recently the maximum penalties prescribed for many of the more common offences were contained in the Consolidating Acts of 1861, or re-enactments of those Acts, and their origins could be traced directly to the terms of transportation established in the 1820s and 1830s as the capital statutes of the eighteenth century were repealed.[4] Such maxima provide no useful indication of a legislative evaluation of different offences in relation to a penal system which has changed fundamentally, and their effect on modern sentencing

---

paint stripper to underwear belonging to his mistress and her husband, causing chemical burns which left no permanent injury. Describing the case as 'most extraordinary', the Court endorsed the sentencer's view that a custodial sentence was necessary to show disapproval of the appellant's conduct, but reduced the sentence from three years to twelve months, on the basis that the appellant intended only to irritate rather than injure.

[1] Writing in 1885, Stephen J. gives an account, with a number of detailed examples, of the 'customary scale of punishments' which had evolved through informal processes of discussion and consultation. See 'Variations in the Punishment of Crime', *Nineteenth Century, 17* (1885), p. 755.

[2] Thus in recent years the Court has developed a series of distinctions to be observed in sentencing offenders for causing explosions; see, in particular, *Byrne* (1975) 62 Cr. App. R. 159.

[3] For an account of the development of legislation governing maximum penalties, see D. A. Thomas, *The Penal Equation*, Institute of Criminology, Cambridge, 1978.

[4] For example, rape was a capital offence until 1840, when 4 and 5 Vic. c. 56 s. 5 substituted a mandatory sentence of transportation for life. Penal servitude for life replaced transportation in the Penal Servitude Act 1857, and the sentencer was first given discretion to impose a lesser term in the Offences Against the Person Act 1861. Penal servitude was merged with imprisonment by the Criminal Justice Act 1948, and the resulting maximum penalty of imprisonment for life was re-enacted in the Sexual Offences Act 1956.

practice is limited.[1] Modern criminal legislation such as the Theft Act 1968 and Criminal Damage Act 1971 allows, as a deliberate policy, equal or in some cases greater scope for judicial discretion in formulating the basis of the tariff.[2] In addition, there remain a significant number of common law offences for which no maximum penalty has ever been fixed by statute,[3] although the sentence for attempt is now subject to the same maximum as that prescribed for the offence attempted,[4] and a similar rule applies to conspiracy to commit a specified offence.[5]

In relation to certain offences—usually those created by statute as new offences since the 1880s—the maximum sentence lies closer to the level of sentence established by judicial practice, and in such cases the general principle relating to the maximum term—that it should be reserved for the worst possible example of the offence concerned—becomes significant. Many illustrations of the application of this principle can be found. In *Smith*[6] the appellant pleaded guilty to three offences of taking a conveyance, in each case a private car, and was sentenced to three years' imprisonment, the maximum term, concurrent on each count. The Court considered that this sentence was not justified, as 'though they were serious offences' it was easy to imagine more serious examples, such as taking a fire-engine or ambulance in circumstances which might endanger the public: 'it is only in cases of real gravity within the class that it is justifiable to impose the maximum sentence allowed by law'. This principle does not mean that the maximum term must never be imposed, nor does it require the sentencer to be unrealistic in considering the relationship of the immediate offence to the general pattern of offences within that category. Upholding the maximum sentence of two years' imprisonment in *Ambler*[7], where the appellant was convicted of bribing a

---

[1] They do however identify the offences for which life imprisonment, now used as an individualized measure to deal with dangerous offenders, is available.

[2] See *Theft and Related Offences*, Eighth Report of the Criminal Law Revision Committees (1966), Cmnd. 2977, paras. 10–12, for a discussion of the issues.

[3] Powers of Criminal Courts Act 1973 s. 18(1) fixes a general maximum sentence of two years' imprisonment for *statutory* offences which authorize the imprisonment for an unspecified term.

[4] Powers of Criminal Courts Act 1973 s. 18(2). The maximum sentence for attempted rape is, anomalously, seven years, although the completed offence is punishable by life imprisonment. See Sexual Offences Act 1956 s. 37 and sch. 2.

[5] Criminal Law Act 1977 s. 3.

[6] 13.2.75, 3669/C/74, [1975] Crim. L. R. 468; see also *Waterfield* 17.2.75, 2787/C/74, (appellant convicted of fraudulently evading the prohibition on the importation of indecent articles and sentenced to the maximum term of two years; as same section applied also to obscene articles, Court held that 'the maximum sentence ought not to have been imposed'); *Wortley* 17.9.76, 2619/B/76 (maximum sentence for obtaining credit while undischarged bankrupt inappropriate, as the money had not 'gone into the appellant's pocket'; although 'this was a bad example of a breach of bankruptcy law', it was 'not the worst kind of offence').

[7] 24.11.75, 3625/C/74, [1976] Crim. L. R. 266.

prison officer to smuggle whisky and hacksaw blades into a prison, the Court stated that while 'it is . . . a principle of sentencing that maximum sentences should only be passed for the worst kind of offence', judges 'should not use their imaginations to conjure up unlikely worst possible kinds of cases'. The maximum, particularly where it was relatively low, was appropriate to the worst example of the offence normally encountered in practice, rather than a hypothetical worst example which might never occur; 'what they should consider is the worst type of offence which comes before the court'. The principle does require the sentencer to consider carefully before imposing a maximum sentence,[1] and it will rarely be appropriate to impose the maximum sentence where the offence has not proceeded beyond an attempt[2] or where there is substantial mitigation.[3]

In most contexts the maximum sentence permitted by law is remote from the levels of sentence normally imposed in practice, and the tariff must be identified in the decisions of the Court of Appeal in dealing with cases within the general category concerned.[4] In relation to each of the main categories of offence with which the Crown Court customarily deals, it is possible to identify a structure of ranges of sentences related to the variations of the particular offence most commonly encountered. Several different terms are used in the judgments of the Court—a sentence may be described as being 'outside the permitted range for the circumstances of the case',[5] 'in keeping with the bracket of sentences clearly adopted for this type of offence',[6] 'really out of pattern with the sentencing practice of this

---

[1] See, for example, *Badharee* 28.11.75, 4581/B/75 (indecent assault on a girl, 20, 'grave assault' with 'terrifying effect', but no violence likely to cause injury; two years reduced to fifteen months, as 'the case did not call for the maximum sentence'); *Money* 5.6.72, 1517/A/72, (indecent assault on girl, 13, involving threats to use razor blade and manual pressure on throat; Court upheld maximum sentence as 'it was as bad a case of indecent assault . . . as it can possibly imagine').

[2] See *Robson* 6.5.74, 5523/B/73 (attempted indecent assault on girl, attempt to persuade girl to enter woods, no physical contact or harm; maximum term not justified despite several previous convictions for sexual violence in past 'it would be . . . unusual that an attempt should be visited with punishment to the maximum extent that the law permits in respect of a completed offence').

[3] See *Shakes* 2.12.75, 3947/B/75 (two years imprisonment for forgery of passport; maximum sentence reduced as there was 'substantial mitigation'); see also *Markus* [1974] 3 W. L. R. 645, below p. 161.

[4] Although there have been cases where the Court has received and acted upon evidence relating to the general level of sentences passed in the Crown Court for the particular offence concerned (see, e.g., *Devito* 14.11.74, 4063/A/74, [1975] Crim. L. R. 175; *Caughie and others* (1969) 53 Cr. App. R. 642), it now seems to be accepted that only sentences which have been approved on appeal are to be considered in determining what is an acceptable level of sentence for a given case; see *Hayes and Reidy* (1976) 63 Cr. App. R. 292 at 294.

[5] *White* 3.7.72, 1319/C/42; see also *Hughes* 1.11.73, 1187/C/73 (sentence 'beyond the limit of the range of sentences normally imposed').

[6] *Hindle* 1.7.75, 899/A/75 (wounding and cruelty to child). See also *Amjad* 6.12.73, 3926/A/73 (sentence 'outside that bracket and excessive').

Court'[1] or 'out of line with the normal sentence passed for such . . . offences'.[2] In other cases the Court may refer to 'the general level of sentences'[3] or 'the general scale of penalties imposed for offences of this character',[4] or may explain the concept more fully. In *Ladd*[5] the Court observed that 'we have to look at the sentences in relation to the various incidents for which the sentences had to be passed . . . and we have to keep the sentences in perspective with sentences that have been passed on other occasions for offences involving criminal activity of this kind, though, of course, varying in their gravity'.

Whatever terminology is used, the central idea is that within the scope of any legal definition a variety of typical factual situations will recur; with each of these typical factual situations there are associated upper and lower limits within which the sentence should normally fall, in the absence of exceptional circumstances in the offence and without regard to mitigating features peculiar to the offender himself. The difference between the upper and lower limits applicable to a particular typical situation constitutes the 'range', 'bracket', 'normal level' or 'pattern of sentence' for that variation of the offence. A sentence above the upper limit will be described as 'excessive', 'out of scale', 'beyond the range', and is normally reduced. A sentence which is within the limits will not be reduced on the ground of disproportion alone,[6] even though it is marginally more severe than the members of the Court might individually have passed;[7] 'the scales of justice are not calibrated in scruples'.[8]

The concept of the tariff is explored in more detail in the following chapter. One illustration at this point may serve to clarify the

---

[1] *Ryan* 18.6.73, 1074/B/73 (wounding with intent).

[2] *King* (1975) 61 Cr. App. R. 316 (tax fraud).

[3] *Rehman Khan* 23.10.73, 2784/A/73 (fraudulently importing cannabis).

[4] *Andrew* 27.1.75, 2377/B/74 (obtaining by deception, forgery).

[5] 14.10.74, 1260/C/74, [1975] Crim. L. R. 50.

[6] See *Vanger* 31.10.77, 2600/A/77 (theft by employee of £70,000; 'in this sort of situation in which tens of thousands of pounds is being stolen over a period of years, it is clear that there is a bracket of sentencing which varies between five years and three years . . . it was for the trial judge to decide, within the bracket . . . what the appropriate sentence should be').

[7] See *Odeku* 1.11.73, 3615/A/73, where the appellant was sentenced to four years for fraudulently importing cannabis. The Court accepted that the case involved 'a commercial transaction . . . to be differentiated from that category of case where sometimes a man is bringing in a portion of cannabis for his own personal consumption and it is also to be differentiated from the organizers of the trade', and having considered a series of other cases decided in the Court of Appeal involving comparable situations observed that 'although . . . a sentence of four years may at the moment be towards the top end of the level of sentences imposed for this offence, it is not so much outside the [level of] sentences which are imposed that we ought to interfere with it'.

[8] *O'Neill* 5.2.76, 1226/B/75.

argument. In *Mohammed*[1] the appellant was sentenced to five years' imprisonment for living on the earnings of prostitution. The Court observed that 'the range of facts covered by this offence is very wide indeed. At one end of the scale are the cases where men get hold of young adolescent girls and by threats and ill treatment put them on the street as prostitutes. When that kind of case comes before the Court heavy sentences are called for. Another kind of case nearly as bad . . . is where the offender attracts some prostitute to his so-called protection and . . . uses force and ill treatment to keep her under his sway. At the other end of the scale are the cases where the prostitute for her own convenience encourages some man to act as her protector . . . the Court has asked itself whereabouts in the scale of offences this case comes'. As there was no evidence of corruption and the evidence of ill treatment was vague and unsatisfactory, the sentence was too severe and the Court reduced it to two years.

As this case indicates, the tariff for any offence may be seen to consist of two parallel scales—one, a scale of factual situations which are typically encountered within the legal definition of the offence, and the other, a scale of ranges (or brackets) of sentences within which the sentence for a case within the corresponding category of situations will normally be expected to fall, excluding consideration of mitigating factors personal to the offender. The bracket of sentences for a particular type of factual situation will allow the sentencer scope to reflect detailed variations within that category of situation: in the case of living on the earnings of prostitution the sentence imposed in a case whose facts fall within the category defined as the second category in the scale would probably vary according to the degree and nature of the violence and ill treatment used. Despite occasional denials of the existence of such structures or patterns,[2] it may be asserted that they can be readily identified in the

---

[1] (1974) 60 Cr. App. R. 141; see also *Russell* 2.4.74, 5083/C/73 ('the offence of living upon the immoral earnings of prostitution is one that can vary considerably in its gravity. There are those sorts of cases where a man forces a girl on to the streets, where a man exercises pressure and violence to drive her to prostitution and then lives on her earnings—that is one end of the scale—and this case is on the other end of the scale . . . there is no suggestion that he has exerted any pressure or even persuasion upon her'; three years reduced to twelve months).

[2] For example, *Jones* 12.5.75, 318/B/75, [1975] Crim. L. R. 203, where the Court upheld a sentence of twelve years' imprisonment for rape with the comment that 'it would be quite wrong to seek to deduce from the facts of individual cases a "pattern" or what is sometimes called a "tariff" of sentences', but then went on to distinguish between cases 'at the one extreme' involving grave violence and the infliction of varying forms of sexual interference, and cases 'at the other extreme . . . in which a young man may perhaps genuinely for a while have thought that the girl was consenting, and then though she has clearly shown she was not, has gone too far'. The latter comments suggest that the Court was prepared to accept the existence of a tariff as that term has been used in this chapter. For examples of the Court carefully distinguishing specific previous decisions, see *Whitfield* 21.3.72, 760/R/75 (distinguishing *Jones* 3.12.71,

Court's decisions (occasionally the Court is prepared to articulate the scale of ranges for a given offence within the course of a single judgment) and form the basis of the Court's approach to the application of the principle of proportionality.

Fixing the Ceiling

Defining the scale of sentences appropriate to the various versions of a particular offence is primarily the task of the Court of Appeal, although the sentencer in the Crown Court, confronted with a unique case, or the first example of a new variety, must initiate the process, subject to appellate correction. The task of the sentencer in the Crown Court in the more typical case, assuming that a tariff sentence is to be imposed, is to relate the facts of the incident with which he is dealing to the established pattern, determine what sentence would be appropriate for that particular set of facts considered in the abstract and then turn his attention to the question of mitigating circumstances peculiar to the offender.[1] The governing principle is that the gravity of the particular incident in the abstract—the relationship of the facts to the established scale of ranges—determines the upper limit of permissible sentences in that case. The tariff fixes the ceiling; it does not indicate what the final sentence will be. The sentencer may reduce the sentence below the level indicated by the gravity of the facts to reflect the presence of mitigating factors in the offender's character or personal circumstances, but no penal objective—general deterrence, preventive custody of a potentially dangerous offender, the protection of society from a persistent recidivist or the treatment of an offender in prison for his own good—justifies the imposition of a sentence which is disproportionate to the facts of the case in the sense that it exceeds the bracket or range appropriate to that variety of the offence concerned. These propositions represent the balance of authority, but as a small number of departures from them can be found it is necessary to examine them in more detail.

THE EXEMPLARY SENTENCE

It has been argued that the objective of general deterrence may justify the choice of a tariff sentence rather than an individualized measure,

---

5081/R/71, [1971] Crim. L. R. 121); *Grant* 10.2.76, 4149/A/75, [1976] Crim. L. R. 640 (distinguishing *Flack* 19.3.68, 6808/67, [1968] Crim. L. R. 339).

[1] See *Lister* 5.10.72, 787/B/72 ('the proper way of sentencing is to look first at the offence itself and the circumstances in which it was committed, then to assess the proper sentence for the offence on the basis that there are no mitigating circumstances; and finally to look to see what the mitigating circumstances are, if any, to reduce the assessed sentence to give effect to the mitigating circumstances').

and it is argued later that the same objective may justify a sentencer in allowing no weight to mitigating factors which would normally result in a significant reduction in sentence; but general deterrence is not held to justify a sentence which is excessive in relation to the facts of the offence concerned. In so far as the term 'exemplary sentence' forms part of the Court's vocabulary, it refers to a sentence which, to serve the purpose of general deterrence, relates strictly to the facts of the offence and makes no allowance for any mitigating factors.[1]

Many cases can be cited in support of the general proposition that a deterrent sentence must not be disproportionate to the offence for which it is imposed. In *Spalding and King*[2] the appellants were each sentenced to fifteen years' imprisonment for wounding with intent and assault to rob. They admitted attacking an elderly blind man at his home, striking him about the head with a wheelbrace. The Court described the offence as 'so repellent that not even the most gruesome-minded of modern authors would dare to attribute the like to sane persons', but reduced the sentence to ten years in each case as 'grim though the case was', it did not qualify for 'that fifteen-year and upward category of sentence that is reserved for the ultimate in criminality when there are large gangs . . . and great sums involved'. In *Langham*[3] the appellant was sentenced to a total of eight years' imprisonment for offences concerning cannabis resin, LSD and heroin. The Court accepted that the appellant was a trafficker in drugs and the sentencer was justified in imposing a deterrent sentence; however, 'the deterrent element in that sentence was excessive' and the sentence was reduced to five and a half years. In *Ladd and Tristam*[4] the appellants were convicted of conspiracy to trespass and causing damage to property on evidence that they had placed one simulated and two real bombs in different consular offices of a foreign state. The Court stated that causing explosions and perpetrating bomb hoaxes were both grave matters and 'clearly a deterrent element has to be involved'. However, it did not necessarily follow

[1] See *Elvin* 14.11.75, 2591/C/75, [1976] Crim. L. R. 204 (four years for arson of school for boy, 17, minor previous convictions, evidence of similar offences in locality; sentence 'entirely appropriate to the gravity of the crime that they committed, quite apart from the fact that this is the classic situation in which an exemplary sentence to discourage other people from . . . committing a particular form of offence which is at the time rife in the locality is justified').

[2] 16.11.71, 2786/B/71; see also *Skinner and O'Donnell* 29.4.74, 415/A/74, (appellants forced their way into a flat, attacked the occupier and killed his dog by stamping on its head; sentence reduced from six years to four, Court commenting that while 'the circumstances of this case are particularly repellant . . . the Court does . . . have to bear in mind the desirability of keeping sentences in some kind of relation to one another').

[3] 13.3.73, 4675/A/72.

[4] 14.10.74, 1260/C/74, [1975] Crim. L. R. 50; see also *Farrell* 15.12.75, 1410/A/75, [1976] Crim. L. R. 318 (bomb hoax; 'people who commit bomb hoaxes must expect to go to prison' but two years 'an excessive sentence'—reduced to twelve months).

that 'on the particular facts very long sentences of imprisonment are justified'; offences of this kind had 'to be kept in their proper perspective'. The sentences were reduced from seven and six to five and four years respectively.

Many further illustrations of this principle are mentioned in the next chapter. Unambiguous departures are rare, but one example is provided by *Raphael*,[1] where the appellant was sentenced to four years' imprisonment for assault occasioning actual bodily harm to a bus conductor, who was bullied and threatened with a knife but did not receive any serious injury. In the light of an increase in the incidence of similar assaults in the city concerned, the sentence was upheld as being 'undoubtedly severe' but 'designedly passed as an exemplary sentence'. It is submitted that this decision is inconsistent with the general body of the Court's decisions.

THE DANGEROUS OFFENDER

The term 'dangerous offender' describes an offender who appears, on the basis of his immediate offence, his previous history and such psychiatric evidence as may be available, to be highly likely to commit grave offences of violence in the future. Such offenders may be dealt with by means of hospital orders or the indefinite sentence of life imprisonment, if they are eligible under the conditions limiting the use of such sentences, which are properly considered individualized measures and as such are not subject to tariff principles. Where an offender who may be classed as 'dangerous' is dealt with by means of a fixed-term sentence, usually because he does not qualify for one of the special measures, the general principle of proportionality applies and the sentence must not exceed the bracket or range appropriate to the facts of the offence he has committed. *Rose*,[2] cited earlier (p. 10), is a strong example of this principle, as is *Coombs*,[3] where a man of 22 was convicted on an indictment for murder of the manslaughter of a child—the daughter of a woman with whom he was living—and sentenced to fifteen years' imprisonment. The sentencer had taken the view that the nature of the violence used against the child, and medical evidence mentioning personality disorder, justified him in the view that the appellant was 'a very dangerous young man to be loose in society'. Reducing the sentence

[1] 9.6.72, 553/C/72, [1972] Crim. L. R. 648.
[2] 20.12.73, 2281/B/73, [1974] Crim. L. R. 266.
[3] 10.10.72, 627/A/72, [1973] Crim. L. R. 65; see also *Robson* 6.5.74, 5523/B/73, above, p. 32 (five years for attempted indecent assault varied to three; although appellant had previous convictions for offences involving sexual violence and could be considered 'a danger to the public', maximum sentence not warranted for attempted offence).

to ten years, the Court stated that there was no evidence to support the making of a hospital order or to justify the view that he was 'a psychopath of a type which can be dangerous over an indefinite period' (in which case life imprisonment might presumably have been justified), and added that 'the right course . . . was to sentence this man for what he had done and not for what the judge thought he might do in the future'. Similarly in *Barnes*[1] the appellant was sentenced to fifteen years' imprisonment for wounding with intent, having been acquitted of attempted murder. The evidence was that he had twice stabbed a man in the heart during a fight in a public house. The sentencer referred to his 'appalling record of violence' and stated that his duty was to pass a sentence which would ensure 'that for a very long time ahead you have no opportunity of repeating your violence'. Endorsing this statement, the Court added 'nevertheless the question remains . . . whether fifteen years is too long'. Accepting that the sentence should be less than would have been appropriate if the appellant had been convicted of attempted murder, the Court reduced the sentence to ten years.

A decision inconsistent with the general body of cases was reached in *Corner*,[2] where a man of 36 was sentenced to four years' imprisonment for indecently assaulting two 9 year-old boys by touching their buttocks over their football shorts. The Court stated that while these were 'trivial homosexual assaults' there was medical evidence 'that this man might become extremely violent', although he did not qualify for admission to hospital and his offences did not allow the indeterminate sentence of life imprisonment to be imposed. Observing that 'all we can do is to pass a sentence which is not unjustly long but will serve to protect the public longer than a sentence solely passed to meet the gravity of the assault', the Court upheld the sentence, together with a consecutive term for an unrelated offence.

As in the case of deterrence, dangerousness may justify the sentencer in his original choice of a tariff sentence and in ignoring mitigating factors which might otherwise lead to a reduction in sentence. In *Wren*[3] a man of 25 with a substantial record, including indecent assault, pleaded guilty to rape. He had abducted a girl in his car and threatened her with a knife, after purporting to engage her as a babysitter. The Court received reports to the effect that the appellant was emotionally immature and of psychopathic personality, and that his behaviour outside prison was unpredictable. The sentencer referred to 'the very real danger that this man

[1] 6.7.72, 5579/A/71.
[2] 10.12.76, 3665/C/76, [1977] Crim. L. R. 300
[3] 1.2.74, 4701/C/73, [1974] Crim. L. R. 322.

constitutes to other girls' and imposed a sentence of eight years' imprisonment. Upholding this sentence, the Court observed that it was 'a very severe sentence' but 'not out of scale'. In another case[1] the prediction of grave offences in the future was based not on psychiatric evidence but on a political statement by the appellants which the sentencer took as evidence that they were 'declared enemies of society'. The Court stated that where 'the evidence establishes that those who have committed the offences charged are dangerous men . . . the Court has no reason for mitigating the penalties in any way . . . it is no good saying they have no previous convictions or that they are still young men . . . the evidence cancels out such mitigation as there is', but concluded that 'the correct principle . . . is to sentence for the offences charged and on the facts proved or admitted'.

THE SOCIAL NUISANCE

A third category of case in which a sentencer may be tempted to impose a disproportionate sentence is that of the offender who may be classified as a social nuisance. Such an offender, frequently suffering from a mild form of personality disorder with a history of intermittent stays in mental hospitals, will usually have made many demands on social service departments and will generally have proved uncooperative and unresponsive to any assistance offered in the past. In addition to a record of minor criminal offences, there will often be a history of disturbing behaviour such as threatened or attempted suicide. The sentencing problem presented by such an offender is not made easier by the triviality of the offence—such as a minor act of criminal damage—for which sentence is to be imposed. Although the authorities are in conflict, it is submitted that the principle is that in such a case the sentencer is not justified in imposing a disproportionate sentence simply because no other alternative is available. This principle was stated with unusual emphasis in *Clarke*,[2] where a woman of 23 was convicted of damaging a flower pot valued at £1. Having suffered serious illness as a child, the appellant had become promiscuous as a teenager, giving birth to at least two illegitimate children, and had committed a variety of offences which the Court described as 'social nuisances rather than serious crimes'. She had been placed on probation, sentenced to borstal training and subjected to a hospital order on the basis of a diagnosis of psychopathic

[1] *King and Simpkins* (1973) 57 Cr. App. R. 696.
[2] (1975) 61 Cr. App. R. 320; see also *Nelson* 18.7.72, 1305/C/72 (three years for smashing window reduced to three months: 'we have not got to the stage . . . where people are locked up merely because they are nuisances . . . they are locked up for the offences which they have committed').

disorder. Having secured her release, she became involved in several disturbances, in the course of one of which she deliberately broke a flower pot. She was subsequently convicted of causing criminal damage and, after an unsuccessful search for a suitable psychiatric disposal, sentenced to eighteen months' imprisonment. The Court stated that the case disclosed that the welfare system made no provision for a person who 'does not require treatment . . . but who cannot live in the community without disturbing others and being a source of danger to herself', but that 'this Court has no intention of filling that gap by sending people to prison when a prison sentence is wholly inappropriate'. The sentence was varied to a fine of £2.

This decision has been endorsed in several subsequent cases.[1] In *Watson*[2] the appellant was sentenced to two years' imprisonment for obtaining a meal valued at 50p by criminal deception, having ordered a meal in a café without the means to repay. In addition to a record of minor offences and periods in mental hospitals, there was a history of 'bizarre behaviour'— throwing things from the balcony of his tenth-floor flat, dressing in women's clothes and minor acts of violence. Efforts by social workers and probation officers to assist had proved 'abortive'. Medical evidence before the sentencer was that although the appellant was probably not suffering from any mental illness, he could not be managed in a non-custodial setting. Referring to the judgment in *Clarke*, the Court stated that 'he is a social nuisance undoubtedly but this Court feels that the sentence for two years cannot possibly stand' and quashed the sentence, having heard that 'suitable arrangements can be made'.

In surprising contrast to these cases is *Arrowsmith*,[3] where an 'inadequate, dangerous, out-of-hand young woman' was sentenced to three years' imprisonment for causing damage amounting to £18 to a flat by flooding it. Her one previous conviction was for throwing a milk bottle through a window, but she had 'a long history of disturbed behaviour' and had experienced care orders and various forms of institutional life. The Court accepted that the sentence was disproportionate, but stated that 'the importance of protecting the public from her and the importance of seeking to alleviate her own condition outweigh any criticism that three years is too long for the offence of which she was guilty.' The sentence was upheld. This case, which is not entirely unprecedented,[4] appears to be irreconcilable

---

[1] For example, *Eaton* 31.7.75, 3182/R/75, [1976] Crim. L. R. 390.
[2] 17.10.75, 1403/A/75.
[3] 2.3.76, 3460/C/75, [1976] Crim. L. R. 636.
[4] See *Horsborough* 30.6.72, 6236/C/71, (man, 59, many previous convictions, three years for throwing a bottle through a plate glass window, causing £60 worth of damage, described as 'an inadequate personality' and 'a confirmed alcoholic', thought unlikely to co-operate with attempts at treatment, no hospital would accept him; Court

with *Clarke* and the cases following *Clarke*, and it must be conceded that there is a conflict in the authorities: it is submitted that the principle in *Clarke* is to be preferred.

THE PERSISTENT OFFENDER

Distinguishable from the previous category of offender is the persistent offender, who over the years has committed a large number of offences, usually not of the highest degree of gravity. It has already been argued that individualized measures will frequently be employed in dealing with offenders in this category. Where confinement is inevitable the sentencer may have the choice between an extended sentence and an ordinary term of imprisonment. The extended sentence is properly classed as an individualized measure and is discussed separately in chapter 8: it is not subject to the governing principle of proportionality of sentence and offence when used as a preventive measure. If the sentencer imposes an ordinary term of imprisonment on an offender with a substantial record, either by choice or because the complex statutory qualifications for an extended sentence are not satisfied, he must observe the ceiling determined by the gravity of the immediate offence. Good character is a substantial mitigating factor which will normally justify a reduction in sentence below the ceiling, and a modest criminal record may leave some room for mitigating effect; but a long record of previous convictions will not justify the imposition of a term of imprisonment in excess of the permissible ceiling for facts of the immediate offence.

This principle has been stated many times and has been recognized by the House of Lords.[1] Many illustrations of its application can be found. In *Marro*[2] a man in his fifties, with many previous convictions

upheld the sentence, accepting that it 'might seem excessive for a comparatively trivial offence . . . but it is right from the appellant's view as offering . . . the best . . . prospect of successful treatment . . . it is also right from the point of view of the public'); see also *Jenkins* 7.3.75, 3910/C/74 (woman, 39, five years for throwing stone through window of bank immediately after release from police station, following violent incident at hospital, long history of minor dishonesty and violence, psychopathic disorder but not suffering from 'dangerous or violent criminal propensities', not suitable either for special or ordinary mental hospital; 'no sentence for a comparatively trivial offence of this kind which involves any substantial term of imprisonment can . . . be related to the gravity of the offence . . . in dealing with an exceptional case of this kind the Court is dealing with the matter more as a precaution for the appellant herself as well as for the public generally', but sentence reduced to two years).

[1] In *D.P.P. v. Ottewell* (1968) 52 Cr. App. R. 679.

[2] 7.10.74, 1402/B/74; see also *Lister* 5.10.72, 787/B/72 (six years' imprisonment on persistent offender for shoplifting property worth £21, fifteen offences, considered 'wholly inappropriate . . . it is manifest that this man was sentenced on his record'; varied to two years); *Thwaites* 25.10.73, 3503/C/73 (four years for theft of suitcase reduced to two: 'it is not right that a court passing a sentence of imprisonment should,

and 'innumerable' sentences of imprisonment, was sentenced to seven years' imprisonment for obtaining and attempting to obtain money by deception—he had obtained various relatively small sums from Chinese restaurant proprietors by pretending to be a collector from the Inland Revenue. Accepting that the appellant was 'a man for whom nothing can be said in mitigation', the Court stated that 'when there is a man in front of the court with a dreadful record, it is imperative, if justice is to be done and to be felt to be done, that he should be sentenced not on his record but on the offences which have brought him to the court'. Accepting 'the need for the public to be protected' and the fact that the offences were serious, 'when one analyses them against the calendar of offences that come before the Crown Court and this Court on appeal, these are not offences which merit seven years' imprisonment'. The Court substituted a term of three years. The principle does not operate only against long sentences; in *Mills*[1] a man of 56 with eighteen previous convictions was sentenced to eighteen months' imprisonment for breaking a glass panel in the door of a cafe. Reducing the sentence to twelve months, the Court stated that while 'a man's record has to be taken into account in imposing sentence, it is always necessary that the sentence should not be excessive in relation to the actual offence committed'. Similarly in *Hyde*[2] a man of 28 years was sentenced to two years' imprisonment for stealing a suit from a shop. Observing that the sentencer had 'paid very great regard to this man's criminal record', the Court reduced the sentence to twelve months with the comment that 'it is an important principle of sentencing that . . . a man should be punished according to the gravity of the offence . . . whereas personal circumstances can be used to mitigate, they ought only in the rarest possible cases be used to increase the penalty . . . Parliament itself has indicated the sort of circumstances in which an extended term of imprisonment may be given'.

---

out of regard for the accused's record and a desire to protect the public, pass a sentence which bears no relation to the particular offence for which he is being sentenced').

[1] 24.5.73, 6436/B/72; see also *Williams* 9.12.76, 1059/A/76 (man, 40, 'in and out of prison time and time again', five years for obtaining pecuniary advantage from hotel 'wrong': 'the fundamentals of sentencing policy are that a man must be sentenced for the offence he has committed and not for his record . . . his conduct merited, apart from his record, a sentence of . . . two years at the most . . . it would be difficult for this Court to find any mitigation on a sentence of that length'; sentence reduced to twenty-one months).

[2] 1.3.73, 3454/A/72; see also *Kesson* 20.11.73, 3848/C/73 (man, 42, thirty-two previous convictions, 'spent more years in prison than the average life sentence'; thirty months for stealing two dresses worth £18 from shop 'out of scale'—reduced to fifteen months); *Croucher* 15.9.76, 1756/B/76 (eighteen months for taking conveyance excessive: 'the Court . . . does not sentence on the accused's record, it sentences for the offence. The existence of the record may make it difficult to find any mitigating circumstances'; sentence reduced).

The cases cited are typical of very many other decisions and clearly illustrate the principle followed in the overwhelming majority of cases in which the issue arises. Despite the emphasis with which the principle is stated in many cases, occasional departures can be found. In *Dunn*[1] a man of 26, with a record of offences dating from his childhood, was convicted of threatening to damage property as a result of giving a false bomb alarm which caused a building to be evacuated. In view of his record of giving false alarms and writing threatening letters, and the evidence that a non-custodial measure could not be made to work, the sentencer imposed a sentence of five years' imprisonment 'not as a punishment' but as 'a sentence that takes you out of circulation'. The Court dismissed the appeal with the comment that the sentencer had taken ' a humane and proper course'. While a tariff sentence will normally be upheld for perpetrating a bomb hoax, the sentence appears to be well above the appropriate bracket[2] and this decision appears to represent a clear departure from the general principle.[3]

The requirement that the sentence should be in proportion to the offence for which it is imposed does not mean that the sentencer must wholly exclude considerations of preventive confinement when determining the length of a sentence, but merely that such considerations do not justify a sentence which is above the range for the offence concerned. So long as the sentence is within the ceiling established by the gravity of the facts, the sentencer may properly give greater weight to the protection of the public against further offences by the offender than to any prospect of rehabilitation through the use of an individualized measure. In *Mikellides*[4] the appellant, sentenced to a total of six years' imprisonment for a series of frauds involving property worth more than £3,000, had a long series of convictions for dishonesty and had served two substantial sentences: his present offences showed that he was 'not just a petty thief but a man who indulges in crime in quite a substantial way'. Despite a social inquiry report which suggested that 'this man has really touched rock bottom' and there was some prospect of a change in his behaviour, the Court stated that 'the preponderant concern is the protection of the public against the depradations of this man' and upheld the sentence. The Court appears to have considered the sentence to be

---

[1] 8.5.75, 5187/C/74.

[2] Compare *Bikram* 16.7.73, 1704/C/73, [1974] Crim. L. R. 55; *Farrell* 15.12.75, 1410/A/75, [1976] Crim. L. R. 318.

[3] See also *Gilmour* 12.10.70, 3024/C/70 (persistent offender; four years for stealing transistor radio upheld in view of Court's 'duty to protect the public'); *Sparrow* 15.1.71, 3980/C/70 (three years for stealing property worth £10 not 'in any way excessive . . . having regard to that record').

[4] 28.11.75, 2098/A/75.

within the permissible limits for the offence, and thus the case does not represent a departure from the general principle. Similarly the need to prevent further offences may justify the sentencer in ignoring any mitigating factors which may be present (although frequently they will be scarce) and imposing the full sentence justified by the facts of the offence. In *Bainbridge*[1] a man of 34 with eleven previous convictions for offences of dishonesty admitted six thefts, some committed while he was on bail awaiting trial for the others. The Court heard that the offences were committed during a period of depression but stated that 'the public interest requires that the appellant should be kept out of harm's way for a considerable period' and that this consideration 'outweighs the sympathy we feel for the appellant, who has had an unhappy life'. Observing that his sentence of two years was 'not an unreasonable sentence in the circumstances of the case', the Court dismissed the appeal.

OFFENDERS LIKELY TO BENEFIT FROM TREATMENT IN PRISON

A sentencer may be confronted with an offender who is thought likely to derive some specific benefit from imprisonment which would not be available under any other form of disposition open to the court; the most typical examples are alcoholics and drug users who have experienced difficulty in overcoming their addiction while at liberty. How far is the sentencer justified in imposing a disproportionate sentence in order to provide a sufficient period of time for the appropriate treatment to take place?

The balance of authority clearly favours the view that the same principle applies in this context as in the other contexts just discussed—the sentencer may impose imprisonment rather than an individualized measure in order to provide an opportunity for treatment, and he may ignore mitigating factors in determining the length of the sentence so as to ensure that the period of confinement is sufficiently long for treatment to take place, but he may not pass a sentence which is disproportionate to the facts of the offence. A clear statement and illustration of this principle is found in *Wilding*.[2] The appellant, who admitted taking a vehicle and possession of a controlled drug, was sentenced to three years' imprisonment, apparently as a result of a medical report relating to his involvement with drugs. The sentence included two years for taking the vehicle. Having referred to earlier decisions on the question whether an excessive sentence was permissible in such cases in the offender's own

[1] 11.10.73, 1715/C/73.
[2] 15.1.74, 4508/A/73.

interests,[1] the Court stated the issue in these terms: 'with his background of drug addiction, is two years within the normal sentencing bracket for the offence in the circumstances in which it was committed in this case? If it is, then . . . the sentence imposed would not be an infringement of sentencing principles . . . but if two years is wrong in principle for this offence . . . then the court has added to what should be the proper sentence an element in the interests of the appellant . . . which was not proper to add'. The sentence for taking a vehicle was 'outside the proper range' and was reduced to twelve months, leaving a total sentence of two years. Similarly in *Janes*[2] a young man with 'a long history of taking drugs' was sentenced to eighteen months' imprisonment for stealing £1 from his mother's gas meter, having previously broken a probation order made for the same offence. Reducing the sentence to nine months, the Court stated that the sentencer 'thought he was imposing a constructive sentence' that 'would help in regard to this man's underlying drug problem', but the principle was that 'where a man is before the Court on a relatively minor offence of dishonesty, it is not right to impose a sentence excessive for that offence, merely because it may have some side-effects on his medical or mental condition'. Similar statements can be found in other cases.[3]

A number of other decisions appear to reflect a contradictory principle. In *Whittaker*[4] a 'chronic alcoholic' was sentenced to two years' imprisonment for assaults on police officers. The Court observed that 'there may be some grounds for saying that two years was excessive in this case' but as the appellant had been selected for psychiatric treatment at Grendon Underwood Prison the Court would not interfere, in the hope that the appellant would 'come out of prison and lead a normal life'. In *Duke*[5] a woman of 23 was sentenced

[1] *Ford* (1969) 53 Cr. App. R. 551; *Moylan* (1969) 53 Cr. App. R. 590.

[2] 23.11.72, 469/B/72. See also *Goodall* 22.4.77, 5638/B/76 ('it was wrong . . . to sentence him so that he might be weaned from his addiction to drugs: he has to be sentenced for these offences').

[3] For example, *Grimes* 14.11.74, 2420/C/74 (three years for various drug offences; sentencer acting 'not by reference to what the proper sentence was for the offences as such but what he thought the proper period of incarceration should be to enable the authorities to treat this appellant for drug addiction . . . if his drug addiction can be treated in prison so much the better, but it is not right to pass a longer sentence because such a longer sentence might enable the drug addiction to be treated'—sentence reduced to eighteen months); *Lightbody* 7.12.71, 2285/A/71 (twenty-one months for burglary of canteen and theft of property worth £22 reduced to twelve, as 'this sentence . . . was imposed for curative purposes and was excessive in relation to the actual offence').

[4] 29.1.71, 3486/B/70.

[5] 1.3.71, 6637/C/70; see also *Eslick* 18.10.71, 1764/R/71, where the Court, dealing with a hospital order on a man convicted of stealing £2 from a hotel, stated *obiter* 'a Court has the power to pass even a substantial term of a custodial kind where it would be best for an accused, for example a drug addict, who might well receive benefit from treatment in prison', and added that the sentencer in the Court below had 'mistakenly

to thirty months' imprisonment for stealing a cheque book and obtaining a bottle of whisky four years previously.[1] In view of evidence that she had been addicted to drugs for several years, the Court took the view that imprisonment was 'the only course' and that 'a fairly long sentence . . . is in this woman's best interest'. The sentence was upheld.

While *Whittaker* may be a weak example, as the Court did not commit itself firmly to the view that the sentence was excessive on the facts, these decisions do suggest that there is some uncertainty about the existence of an exception to the general principle that a disproportionate sentence may not be imposed to provide a basis for treatment. The existence of such an exception, allowing a disproportionate sentence in cases of drug addiction but not alcoholism, would be consistent with earlier decisions such as *Ford*.[2] It is not supported by *Whittaker*, which involved alcoholism rather than drug addiction, a condition which was held in *Ford* not to justify a disproportionate sentence. Later cases such as *Wilding* and *Janes*, both of which involved drug addiction, appear to contradict the existence of such an exception, and as in *Wilding* at least the Court considered itself to be applying the principles expressed in *Ford*, it may be safe to conclude that those decisions represent the current view of the Court and that the correct principle is now that the fact that the offender is a drug addict does not justify the sentencer in imposing a sentence which is out of proportion to his offence in order that he may undergo treatment in prison.

The Effect of Mitigation

The final step in the process of calculating the length of a tariff sentence is to make allowance for mitigation, reducing the sentence from the level indicated by the facts of the offence by an amount appropriate to reflect such mitigating factors as may be present. Mitigating factors exist in great variety, but some are more common and more effective than others. They include such matters as the youth and previous character of the offender, the pressures under

---

thought that it would not be in order, having regard to the comparative triviality of the present offence, to impose a substantial term of imprisonment'; *Riley* 1.3.74, 5474/A/73, where the Court varied a sentence of life imprisonment to three years, observing that if there had been 'no mental element involved', the sentence would probably have been 'of the order of eighteen months to two years'.

[1] She had been subject to a series of fresh probation orders made in respect of the original offences as a result of failing to comply with the requirements of residence and notification of change of address.

[2] (1969) 53 Cr. App. R. 551; see also *Glasse* (1968) 53 Cr. App. R. 121, and *Simone* 14.3.68, 5326/67.

which he committed the offence and the incidental losses which he has suffered or will suffer as a result of his conviction. They are not limited to matters connected with the offence, as the court may take into account creditable conduct on the part of the offender which is wholly unrelated to the incident which has brought him before the court.

A detailed analysis of the significance of the factors most. commonly encountered is attempted in chapter 4. At this point it is sufficient to mention the general principle that credit for mitigating factors is not an entitlement of the offender, as the sentencer is permitted to refrain from making an allowance for mitigating factors in order to achieve a recognized penal objective, such as general deterrence, the prevention of further offences for the duration of the sentence or the provision of appropriate treatment for the offender. As has been argued, these considerations are not normally held to justify a sentence which is disproportionate to the immediate offence, but they may justify the sentencer in ignoring mitigating factors and giving no credit for them.[1] The effect of the principle allowing the sentencer to disregard mitigating factors in order to emphasize general deterrence or to achieve some other penal objective is most clearly seen where a number of offenders with different histories are involved together in an offence of substantial gravity. The principle allows the sentencer to refrain from making distinctions between the offenders on the basis of their individual records and circumstances, but distinctions should still be made to reflect different degrees of responsibility in the commission of the offence. The point is illustrated by *Turner and others*,[2] where a large number of appellants were sentenced to long terms of imprisonment for participating in a series of armed bank robberies. The Court declined to take account of variations in record which would normally be a basis for distinguishing between different participants—'the fact that a man has not much of a criminal record, if any at all, is not a powerful factor to be taken into consideration when the Court is dealing with offences of this gravity', but made reductions in some of the sentences to reflect variations in the degree of involvement and responsibility.

Where there is no specific justification for withholding credit for mitigating factors the sentencer will normally be expected to make an appropriate reduction. Denying credit for mitigation. is an exceptional course limited to cases where a particular emphasis on

[1] See, for example, *Bradley* 14.10.69, 3275/69, [1970] Crim. L. R. 171 (baggage master at London Airport conspiring to receive foreign currency stolen while in transit: 'a deterrent sentence was called for, and when a court finds that its duty is to pass a deterrent sentence, considerations of the particular prisoner's past good character . . . are of much less moment than normally would be the case'); see also *Inwood* (1974) 60 Cr. App. R. 70, p. 198 below.
[2] (1975) 61 Cr. App. R. 67 at 91.

deterrence is justified, or where considerations such as the prevention of further offences are unusually compelling. In what may be considered the general run of cases a sentence which fails to reflect the presence of recognized mitigating factors will be reduced on appeal.

Secondary Tariff Principles

THE EFFECT OF REMISSION AND PAROLE

The imposition of a sentence of imprisonment for a specified period does not mean that the offender will necessarily be confined for that length of time. The sentence passed by the court will be treated as reduced by any period spent in custody under the order of any court in the course of proceedings relating to the offence for which the sentence is imposed,[1] and one-third of the nominal term will be remitted unless the offender suffers loss of remission as a disciplinary sanction in prison.[2] Additionally, after serving one-third of the sentence the offender will be eligible for release on licence on the recommendation of the Parole Board, provided that he has served at least twelve months.[3] Release on licence is discretionary; if the offender is released he remains on licence and subject to recall until the time when he would, apart from his release on licence, have been released from the sentence with remission. Offenders under 21 when sentenced and offenders subject to an extended-sentence certificate may be detained for the whole nominal period of the sentence, and if released on licence, may be subjected to the licence and the possibility of recall for the whole of that period.[4]

The general principle is that in determining the length of a fixed-term sentence of imprisonment, the sentencer should not have regard to remission[5] or the possibility of release on licence.[6] The only

[1] Criminal Justice Act 1967 s. 67. This provision does not apply to periods of custody abroad in connection with extradition proceedings (see *Bennet* 4.2.75, 3837/B/74, [1975] Crim. L. R. 654), nor to custody prior to the imposition of a non-custodial sentence or suspended sentence. Where an offender has spent a significiant period in custody and then receives a suspended sentence, the sentencer should reflect the period already spent in custody in the length of the suspended sentence; see *Pollitt* 13.4.70, 6661/69; *Deering* 10.2.76, 3218/A/75, [1976] Crim. L. R. 638, p. 251 below.

[2] See Prison Rules 1964, r. 5 (as amended).

[3] Criminal Justice Act 1967 s. 60. For a detailed analysis of the effect of these provisions, see Zellick, *Calculating the Parole Eligibility Date* [1976] Crim. L. R. 241.

[4] Criminal Justice Act 1967 s. 60 (3).

[5] *Maguire and Enos* (1956) 40 Cr. App. R. 92, followed in *Jarrett* 25.9.73, 2092/C/73 (wrong to calculate sentence by determining minimum period to be served after allowing for remission and adding appropriate period to ensure minimum would be served; explanatory reference to effect of remission not necessarily fatal, but better course to leave explanation to defendant's legal advisors or prison authorities).

[6] See *Black* 13.11.70, 631/B/70, [1971] Crim. L. R. 109.

exception appears to be that the sentencer may consider the effect of normal remission when determining the length of a sentence imposed with the object of providing treatment for the offenders,[1] so long as the nominal sentence is not disproportionate to the offence for which it was imposed.[2]

An illustration of these principles is provided by *Peace and Penwill*,[3] where the appellants were sentenced to terms totalling three years' imprisonment for burglary and possession of controlled drugs. The Court stated that the sentences as passed were not excessive in relation to the offences, and the appellants had no cause for complaint on the ground of disproportion. However, the sentencer had calculated the sentence on the basis that the appellants should spend at least twelve months in custody in order to receive treatment in connection with drug taking and had allowed for the possibility of their release on parole. This approach was incorrect: the sentencer should have disregarded the possibility of parole but was entitled to bear in mind that the appellants would almost certainly become entitled to remission. The correct sentence to reflect the sentencer's intentions was eighteen months, and the sentences were reduced to this total.

The principle that the sentencer should disregard the possibility of parole when deciding the length of a sentence does not mean that he should pretend that it does not exist, or that a reference to the possibility of parole when passing sentence will inevitably lead to the sentence being quashed on appeal. So long as the sentence is justifiable without reference to the possibility of parole, it is not necessarily improper to mention the possibility of parole to 'give . . . a ray of light' to the offender,[4] although such references are best avoided as a general rule.[5]

---

[1] *Turner* (1966) 51 Cr. App. R. 72.

[2] This conclusion follows from the cases cited previously, and neither the facts nor the Court's observations in *Turner* are inconsistent with it.

[3] 4.11.74, 2851/A/74; see also *Gisbourne* 14.3.77, 3501/B/76 (youth, 20, sentenced to three and a half years' imprisonment, judge expressing wish 'to benefit this appellant by giving him the opportunity of the support of the probation service when he was released on parole'; this approach 'erroneous': 'the correct course for the judge was to pass a sentence which he thought appropriate for the offence, not to concern himself . . . with the possible question of parole').

[4] *Black* 13.11.70, 631/B/70, [1971] Crim. L. R. 109; see also *Biggs* 27.6.74, 969/C/74 (youth, 17, long record of institutional confinement, seven years' imprisonment for 'as grave an offence of arson as it is possible to conceive'; Court considered sentence 'in no way wrong in principle' and had the advantage of 'preserving the maximum degree of flexibility for the future'); *Lowry* 15.11.74, 756/A/74 ('the granting of parole has nothing whatsoever to do with this Court . . . it may be that at an early date favourable consideration may possibly be given to an application by him for parole . . . all this Court can say is that this sentence was . . . the proper sentence').

[5] *Glease* 9.12.77, [1978] Crim. L. R. 372.

THE RELEVANCE OF THE OFFENDER'S CONDUCT DURING THE PROCEEDINGS

The principles governing the extent to which a sentencer may take into account the offender's behaviour during the course of the proceedings against him are well settled. A plea of guilty may properly be treated as a mitigating factor, indicating remorse, and will justify a reduction in the sentence below the level appropriate to the facts of the offence; but the defendant who contests the case against him, while not entitled to that mitigation, may not be penalized for the manner in which his defence has been conducted by the imposition of a sentence above the ceiling fixed by the gravity of the offence. Upholding a sentence on an appellant whose co-defendant had been sentenced less severely, the Court stated that 'there is no suggestion that the judge was imposing on this appellant, because he had contested his guilt, anything beyond what was the full, appropriate sentence for the offences of which he was convicted; but there is no doubt at all that he was entitled to give very substantial weight in the scale to [the co-defendant's] plea of guilty which has saved any trial . . . and which demonstrated, as plainly as anything could, his remorse and regret for what he had done'.[1] Many similar statements can be found; the Court has frequently stated that 'it is not right to impose a heavier sentence because a person exercises his right to plead not guilty and require the prosecution to prove the charge',[2] but that 'it is a well recognized practice of the courts wherever possible to give some degree of credit in the case of somebody who pleads guilty'.[3]

Where a sentencer reacts to the manner in which the defence has been conducted by imposing a sentence in excess of what the facts of the offence warrant, the Court will normally reduce the sentence. In Martin[4] the appellant was sentenced to three months' imprisonment for driving with a blood alcohol content slightly in excess of the permitted limit. At his trial he denied that he had been the driver of the vehicle concerned. Quashing the sentence the Court stated that 'if he was rightly convicted he lied to the police and the court which

---

[1] *Hickman* 20.11.75, 1875/B/75; see also *Cugullere* 25.10.71, 661/C/71 ('he could not pray in aid in mitigation a plea of guilty because he fought the case tooth and nail . . . that, of course, is no ground for increasing the sentence but it deprived him of what was really about the only form of mitigation that was open to him'); *Daisley* 6.10.72, 5207/B/71 (co-defendant 'could reasonably expect some degree of discount for the fact that he pleaded guilty. One who does not plead guilty can only expect to have the full sentence appropriate to that class of case').

[2] *Lee* 22.1.73, 6303/C/72.

[3] *Bhatti, Bhatti and Gill* 6.5.74, 901/C/74.

[4] 1.8.73, 780/C/73.

convicted him . . . this is a reason for not being especially lenient or merciful, and it might even be a reason for proceeding against him for perjury . . . but it is not a good reason for sending him to prison where the other circumstances of the case did not warrant such punishment'. In a case where the sentencer, imposing nine months' imprisonment for a similar offence, referred to the appellant's 'perjury in the witness box' as a factor which 'aggravates the offence', the Court quashed the sentence with the comment that 'it is now a well established principle . . . that behaviour of a defendant . . . such as attacking a prosecution witness's character or giving evidence which is or may amount to perjury is not a basis upon which what would otherwise be an appropriate sentence may be increased'.[1] The same principle applies to other aspects of the conduct of the defence, such as a refusal of consent to summary trial in a case which might otherwise have conveniently been tried in the magistrate's court,[2] and discourteous behaviour towards the court.[3]

It is not possible to identify any scale establishing the precise extent to which a sentence may be reduced to reflect the presence of a plea of guilty, as frequently the plea will be one of a number of factors advanced as reasons for a reduction, and its main effect may be to enhance the influence of other factors rather than as an independent consideration.[4] In a number of cases the Court has reduced a sentence, or justified a differential between sentences imposed on co-defendants, by reference only to a guilty plea, and these cases give an indication of the scale of reduction which may properly be made. In

---

[1] *Cash* 25.5.73, 1398/A/73; see also *Khaliq* 6.12.73, 1527/A/73 (sentencer not to 'sentence for a lying, disgraceful defence which has been put forward but for the crime which has been committed').

[2] See *Jamieson* (1975) 60 Cr. App. R. 318 (fine of £300 for stealing half bottle of whisky worth £1.55 varied to conditional discharge: 'a man should not be sentenced more heavily merely because he exercises his right to trial by jury . . . it does not accord with justice . . . that a man should run any risk of heavier penalty in such circumstances, if the offence does not warrant the sentence passed'). For the application of this principle to orders relating to costs, see p. 340 below.

[3] See *Ford* 5.2.74, 4771/C/73 (late arrival at court irrelevant). For stronger examples, see *Jacka* 6.10.66, 2304/66, [1966] Crim. L. R. 692; *Aston* [1948] W. N. 252. In a case of grave misconduct in the face of the Court, the proper course is to pass a separate sentence for contempt, which may be consecutive to the principal sentence. See *Greenberg* 8.4.74, 4578/R/73; *Aquarius* (1974) 59 Cr. App. R. 165.

[4] See *McAleny and Griffiths* 5.12.75, 965/B/75 ('a plea of guilty is the best demonstration that a guilty man can give . . . of his genuine remorse . . . a plea of guilty is for that reason of itself a very substantial mitigating factor, but of course it goes beyond that, because the very act of pleading guilty gives to a guilty man the opportunity to bring to the court whatever other mitigating factors there may be'); see also *Burke* 1.2.74, 33/C/74 (six months for student, two previous convictions, not inappropriate or excessive for shoplifting; interruption of studies and damage to career regrettable, but 'difficult to suspend a sentence . . . when the accused has elected trial and given evidence denying the offence, which has been rejected by the jury'—sentence reduced 'in mercy').

one example[1] a first offender was sentenced after a contested trial to four years' imprisonment for his part in a substantial fraud involving large numbers of stolen traveller's cheques; co-defendants whose responsibility and previous histories were similar received three years on their pleas of guilty. The Court justified this distinction as 'a discount on a sentence on account of a guilty plea', which was 'well established' as a 'perfectly proper approach to sentencing'. In another case[2] the appellant was sentenced to seven years' imprisonment for a large number of thefts of company funds involving over £250,000. The Court stated that 'if the case had been fought, the sentences could not have been interfered with by this Court', but added that 'these sentences, though not above the tariff for frauds of this magnitude, did not take sufficient account of the fact that the appellant had pleaded guilty' and 'for this reason only' reduced the sentence to five years. In a third example[3] three appellants were sentenced to varying terms for handling stolen property, following their convictions by the jury. One complained that his sentence of five years was excessive by comparison with that of a fourth co-defendant, who was described as 'the brains behind this criminal enterprise' but received only three and half years' imprisonment. Justifying this differential the Court stated that 'it has long been a principle in our courts that the man who pleads guilty can expect less severe punishment than one who pleads not guilty', and that in the case of the appellant the sentencer 'was not adding, he was just not taking off'. These cases suggest that a bare plea of guilty, without any further mitigation, may justify a reduction in sentence of between one-quarter and one-third of the net figure established by reference to the facts of the offence. The cases do not suggest that it is proper to reflect a plea of guilty by anything other than a reduction in the *quantum* of the sentence; a bare plea of guilty would not (it is submitted) justify suspension of a sentence which would otherwise be immediate.

Concurrent and Consecutive Sentences

The question whether sentences of imprisonment should be ordered to run concurrently or consecutively arises in a variety of different ways. The offender may be convicted of several counts in the same indictment, or of several offences charged in different indictments; he may already be serving a term of imprisonment with a substantial

[1] *Drummond* 4.7.72, 2556/C/71.
[2] *House* 18.1.74, 1186/C/73; see also *Downs* 10.5.76, 5595/C/75 (eight years for rape 'does not reflect the mitigation to which he can reasonably lay claim for his plea of guilty'—reduced to six years).
[3] *Gomez, Cooper and Bovington* 5.10.72, 5238/B/71.

unexpired portion, or have received such a sentence from another court in the recent past. The sentencer may have to consider the enforcement of a suspended sentence or to deal with the offender in respect of earlier offences for which he was subjected to probation or conditional discharge. In all of these cases the sentencer has power to order any sentences of imprisonment which he may impose to run consecutively with each other or concurrently, although he may not antedate the commencement of a sentence.[1] The power to order sentences to run consecutively is subject to two major limiting principles, which may be called the 'one-transaction rule' and the 'totality principle'. A number of detailed rules relating to particular questions have also developed.

THE ONE-TRANSACTION RULE

The one-transaction rule can be stated simply: where two or more offences are committed in the course of a single transaction, all sentences in respect of these offences should be concurrent rather than consecutive. Difficulty lies in establishing a sufficiently precise definition of the concept of a single transaction. Apart from occasional inconsistencies on specific applications,[2] the Court sometimes upholds consecutive sentences which appear to offend the concept, on the ground that the totality of the sentence is correct and that no purpose would be served in making a formal variation which would leave the effective sentence unchanged, and from time to time varies a sentence with a reference to the single-transaction principle when that principle does not appear to have been infringed and the real ground of the reduction is that the totality of sentence is excessive. For these reasons the exact limits of the concept are difficult to identify.

The essence of the one-transaction rule appears to be that consecutive sentences are inappropriate when all the offences taken together constitute a single invasion of the same legally protected interest. The principle applies where two or more offences arise from the facts—as when the same series of blows constitutes assault occasioning actual bodily harm and wilful ill treatment of a child,[3] or malicious wounding and indecent assault[4]—but the fact that the two

[1] See *Gilbert* (1974) 60 Cr. App. R. 220.
[2] See below, p. 55.
[3] See *Cripps* 19.12.75, 4579/B/75; see also *Parker* 11.10.73, 3736/B/73 (maliciously inflicting grievous bodily harm and assaulting police officer in execution of duty, single attack on one victim; consecutive sentences 'wrong in principle').
[4] See *Giffin* 8.7.74, 1447/B/74 (single attack, violent and indecent; 'really one incident . . . even though it may constitute a breach of the criminal law in a variety of ways'); see also *Turpin* 28.6.71, 392/71. In *Howard* 5.6.75, 683/B/75 it was held that two

offences are committed simultaneously or close together in time does not necessarily mean that they amount to a single transaction. Consecutive sentences have been upheld for taking a vehicle without consent and driving it dangerously,[1] and for driving with an excess blood alcohol level and attempting to bribe a police officer to refrain from administering a breath test.[2]

The concept of 'single transaction' may be held to cover a sequence of offences involving a repetition of the same behaviour towards the same victim, such as a series of sexual offences with the same partner,[3] a number of frauds on the same victim[4] or several perjured statements made in the course of the same trial,[5] provided the offences are committed within a relatively short space of time.[6] The concept will not normally apply to a series of similar offences involving different victims, even though the offences are of a similar character. In *Birch*[7] the appellant was convicted of three offences of indecent assault and two of assault occasioning actual bodily harm on evidence that he had indecently accosted three women on different occasions, using violence towards two of them. The Court considered that the sentences for the offences of assault occasioning actual bodily harm should be concurrent with the sentences of indecent assault affecting the same victim, as each incident was properly considered to form one transaction: however, the combined sentences arising from each incident were properly made consecutive with each other, as the three incidents were separate.

The application of the principle can be traced in relation to a number of recurring situations. Burglary accompanied by violence towards the occupier of the premises does not form a single

---

separate attacks on the same woman within a short space of time, one indecent and the other violent, did not form part of the same incident.

[1] *Newbury* 21.1.75, 4205/C/74, [1975] Crim. L. R. 295 (taking vehicle and almost immediately afterwards driving dangerously 'entirely separate offences . . . a consecutive sentence is right'); see also *Howison* 12.3.74, 5046/C/73; *Fogarty* 5.5.75, 4953/B/74.

[2] *Whitcomb* 30.10.73, 3119/B/73 (individual sentences of eighteen months and two years each excessive, but properly consecutive; reduced to six months and six months consecutive).

[3] See *Lewis* 3.7.72, 5944/A/71 (sentences for buggery and indecent assault on same boy, 'all acts under the same association and within the same period', properly concurrent).

[4] See *Paddon* 3.3.71, 5740/B/70.

[5] See *Gordon* 29.3.71, 5282/A/70, where consecutive sentences were upheld, despite being considered to form part of one transaction.

[6] See *Randall* 15.5.73, 1035/A/73 (consecutive sentences upheld for thefts from mail by postman as 'offences were spread over a substantial period of time'); *Palmer* 29.7.74, 670/C/74 (three attempts at incest over period of two years; consecutive sentences correct in principle.)

[7] 27.4.71, 5800/C/70.

transaction,[1] and violent resistance to arrest does not form part of the same transaction as the offence for which the arrest is being attempted.[2] In each case consecutive sentences are appropriate. The rule does appear to cover burglary committed in conjunction with going equipped for theft[3] and offences of violence accompanied by possession of an offensive weapon,[4] although conflicting decisions can be found in each case.[5]

Apart from these cases, many applications of the rule can be found which do not lend themselves to any generalization. Simultaneous assaults on a number of different people in the course of the same fracas are likely to be treated as a single transaction,[6] and the term covered a case where the appellant assaulted a man in the street and stole his shopping, in circumstances not constituting robbery.[7] Unlawful possession of a forged banknote and uttering the same note were covered by the term,[8] but the Court refused to treat as one transaction a case where the appellant forged an entry in the log-book of a car and subsequently used the log-book as a means of obtaining by deception.[9] Stealing a car and its contents was held to constitute a single transaction[10] but obtaining money by deception by agreeing to sell a stolen car was not so closely related to the theft as to require concurrent sentences—the offences of deception 'comprised different types of harm from . . . the thefts and the harm caused was to a different person'.[11] A series of thefts in different shops in the course of one afternoon formed part of 'a single shoplifting expedition' for which consecutive sentences were held to be incorrect,[12] and burglary

---

[1] *Bunch* 6.11.73, 2383/C/75 (five years for serious burglary 'right and it was obviously right that the sentence for assault on the householder should be made consecutive'); *Jones* 15.12.75, 2154/B/75 (violent attack on householder during burglary 'over and above that offence and involving a totally different degree of criminality').

[2] *Kastercum* (1972) 56 Cr. App. R. 298 (consecutive sentence 'generally preferable to emphasize the gravity of assaulting the police as a means of escape'); *Jones* 14.1.72, 3372/A/71; *Kelly* 19.11.73, 2554/B/73.

[3] See *Corby* 13.3.73, 1537/B/72; *Cohen and Humphries* 18.5.73, 5518/C/72 (attempted burglary); *Gibson Forbes* 23.4.70, 8130/C/69.

[4] See *Willis* 29.3.72, 4677/A/71.

[5] For burglary and going equipped, see *Ferris* 5.6.73, 1243/C/73, [1973] Crim. L. R. 642 (where the Court appears to have treated the case as an exception to the general principle) and *Shanley* 4.6.70, 1953/70. For violence and possession of an offensive weapon, see *Woollard* 1.5.72, 5487/A/71; *Scales* 7.5.74, 1239/C/74.

[6] *Burns* 4.5.73, 6536/C/72; see also *Williams* 15.11.75, 4273/B/75 (consecutive sentences for assaults committed in course of one fracas 'unorthodox' but upheld because total not excessive).

[7] *Little* 28.10.75, 3523/A/75.

[8] *Lewington* 23.1.73, 2672/A/72.

[9] *Bennett* 20.6.72, 1009/A/72.

[10] *Linwood* 27.10.72, 2725/A/72.

[11] *Bishoppe* 23.2.73, 3333/C/72, [1973] Crim. L. R. 583.

[12] *Lyons* 10.11.75, 2774/B/75.

of a chemist's shop has been held to form part of the same transaction as the subsequent unlawful possession of controlled drugs.[1]

In certain cases consecutive sentences are not merely permissible but expected. The Court has stated that consecutive sentences should normally be imposed where robbery is committed by persons in possession of firearms, irrespective of whether the unlawful possession of the firearm constitutes part of the same transaction as the robbery.[2] A similar presumption in favour of consecutive sentences applies where one offence is committed while the offender is on bail in the course of proceedings for another offence,[3] where the court imposes a sentence of imprisonment for an offence in respect of which the offender has been subject to a probation order or conditional discharge[4] or where the court enforces a suspended sentence.[5]

THE TOTALITY PRINCIPLE

The effect of the totality principle is to require a sentencer who has passed a series of sentences, each properly calculated in relation to the offence for which it is imposed and each properly made consecutive in accordance with the principles governing consecutive sentences, to review the aggregate sentence and consider whether the aggregate is 'just and appropriate'.[6] The principle has been stated many times in various forms: 'when a number of offences are being dealt with and specific punishments in respect of them are being totted up to make a total, it is always necessary for the court to take a last look at the total just to see whether it looks wrong;[7] 'when . . . cases of multiplicity of offences come before the court, the court must not content itself by doing the arithmetic and passing the sentence which the arithmetic produces. It must look at the totality of the criminal behaviour and

[1] *Smith and Davison* 10.2.75, 4417/B/74. A contrary view was taken in *Orrell and Woods*, 16.6.70, 9342/B/69 (consecutive sentences upheld for handling and possessing stolen drugs: 'it is not merely handling something which has been stolen, it is also a quite separate offence that that thing is something it is unlawful to have in your possession anyway, whether it is stolen or not').

[2] See *Faulkner* (1972) 56 Cr. App. R. 594; *Lydon* 18.1.74, 4577/A/73; *Baldessare* 9.5.75, 4767/B/74.

[3] See, for example, *Young* 16.3.73, 2509/C/72, [1973] Crim. L. R. 585 (consecutive sentence for theft committed while on bail pending trial for uttering forged banknotes: 'it would be a very wrong form of sentencing to give people who are . . . allowed bail any sort of idea that they can then commit another offence without . . . getting any additional penalty'—sentence upheld); *Henderson* 29.3.72, 260/C/72 (minor frauds; total sentence of three years excessive, individual sentences reduced, but still consecutive; fact that one offence committed after being bailed 'a very good reason . . . for making the sentence consecutive').

[4] *Webb* [1953] 2 Q. B. 390.

[5] *Ithell* (1969) 53 Cr. App. R. 210.

[6] *Smith* 26.11.71, 1895/C/71, [1972] Crim. L. R. 124.

[7] *Haslam* 24.11.72, 4151/B/72.

ask itself what is the appropriate sentence for all the offences'.[1]

The principle applies to all situations in which an offender may become subject to more than one sentence: where sentences are passed on different counts in an indictment[2] or on different indictments,[3] where the offender is subject to a suspended sentence[4] or probation order,[5] where he is already serving a sentence of imprisonment[6] or makes appearances in different courts within a short space of time.[7] In all such cases 'the final duty of the sentencer is to make sure that the totality of the consecutive sentences is not excessive'.[8]

Where the totality of the sentences does appear to be excessive and some adjustment is necessary, it is usually preferable to make the adjustment by ordering sentences to run concurrently, rather than by reducing the length of individual sentences and allowing them to remain consecutive. The Court has stated that a series of short consecutive sentences adding up to a substantial total is generally inappropriate; 'it is better to pass . . . an appropriate sentence on each count and make those sentences run concurrently'.[9] Where concurrent sentences are passed for offences of differing gravity, the sentences imposed for the less serious offences should not be disproportionate to the particular offences for which they are imposed, even though the length of these sentences will not affect the total period for which the offender is liable to be detained.[10]

The many decisions of the Court in which the totality principle has been applied to explain the reduction of a cumulative sentence made up of correctly calculated individual parts suggest that the principle has two limbs. A cumulative sentence may offend the totality principle if the aggregate sentence is substantially above the normal level of sentences for the most serious of the individual offences involved, or if its effect is to impose on the offender 'a crushing

[1] *Barton* 6.10.72, 1546/B/72.

[2] *Bodycombe* 21.1.74, 4702/C/73.

[3] *Andrew* 27.1.75, 2377/B/74.

[4] *Bocskei* (1970) 54 Cr. App. R. 519; *McGlinchey* 3.10.74, 1811/C/74.

[5] *Winthrop* 27.11.72, 2111/C/72.

[6] *Schallamach* 3.7.73, 5872/B/72.

[7] *Cox* 12.2.74, 2629/C/73. Where an offender appears before two or more courts in quick succession, the sentencer dealing with him last should adjust the sentence he imposes so that the accumulated sentences conform to the principle.

[8] *Bocskei* (1970) 54 Cr. App. R. 519.

[9] *Simpson* 1.2.72, 4470/B/71; see also *French* 26.6.75, 497/C/75; *McGuire* 24.9.75, 603/C/75; *Bainbridge* 11.10.73, 1715/C/73.

[10] See *Smith* 13.2.75, 3669/C/74, [1975] Crim. L. R. 468 ('where there are a large number of offences proved . . . a whole series of short consecutive sentences should be avoided. When the offences charged vary in gravity from the trivial to the comparatively serious, it is wrong as a general rule to impose concurrent sentences of equal or comparable length . . . the overall sentence should reflect the total appropriate to the course of criminal conduct revealed by the charges . . . it is fairer . . . to impose the total sentence in respect of one, perhaps the most grave, of the offences and then to impose lesser sentences in respect of the other offences').

sentence'[1] not in keeping with his record and prospects. The first limb of the principle can be seen as an extension of the central principle of proportionality between offence and sentence, while the second represents an extension of the practice of mitigation.

Many illustrations can be found of the Court reducing an aggregate sentence on the grounds that the total bears no relationship to the inherent gravity of the individual offences. In *Andrew*[2] a man with fifteen previous convictions was sentenced to a total of seven years' imprisonment for a series of offences of dishonesty involving obtaining money from a woman and stealing fur coats from his employer. Varying the sentence, the Court stated that 'grave as the offences are, we have to bear in mind the general scale of penalties imposed for offences of dishonesty of this character', and that 'a total of five years would be about right for both indictments'. In *McGready*[3] the appellant was sentenced to three consecutive terms of two years' imprisonment for three offences of taking a vehicle without consent; the Court considered that although the sentences are properly made consecutive, the total of six years was 'excessive . . . the offences did not merit such a substantial term'. The sentence was reduced to three years. In *Holderness*[4] the appellant received sentences totalling four years' imprisonment for a variety of charges, primarily motoring offences. The Court stated that the sentencer had failed to 'take the step . . . of standing back and looking at the overall effect of the sentences', and that if he had done so, 'he would have at once appreciated that he was imposing the kind of sentence which is imposed for really serious crime'. The sentence was reduced to twenty-seven months.

The principle is not confined to relatively long sentences. In *Hynes*[5] the appellant, convicted on three separate indictments of assaulting a police officer, driving while disqualified and theft of £3, received sentences totalling twelve months' imprisonment. None of the sentences was 'erroneous in principle' in relation to the offence for which it was imposed, but 'at the end of the day . . . this man faced a term of imprisonment which, taking account of the three offences, his record and background . . . was altogether excessive'. The sentence was reduced to six months.

Precise formulation of the first limb of the totality principle

---

[1] *Raybould* 1.6.70, 192/70.

[2] 27.1.75, 2377/B/74.

[3] 15.1.76, 3883/B/75.

[4] 15.7.74, 1346/A/74; see also *Adair* 8.3.73, 6125/A/72 (sentences totalling forty-five months for driving while disqualified and related offences: 'nothing wrong with the sentences considered separately' but 'the total is excessive'—reduced to thirty-three months).

[5] 13.11.73, 3988/B/73.

presents difficulty, particularly as the Court has on occasion upheld consecutive sentences amounting to a total in excess of the statutory maximum for the individual offence concerned,[1] and even consecutive maximum sentences,[2] but the essence of the principle appears to be that the aggregate sentence should not be longer than the upper limit of the normal bracket of sentences for the category of cases in which the most serious offence committed by the offender would be placed. This formulation would allow an aggregate sentence longer than the sentence which would be passed for the most serious offence if it stood alone, but would ensure that the sentence bore some recognizable relationship to the gravity of that offence.

The second limb of the totality principle represents an extension of the practice of mitigation. This part of the principle appears to require a sentencer who imposes a series of consecutive sentences to consider the mitigating factors in relation to the totality of the sentence, even though they have already been considered in relation to the individual component parts. A factor which has carried no weight in relation to the component sentences may justify some reduction in the totality, and a factor for which allowance has been made in calculating the length of the component sentences may have further value when considered against the combined length of all the sentences.

Many cases illustrate these propositions. In *Lane*[3] a man of 24 was sentenced to terms of imprisonment totalling six years for a variety of offences including robbery and burglary. The Court stated that 'taking these offences as individual offences on their own facts, the separate sentences . . . were not wrong in principle and not excessive', but the sentencer should 'have regard to the overall total . . . particularly in the case of younger men who are serving their first sentence of imprisonment'. The sentence was reduced to four years. In *Wickwar*[4] a youth of 21 received sentences totalling three and a half years for 'a very large number of extremely varied offences'; looking at the sentences individually the Court considered that 'not one of them is other than exceedingly moderate for the offence for which it was imposed'. However, the question of the

---

[1] See, for example, *Knott* 19.6.72, 5301/B/71 (consecutive sentences of nine months upheld for two offences of driving while disqualified, although maximum twelve months for single offence); *Palmer* 29.7.74, 670/C/74 (consecutive terms totalling four and a half years upheld on three counts of attempted incest, although maximum for single offence two years).

[2] See, for example, *Perry* 14.12.76, 686/C/76 (indecent assault).

[3] 4.11.75, 1563/B/75.

[4] 12.11.73, 4113/B/72; see also *Morgan* (1971) 56 Cr. App. R. 181 (youth, 19, fourteen years for burglary, robbery, impeding apprehension of suspected murderer: 'grave offences . . . sentences . . . individually right and ought to be made consecutive' but reduction in total justified by youth—varied to eleven years).

totality remained: 'is it right . . . that on his first occasion going to prison, he should go for three and a half years?' The Court decided to 'give him the benefit of his youth' and reduced the sentence to two years.

While it is in cases of younger men facing their first sentence of imprisonment, or their first sentence of substantial length,[1] that the second limb of the totality principle is most frequently encountered, it is not limited to that context. The principle is also seen in cases of offenders of more mature years receiving their first custodial sentence, the length of which is often enhanced by the enforcement of an accumulation of suspended sentences and the imposition of sentences for offences for which probation orders have previously been made,[2] or of persistent offenders faced with long periods of almost continuous imprisonment.[3] Other illustrations are cases where the appellant faces a long term of imprisonment for an offence in the first order of gravity and one or more shorter consecutive terms for lesser unrelated offences.[4] The principle appears to be a general one, applying wherever mitigating factors are to be considered. In *Lowther*[5] a man of 28 received sentences totalling five years for unrelated offences of theft, going equipped for theft and obtaining by deception. He had served a number of terms of imprisonment, the

[1] *Davis* 15.10.73, 1659/C/73 (five years for robbery and two years consecutive for other offences for man, 23; 'sentences totalling seven years are excessive in the case of this young man who has not previously received longer sentences than twelve months and whose record does not show him by any means to be a hopeless case'; sentences made concurrent); see also *White* 22.1.73, 2493/C/72 (five years for large number of burglaries involving small amounts by man, 24, eight previous convictions; 'time had not yet come, having regard to his youth and the fact that he had only had one previous sentence of imprisonment, for a sentence of the length which was . . . imposed'— varied to three years).

[2] See *Alford* 14.4.75, 4366/A/74 (woman, 35, six months for handling, suspended sentences totalling eighteen months enforced consecutively; handling sentence 'cannot be described as severe' but 'nine months would be sufficient for her first custodial sentence'). In *Smith* 26.11.71, 1895/C/71, [1972] Crim. L. R. 124, where the appellant was subject to suspended sentences totalling thirty months, the Court stated that 'circumstances in which a number of suspended sentences are allowed to accumulate' should be avoided, as 'on the final day of reckoning the total of imprisonment which appears to be appropriate is excessive having regard to all the circumstances'.

[3] See *Dance* 22.7.75, 2035/A/75 (man, 37, nineteen years spent in prison under previous sentences; sentences totalling nine years for theft and fraud 'excessive for a man who has spent so long of his time in prison already'—varied to six years).

[4] See *Greenfield and others* (1973) 57 Cr. App. R. 849 (ten years for conspiracy to cause explosions and thirty months consecutive for cheque frauds involving £1,100; judge imposing second sentence 'took . . . the copybook approach' but 'did not perhaps appreciate that . . . it is always necessary . . . to have a last look at the result which has been produced'; sentences made concurrent).

[5] 19.11.73, 1733/C/73; see also *Robson* 9.4.73, 3820/C/72 ('it is . . . in a sense illogical, when faced with a whole range of miscellaneous criminal activity, to pay regard to the total effect of the sentences imposed rather than to the individual crimes . . . it is an act of mercy'; six and a half years 'too much for this man to have to face'—reduced to four years).

longest of which was eighteen months. The Court considered that none of the individual sentences 'was in any sense wrong in principle or excessive for the particular offence' and the offences were not 'the product of a single transaction . . . on the face of it, one has proper sentences, properly made consecutive'. However, taking 'a last look . . . to see whether the total is or is not excessive for the case as a whole', the Court decided 'on . . . a narrow balance' to reduce the sentence to three years, as the appellant had been about to marry his fiancée and 'in the end society may suffer less if this sentence is reduced and she be given a more proximate opportunity of using her influence upon him'.

It has been argued that a sentencer may ignore mitigating factors but not the general requirement of proportionality between offence and sentence, if the offender appears to require a substantial period of custody for the purposes either of preventive confinement or of treatment. These qualifications appear to apply to the totality principle, although their precise scope is not yet settled. The cases do indicate that a sentencer may ignore the second limb of the totality principle and give full effect to a series of consecutive sentences where there is a specific reason for doing so and other requirements relating to consecutive sentences are met. In *Kenny*[1] a man of 37 with a long record of convictions for violence received sentences totalling nine years for three attacks on his wife committed over a period of several months. It was claimed that the total sentence was excessive, particularly in relation to such mitigating factors as his pleas of guilty, the presence of some provocation and the danger of his becoming institutionalized. The Court refused to vary the sentences, which were 'appropriate in the case of a very dangerous man'. In *Cotterill*[2] a man of 42 with many previous convictions for dishonesty was sentenced to a total of seven years, made up of consecutive periods of one, two and three years, for a series of frauds which began within a few weeks of his release from prison. The sentence was upheld 'not in anger . . . but in sorrow' as 'it was necessary for the protection of society to keep this man in custody for a long period'. While it could be argued that this decision does conflict with the first limb of the totality principle as formulated earlier, as the individual frauds involved relatively small amounts, it also illustrates that the second limb of the totality principle may be overriden where there is a particular need for preventive custody.

[1] 16.1.76, 3660/B/75.
[2] 6.5.75, 4578/C/74; see also *Lightbody* 3.3.77, 5317/B1/76, [1977] Crim. L. R. 626.

COMBINING DIFFERENT FORMS OF CUSTODIAL SENTENCES

Problems may arise where an offender is subject to a fixed term of imprisonment and some other form of custodial sentence at the same time, such as life imprisonment, an extended sentence or borstal training.

It is well settled that a sentence passed consecutively to a life sentence, or expressed to begin at the expiration of a life sentence to which the offender is subject, is void in law.[1] Where an offender serving a fixed-term sentence is to be sentenced to life imprisonment, the life sentence should take effect immediately rather than consecutively to the fixed term sentence.[2] Where a sentence of life imprisonment is imposed at the same time as one or more fixed-term sentences to provide a basis for preventive confinement of a dangerous offender, the fixed-term sentences should normally be concurrent with each other and not disproportionate to the offences for which they are imposed. It is incorrect to attempt to restrict the possibility of the release on licence of a person subject to a discretionary sentence of life imprisonment by imposing excessively long concurrent fixed-term sentences.[3]

A considerable number of cases have been concerned with the problems of imposing ordinary terms of imprisonment consecutive to extended terms. The appropriate principles were considered by a court of five judges in *Jackson*,[4] in which several previous decisions[5] were overruled. The Court stated that it is wrong to impose on the same occasion an extended term of imprisonment and a non-extended term consecutive to the extended term. Equally, it is incorrect to impose on the same occasion an extended term and a concurrent non-extended term of greater length. Where an offender already subject to an extended term falls to be sentenced on a later occasion, there is no objection to the imposition of a term of imprisonment, not certified as extended, to run consecutively to the existing extended term. In this event the sentencer should use the formula that the later sentence is 'to run from the date upon which but

[1] *Foy* (1962) 46 Cr. App. R. 290.
[2] *Jones* (1961) 46 Cr. App. R. 129.
[3] *Stanford* 3.7.72, 708/A/72; see also *Skelding* (1973) 58 Cr. App. R. 313 (life imprisonment upheld for series of homosexual offences against boys; appellant 'dangerous' but not within scope of Mental Health Act 1959 s. 4; concurrent sentences of five years reduced as 'it would be wrong if this man's condition improved in a shorter time than anybody at present anticipates, that there should be any possibility of his release being hampered by the existence of those five-year sentences').
[4] (1973) 58 Cr. App. R. 405.
[5] *Barratt* (1969) 53 Cr. App. R. 531; *Horner* (1971) 55 Cr. App. R. 366.

for the imposition of this sentence, you would be released from prison either on licence or finally'. Earlier decisions indicate that there is no objection to imposing an extended term to run consecutively to an ordinary term,[1] and consecutive extended terms are not necessarily wrong in principle.[2]

Where the offender is already serving a term of imprisonment but has been released from that sentence on licence by the Home Secretary on the recommendation of the Parole Board, the sentencer may disregard the existing sentence and impose a fresh sentence for the latest offence taking immediate effect. If he wishes the sentence to take effect at the conclusion of the existing sentence, he should first exercise his statutory power to revoke the licence[3] and use the normal formula that the subsequent sentence will be 'consecutive to the total period of imprisonment to which you are already subject'.[4] (The sentence for the later offence should not be inflated on the ground that it was committed while on parole.)[5]

Sentences of borstal training and detention in a detention centre should not be combined with terms of imprisonment, unless the sentence of imprisonment is a concurrent term of nominal length imposed to terminate a pre-existing probation order or conditional discharge made for an offence for which borstal training or detention cannot be used. An immediate term of imprisonment should not be imposed consecutively to a sentence of borstal training[6] or detention in a detention centre,[7] nor should a sentence of borstal training or detention be ordered to commence at the expiration of a sentence of imprisonment.[8] Where an offender already subject to a sentence of borstal training or detention in a detention centre is liable to be sentenced for other offences, the sentencer may (if his powers allow him to do so)[9] impose concurrent sentences of borstal training or detention, as the case may be, or a concurrent nominal sentence of

---

[1] *Stewart* 16.3.71, 5771/B/70, [1971] Crim. L. R. 296.

[2] See *Francis* 25.2.74, 4090/B/73.

[3] Criminal Justice Act 1967 s. 62(7); see *Practice Direction* (1975) 62 Cr. App. R. 131.

[4] See *Shard* 21.4.72, 5119/A/71, [1972] Crim. L. R. 445. Failure to revoke the licence in such circumstances could, on one view, leave the offender at large, as the new sentence imposed by the court would not commence until the expiration of the parole period, during which the offender would be entitled to continue at liberty.

[5] *Fletcher* 16.10.74, 3731/C/75.

[6] See *Stuart* (1964) 49 Cr. App. R. 17.

[7] *Raisis* (1969) 53 Cr. App. R. 553.

[8] See *Donaghue* 25.2.63, 2497/63, [1963] Crim. L. R. 375.

[9] Problems arise where the offender is subject to a probation order or conditional discharge made at a magistrates' court, in which case the Crown Court will not have power to impose borstal training unless the offender has been specifically committed in respect of the original offence under Magistrates' Courts Act 1952 s. 28 or 29. Where the offender is under 17, the second alternative of a nominal term of imprisonment is also precluded.

imprisonment;[1] alternatively, if the gravity of the instant offence justifies such a course, he may pass a sentence of imprisonment of substantial length taking immediate effect, which will absorb the unexpired portion of the sentence of borstal training or detention.[2] Sentences of borstal training may not be ordered to run consecutively to each other,[3] although a court dealing with an offender already subject to a borstal sentence may impose a further sentence of borstal training taking immediate effect,[4] or (if the offender has been released on licence) order him to return to borstal.[5] Consecutives sentences of detention in a detention centre may be imposed, so long as the aggregate of the sentence does not exceed six months (if the orders are made on the same occasion).

Similar principles apply to suspended sentences of imprisonment. It is inappropriate to impose a suspended sentence on the same occasion as an immediate sentence of imprisonment,[6] or on a person who is subject to a sentence of imprisonment[7] or borstal training, at least prior to his release on licence.[8] Where suspended sentences are imposed on one occasion in respect of a number of offences, it is the duty of the court imposing the sentences to determine whether they will take effect, if enforced, as concurrent or consecutive sentences.[9] If suspended sentences are passed on the same offender on different occasions so that he becomes subject to more than one such sentence, the decision whether they should be served concurrently or consecutively is the responsibility of the court ordering them to be served, if they come to be enforced.[10] Where an offender subject to a suspended sentence is subsequently sentenced to borstal training, he ceases to be liable to be dealt with in respect of the suspended sentence and no question of concurrence arises.[11]

Disparity of Sentence

Where two or more offenders are concerned in the same offence or series of offences, a proper relationship should be established between the sentences passed on each offender. If their responsibility

1 See *Stuart* (1964) 49 Cr. App. R. 17.
2 See *Skonnemand* 7.4.67, 185/67.
3 See *Elliott* 16.12.74, 3012/C/74, [1975] Crim. L. R. 174; *Bennett* 8.11.76, 1136/B/76.
4 Where this course is taken, the court may indicate that it does not wish the second sentence to interfere with the release of the trainee at the optimum time as if only the first sentence were in effect; see *Evans* (1972) 56 Cr. App. R. 854.
5 Criminal Justice Act 1961 s. 12(1).
6 *Sapiano* (1968) 52 Cr. App. R. 674.
7 *Fitzgerald* (1971) 55 Cr. App. R. 515.
8 *Dick* 20.9.71, 2249/C/71, [1972] Crim. L. R. 58; *Baker* 25.1.71, 4633/C/70.
9 *Wilkinson* (1970) 54 Cr. App. R. 437.
10 *Blakeway* (1969) 53 Cr. App. R. 498.
11 Powers of Criminal Courts Act 1973 s. 22(5).

in the commission of the offences and all other relevant factors are indistinguishable, the same sentence should be passed on each. A difference in the degree of culpability, or the presence of mitigating factors affecting one offender only, should be reflected in a distinction between their sentences. In appropriate circumstances the sentencer may deal with one offender by means of an individualized measure, while following tariff principles in sentencing his co-defendant; as different approaches have been adopted, no question of disparity arises in such a case.

The use of an individualized measure to deal with an offender whose co-defendants are to be sentenced to fixed terms of imprisonment may be justified, in a case where their involvement in the commission of the offence is equal, by circumstances indicating that one offender may be particularly amenable to the use of the individualized measure intended. In *Chapman*[1] two men with substantial records admitted ten burglaries. The appellant was sentenced to five years' imprisonment; his co-defendant, who was older with 'possibly a worse record', was made the subject of a probation order with a condition of residence in the hope that this course would enable him to overcome 'a very serious alcoholic problem'. The Court upheld the appellant's sentence, saying that there was no reason to believe that a variation in his sentence would lead to a change in his behaviour, and that there was no ground for a complaint based on disparity: 'the two disposals were each appropriate along two different lines, but that does not produce disparity in the true sense of the word'. Similarly in *Rowe*[2] a youth of 19, who had previously experienced borstal training, received sentences totalling thirty months for various offences concerning motor vehicles; his co-defendant, who had been equally involved in the offences, was put on probation. Upholding the sentence, the Court stated that the appellant had no justification for a sense of grievance; the co-defendant was younger, did not have the appellant's 'dreadful record', was not subject to an existing suspended sentence and had

[1] 17.7.75, 1855/B/75; see also *Galloway* 13.1.75, 3250/B/74 (two years for handling upheld, despite probation order for co-defendant, similar age and record; co-defendant alcoholic, probation intended to help him 'come to terms with drink problem'; no similar treatment for appellant possible: 'the disparity of the sentences between the two does reflect a real difference in their circumstances'); *Taylor and Handleigh* 23.9.76, 4436/A/75 (four years for series of burglaries varied to probation for one appellant, in view of medical and other evidence; similar sentence on co-defendant approved in principle, as 'there are differences between the cases', but reduced to two years 'to do justice' between the appellants).

[2] 10.5.74, 5524/B/73; see also *Wohlman and Cole* 29.7.71, 2194/C/71 (borstal training varied to probation for youth, 19, no previous convictions, 'a stable and apparently decent young man . . . led by a man with a criminal record into offences which he would otherwise have shrunk from taking part in'; five years for older co-defendant upheld).

survived two months' deferment of sentence before the probation order was made.

Alternatively, both defendants may have equal prospects of deriving benefit from an individualized measure, but a difference in their respective responsibilities for the offence will mean that the competing demands of the tariff outweigh the case for individualized treatment for one offender but not the other. Two drug addicts sentenced to two years' imprisonment for stealing a quantity of drugs from a chemist's shop were each considered to have 'a good prospect of rehabilitation'; the Court refused to vary the sentence of one appellant, who was considered 'the moving spirit', but substituted a probation order requiring psychiatric treatment in the case of the other.[1] This approach is only permissible where there is a significant difference either in the respective degree of responsibility of the offenders or in their amenability to treatment under an individualized measure. If their complicity and circumstances are substantially the same, it is improper to attempt to achieve different penal objectives by adopting conflicting approaches in relation to each defendant.[2]

Frequently the offender who has received an individualized measure will advance disparity between his sentence and that of his co-defendant as a ground for variation, as the individualized measure will involve the possibility of a longer period of custody than this co-defendant's tariff sentence. Provided that the individualized measure was properly imposed, the Court will not normally interfere. In *Ash*[3] a youth of 18 was sentenced to borstal training for stealing a motorcycle; his co-defendant, a man of 29, received four month's imprisonment. Having reviewed the appellant's history and circumstances the Court upheld his sentence, stating that borstal training was the most appropriate sentence for him, and that the argument that he had a grievance over the older man's sentence 'entirely ignores the fact that where a young man is sent to borstal training because he requires training, it is necessary that he be sent for a sufficient period for that training to be effective. It is not . . . comparing like with like to compare the sentence of training imposed on him with a sentence of imprisonment' imposed on his co-defendant.

Where each co-defendant is to receive a tariff sentence, the sentencer should take into account differences in their respective responsibilities for the offence. A distinction should be made between the sentences of those who have planned or initiated offences and

---

[1] *Boggis and Debski* 18.8.75, 1533/B/75.

[2] See *Milburn* 2.4.74, 5314/C/73, [1974] Crim. L. R. 434.

[3] 10.2.70, 5451/69; see also *MacLachlan* 1.2.73, 5365/B/72 (borstal training justified although co-defendants received suspended sentences, as 'it is not always the case that sentences are imposed simply as a punishment; they are often imposed in the interests of the persons concerned').

those who have followed their lead[1] or joined in existing criminal enterprises.[2] If involvement in the commission of the offence constitutes an abuse of trust by one defendant, this aggravating feature should be reflected in the relationship of his sentence to that of his co-defendant.[3] In more spontaneous offences variations in the degree of immediate participation by different offenders should be marked in their sentences, so that the use of a weapon by one offender in the course of a fight,[4] or the intentional infliction of more serious injury, will attract a longer term. In *Hutchinson and Hutchinson*[5] two brothers were convicted of wounding with intent and attempting to wound with intent respectively. The evidence was that in the course of a disturbance at a drinking club, the younger brother had twice struck a man in the face with a glass, causing injury; the elder brother had subsequently struck the same man with a chair as he lay on the ground. The Court held that the sentence of four years on the younger brother was 'perfectly proper', but the difference between that sentence and the three years imposed on the elder brother for attempting to wound did not reflect the fact 'that the degree of his responsibility is considerably less' or 'the possibility . . . that he was drawn into this by his brother'. His sentence was reduced to eighteen months.

[1] See, for example, *Wilson* 25.1.73, 5046/B/72 (eighteen months for going equipped and attempted theft at telephone kiosk justified, although co-defendant received only three months; appellant 'the leader', co-defendant, 'a hanger-on and certainly not such an active participant'); see also *O'Brien and Noonan* (1975) 61 Cr. App. R. 177 (seventeen years and fifteen years for manslaughter in course of robbery reduced to twelve and ten respectively; original sentences 'over-severe' but 'there must be a difference' between sentences to reflect the finding that one appellant had planned the robbery).

[2] See, for example, *Bernard and others* 29.10.73, 3619/A/73 (two years for handling stolen paper reduced to twelve months, as 'there should be some differentiation' between sentences on secondary receivers and 'the prime mover . . . who quite obviously was making a business of disposing of these stolen goods' but received the same sentence); see also *Albiston and others* 1.11.74, 1875/C/74 (three years for substantial thefts of company property over period of time 'not out of line'; upheld for defendants involved from early stages; reduced to twelve months for those becoming involved only at late stage).

[3] See, for example, *Warton* 24.11.75, 3735/C/75, [1976] Crim. L. R. 520 (longer sentence on appellant for theft of agricultural merchandise justified, as 'he had by far the most responsible position when comparison is made with his co-defendants'); see also *Burton and Nightingale* 18.2.72, 5541/A/71 (nine months for burglary of factory upheld for appellant, employee of company; suspended for co-defendant).

[4] See, for example, *Carberry* 27.2.73, 2662/A/72 (four years for wounding with intent, involving stabbing, upheld; no disparity with twelve months imposed on co-defendant convicted on unlawful wounding in same incident, as co-defendant used fists and the offences were 'completely different'); see also *Freeman and Bircham* 7.3.72, 4415/A/71 (five years for wounding with intent upheld for defendant using knife, reduced to three years for co-defendant using only feet and hands).

[5] 28.10.74, 886/B/74; see also *Quinn and others* 2.3.72, 2461/B/71 (manslaughter by striking victim on head with hammer; ten years for principal who inflicted blow, eight years for co-defendant who participated by grappling with victim, five years for third who withdrew from planned 'sorting out' before violence began; all upheld).

The relationship between the sentences imposed on co-defendants should also reflect the presence of mitigating factors applying to them individually. Differences in age[1] between offenders—at least where one is not yet too old to expect mitigation on the ground of youth and the other has passed that point—or in the number and quality of their previous convictions[2] will normally result in a difference in their sentences. The fact that one defendant has pleaded guilty[3] or given information or evidence which has led to the prosecution of his accomplices[4] will justify a differential; the same will be true wherever any mitigating factor applies to one defendant only. In *Keightley*[5] two appellants, father and son, were sentenced to eighteen months' imprisonment for conspiracy to defraud an insurance company by making false claims following a burglary at their business premises. The Court took the view that the son was no less responsible than his father and that the sentences in each case were lenient; however, a few months before the trial the son had, 'with great gallantry', saved a child from drowning in a river. To recognize this 'act of heroism' the Court reduced the son's sentence to allow his immediate release, while dismissing the father's appeal against conviction with an order that forty days spent in custody pending appeal should not count towards his sentence.

As was argued earlier, allowance for mitigation is not considered an entitlement, and mitigating factors may be ignored where there is a particular emphasis on deterrence or some other specific penal objective. In such a case discrimination between offenders on grounds of age, record or other circumstances going to mitigation is not necessary, but it is still appropriate to reflect differences in degrees of responsibility in the commission of the offence.[6]

In the process of establishing a proper relationship between the sentences passed on individual co-defendants, a factor affecting the responsibility of one defendant may be set against a different factor affecting the other, with the result that similar sentences may be

[1] See, for example, *Turner* 4.10.76, 2059/B/76 (two men, aged 39 and 22 respectively, convicted of joint participation in two assaults; longer sentence on older appellant justified as 'there is . . . a world of difference in the responsibility to be attached to two men of these very different ages').

[2] See, for example, *Straker* 8.2.73, 3605/A/72 (two years for blackmail and assault— enforcing payment to prostitute—excessive as 'he received the same sentence as the woman . . . with five previous convictions, whereas he was a man with none'; reduced to twelve months).

[3] See, for example, *McAleny and Griffiths* 5.12.75, 965/B/75 (difference between ten years and six years for robbery substantial, but justified by plea of guilty and other mitigating factors); see also *Hickman* 20.11.75, 1875/B/75, p. 50 above.

[4] See, for example, *Clarke* 24.7.75, 5125/C/74 (six years for robbery and burglary reduced to four to reflect guilty plea and 'the assistance that he gave in the administration of justice' by giving evidence against accomplice sentenced to six years).

[5] 20.12.71, 4080/C/71, [1972] Crim. L. R. 272.

[6] See *Turner and others* (1975) 61 Cr. App. R. 67 at 91.

imposed in both cases. In *Spratley*[1] a hotel porter participated in a robbery in which the hotel manager was attacked and the hotel payroll stolen; his co-defendant, not an employee of the hotel, used a degree of violence in carrying out the robbery which went beyond the appellant's expectations. Upholding seven years' imprisonment, the same sentence as imposed on the co-defendant, the Court endorsed the trial judge's view that the appellant's abuse of trust in providing information was equivalent to his co-defendant's use of grave violence, and 'when one adds up and balances the part' each had played there was really 'no distinction'. In other cases the effect of mitigating factors peculiar to one defendant may be cancelled out by other considerations enhancing his responsibility, with the result again that no discrimination will be apparent in the eventual sentences. In *Hawkins*[2] a man of 22 was sentenced to five years' imprisonment for a series of burglaries committed in company with a youth of 19, who had taken the leading part; balancing the co-defendant's greater responsibility against the mitigating effect of his age, the Court decided that the same sentence was appropriate in each case, and reduced the appellant's sentence to three years. Similarly where four prisoners were indicted for attacking a fifth, it was held that the sentence on one who pleaded guilty to wounding with intent should not be greater than those imposed on the three convicted by the jury of the lesser offence of unlawful wounding. Allowing for the greater gravity of his offence, he 'did not put the court and country to the trouble of a longish trial . . . they should all have received the same sentence'.[3]

The problem of establishing a proper relationship between sentences passed on co-defendants becomes more difficult when one or more of them is sentenced to borstal training. It was argued earlier[4] that borstal training had acquired a dual status and could be used interchangeably as an individualized measure or as a tariff sentence, its propriety in a particular case depending on the intention with which it was imposed. The duality in the status of borstal training complicates arguments relating to disparity. The cases appear to support a series of propositions. Where borstal training is imposed as an individualized measure, comparison with a fixed term of imprisonment, whether involving a longer or shorter period of custody, is inappropriate; no question of disparity between the sentences arises and the issue is whether borstal training is the best disposal for the offender concerned.[5] Where borstal training is imposed as a tariff

[1] 22.6.71, 610/C/71.
[2] 19.10.70, 2250/C/70.
[3] *Tidd and others* 25.9.73, 1507/B/73.
[4] See above, p. 12.
[5] *Ash* 10.2.70, 5451/69; *Huntley* 4.11.75, 4015/C/75, p. 284 below.

sentence, questions of disparity may arise between the offender sentenced to borstal training and other offenders sentenced to fixed terms of imprisonment,[1] or between different offenders each sentenced to borstal training as a tariff sentence.[2] The sentences should reflect varying degrees of responsibility and mitigating factors peculiar to one co-defendant, in so far as the statutory provisions permit.[3] (For the purposes of comparison, borstal training should be treated as equivalent to a sentence of between nine and eighteen months.)[4] It follows that where two or more defendants are sentenced to borstal training as an individualized measure, no question of disparity arises, and the propriety of the sentence in each case depends on the circumstances and likely response of the individual offenders. Where two or more offenders are sentenced to borstal training, one as an individualized measure and the other as a tariff sentence, again no question of disparity arises.

Similar complexities arise where one defendant is sentenced to an immediate term of imprisonment and the other receives a suspended sentence. The sentencer must consider the length of sentence and the decision to suspend separately. The fact that one sentence has been suspended does not in itself justify a longer term. A sentence of twelve months' imprisonment suspended for two years was reduced to nine months suspended as the appellant was considered to have been only the 'front man' in a business selling obscene books, while the principal in the enterprise, who had restocked the shop after a series of raids and forfeiture proceedings, received nine months' immediate imprisonment; the Court commented that 'it is wrong that his sentence of imprisonment should be twelve months whereas [his co-defendant's] was only nine months, even though his sentence was

---

[1] See *Neary* 9.4.74, 609/C/74, where a girl of 19 with no previous convictions was put on probation for being concerned in taking a conveyance; her co-defendants, each with records, were sentenced to short terms of imprisonment. The appellant subsequently broke the terms of the order and was sentenced to borstal training. Judged as a tariff sentence, this sentence 'was considerably longer than either of her co-defendants had received although they had criminal records and the part they played was more culpable'; accordingly the 'only possible justification' for the sentence was as a training measure, but on this basis the sentence was inappropriate, as the appellant 'had exhibited no criminal tendencies of any sort before'. A further probation order was substituted.

[2] See *Morrell* 6.8.74, 2667/B/74 (borstal training for girl, 20, no previous convictions, for cheque and credit card frauds; varied to probation; co-defendant involved in far greater number of offences over longer period received same sentence and 'the disparity between the two cases, and that two of them should have received the same sentence, is undoubtedly a source of grievance').

[3] Where some degree of disparity is inevitable as a result of Criminal Justice Act 1961 s. 3, the Court will not necessarily reduce the longer sentence; see *Devaney* 25.9.73, 2431/A/73.

[4] See *Bikram* 16.7.73, 1704/C/73, [1974] Crim. L. R. 55; *Roderick* (1967) 51 Cr. App. R. 70.

suspended'.[1] At the same time, the decision to suspend sentence in one case and not the other must be justified by the presence in the case concerned of factors relevant to the decision to suspend which are not present in the other. In *Cruickshank*[2] a man of 23 with 'an appalling record' was sentenced to three years' immediate imprisonment for three burglaries and taking a conveyance; his co-defendant in respect of two of the burglaries received a sentence of two years' imprisonment suspended. The Court stated that the difference in the lengths of their sentences was justified by the fact that the appellant was dealt with for more offences than his co-defendant, while the decision to suspend in the case of the co-defendant was explained by the fact that 'despite a very bad start' the co-defendant had 'made an attempt to mend his ways . . . on coming out of prison'. There was 'some hope that he might be able to put crime behind him'; he had obtained and stayed in regular employment, 'something which this appellant has never done'. The appeal was dismissed with the comment that if the appellant 'has a sense of grievance it is not based on reasonable grounds'.

DISPARITY OF SENTENCE AS A GROUND OF APPEAL

Disparity of sentence may take several forms. It may be claimed that the sentencer has without proper reason imposed a more severe sentence on the appellant than on his co-defendant,[3] or that in imposing the same sentence in each case he has ignored factors which warrant a differential in favour of the appellant.[4] Alternatively, it may be asserted that although a distinction in favour of the co-defendant is justified, the distinction that has been made is excessive.[5] A fourth version is that the distinction which the sentencer has made in favour of the appellant is inadequate to recognize the difference between their cases.[6] Whichever variety is present, the main value of an argument based on disparity between the sentences passed on co-defendants is the force it may add to the claim that relevant considerations affecting the individual appellant have been ignored. Disparity of sentence will rarely be effective as an independent argument.

[1] *Pitblado and Kelly* 10.2.75, 3921/C/74, [1975] Crim. L. R. 471.
[2] 17.1.75, 3662/C/74.
[3] See *Tidd and others* 25.9.75, 1507/B/73, p. 69 above.
[4] See, for example, *Straker* 8.2.73, 3605/A/72, p. 68 above.
[5] See, for example, *Beere* 22.11.74, 4647/B/73 (six years for arson for appellant, six previous convictions, on parole at time of offence; co-defendant, equally implicated, no previous convictions, sentenced to eighteen months; 'ample reason for making a difference between the two . . . but not sufficient justification for imposing . . . on one a sentence four times as long as that imposed on the other'; reduced to three years).
[6] See, for example, *Hutchinson and Hutchinson* 28.10.74, 909/C/74, p. 67 above.

In some cases the Court is confronted with an appellant whose sentence appears to be correct in every respect, but whose co-defendant has received a sentence which is in the Court's view unduly lenient. The Court has no power to increase the co-defendant's sentence, whether or not he has appealed,[1] and is therefore faced with the choice between upholding the sentence and leaving the appearance of injustice or reducing the sentence to what it considers an inappropriate level.[2] In such a case the practice of the Court is to reduce the more severe sentence only if there is 'such a glaring difference between the treatment of one man as compared with another that a real sense of grievance would be engendered'.[3] Many illustrations of this practice can be found. In *Stephens*[4] the appellant was sentenced to seven years' imprisonment for 'a very unpleasant robbery'; his co-defendant, tried earlier, received 'an extraordinarily lenient sentence' of two years. Although the longer sentence was 'perfectly proper', the Court considered that 'the disparity is so startling' that it was bound to make some reductions in the sentence, which was varied to five years. The practice is not confined to cases involving long sentences. In *Street*[5] the appellant was sentenced to twelve months' immediate imprisonment for handling stolen television sets; another man convicted of handling substantially more property stolen by the same burglar received a suspended sentence. The Court stated that both men should have received immediate imprisonment and that the second receiver had been treated 'with a leniency which we are at a loss to understand'; however, the resulting disparity was so great as to amount to 'a denial of justice', leaving the appellant 'suffering from a very real sense of grievance'. The sentence was suspended.

It is impossible to quantify precisely the degree of disparity which will be sufficiently gross to justify the reduction of an otherwise appropriate sentence. In deciding whether a gross disparity of sentence exists, the Court normally has regard only to comparisons with offenders who have participated in the same offence as the

[1] Criminal Appeal Act 1968 s. 11(3).

[2] See, for example, *Bishop* 8.6.73, 1395/A/73 ('if justice is to be even-handed, then this man would have less than he deserved . . . if this man is to get the penalty appropriate to the merits of his offence, then he may . . . well feel that he has suffered an injustice when compared with the fate of his comrades in the crime').

[3] *Brown and others* 28.11.74, 3450/A/74, [1975] Crim. L. R. 177.

[4] 30.11.72, 3980/A/72; see also *Slater* 7.10.71, 4294/C/70 (seven years for robbery not excessive, but co-defendants received suspended sentences; appellant 'might have a very real sense of grievance if this discrepancy was allowed to stand'; reduced to five years).

[5] 18.12.73, 4700/C/73, [1974] Crim. L. R. 264; see also *Russell* 8.3.74, 355/C/74 (six months' detention for burglary varied to a fine of £50; 'sentence was in isolation justifiable . . . the others, who ought to have received immediate sentences, got away with suspended sentences and fines').

appellant. While it is a common practice to cite decisions of the Court of Appeal in order to establish the limits of the range of sentences permissible in a given case, and the Court has occasionally on its own initiative obtained schedules of its own previous decisions in a particular context, it is generally considered inappropriate to seek to establish a disparity between the sentence imposed on the appellant and a sentence imposed in the Crown Court, not tested on appeal, in a different case with which he has no connection.[1] In one decision the Court appears to have extended this limitation by stating that 'an argument based on disparity should be based on the circumstances prevailing when the sentence attacked was itself passed, and we do not think, save in the most exceptional circumstances, that it should ever be proper for the Court to listen to an argument based on disparity which involves bringing in subsequent sentences passed on other people before a different judge in another court'.[2] This statement appears to represent a significant restriction of the scope of the disparity argument, as the most serious examples of disparity are likely to be found where offenders involved in the same offence are sentenced in different courts or on different occasions,[3] particularly where one is dealt with summarily and one on indictment.[4] Occasionally the Court has reduced a sentence for the sole reason that its own decision to reduce the sentence on a co-defendant has created an unjustifiable disparity which did not exist at the time of the original sentence.[5] It is submitted that the statement cited should be qualified so as to allow comparisons with sentences passed in other courts or on persons concerned in the same offences as the particular appellant; otherwise an artificial distinction will arise between cases where the unduly lenient sentence is passed before the sentence subject to appeal (where the comparison will be permissible) and cases where the unduly lenient sentence is passed subsequently (where the comparison will be inappropriate). This difference is not likely to affect the offender's sense of grievance or the appearance of a denial of justice.[6]

[1] See *Hayes* (1976) 63 Cr. App. R. 292.
[2] *Brown and others* 28.11.74, 3450/A/74, [1975] Crim. L. R. 177.
[3] See, for example, *Slater* 7.10.71, 4294/C/70, p. 72 above.
[4] See, for example, *Baker* 21.11.72, 3332/C/72 (two years for indecent assault on boy of 15 'grossly disparate' with fine of £30 imposed on man tried summarily for offences against same boy; reduced to twelve months).
[5] See, for example, *Smith* 12.6.75, 2242/C/75; *Singh* 17.6.75, 2507/B/75.
[6] Subsequent decisions suggest that comparisons with accomplices sentenced later than the appellant and in different courts are permissible (see *Potter* 15.9.76, 1784/B/76, [1977] Crim. L. R. 112) but the limitation to comparisons with sentences passed at the same time as the sentence subject to appeal was restated in *Stroud* (1977) 65 Cr. App. R. 150.

3

The Substance of the Tariff

Section 1: Offences Resulting in Death

MURDER

A person over the age of 18 convicted of murder must be sentenced to life imprisonment.[1] A sentencer imposing life imprisonment for this offence may make a recommendation that the offender should not be released on licence until a specified period of time has elapsed.[2] A recommendation, if made, is not binding on the Home Secretary and should not normally be for a period of less than twelve years.[3] Neither the sentence of life imprisonment[4] nor the recommendation[5] is subject to appeal.

Where a person under the age of 18 is convicted of murder, the sentencer must order him to be detained in accordance with Children and Young Persons Act 1933 s. 53(1).[6] In this case no period of detention is specified and there is no power to recommend that a specified period should elapse before the offender is released from custody.[7]

MANSLAUGHTER

'Manslaughter' is a generic term for a group of offences with different definitions, linked only by the common requirement of a death. Within the legally distinct categories of manslaughter it is possible to identify varying patterns of factual situations which provide a basis for discussion of the Court's sentencing policy.

---

[1] Murder (Abolition of Death Penalty) Act 1965 s. 1(1).
[2] *Ibid.*, s. 1(2).
[3] See *Flemming* 22.2.73, 2914/C/72.
[4] See Criminal Appeal Act 1968 s. 9.
[5] *Aitken* (1966) 50 Cr. App. R. 204; *Sewell* 5.12.72, 1686/C/72.
[6] The form of sentence is that the offender be detained 'during Her Majesty's pleasure'.
[7] See *Flemming* 22.2.73, 2914/C/72, decided on s. 53(2).

Manslaughter by reason of diminished responsibility

A person convicted of manslaughter by reason of diminished responsibility is one who has killed in circumstances which would amount to murder but for the fact that 'he was suffering from such abnormality of mind . . . as substantially impaired his mental responsibility for his acts and omissions'. Offenders in this group fall within the wider category of mentally abnormal offenders, and sentencing in diminished responsibility cases is an application to a particular context of the principles governing the sentencing of mentally abnormal offenders generally (discussed in chapter 7). As has been shown, in dealing with mentally abnormal offenders the Court favours the use of individualized measures, and in cases of manslaughter by reason of diminished responsibility, where the condition of the offender is appropriate and suitable facilities are available, a hospital order (usually accompanied by an indefinite restriction order)[1] or a probation order requiring submission to psychiatric treatment[2] will be made. Where the untreatability of the appellant's disorder makes a hospital order unsuitable[3] or accommodation is not available in a hospital offering sufficiently secure conditions,[4] the usual sentence is life imprisonment. This sentence is normally preferable to a long fixed term, as the fully indefinite sentence allows earlier release if changes in the offender's condition make this course possible[5] or continued detention if he remains likely to commit grave offences in the future.[6]

Fixed-term sentences are considered appropriate only in exceptional cases, usually where the offender has recovered by the time of the trial from the condition which affected his responsibility at the time of the offence. If he is neither in need of psychiatric treatment

[1] See, for example, *Parker* 17.4.75, 248/R/75; *Stoby* 13.12.71, 2857/C/71.

[2] See, for example, *Griffith* 1.5.75, 3537/C/74, p. 11 above.

[3] See, for example, *Adams* 11.4.75, 3291/B/74 (offence committed under profound reactive depression, not presently suffering from treatable illness, uncertainty about future behaviour); *Swann* 30.7.71, 3261/C/70, [1971] Crim. L. R. 660 (offence committed under emotional strain, varying diagnoses, no treatment recommended); *Wilkins* 18.3.74, 3917/A/73 (psychopathic disorder, not susceptible to treatment).

[4] See *Rainbird* 21.3.75, 837/R/75, where the administrative aspects of the problem are discussed in detail. The reason given for upholding a sentence of life imprisonment in preference to a hospital order in *Harvey* 16.7.71, 753/A/71, [1971] Crim. L. R. 664, that the patient might be discharged from hospital if treatment proved impracticable, although still a danger to others, appears to ignore the power to impose a restriction order under Mental Health Act 1969 s. 65 (see below, p. 295).

[5] See, for example, *Swann* 30.7.71, 3261/C/70, [1971] Crim. L. R. 660 ('the basic reason why . . . cases . . . of manslaughter on the grounds of diminished responsibility so frequently lead to an indeterminate sentence is that in mercy the accused man may not be kept in detention a day longer than the authorities think is right, having regard to his progress and his recovery').

[6] See, for example, *Farrell* 16.11.70, 2926/B/70 (life imprisonment upheld 'in justice . . . to the public, whose safety must always be borne in mind').

nor likely to behave violently in the future, and the offence was committed while his mental processes were gravely affected, the proper course may be a discharge or nominal sentence of imprisonment. In *Davies*[1] the appellant had developed 'severe depression of psychotic intensity' as a result of a long period of business anxiety and serious domestic problems arising from his wife's mental ill health. He decided to commit suicide but, concerned that his wife would be unable to fend for herself after his death, took her life before making a determined but unsuccessful attempt on his own. Hearing that the appellant's responsibility for his actions was 'not only diminished . . . but almost extinguished', but that in the changed circumstances there was no need for psychiatric treatment and no risk of future homicide, the Court reduced his sentence of two years' imprisonment to allow his immediate release. Where the offender at the time of trial is neither in need of treatment nor dangerous, but the extent to which his mental processes were affected at the time of the offence was not so great as to exclude some responsibility for his actions, a fixed-term sentence of intermediate length may be upheld. In *Tenconi*[2] the appellant admitted manslaughter of the woman with whom she had been living when the victim broke off their relationship. The plea had been accepted on the basis that the appellant was suffering 'from a mild degree of depressive illness' at the time of the killing, but there was no justification for a hospital order by the time of the trial (although it was suggested that psychiatric probation order might be made). In view of 'the measure of deliberation' with which the offence had been committed, the Court upheld the sentence of three years' imprisonment.

Manslaughter by reason of provocation

Many cases of manslaughter by reason of provocation arise out of the deterioration of emotional relationships; commonly the victim is the wife or husband of the offender, or a third party who has become involved with one of them. The scale of sentences appears to extend from about three years' to about seven years' imprisonment. Sentences within the higher range of six or seven years' imprisonment will be upheld in cases where the degree of provocation is limited and there is some evidence of deliberation. In *Hamerton*[3] the appel-

[1] 16.12.74, 3863/B/74.
[2] 9.3.72, 6041/A/71; see also *Fulker* 3.7.72, 6086/B/71, [1972] Crim. L. R. 579 (manslaughter of wife while depressed and under grave provocation, no mental illness at time of trial; five years reduced to three); *Spencer* 12.8.76, 2088/B/76 (manslaughter of wife, depression and provocation, but killing deliberate'; seven years reduced to four).
[3] 14.10.74, 1913/A/74; see also *Hodgson* 17.6.71, 4818/A/70 (appellant stabbed man found in bedroom with wife, after marriage treated as finished following adultery by

lant stabbed his wife when she received a telephone call from a man with whom she had behaved 'in a provocative, flirtatious manner' at a party. Although there was a lengthy history of matrimonial discord, there was no suggestion of adulterous relationships, and the husband's behaviour in going downstairs, taking a knife from the kitchen into another room and stabbing his wife left him 'time . . . to reflect on what he was doing'. The Court considered that the case was 'on the borderline' and could not be treated as an example of 'gross provocation'. The sentence of seven years was upheld. A sentence much longer than this is unlikely to be upheld, even where the provocation is not grave. In *Beard*[1] the appellant strangled his wife after finding letters from another man with whom he had known for some time she was having an affair; the appellant had previously committed adultery with a number of women, including the wife of his wife's lover. The Court considered that the appellant was probably 'fortunate in his verdict' and that the case could not be regarded as one of 'such sudden and extreme provocation as could reduce this case to a comparatively minor case in its class'; however, the sentence of ten years' imprisonment did not 'give sufficient weight to the jury's view that this was manslaughter on the ground of provocation' and it was reduced to seven years.

Sentences at the lower end of the scale, within the bracket of three to five years, are likely to be considered appropriate where the provocation is grave and its effect on the offender immediate. Given a high degree of provocation, sentences vary within this bracket in accordance with the nature of the violence used. A sentence of about five years may be upheld where after grave provocation death is caused by a sustained course of violent conduct. In *Parkinson*[2] the appellant returned from night work to find his wife with another man; in the course of subsequent arguments she claimed that he was not the father of one of her children, who had died some time previously. The Court accepted that the case was one of 'extreme provocation', but that the nature of the appellant's reaction had also to be considered. He had apparently partially strangled his wife, tied her up on a bed and struck her on the head with a heavy hammer. The Court accepted that while there was no suggestion of a 'predisposition to the use of

---

both parties; case 'near the borderline between manslaughter and murder'; seven years upheld); *Arnold* 2.6.72, 4859/B/71 (appellant stabbed wife after threats to commit adultery in future; seven years upheld).

[1] 11.6.71, 1012/C/71.

[2] 21.2.74, 3226/C/73; see also *Ditta* 23.7.70, 1941/B/70 (wife killed with repeated axe blows in 'frenzied attack by a man completely out of control', appellant 'driven beyond restraint' by cumulative affect of persistent provocation; life imprisonment inappropriate, as no evidence of instability—varied to five years).

violence, which often attracts sentences at the higher end of the scale for cases of manslaughter under provocation', the degree of violence used by the appellant could not be considered irrelevant. His sentence was reduced from eight years' imprisonment to five. By contrast, in *Carvell*[1] the appellant strangled the woman whom he had planned to marry, following several days of 'incessant quarrels' during which she had expressed violent hostility towards his small son and made allegations that the appellant had slept with her mother. The killing was sudden and virtually instantaneous; the Court accepted that the appellant had been 'taunted beyond endurance in a malicious manner on sensitive matters' until 'his self control snapped'. His sentence was reduced from six years' imprisonment to three.

Sentences of less than three years' imprisonment for manslaughter by reason of provocation in domestic cases will rarely be considered appropriate unless there is substantial mitigation in addition to the provocation. In *Mason*[2] the appellant killed his wife following a period of 'non-stop nagging' accompanied by neglect of her household responsibilities and allegations that his inability to work was due to malingering, when he was actually suffering from disorders of the heart and circulatory system. The incident happened when he 'suddenly . . . lost his temper' when she started nagging him one morning after he had taken her a cup of tea in bed. The Court stated that the sentence of four years' imprisonment was not 'wrong in principle or excessive' but solely in view of the appellant's deteriorating physical condition, it was varied to a conditional discharge.

The pattern of sentences in other cases of manslaughter by reason of provocation reflects that of the domestic cases. Cases where the provocation is less than extreme and the killing accompanied by some degree of deliberation will justify a sentence of about seven years' imprisonment. In *Stone*[3] the appellant used a kitchen knife to stab a man who had called on him to collect some money which the appellant owed him. Accepting the jury's finding that the appellant had been provoked, the Court pointed out that after the provocation had ceased the appellant had 'armed himself with a knife and

[1] 26.7.71, 702/C/71; see also *Cooper* 18.5.73, 5885/B/72 (mother stabbed once by son with bread knife he was using at time, death result of gross verbal provocation after long period of behaviour which had led to breakdown of son's marriage and made 'life in this house . . . a hell upon earth'; five years reduced to three); *Dowding* 29.11.73, 1404/A/73 (conviction for murder reduced on appeal to manslaughter, evidence that wife taunted appellant in relation to sexual difficulties, strangulation; three years imposed).

[2] 19.2.73, 5512/B/72; see also *Liddell* 4.12.75, 3129/C/75 (wife stabbed with potato peeler and screw driver after gross provocation received with great restraint until appellant 'lost control of himself', attempting suicide following killing; thirty months reduced to twelve in view of effect of episode on young children of marriage).

[3] 27.4.71, 57/C/71.

followed the deceased man out of the house'. His sentence of seven years' imprisonment was upheld. A lower sentence was imposed in *McAuliffe*,[1] where a man was stabbed to death with a pair of scissors in a fight following a party at which the deceased had been 'vociferous, threatening and insulting'. Accepting that the deceased 'had been asking for trouble' and that the appellant had not taken the scissors with the intention of using them as a weapon, the Court reduced his sentence from eight years' imprisonment to five.

Manslaughter by an unlawful and dangerous act

The pattern of sentences imposed in the wide variety of cases falling within the general category of involuntary manslaughter may be identified if cases are divided into a number of subcategories based on the most common factual situations.

Manslaughter of small children by parents and quasi-parents A significant proportion of the 'unlawful act' manslaughter cases which came before the Court concern the deaths of small children killed either by a parent or by a person living with the parent and assuming some parental responsibilities—sometimes described as 'battered baby' cases. Occasionally the offender in such a case will be found to be suffering from a mental disorder requiring psychiatric treatment under either a hospital order[2] or a psychiatric probation order,[3] but in many cases a sentence of imprisonment will be upheld. The scale of sentences appears to extend from about three years to about seven years, although in a few exceptional cases sentences of greater length have been upheld.[4] More commonly, the Court will consider a sentence within the range of six to eight years appropriate for the most serious examples of this kind of offence, where death has been caused by grave violence carried out over a period of time. In

---

[1] 2.12.74, 1431/B/74.

[2] See, for example, *Gentle* 12.3.71, 5596/A/70, where the charge was infanticide.

[3] See, for example, *Clemence* 25.7.75, 1051/C/75 (manslaughter of new-born baby by neglecting to make any arrangements for confinement, previous similar incident, appellant 'immature, dependent personality', case called 'not . . . so much for punishment as assistance and help'; four years varied to probation requiring submission to psychiatric treatment).

[4] See *Galloway* 20.9.71, 5888/C/70 (manslaughter of stepdaughter aged 2½ by series of punches all delivered on same occasion, appellant sub-normal but not requiring treatment; ten years upheld); *Cleaver* 3.12.71, 2421/B/71 (manslaughter of eight-week-old baby by striking on head with a plaster cast, serious injuries inflicted on other twin; appellant considered to be untreatable psychopath; ten years upheld partly as 'offenders of this kind must be sentenced in such a way as to put the person . . . in a position where he cannot repeat these offences'). Both cases seem to be inconsistent with later decisions, particularly *Coombs* 10.10.72, 627/A/72, [1973] Crim. L. R. 65, cited at p. 37 above, in so far as they appear to approve the imposition of a sentence beyond the normal scale on preventive grounds.

Roberts[1] the appellant was sentenced to ten years' imprisonment for manslaughter of his five-month-old son, having previously been put on probation for neglect of the same child. The post-mortem examination disclosed 'numerous injuries of different ages' to the head, including fractures of the skull inflicted on three separate occasions. The appellant, who admitted banging the child's head on the wooden arm of a settee on two occasions, was described as a person of low intelligence, although he was not mentally ill and knew that he should not have treated the child in this way. The Court considered the case 'an extremely bad case of its kind' which 'requires to be marked by a very substantial . . . sentence', but the sentence of ten years' imprisonment was above the level required; the sentence was reduced to seven years. In *Busby*[2] the appellant killed his fortnight-old baby with a punch which was 'the culmination of several days of ill treatment'; despite his good character the Court upheld a sentence of seven years' imprisonment.

Sentences in the lower bracket, between three and five years, are considered appropriate for cases where the death of the child is the result of the use of violence on an isolated occasion. In *Hughes*[3] the appellant was convicted of manslaughter of the eleven-month-old son of the woman with whom he was living. The child died from a number of blows to the head inflicted in 'a sudden uncharacteristic bout of temper', and there was no suggestion of any previous violence towards the child, whom the appellant had previously treated 'with kindness and consideration'. In view of this background, although the appellant had used 'extreme violence' on the occasion of the child's death, the sentence of seven years was 'beyond the range of . . . sentences normally imposed' and was reduced to five years.

[1] 9.12.75, 3425/C/75; see also *Kepple* 19.7.73, 2365/C/73 (child of 8 killed by blow from stepfather, evidence of injuries inflicted over period of a week prior to death; conviction for murder reduced to manslaughter, eight years imposed); *Thorpe* 20.3.75, 5048/B/74 (child of fourteen months killed by man living with mother, variety of injuries apparently inflicted over period of three weeks; twelve years reduced to six); *Taylor* 24.1.75, 3311/C/74 (death resulting from series of injuries inflicted on one occasion; ten years reduced to six); *Silman* 14.6.76, 124/A/76 (death of six-week-old baby from pressure applied to face; admission of previous acts of violence towards child; ten years reduced to seven); see also *Coombs* 10.10.72, 627/A/72, [1973] Crim. L. R. 65, p. 37 above.

5.10.71, 2742/B/71; see also *Fitzgerald* 26.2.70, 7046/C/69, [1970] Crim. L. R. 357 (six years upheld for manslaughter of 3-year-old by stepfather, 'evidence of a course of cruel conduct' over period of several weeks before death).

[3] 1.11.73, 1187/C/73; see also *Adesokan* 26.2.70, 7644/C/69, [1970] Crim. L. R. 357 (death of child of 2 from series of blows inflicted by father on single occasion, no evidence of previous violence; five years upheld); *Bailey* 27.1.72, 6676/A/70 (youth, 20, causing death of child for whom he was babysitting, several blows on single occasion, had previously looked after child with no sign of aggression; four years imposed on substitution of conviction of manslaughter for murder); *Hurst* 16.3.76, 5116/B/75 (death of four-week-old baby following four slaps on single occasion; no evidence of other violence; seven years reduced to four).

A lower sentence will be approved where, in addition to the absence of a background of violent behaviour towards the child, the death is the result of a single blow. In *Rhodes*[1] the appellant killed the eighteen-month-old son of the woman with whom he was living by a single blow which caused the child's head to strike the wall behind it; death resulted from a fractured skull. Accepting that the appellant had previously behaved as 'a loving father' to the child, who was 'in the habit of screaming and crying', without any sign of violence, and that death resulted from 'one blow only . . . struck in exasperation and in a temper' which had unfortunate and unintended consequences, the Court considered the sentence of five years 'too heavy' and reduced it to three. Similarly in *Power*[2] the Court reduced to three years a sentence of six years' imprisonment imposed on the father of a 2-year-old boy who had thrown the child in the air while leaning over the second-floor balcony of a block of flats. It was accepted that the father intended to catch the child and had thrown him in the air in order to put pressure on his wife, who was in the act of leaving him. The child's death as a result of falling to the ground was the result of 'gross negligence of a criminal nature', and there was no suggestion of 'any previous ill-usage of his child'.

A sentence much lower than three years will not normally be justified in the absence of substantial mitigation going beyond the usual circumstances of loss of sleep, exasperation and depression seen in most cases of this kind.[3] In *Whitcombe*[4] the appellant was sentenced to four years' imprisonment for manslaughter of his eight-month-old daughter. The Court accepted that death was the result of a blow on an isolated occasion which had thrown the child against a wall, causing her to sustain a fractured skull from which she died, and that at the time of the incident the appellant was depressed and tired and prevented from sleeping by the child's crying. There was no suggestion that the appellant had previously used violence towards the child, who had been 'treated properly by its parents'. Despite these considerations the Court considered it necessary to 'give effect to the public revulsion that arises in this sort of crime' and upheld the sentence.

[1] 15.11.73, 3348/A/73; see also *Jones* 17.5.73, 390/B/73 (death of child caused by being thrown against floor, difficult home conditions due to inadequacy of appellant and wife; six years reduced to three).

[2] 22.3.71, 5686/B/70, [1971] Crim. L. R. 432.

[3] See, for example, *Pyle* 3.12.76, 4042/A/76 (death of child following inhalation of vomit after being shaken by 'loving and dedicated' father, shaking 'a little over what a normal father might do in a lawful way . . . a very minor breach of the law', substantial other mitigation; twelve months varied to conditional discharge).

[4] 16.10.70, 3744/A/70, [1971] Crim. L. R. 51.

Manslaughter in the course of robbery Cases of manslaughter arising out of robbery appear to be divisible into two subcategories—those where the degree of force actually used (or intended by the particular defendant) was such that death was an unlikely consequence of the assault, and those where the nature of the violence offered was such that serious injury or death was a probable consequence, even though the defendant was not proved to have foreseen it.

In cases within the first category, the proper approach appears to be to assess the sentence which would have been appropriate for the robbery if death had not occurred, and to increase that sentence by a modest amount to reflect the fact that death has resulted. In *Edwards*[1] the appellant was sentenced to ten years' imprisonment for manslaughter and conspiracy to rob a rent collector; his co-defendant, who had attacked the rent collector, striking him on the head with a hammer, was convicted of murder. The Court interpreted the jury's verdict to mean that although the appellant had taken part in planning the robbery, he did not anticipate that his co-defendant would carry a weapon or use a degree of force likely to cause grave injury. In these circumstances, 'the Court has to ask itself this question: had there not been a death, what would the appropriate sentence have been for counselling or procuring the robbery and, secondly, to what extent does the fact that the victim died make any difference to the appropriate sentence?' The sentence was reduced to five years, a term which would probably not have been considered excessive for the robbery in isolation (see below, p. 142). In another case[2] two young men attacked a man they met in a public lavatory, punching him in the face and holding him by his braces; there was some suggestion of kicking, but the medical evidence was that the cause of death was the inhalation of vomit while unconscious and that the deceased's injuries were the result of fist blows. The sentences were reduced from six years to three, partly because of the appellants' ages and the fact that 'the result was far graver than they ever contemplated'. In a third example[3] two men were convicted of the manslaughter of an older man with whom one of them had become acquainted. The appellants gained access to the deceased's house and tied him to the floor by his wrists and ankles, after causing lacerations to his head which 'were not injuries which anyone could have expected would have caused death'. Death was the result of the 'unlucky accident' that the deceased had inhaled blood flowing from

---

[1] 22.2.72, 6105/C/70.
[2] *Robson and Murray* 19.7.71, 56/C/71.
[3] *O'Brien and Noonan* (1975) 61 Cr. App. R. 177. The sentence of sixteen years upheld in *Mann* 30.6.72, 3767/A/71, where an elderly woman died of heart failure after being tied up by two men who gained access to her house, appears to be inconsistent with the proposition formulated in the text.

cuts on his lips. In view of this evidence the Court considered that although 'it was a very grave manslaughter', it was 'not the most serious of its kind' and reduced the sentences of seventeen and fifteen years respectively to ten years. While this sentence is considerably longer than the sentences approved in the other cases cited, it is comparable to the sentences upheld in cases where a robbery is accompanied by violence against a householder in his own house (see below, p. 141).

In the second group of cases, where death results from a degree of violence intrinsically likely to cause death or serious injury, the circumstances of the robbery are of less importance, and a substantial sentence more directly related to the act of violence itself will be upheld. In *Hughson*[1] the appellant and his co-defendant lured the deceased to a derelict school under the pretence of being able to supply him with cannabis; their intention was to rob him of the substantial amount of cash he was to pay for the drug. In the course of the robbery the appellant stabbed the deceased in the stomach. Observing that the case 'came as near to murder as a case of manslaughter could possibly come', the Court upheld the sentence of ten years. Similarly in *Naishmann*[2] the appellant participated in the robbery of an 80-year-old newsagent who died after being severely beaten and probably kicked; a sentence of ten years was upheld.

Manslaughter arising out of an assault In a further category of cases, death occurs as the unintended consequence of an assault, often committed in the course of a fight between the deceased and the victim. As in the robbery cases, the Court's approach is to relate the sentence to the gravity of assault, although it may be aggravated if the possibility of death or bodily injury should have been apparent to the accused at the time. In *Unsworth*[3] a man of 36 slapped the face of an elderly woman who had slapped his face in the course of an argument between him and her husband. In falling she struck her head on a bar rail and sustained a fracture of the skull from which she died. The Court stated that the appellant had used 'aggressive violence', although 'not a very serious kind', and it was necessary 'to treat death arising from an unlawful act in a more serious way than an unlawful act of the same kind which does not result in death', particularly as some risk of injury was forseeable 'if a healthy building worker strikes

[1] 29.1.71, 3817/B/70.
[2] 14.1.70, 2478/69.
[3] 22.11.73, 3482/B/73. The Court distinguished *O'Neill* (1966) 51 Cr. App. R. 241, on the ground that in the latter case there was an element of self-defence. See also *Mallett* 21.12.71, 5073/A/71, [1972] Crim. L. R. 260 (punch in mouth, causing deceased to fall over dog lead, striking head on pavement; eighteen months not excessive as assault was unprovoked, but sentence suspended).

an elderly woman with his hand'. The sentence of two years' imprisonment was however too severe and a sentence of six months was substituted. This sentence would be within the range of sentences for common assault, assuming a custodial sentence to be appropriate. Where the nature of the assault is such that a more serious charge would have been supported, a more substantial sentence will be upheld. In *Monnax*[1] the appellant engaged in a fist fight with the deceased, in the course of which he banged the deceased's head against a wall. The prosecution accepted his plea to manslaughter on the basis that there was no intent to inflict serious injury, no weapon was used and the deceased's skull was such that he was more susceptible to brain damage than the average person. Accepting that 'very considerable violence must have been used', the Court reduced the 'unduly lengthy' sentence of six years to three.

The use of a weapon in circumstances which would justify a conviction for maliciously inflicting grievous bodily harm will lead to a longer sentence, within the range of four to six years. In *Whittle*[2] a quarrel in a public house led to an exchange of blows in which the appellant struck the deceased in the neck with a beer glass, severing a blood vessel in the neck. The Court held that the sentencer was justified on the evidence in concluding that the appellant was aware of the glass in his hand when he struck out, and upheld the sentence of five years' imprisonment. Sentences in this range are likely to be upheld where the accused has unintentionally choked the deceased to death by applying pressure to the throat,[3] or engaged in other violence intrinsically likely to cause injury of a serious nature, even where no weapon has been used. In *Freer*[4] the appellant was convicted of the manslaughter of his wife, who died from a fractured

[1] 2.12.75, 4098/C/75; see also *Bates* 22.11.74, 893/B/74 (deceased's head banged against pavement several times in course of fight, but no premeditation or weapon; six years reduced to four); *Culhane* 25.11.75, 2204/C/75 (deceased struck single blow to head with beam of wood, some provocation, no intent to inflict serious injury; eight years reduced to three); *Morton* 4.3.77, 5055/B2/76 (death arising from kicking in course of brawl, deceased's unknown poor state of health a major contributory factor, no premeditation; seven years 'excessive' – reduced to three). The sentence of seven years substituted by the Court in *Nicholson* 7.6.73, 405/B/73, where the deceased inhaled vomit after being knocked unconscious by the accused, appears to be inconsistent with the general pattern.

[2] 30.4.74, 5274/B/73, [1974] Crim. L. R. 487; see also *Baines* 2.5.75, 337/B/75 (appellant armed with knife and axes after fight, deceased colliding with appellant and impaling self on knife; appellant 'asking for trouble'—six years upheld); *Roche* 21.12.71, 2692/C/71 (knife and broken bottle used in affray; five years for manslaughter upheld).

[3] For example, *Smith* 9.4.74, 102/A/74, (death caused by brief pressure to throat leading to vagal inhibition; five years upheld); *Atkinson* 5.4.73, 5761/A/72 (death caused by pressure to throat in attempt to stop landlady shouting and screaming—life imprisonment inappropriate as no evidence of continuing dangerousness—seven years substituted).

[4] 10.10.74, 1180/B/74, [1975] Crim. L. R. 52.

skull following a fall down a flight of stairs. The Court interpreted the jury's verdict to mean that the appellant, in a 'raging temper', had pushed or assaulted his wife at the top of the staircase 'with a reckless disregard as to what might happen if she should fall down'. The sentence of six years was upheld.

Sentences at the upper limit of the scale for 'unlawful act' manslaughter, which appears to be about ten years' imprisonment, will be reserved for cases where the accused has taken part in an enterprise where grave violence was in contemplation, but has escaped conviction for murder because the principal has gone beyond the scope of the common purpose. In *Harold and others*[1] a number of men attacked the deceased, threatening him with an axe; the cause of death was a wound, apparently inflicted by one of the accused with a knife without the knowledge of his co-defendants. The principal was convicted of murder; other defendants who had taken part in the attack received sentences ranging between seven and ten years, which were upheld with the comment that it was 'manslaughter of a very grave kind'.

PROCURING ABORTION

Although the number of appeals involving cases of using an instrument with intent to procure miscarriage have declined, the Court appears to have maintained the view that this offence normally calls for a tariff sentence, the length of which will be governed primarily by the extent to which the offender can be considered a professional. In *Ramsey*[2] the Court observed that 'the legislature having made provision for abortion under the National Health Service it makes it . . . even more important that the law should be strictly and fully enforced against the carrying out of illegal abortions, with all the appalling dangers that are involved'. A similar view was expressed in *Scrimaglia and Young*,[3] where the Court observed that abortionists might be divided into 'three classes . . . women who do it on one isolated occasion, those who are real professionals making a business of it, and some in between who on more than one occasion but not regularly have conducted this operation and do it out of kindness albeit for money'.

The range of sentences for those in the first category, the 'real professionals', appears to lie between five and eight years' imprison-

[1] 7.3.74, 3268/B/73.
[2] 22/6/70, 2918/B/70.
[3] (1971) 55 Cr. App. R. 280 ('the usual argument that prevailed, that abortion was done out of pure kindness, there being no legal means of doing it, now does not avail anybody . . . an offence of this sort, particularly today, does call for a period of imprisonment').

ment. A sentence of eight years was upheld in the case of a man convicted of 'conducting a very substantial business in abortions', in addition to other offences of indecent assault,[1] and a sentence of five years was upheld on a 'professional abortionist' who admitted eighty offences committed over a period of about six years,[2] the Court observing that the sentence 'gave full effect to this man's confession of . . . guilt' and might otherwise have been longer.

The bracket of sentences for the offender who occasionally performs abortions for payment but does not make it a regular business appears to be between two and three years. In *Hill*[3] the Court stated that 'there is a distinction between the full-scale professional abortionist who performs illegal abortions as a business and the abortionist who is described as a semi-professional . . . it is not always easy to draw the line between these two'. As the evidence did not establish that the appellant fell into the first category, his sentence was reduced from five years' imprisonment to three. In another case[4] the appellants were considered on the available evidence to fall 'into the upper ranks of the second category . . . they are very nearly professionals if not quite'; their sentences were reduced to two years. Similar sentences have been approved in comparable cases.[5]

For offenders in the third category, the casual abortionists who commit the offence on an isolated occasion for motives which are not primarily financial, a sentence in the region of twelve months may be upheld. In *Ramsey*[6] the appellant attempted to abort a girl who had become pregnant as a result of her relationship with the appellant's son. The attempt was unsuccessful and the girl suffered no injury. Despite the appellant's good character, commendable work record in an important public service and the fact that he had not acted for gain, the Court upheld his sentence of twelve months' imprisonment.

The Court has had few opportunities to consider the case of abortions performed by qualified medical practitioners in appropriate clinical surroundings but in circumstances not covered by the Abortion Act 1967. In one such case[7] the Court upheld a sentence of

---

[1] *Okenarhe* 15/3/71, 4385/A/70.
[2] *Odiachi* 12/5/70, 9363/B/69.
[3] 22/7/71, 6388/B/70.
[4] *Massaquoi and Massaquoi* 7/12/71, 3262/C/71, [1972] Crim. L. R. 190.
[5] See, for example, *Leo* 15/2/73, 6445/C/71 ('back-street abortionist . . . she did this for reward and . . . it was not the first time'; twenty-one months upheld); *Scrimaglia and Young* (1971) 55 Cr. App. R. 280 (appellants 'not regularly professionals' but 'this has happened before'; three years reduced to two). A sentence of four years was upheld in *Hilliat* 5/10/71, 966/B/71, where the appellant, who charged £80 for his services, had previously been sentenced to three years for a similar offence.
[6] 22/6/70, 2918/B/70.
[7] *Smith* (1973) 58 Cr. App. R. 106.

twelve months' imprisonment suspended for two years, but reduced a fine from £5,000 to £1,000, in view of the changed financial circumstances of the appellant. It is not clear whether this case is a basis for generalization.

A further group of cases concerns the position of offenders who play a secondary role in procuring an abortion, either by acting as a go-between for the abortionist and the pregnant woman or by assisting in some other way, such as by making premises available for the operation. Although the Court has described sentences of imprisonment of up to two years as not necessarily 'wrong in principle', it generally appears to be ready to give great weight to mitigating factors in this context, particularly where the offender can be shown not to have acted simply for financial gain. In several such cases the Court has reduced a sentence to allow the immediate discharge of the appellant[1] or has suspended the sentence.[2]

CAUSING DEATH BY RECKLESS DRIVING[3]

The principal problem of the sentencer in cases of causing death by dangerous driving is to decide whether the offence is sufficiently grave to require a custodial sentence. In *Guilfoyle*[4] the Court distinguished between 'two broad categories' of cases causing death. For those 'in which the accident has arisen through momentary inattention or misjudgement' a fine coupled with disqualification from driving was normally appropriate. Custodial sentences were properly reserved for 'those who have caused a fatal accident through a selfish disregard for the safety of other road users or their passengers, or who have driven recklessly'. The latter category included 'cases in which an accident has been caused or contributed to by the accused's consumption of alcohol or drugs'.

Many cases illustrate the application of this distinction in a variety of contexts. Some clearly fall into the category for which custodial sentences are appropriate, such as where it is established that the

---

[1] See, for example, *Curtin and Griffiths* 28/5/71, 494/71 (father of twin daughters arranging abortions for both, friend of family arranging introduction with abortionist; twelve months and fifteen months respectively reduced to equivalent of six); *Aubry* 13/5/71, 503/B/71, [1971] Crim. L. R. 490 (woman allowing use of flat for three separate operations on same woman, no direct participation or financial gain; eighteen months in prison 'not wrong in principle' but reduced to nine).

[2] See, for example, *Mahati and Saunders* 20/6/74, 1074/A/74 (two years for nurse assisting medical practitioner in performance of illegal operations and for medical centre employee referring potential patients, no substantial financial gain in either case; sentence not 'in any way wrong', but suspended in each case).

[3] This offence, originally causing death by reckless or dangerous driving, is redefined by Criminal Law Act 1977 s. 50 to apply to 'reckless' driving only.

[4] (1973) 57 Cr. App. R. 549.

offender was engaged in racing on the highway[1] or was a completely inexperienced driver driving without proper supervision.[2] In other cases the criteria for the imposition of a custodial sentence have been satisfied by evidence of reckless overtaking or driving at a grossly excessive speed. In *Dutton*[3] the appellant was alleged to have attempted to overtake a line of seven vehicles travelling on a single carriageway at a point where the road was narrow and curved to the right. The appellant admitted that he had pulled out in hope of finding a gap between the vehicles he was overtaking, if it became necessary for him to return to the left-hand side of the road. He collided with a car coming in the opposite direction, causing the death of a woman travelling with her children. The Court upheld a sentence of nine months' imprisonment with the observation that 'although this appellant is a man of excellent character and has considerable experience as a driver, he did in this case take a deliberate risk'. In *Lyons*[4] a young man went for a drive with four friends at such a speed that his passengers were frightened and shouted to him to slow down. Eventually he lost control of the vehicle in attempting to negotiate a bend at 'a wholly excessive speed' and in the ensuing accident one of his friends was killed. The Court described the offence as 'very serious' and added that 'the proper sentence of imprisonment was something of the order of twelve to eighteen months'. (In view of complexities arising under Criminal Justice Act 1961 s. 3, the sentence was reduced to six months). In *Brown*[5] a corporation bus driver was alleged to have driven his bus down a street crowded with workers leaving a shipyard so close to the pavement and so fast that pedestrians had jumped out of the way. Two passengers on the bus became anxious about the manner of the appellant's driving before he collided with a pedestrian, who died as result of the accident. The Court stated that this was a bad case of causing death by dangerous driving' but reduced the sentence from twelve months' imprisonment to six in view of various mitigating factors.

[1] See, for example, *Thistlethwaite* 24.7.73, 1285/C/73 (youth, previous good character, racing against other youths on motorcycle, pedestrian killed on zebra crossing; borstal training upheld).

[2] *Hallifax* 1.12.72, 2803/B/73, [1973] Crim. L. R. 190, p. 90 below.

[3] 31.1.72, 234/B/72, [1972] Crim. L. R. 321; see also *Bowerman* 15.10.74, 1827/C/74 (crossing continuous white line to overtake long vehicle, visibility restricted; imprisonment justified but twelve months excessive—reduced to equivalent of nine); *Thomas* 16.3.70, 8214/69 (overtaking at 75 mph on left-hand bend despite continuous white line: 'prison sentence . . . inevitable'; fifteen months reduced to nine).

[4] (1971) 55 Cr. App. R. 565; see also *Briggs* 23.6.75, 1188/A/75 (car driven at 60 mph through bend subject to 30 mph advisory limit, control lost; twelve months upheld).

[5] 8.2.74, 4971/B/73; see also *Cox* 25.9.73, 2920/C/73 (car driven at excessive speed on road subject to repairs, despite protests of passengers; left road after hitting bump, one passenger killed; 'custodial sentence was appropriate' but eighteen months excessive—reduced to twelve).

These cases may be contrasted with *Fulcher*,[1] where a lorry driver following a bus loaded with children down a hill was alleged to have allowed his attention to wander. As a result he was unable to stop when the bus driver braked sharply and, in swerving to avoid a collision with the bus, collided with a car coming in the opposite direction, causing the death of the driver. The Court stated that as the case had been 'presented as a case of momentary inattention leading to death', it did not justify a custodial sentence, either immediate or suspended, and the sentence of two months' imprisonment was varied to a fine of £50.

In many cases of causing death by dangerous driving it is established that the offender's capacity to drive was impaired by alcohol. In such cases a sentence of imprisonment will normally be upheld, if the degree of impairment was substantial and the accident attributable to it. In *Court*[2] the appellant spent some hours drinking 'the major part of a bottle of whisky' before driving at an excessive speed into a junction, entering the wrong lane of a dual carriageway and running down a lady crossing the road on foot. Observing that the appellant's blood alcohol concentration was 208 milligrammes per 100 millilitres, the Court commented that it was 'a bad case made worse by the fact that the dangerous driving was clearly a result of having taken far too much alcohol', but reduced the sentence from four years' imprisonment to twelve months'. In *Foster*[3] the appellant overtook a vehicle which had stopped at a pedestrian crossing to allow a child to cross the road; the child was killed when she emerged from behind the car which had stopped. Lengthy skid marks were held to justify the inference that the appellant 'was driving at a dangerously fast speed', and a blood test taken nearly an hour after the accident revealed a blood alcohol concentration of 128 milligrammes per 100 millilitres. Upholding a sentence of nine months' imprisonment, despite the 48-year-old appellant's good character and service record and a petition signed by many of his friends and colleagues, the Court stated that as the appellant was driving 'at a dangerous speed, with a high concentration of alcohol in his blood . . . it was a case for a prison sentence'.

The cases do not suggest that a custodial sentence is automatically required wherever there is any evidence of the consumption of

[1] 31.1.74, 4805/A/73; see also *Bramham* 25.6.70, 3062/A/70 (manager of pop group falling asleep while returning from evening engagement, after stopping twice to take fresh air; six months varied to fine of £100); *Barton* 20.1.77, 5797/C/76 (death of elderly couple on pelican crossing arising from 'very bad error of judgement'; custodial sentence unnecessary, six months' detention varied to conditional discharge).

[2] 2.5.74, 1001/A/74; see also *Sullivan* 30.10.73, 4220/A/73, [1974] Crim. L. R. 56 (pedestrian killed by driver with 'gigantic' blood alcohol content after extensive drinking; eighteen months 'justified to the last day').

[3] 17.1.72, 5464/A/71.

alcohol prior to the accident. The question is whether the driving generally fell into the category of selfish disregard for others or deliberate risk taking, and the presence of a high blood alcohol concentration is probably relevant primarily as an explanation of the offender's conduct or as a rebuttal of some alternative explanation of the accident. Where a minor lapse leads to fatal consequences, the fact that the offender's blood alcohol concentration is marginally over the permitted limit does not necessarily require the Court to impose a custodial sentence. In *Finnimore*[1] the appellant had consumed some alcohol with a meal. While driving to work he took a bend at an excessive speed, lost control of the car and collided with a motor scooter coming in the opposite direction, killing the driver. The evidence showed that the appellant's blood alcohol level was 88 milligrammes per 100 millilitres; the Court observed that 'that was a small matter, and had that offence stood by itself clearly a custodial sentence may not have been appropriate'. However, considering other circumstances, in particular the excessive speed and evidence that the vehicle had been so badly maintained as not to be in a fit state to be driven, the sentence of nine months' imprisonment was upheld.

For those examples of causing death by dangerous driving which fall into the category for which a custodial sentence is appropriate, the range of sentences is relatively narrow. The Court is clearly reluctant to uphold a sentence in excess of two years' imprisonment, even where the driving is particularly bad, and the majority of sentences of imprisonment are for periods of less than twelve months. In *Court*[2] (see above, p. 89) the Court considered that a sentence of four years' imprisonment was 'manifestly excessive', although a custodial sentence was necessary; a sentence of twelve months' imprisonment was substituted. In *Lyons*[3] (see above, p. 90), although the facts were held to justify a custodial sentence, three years' imprisonment was considered excessive and was reduced. In *Hallifax*[4] a young woman, who had driven on only two previous occasions and did not hold a licence, took over a car when her companion became unfit to drive through drink. She admitted driving at a high speed and killing a child who was crossing the road at a pedestrian crossing. The Court held that the sentence of three years'

[1] 26.2.74, 117/A/74; see also *Dalton* 14.3.77, 999/B/77 (young driver, loss of control as a result of excessive speed on bend, passenger killed; custodial sentence not required, although blood alcohol level 144/100—nine months varied to allow immediate release).

[2] 2.5.74, 1001/A/74.

[3] (1971) 55 Cr. App. R. 565.

[4] 1.12.72, 2803/B/72, [1973] Crim. L. R. 190; see also *Selsby* 11.12.70, 4779/A/70, [1971] Crim. L. R. 178 (three years for killing mother and child on pedestrian crossing while affected by anti-depressant tablets; reduced to eighteen months, partly in view of mitigating factors).

imprisonment imposed by the sentencer was 'an excessive sentence' and although the case 'did call for a custodial sentence', the sentence should not have been more than eighteen months' imprisonment; as the appellant was under 21 years old the sentence was varied to borstal training. In *Heath*[1] the appellant caused the death of a passenger in a vehicle with which he collided head-on as a result of attempting to overtake two cars 'when it was clearly and obviously unsafe for him to do so'. Although the Court considered that an immediate prison sentence was justified for 'a bad case of dangerous driving', in which 'drink played a part', the sentence of three years' imprisonment was 'out of scale for an offence of this kind'. A sentence of twelve months' imprisonment was substituted. In other cases, initial sentences of twelve months or less have been reduced to reflect the presence of mitigating factors.[2]

Section 2: Non-fatal Offences of Violence

ATTEMPTED MURDER

The majority of the relatively small number of cases of attempted murder which come before the Court arise out of violence committed within an established relationship—the most common example involves an attack by a husband on his wife. For cases of this kind, in which there is often some degree of provocation in addition to other mitigating factors,[3] the usual bracket of sentences appears to be between five and seven years' imprisonment. In *May*[4] the appellant and his wife had separated after eight years of 'stormy marriage', and his wife had begun to associate with another man. Having heard that this man had uttered threats against him, the appellant equipped himself with an axe when visiting his children, who were living with his wife. A fight developed between the appellant and his wife's friend, and when the appellant had chased the friend from the house he turned on his wife, striking her several blows to the head but not causing any permanent injury. Observing that any attempted murder

[1] 16.11.72, 1940/A/72.
[2] For example, *Hetta* 15.3.74, 517/B/74 (accident caused by excessive speed and dangerous overtaking; six months 'perfectly right', but reduced in view of good character, previous good driving record, and plea of guilty).
[3] A sentence of twelve years was upheld in the 'unusual' case of *Goode* 28.6.76, 267/B/76, where the appellant made three 'planned and deliberate' attempts to poison his wife.
[4] 5.11.74, 642/C/74; see also *Sapsford* 20.4.70, 8561/69 (eight years for stabbing sleeping wife following matrimonial difficulties 'too hard' for man of good character 'with excellent work record'—reduced to six); *Phillips* 4/10/71, 855/B/71 (seven years for stabbing common law wife 'severe' but not excessive); *Evans* 25.1.72, 3431/A/71 (six years for stabbing girl following matrimonial difficulties 'lenient').

was necessarily 'a grave offence', as an intention to kill was necessarily involved, the Court stated that 'giving full weight . . . to the general background against which this offence was committed' and to the appellant's relatively good record, the sentence of nine years' imprisonment was 'too long'. A sentence of six years was substituted. In *Beever*[1] the appellant admitted attempting to murder his son and wounding his wife with intent. His marriage had broken down after sixteen years and he had decided to kill his family before taking his own life. Having attacked his son and wife with a hammer, the appellant made a determined attempt at suicide. All three survived, and the appellant was sentenced to life imprisonment. In view of medical evidence that the appellant was not suffering from any mental disorder, the Court considered that 'there is no ground here for the imposition of a life sentence', and substituted a sentence of seven years' imprisonment.

The lower limit of the sentencing bracket for cases of this kind appears to be about five years' imprisonment, and sentences below that level would normally reflect the presence of exceptional mitigation. In *Bullman*[2] the appellant met his wife by appointment some time after she had left him, following a violent incident involving their daughter. When the wife disclosed her intention to institute matrimonial proceedings against him, the applicant seized her and attempted to cut her throat with a carving knife, subsequently claiming that he intended to commit suicide thereafter. The appellant, 'a man of exemplary character' with 'a very good work record', was sentenced to five years' imprisonment; observing that 'this was as near murder as one could get', the Court upheld sentence.

The small number of cases of attempted murder committed in other circumstances prevents any useful generalization about the level of sentences likely to be considered appropriate where the offence is committed in a different context. As it would normally be appropriate to ensure some distinction between those convicted of the complete offence of murder and those convicted of attempt, even though the intention required for attempt is more strictly defined than in the case of murder, it may be that the upper limit of the scale for attempted murder would be in the region of fourteen years, and that a sentence of this level would be reserved for a deliberate attempt at murder with

---

[1] 3.5.71, 144/A/71, [1971] Crim. L. R. 492.

[2] 19.3.71, 5505/C/70; see also *Alchin* 18.1.72, 3582/B/71 (wife attacked with hammer following separation and association with other men, subsequent attempt at suicide by appellant; four years 'a very lenient . . . sentence'); *Sloan* 21.5.76, 49/C/76 (wife stabbed with scissors after long period of matrimonial difficulty, 'a crime of passion quite unpremeditated' committed by 'man of good character . . . a hard worker'; severe sentence necessary as attack was sustained, but seven years reduced to five).

no real provocation. In *Hekker*[1] the appellant fired a number of shots at police officers and a neighbour after spending the evening consuming 'an enormous amount of alcohol'. On two counts of attempted murder and other lesser offences the appellant was sentenced to a total of eighteen years' imprisonment. Accepting that this was not 'the type of case where a man goes out in revenge to kill another' and accordingly 'cannot be regarded as the most serious of its kind', the Court reduced the sentence to twelve years' imprisonment.

WOUNDING OR CAUSING GRIEVOUS BODILY HARM INTENT

In the overwhelming majority of appeals involving sentences for offences under Offences Against Persons Act 1861 s. 18, the Court approves the imposition of a tariff sentence. Individualized measures are rarely endorsed on appeal except in cases where the offender is in need of psychiatric treatment[2] or falls within the conditions of eligibility for life imprisonment.[3] Exceptional circumstances may justify suspension of a term of imprisonment[4] or, in the case of a young adult offender, the preference of borstal training to imprisonment.[5] The scale of fixed-term sentences of imprisonment extends from about three years' to an upper limit of about twelve years' imprisonment.

Sentences shorter than three years will normally be found only where unusually strong mitigating factors are present, or where the

[1] 9.10.72, 1846/A/72, [1973] Crim. L. R. 128; see also *Morris* 24.5.76, 4209/B/75 (attempt by burglar to murder hotel guests following discovery, no history of violence; twelve years upheld, consecutive terms for unrelated offences made concurrent under totality principle).

[2] See, for example, *Hayes* 29.1.74, 3658/A/73 (three years for attack on wife with penknife varied to probation with condition of submission to psychiatric treatment as in-patient for three years); *Smith* 17.6.71, 448/A/71 (wife stabbing sleeping husband with kitchen knife; three years varied to psychiatric probation in view of medical evidence).

[3] For example, *Crout* 5.11.73, 3170/B/73; *Buchanan* 16.6.75, 4783/B/74; *Chaplin* 4.12.75, 3985/B/75, [1976] Crim. L. R. 320.

[4] For example, *Jackson* 29.8.74, 264/B/74, [1974] Crim. L. R. 718 (wife attacking husband with knife in immediate presence of police officer, while 'beside herself' following long period of subjection to 'greatest cruelty'; two years immediate imprisonment varied to two years suspended, case not to be treated as indication that court 'looks with complacency upon the use . . . of lethal weapons by one spouse against another'); *Parker* 15.4.75, 5280/A/74 (husband throwing domestic cleaning fluid at wife, 'isolated incident arising as a result of an unhappy and frustrated marriage', no significant injury caused, 'excellent record'; two years immediate imprisonment varied to two years suspended, decision not to indicate 'that husbands who throw corrosive liquid over their wives are not to be treated with gravity').

[5] For example, *Gordon* 18.2.74, 5514/B/73 (fist blows to face of police officer, causing fractured nose and lacerations; three years varied to borstal training in view of particularly good record during apprenticeship).

facts of the offence, while satisfying the formal requirements of the definition, do not fall within the usual pattern. In *Allen*[1] a man of 21, with 'an excellent character and work record' visited at her home his former girlfriend, who had recently broken off their relationship. In the course of the quarrel the appellant took a carving knife from the sideboard and attacked her with it, causing a number of cuts but no wounds 'of any particular seriousness'. Observing that the appellant's sentence of three years' imprisonment was 'at the lower end of the normal bracket for this kind of offence' and was 'the type of sentence which is normally passed in this class of case', the Court stated that 'the fact that this was a momentary loss of control amounting to frenzy' justified a reduction of the sentence to two years. In *Boughen*[2] the appellant was challenged to a fight by his eventual victim; in the course of the fight the appellant struck the victim with a fishing knife he happened to be carrying at the time. Accepting that the appellant, who had no previous convictions and a 'quite favourable background', had acted under provocation, the Court decided that 'a degree of leniency can be extended' and reduced his sentence from three years' to eighteen months' imprisonment. In a third case the violence arose out of a dispute between the landlord of a house let out in flats and one of his tenants, in the course of which the landlord struck at the tenant with a kitchen knife, inflicting a slight cut to the tenant's thumb and receiving himself various bruises in return. Observing that with one exception 'he had been an exemplary member of the community', the Court stated that 'thirty months is greater than is required for either the offence or for the offender' and reduced the sentence to eighteen months.[3]

Cases such as these can probably be regarded as exceptional, and more commonly an impulsive act of violence involving the use of a weapon or the intent to inflict serious injury will attract a sentence within the bracket of three to five years. In *Mack*[4] the 20-year-old mother of two young children intervened in a fight between her common law husband and another couple who lived in the same building by throwing a pan full of hot cooking oil over one of them, causing serious burns. Despite the appellant's 'completely clean record', the Court stated that the sentence of three years' imprisonment was 'not excessive' and upheld it. In *Jones*[5] a youth of 20 with no

[1] 24.3.72, 5197/B/71; see also *Jackson* 23.3.73, 153/C/73 (man, 29, no previous convictions or acts of violence, seizing by throat woman with whom he had previously lived, after breakdown of relationship, 'spontaneous impulsive act' causing only minor injuries'; three years for attempting to cause grievous bodily harm reduced to eighteen months).

[2] 2.11.71, 3662/C/71.

[3] *Tsagaris* 27.6.72, 1407/C/72.

[4] 2.7.74, 1384/A/74, [1974] Crim. L. R. 557.

[5] 3.3.72, 5287/B/71; see also *Morris* 16.7.71, 1190/A/71 (man, 21, 'with no previous

previous convictions used a glass beer mug to strike the head of the landlord of a public house who had intervened in an argument among customers. A sentence of three years' imprisonment was upheld. In *Purves*[1] the appellant attacked with a hammer a man whom he found in bed with a woman who had lived with the appellant for fourteen years. Accepting that this 'was an extreme example of provocation' and that the appellant had 'no record of violence at all', the Court upheld a sentence of three years' imprisonment with the observation that 'had these mitigating features not been present this offence would have merited a very long term of imprisonment indeed'.

Within the bracket of three to five years' imprisonment, the sentence will vary according to such factors as the nature of the weapon used, the degree of the injury intended, the actual injury inflicted and the degree of provocation, if any. Evidence of any significant degree of deliberation, such as the acquisition or possession of a dangerous weapon, may justify a sentence at the upper extreme of the bracket. In *Gunn*[2] a 'bouncer' at a dance hall was sentenced to five years' imprisonment for wounding with intent a man involved in a fight on the dance floor. It was alleged that the appellant deliberately broke a glass tankard and used the jagged edge of the broken glass as a weapon. His sentence was upheld. In *Louis*[3] the appellant attacked a fellow workman, without any apparent provocation, stabbing him several times in the back and on the scalp. The appellant claimed that he believed the victim was preparing to attack him on behalf of a third person, but this account was apparently rejected by the jury. His sentence of five years was upheld. Similar sentences are likely to be upheld where the appellant, although unarmed, clearly intends to inflict injury of the gravest kind. In *Crozier*[4] the appellant attacked a police officer who was attempting to arrest him, making a determined attempt to gouge out the officer's eye with his thumbs. His sentence of five years' imprisonment was upheld,

---

convictions and a good work and social record', striking landlord with broken beer glass, causing injury to arm; three years upheld).

[1] 18.10.73, 2177/A/73; see also *Tan* 14.12.71, 4455/B/71 (knife attack by 'excellent worker' with no previous convictions on man found in bed with appellant's wife, multiple stab wounds; fifteen months 'a very light sentence'); *Woodward* 17.6.71, 849/A/71 (appellant stabbed man he found sleeping with his wife some months after the marriage had broken down; three years upheld).

[2] 25.4.72, 4/B/71; see also *Brown* 23.11.72, 3345/C/72 (man, 34, no previous good character, slashing barman with razor following ejection from club, victim chased around car; four years upheld.)

[3] 18.1.72, 2436/B/71; see also *Blandford* 14.3.72, 3506/B/71 (youth, 20, no previous convictions, stabbing wife with butcher's knife apparently carried for the purpose; five years upheld); *Spears* 2.7.73, 1796/A/73 (youth, 18, apparently premeditated attack on elderly relative with sheath knife; five years upheld).

[4] 19.11.71, 1667/A/71.

as was a similar sentence in *Kennedy*,[1] where the appellant participated in an unprovoked attack on an off-duty police officer, butting
him in the face and kicking him while on the ground (in both cases the
appellant had previous convictions for offences of violence).

Sentences at the lower limit of the range will be approved where,
although the intention to inflict grievous bodily harm is established,
the element of deliberation is lacking. In *Chubb*[2] the appellant
stabbed his friend during a struggle following an argument. The
Court accepted that the wounds were inflicted with a fishing knife
which the appellant had found in his pocket at the time of the incident
and had not been carrying with a view to violence. In view of his good
character and genuine remorse his sentence was reduced from four
years' imprisonment to two. Alternatively, a sentence at the lower
limit may be approved where there is a premeditated attempt to inflict
a degree of harm which, while still 'grievous', is less serious than is
typical. Two appellants, each of good character engaged in an
apparently premeditated assault on the tenant of house belonging to
one of them, using a piece of plastic piping to beat him on the back.
The Court observed that although it was a 'cowardly attack', the
weapon used (which was described by one witness as 'resilient' and
'rather soft') was 'not as terrible . . . as a knife or a broken bottle
which sometimes are the instruments used to inflict a grievous injury'.
The sentences were reduced in each case from five to three years'
imprisonment.[3]

The next range of sentences, from five up to eight years' imprisonment, is reserved for cases exhibiting a combination of aggravating
features. Cases for which sentences in this bracket are upheld usually
involve the premeditated infliction of grave injury, the use of a lethal
weapon and the absence of any real provocation or other mitigation.
An example is *Showers*,[4] where a man of 25 with 'a bad previous
record for violence' knocked at the door of a club and, when the door
was opened, discharged a sawn-off shot-gun at the legs of the club
manager from a range of about six feet. His sentence of seven years'
imprisonment was upheld. In *Keleman*[5] the appellant equipped

[1] 26.2.73, 2682/A/72.

[2] 21.1.71, 3151/A/70. Compare *Ambrose*, 25.11.71, 3902/B/71, where a youth of 20
with previous convictions for offences of violence, including possession of an offensive
weapon, drew a knife in a public house to threaten other customers and subsequently
stabbed one of them; four years upheld for 'an entirely unprovoked and grave attack
with a knife'.

[3] *Stewart and Stewart* 23.2.73, 2804/B/71.

[4] 25.2.71, 4081/A/70; see also *Hill* 30.1.71, 1587/C/74 (young man imprisoned and
subjected to severe beatings, burning with cigarette ends and cutting, apparently in
retaliation for non-payment of debt arising out of dealing with drugs; seven years
upheld).

[5] 30.4.71, 5990/A/70; see also *Johnstone* 4.10.71, 1257/A/71 (appellant stabbing
woman with whom he had previously lived after waiting for several hours outside her

himself with a loaded pistol and waited for four hours outside a house where the woman with whom he had previously been living was staying. When the woman had returned to the house, the appellant gained access and subsequently shot both the woman and her mother, although in neither case was the injury fatal. The Court accepted that the appellant had for a long time 'lived a very disturbed and turbulent life' with the woman, but in view of the deliberate use of a gun the sentence of seven years could not be considered excessive. In *Moxham*[1] a youth of 18, following a pre-arranged plan in which a friend acted as a decoy, attacked another youth, knocking him to the ground, kicking him in the face and subsequently banging his head on the pavement for a period of several minutes. The victim suffered a fractured skull with underlying brain damage, resulting in paralysis of the limbs and loss of speech. The sentence of seven years' imprisonment, although 'a terrible sentence to pass upon a young man', was upheld.

Sentences in this bracket are less likely to be upheld where the offence is clearly unpremeditated, even though it has other aggravating features. In *Lawrence*[2] the appellant received seven years' imprisonment for wounding his wife with intent. The marriage had deteriorated to the point where the wife had obtained an injunction forbidding him to have any contact with her, and he had already been committed for a breach of that injunction. He subsequently returned to the matrimonial home, claiming that his intention was to attempt a reconciliation; a quarrel arose when he learned that his wife had disposed of some of his property, and he took a carving knife from the kitchen and stabbed his wife with it. The Court stated that 'this was clearly a passionate outburst' and that 'seven years' imprisonment was of unnecessary severity'. A sentence of five years was substituted. In *O'Rourke and O'Rourke*[3] a quarrel developed in a public house following a complaint about the quality of the beer. Having been

flat, 'strong emotional stresses' arising from disputed access to child; ten years 'more appropriate to . . . attempted murder'—reduced to seven years).

[1] 26.6.75, 205/A/75, [1976] Crim. L. R. 80; see also *Hill* 29.4.75, 3974/C/74 (burglar striking police officer while resisting arrest, serious facial injuries possibly caused by use of brick or concrete block; seven years upheld).

[2] 14.7.75, 1883/B/75; see also *Walters* 29.7.71, 6470/B/70 (attack on common law wife found in bed with other man, various injuries including fractured rib; seven years 'too much'—reduced to five); *Simpson* 26.1.71, 3143/A/70 (attack on wife with bottle and axe, minor injuries only, offence 'happened in the heat of the moment under . . . great provocation'; seven years 'quite disproportionate'—reduced to three).

[3] 30.11.72, 1575/B/72; see also *Owens* 29.10.73, 698/B/73 (fight in public house, beer glass pushed into victim's face; eight years 'beyond the reasonable scale for the particular incident', despite gravity of offence and previous convictions for violence; reduced to five years).

ejected, one of the appellants seized a customer who had assisted the landlord, while the other slashed at him with a knife, causing wounds to his neck and arm. The Court observed that 'the use of a knife . . . must be visited by a substantial sentence' but 'seven years was somewhat excessive in the circumstances'. A sentence of five years was substituted in each case. In *Hall*[1] a man of previous good character was stopped by two plainclothes police officers while walking home late at night. He took a knife from his pocket and struck at one of the officers, causing an injury to his arm. He subsequently claimed that he did not appreciate that the two men were police officers and reacted in panic as he thought they were about to attack him because he was an immigrant. Accepting this explanation, the Court reduced his sentence from six years' imprisonment to three.

Sentences above the level of eight years' imprisonment are upheld in relatively few cases, usually where grave injuries are deliberately inflicted in the course of some otherwise criminal purpose, such as robbery or blackmail. In *Sheppard*[2] the appellant and his brother were involved in two robberies, in the course of one of which the victim received blows to the head from a weapon—possibly a lead pipe filled with concrete—which caused brain damage leading to permanent disability. The Court upheld a sentence of ten years' imprisonment. The same sentence was upheld in *Ravenhill*,[3] where a youth of 20 resisted arrest on three separate occasions, using a large spanner, scissors and a hammer to attack the officers concerned, one of whom received a neck wound which was nearly fatal. In *Jacobs*[4] a sentence of twelve years' imprisonment for conspiracy to cause grievous bodily harm was upheld on the basis of allegations that the appellant had led a punitive expedition against a man who had 'offended against the rules of the society in which he operated' by making 'certain demands' of the licensee of a public house.

Sentences in the bracket of eight to twelve years are not likely to be upheld in cases which do not possess this combination of grave aggravating features, even though they have serious aspects. In *McDonald and Mitchell*[5] two men made a 'deliberately planned' and 'unprovoked' attack on a third with a hammer and a crowbar, striking him a series of blows to the head and back which caused a

---

[1] 25.5.71, 409/C/70; see also *Bogle* 5.4.74, 4307/B/73 (knife used in fight following argument in club, some provocation, superficial wounds; six years 'too severe'—reduced to four years).

[2] (1970) 54 Cr. App. R. 383; see also *Scholey* 20.2.70, 4763/69 (woman of 89 knocked down cellar steps and left barricaded and injured in burning house; nine years upheld).

[3] 5.11.73, 3668/A/73.

[4] 18.3.74, 3259/B/72.

[5] 26.1.71, 2181/C/70; see also *Lynch* 13.5.77, 5112/C/76, [1977] Crim. L. R. 757.

variety of wounds but no serious fractures. The Court considered that 'grievous as the offences were', the sentences of ten years' imprisonment were 'not only unusually severe but . . . really out of pattern with other offences of violence' and reduced them to six years. In *Luttman*[1] a youth of 19 discharged a shotgun in the course of 'an arranged battle' between rival gangs of youths, causing almost fatal injuries to another participant. Observing that while in such cases 'a long sentence . . . is called for quite regardless of the age of the assailant', the Court held that as the appellant had been acquitted of attempted murder and was entitled to some credit for surrendering to the police on his own initiative; in these circumstances the sentence of twelve years' imprisonment was 'too great' and a sentence of eight years was substituted.

Twelve years' imprisonment probably represents the upper limits of the scale of sentences for offences under section 18;[2] longer sentences have been reduced in cases possessing the gravest aggravating features, on the ground that some room should be left for cases of attempted murder where the intention to kill is established.[3]

UNLAWFUL WOUNDING OR MALICIOUSLY INFLICTING GRIEVOUS BODILY HARM

Offences under section 20 of the Offences Against the Person Act 1861 differ from those under section 18 primarily in the intent which must be established in each case. As the graver charge under section 18 requires proof of an intention to do grievous bodily harm, a conviction under section 20, whether by plea or verdict, implies that that intention was not established. The offender must be sentenced in the light of that determination.[4] Quashing a conviction under section

[1] 9.10.72, 5246/B/71, [1973] Crim. L. R. 127.

[2] In *Smith* 7.5.71, 4282/C/70, the Court upheld a sentence of fifteen years on a 'wickedly dangerous man' convicted of stabbing two people, apparently with premeditation, commenting that life imprisonment would have been more appropriate in view of his previous conduct and likely future behaviour. It could be argued that this sentence should have been reduced following the principle in *Rose* 20.12.73, 2281/B/73, [1974] Crim. L. R. 266. p 10 above.

[3] See, for example, *Barnes* 6.7.72, 5579/A/71, discussed at p. 38 above; *Spalding* 16.11.71, 2786/B/71, discussed at p. 36 above.

[4] See, for example, *Thomas* 14.3.74, 5141/A/73 (victim attacked with boiling water and spade while asleep, appellant acquitted of attempted murder and causing grievous bodily harm with intent, convicted under s. 20; sentencer apparently considered that 'the jury had reached a verdict which was merciful', imposed sentenced appropriate to conviction under s. 18; sentence reduced as 'the judge, despite his own views as to what the jury should have done, was . . . bound in law to sentence this man on the basis that he was not proved to have intended to do any of the harm which was in fact done'); *Donnelly* 30.11.76, 1974/A/76 (victim struck in face with beer mug, serious lacerations, plea of guilty under s. 20 accepted after trial under s. 18 part heard; Court 'accepted . . . that this appellant did not address his mind to the consequences', five years excessive although no personal mitigation, reduced to three).

18 and substituting a conviction under section 20, the Court observed that 'there is a world of difference in wickedness and culpability' between the two offences.[1] This principle clearly applies whether the indictment originally charges an offence under section 18 or not.[2]

The normal scale of sentences for offences under section 20 does not extend beyond three years, although occasional examples of longer sentences will be found.[3] In *Coffey*[4] the appellant, engaged in a public house fight, seized a table leg and swung it backwards to aim a blow at an assailant, unintentionally striking a bystander on the head, causing disfigurement and the loss of an eye. The Court accepted that in the light of the jury's verdict the injury could not be treated as intentional although 'it was undoubtedly recklessness of a very high order'; the sentence was reduced from four years' imprisonment to three. Similarly in *Baynes*[5] the appellant struck his opponent with a beer bottle in the course of a fight outside a public house; it was accepted that the bottle was not broken when the blow was struck but broke on impact with the victim's head. The sentence was reduced from four years' imprisonment to two.

Sentences of three years' imprisonment are commonly upheld for offences of malicious wounding where the attack is unprovoked and involves the use of a weapon such as a bottle, boots or bicycle chain. In *Hickling*[6] the victim intervened when a group of youths began to molest two younger boys; the appellant struck him several times with a bicycle chain and subsequently punched and kicked him while he lay on the floor. Despite the appellant's youth (he was 20) and the absence of significant previous convictions, the sentence of three years' imprisonment was upheld. In *Dyer*[7] a soldier, who was found to have offered no provocation, suffered a fractured jaw as the result of being kicked in the face by the 17-year-old appellant, after being knocked to the ground in the course of a fracas in a garrison town. The Court upheld the sentence of three years' imprisonment. In

[1] *Longworth* 26.2.76, 3077/B/75.
[2] See the general discussion at p. 366.
[3] For example, *Ali* 22.2.72, 4070/C/71 (blow struck with broken glass in course of 'deliberate sortie to this public house . . . to cause trouble by violence', blow struck intentionally although intention to cause grievous harm not proved; four years upheld); *Day* 18.1.74, 4364/A/73 (victim stabbed with six-inch knife during fight, appellant claiming stabbing accidental, case 'on the borderline between wounding with intent and unlawful wounding'; five years upheld).
[4] 15.11.74, 1849/C/74; see also *Woods and Frewer* 5.4.73, 4830/C/72 ('violent and unprovoked attack on an innocent individual' with bottle, head wound requiring nineteen stitches; three years upheld); *Donnelly* 30.11.76, 1974/A/76 (n. 4, p. 99 above).
[5] 11.11.74, 3340/C1/74.
[6] 6.3.72, 5561/A/71. See also *Isaacs* 1.3.71, 5379/B/70 (three separate unprovoked attacks on women encountered in street, various injuries including fractured cheek bone, broken teeth, concussion; three years upheld).
[7] 28.6.74, 633/C/74.

Walters[1] a man of 35 used an iron bar to hit on the head a man who approached him to complain of a remark the appellant had earlier made to the victim's wife; the jury were taken to have rejected the appellant's story that the victim and a companion had initiated the violence. The sentence of three years was upheld.

As in other cases of violence, the presence of provocation or other circumstances leading to impulsive action will justify a substantial reduction in sentence. In *Parsons*[2] the appellant, in an attempt to restore order in a club of which he was the senior member present, struck a man in the face with a hand holding a beer glass, causing lacerations to his face. The Court considered that the sentence of eighteen months' imprisonment was 'the appropriate sentence . . . in the ordinary way', but reduced it to allow his immediate discharge in view of strong personal mitigating factors. In *Rai*[3] a dispute between tenants over the use of a shared kitchen led to a fight in which the victim suffered an eye injury resulting in a permanent impairment of vision. Accepting that the offence was unpremeditated, provoked in part by the victim swearing at the appellant's wife and did not involve the use of a weapon, the Court reduced the sentence from three years' imprisonment to two.

As these cases indicate, personal mitigating factors assume greater significance as the inherent gravity of the offence declines, and the fact that the definition of the offences under the section can include cases of relatively minor violence makes identification of the lower limit of the scale of sentences difficult. Several decisions suggest that in the least serious examples of unlawful wounding, where relatively minor injuries are inflicted without intention in the strictest sense, a sentence of between six and twelve months will be upheld by reference to the facts of the offence considered in isolation, and reduction below this level (or suspension of the sentence) depends on mitigating factors

[1] 21.7.75, 1474/A/75.

[2] 7.6.73, 1037/A/73; see also *Newman* 22.6.73, 2320/C/73 (appellant coming to aid of licensee fighting with customer, striking one with beer glass causing minor injuries; in view of 'excellent character' and fact that offence committed in attempt to assist in restoration of order, 'some punishment was called for, but not a heavy one'; twelve months reduced to allow immediate discharge); *James* 28.8.74, 2114/C/74 (official at darts tournament striking spectator with beer glass, causing lacerations to ear, some evidence that blow struck in apprehension of attack by victim; eighteen months reduced to twelve and suspended).

[3] 16.10.73, 1758/A/73; see also *Evans and McLoughlin* 29.3.73, 5240/A/72 (attack on club doorkeeper by persons refused admission, some kicking but no permanent injury, case 'an example of men who had not come looking for trouble suddenly losing their head'; eighteen months reduced to twelve, partly in view of good character); *Ali and Fatik* 29.10.73, 2503/B/23 (dispute in restaurant over unpaid bill, victim hit with chapatti maker and other kitchen implements, laceration to head requiring seven stitches, violence 'erupted suddenly' and did not involve knife; two years reduced to twelve months, partly to reflect mitigating circumstances).

rather than the inherent gravity of the offence. In *Booth*[1] a man of 43 with numerous previous convictions admitted throwing a missile through the window of a house for no particular reason while in a 'drunken state'. A person in the house was struck by the missile and suffered an injury to the nose which left some permanent scars. The Court accepted that there was no intention to cause injury and, despite the appellant's 'appalling record', concluded that his sentence of fifteen months' imprisonment represented 'excessive harshness'. A sentence of nine months was substituted. In *Barker*[2] a fight broke out in a police cell between two persons who had been arrested for drunkenness; the appellant punched and possibly kicked the victim causing bruising and minor facial cuts. The Court observed that 'unlawful wounding is a serious offence and is rightly visited in most cases by terms of imprisonment', but as no weapon was used and no serious injury was caused, the sentence for 'a drunken brawl which got out of hand' was reduced from two years to the equivalent of ten months.

ASSAULT OCCASIONING ACTUAL BODILY HARM

The imprecise distinction between the offences of unlawful wounding (or maliciously inflicting grievous bodily harm) and assault occasioning actual bodily harm is one of the least satisfactory features of the criminal law. As the proof of an offence under section 20 of the Offences Against the Person Act 1861 requires evidence either of a wound or of grievous bodily harm, many cases where a moderate degree of injury is caused, either intentionally or recklessly, without a sufficient break in the skin to satisfy the definition of 'wound', fall outside the scope of that section and are presented under section 47 as assaults occasioning actual bodily harm. While formal proof of this offence does not require evidence of any intention to inflict injury, the offence cannot be considered in all cases to be less serious than an offence under section 20. The principles governing the drawing of inferences for the purpose of sentence appear to allow a sentencer dealing with an assault occasioning actual bodily harm to infer the existence of an intent to injure, where the nature of the injury actually inflicted would not suffice for a charge under section 20. Where the offender has inflicted a wound or grievous bodily harm, and an offence under section 20 would be established if the required mental state could be proved, it is submitted that a conviction under section 47, whether by plea or verdict, implies that no intent to injure was present and the offender should be sentenced on that basis.

[1] 29.8.74, 1474/B/74.
[2] 17.12.74, 2081/B/74.

The scale of sentences for assault occasioning actual bodily harm runs parallel to that for unlawful wounding. Sentences in excess of three years' imprisonment will rarely be upheld. In *Reed*[1] a man of 33 with four previous convictions for offences of violence 'laid an ambush' for the victim, who had earlier remonstrated with him for his behaviour at a dance. The victim, who was knocked to the ground and kicked about the head and body, suffered minor injuries, chiefly grazes and bruises. Although it was 'a most deliberate offence', the Court considered the sentence of four years' imprisonment 'extremely severe' and reduced it to three. In *Callaghan*[2] a man of 46 with 'a substantial number of previous convictions' was involved with others in resisting arrest. The officer concerned was punched 'heavily' in the face several times and suffered bruising (in addition to other injuries for which the appellant was not responsible); the Court considered that the sentence of four years' imprisonment went 'somewhat beyond the offences, serious as they were, should properly justify'. The sentence was reduced to three years. Sentences at this level are frequently upheld where there is an unprovoked attack, involving butting, kicking or the use of a blunt weapon, which causes moderate injury. In *Welsh*[3] a youth who was induced to leave a public house by a trick and attacked by a group of youths, including the appellant, was knocked to the ground and kicked, suffering extensive bruising to the head. The sentence of three years was upheld. In *Fisher*[4] a youth of 18 with no previous convictions attacked a bus passenger who had protested when the appellant forced his way to the front of the queue. The victim was punched several times and subsequently kicked after he had fallen to the floor, but suffered only minor injuries. A sentence of three years was upheld. The same sentence was upheld in *Aston*[5] where the appellant punched a traffic warden who was noting particulars of his car, and then twice drove the car at the warden, who was able to escape.

[1] 11.1.71, 2347/A/70; see also *Bull* 6.12.71, 1830/C/71 (knife brandished in dispute between drivers, minor cut to finger; 'appalling record for violence' but four years 'more appropriate to the deliberate use of a knife'—reduced to two); *Parker* 21.6.73, 978/A/73 (schoolgirl attacked in street, knocked to ground, bruises and grazes suffered; five years 'unnecessarily harsh' despite previous convictions for indecent assault and rape—reduced to thirty months).

[2] 26.2.71, 3572/C/70. A sentence of four years was substituted in *Hayes* 3.3.72, 1347/B/71, for the original sentence of five years; an officer was hit with a bar stool and beer bottle, choked with the cord of his radio set and then pelted with beer glasses. Although it was 'a very bad case' and the appellant had thirteen previous convictions, the maximum sentence was not justified.

[3] 11.1.73, 3925/A/72; see also *Romain* 15.11.71, 1657/A/71 (girl punched by appellant making advances, front teeth broken, several previous convictions for violence; three years upheld); *Cairns* 2.4.73, 2577/C/72 (woman of 62 punched in mouth, two days in hospital; three years upheld).

[4] 28.4.75, 5075/B/74.

[5] 22.4.71, 5594/A/70.

As in the case of malicious wounding, considerably shorter sentences will be found where the violence is the result of provocation. In *Collins*[1] the deputy superintendent of an old people's home attacked an elderly inmate, striking a number of blows. The Court accepted that while the offence constituted a breach of trust, it was an isolated incident involving 'a substantial element of provocation', and reduced the sentence from two years to twelve months. Shorter sentences will also be expected where the violence, although not provoked, is of a relatively minor kind. In *Johnston*[2] a man of 29 with several previous convictions for violence was sentenced to thirty months' imprisonment for an assault on a girl who protested when he abused her friend, who had refused to dance with him at a night club. The Court stated that the sentence was 'excessive' for 'a slap in the face causing an abrasion' and reduced the sentence to twelve months.

As these cases suggest, a sentence of between six and twelve months' imprisonment will not necessarily be considered excessive for even the least serious instances of assault occasioning actual bodily harm, by reference to the facts of the offence alone. Reduction of a sentence below that level or the use of alternative measures will usually reflect the presence of personal mitigating factors. In *Shanks*[3] a taxi driver, with previous convictions some years earlier, punched once a pedestrian who had banged the top of the taxi when it failed to stop at a pedestrian crossing; the victim suffered a cut lip requiring stitches. The Court refused to vary or suspend the sentence of six months' imprisonment.

COMMON ASSAULT

The difference between common assault and assault occasioning actual bodily harm depends on the nature of the consequences suffered by the victim, rather than the inherent quality of the violence, and for this reason an offence of common assault may be treated as seriously (within the limitations of the maximum penalty) as an assault occasioning actual bodily harm, where other circumstances are equal. In *Morley*[4] the appellant was convicted of common assault

[1] 6.2.73, 4976/A/72.
[2] 15.12.72, 3135/A/72; see also *Skidmore* 21.6.71, 1907/C/71 (fist blows causing black eye and bruises, previous convictions for violence, some provocation; fifteen months reduced to nine); *Lamberth* 3.11.72, 1675/C/72 (two blows with fist in course of dispute, minor injury not requiring treatment, 'too much attention was paid to the man's previous record and not enough to the comparatively minor extent of the injuries inflicted'; three years reduced to twelve months).
[3] 4.2.75, 4692/A/74; see also *Lodge* 23.8.72, 3495/A/72 (assault by passenger on taxi driver after dispute over fare, no serious injury, not premeditated; 'isolated incident and out of character'—twelve months reduced to six).
[4] 2.7.73, 861/C/73.

on an indictment for assault occasioning actual bodily harm, following evidence that he had participated in a fracas and kicked out several times in the direction of the victim as he lay on the ground. Although the victim received a number of injuries, the Court accepted that the jury had decided that the appellant's kicks had not connected; nevertheless the maximum sentence of twelve months' imprisonment was upheld as 'entirely appropriate' for 'the kind of assault from which serious injury might very well result'. A sentence of imprisonment is not necessarily wrong in principle even where the assault is not of the most serious kind.[1] Examples of common assault for which sentences of imprisonment have been upheld (usually in the absence of any personal mitigating factors) include threatening a landlord with a knife without striking a blow,[2] punching and kicking, without causing injury, a stranger who had offered no provocation[3] and pulling a girl into an alley and making an indecent proposition.[4] In other cases the Court has approved the imposition of a sentence of imprisonment in principle, but varied or suspended it because of mitigating circumstances,[5] which are likely to be of more significance in cases of relatively minor violence than in the more serious instances.

ASSAULTS ON POLICE

The use of violence against police officers will often result in charges of wounding with intent, malicious wounding or assault occasioning actual bodily harm. The decisions of the Court suggest that in such cases the sentencer should apply the same criteria as in other examples of those offences: the nature of the injury intended, the degree of premeditation and the extent of any provocation which may have existed. The fact that the victim is a police officer does not appear to be a significant aggravating factor in relation to the length of sentence imposed for such offences, although it may extinguish

[1] See *Joseph* 7.11.72, 2831/B/71, [1973] Crim. L. R. 188.
[2] *Gilbert* 4.4.74, 4400/C/73 (nine months); see also *Ryle* 7.3.72, 4795/B/71 (diner in restaurant unable to pay bill, threatening waiter with steak knife and broken wine glass; twelve months upheld).
[3] *Doyle* 12.10.71, 2202/C/71 (twelve months).
[4] *Miller* 9.12.71, 4410/A/71 (twelve months); see also *Odejinmin* 8.5.70, 8456/69 (woman seized and pushed to ground by stranger, no ulterior motive established; twelve months upheld).
[5] For example, *Waclawski* 26.9.72, 4199/C/72 (chauffeur bumping traffic warden with car; nine months 'by no means wrong in principle', sentence suspended as act of mercy); *Lucas* 5.12.74, 3632/C/74 (use of fists in free-for-all in restaurant, appellant not responsible for causing injury; six months reduced in view of delay before trial, birth of child, promising career as skilled workman).

whatever chance of a non-custodial sentence might otherwise have existed.[1]

Where the offence is charged as assault on a constable under the Police Act 1964, in cases which would otherwise amount to common assault, some difference in the Court's approach is apparent. The status of the victim will justify the sentencer in taking a more serious view of the offence than would be appropriate if the assault is committed against a private person. A custodial sentence may be justified for an assault which, if committed on a private person, might attract a non-custodial sentence, and some difference in the length of custodial sentences is also apparent; in both cases the difference may possibly be explained as the result of a greater reluctance to give effect to mitigating factors in the case of assaults on police than in other assaults.

The Court has frequently emphasized that a sentence of imprisonment should normally be imposed where an assault on a constable involves the deliberate use of force against an officer even though the degree of violence is moderate. In *Bell*[2] the appellant resisted arrest by striking the officer in the chest with his knee, apparently causing no injury. The Court stated that 'whenever there is a deliberate assault on a police officer such as this, the normal sentence is a loss of liberty' and upheld the sentence of two months' imprisonment with the comment that the appellant was 'exceedingly lucky' that it was not longer. In *Mackinnon*[3] a man of 'excellent character' was convicted of assaulting a constable in the execution of his duty, but acquitted of assault occasioning actual bodily harm on the same occasion; he had resisted arrest in the course of a meeting which had led to an obstruction of the highway, but it was uncertain whether he had punched the officer. The Court upheld the sentence of three months' imprisonment with the observation that the appellant 'could not well have complained if the sentence had been longer'. (Where an offender is sentenced to imprisonment for the offence for which he was being arrested at the time of the assault, the sentences should normally be consecutive.[4] The fact that the primary offence does not justify a sentence of imprisonment,[5] or that the offender is eventually

---

[1] See, for example, *Coleman* (1975) 61 Cr. App. R. 206 (student, no previous convictions, assaulting two officers, causing actual bodily harm by kicking with 'heavy boots'; both officers off-duty for several weeks; custodial sentence appropriate in cases of violence against police, except where mitigation 'wholly exceptional'; length of sentence to depend on age of accused and degree of violence used; eighteen months upheld).

[2] 19.12.72, 4998/B/72, [1973] Crim. L. R. 318.

[3] 17.3.72, 623/C/72.

[4] *Kastercum* (1972) 56 Cr. App. R. 298; *Jones* 14.1.72, 3372/A/71.

[5] See *Williams* 17.10.75, 3114/C/75 (three months for driving with excess blood alcohol quashed, six months for assault on constable upheld).

acquitted of an offence for which he was being lawfully arrested at the time of the assault,[1] does not affect the gravity of the assault on the constable.)

The range of sentences for assaults on police officers not resulting in injury sufficient to justify conviction for a more serious offence appears to extend from about six months' to the maximum of two years' imprisonment. Within this bracket the nature of the violence, the circumstances in which it came to be offered and the extent of premeditation will be relevant. Cases have already been cited in which sentences of less than six months for relatively minor assaults on constables, committed without obvious premeditation, have been described as lenient. Longer sentences have been upheld in cases involving a greater degree of violence. In *Henstock*[2] a 'hard-working and reliable' young man with no previous convictions jumped on the back of an officer in the course of a disturbance outside a club, knocking him to the ground and possibly kicking him in the back. The sentence of twelve months' imprisonment was upheld. In *Bell*[3] a man of 33 of good character fought with two officers who had been called to a party at a public house (minor cuts suffered by one officer resulted in a charge of assault occasioning actual bodily harm in respect of one of them). Declining an invitation to suspend the sentence as 'the assaults were committed on police officers', the Court upheld the sentence of fifteen months' imprisonment. Sentences of eighteen months and two years have been upheld in cases aggravated by the use of weapons[4] or the unfulfilled intention to cause injury.[5]

The strict view generally taken by the Court of this offence, and the reluctance to approve non-custodial measures except in exceptional cases or those where the assault is minimal or unintentional, does not mean that mitigating circumstances have no effect, although they may have less effect than in other cases. In a case where the appellant came to the aid of his brother who was struggling with officers called to a disturbance at a farewell party intended to mark the appellant's emigration to Canada, the Court treated the fact that the conviction

[1] See *Stewart* 20.12.71, 4964/C/71 (officer punched in attempt to resist arrest for driving with excess blood alcohol, 'comparatively trivial' injuries, offender acquitted of driving offence; eighteen months upheld).
[2] 24.7.73, 1996/C/73.
[3] 28.1.74, 5190/A/73.
[4] See, for example, *Kentish* 16.1.73, 2059/B/72 (eighteen months for threatening officers with hammer, seizing one by throat; upheld, despite acquittal of offence for which arrest was attemped); *McFarlane* 8.5.72, 644/A/72 (young man, 'affirmative good character', striking officers with fists, passing stick to accomplice; two years upheld).
[5] See, for example, *Green* 13.3.75, 3875/B2/75 (officers kicked, bitten and butted in removing appellant from courtroom; eighteen months upheld).

would probably prevent or substantially delay the appellant's departure, and thereby cause him heavy financial loss, as grounds for reducing the sentence from nine months' imprisonment to six.[1]

VIOLENCE AGAINST YOUNG CHILDREN

Acts of violence against children committed by their parents or by other persons responsible for their care, may result in charges under those sections of the Offences Against the Person Act 1861 used to deal with offences of violence in general, or section 1 of the Children and Young Persons Act 1933. This section covers a wide range of behaviour, including cruelty and ill treatment, and overlaps with the definition of assault occasioning actual bodily harm. There appears to be no basis for arguing that a conviction under section 1 of the 1933 Act involves the conclusion that facts which would prove the more serious offence have not been established. The Court has held that the maximum penalty of two years' imprisonment under the 1933 Act does not restrict the power of the sentencer in dealing with cases of violence to children under 16 where the offence is charged under other provisions.[2]

Speaking generally of cases of violence to children, the Court observed that few cases presented greater difficulties in sentencing; 'at one extreme they reveal utter brutality which must be dealt with very severely . . . at the other extreme one gets cases of undoubted maltreatment . . . where the explanation is to be found in social inadequacy or momentary loss of temper'.[3] In cases in the latter category an individualized measure may be approved, provided that the degree of violence used against the child is not grave and arrangements can be made for sufficient support and supervision to make recurrence of the offence unlikely. In one such case[4] the mother of a family living in 'very cramped' conditions admitted inflicting grievous bodily harm on her second child by shaking him and pulling him out of his cot by an arm and a leg. The incident took place within a few weeks of the birth of the child, during a period of matrimonial difficulty and general anxiety which had led to the appellant discharging herself from a hospital against medical advice; the child

---

[1] *Bell, N. J.* 28.1.74, 5190/A/73.
[2] *Beanland* (1970) 54 Cr. App. R. 289.
[3] *Cripps* 19.12.75, 4579/B/75.
[4] *Bonner* 7.10.75, 4323/C/75; see also *Whitney* 10.10.72, 4715/B/72 (assaults by girl, 19, on baby during first three months of life, marriage in difficulties, baby in care; six months' imprisonment varied to probation for three years); *Layne* 20.12.74, 3886/B/74 (young children suffocated by smoke after being left alone overnight, evidence that appellant generally cared well for children; twelve months' imprisonment varied to probation).

was now in care and there were prospects that the marriage would be re-established. The Court varied the sentence from eighteen months' imprisonment to probation for three years.

Where exceptional mitigation is not present, or the violence is of a higher degree or carried on over a more substantial period of time, a custodial sentence is likely to be upheld. In *Doherty*[1] a man of 23 began to live with a woman who had four children and assumed the role of father to them. On two occasions the appellant lost his temper with one of the children, who was eighteen months old; on the first occasion he shook or pulled him, causing a fracture of the radius and ulna, and on the second he struck the child and bit his arm. Declining to consider suspension of the sentence, the Court indicated that it was necessary to mark 'the disapproval of the public for this vicious type of behaviour', but added that the appellant's lack of previous convictions for violence and the fact that 'the acts of violence . . . were not of the more serious kind which . . . occur in cases of this sort' allowed the Court to reduce the sentence from four years' imprisonment to two. In *Harris*[2] the appellant was convicted of assault occasioning actual bodily harm to the 3-year-old daughter of a woman with whom he was living. It was alleged that in the course of a quarrel with her mother the appellant picked the child from her push-chair and threw her against a refrigerator, causing extensive bruising. Treating the appellant as a man of previous good character, and accepting that the assault was an isolated incident, the Court concluded that 'a custodial sentence . . . was inevitable' and that two years' imprisonment was not 'manifestly excessive'.

The range of sentences for cases not involving the deliberate infliction of serious injury extends from about six months' imprisonment to three years, although a few longer sentences can be found[3] (examples of more serious violence leading to death were given earlier).[4] In *Kennedy*[5] the appellant inflicted minor injuries on the 3-year-old son of the woman with whom he was living by throwing a shoe at him and subsequently slapping his legs with it. The

[1] 25.10.74, 2206/A/74.

[2] 14.6.74, 982/C/74; see also *Taylor* 31.10.74, 2110/C/74 (eighteen months' imprisonment for abuse of baby over several months by youth, 19, not excessive; consecutive sentences for unrelated offences satisfying Criminal Justice Act 1961, s. 3); *Aplin* 17.11.75, 3211/A/75 (blows with back of hand to face of 2-year-old child, bruising but no serious injury; three years reduced to two).

[3] See, for example, *Downes* 11.1.71, 1633/C/70 (blows causing child, 3, to strike head against wall, resulting in brain damage, earlier incident causing fractured shin; sentences totalling five years upheld: 'Court should pay regard to . . . public revulsion'); *O'Brien* 4.3.77, 4160/B2/76 (child 'grossly ill-treated . . . over a period of weeks', extensive bruising and damage to genital area, appellant several previous convictions for violence; sentences totalling six years reduced to four).

[4] See p. 79 above.

[5] 17.2.75, 4319/A/74.

Court stated that while 'an assault upon a young child which causes that child injury could in no way be condoned', the nature of the injuries indicated that the case was 'at the lowest end of the scale for this particular type of offence'. The sentence was reduced from eighteen months' imprisonment to six. By contrast in *Hindle*[1] a foster parent was sentenced to three years' imprisonment for wounding a 3-year-old child, who was subsequently found to have forty-five bruises and a head wound caused by a blow with a slipper. Despite the appellant's 'excellent character', the Court considered the sentence of three years' imprisonment to be within 'the bracket of sentences . . . adopted for this type of offence' and upheld it. The cases, viewed collectively, suggest that the criteria for determining the appropriate sentence within this range include the degree of violence offered, the extent to which the incidents charged reflect a pattern of violence and neglect, and the existence of pressures arising from overcrowded accommodation and other social disadvantages. In *Bull*[2] a child of six months was beaten by her father in such a way as to cause fractures of an arm and a leg and extensive bruising on different parts of the body; she had however completely recovered from her injuries. The appellant was depressed and physically unwell at the time of the offence and had had very little sleep during the preceding two days. Taking the view that 'this is a single violent loss of temper' rather than 'a progressive . . . campaign of cruelty', the Court reduced the sentence from three years' imprisonment to two.

RIOT AND AFFRAY

The definitions of the principal offences against public order cover a wide variety of situations, varying from major disturbances involving hundreds of people to fights involving three or four. The level of violence used, the scale of the affray and the extent to which it is premeditated or spontaneous appear to be the most important criteria in determining the length of sentence. A major problem in sentencing in this context is that of determining the individual responsibility of particular defendants. Frequently individual offenders who have participated in an affray or riot will be charged additionally with such offences as wounding with intent or possessing an offensive weapon, which will provide a basis for drawing inferences either against them or (if acquitted) in their favour; but the Court has stated that participation in an affray itself is a grave matter, even though the acts of the particular defendant were not in

[1] 1.7.75, 899/A/75, [1976] Crim. L. R. 322.
[2] 22.2.77, 5074/B/76.

themselves extremely violent: 'those who take part in affrays . . . take on a measure of responsibility for the conduct of those others with whom they are acting jointly in the affray'.[1]

Analysis of the appropriate sentencing brackets is made easier if cases are divided into premeditated affrays—ranging from pitched street battles between rival gangs to ambushes of individuals for the purpose of revenge—and spontaneous affrays, where general fighting breaks out in response to an unforeseen incident. Sentences for affrays in the first category vary from an upper level of about eight years to a lower point of about three years, depending on the level of violence and the number of persons involved. In one case two groups of youths fought 'an arranged battle' in a city street; over one hundred people were involved and a variety of weapons, including shotguns, bicycle chains and iron bars, were used. One young appellant, convicted of affray and wounding with intent after firing a shot-gun, was sentenced to twelve years' imprisonment; the Court accepted that 'long sentences of imprisonment should be passed upon a gang leader who goes armed to battle' but decided that the sentence could be reduced to eight years.[2] In a second case of 'planned affray' six men using a variety of weapons attacked a seventh who had allegedly threatened one of them on a previous occasion; the victim was left lying in the road and was killed by a vehicle driven by the principal defendant, who was convicted of murder.[3] The Court considered that a sentence of ten years on one appellant who took a leading part in the fighting, while not necessarily 'excessive in the circumstances of the case', could be reduced to eight years, partly in view of mitigating factors.

Where the general level of violence is lower, sentences of three or four years may be appropriate. In *Lovett and another*[4] a group of youths who had been refused entry to a club started a fight, swinging crash helmets and heavy chains in the air. One serious injury resulted in a separate conviction for causing grievous bodily harm, but the Court upheld sentences of three and four years' imprisonment on several defendants convicted only of affray, observing that although

---

[1] *Avison and others* 24.4.75, 5030/B/74; see also *Caird and others* (1970) 54 Cr. App. R. 499 at 507 ('it is a wholly wrong approach to take the acts of any individual participator in isolation. They were not committed in isolation and . . . it is that very fact that constitutes the gravity of the offence').

[2] *Luttman and others* 9.10.72, 5246/B/71, [1973] Crim. L. R. 127.

[3] *Bogan and others* 12.6.72, 3319/A/71.

[4] 27.6.75, 840/A/75. Sentences of three years were reduced to borstal training in comparable circumstances in *Avison and others* 24.4.75, 5030/B/74, as a result of problems arising from disparities; apart from this the Court stated that 'the appellants . . . would have had difficulty in persuading this Court to reduce the sentences of three years' imprisonment'. See also *Warren and Tomlinson* 29.10.74, 111/R/74, [1975] Crim. L. R. 111.

one defendant was only 19, 'a sentence of borstal training would not have been appropriate in this case . . . three years' imprisonment was correct both in principle and extent'. In another case[1] three men attacked a fourth who had allegedly been responsible for an assault on a woman acquaintance. The victim was threatened with a knife and bystanders (including several children) were 'reduced to a state of hysteria', although no actual injuries were inflicted. The sentences of three years imposed on two appellants were upheld.

Where the affray develops spontaneously, the bracket of sentences is rather lower, unless exceptionally grave violence is used.[2] In *Long and others*[3] about seventy young people fought in the street, the affray lasting about twenty minutes, but the Court accepted 'this was not one of those cases in which a number of young people band together to go and fight by way of reprisal'; for this reason the sentences of three years were excessive and were reduced, the Court observing that the appropriate sentence would have been about eighteen months. In *Kennedy and Kennedy*[4] the appellants and a third man fought in the street after an incident in a public house; although members of the public were frightened by the incident, no serious injuries were caused. The Court accepted that 'in a case of public violence and disorder of this sort there should be an immediate sentence of imprisonment' but that 'a substantially shorter sentence' than the term of three years imposed by the sentencer would have been sufficient; a sentence of twelve months was substituted.

Section 3: Sexual Offences

RAPE

In the overwhelming majority of cases of rape which come before the Court, a tariff sentence is upheld. Individualized measures, other than life imprisonment[5] or a hospital order,[6] are rarely seen, and a

---

[1] *Summers and others* 15.5.72, 5533/A/71.

[2] See, for example, *Gleaves and others* 18.3.71, 4558/B/70 (knives used in racial fight; three years upheld).

[3] 18.10.71, 1552/C/71.

[4] 15.3.74, 5171/A/73; see also *Sargeant* (1974) 60 Cr. App. R. 74 (fight at discotheque following use of excessive force by bouncer; two years reduced to equivalent of nine months).

[5] See, for example, *Panayiotou* 12.4.73, 6540/C/70 (life imprisonment upheld for man, 38, two rapes and one attempt, four previous convictions for rape, violence used in some cases, psychiatric evidence that further assaults likely); *O'Rourke* 27.11.72, 3920/A/72 (rape of 8-year-old child, grave violence, evidence of continuing dangerousness; life imprisonment upheld). For cases where life imprisonment has been varied to a fixed term on the ground that the dangerousness of the offender was not established, see *Lewis* 14.1.74, 2845/B/73 (rape of 14-year-old with violence, conflicting views on risks of repetition; life imprisonment varied to five years); *Wheal* 7.10.74, 2781/C/74

sentence of borstal training is more usually used as the equivalent of a sentence of imprisonment within the limits imposed by Criminal Justice Act 1961 s.3 than as a training measure.[7]

The scale of sentences extends from a usual minimum of two years to an upper limit of twelve years, although sentences both shorter[8] and longer[9] are occasionally seen. The factors which advance the sentence within this scale include the degree of violence used or threatened in the course of committing the act, the infliction of other forms of sexual abuse, the involvement of more than one defendant and the forcible abduction of the victim or the invasion of the victim's house. Conduct on the part of the victim which increases the risk of rape, such as willing participation in minor sexual activity or (to a lesser extent) imprudent behaviour such as accepting a lift in a car from strangers, is usually treated as a reason for some reduction in sentence. The age of the victim does not appear to have any substantial significance (except that the rape of a young child or an elderly woman may be an indication of the need for psychiatric investigation). The victim's previous sexual experience is not a major factor. The Court has said that 'it is not to be thought that whenever the victim of a rape is a woman of experience or of dubious moral standards it is any less an outrage to take that which the woman is not willing to give', although it is relevant to consider the extent of any physical or traumatic injury caused by the offence.[10] The fact that the victim has forgiven the offender is not necessarily relevant.[11]

(rape of elderly woman with threats of violence, apparent risk of repetition insufficient to justify indeterminate sentence; life imprisonment varied to six years); *Waterman* 5.10.70, 1370/B/70 (rape and two indecent assaults with knife threat, medical evidence that no abnormality or mental disorder present; life imprisonment varied to six years). Difficulties arise where the offender is convicted of attempted rape, for which the maximum sentence is anomalously limited to seven years; see *Scott* 15.5.70, 8885/69.

[6] For example, *John* 27.7.71, 138/A/71 (ten years for two attempted rapes and other offences varied to hospital order with indefinite restriction, diagnosis of paranoid schizophrenia).

[7] See, for example, *Broadhurst* 28.2.75, 4533/C/74 (p. 271 below); *Docherty* 27.6.75, 1015/C/75 (rape of girl after 'relatively mild' intimidation, no evidence of physical or mental injury, appellant 17 with 'exemplary character'; three years' imprisonment varied to borstal training).

[8] For example, *Taylor* 11.4.72, 5484/A/71 (rape of young married woman by friend, no violence or injury, previous belief that advances would be welcome, offence discontinued after initial penetration, immediate confession to police; three years reduced to twelve months in view of 'unusual features').

[9] For example, *O'Dwyer* 17.1.75, 1596/C/74, [1975] Crim. L. R. 247 (child of 11 forcibly abducted and raped, many previous convictions including previous rape of child; life imprisonment probably more appropriate—fifteen years upheld).

[10] *Docherty* 27.6.75, 1015/C/75; see also *Christoforou* 8.7.70, 1256/A/70 (borstal training for youth, 20, no previous convictions, aiding and abetting rape of admitted prostitute; upheld).

[11] See *Pritchard* (1973) 57 Cr. App. R. 492 ('the complainant's subsequent attitude . . . to the sentence is a completely irrelevant consideration').

Sentences in the lowest bracket of two or three years' imprisonment (or borstal training in the case of offenders under 21) are most commonly found where a relatively young man has raped a woman in the same age group with minimal force and the victim's consent to some degree of familiarity. In *Lynch*[1] two girls on the way home from a dance accepted a lift from two men in their early twenties, who were subsequently convicted of attempted rape and indecent assault respectively. The Court took the view that the girls consented to some sexual familiarity, that no violence was used and that the co-defendant's threat to use ammonia was empty as he had none with him, but considered that three years' imprisonment was 'not excessive' for the attempted rape (the sentence was reduced to two years because of an unjustified disparity between that sentence and the co-defendant's 'unduly lenient' sentence of two years for indecent assault). In *Broadhurst*[2] a youth of 19 was allowed to accompany an 18-year-old girl to her flat, where she was 'not . . . reluctant to join in the preliminary lovemaking' but refused to have intercourse; the appellant then raped her, using 'a certain amount of force' but causing no significant injury. The sentencer imposed three years' imprisonment, which the Court considered 'too long, having regard to the age of the parties and . . . the degree of encouragement which the girl gave', and as there was 'no question of . . . a sentence of detention or probation' the sentence was varied to borstal training. In *Miller*[3] a single woman of 31 accepted a lift, late at night, from the appellant, a stranger, and was subsequently induced to enter a flat where the appellant raped her, using force but not apparently causing or threatening injury. The Court, accepting that the offence was 'out of character' and that the appellant had provided valuable public service in a voluntary capacity, reduced the sentence from five years' imprisonment to three, 'as an act of mercy, but without criticizing the sentence that was . . . passed'. As this case indicates, the location of a sentence in the lowest sentencing bracket may reflect personal mitigating factors rather than the inherent quality of the offence.[4]

In cases not distinguished either by aggravating features or by the

[1] 19.1.70, 2368/69.

[2] 28.2.75, 4533/C/74; see also *Docherty* 27.6.75, 1015/C/75 (p. 113 above); *Smith* 24.6.71, 655/C/71 (youth, 19, used 'a certain degree of violence' against a girl of 17 who had permitted a degree . . . of familiarity' but then went 'far beyond [what] the girl had intended'; three years upheld); *Williams* 11.2.72, 4854/B/71 (three years for attempted rape of 15-year-old girl by 18-year-old youth in company with others upheld; girl previously 'flaunting herself' in front of hostel where appellant living, previous intercourse with appellant).

[3] 3.7.73, 5226/A/72.

[4] See, for example, *Pritchard* (1973) 57 Cr. App. R. 492 (four years for violent rape of sister-in-law not excessive; reduced to three as 'an act of mercy', as appellant now realized 'the full implication of the disaster . . . he has brought upon his own family'); *Bell* 30.11.72, 4617/A/72 (rape of young woman in ladies' lavatory, immediate

characteristics just described, the Court will normally uphold a sentence of between three and five years' imprisonment. Many examples can be found. In *Abbasi*[1] a man of good character was convicted of raping a foreign girl whom he had induced to enter his car and subsequently threatened; accepting that it was a case of 'rape by fear rather than by force', the Court upheld four years' imprisonment. In *Slade*[2] the appellant met a young woman walking on a cliff path; after walking together for some time they entered a cave to examine a rock formation, where the appellant raped her after threatening to kill her. The victim suffered no direct physical injury but was in a state of clinical shock some hours after the event. The sentence of five years was upheld. In *Vivian*[3] a youth of 18 accosted a nurse who was returning late at night to a nurses' home, threatened her with a knife and demanded intercourse; he desisted on discovering that she was menstruating at the time. A sentence of four years for attempted rape was upheld.

Longer sentences, within the bracket of five to eight years' imprisonment, will usually be upheld where the offence is accompanied by aggravating factors. The rape of a girl by a group of men will be held to justify a sentence in this range, as in *Hume and others*,[4] where eight youths of previous good character were each convicted of raping (or attempting to rape) a 17-year-old girl and (with one exception) aiding and abetting the others. It was alleged that the girl had been accosted by the youths in a street one evening, dragged to a field and subjected to a 'mass assault' involving several acts of

---

confession, 'absolutely clean record', marriage recently broken up; five years reduced to three).

[1] 21.5.73, 339/A/73; see also *Clark* 11.10.71, 3281/C/71 (rape of defective 16-year-old girl, force used but no serious injury; five years upheld).

[2] 12.3.74, 4881/A/73; see also *Groves* 22.10.71, 598/C/71 (rape of woman found in broken-down car with children, 'comparatively little physical violence used . . . victim overpowered by fear rather than actual force'; five years upheld).

[3] 1.2.71, 4092/A/70; see also *Price* 15.10.71, 1438/B/71, [1972] Crim. L. R. 57 (attempted rape of woman having trouble with car, victim punched and thrown to ground, attack interrupted by arrival of dog walker; five years upheld); *Potter* 13.11.73, 3760/B/73 (attempted rape by acquaintance in company with two other youths, no penetration or substantial injury, 'terrifying experience'; five years upheld); *Maynard* 22.2.71, 5356/B/70 (schoolgirl attacked when walking home from cinema, dragged into alley, knocked to ground, attack interrupted, no serious damage; five years for youth, 20, upheld).

[4] 8.12.72, 5447/C/72, [1972] Crim. L. R. 320; see also *Remie* 19.10.71, 6015/B/70 (girl abducted from park by four men, subjected to rape and attempted rape; six years upheld); *Gilligan* 11.1.71, 5221/A/70 (16-year-old babysitter raped by two men; seven years upheld); *Julien and others* 11.11.70, 2763/C/70 (girl imprisoned in house, raped by seven men; six years upheld, nine years on one appellant convicted of additional offences); *Frayne and Winter* 17.6.76, 5656/A/75 (courting couple surprised by three men, man held at point of screwdriver, girl raped by two of the attackers; five years and six years respectively upheld).

intercourse and other indecencies. Sentences of seven years' (in one case, six years') imprisonment were upheld. Abduction or imprisonment of the victim will justify a sentence at this level, as in *Wren*,[1] where the appellant induced a foreign student to enter his car after earlier purporting to engage her as a babysitter; the girl was driven to a lonely place, threatened with a knife, raped and abandoned. The sentence of eight years' imprisonment was upheld.

Other aggravating features which will support a sentence in excess of five years include the use of a high degree of violence, in addition to the force required to perpetrate the rape,[2] or the infliction of sexual indignities other than intercourse. In *Birch*[3] a man of 24 with several previous convictions for indecent assault attacked a nurse who was walking to a bus stop late at night. The victim was subjected to violence causing an injury to her nose, raped, and forced to submit to oral intercourse; the incident lasted over an hour. The Court upheld a sentence of eight years' imprisonment. The rape of a woman by an intruder in her home will frequently attract a sentence in the higher bracket. In *Drever*[4] the appellant forced his way, in the small hours of the morning, into a house occupied by a single woman in her fifties, dragged her from the bathroom into a bedroom and raped her with some force. Despite the appellant's good character and 'genuine

---

[1] 1.2.74, 4701/C/73, [1974] Crim. L. R. 322; see also *Roberts* 15.6.72, 861/C/72 (car containing sleeping woman taken from the car park, driven to lonely place, woman raped and subjected to other indecencies; seven years reduced to four solely on account of age of appellant, just 17 at date of sentence); *Gibson* 4.3.71, 3225/B/70 (young woman lured to flat on pretext of availability for lease, detained and raped; six years upheld); *Khan* 6.6.74, 1428/B/74 (victim abducted while drunk from club known as resort of prostitutes, raped by two men of good character; seven years reduced to five, partly as victim had 'put herself at risk'); *Jones* 31.7.73, 1133/B/73 (girl of eighteen forced into a car and indecently assaulted, managed to escape before being raped; four years upheld).

[2] See, for example, *Partridge* 13.5.74, 952/C/74 (woman kicked in head in attempt to rouse her from drunken stupor after rape; nine years for rape and manslaughter upheld).

[3] 11.4.75, 4815/C/74; see also *Findlay* 8.5.72, 512/C/72 (young typist attacked in office during lunch-hour by 19-year-old youth, raped, subjected to oral intercourse, no extreme violence; seven years reduced to five because of age).

[4] 25.4.72, 5587/A/71; see also *Rhodes* 17.4.72, 42/A/72 (appellant forcing entrance to house during evening, raping 16-year-old babysitter with considerable force, injuries inflicted; seven years upheld); *Thompson* 15.11.73, 2296/B/73 (woman accosted in lift in block of flats, taken to own flat, raped, subsequently bound and gagged; eight years upheld); *Bex* 5.6.75, 4548/C/74 (appellant gaining entrance to houses by fraud, threatening women with knife, attempting rape; sentences totalling eleven years excessive under totality principle—reduced to total of seven years); *Aldred* 8.5.70, 206/A/69 (man entering house by window, threatening harm to children; twenty years reduced to eight); *Jones* 21.2.77, 5971/A2/75 (pregnant woman raped by burglar, ten years 'somewhat too long'—reduced to eight). In *Jason* 20.2.76, 3795/C/75 sentences totalling twelve years were upheld for four rapes or attempts on women attacked in their own homes, partly in view of the risk of repetition. The case may be seen as a refusal to apply the totality principle in the case of a dangerous offender; compare *Kenny* 16.1.76, 3660/B/75 (p. 61 above).

contrition', the sentence of seven years' imprisonment was upheld.

Where aggravating factors such as these are not present, a sentence much in excess of five years is unlikely to be upheld. In *Brimacombe*[1] a man of 28 raped an 11-year-old schoolgirl whom he encountered on her way home from school. Although it was 'a serious rape', no weapon or grave violence was used, and hearing that the offence was related to a period of matrimonial difficulty, the Court reduced the sentence from eight years' imprisonment to five.

Sentences in excess of eight years' imprisonment are clearly reserved for cases exhibiting a combination of aggravating features in their strongest form, and twelve years appears to represent the upper limit of the scale. This sentence was upheld in *Jones,*[2] where the appellant forced his way into the victim's car, constricted her throat on several occasions so that she lost consciousness, raped and buggered her more than once, subjected her to oral intercourse, attempted to strangle her with a piece of string and finally left her naked in a ditch. In view of the 'horrifying features' of the case the sentence of twelve years was upheld.

INCEST

Almost all cases of incest which come before the Court involve intercourse between father and daughter, usually while the daughter is in her early teenage years and still under the protection of her parents. Frequently the facts of the offence will be disputed, and a plea of guilty to one or more counts may not resolve the question whether the counts charged represent isolated incidents or a regular pattern of behaviour. The Court has held that where the accused pleads guilty or is convicted in respect of specified occasions and denies any other instances, he must be sentenced on the basis that no other acts of incest have occurred, unless further counts are added to the indictment and proved in the normal way.[3] It is submitted that a similar principle applies to allegations that the daughter did not consent; the sentencer should not proceed on the basis that the

---

[1] 20.4.71, 3783/B/70; see also *Cleary* 8.6.70, 9613/69 (rape of 15-year-old girl with considerable force; eight years 'out of line even for such a bad rape as this one'— reduced to six); *Peel* 25.1.72, 2330/A/71 (woman going for car ride at 2 a.m., after some 'kissing and cuddling' threatened with knife and kicked to ground; ten years reduced to six); *Downs* 10.5.76, 5595/C/75 (12-year-old girl induced to enter car, raped under threats; eight years reduced to six, primarily to reflect plea of guilty).
[2] 12.5.75, 318/B/75, [1976] Crim. L. R. 203; see also *Lashley* 14.1.71, 299/C/70 (woman almost strangled prior to rape; sentences totalling twelve years upheld); *Gibson* 1.3.76, 3587/A2/75 (forcible rape and buggery of 8-year-old, serious injuries inflicted; twelve years upheld).
[3] *Huchison* (1972) 56 Cr. App. R. 307.

offence was aggravated in this way unless a count for rape is included in the indictment and proved or admitted.

While the Court has occasionally substituted non-custodial sentences on appeal in cases of incest between father and daughter,[1] a tariff sentence is upheld in the majority of cases. Frequently the appellant has a number of substantial mitigating factors in his favour, and the weight which the Court usually gives to these makes difficult the precise definition of the limits of the normal range of sentences considered in relation to the facts of the offence in the abstract.

Sentences of five years' imprisonment or longer are likely to be upheld where the father deliberately exploits his position in the family by systematically seducing his daughter over a period of time, usually by a series of acts of increasing indecency until the process is completed. Often in such cases more than one daughter is involved, and occasionally the process may spread outside the family to include friends of the daughter. In the worst cases the offender will involve other males, even his own sons, in the activities.[2] In *Forster*[3] the appellant was convicted of four counts of incest with his 11-year-old daughter. It was alleged that having decided that the child was old enough to be initiated into sexual activities, he had committed incest

[1] For example, *Landall* 4.12.75, 2889/C/75 (two years for incest with daughter, apparently about 18 'entirely appropriate' but varied to probation in view of 'special considerations'—offences stale, partly provoked by daughter, some committed after daughter had established independence); *Hawes* 19.10.73, 1347/A/73 (incest with daughter from age 16, already pregnant by another person; three years 'fully justified' but varied to probation in view of deteriorating medical condition of appellant); *Smith* 15.3.74, 5469/A/73 (incest with 13-year-old after separation for twelve years, appellant and daughter 'to all intents and purposes strangers to each other', daughter already 'accustomed to fairly regular sexual intercourse'; offence 'serious' and three years 'not surprising', but varied to twelve months suspended); *Glynn* 30.1.70, 4592/C/69, [1970] Crim. L. R. 293 (four years for attempted incest with daughter, 8, appropriate, but varied to probation in view of various mitigating circumstances, including attitude of wife and children); *Cooke* 26.11.76, 2436/C/76 (four years for incest with two daughters 'eminently right', but varied to two years suspended in view of attitude of family and other mitigation); *Taylor* 29.3.76, 529/B/76 (two years varied to probation in view of 'exceptional grounds').

[2] See *Grant* 10.2.76, 4149/A/75, [1976] Crim. L. R. 640 (father of five daughters and two sons, commencing incest with each daughter at age 7 or 8, regular offences over period of ten years, other offences of indecent assault and buggery, sons encouraged to indulge in sexual activity with sisters; offences 'outside the normal scale'—fifteen years upheld to 'mark the horror and disgust of every right-thinking person' and to 'give a chance to the family to make a new life for themselves'; *Flack* 19.3.68, 6808/67, [1968] Crim. L. R. 339, distinguished on facts); see also *Dye* 11.3.77, 1849/C/76 (ten years for incest and indecent assault on daughters and son reduced to seven in view of low intelligence).

[3] 21.1.72, 4727/A/71; see also *Curtis* 26.6.73, 1515/B/73 (incest, indecent assault and buggery of own three children and niece, 15, 11, 8, 7, appellant 'not the most intelligent of persons'; ten years reduced to seven); *Flack* 31.10.77, 3536/A/76 (incest with youngest daughter by man previously sentenced for incest with other daughters; nine years reduced to seven).

with her and introduced another man into the house with a view to
intercourse with her. His sentence of seven years' imprisonment was
upheld. In *Palmer*[1] the appellant admitted three offences of attempted incest against his daughter over a period of two years, beginning
when she was fourteen. On the first occasion he had deliberately made
her drunk before attempting the offence. Observing that the maximum sentence for attempted incest was two years' imprisonment (by
contrast with seven years for the completed offence)[2] and that pleas
to attempt should not be accepted where there was evidence of
sufficient penetration to establish the full offence, the Court upheld
consecutive sentences totalling four and a half years.

Although in cases not exhibiting these aggravating factors sentences of five years or more have been approved as correct in principle
and reduced only because of the presence of personal mitigating
factors,[3] the usual range of sentences for the more typical cases of
incest (involving a series of acts over a short period of time, often
within a family living in cramped conditions, and a father whose
normal sexual relationship with his wife has been interrupted)
appears to extend from two to four years' imprisonment. In *Varcoe*[4] a
man of 41 with no previous convictions, described as 'a very good
provider for his family' although 'of rather dull mentality', admitted
about ten acts of incest with his 13-year-old daughter over two
months, following a period of matrimonial difficulty; the sentence of
four years was upheld. In *Donkin*[5] a man of forty with 'a clean record'
admitted two charges of incest and two of attempted incest in respect

[1] 29.7.74, 670/C/74; see also *O'Dell* 16.11.71, 1774/B/71 (sentences totalling eight
years excessive for incest with daughter and indecent assault on various other children;
reduced to five years by making all sentences concurrent; five years for incest upheld);
Fry 28.10.75, 3515/A/75, [1976] Crim. L. R. 266 (incest with granddaughter, 13, part of
'course of conduct over longish period' involving indecent assault; five years upheld);
Leadbeater 14.6.76, 140/A/76 (sentences totalling eight years for attempted incest and
indecent assault on daughter between ages of 8 and 10, appellant 'did not appear to
understand the gravity of what he was doing'; reduced to five years); *Stanier* 21.10.77,
1151/A/77 (attempted incest and other offences against daughter, 12; ten years
aggregate 'more severe than one would expect', reduced to total of six years).
[2] Higher maxima apply in each case where the daughter is under 13; see Sexual
Offences Act 1956 s. 37 and sch. 2.
[3] For example, *Phillips* 10.11.72, 1284/C/72 (appellant sentenced to six years on
basis of incest with two daughters following admission of incest with one, counts
relating to others to lie on file; sentence would have been 'appropriate' if all offences
established, but reduced to two on basis of single count admitted); *Bates* 2.4.73,
734/B/73 (six years for incest with daughter, 10, reduced to four in view of
'unblemished record' and plea of guilty); *Roberts* 22.3.73, 2962/C/72 (five years for
single act of incest with 15-year-old 'did not err in principle'—reduced to three years in
view of loss of career, gratuity, pension rights and other mitigating factors); *Stevens*
5.5.70, 116/B/70 (six years 'not . . . an outrageous sentence' for incest and buggery
with daughter; reduced to four in view of attitude of wife and daughter).
[4] 19.2.76, 5401/B/75.
[5] 7.11.75, 4451/B/74, [1976] Crim. L. R. 266; see also *Kelly* 6.6.72, 5763/B/71 (man,
51, no previous convictions for sexual offences, two counts of incest with daughter, 12;

(apparently) of two of his seven children, with whom he and his wife were living in 'congested . . . conditions'. The offences had taken place within a period of a few weeks and although the daughters were not willing participants, they were not disclosed until a year after they had occurred. Sentences totalling four years' imprisonment were upheld. In *Casey*[1] the appellant's wife died and his 21-year-old daughter, who had no previous sexual experience, assumed responsibility for running the household. She reluctantly engaged in intercourse with her father on several occasions and eventually became pregnant. The father's sentence of four years' imprisonment was upheld.

Apart from mitigating factors personal to the offender, some characteristics of the offence may justify a lower sentence. The age of the daughter does not appear to be a critical factor, unless she is very young,[2] but the fact that she has previously had sexual experience with another man[3] or has established some degree of financial or domestic independence may be significant. In *Grimbleby*[4] the appellant's marriage broke down and his eldest daughter went to live with his wife at the age of 6; eleven years later, when his second liaison collapsed, the daughter, now nearly eighteen and with 'considerable sexual experience', came to live with the appellant to act as housekeeper and look after the younger children. Intercourse took place several times with the daughter's full consent, after they began to share a bed for convenience in view of the 'very overcrowded' living conditions. The appellant, who had no previous convictions and an 'exemplary work character', admitted the offences immediately after they were discovered. His sentence was reduced from four years' imprisonment to two. A shorter sentence may also be appropriate where only a single act of incest can be established. In *Humphrey*[5] a man of 'limited intelligence' admitted a single offence,

---

four years upheld); *Daniel* 22.11.71, 1978/A/71 (single count of incest with daughter, 15, acquitted of other counts of incest and rape; four years upheld); *Elsworth* 7.7.77, 5877/A/76 (attempted incest with grand-daughter, 10; four years upheld).

[1] 1.3.71, 6110/B/70.

[2] See, for example, *Hampton* 8.5.70, 205/70 (three years for three counts of incest with 9-year-old daughter upheld, sixty-three days not to count).

[3] See, for example, *Moore* 20.11.75, 2099/A/75 (four counts of incest or attempt with 'overdeveloped' 16-year-old daughter with previous sexual experience; four years reduced to eighteen months); *Tharby* 21.1.71, 4446/A/70 (incest with experienced 18-year-old daughter with full consent; sentence 'properly a comparatively small one', concurrent with three years for incest with 15-year-old daughter).

[4] 23.11.72, 4000/A/72; see also *Wilson* (1973) 58 Cr. App. R. 304 (incest with daughter living in her own flat, daughter 'reluctantly submitted' after father's threat of suicide; five years reduced to three).

[5] 16.1.76, 3426/C/75; see also *Huchison* (1972) 56 Cr. App. R. 307; *Phillips* 10.11.72, 1284/C/72 (above, p. 119). Longer sentences were upheld, or considered appropriate for single acts of incest in *Roberts* 22.3.73, 2962/C/72 (above, p. 119) and *Daniel* 22.11.71, 1978/A/71 (above, p. 120).

involving 'nominal penetration', with his sub-normal 14-year-old daughter; the sentence of five years' imprisonment was reduced to thirty months.

Apart from these considerations, the most common reason for the reduction of a sentence below the level of three to four years is the presence of personal mitigating factors, which may carry greater weight in this context than in cases of sexual violence.[1] In one such case[2] the appellant admitted regular acts of intercourse with his 18-year-old daughter over a period of six months. The Court, referring to several mitigating factors, including the appellant's previous good character, his record of thirty years' work for one employer and the fact that the offence had led to divorce proceedings, reduced the sentence to thirty months' imprisonment, 'in the special circumstances of this case . . . without in any way seeking to fault a sentence of four years for incest'.

Incest between brother and sister, although very rarely the subject of an appeal against sentence, is clearly treated as an offence very different from incest between father and daughter. In the two cases of this kind before the Court in recent years, a non-custodial sentence has been substituted.[3]

UNLAWFUL SEXUAL INTERCOURSE WITH GIRLS OVER 13 AND UNDER 16

The most significant sentencing consideration in cases of unlawful sexual intercourse with girls between 13 and 16 is the age difference between the parties.[4] Where the offender is himself only a few years older than the girl concerned the usual sentence is a fine or conditional discharge,[5] although an individualized measure such as

[1] See, for example, *Brignull* 16.10.75, 2574/C/75 (four years for incest with daughter, 12, 'correct sentence'; reduced to thirty months in view of good record, loss of pension rights, plea of guilty and deterioration of character in prison); *Perkins* 23.8.72, 1950/A/72 (three years for incest with daughter originally 13, reduced to equivalent of eight months, although 'not . . . wrong in principle or . . . excessive', because 'the family unit will reunite if this man is allowed to return'); *Carter* 18.2.75, 4040/A/74 (five years for several acts of incest with 13-year-old daughter after breakdown of marriage 'unnecessary', as 'he punished himself more effectively than any court could punish him' and 'the chances of a repetition . . . are absolutely nil'; reduced to eighteen months); *Webb* 2.3.76, 3899/A2/75 (four years 'difficult to criticize' but reduced to thirty months because of mitigating circumstances).

[2] *Holmes-Parker* 30.1.73, 4002/A/72.

[3] See *George* 24.6.71, 2390/B/71 (youth, 16, incest and attempt with younger sisters, all children sharing same bedroom, borstal training varied to probation); *Winch* 2.5.74, 704/A/74, [1974] Crim. L. R. 487 (man of 33 living with sister, 34, as man and wife; two years suspended varied to conditional discharge).

[4] For a general discussion, see *Taylor* (1977) 64 Cr. App. R. 182.

[5] See, for example, *Chambers* 10.5.71, 1201/A/71 (youth, 19, no previous sexual offence, 'entirely willing and sexually experienced girl of 14'; borstal training varied to fine, 'in such cases the normal disposal . . . is a conditional discharge or a fine').

probation will be considered appropriate if the general circumstances indicate a need for training or supervision.[1] A custodial sentence is likely to be upheld, despite the proximity of the ages of the parties, where the appellant has deliberately flouted the law by committing the offence with full knowledge of the circumstances and after appropriate warning. In *Farrall*[2] a man of 22 was sentenced to eighteen months' imprisonment for abducting and having unlawful intercourse with a girl of 14. Shortly before the offences were committed he had received a suspended sentence of six months for similar offences with the same girl; this sentence was brought into effect. Observing that 'what worries this Court is the defiance which the appellant displayed towards the law', the Court was able to extend 'a measure of mercy' by reducing the sentences to a total of eighteen months. Other aggravating factors may justify a sentence of imprisonment, despite the absence of a substantial difference in age.[3]

Offenders beyond their early twenties are more likely to receive a sentence of imprisonment. In *Rathbone*[4] a divorced man of 26 admitted intercourse with a girl of 15 and attempted intercourse with her friend. The Court stated that although both girls 'had a taste for sexual intercourse which was not seemly for their ages', the law intended that 'girls under 16 should be protected from men and from themselves'; in view of the ten-year difference in the ages of the parties the sentence of nine months' imprisonment was upheld. Unless aggravating features are present, the sentence in such cases will rarely exceed twelve months' imprisonment. In *Waters*[5] a married man of 27

[1] See, for example, *Eccles* 24.2.72, 5835/C/71 (borstal training for youth, 19, previously conditionally discharged for offence with same girl; varied to probation); *McKay* 23.9.74, 1552/C/74 (youth, 19, girl, 14, offence committed in presence of others; borstal training varied to probation); *Barnes* 17.2.77, 413/C/77 (youth, 18, several convictions; three months' detention upheld); *Wilson* 1.11.76, 4734/B/76 (youth, 16, previous convictions for variety of offences, including unlawful sexual intercourse, 'a young man who pays no regard to the law'; borstal training upheld).

[2] 20.7.71, 5813/C/70; see also *Sutton* 29.1.71, 6017/B/70, [1971] Crim. L. R. 301 (man, 22, previously fined for similar offence with different girl; nine months for offence with girl, 14, upheld: 'this man . . . did what he did . . . with full knowledge that it was an offence . . . for which he had already been punished, and . . . he flouted the law').

[3] See, for example, *Planas* 4.6.74, 1774/B/74 (youth, 20, houseparent at children's home, offence with girl, 15, in care; six months immediate varied to six months suspended).

[4] 20.2.76, 5519/C/75, [1976] Crim. L. R. 521; see also *Larby* 5.2.71, 6069/B/70 (man, 39, girl, 14; twelve months 'fully within the normal limits'—upheld); *Lane* 5.9.73, 3190/B/73 (man, 32, girl becoming pregnant after warnings from parents and police; twelve months upheld); *Hayes* 6.2.75, 4571/C/74 (man, 33, intercourse with friend of daughter; nine months upheld, despite other serious consequences of offence to appellant). *Griffiths* 5.5.75, 5188/C/74, where the Court considered a sentence of imprisonment 'excessive' for a man of 29, appears to represent a departure from the normal pattern.

[5] 22.2.74, 5243/B/73; see also *Tung* 4.10.76, 2770/C/76 (man, 27; two years excessive—reduced to equivalent of eight months); *Taylor* 15.3.77, 6205/B1/76 (man,

admitted several offences with a 'willing' girl of 13 who had previous sexual experience; the sentence was reduced from eighteen months' imprisonment to nine. The Court is often prepared to give substantial effect to personal mitigating factors in cases where imprisonment is justified on the facts of the offence, either by reducing[1] or suspending[2] what would otherwise be the appropriate sentence.

Sentences in excess of twelve months' imprisonment are likely to be upheld where, in addition to the difference in ages between the parties, the offence is aggravated by the existence of a relationship between them casting some obligation of care on the offender. In *Roper*[3] a man of 46 was sentenced to consecutive terms of two years' imprisonment for two offences with a girl who regarded him as a friend of the family and called him 'uncle'; the Court considered it 'a bad case' of 'breach of trust', but varied the sentences to two years concurrent. In *Boyd*[4] a sentence of eighteen months' imprisonment passed on a man of 34 for intercourse with his 14-year-old stepdaughter was upheld, and a similar sentence was upheld on a man of 32 who committed the offence with the 14-year-old daughter of the family with whom he had lodged for some years.[5] Sentences of this length have also been upheld where the circumstances of the offence indicate unusual depravity[6] or indifference to the welfare of the girl concerned.[7]

21, girl, 15; twelve months excessive—reduced to three).

[1] See, for example, *Dodds* 21.8.72, 3065/A/72 (man, 33, girl, 15; sentencer 'might very well . . . have passed a longer sentence' than six months, but sentence reduced to allow immediate release, as appellant 'has made a real effort . . . to live down a chequered and criminal past'); *Handley* 7.5.73, 1182/C/73, (man, 36, girl, 14; twelve months varied to three months with fine, in view of good character and effect of sentence on wife and family); *Gill* 8.7.74, 2149/C/74 (man, 33, girl, 15 'keen and willing', appellant admitted offences on own initiative; nine months reduced to allow immediate release); *Shuck* 9.2.76, 5241/C/75 (man, 32, 'of sterling qualities apart from this . . . episode', girl becoming pregnant; twelve months 'not too severe' reduced to six because 'his background speaks so well for him').

[2] See, for example, *Green* 4.6.74, 1735/B/74 (man apparently in thirties; twelve months for single act with girl, 15, appropriate in length, but suspended in hope that appellant would be able to resolve matrimonial problems); *Doman* 28.2.75, 264/A/75 (man, 62, girls, 13 and 15, nine months immediate varied to nine months suspended in view of 'the girls' depravity').

[3] 19.7.74, 868/B/74; see also *Strickland* 7.5.73, 1263/C/73 (man, 53, intercourse with friend of disabled daughter staying with family; eighteen months reduced to nine to allow appellant to care for daughter, Court 'moved not so much by sympathy for appellant, whose offences were disgraceful, as by sympathy with daughter'); *Young* 29.4.76, 4193/75 (man, 41, seduction of daughter of friend over period of months; two years not 'too severe' for offences against 'the girl in the position of one of the family').

[4] 13.1.72, 3787/A/71.

[5] *Cochrane* 15.6.71, 927/B/71; see also *Blakeley* 22.3.71, 5467/C/70 (single offence with 15-year-old girl engaged as babysitter for appellant's children; fifteen months upheld).

[6] See, for example, *Eyre and Bowler* 30.7.70, 308/C/70 (photographs taken while offence in course of commission; eighteen months upheld).

[7] See, for example, *Wesson* 27.7.72, 832/C/72 (man, 43, divorced and two liaisons

UNLAWFUL SEXUAL INTERCOURSE WITH GIRLS UNDER 13

Although a few cases can be found where the offender is under 21,[1] the typical appellant in cases of unlawful sexual intercourse with girls under 13 is an older man, often in his fifties or sixties. In most cases the Court upholds a tariff sentence (although presumably psychiatric measures would be approved in appropriate cases), and the normal sentencing bracket seems to be between three and five years, although longer sentences are occasionally upheld.[2] In *Prescott*[3] a man of 62 admitted intercourse and indecency with an 11-year-old girl who had come to his house to play with his granddaughter. The Court considered that in view of his character and the probability that no further offences would be committed, the sentence could be reduced from five years to three. In *Major*[4] a man of 62 admitted a number of offences of unlawful sexual intercourse and indecent assault committed over a period of years with a girl between the ages of 6 and 10. The Court stated that a sentence of imprisonment was necessary to ensure 'the protection of young members of the public and . . . demonstrate the public's revulsion at the type of crime committed', but that the total of six years' imprisonment was 'longer than was necessary for a person of the age of this appellant'. Sentences totalling four years were substituted. In *Clarke*[5] a man of 54 admitted several acts of intercourse and indecency, committed over a period of time with a girl between the ages of 8 and 15, who was the daughter of a woman with whom he had been associating. The Court said that although 'severe sentences' were necessary in cases of this kind to indicate 'society's abhorrence of such matters', nine years' imprisonment was too long, and sentences totalling five years were substituted. These cases appear to indicate that the frequency of the acts and the duration of the relationship are the significant criteria, and that the

---

'leaving a trail of . . . six children . . . with large arrears of maintenance and affiliation', intercourse with 11-year-old leading to pregnancy; eighteen months upheld); *Edwards* 27.5.76, 1521/C/76 (divorced man, 36, several children, series of offences with girl, 15, leading to pregnancy; fifteen months upheld).

[1] For example, *Rayasat* 24.6.71, 53/C/71; *Uddin* 5.10.70, 2891/B/70; *Dillon* 5.5.75, 4909/A/74. In each case the Court upheld, substituted or would have preferred borstal training.

[2] See, for example, *Crowther* 14.3.75, 5187/A/73 (man, 45, intercourse with 9-year-old daughter of couple who had taken him into their home and treated him as member of family; ten years 'too severe'—reduced to seven).

[3] 25.2.74, 4610/B/73.

[4] 12.5.72, 5041/B/74; see also *Dean* 16.6.72, 1295/C/72 (widower, 63, attempted intercourse with 'extremely precocious' girl, 12; three years upheld).

[5] 2.5.75, 4881/C/74.

offence will be aggravated where the offender takes advantage of some relationship with the child or the confidence of the parents to commit the offence.[1]

INDECENT ASSAULT ON FEMALES

The term 'indecent assault', even when limited to females, covers a wide range of behaviour. At least three different kinds of incident commonly result in prosecutions for this offence, and it is necessary to distinguish between them in order to examine the sentencing practice of the Court. The three categories of indecent assault on females into which most cases can be placed are aggressive assaults on mature women and girls falling short of attempted rape, technical assaults on consenting adolescent girls under 16 in circumstances not amounting to unlawful sexual intercourse, and offences of indecency with younger children (including some offences charged under the Indecency With Children Act 1960). The problems of sentencing in cases of indecent assault are aggravated by the structure of maximum penalties for the offence, which are two years' imprisonment if the victim is 13 years old or over and five years if she is below that age.[2] These maxima, unlike those applicable to most offences, leave little room for manoeuvre in cases exhibiting aggravating features, with the consequence that additional charges (such as assault occasioning actual bodily harm) are often included in indictments. This practice can cause difficulty in relating the sentences on the different counts to each other (particularly where the offender is under 21 and thus subject to the restrictive provisions of Criminal Justice Act 1961 s.3)[3]

[1] See, for example, *Obado* 11.3.71, 4616/C/70 (intercourse and other offences by man, 31, with illegitimate daughters of wife; five years upheld); *Thomas* 26.4.71, 4160/B/70 (intercourse leading to pregnancy with 11-year-old daughter of woman with whom appellant living; five years upheld); *Wetherell* 24.2.77, 54/B/77 (man, 31, intercourse with 12-year-old daughter of friend, photographs taken, other children involved; five years reduced to four).

[2] Sexual Offences Act 1956 s. 37 and sch. 2.

[3] See, for example, *Blake* 15.5.72, 1474/A/72, where a youth of 17 entered the bedroom of a woman of 74, indecently assaulted her in a serious manner and incidentally caused some bruising and a minor cut. He was sentenced to six months' imprisonment (the maximum permissible under Criminal Justic Act 1961, s. 3) for the indecent assault, and three years for assault occasioning actual bodily harm. The Court considered that the indecent assault was the 'serious feature' and justified a sentence of imprisonment 'of substantial proportion', while the assault occasioning actual bodily harm was 'by comparison of a minor character'. Describing the outcome as 'incongruous' and attributing 'these disparate and incomprehensible sentences' to the effect of the 1961 Act, the Court held that as the assault occasioning actual bodily harm would not in itself justify three years' imprisonment, the proper sentence was borstal training, following the principle in *Lowe* (1964) 48 Cr. App. R. 165. Where the violence is the principle gravamen of the offence, it is appropriate to impose a longer sentence for the non-sexual offence; see *Compton* 13.5.75, 4776/B/74 (girl partly strangled; three years for assault occasioning actual bodily harm upheld).

and may lead to departures from the principle requiring concurrent sentences for offences forming part of a single transaction.[1] There is clearly an urgent need for a legislative revision of this area of the criminal law which would distinguish between forms of behaviour which are really quite different and provide scope for an approach to sentencing more consistent with the Courts general policy.

Agressive assaults on mature women and girls

While individualized measures have been substituted on appeal in cases of indecent assault falling within this category where a particularly strong case could be made,[2] the general preference of the Court is for a tariff sentence. As the victim in most cases within this category is over the age of 13, the maximum sentence is limited to two years' imprisonment. This term has been upheld in several cases where the victim was subjected to substantial indecency and some degree of violence, with no provocation or other behaviour which could be interpreted as an invitation to familiarity. In *Weston*[3] a man of 'completely unblemished record' seized a young woman (who was unknown to him) in the street, threw her to the ground, pulled some of her clothing off, bit her breast and inserted his fingers into her private parts. He was convicted of malicious wounding and indecent assault and sentenced to eighteen months' and two years' imprisonment consecutively; the Court accepted that the episode amounted to 'one incident of considerable gravity' and varied the sentences to two years on each count concurrent. Where the degree of indecency or physical violence is slightly less, a sentence below the maximum will

1 See, for example, *Griffin* 8.7.74, 1447/B/74, where the appellant entered his cousin's bedroom and struggled with her while handling her indecently; the girl suffered several bruises. He was sentenced to two years for indecent assault and two years consecutive for assault occasioning actual bodily harm. The Court commented that the events constituted 'one incident' and that while 'the maximum sentences . . . sometimes leave the Court with the feeling that its powers of punishment are inadequate, feelings of frustration must not . . . be obviated . . . by the imposition of consecutive sentences'. The sentence on the second count was reduced to one year, still consecutive. Where the violence is distinct from the indecency, consecutive sentences may be appropriate, as in *Howard* 5.6.75, 683/B/75, where the victim was first indecently assaulted in a serious manner, and then, after an interval, beaten about the head with a brick.

2 See, for example, *Miller* 28.1.75, 5105/C/74 (serious indecent assault on girl being taken home from club after some familiarity, appellant married later same day; offence 'did merit a sentence of imprisonment', but suspension justified in view of exceptional circumstances); *Coe* 28.1.75, 2791/C/74 (eighteen months for indecent assault 'certainly not inappropriate to the offences'—varied to psychiatric probation order).

3 30.4.74, 3010/A/73; see also *Money* 5.6.72, 1517/A/72 (girl of 13 pushed to ground, threatened with razor blade, private parts handled: 'as bad a case of indecent assault . . . as [the Court] possibly can imagine'; two years upheld); *Brown* 7.7.75, 486/C/75 (woman seized from behind, subjected to pressure on back, breasts handled; two years upheld); *Perry* 14.12.76, 686/C/76 (three violent assaults on different occasions; three consecutive terms of two years upheld).

be appropriate. In *Clouthier*[1] the appellant assaulted three women on separate occasions, in each case seizing the woman from behind and putting his hand up her skirt, but not persisting in the face of resistance. The Court considered that although they were 'serious matters', the violence was of a kind unlikely to result in 'physical harm as distinct from shock and fear' and the sentences could be reduced from two years in each case consecutive to eighteen months in each case consecutive. Sentences between nine and eighteen months are typically upheld in comparable cases.[2] A sentence below this level will be appropriate where the degree of indecency and violence is minimal, as in *Marshall*[3], where the appellant walked alongside a woman in the street and when she stopped to look in a shop window, put his hand up her skirt; the Court considered that while the offence was 'regrettable', it was not 'a particularly serious matter as offences go'. The sentence was reduced from eighteen months' to six months' imprisonment (consecutive to other terms for unrelated offences).

Technical assaults on consenting adolescent girls

Very few cases in this category come before the Court, but those that do suggest that the proper approach to sentencing in these cases reflects that evident in cases of unlawful sexual intercourse with girls between 13 and 16. In a case where a group of youths aged between 16 and 18 admitted being involved in various forms of indecent behaviour with two girls aged about 14 who consented to their attentions, the Court stated that 'when youths of this age commit indecent assaults in such circumstances . . . it is seldom that . . . a custodial sentence is appropriate. In the absence of aggravating features the choice might well lie in a fine or discharge or probation'. However, in the present case the offence was aggravated by the fact that the appellants had acted as a group, and custodial sentences of

[1] 14.6.74, 1049/A/74; see also *Badharee* 28.11.75, 4581/B/75 (struggle with girl, attempt to remove clothing and handle private parts, person exposed; case 'did not call for the maximum sentence—two years reduced to fifteen months).

[2] See, for example, *Turpin* 28.6.71, 392/71 (girl, 19, at party, pulled into bedroom, punched and threatened, made to remove clothing, handled indecently; 'serious assault' but wrong to pass consecutive sentences for indecent assault and assault occasioning actual bodily harm—sentence varied to six and fifteen months concurrent); *Ibrahim* 18.1.74, 3569/C/73 (chambermaid seized in hotel bedroom, pushed on to bed, unsuccessful attempt to remove clothing; offence 'commanded a substantial immediate prison sentence', but eighteen months reduced to twelve in view of good character); *Hardiman* 19.6.70, 953/70 (girl of 13 seized from behind, pulled into garden, threatened with knife, clothing torn, breasts and private parts handled; twelve months upheld for 'man of positively good character', longer sentence would have been justified).

[3] 20.11.70, 3591/C/70, [1971] Crim. L. R. 105.

three or six months' detention were upheld, despite the fact that the prosecution had accepted that the appellants believed the girls to be over 16.[1] Where there is a substantial difference in age between the parties, a custodial sentence is more likely to be upheld, although not one of substantial length. In *Ezekiel*[2] a married man of 31 became involved with a girl of 15 and lived with her for some weeks, engaging in 'intimacy falling short of intercourse'. He was sentenced to two years' imprisonment. The Court stated that although 'conduct of this kind is to be very strongly discouraged', the offence took place in the context of a relationship of mutual affection and the sentence could be reduced to allow the appellant's release after serving the equivalent of nine months' imprisonment.

Indecency with small children

Individualized treatment in cases of indecent assault on small girls is generally limited to psychiatric measures such as hospital orders[3] or psychiatric probation orders;[4] occasionally an extended sentence will be upheld where there is a long record of similar conduct in the past.[5]

Although in cases of indecent assault on small children it is common to find a considerable number of counts in the indictment, often relating to more than one child, the Court will seldom uphold sentences totalling more than five years, the maximum sentence for a single offence, unless exceptional circumstances are present.[6] The length of sentence, within the range of twelve months to five years, appears to depend more on the number of offences committed on the present occasion and the offender's previous history of similar behaviour than on the inherent gravity of the individual assault. In *Lovelock*[7] a man of 48 with five previous convictions for indecent assault, convicted of indecently assaulting a girl of 11 by touching her private parts through her clothing and, on a second occasion, exposing himself to her, received sentences totalling six years' imprisonment, which were upheld. By contrast, in *Couzens*[8] a man of 44 with no previous convictions was convicted of offences against

---

[1] *Green and others* 9.3.71, 295/C/71, [1971] Crim. L. R. 299.

[2] 24.3.72, 4020/B/71.

[3] See, for example, *Rose* 15.5.70, 550/A/70.

[4] See, for example, *Goodwin* 21.12.71, 3129/B/71; *Fletton* 6.9.71, 3101/B/71; *Watkins* 17.1.72, 4357/A/71; *Woolman* 9.8.74, 432/B/74.

[5] See, for example, *Nicholls* (1970) 55 Cr. App. R. 150 (serious indecent assault on girl of 7, 'horrifying' record of similar offences over period of eighteen years; ten years extended sentence upheld).

[6] See, for example, *Napier* 8.10.71, 2814/C/71 (man, 57, organizing 'children's brothel', although not for financial gain, variety of offences against children of both sexes; nine years reduced to seven).

[7] 10.11.72, 1023/A/72.

[8] 24.5.71, 6548/70.

three girls, which involved placing his person between their legs and handling their private parts; the offences were committed in premises which were described as a 'children's brothel'. His sentence was reduced from six to three years' imprisonment.

Sentences of two to four years' imprisonment are commonly upheld where the offender has committed several assaults of a serious nature (not amounting to intercourse) but has no record of similar offences in the past. In *Griffiths*[1] a man of 31 admitted several serious assaults against a boy and girl aged 9 and 8 respectively, committed in their own house, where he was welcome as a friend of the family; he also admitted attempting to entice two girls into his car on a different occasion. In view of the appellant's previous good character the Court considered the sentences totalling five and a half years' imprisonment too long and reduced them to a total of four years. In *Wilkinson*[2] a man of 60 admitted several charges of indecent assault (and one of sexual intercourse) with his grandnieces over a period of four years, beginning when the oldest was 8 years old. The Court said that a 'substantial custodial sentence' was inevitable, but that five years did not make sufficient allowance for mitigating circumstances, particularly his age. The sentence was reduced to three years. In *Beech*[3] the appellant admitted a series of offences of indecent assault and gross indecency, involving masturbation and handling of private parts, committed against his daughter between the ages of 11 and 13; the offences had ended two years before the trial. The Court held that sentences totalling five years were 'altogether inordinate', and that sentences totalling two years were sufficient.

Even where the offender has a record of similar offences in the past, a sentence much in excess of three years' imprisonment is unlikely to be upheld (except, where appropriate, as an extended sentence)[4] for a single offence. In *Foster*[5] a man of 45, who had been convicted of indecent assault on several previous occasions (at considerable intervals), took home a girl of 4 whom he found playing in a park and subjected her to a serious indecent assault. The sentence of five years

[1] 21.4.75, 4682/A/74; see also *Jennings* 11.12.70, 4150/B/70, [1971] Crim. L. R. 179 (man, 55, no previous convictions, serious indecent assaults on girls aged 9 and 11; four and a half years upheld).

[2] 14.11.74, 3025/C/74; see also *Good* 29.4.76, 5809/C/75 (three years for 'school master, 60, for indecent assaults on two girl pupils visiting him at home 'by no means . . . excessive' on facts; reduced to eighteen months in view of extensive mitigation).

[3] 6.9.71, 725/A/71; see also *Scheller* 13.7.72, 1893/A/72 (man, 62, indecent assault and attempted intercourse with girls, 11 and 13; four years 'excessive'—reduced to two).

[4] See *Nicholls* (1970) 55 Cr. App. R. 150.

[5] 16.10.70, 3462/B/70; see also *Robson* 6.5.74, 5523/B/73 (man, three previous convictions for indecent assault or attempted rape, attempting to persuade girl of twelve to enter woods; five years for attempted indecent assault reduced to three).

was reduced to three. For a man with no previous history of sexual misconduct with children the sentence for an isolated assault—or for a very small number of assaults—is not likely to exceed eighteen months' imprisonment and may be reduced where substantial mitigation is present.[1] In *Rowley*[2] a 'thoroughly satisfactory citizen' of 45 admitted four assaults on an 8-year-old friend of his daughter; accepting evidence that there was very little chance that the behaviour would be repeated, the Court reduced the sentence from three years to eighteen months.

In all of these cases, the indecency involved was of a substantial nature, usually involving the removal of clothing, touching of private parts and exposure of the person, or some of these elements. Where these elements are not present and the degree of indecency is trivial, a much shorter term or non-custodial sentence will be appropriate. In *Moon*[3] a music teacher kissed a 13-year-old pupil against her will and subsequently 'held her tightly'; the Court stated that the sentence of twelve months' imprisonment, notwithstanding the relationship of teacher and pupil, was 'out of proportion to the gravity of the offence', and ordered his immediate release.

LIVING ON THE EARNINGS OF PROSTITUTION

In most cases of living on the earnings of prostitution (or, if the offender is a woman, exercising control over a prostitute) the Court is prepared to uphold a sentence of imprisonment. The normal scale extends from twelve months to five years, although it is likely that sentences up to the maximum of seven years would be upheld where there are grave aggravating features. Sentences within the bracket of four to five years are usually approved where the offender has coerced the woman concerned into becoming or remaining a prostitute, and has exercised a significant degree of control over her activities. In

[1] As in *Coote* 28.1.71, 5116/B/70 (man, 50, clean record, unintentionally exposing himself to child, subsequent assault; offence 'calls for imprisonment' but twelve months reduced to equivalent of eight); see also *Burke* 14.12.71, 3908/B/71.

[2] 5.3.71, 6289/A/70; see also *Tasamulug* 29.4.71, 5881/A/70 (indecent assault on girl of 9 by friend of family, no previous convictions, isolated incident; eighteen months upheld); *Woods* 13:7.71, 6788/B/70, [1971] Crim. L. R. 659 (man, 23, no previous convictions, single assault on girl of 7 found playing; eighteen months upheld). In each of these cases the assault took the form of removing the child's underclothes and placing the person between the thighs. See also *Key* 10.11.75, 3122/C/75 (man, 36, one similar offence ten years earlier, several acts of indecency, but not 'the most serious offences of this kind', with girls, 11 and 12; three years excessive—reduced to eighteen months).

[3] 11.1.72, 4695/A/71; see also *Daltrey* 10.12.76, 3158/A/76 (hospital porter touching lower part of child's leg under bedclothes; nine months 'far too long'—reduced to equivalent of two months).

Wilkie[1] the offender was convicted of living on the earnings of a woman who had been a prostitute for some years before they met; when she decided to give up prostitution the appellant forced her to continue for a period of about six months by a combination of actual violence and threats to her family. The Court upheld a sentence of five years as 'right and proper'. In *Burke*[2] the appellant went to live with 'an acknowledged prostitute' and for a period of two months 'subjected her to a life of slavery by the violence and brutality he employed against her', forcing her to 'almost continuous' activity and receiving the greater part of her earnings. The Court considered the sentence of four years' imprisonment 'well deserved'.[3]

Where the element of coercion is lacking but the offender relies on the earnings of the woman as his main source of income, the appropriate sentence is more likely to be within the range of two to three years' imprisonment. In *Brown*[4] a man with previous convictions for the same offence lived with a woman for some years, receiving part of her earnings and treating them as his principal means of support; there was no evidence that he had induced her to become a prostitute or to continue to act as one against her will. For this reason the sentence was reduced from five years' imprisonment to three. Similarly in *Gomez*[5] a man of previous good character was convicted of living on the earnings of a prostitute over a period of about twelve months; although there were at least three violent incidents during this time, the Court accepted that the assaults arose out of jealousy

---

[1] 13.5.74, 648/C/74; see also *Jones* 16.12.74, 1653/A/74, [1975] Crim. L. R. 179 (woman inducing girls to take part in call-girl service; sentence of five years appropriate because 'these girls were dragged into . . . service by false promises, and . . . they were intimidated when they sought to get out'); *Dennis* 9.10.70, 6242/A/69 (man, 33, two previous convictions for same offence, living on earnings of woman at intervals over two years, some violence during early stages but woman returned voluntarily at later stage after leaving; seven years reduced to five).

[2] 28.9.70, 1674/A/70; see also *Julienne and Weaver* (1971) 55 Cr. App. R. 426 (men living on earnings of three women, evidence of control and some violence; six years reduced to four).

[3] The sentence was reduced by three months, as the appellant had previously served that term for assaulting the woman.

[4] 26.9.73, 1273/C/73; see also *Stewart* 25.1.74, 3635/A/73 (youth, 20, living on earnings of girl, 15, already initiated; no evidence of corruption or violence; four years reduced to three); *Morrison* 4.7.75, 971/B/75 (man, 31, previous conviction for similar offence, living on earnings of prostitute, no evidence of violence or active involvement; three years upheld).

[5] 21.6.74, 1321/C/74; see also *Mohammed* (1974) 60 Cr. App. R.\141 (man living on earnings of experienced prostitute, 'large sums' of money received but no evidence of violence or coercion; five years reduced to two); *Morgan* 8.7.71, 1416/C/71 (living on earnings of woman, no compulsion, previous convictions seven years earlier for living on earnings of same woman; two years 'a moderate and entirely fair sentence'); *Edwards* 19.11.70, 3665/C/70 (man, 36, living on earnings of woman with whom living, no violence or coercion; sentences totalling four years reduced to two); *Callegia* 18.1.73, 4389/A/72 (two previous convictions in distant past, living on earnings over short period, 'no element of coercion'; two years upheld).

and were not part of a pattern of behaviour intended to force her to continue to act as a prostitute. The sentence was reduced from five years to three.

Sentences in the lowest bracket, between twelve and eighteen months' imprisonment, are likely to be found where the offender receives money from the woman concerned but the relationship cannot be characterized as one of exploitation. In *Russell*[1] the appellant received a sentence of three years for living on the earnings of a woman who was a prostitute before they met; although there was evidence that the appellant had received money from the woman during a period of unemployment, most of this had been spent on their joint living expenses. Stating that 'there is no suggestion that he has exerted any pressure or even persuasion upon her to indulge in prostitution' and that 'the picture is one of two people who set up a home together', the Court reduced the sentence to twelve months. In *Girling*[2] a man of 29 received sentences totalling three and a half years' imprisonment for living on his wife's earnings. Accepting evidence that the appellant was 'dominated by his wife's stronger personality', the Court reduced the sentences to a total of fifteen months.

BUGGERY

Almost all cases of buggery which come before the Court concern buggery of a young male.[3] Individualized measures are usually limited to cases where there is mental disturbance or abnormality, and may take the form of a psychiatric probation order,[4] simple probation order,[5] hospital order or sentence of life imprisonment.[6]

[1] 2.4.74, 5083/C/73; see also *Quinn*, 22.7.77, 116/C/77 (man living on earnings of wife, experienced prostitute before marriage, 'not the usual type . . . of case', thirty months reduced to twelve).

[2] 16.12.74, 4118/B/74; see also *Miller* 13.5.76, 5634/A/75 (man of good character, associating with girl for 'weeks rather than months', no evidence of coercion; three years reduced to eighteen months).

[3] For a rare case of buggery with a consenting woman, see *Harris* 23.2.71, 6507/B/70, [1971] Crim. L. R. 292; most cases of buggery of a woman occur as part of a sequence of events including rape. For buggery of an animal, see *Williams* 3.5.74, 1454/B/74, [1974] Crim. L. R. 558.

[4] See, for example, *Abbott* 12.6.70, 284/70.

[5] See, for example, *Anderson* 5.6.73, 1149/B/73 (single act with boy, 15, after period of 'acute depression', supportive friends and psychiatric treatment available; eighteen months varied to probation); *Mountford* 6.12.73, 3976/A/73 (man, 51, borderline subnormal, series of acts with 'assertive' boy, 15; two years' imprisonment varied to probation).

[6] See, for example, *Skelding* (1973) 58 Cr. App. R. 313; *Bringins* 5.5.75, 421/C/75 (man in early twenties, single act against small boy, history of 'mental and emotional backwardness', prognosis of further similar behaviour; life imprisonment upheld). In *Dearden* 11.2.74, 3414/B/73 a man of 55 with a long record of indecent assault on males was sentenced to life imprisonment for buggery with a boy of 12; accepting the

The scale of fixed-term sentences extends from three years' imprisonment to an upper limit of about ten years, although in the majority of cases a sentence between three and five years will be appropriate. Longer sentences are likely to be upheld where the offence is aggravated by such elements as force or coercion,[1] systematic seduction over a period of time,[2] abuse of parental or other authority,[3] or the extreme youth of the victim.[4] Where factors such as these are present, either singly or in combination, sentences up to ten years have been upheld, but more usually the sentence does not exceed seven years' imprisonment. Even when cases are not aggravated by these elements, the Court will sometimes uphold a sentence in the upper bracket where the offender has a record of similar offences over a substantial period of time and appears likely to repeat the offence in the future.[5] The imposition of long fixed-term sentences in such cases, at least where the facts of the immediate offences do not fall into the aggravated category, may be seen as a departure from the general principles discussed earlier, and it is submitted that the proper course in such cases is to impose either life imprisonment or an extended sentence, for which many such offenders will qualify.

In the more typical case, where the victim is a willing adolescent and the offender, although not necessarily a first offender, does not have an extensive record, the appropriate sentence is more likely to fall within the bracket of three to five years' imprisonment. In *Bradley*

---

propriety of life imprisonment in such circumstances for a younger man, the Court reduced the sentence to ten years as 'his urges . . . are likely to be on the wane in a few years' and the fixed term would provide adequate protection in the interim. This decision is difficult to reconcile with the Court's general approach to the use of life imprisonment, which is often justified, by reference to the absence of any minimum period to be served before the offender may be considered for parole, as an 'act of mercy' by comparison with a long fixed-term sentence.

[1] See, for example, *Stewart* 16.11.72, 2223/A/72, [1973] Crim. L. R. 319 (man, 28, previous convictions for buggery and indecent assault, buggery of boy, 14, by intimidation; ten years upheld).

[2] See, for example, *Nicholls* 27.6.75, 1233/B/75 (man, 62, systematic seduction of four brothers over period of time; ten years justified on facts—reduced to six years because of age).

[3] See, for example, *Hackley* 1.2.73, 2830/B/72 (buggery of son, 10, and stepson, no previous convictions; seven years upheld, 'substantially longer sentence' would have been justified); *Hillington* 11.6.70, 5652/69 (buggery with son 11, indecency with son, 7; six years upheld); *Walker* 7.7.77, 6095/C/76 (buggery of boy by child care officer at residential school; five years upheld).

[4] See, for example, *Morris* 2.11.72, 2278/A/72 (man, 26, buggery of boy, 8, other similar offences over period of nine years; seven years upheld; 'the protection of small boys comes before the individual interests of the appellant').

[5] See, for example, *Bushell* 18.11.71, 6775/B/70 (man, 33, six previous convictions for offences against boys, recently on probation, no treatment available: 'there is nothing to do except to remove him from a life of freedom in the interests . . . of boys of this age'); see also *Johannsen* (1977) 65 Cr. App. R. 101.

and Moore[1] two men aged 24 and 46 respectively, each with no previous relevant conviction, received seven years' imprisonment for buggery of a 14-year-old boy who had been paid a few pounds. The Court stated that although it was 'a grave offence . . . meriting severe punishment', there was no aggravating feature such as abuse of parental authority, and for this reason 'the term of seven years' imprisonment is too long'. A sentence of five years was substituted. In *Jones*[2] a milkman admitted one offence of buggery and several offences of indecency with a number of boys between the ages of 9 and 15. The Court accepted that 'there was an element of corruption' as the boys had no previous knowledge or experience of such activities, but sentences totalling six and a half years were 'far too long'; the total was reduced to three years.

The factors which should govern the length of sentence within this bracket were considered in general terms in *Willis*[3] and are illustrated in other cases. In *Keefe*[4] a man described as 'in all other respects . . . a first-rate citizen' admitted a series of offences with a boy of about 15 whom he had met in the course of his activities as a swimming instructor. The offences were committed during a relationship which began shortly after the appellant's release from a sentence of nine months' imprisonment for offences with a different boy. Although it was a 'sad and tragic case', in that the original offences began only when the appellant's common law wife died, the Court upheld a sentence of five years' imprisonment. The important factors in this case were the previous convictions, the corruption of the boys concerned and the likelihood of other boys being seduced in the future. Where the offence can be seen as an isolated aberration by a man with no long-standing pattern of abnormal sexual behaviour, a sentence nearer three years may be appropriate. In *Hennessy*[5] a man of 35 admitted two offences against the 12-year-old son of the family with whom he lodged. The Court observed that they shared the same

[1] 24.2.72, 5352/C/71; see also *Wrigley* 22.1.74, 2087/C/73 (man, 30, no previous relevant convictions, buggery of boys aged between 14 and 17; eight years reduced to five).

[2] 14.12.73, 1674/C/73.

[3] (1974) 60 Cr. App. R. 146.

[4] 23.4.70, 8407/A/69. Compare *Smith* 5.11.73, 3227/C/73 (man, 58, buggery with two boys, 13 and 14, 'not a case of a man . . . seeking to corrupt young boys; succumbed to temptation . . . when he was lonely', no previous convictions; sentences totalling four years reduced to three); *Murphy*, 2.10.73, 3312/A/73 (five years for buggery of two boys, 16 and 12, 'too much' for man with no previous conviction for indecency; reduced to three and a half years).

[5] 10.7.72, 1907/A/72; see also *Riley* 13.7.72, 1491/A/72 (man, 31, single act with boy, 15, following chance meeting, case treated as 'isolated . . . offence' following 'sudden temptation', despite earlier convictions; six years varied to thirty months); *Mooney* 8.3.74, 209/B/74 (man, 32, single act of buggery of 10-year-old boy for payment, one previous conviction for inviting gross indecency, no violence or physical injury; four years reduced to three).

bedroom and the offence 'sprang out of affection for the child'; there was a 'complete absence of some of the crudities that are so manifest in cases of this kind'. Accepting that the offences did not reflect a regular pattern of behaviour and that the appellant was 'most remorseful', the Court reduced the sentence from four years' imprisonment to three.

A sentence of three years' imprisonment appears to represent the lower limit of the normal sentencing bracket. In *Solomon*[1] a man of 44 admitted one act of attempted buggery with a youth of 16 who was 'known to be . . . susceptible to homosexual advances'; the boy's father had asked the appellant to keep an eye on the boy, who was living alone. The sentence of three years was upheld. Lower sentences than this will usually be considered appropriate only where the offence is committed in circumstances most favourable to the accused and substantial personal mitigating factors are present. In *Ibrahim*[2] a man of previous good character received two years' imprisonment for a single act of buggery with a youth of 16. The Court accepted that the offence took place at the boy's instigation, that the boy was not corrupted and that the appellant was 'lonely and . . . frustrated' at the time. The sentence was reduced to the equivalent of eight months' imprisonment.

INDECENT ASSAULT ON MALES[3]

The Court's policy in cases of indecent assault on males reflects that seen in the buggery cases; individualized measures, usually providing psychiatric treatment,[4] are approved in appropriate cases, and preventive sentences may be upheld where there is a long history of indecent assaults of a serious nature.[5] (The maximum sentence is ten

[1] 2.4.73, 5405/B/72.

[2] 28.2.72, 4453/B/71; see also *Lewis* 3.7.72, 5944/A/72 (man, 22, three acts of buggery and other indecency with boy, 12, previous experience, 'no element of seduction and . . . corruption was of a minimal kind', appellant only 20 when offence committed; four and a half years reduced to thirty months).

[3] For a rare case of indecent assault on a boy of 14 by a woman, see *Faulkner* 8.8.72, 3193/B/72, [1972] Crim. L. R. 793.

[4] See, for example, *Ferris* 7.10.75, 706/C/75 (hospital order); see also *Farmborough* 13.3.70, 6735/69, where a man with a long history of similar offences was bound over to come up for judgement for five years, on condition of submitting himself to specified treatment (the longest period of treatment which could be required at that time as a condition of a probation order was twelve months).

[5] See, for example, *Dillon* 11.12.70, 1524/C/70 (man, 38, history of long sentences for indecent assault, serious indecent assault on boy, 10, ten years' imprisonment upheld: 'the main . . . consideration is the prevention of this sort of offence by this man'). It is submitted that the sentence should have been certified as extended; compare *Lundbech* 4.6.70, 5471/69 (single indecent assault on boy, 'not the worst kind of indecency', long record of indecency with boys; ten years might have been appropriate as extended term, but 'we have to deal with him for the offence to which he pleaded guilty' — sentence reduced to five years).

years' imprisonment and accordingly the indeterminate sentence of life imprisonment is not available).

Although 'it is not the label of indecent assault which is important but the nature of the fact',[1] the normal range of sentences for indecent assault on males is rather lower than the range in cases of buggery. Sentences in excess of five years' imprisonment are rarely upheld. In *Greenlees*[2] a man of 62 with no previous convictions admitted a series of offences of indecency with boys aged apparently about 13 and was sentenced to six years' imprisonment, with four years consecutive for offences against girls of similar age. The Court considered that while 'an immediate custodial sentence . . . of considerable severity . . . is inevitable', ten years was excessive; the sentences for indecent assault on the boys were reduced to three years and the other sentences were reduced to the same term and made concurrent. Sentences in excess of three years are usually upheld only where there are aggravated factual circumstances—the corruption of previously inexperienced children, inherently grave assaults, or the involvement of a large number of children—or where the offender has a substantial record of similar behaviour in the past. In *Cox*[3] a man of 37 admitted indecent behaviour over a period of two years with six boys between the ages of 9 and 12 who lived on the same housing estate. The appellant initiated the offences by showing the boys indecent pictures and had paid them after each act; the assaults consisted chiefly of masturbation but at least one instance of oral contact was admitted. The Court accepted that there was no evidence of physical violence or buggery, but it was 'a very bad case' and the sentence of four years' imprisonment 'cannot be faulted'.

Where the assaults themselves are of a less serious character, involve fewer children or are committed over a shorter period of time, the appropriate sentence will fall within the bracket of eighteen months to three years. In *Spicer*[4] a man of 31 with three previous

---

[1] *Willis* (1974) 60 Cr. App. R. 146.

[2] 11.2.75, 4456/B/74; see also *Ramsay* 21.2.75, 1029/A/74 (man, 41, six previous convictions for offences against children, indecent assault on boys, 9 and 10, within two months of release from prison; seven years reduced to five in view of possibility of anti-libidinal drug treatment on release).

[3] 27.6.75, 1326/C/75; see also *Tannock* 19.1.70, 5484/69 (man, 36, no previous convictions, marital and financial problems, seven indecent acts towards children including own son and daughter; four years upheld); *Bell* 26.2.73, 5146/C/72 (indecent assaults on children, 5 and 6, oral contact, previous conviction for indecent exposure and indecent assault; sentences totalling eight years reduced to four).

[4] 23.11.72, 3926/A/72; see also *Green* 19.1.73, 4690/A/72 (man, 31, indecent assaults, 'not the most serious of their sort', on two boys, 12 and 13, several previous convictions for indecency; four years reduced to two); *Sheppard* 22.1.71, 5553/A/70 (man, 38, no previous convictions, indecency with two boys, 12 and 16, involving mutual masturbation; 'immediate imprisonment is called for . . . the total of four years is high'—thirty months substituted); *Ringham* 24.4.75, 4900/A/74 (school caretaker and cub leader indecently assaulting boys between 9 and 11, indecent pictures shown and

convictions for similar offences received four years' imprisonment for two indecent assaults on a boy of 9. As the assaults were 'of a very slight character' and 'lacked many of those grave features which leave a psychological mark upon the victim', the sentence was 'intrinsically . . . wrong in principle'; a sentence of two years was substituted. In *Warren*[1] a man of 26 with no previous convictions admitted a number of indecent assaults on three boys who were related to him by marriage; the offences, which occurred during a period of marital difficulty, including placing the person in contact with the boys' bare buttocks, although there was apparently no allegation of attempted buggery. The Court stated that although a custodial sentence was necessary, five years' imprisonment was 'out of scale' and 'beyond that which is appropriate to offences of this sort in these circmstances'. A sentence of thirty months was substituted.

Sentences of less than eighteen months' imprisonment will usually be approved in cases (apart from those where extensive personal mitigation is available) involving a small number of assaults not of the most serious nature on the same boy over a short period of time. In *Riley*[2] a man of 48 with no previous convictions received a sentence of two years' imprisonment for a single offence against a boy of 13, who had apparently consented to being handled; the Court considered the sentence of two years' imprisonment 'excessive . . . for this single offence' and reduced it to nine months. In *Cavey*[3] a man of 59, who had been fined many years previously for indecent assault, received a sentence of twelve months' imprisonment for indecently touching a boy of 11 in the changing-room of a public swimming-pool. Although it was not appropriate to suspend the sentence, the Court considered twelve months too long for an offence which was 'not a particularly serious example of its kind', particularly as 'the step from a relatively small fine to twelve months' imprisonment was too great'. A sentence of six months was substituted.

GROSS INDECENCY

Although some cases involving younger people lead to charges of committing an act of gross indecency, most examples of this offence

---

money paid, nature of the assaults 'while not at the bottom of the scale . . . certainly not at the top'; sentences reduced from three years to two).

[1] 9.10.70, 1108/A/70.

[2] 10.7.72, 395/B/72; see also *Baker* 21.11.72, 3332/C/72 (two indecent assaults on 'thoroughly corrupted' boy, 15; two years not excessive, but reduced to one year because of disparity with 'astonishing' fine of £30 imposed on co-defendant on summary conviction).

[3] 24.6.75, 2473/B/75; see also *Woods* 14.10.74, 2890/A/74 (officer in Boy Scout movement, single indecent act with boy at scout camp, assault 'not the most serious of

involve a youth between 16 (the age at which his consent prevents conduct from constituting an assault) and 21. Sentences of imprisonment have been upheld where aggravating features were present,[1] but non-custodial sentences appear to be appropriate in more typical cases. In one case a man of 39 with no previous convictions engaged in 'a little mutual sex play' in a car with a youth he had met in a public house; accepting that the appellant believed the youth to be over 18, the Court observed that a sentence of immediate imprisonment was unnecessary and that 'it would have been more appropriate to have dealt with this breach of the law by way of a financial penalty'.[2]

Section 4: Theft and Related Offences

ROBBERY

The offence of robbery covers a variety of situations and the relevant scales of sentences can best be identified by reference to the different forms which robbery may take.

Large-scale organized robbery

A robbery in this category typically involves a gang of men, armed with weapons such as sawn-off shotguns or pickhandles, attacking premises or a vehicle in the hope of stealing very large sums of money or valuable property. Usually the assault will be preceded by careful research and planning and stolen cars used to escape from the scene. Grave violence may be used or threatened. For robberies in this category the Court has stated that 'the ordinary penalty . . . is nowadays about fifteen years'.[3] A sentence of this length was upheld

---

this type of . . . offence', although aggravated by position of trust; 'immediate operative term of imprisonment' necessary, despite 'powerful mitigating factors', but nine months reduced to equivalent of six); *Thompson* 14.2.75, 5014/B/74 (man, 40, previous convictions for indecency, attempting to procure indecency with boys, 11 and 13, by offering money; twelve months upheld).

[1] See, for example, *Lyons* 10.6.75, 1672/C/75 (clergyman attending 'orgy' with boys, 16 and 18, both with 'considerable sexual experience of this sort', not connected with appellant's church; two years upheld); *Eustice* 21.1.75, 4554/C/74 (departmental manager accosting junior employee in staff lavatory, indecent touching and suggestion, single offence many years previously; six months immediate varied to six months suspended).

[2] *Massetti* 11.2.75, 4700/B/74; see also *Neefjes* 3.10.72, 807/B/72 (act of gross indecency in cubicle of public lavatory; fine of £50 'appropriate . . . for any offence of this kind'—upheld); *Malins* 18.11.76, 5221/A/76 (man of previous good character, mutual masturbation with youth, 17, with 'considerable experience', no question of corruption or payment; eighteen months immediate imprisonment 'manifestly excessive', varied to conditional discharge.)

[3] *Kerr and Smith* 12.12.75, 872/A/75.

on a man convicted of a single offence of this kind.[1] Sentences of ten years, imposed on two men in their early thirties, each with an impeccable past record, who used an imitation pistol to commit a bank robbery which had been planned with 'great care and attention to detail', were upheld with the comment that they 'generously' reflected the available mitigation.[2] A sentence of eight years' imprisonment imposed on one of four men who robbed a security van which was delivering cash to a bank was described as 'inadequate', even though followed by a consecutive term of four years for using a revolver in the same robbery.[3] In a typical example of this class of case five men were convicted of conspiracy to rob or robbery following an armed raid on a Post Office van, in the course of which £10,000 was stolen. The Post Office van was rammed by a car and men from another van, wearing balaclava helmets, threatened the driver with a sawn-off shotgun and an axe. Telephone wires in the vicinity had been cut and a third vehicle was used as a get-away car. The Court upheld sentences of twelve years on those convicted of conspiracy only and fifteen years on those convicted of participation in the actual robbery, with the comment that the sentences 'were at the lowest end of the range of sentences that are meted out to those who are convicted of armed robbery'.[4] Many comparable cases can be found.[5] The particular problems arising in cases involving a series of robberies, each of which would individually justify a sentence of about fifteen years, were considered in *Turner and others*,[6] where the Court stated that 'something must be added to the basic sentence . . . on those who committed more than one robbery,' but that the aggregate sentence should not normally exceed eighteen years, unless the offences came into a category which could be considered 'wholly abnormal'.[7]

The position of minor participants in major robberies has been considered on several occasions. The Court has stated that as a general rule all active participants in the robbery should be sentenced

[1] *Dallison* 17.2.75, 2453/B/74 (attack on security van, shots fired from shotgun, £20,000 stolen).
[2] *Kerr and Smith* 12.12.75, 872/A/75.
[3] *Baldessare* 9.5.75, 4767/B/74.
[4] *Blackford* 29.3.72, 2445/C/72.
[5] See, for example, *Downs and others* 28.10.75, 5040/B/74 (armed robberies at post offices and business premises; fifteen years upheld); *Stocker and Cain* 25.7.74, 5156/A/73 (robbery of Post Office van by men armed with shot-guns and wearing stocking masks; fourteen and twelve years not too severe, but reduced to remove possible sense of grievance over procedural slip); *Mills* 5.4.73, 6042/A/71 ('well planned' robbery at jeweller's shop by gang of six, some carrying pick handles, goods worth £26,000 stolen, violence used on assistants; sentences of twelve, ten and nine years on various participants upheld).
[6] (1975) 61 Cr. App. R. 67 at 92.
[7] As, for instance, where hostages were taken and held for several days: see *Termine and others* (1977) 64 Cr. App. R. 299.

on the same basis—'this Court . . . does not normally stop to consider whether a particular prisoner actually held up the cashier . . . had a gun or . . . an iron bar, or was the driver standing outside ready to drive away. All are equally guilty because without each playing his full part the crime could not be perpetrated'.[1] Secondary participants, such as those who supply information essential to the planning of the robbery, will receive severe sentences, but at a significantly lower level. A bank clerk who supplied information to a group of robbers who subsequently attacked the bank was sentenced to five years' imprisonment, which the Court upheld despite his youth and good character;[2] a bank messenger who gave information about the movement of money between different branches of his bank and subsequently lent his keys for copying, was sentenced to ten years' imprisonment, which the Court considered excessive, partly because of his good character and assistance to the police, and reduced to six years.[3]

The cases indicate that the characteristics of the offence which justify the long sentence are the elements of organization, planning and violence, rather than the nature of the premises attacked. In *Bell*[4] the appellant went alone into a branch bank and threatened a cashier with an imitation firearm; he ran out of the bank with £500, but was detained after a chase by two bank employees. The Court stated that although the offence was 'very serious', it could not be classed as 'organized . . . or professional crime'. The appellant had made no plans for a get-away, and his offence was described by the prosecution as 'amateurish and spontaneous'. Although the offence 'merited serious punishment', the sentence of nine years' imprisonment appeared to be 'out of scale' if 'measured against the gravity of other bank robberies'; a sentence of six years was substituted. Similarly, the fact that a number of offenders are involved does not necessarily mean that a term of fifteen years is the correct starting point for the consideration of the appropriate sentence in all cases of violent robbery. In one case[5] three men in their early twenties robbed the proprietor of an off licence of £25, threatening her with a

---

[1] *Brett and others* 28.7.75, 5289/B2/73 (robbery of bullion van 'organized . . . with almost military precision on a most elaborate scale', serious violence used; fifteen years upheld on active participants).
[2] *Holt* (1975) 61 Cr. App. R. 67 at 94.
[3] *Jolly* 8.3.73, 5331/A/72.
[4] 13.1.75, 3801/B/74; see also *Ayres* 11.2.77, 3657/C/76 (robberies at banks by man acting alone, imitation firearm used, about £10,000 stolen; twelve years excessive though 'a deterrent sentence is necessary'; reduced to eight years).
[5] *Whittaker and others* 14.1.77, 2946/B/76; see also *Byrne* 10.2.77, 3156/A/76 (two men robbing village store, threatening manager with unloaded gun, fifteen-year guideline 'not . . . a starting point in all cases of armed robbery'; ten years reduced to eight).

sawn-off shotgun and wearing masks, and were sentenced to terms of thirteen and twelve years' imprisonment respectively. The Court observed that the offence lacked the characteristics of careful planning—having been arranged only the previous day—the expectation of large amounts of money and the determination to use grave violence in an inevitable confrontation with security guards. For these reasons it was incorrect to equate the offence with highly organized robbery for which such terms were appropriate, and sentences of nine years and eight years respectively were substituted.

Other decisions indicate that the sentence of fifteen years should not be imposed mechanically even in those cases where the offence exhibits the characteristics of 'first division' robbery.[1] 'If one takes fifteen years as the starting point there must be room for differentiation', according to such factors as the degree of sophistication shown in the execution of the robbery, whether firearms were loaded, whether they were fired to injure or to frighten and whether there was a plea of guilty.[2] In one case[3] several men attacked a wages office, threatening the cashiers with a gun and other weapons, and stole £1,900. The offence had been planned some weeks previously with the aid of information from an employee who had been bribed. The Court observed that the offence was not sufficiently 'different in kind and scale and in the degree of danger to the public' to make fifteen years an inappropriate starting point, but that although this sentence was in the correct bracket, there was room to reflect the fact that the robbery was 'a fairly amateurish and unsophisticated operation' by comparison with the robberies involved in such cases as *Turner*; the sentences of twelve years actually imposed did 'not allow sufficient scaling down from the starting point of fifteen years'. Sentences of ten and nine years respectively were substituted for the active participants.

Violent burglary

A second distinct category of robbery may be described as violent burglary. In this class of case a gang of men enter a house, often in a relatively isolated place, subject the occupants to violence or threats, often tying and gagging them, and steal substantial amounts of cash or valuable property. In the absence of exceptional mitigating factors, sentences for robberies in this category are likely to fall between five and ten years, depending on the degree of violence used

[1] *Ward and others* 20.1.77, 769/A/76.
[2] *Ward and others, ibid.*
[3] *Ward and others, ibid.*

to the occupants of the premises concerned. In *Power*[1] the appellant and another man entered the bedroom of premises occupied by a couple in their seventies and attacked them with a stick as they slept; the wife was subsequently attacked a second time by the appellant, suffering lacerations and bruising. Sentences totalling ten years' imprisonment were upheld. Similar sentences were upheld in a case where two men committed a series of burglaries at the homes of small tradesmen, in which the victims were subjected to violence, tied up and gagged; although the appellants were in their early twenties, the Court considered that the sentences 'were not too severe'.[2]

Considerably shorter sentences are likely to be approved where the degree of violence offered to the occupant is much less. In *Fielding and others*[3] four men broke into a house where they believed £4,000 in cash was kept. The sole occupant, a woman, was seized and told not to struggle, but no serious violence was used; the victim was made to sit in an easy chair with a towel over her head during the course of robbery. In view of the fact that 'the minimum of force' was used and all the appellants pleaded guilty, the Court reduced their sentences from seven years (in the case of the instigator) to four, and proportionately in the case of the other appellants. In another case[4] four men broke into premises which they believed to be unoccupied at the time; finding a lady of 92 watching television, they tied her up 'loosely' before leaving the building. The Court held that although the sentence of six years on one appellant was 'right in principle', it failed to reflect certain mitigating factors in the appellant's personal history, which justified a reduction to four years.

Robberies of tradesmen and small business premises

In some respects robberies in this category resemble bank raids, in that they usually involve some element of planning and observation, but they are typically on a much smaller scale, involving fewer

---

[1] 29.3.73, 6253/C/72; see also *Noone and others* 21.7.77, 6154/A/76 (elderly couple attacked at home, beaten and threatened with knife, £5,000 stolen; ten years 'entirely proper'; reduced to seven on one appellant to reflect mitigation).
[2] *Sweeting and Oldham* 7.7.75, 4718/B/74, [1976] Crim. L. R. 81; see also *McAleny and Griffiths* 5.12.75, 965/B/75 (robbery at house of company director, occupants threatened with revolver, bound and gagged; ten years on principal upheld); see also *Wong* 16.5.75, 4463/B/74 (two attacks on householders at night, serious violence and tying up; eight years 'erred, if . . . at all, on the side of moderation'); *Ord and Hammond* 19.1.73, 3600/B/72 (tradesman, 60, attacked at home with ammonia and bat, tied up with prepared cord and gagged with plaster; six years upheld, allowing for mitigation). The reduction of a sentence of ten years in *Fidler* 2.4.73, 4666/A/72, where two elderly women were 'terrorized' in their home, was probably based on the totality principle, as the appellant was subject to other sentences for unrelated offences.
[3] 2.5.74, 423/A/74.
[4] *Clarke* 24.7.75, 5125/C/74.

participants, a lesser degree of violence and the theft of much smaller sums. Examples include robberies of garage forecourt attendants, tradesmen or rent collectors carrying substantial sums of cash in the street, or of small shopkeepers. Sentences for offences in this category will usually fall within the range of three to seven years according to the degree of organization involved and the nature of the violence used.[1] In *Kenneth*[2] the appellant and another man attacked the proprietor of a jeweller's shop as he walked home from work, stabbing him in the face with a small knife and kicking him about the face and body. The Court upheld a sentence of seven years' imprisonment for 'a terrible piece of premeditated violence'. In *Sparrow*[3] the appellant armed himself with a carving knife before hiring a taxi and instructing the driver to take him to a remote place, where he stabbed the driver in the arm and neck before stealing a quantity of cash. A sentence of six years was approved, although the appellant was only 19.

Rather lower sentences will be approved where the degree of violence is substantially less. In *Ritchie*[4] a woman carrying her firm's wages was attacked by two men who pushed her down and stole a bag containing about £700. The Court reduced the sentence from five years to three, partly on account of mitigating factors in the appellant's background. In another case[5] the appellant entered a hotel and asked to speak to the manager; when the manager appeared he was threatened with an air pistol and ordered to hand over the contents of the hotel safe and his wristwatch. Eventually the appellant surrendered when another hotel employee intervened. The Court considered the sentence of four and a half years 'fully justified . . . considering the offence alone' but in view of its 'amateurish nature' felt able to take account of personal mitigating circumstances which enabled it to reduce the sentence to three years.

---

[1] Sentences of nine years were upheld in *Jenner and others* 15.3.77, 5181/C/76, where three men used unloaded firearms in robbing a garage and a betting shop.

[2] 17.7.74, 946/C/74.

[3] 5.6.75, 964/B/75; see also *Jenkins* 30.10.73, 1417/A/73 (attack by two men on garage forecort attendant, victim knocked down with large stick; six years upheld); *Leary* 20.10.75, 2551/C/75 (attack on elderly manager of jeweller's shop, victim subjected to violence, £450 stolen; seven years 'within the range of sentences which are passed for this type of offence', but reduced to five on account of mitigating circumstances); *Davis* 15.10.73, 1659/C/73 (robbery at garage, attendant threatened with air pistol pressed against head, £200 stolen from till; five years upheld, consecutive sentences for other unrelated offences made concurrent under totality principle).

[4] 1.11.73, 904/C/73.

[5] *Spain* 19.11.74, 2684/B/74; see also *Street and Gray* 3.10.74, 2844/A/74, (small amounts of goods or cash stolen from shops, assistant and customers threatened with knife but no actual violence; four years reduced to three on account of age (17 and 19) and (in one case) previous good character).

Mugging

The term 'mugging' describes a robbery in which the victim is attacked in the street or some other public place, subjected to whatever violence is necessary to overpower him and deprived of his wallet, watch and any other items of value which he may have on him at the time. Frequently the offence is committed by an offender on his own, or in company with one other, and may be a spontaneous reaction to a sudden opportunity; robberies in this category will rarely be accompanied by the kind of careful planning seen in varying degrees in the categories already described. The appropriate bracket of sentences for offences in this category appears to extend from two years to about four years, although longer sentences are upheld where there is unusually serious violence. The fact that many offenders committing offences of this kind are in their early twenties or younger, and are therefore entitled on normal principles to some mitigation, may affect the general level of sentences seen in the majority of cases, and longer sentences may be appropriate where the offence is committed by offenders with no claims to mitigation.[1]

An example of a case at the upper limit of the range is *Burke*,[2] where a man of 21 with a substantial record assaulted a partially sighted person at an underground station, threatened him by pressing a knife against his throat and stole a small amount of cash, credit cards and other items. The sentence was reduced from six years' imprisonment to four. In *Naraine*[3] the appellant and another man followed the victim into the lavatory of a public house, punched and kicked him and his companion and stole about £20. The Court considered that although 'this was an unpleasant offence . . . it did not merit a sentence as severe as five years' imprisonment'; a sentence of three years was substituted. Sentences of three years have been upheld in a number of cases where a moderate amount of violence has been used, even though the amounts stolen were relatively small.[4] In

[1] See, for example, *Howarth* 19.2.73, 1758/C/72 (man, 34, sixteen previous convictions, stealing £4 from drunk, two fist blows to face, no serious injury; seven years reduced to five).

[2] 7.3.74, 4332/B/73.

[3] 15.11.73, 6635/A/72; see also *Hibbert* 27.2.73, 5959/C/72 (middle-aged man attacked outside public house, knocked to ground, punched and kicked, £2 and other property stolen; four years 'a little too severe' for youth, 20, substantial record; reduced to three, partly on grounds of disparity). In *Snaith* 31.1.77, 3437/A/76 a sentence of four years was upheld for a man of 20 who knocked an elderly lady to the ground and stole her handbag.

[4] See, for example, *Webster* 5.2.73, 5299/A/72 (woman attacked 'on sudden impulse', struck on head but not seriously injured, nothing stolen; three years upheld for assault with intent to rob); *Denby* 19.7.73, 1173/C/73 (disabled victim attacked at home, no grave violence, wallet containing £15 stolen; three years upheld); *Flavius* 3.2.77, 3683/C/76, [1977] Crim. L. R. 629.

Taylor[1] a young man of good character participated in a robbery in which three youths chased a fourth until he fell, kicked him while he lay on the ground and stole about £80. The Court upheld the sentence of three years with the comment that the case was of a 'horribly common' kind.

Sentences of three years' imprisonment are unlikely to be upheld, at least in the case of relatively young offenders, where the robbery is committed by threats rather than force, or the degree of violence is minimal. In one case two brothers aged 19 and 17 accosted a youth on the street, threatened him with something which looked like a gun and stole £5. On a second occasion £20 was stolen in a similar manner from another man. Observing that 'it was not one of the more serious types of mugging in that no violence was used', the Court reduced the sentence from three years to borstal training.[2] In *Davis*[3] a youth of 20 approached a young couple in the street late at night, prodded one of them in the back and induced them to part with about £4. The Court stated that although the offence 'plainly merited a custodial sentence', it would not justify a sentence, at least on a young man, in excess of two years' imprisonment; the sentence of three years was accordingly varied to borstal training.

In a small number of cases where the Court has considered muggings carried out by groups of girls or young women, it has been made clear that such cases should not be treated differently from the more usual kind. In *Togneri*[4] three teenage girls assaulted a woman who was waiting at a bus stop, stealing her watch and knocking her to the ground. Although the appellant had no previous convictions, the Court upheld a sentence of borstal training as 'a perfectly proper deterrent sentence'. In *Hodgson*[5] two young women attacked an elderly lady in a public lavatory, stealing her handbag containing £38 in cash. The Court upheld a sentence of eighteen months on one woman aged 26 with no previous convictions, observing that 'the fact that this was carried out by two women and one youth . . . does not

---

[1] 13.1.75, 2657/B/74.

[2] *Sparkes and Sparkes* 3.11.75, 2847/C/75.

[3] 16.11.73, 3994/A/73; see also *Love* 26.7.74, 1486/B/74 (youth, 17, accosting two men, stealing 50p; no serious injury inflicted or weapon used; three years varied to borstal training); *Bodycombe* 21.1.74, 4702/C/73 (man 26, no relevant previous convictions, robbing boy of 12 of very small sums by threats; three years reduced to two); *Barton* 5.4.73, 552/A/73 (various people threatened with knife, £2 and a tie stolen; four years varied to borstal training).

[4] 16.2.73, 4944/A/72. In *Wells and others* 6.3.73, 46/B/73, where sentences of borstal training imposed on three teenage girls who forcibly stole a handbag from a 15 year-old were varied to probation, the degree of violence used was apparently modest and the Court would have preferred detention in a detention centre if such a sentence had been available.

[5] 27.10.75, 3213/A/75, [1976] Crim. L. R. 204.

make it any better than the normal type of mugging . . . carried out exclusively by men'.

BLACKMAIL

Most cases of blackmail which came before the Court fall into one of two categories—demanding money under a threat to expose or accuse the victim, and demanding money under an immediate threat of violence.

Cases in the first category are almost invariably treated seriously and will often attract a sentence of three years' imprisonment even where there is substantial mitigation. In *Cole*[1] a man aged 52 of 'perfectly good character' demanded £2,000 from his former employers under the threat of accusing them of fraud in connection with tax returns. The Court stated that the sentence of four years' imprisonment was not excessive on its face, but in view of 'exceptional . . . mitigating factors'—including the facts that the appellant was under severe financial pressure and had a grievance against the employers over his dismissal—reduced it to three years. A youth of 18 who demanded several hundred pounds from an older man with whom he had engaged in homosexual activities was sentenced to three years' imprisonment, which the Court considered, despite his age, 'neither wrong in principle nor by any means excessive'.[2] Considerably longer sentences have been upheld where the threats were made over a period of time with no mitigation. In *Costello*[3] a man with several previous convictions for offences of dishonesty demanded considerable sums over a period of three years from a young woman, under the threat of disclosing to her family that he had arranged an unlawful abortion for her some years previously. The sentence of seven years' imprisonment was upheld. Sentences totalling six years and seven years respectively were upheld on two police officers convicted of conspiracy to commit blackmail and pervert the course of justice by threatening to accuse persons of crimes they had not committed unless payments were made.[4]

The second category of blackmail, demanding money under the threat of immediate violence or damage to property, is analogous to

[1] 20.3.75, 5214/A/74. In *Wright* 22.1.74, 5262/B/73 the appellant demanded £500 'compensation' from his wife's employer with whom she had had an affair; the Court reduced and suspended the sentence 'as an act of mercy in peculiar circumstances'.
[2] *Wray* 9.5.74, 870/B/74; see also *Powell and Barford* 9.5.75, 398/B/75 (youths of 18 and 20, demanding money and use of car from older man after homosexual activity; three years upheld in each case).
[3] 30.6.75, 931/B/75, [1975] Crim. L. R. 724; see also *Kelvie* 19.10.73, 3009/A/73 (man, 21, demanding £800 over several months from youth, 16, to refrain from disclosing youth's thefts from father's business; five years upheld).
[4] *Harris and Robson* 26.6.73, 1068/R/72.

robbery and attracts sentences between twelve months and seven years, according to the nature of the threat and the nature of the demand. A sentence of seven years was upheld on an appellant who demanded £15,000 from a bank by displaying an imitation bomb.[1] In a case where a garage proprietor was threatened with damage to his car and premises if he did not discharge a debt contracted by his son, a man in his thirties, the Court considered that eight years' imprisonment was higher than was justified for 'the use of strong-arm tactics to recover money', and substituted sentences totalling six years.[2] In *McCauley*[3] the appellant demanded money from his elderly father, threatening violence and doing actual damage to equipment within the house. The Court considered the sentence of three years' imprisonment 'entirely proper'. A man of previous good character who punched and struggled with a prostitute's client who refused to pay the agreed fee, having decided not to avail himself of her services after making an appointment, was sentenced to two years' imprisonment; this sentence was considered 'unnecessarily severe' in view of his good character and other mitigation, and a sentence of twelve months was substituted.[4]

BURGLARY

Identifying the ranges of sentences for burglary presents a number of difficulties. The definition of the offence covers a wide variety of factual situations; offenders are frequently convicted of a large number of offences on the same occasion; and mitigating factors carry greater weight in this context than in many others. The cases do however provide some guidance.

Sentences in excess of seven years are generally reserved for carefully planned burglaries which involve large amounts of property or cash, are carried out with determination and skill and often require the use of explosives or sophisticated techniques for defeating security devices. In one such case[5] a group of men tunnelled from the basement of a shop, which had allegedly been acquired for the

[1] *King* 4.11.75, 1803/B/75, [1976] Crim. L. R. 200; see also *Drayson* 12.10.73, 2836/B/73 (demanding £20,000 from bank manager by means of note threatening to explode bomb, no actual or imitation bomb, threat not taken seriously; four years not excessive but reduced to thirty months in view of 'special personal circumstances').
[2] *Parkes and Pressley* 24.1.74, 1858/B/73.
[3] 30.7.75, 3721/A/74; see also *Reid* 8.5.73, 5824/B/72 (demanding £4 as compensation for allegedly broken window, threats to beat victim up, accompanied by minor violence; eighteen months upheld).
[4] *Straker* 8.2.73, 3605/A/72; see also *Akers* 17.6.74, 1445/B/74 (serviceman using violence to collect money owed to him for cannabis supplied; nine months upheld despite loss of career).
[5] *Wolfe and others* 23.5.74, 730/B/73.

purpose, to the strongroom of a bank situated some distance away, used gelignite to gain access to the vault and stole property worth over £1,500,000. Sentences of twelve years were upheld on several participants. In a second case involving 'a highly professional well-planned conspiracy to break into and steal from sub-post offices' in which safes were opened with explosives, the Court considered that a sentence of fourteen years did not allow sufficient credit for the fact that no physical violence was used or intended; a sentence of twelve years was substituted.[1]

Sentences in this bracket are not likely to be upheld for burglaries on a more modest scale, even if committed in large numbers by an offender with a long record. In *Craig*[2] a man with 'an enormous list of previous convictions' was sentenced to ten years' imprisonment for forty-two burglaries of schools, having been convicted of similar offences on at least five previous occasions. The individual offences involved modest amounts of cash or property, totalling about £470. The Court commented that although the appellant could be described as a 'professional', it was necessary to consider the nature of the individual offences, which did not involve violence or disturbance of householders. Observing that 'the sentence for such offences does not necessarily involve a steady progression up the scale', the Court reduced the sentence to five years.

For burglaries lacking the elements of careful planning, the participation of a group of men and sophisticated techniques of entry, the Court is not normally prepared to uphold sentences in excess of seven years,[3] although sentences at this level have been upheld where large numbers of unambitious burglaries have been committed by men with little to offer by way of mitigation. In *Rudman*[4] the appellant admitted twenty-four burglaries of houses, in the course of which he had stolen cash and portable property amounting in all to £1,300. The offences began within two weeks of the imposition of a suspended sentence for earlier burglaries. The Court held that the six years' imprisonment was justified by reference to the large number of offences committed within a relatively short period, and the appellant's record, which made it 'perfectly clear that this man is a persistent burglar', indicated that 'there is no ground for mitigating in any way what would otherwise be the penalty'. In

[1] *Dachey* 21.10.74, 5950/B/72; see also *Toms* 3.10.74, 1904/A/74 (burglaries 'done with considerable skill and . . . a good deal of preliminary reconnaissance', carried out by gang over period of two years; ten years upheld; but consecutive suspended sentence ordered to run concurrently).

[2] 19.11.74, 2079/B/74.

[3] For an exceptional decision see *Lightbody* 3.3.77, 5317/B1/76, [1977] Crim. L. R. 626.

[4] 27.9.73, 1602/C/73.

Busby[1] a man of 31 who had served five previous sentences of imprisonment for breaking offences admitted twenty-three burglaries of houses and other premises, involving property worth about £3,000. As the appellant was 'rightly described . . . as a professional burglar', the sentence of seven years was not considered 'in any way excessive'.

Where the records or age of the offender leave some scope for mitigation, the appropriate sentence for a series of burglaries will probably be in a lower bracket, between three and five years. In *Kincaid*[2] a man of 25 with twelve previous convictions for offences of dishonesty, including burglary, admitted fifteen burglaries of houses. The Court felt that although 'a substantial sentence was called for', the sentence of six years was excessive in view of his age and an earlier sentence of eighteen months to which the present sentence was consecutive; a sentence of four years was substituted. In *Jarrett*[3] the appellant was young (21) but admitted an unusually large number of offences (sixty-four); he had previously undergone borstal training but his record was 'not a very bad one by the standards of today'. In these circumstances the Court considered that six years was too much for 'a large series of petty burglaries', and substituted a term of four years.

Equally, sentences exceeding five years are unlikely to be upheld even on experienced offenders where the number of the immediate offences is small. In *Sibley*[4] a man of 34, who had served six previous sentences of imprisonment for burglary, received a sentence of seven years for breaking into two bungalows, causing extensive damage and stealing property worth about £300. The Court observed that as the offences were 'the repetition of a well established pattern of previous offences of the same sort', it was impossible to give the appellant a 'young old-lag's chance', but that, 'even having regard to this man's record', seven years was 'too much for these particular offences'; a sentence of five years was substituted. In *McGarrity*[5] a 'professional burglar' with 'an appalling record' was sentenced to seven years' imprisonment for a single burglary of a house in which some silverware was stolen; the Court considered that the sentence was 'too high', particularly as there was some mitigation, and reduced the sentence to three years.

Sentences between three and five years are commonly upheld

[1] 15.2.73, 3686/B/72; see also *Dodds* 1.12.75, 1268/B/75 (thirty burglaries of houses, antiques and silver stolen, systematically sold through dealer; 'large scale professional burglaries in respect of which there were no mitigating factors'—seven years upheld).
[2] 17.4.73, 4139/B/72.
[3] 26.4.74, 5458/A/73.
[4] 17.1.75, 3680/C/74.
[5] 22.5.75, 902/B/75.

where the offender is in his mid-twenties or older, has committed several burglaries and has a significant record.[1] Sentences of three years have been upheld on offenders in this category convicted of an isolated burglary of a modest nature, as in *Gluckstead*,[2] where a man of 27 with several convictions for offences, including burglary broke into a house and stole the contents of the gas meter and two Post Office savings books. The Court said that the sentence of three years' imprisonment was 'not . . . improper'. In *Cashmore*[3] a man of 33 with three previous custodial sentences for dishonesty (including two breaking offences) broke into an inhabited public house at night with intent to steal. Although the appellant had committed no offence for over two years since his last release from prison, the Court upheld three years' imprisonment as 'appropriate to the circumstances' and could find 'no grounds justifying any reduction in it'. The sentences were upheld in each case.

Decisions such as these suggest that a sentence of three years will not necessarily be considered excessive on the facts for a single burglary, at least of a private home, and sentences below this level reflect the presence of mitigating factors rather than the inherent gravity of the offence. Even where there is some mitigation, sentences between twelve months and two years are commonly upheld for single offences of burglary. In *Webb*[4] the appellant was 24 and had not committed any significant offence since his marriage three years previously; the Court upheld a sentence of eighteen months for breaking into a garage and stealing £750 from the safe as 'well deserved . . . on the facts of the case'. In another case [5] the appellant, a man of good character, went with two others to a house believed to be empty and knocked at the door to confirm their belief; all fled when the owner returned unexpectedly. Upholding a sentence of twelve months for attempted burglary the Court commented that 'the gravamen in burglary or attempted burglary . . . is the terror which is instilled into people' and that the sentence was 'appropriate'.

---

[1] See, for example, *Lowther* 12.2.73, 3946/A/72 (man, 25, previous sentences of borstal training and imprisonment; five years for three burglaries involving £2,500 upheld, together with consecutive terms for other offences); *Armstrong* 26.1.73, 4702/B/72 (man, 28, 'substantial number of previous convictions', seventeen burglaries admitted, modest amounts stolen; four years upheld).

[2] 24.7.75, 1044/C/75.

[3] 10.4.73, 2607/A/72; see also *Best* 5.11.73, 3557/C/73 (breaking into flat in afternoon while occupier away, £10 stolen; long record of similar offences 'weighed . . . too heavily in the scales'—four years reduced to two).

[4] 5.6.75, 1508/B/75; see also *Hanlon* 22.1.73, 4598/C/72 (man, 27, one previous conviction for office breaking, single burglary, offence not pre-planned and committed while 'substantially under the influence of drink'; eighteen months upheld).

[5] *Davey* 5.6.75, 1248/B/75; see also *Daly* 29.4.71, 5085/C/73 (man, 29, 'some previous record but not a very bad one', burglary of flat and theft of property worth £230; twelve months 'a mild sentence'—upheld).

The weight attached to mitigating factors in burglary cases, particularly of the less serious kind, prevents a precise identification of the lower limit of the scale of sentences for single examples of burglary of the least serious kind, but the cases suggest that a sentence in the region of twelve months will not necessarily be considered excessive on the facts for the most minor form of burglary, where there is no scope for mitigation. In *Mansell*[1] a man of 30 with 'a very bad record' broke into a school sweet shop and stole sweets worth £25, for which he received two years' imprisonment. The Court observed that 'men are not sentenced on their records; they are sentenced for what they have done', and 'the maximum sentence which should have been imposed on him . . . on the facts' was twelve months. As there were no mitigating circumstances justifying a reduction in the sentence appropriate to the facts, that sentence was substituted. In *McIntosh*[2] the appellant broke into a tobacco kiosk and stole chocolate and matches worth £3. The Court observed that the sentencer's remarks about the community's need for protection from the appellant were inappropriate, despite his 'many previous convictions', as the sentence was not an extended sentence; the sentence was reduced from three years to twelve months.

THEFT

As in the case of robbery, the sentencing brackets for theft can best be identified if the offence is divided into a number of categories based on the most common factual situations.

Hijacking

Hijacking—the theft of a lorry together with a valuable load—is an offence usually carried out by a group of men following a carefully prepared plan. It exhibits those characteristics of organization and premeditation which generally attract longer sentences wherever they occur. Sentences upheld on the principal participants in a well planned hijacking involving a substantial amount of valuable property are often within the bracket of five to seven years, although shorter sentences will be appropriate for those who have played minor parts on the margins of the enterprise. In one such case a group

[1] 4.12.75, 2255/C/75.
[2] 27.11.73, 2639/C/73. Compare *Sheldon* 20.1.75, 2982/B/74 (entering shop through front window, arrested on premises in possession of goods worth £17, twenty previous convictions, but 'the sentence . . . had to be geared to the circumstances of the offence itself'; eighteen months reduced to equivalent of six, with consecutive suspended sentence).

of men stole a trailer loaded with whisky worth £30,000 from a lorry park; sentences of seven years were upheld on those appellants who were considered to have taken leading parts.[1] A sentence of six years was upheld on an appellant who planned the successful theft of a lorry-load of whisky from a dock.[2] Two men who stole a lorry loaded with carpets worth £28,000 received sentences of seven years' imprisonment, which were reduced on appeal to five years, apparently because the offence did not involve the same degree of organization or the participation of such a large number of persons as the more typical hijacking.[3]

Rather shorter sentences may be approved for those who have played lesser parts in the enterprise, but an offender who has taken an active part, even though a minor one, will be fortunate to receive a sentence of less than about three years. In *Nevin*[4] the appellant obtained work as a driver at the instigation of another man and abandoned his vehicle, together with its valuable load, in order to allow the other man to remove it. In the event the attempt was unsuccessful and all the property was recovered. Apparently accepting that the appellant had been 'a reluctant participant in this dishonest scheme' and had been subjected to some pressures and threats, the Court upheld a sentence of three years' imprisonment.

Thefts by employees and persons in positions of trust

The considerable volume of cases of theft by employees or other persons in positions of trust provides a useful guide to the appropriate sentencing brackets for cases of theft generally. The substantial mitigation often seen in cases of this kind, where a man of good character may stand to lose as a result of his conviction his career, pension rights and possibly his home, is often balanced by the aggravating effect of the abuse of trust which the offence constitutes.

The scale of sentences appears to extend to about seven years' imprisonment, but sentences in the highest bracket, between five and seven years, are reserved for cases involving extremely large sums of money. In *House*[5] the appellant admitted over two hundred thefts of the funds of a company of which he was a director and major shareholder. Over £270,000 was stolen over a period of five years and the company was eventually wound up with a deficit of £150,000. The money was spent in part to meet the appellant's 'grandiose' living

---

[1] *Galvin and others* 21.1.74, 3362/A/73.

[2] *Sullivan and others* 21.3.75, 3108/B/74.

[3] *Smith and Eastop* 17.10.75, 4995/A/74; see also *Thomas* 23.4.74, 5362/C/73 (theft of jewellery worth £20,000 from boot of parked car, two men involved; five years upheld).

[4] 17.1.74, 3577/C/73.

[5] 18.1.74, 1186/C/73.

expenses. The Court held that the sentence of seven years was not excessive in relation to the facts, but could be reduced to five years in view of the appellant's plea of guilty. By contrast in *Cunningham*[1] the appellant admitted twenty-two offences involving the misappropriation of about £13,000 belonging to his employers and was sentenced to six years' imprisonment, with a suspended sentence for other offences activated consecutively. The Court observed that while precise figures were not critical, it was essential 'to place the offences in the right perspective within offences of this type'. This was not a case of a man defrauding his employer of hundreds of thousands of pounds, but it could not be equated with that of a man who appropriated a few hundred pounds. The case accordingly fell 'within the middle range'; a sentence of three years was appropriate (together with the activated suspended sentence). Many comparable cases can be found.[2] In *Albiston and others*[3] five men, all of good character, were each sentenced to three years' imprisonment for conspiring to steal tyres from their employer; goods worth about £14,000 were stolen over a period of just over a year. The Court considered that sentences of three years were 'not out of keeping . . . with the sort of sentences that are passed for . . . serious offences of dishonesty . . . on the part of employees', and upheld the sentence on the appellants who had initiated the scheme, making various reductions in the sentences of those who had taken part at later stages. In *Hunter*[4] the treasurer and secretary of a club misappropriated about £10,000 of the club's funds over a period of fifteen months; almost all the money was lost in gambling. Accepting that it was 'in many ways a tragic case' in view of the appellant's 'hitherto exemplary character', the Court upheld the sentence of three years with the comment that 'others faced with a similar temptation . . . must . . . be fortified by knowing that the penalty

---

[1] 21.4.75, 3561/B/74.

[2] See for example, *Jeyes and others* 17.3.77, 5348/B/76 (theft of tyres by depot manager and sale of tyres stolen from manufacturer, over £13,000 involved; four years upheld on man of good character); *Ragoonan* 13.4.73, 575/A/73 (£31,000 stolen, all invested, almost complete restitution; five years for 'very grave . . . breach of trust' reduced to three); *Gernat* 23.11.73, 3104/B/73 (solicitor misapplying £17,000 of client's funds, complete restitution made before criminal proceedings instituted, long delay between discovery and trial; four years reduced to two in view of mitigation, otherwise 'there could be no criticism' of original sentence); *Wilshere* 11.12.75, 2683/A/75, [1976] Crim. L. R. 458 (fraudulent practices by stockbroker, over £20,000 involved, substantial restitution; four years 'in the lower range . . . for offences of this gravity').

[3] 1.11.74, 1875/C/74; see also *Vanger* 31.10.77, 2600/A/77 (office manager defrauding company of £70,000 over several years, significant restitution made, four years within correct bracket, upheld).

[4] 18.11.76, 1989/A/76. Compare *Parker* 12.5.75, 122/C/74 (club secretary misappropriating £6,400, exemplary character, three years 'a thoroughly appropriate sentence for this class of case', but reduced to eighteen months in response to petition for leniency by substantial proportion of club membership).

for committing a breach of trust is bound to be . . . a sentence of substantial duration'.

As the amount stolen begins to be measured in hundreds rather than thousands, the level of sentences descends correspondingly; in the absence of unusual aggravating features sentences in such cases will rarely exceed two years' imprisonment. In *Berry*[1] the manager of a butcher's shop stole about £970 in small amounts over about nine months, and was sentenced to two years' imprisonment. The Court observed that although the breach of trust was aggravated by the facts that the offences were 'spread over quite a considerable period of time' and that the money was spent on gambling and drinking, the sentence could be considered 'too severe'. A sentence of fifteen months was substituted. In *Craik*[2] the manager of a newsagent's shop stole about £375 from the till over a period of about six months and was sentenced to two years' imprisonment; the Court stated that while 'a man who commits systematic breach of trust in this way cannot hope . . . to avoid a sentence of immediate imprisonment',[3] it was 'not necessary either for the protection of the public, to deter others or to punish this man' that the sentence should be so long. The sentence was reduced to twelve months. In another case[4] a woman clerk stole small amounts from coin boxes which it was her duty to empty; over a period of two and a half years the total taken amounted to about £685. The Court held that the sentence of nine months' immediate imprisonment was neither inappropriate nor excessive.

In all of these cases the appellants were people of previous good character, or with no more than minor convictions in the distant past, and the sentences approved by the Court presumably make the normal allowance for this factor. Where the offender who steals in breach of trust has no such mitigation in his favour, a rather longer sentence than those exemplified above may be appropriate.[5]

[1] 1.3.77, 4956/A/76; see also *Sidebotham* 9.5.75, 4948/A/74 (salesman stealing £1,280 from employer; eighteen months 'does not seem out of keeping with the sentences that are passed . . . for this type of offence on this scale', but reduced to twelve months in view of possible misunderstanding by sentencer of appellant's status in company at time of offence); *Le Masurier* 10.12.76, 4848/C/76 (savings club secretary misapplying about £1,200 belonging to club members; two years upheld).

[2] 8.4.75, 4236/C/74; see also *Taylor* 9.10.73, 3481/B/73 (manageress of take-away restaurant stealing £490 in one week; twelve months upheld); *Uche* 6.5.75, 1202/B/75 (railway employee stealing goods in transit, property worth about £300; twelve months upheld).

[3] The Court referred to the appellant's single previous conviction for theft eight years previously as reinforcing the justification for an immediate sentence.

[4] *Dzienisz* 4.2.74, 5220/B/73.

[5] See, for example, *Stewart* 19.12.74, 4012/A/74 (man, 40, seventeen previous convictions for dishonesty, several previous custodial sentences, stealing £800 from employer's safe; five years 'quite justifiable' but reduced to four in view of guilty plea); *Willis* 16.3.73, 5362/B/72 (building worker, eighteen previous convictions, stealing equipment worth about £200 from site; two years upheld).

One category of case which justifies attention is that of the postman stealing mail. The Court generally expects a sentence of immediate imprisonment to be imposed in such cases, despite the usual mitigating factors of good character, loss of position and other indirect consequences. While the precise scope of the sentencing bracket is not easy to identify, often because the amount of the thefts is uncertain,[1] a sentence of twelve months may represent the lowest point in normal circumstances. In *Greenwood*[2] a postman aged 23 stole a number of packets during the first two weeks of his employment and received eighteen months' imprisonment; the Court observed that while 'the case required an immediate custodial sentence', twelve months was sufficient. In *Cook*[3] a sorter aged 56 was sentenced to nine months' imprisonment for stealing a ring and two counts of opening a postal packet. In view of certain personal mitigating factors the Court stated that the sentencer was 'justified in not imposing the normal length of sentence for this kind of criminal conduct', and upheld the sentence, which was thought to 'reflect all the mitigating circumstances'. Rather longer sentences will be upheld where larger numbers of letters are stolen over a substantial period of time. A sentence of four years was upheld on a postman who admitted stealing over one thousand letters in the course of 'a series of systematic and deliberate interferences with the mail',[4] and a sentence of twenty-seven months was considered 'severe' but not 'excessive' for stealing thirty-seven packets worth about £477.[5] In *Baker*[6] a sorter aged 27 admitted stealing two packets containing a total of about £390, while in financial difficulties. The appellant admitted the offences as soon as he was challenged and pleaded guilty, but the Court considered that the sentence of twenty-one months made 'a substantial reduction' to reflect the 'very weighty matters of mitigation' and upheld it.

Shoplifting

Although the overwhelming majority of shoplifting cases are tried summarily, sufficient numbers of shoplifting cases come before the Court of Appeal following proceedings in the Crown Court to enable the outlines of a sentencing policy to be identified.

[1] See *Rendall* (1973) 57 Cr. App. R. 714 (postman stealing mailbag containing thirty-four registered packets, other offences, precise value uncertain, but this 'not necessarily a conclusive yardstick'; three years not 'manifestly excessive' for offences spread over substantial period of time).
[2] 13.10.75, 1750/A/75.
[3] 10.12.73, 4399/B/730.
[4] *Courts* 22.7.74, 1590/C/74.
[5] *Cheney* 4.5.73, 732/B/73.
[6] 15.11.76, 4172/B/76.

A number of cases suggest that a sentence of imprisonment will rarely be appropriate for the shoplifter with no previous convictions, although the Court has indicated that there is no set minimum number of convictions which must occur before imprisonment may be considered.[1] In *Patel*[2] a married woman with no previous convictions, found guilty of three thefts committed on the same day in two different shops, was sentenced to six months' imprisonment suspended for two years. The Court heard that the appellant had been under treatment for depression, and observed that 'albeit that this type of offence is far too prevalent' a sentence of imprisonment, either immediate or suspended, was inappropriate 'in the light of the relatively minor nature of the particular offences'. The suspended sentence was accordingly quashed. In *Mark*[3] a woman of previous good character accompanied a friend on a shopping expedition; the friend, who had previous convictions for shoplifting, committed a series of thefts in the presence of the appellant, who eventually joined in and stole goods worth £15. The friend received an immediate sentence of fifteen months' imprisonment; the appellant was sentenced to six months' imprisonment suspended for two years and fined £250. Observing that the two cases were 'entirely different', the Court held that the sentences imposed on the appellant (which included other financial orders) were 'wrong in principle, grossly excessive and harsh'. The suspended sentence was quashed and the fine reduced to £45. Although occasional inconsistent decisions can be found,[4] these cases appear to indicate the Court's view of the proper approach to sentencing the casual shoplifter.

More commonly, the defendant in a shoplifting case which comes before the Court is a persistent offender with a long record of various offences of dishonesty. In such cases a custodial sentence will normally be upheld, although the sentencer is bound by the normal principle requiring proportionality between offence and sentence, and the appropriate sentence will often be relatively short.[5] On a number of occasions in shoplifting cases the Court has restated the principle that a disproportionate sentence of imprisonment is not justified by the offender's record; if the sentencer wishes to impose a preventive sentence of greater length than the facts of the offence warrant, the sentence must be certified as an extended sentence in

---

[1] See *Bailey* 22.8.77, 3993/B/77, [1978] Crim. L. R. 53.

[2] 24.2.77, 3949/C/76.

[3] 15.10.74, 2408/C/74; see also *Norman* 11.10.77, 4287/B/77 (one months' imprisonment for woman, 20, no previous convictions, stealing clothing worth about £60, 'wrong in principle'; varied to fine of £50).

[4] For example, *Penny* 5.4.71, 484/A/71, [1971] Crim. L. R. 435; *Partridge* 19.1.76, [1976] Crim. L. R. 641.

[5] See *Anderson* (1972) 56 Cr. App. R. 863.

accordance with the statutory procedure.[1] Although occasional
sentences of two years have been upheld for relatively minor offences
of shoplifting committed by offenders with extensive records of
similar offences,[2] the more usual bracket appears to lie between nine
and fifteen months' imprisonment. In *Kesson*[3] a man of 42 with thirty-
two previous convictions was sentenced to thirty months' imprisonment for stealing two dresses worth £18 from a department store. The
Court considered whether 'it would be worth taking a risk' with a
probation order, but decided against that course in the light of the
social inquiry report; accepting the inevitability of imprisonment, the
Court concluded that the sentence was 'out of scale for this offence'
and reduced it to fifteen months. In *Anderson*[4] a woman of 34 with six
previous convictions for shoplifting or similar offences received
sentences totalling twelve months for stealing tins of salmon from a
supermarket and other similar offences for which she had earlier been
put on probation. The Court accepted that in cases of repeated
shoplifting 'a custodial sentence is called for', but the sentence should
not necessarily be a long one; in the present case the sentence was
reduced to the equivalent of about five months' imprisonment. These
cases suggest that where the offender can be considered a persistent
shoplifter, the length of sentence, subject to an upper limit of about
eighteen months, will vary in accordance with the record and
prospects of the offender rather than the details of the items stolen. In

[1] See, for example, *Haines* 30.11.73, 3485/B/73 (stealing various items worth £7 in all
from supermarket, attempt to escape when challenged: 'bad record . . . played . . . an
undue part in the assessment of his sentence . . . a man should not be sentenced to
more than the gravity of the offence demands merely because he has a bad
record . . . if he has a bad record, then the gravity of the offence stands out as the start
criterion for the scale of punishment'; four years reduced to two); *Ashworth* 2.7.73,
41/B/73 (theft of two turkeys and three cardigans, seven blouses stolen subsequently
while on bail, many previous convictions; five years might have been appropriate as
extended sentence, but as ordinary sentences 'out of proportion to the charges'—
reduced to total of thirty months). See also *Lister* 5.10.72, 787/B/72 (n. 1, p. 35 above).
In *Morley* 23.3.73, 6251/A/72 a sentence of three years for shoplifting was upheld, the
Court observing that 'it may be that an extended sentence would have been
appropriate').

[2] See, for example, *Rice* 5.4.74, 343/C/74 (two offences of shoplifting involving
property worth £6, thirty-six previous convictions; sentences totalling two years
including activated suspended sentence upheld); *Lister* 5.10.72, 787/B/72 (n. 1, p. 35
above); *Prior* 24.10.77, 2380/A/77 (shoplifting goods worth £8 by man with 'very poor
record'; three years 'disproportionate to the gravity of the offence', reduced to eighteen
months).

[3] 20.11.73, 3848/C/73; see also *Leadley* 8.11.76, 1099/A/76, [1977] Crim. L. R. 369.

[4] (1972) 56 Cr. App. R. 863; see also *Parker* 26.4.74, 847/B/74 (woman, 39, nine
previous convictions, stealing clothing from department store while on probation for
similar offence; six months upheld); *Kearns* 21.6.74, 945/C/74 (eight months for
'exceptionally clumsy shoplifting of a pair of underpants', with four months'
suspended sentence activated, excessive—reduced to equivalent of six months); *Jones*
16.12.76, 3658/C/76 (fifteen months for 'persistent shoplifter' for theft in supermarket
excessive, nine months would have been appropriate; sentence reduced to allow
immediate release as 'act of mercy').

Roberts[1] the appellant and a companion stole four items of clothing from a shop and received a sentence of eighteen months' imprisonment. The Court observed that although the sentence was 'high up the scale for this type of offence, it cannot be said to be so excessive that in the ordinary course of events this Court would interfere'; however, although the appellant had 'a bad record', there was room for some mitigation and the sentence could be reduced to twelve months.

In a few cases the appellant clearly falls between the extremes of the persistent shoplifter for whom a sentence of imprisonment will normally be appropriate (at least in the absence of reasons for experimenting with probation or another individualized measure), and the first offender for whom the appropriate sentence will normally be a fine or conditional discharge. In the case of what may be called the irregular shoplifter—the offender with several convictions spread over a long period of time, with substantial intervals between them—the decisions of the Court suggest that if a sentence of imprisonment is imposed, it should be of very short duration, such as three months. In *Boath*[2] a man of 54 was sentenced to nine months' imprisonment for stealing two pipes worth £1.52. He had four previous convictions for similar offences spread over a period of fourteen years, the last one over seven years earlier. The Court considered that in view of this fact and other mitigating circumstances the sentence was 'out of proportion' and substituted a sentence of three months.

All the cases cited involve the theft of small amounts of property worth a very modest amount. Where the offence, although capable of being characterized as shoplifting, involves the determined theft of substantial quantities of valuable property, different considerations will apply. In *James*[3] three appellants took part in a 'shoplifting spree' in which a variety of relatively expensive items, including two shotguns worth over £3,000, were stolen. All the appellants had modest records. The Court considered that the sentences of three years' imprisonment were 'excessive', although 'imprisonment was right'. Sentences of eighteen months were substituted in each case.

Other thefts

The enormous variety of other forms of theft, and the weight given to

[1] 16.11.76, 1289/C/76.
[2] 1.2.74, 5425/A/73; see also *Sweeney* 8.8.73, 2850/B/73 (woman, 51, theft of two packets of pigs' hearts, several previous convictions but none within about five years of present offence; three months 'entirely right' but suspended as appellant on bail pending appeal).
[3] 8.11.76, 1376/A/76.

mitigating factors where the offence is not aggravated by violence, entry of premises or breach of trust, prevent precise formulation of a scale of sentencing brackets for thefts not falling within the categories discussed. While the value of the property stolen is an indicator of the gravity of the offence, it is not the only one. The theft of property of little intrinsic value may be aggravated by such factors as the vulnerability of the owner[1] or the systematic execution of the theft;[2] theft from the person in the form of bag-snatching or pocket-picking will usually justify a sentence not necessarily limited strictly by reference to the value of the property stolen.[3] The upper extreme of the scale may be indicated by *White*,[4] where a 'professional thief of a very high efficiency' stole a ring worth about £30,000 from a jewellery department and attempted to repeat the offence on a later occasion. The Court observed that while such offences attracted a substantial penalty, the sentencer had 'put this appellant into a higher bracket than the class of offence deserves' in imposing sentences totalling ten years' imprisonment. The total was reduced to six years (three years on each count). At the other extreme, a very minor theft may justify a sentence as high as twelve months where there is no possible scope for mitigation of any kind. In *Walker*[5] a man of 40 with an 'exceptionally bad record' stole envelopes containing £3.52 from a drawer in an office where he was left alone. The Court considered that the sentence of twelve months imposed for this offence was not excessive and that the two suspended sentences to which the appellant was subject at the time of the offence were correctly activated consecutively. In *Chivers*[6] a man of 58 with 'a very bad record for petty crimes' stole a ladder 'blatantly and in full view of the public' within a few weeks of his release from an earlier sentence. The Court considered that the sentence of two years' imprisonment was 'too much' and substituted a term of nine months.

[1] See, for example, *Jugdaohsingh* 11.2.77, 607/B/77 (attempt to steal £20 from paralysed hospital patient; six weeks' imprisonment upheld); *Chapman* 3.5.74, 174/A/74 (theft of antique from aged person under pretext of purchase, object worth only £3.50 in event; three years reduced to equivalent of eight months).

[2] See, for example, *Attarde and Waterfield* 18.2.75, 4680/A/74, [1975] Crim. L. R. 729 (theft of petrol from parked cars, appellant's car equipped with additional petrol pump to facilitate siphoning; imprisonment appropriate for 'determined and sophisticated' theft but three years reduced to two).

[3] See, for example, *Uter* 29.4.74, 467/A/74, [1974] Crim. L. R. 484 (youths, 19, stealing purse from bag carried by railway passenger, several previous convictions; three years upheld); *Goodchild* 13.12.76, 3323/C/76 (woman, 21, attempting to take purse from shoulder bag carried by pedestrian, three accomplices; twelve months upheld).

[4] 4.2.77, 2872/A/76, [1977] Crim. L. R. 433.

[5] 16.1.75, 3482/A/74.

[6] 21.1.77, 4567/C/76.

FRAUD

The expression 'fraud' can be used to cover various kinds of activities which may result in charges of obtaining by deception, conspiracy to defraud, forgery or occasionally offences under such legislation as the Prevention of Fraud (Investments) Act 1958. As in the case of robbery and theft, the Court's approach to sentencing in this context can best be illustrated by dividing cases into categories based on the most common factual situations, rather than on legal definitions.

Long firm frauds

The essence of a long firm fraud is relatively simple. A business is established—or an existing business is taken over—and conducted with apparent honesty for so long as is necessary to establish credit with the suppliers of various kinds of goods necessary to the conduct of the business. Once the confidence of the suppliers has been obtained, the fraudsmen place large orders with the suppliers, take delivery of the goods on credit, sell them and disappear with the proceeds. In practice long firm frauds are carried out with varying degrees of sophistication and on varying scales; in some cases the enterprise is fraudulent from the start, while in others the offender resorts to fraud in the hope of keeping alive a failing business, with the intention of paying off his creditors when better times return. For a case falling within the first category, a deliberately planned long firm fraud, a sentence of five years' imprisonment will not normally be considered excessive for those who have taken a significant part, even where the fraud is on a moderate scale by comparison with other cases. In one such case[1] the appellants perpetrated 'a classic long firm fraud' over a period of a few months by ordering goods on behalf of a company dealing in china and disposing of them without paying for them. As a result of the fraud 'a considerable number of honest traders . . . lost a lot of money'. Sentences of five years imposed on the principals were upheld, the Court observing in relation to one appellant that 'the gravity of the offence outweighs any mitigating factors that one can discover in his personal situation'. In another

[1] *Bennett and others* 16.12.76, 5798/B/75; see also *Falco and Caldori* 14.3.74, 3696/A/73 (long firm fraud 'of a familiar type', legitimate business taken over and 'used as a vehicle in the fraud', losses to suppliers at least £27,000, possibly much higher; five years 'customarily imposed for offences of this sort', sentencer reflecting mitigating factors by imposing three years only, sentences reduced to two years as particular appellants played 'comparatively minor parts'); *Smith* 16.5.74, 3973/A/73 (long firm fraud causing losses of £30,000, particular appellant playing secondary part; four years reduced to three).

case[1] the appellants acquired control of a 'perfectly reputable and honest company' which was used as the basis for a long firm fraud in which the company 'incurred debts in the ordinary way by ordering goods at a great rate and to a very considerable value' and then disposing of them without documentation, leaving the suppliers substantially unpaid. The principal appellant, who was considered to have 'organized and controlled' the enterprise, was sentenced to nine years' imprisonment on the basis that the total losses inflicted on suppliers were excess of £60,000. Accepting that the true losses were very much smaller, and that the case was 'not an exceptionally bad long firm fraud; it was a ordinary long firm fraud', the Court reduced this sentence to five years, with the comment that the original sentence was 'much too high'.

Rather shorter sentences may be appropriate where the business is begun with honest intentions but becomes fraudulent in the face of difficulties. In one such case[2] the two appellants were sentenced to five years' imprisonment for a series of offences involving the purchase and subsequent sale of second-hand cars. The Court accepted that the appellants began to operate as dealers in second-hand cars without any fraudulent intentions, but 'turned their hand to fraud in order to keep solvent in a business that was hopelessly under-capitalized'. About £20,000 had been lost, the greater part by finance companies whose outstanding accounts in the cars were not settled, the rest by owners of cars who entrusted them to the business on a sale-or-return basis but never received the proceeds of the sale. The Court considered that although the case involved 'systematic fraud' the sentences were 'not only severe, but . . . excessive'. Terms of three years were substituted.

Frauds on financial institutions

In this category are cases where a lending institution, such as a bank, finance company or building society, is induced to lend money against the security of property which is either grossly overvalued for the purpose of the loan or non-existent. Although a variety of different kinds of transaction come within this category, the most common example is that of obtaining money from a finance company

[1] *Green Lucas and Schallamach* 24.3.72, 3463/A/71; see also *Markus* [1974] 3 W. L. R. 645 (fraudulently inducing investments in international agricultural business; seven years not excessive, but reduced as statutory maximum under the Prevention of Fraud (Investments) Act 1958 inappropriate for first offender).

[2] *Rhys-Griffiths and McAlpine* 4.7.75, 4254/C/74; see also *Hassan* 6.6.74, 836/B/74 (travel agency conducted fraudulently after difficulties encountered, money accepted for tickets but tickets not provided, losses of about £2,500 caused to private individuals; two years upheld).

by means of a fraudulent hire purchase agreement relating to non-existent cars or other goods. The appropriate sentencing bracket will depend on the amount obtained by the fraud, the sophistication with which it was carried out and the length of time over which it extended. In one instance,[1] described by the Court as 'a typical case of a person engaged in a motor business making use of hire purchase facilities in respect of vehicles that did not exist', in which finance companies lost about £16,000, the Court upheld a sentence of five years and three months' imprisonment with the comment that 'the amount of money involved is only of comparatively minor significance; it is really the quality of the transactions that matters'. As the present case involved 'a considerable number of transactions deliberately dishonestly undertaken', the sentence was not excessive. A dealer in diamonds[2] defrauded a bank which had allowed extensive overdraft facilities on the security of diamonds deposited with the bank by gradually replacing the diamonds with stones of much lower value, causing the bank to lose over £200,000. The Court observed that 'businessmen who indulge in this kind of fraud . . . which clogs the wheels of commerce . . . must expect . . . severe sentences'; the total sentence of four years' imprisonment was not excessive, but as it was made up of inappropriate consecutive terms of three years and one year, it was reduced to three years on all counts concurrent.

A lower level of sentence may be appropriate where either the amounts involved in the fraud are substantially less[3] or the fraud is not intended to damage the lender's interests. In *Skinner*[4] a farmer of 'excellent character in a good honest way of business' required financial support to extend certain buildings. The finance company to whom he applied for a loan was not empowered to lend money for building, but the appellant was persuaded by their agent to submit an application for a loan to cover the cost of the equipment needed for the building, inflating the amount requested by the amount needed for the building operation. The application was supported by falsified invoices; a total of about £22,000 was obtained, which the appellant intended and expected to repay within the term of the loan. When the appellant's company failed, the finance company was left with a loss of about £4,000, having taken other security as collateral. The Court

---

[1] *Pathak* 3.12.73, 3062/A/73.
[2] *Mehta* 26.4.74, 2937/C/73.
[3] See, for example, *Frugtniet* 18.2.75, 2902/R/74 (fraudulent applications for loans, signatures on applications forged, about £1,000 obtained, several previous convictions; two years not excessive although case 'falls within the less serious category of offences of fraudulently obtaining monies from finance houses').
[4] 16.3.73, 4290/C/72; see also *Dibley* 24.1.75, 5150/C/74 (application for hire purchase agreement on car, signature of guarantor forged, payments maintained until financial difficulties arose, subsequent fraudulent transaction over second car; nine months 'appropriate and right').

held that an immediate sentence of imprisonment was justified, but that the term of three years imposed by the sentencer was excessive; a sentence of twelve months was substituted. In *Cranshaw*[1] the appellant submitted a proposal form for a credit sale agreement relating to a car, in which certain particulars were mis-stated; the Court, accepting that the appellant was 'cutting the corners of his credit' and intended to repay the loan within the agreed period, decided that the sentence of twelve months imposed by the sentencer could be varied by being suspended.

On a number of occasions the Court has considered the problem of fraudulent applications for mortgages, where the lender's interest is properly secured on the house but the borrower overstates his income to overcome the lender's status requirements. In one such case,[2] where several appellants, one an officer of the lending institution, arranged for a number of mortgage applications to be supported with false documentary evidence of income supplied by a non-existent employer, charging a fee to the applicant for their assistance, the Court upheld sentences of eighteen months' imprisonment despite the good character of all concerned. In a similar case[3] where the false evidence was supplied by an estate agent on behalf of clients whose applications were otherwise 'genuine applications' for 'genuine properties', the Court held that the excellent previous character of the appellants allowed it to take 'a more merciful view of the matter than would ordinarily be possible in a case of this kind'. The original sentences of eighteen months were suspended. These cases suggest that where the fraudulent applications are the result of a conspiracy or course of conduct involving persons familiar with the procedures for obtaining mortgages, sentences of the order of eighteen months will not be excessive, although the question of suspension may arise in appropriate circumstances. Presumably a shorter sentence would be appropriate for the fraudulent applicant who falsifies his own income, with the expectation of being able to meet the repayments.

Cheque frauds

A typical cheque book fraud involves the use of a stolen cheque-book to obtain cash, goods or services in return for forged cheques; a more modern variation is the credit card fraud involving the use of a stolen credit card. Frauds in this category are carried out on varying scales and with varying degrees of sophistication. For the most ambitious

[1] 28.1.74, 5148/A/73.
[2] *Duru and others* (1973) 58 Cr. App. R. 151.
[3] *Sarin and Zaidi* 14.3.74, 5189/A/73; see also *Weston* 4.9.73, 2752/A/73 (false reference provided to mortgage applicant, loan fully secured; nine months upheld).

versions, involving large numbers of documents and substantial sums of money, sentences between five and seven years may be upheld. in *Spring*[1] the appellant, together with others, obtained £36,000 by the use of cheque-books and banker's cards obtained by opening bank accounts in fictitious names; the Court upheld seven years' imprisonment as 'richly deserved'. In *Dare*[2] the appellant received a sentence of five years' imprisonment for his part in a conspiracy in which forged cheques drawn on English banks were cashed at banks in various parts of Europe, causing a loss of £56,000 to the banks. Observing that the appellant was 'at the very centre of . . . an enterprise which required daring, resource and determination', the Court upheld the sentence.

Where the element of organization is lacking and the amount obtained is substantially less, the appropriate sentencing bracket may be between two and four years. In *Allison*[3] a man with several previous convictions admitted over sixty offences involving the use of various stolen credit cards to obtain a total of about £1,000. The Court considered that the 'very substantial' sentence of five years should be reduced to three. In *Oddy*[4] the appellant admitted obtaining property and cash worth more than £5,000 in the course of over thirty cheque frauds involving four bank accounts opened for the purpose, and related offences of obtaining a passport by false statements; sentences totalling thirty months were upheld. In another case,[5] where the total amount obtained by two men (each with several previous convictions) by means of a stolen cheque book was about £200, the Court reduced the sentence from three years to two. A sentence of two years was upheld on a young woman of previous good character who admitted over fifty cheque frauds, some with her own and some with a stolen cheque-book, the Court observing that the sentence was not excessive for 'a deliberate course of fraudulent conduct'.[6] In a further example[7] the Court described a sentence of

---

[1] 4.9.73, 3065/A/73; see also *Browne* 30.11.73, 4162/C/73 (seven years for 'front man' in large-scale cheque fraud involving losses of £11,000; sentence more appropriate to principal, reduced to four years for 'labourer' used by others to cash cheques stolen by them).

[2] 27.11.75, 734/C/75.

[3] 18.12.75, 1908/C/75; see also *Hourihan* 23.10.73, 1748/A/73 (ten offences involving stolen cheques; six years aggregate too long, reduced to three); *Green and Delooze* 15.10.74, 2518/A/74 (three years and two years consecutive for two series of cheque frauds, substantial amount of property obtained from shops; sentences, properly made consecutive as second series of offences committed while on bail for first, upheld).

[4] (1974) 59 Cr. App. R. 66; see also *Matthews* 15.12.75, 3366/B/75 (160 offences, over £4,000 obtained; eighteen months 'very lenient'); *Hughes* 20.1.75, 2017/B/74 (eleven offences of obtaining total of £1,500 with cheques stolen from former employer; sentences totalling two years 'merciful').

[5] *Thomas and Richardson* 23.3.73, 5197/C/72.

[6] *Oakham* 25.11.76, 1660/A/76; see also *Novelli and Faulkner* 11.2.75, 3664/C/75 (forty-eight cheque frauds by man of good character, £1,300 obtained; eighteen

eighteen months, imposed on a man of good character who obtained a cheque book in another person's name and drew on his account until it was exhausted, subsequently attempting to repeat the process with another bank in the name of one of their customers, as 'the minimum sentence that could properly be passed'. These cases suggest that where there is a series of cheque frauds carried on with some degree of deliberation and several hundred pounds are involved, a sentence much less than two years will owe more to mitigating factors than the inherent quality of the offence, although presumably a sentence at this level would be inappropriate for an isolated cheque fraud unless the amount concerned was unusually large or other aggravating circumstances were present.

Post Office frauds

The most common fraud on the Post Office is committed by obtaining one or more savings bank deposit books, forging entries recording deposits and then making withdrawals against the deposits. Very large numbers of offences may be involved in particular cases, and the offender in this category of case is more likely to have a substantial record than in the other categories of frauds. Occasionally an extended sentence will be imposed,[8] and in one case, where a Post Office employee was involved in a scheme by which the Post Office was defrauded of over £130,000 by extensive and sophisticated forgery, a sentence of twelve years was upheld.[9] More commonly however the sentence on an offender with no significant mitigation and a substantial series of offences will be between four and seven years. In Cullen[10] a man with a substantial record was convicted of conspiracy to defraud the Post Office by means of forged pension books, of which three thousand had earlier been stolen in a burglary by another person. The Court held that the sentence of seven years was not excessive for the offence, but ordered it to run concurrently with a sentence imposed earlier for unrelated offences to avoid an excessive aggregate. In Smith[11] the appellant admitted twenty-four frauds on the Post Office and received a sentence of seven years' imprisonment; the Court accepted that although the sentence was not

---

months not excessive for 'persistent frauds carried out on a substantial scale').

[7] Warburton 3.11.75, 2498/B/75.

[8] See, for example, Thomson 10.6.74, 5031/C/73 (150 Post Office frauds involving £33,000; ten years extended upheld); Grimwood 25.1.73, 4035/B/72 (seven offences, long record; six years extended upheld).

[9] Murray 20.12.73, 3649/C/72, [1974] Crim. L. R. 266.

[10] 23.1.75, 1135/B/74.

[11] 16.5.74, 4882/A/73.

necessarily excessive, the sentencer might have attributed to the appellant his co-defendants' greater number of offences. The sentence was reduced to five years 'on the footing that something has gone wrong'. In a third case[1] the appellant was sentenced to six years' imprisonment for his part in eight offences; although he had a 'shocking record', the Court reduced the sentence to four years, partly to reflect his eventual plea of quilty.

Sentences in this range are clearly reserved for systematic forgeries carried out with determination and some degree of skill; much lower sentences will be appropriate where the offence can be seen as casual or opportunistic. In *O'Rourke*[2] a women of 30 with ten previous convictions, who was on probation for other offences, obtained about £25 by forging her landlady's signature on her pension book. Partly in view of personal mitigating factors the Court reduced the sentence to a total of twelve months.

Confidence tricks

Frauds on private individuals occur in many different forms, but it is possible to identify two broad categories. The first is the case where a particular individual is defrauded of a very substantial amount of money as a result of an elaborate deception carried out over a period of time; the second involves an offender who carries out a whole series of relatively minor frauds by repeating the same simple deception with large numbers of people and obtains as a result a very substantial amount in total.

Sentences for cases falling within the first category will vary according to the amount obtained, the nature of the deception and the damage, economic and emotional, suffered by the victim. In *Andrew*[3] a man of 50 with many previous convictions for dishonesty admitted defrauding a widow by persuading her to entrust him with her savings for investment, spending the money in the course of an affair with her. The Court considered that a total of five years' imprisonment was 'about right' for these offences and several

---

[1] *Wiggans* 6.4.72, 6041/C/72; see also *Kellier* 2.4.73, 3012/C/72 (woman, 29, several previous convictions, eighty-five offences involving £3,800; four years upheld; no appeal by principal against sentence of six years).

[2] 4.6.74, 1702/B/74.

[3] 27.1.75, 2377/B/74; see also *Meischel* 6.4.73, 5200/C/72 (widow defrauded of £3,700 over period of several months; five years 'in no way wrong in principle or excessive', but reduced to three in view of attitude of victim); *Waterson and Cockayne* 17.5.74, 4418/C/73 (woman defrauded of £1,500 in sale of rings; five years 'perfectly proper' for principal offender, but reduced to three in view of delay in case coming to trial); *Waterfall* 24.11.75, 4321/C/75, [1976] Crim. L. R. 203 (forgery of will of elderly person, potential gain of £6,500; two years' imprisonment made adequate allowance for age (70) and good character of appellant).

independent thefts. In another case[1] the appellant persuaded a shopkeeper to invest over £5,000 in a scheme to install breath-test machines in public houses; a second victim was defrauded of over £3,000 in connection with a plan to install coffee machines. The sentencer imposed an extended sentence of eight years, but as the statutory notice was defective, although the appellant had 'a very long record', the Court had to consider whether eight years was 'an excessive sentence when looked at not as an extended sentence but as an ordinary sentence'. The Court concluded that, as the sentence would be 'at the top of the appropriate range', some allowance could be made for the appellant's ill health and other mitigating circumstances of a personal nature. A sentence of four years was substituted.

Shorter sentences will be appropriate where the sums involved are significantly lower. A sentence of fifteen months was upheld on a young married man who defrauded a young woman of £770 by pretending an intention to marry her,[2] and a home help who forged a signature to withdraw £90 from the savings account of an elderly client received twelve months' imprisonment.[3] In *Morson*[4] a man with 'a long record' obtained £60 for an elderly car by describing it in terms know to be false and providing a false log-book and test certificate. The Court considered his sentence of two years 'excessive' and substituted a term of twelve months.

Examples of the second category of confidence trick, where large numbers of people are defrauded of relatively small amounts by a repeated false pretence, include *Ruff*,[5] where a man with many previous convictions called on elderly people, pretending to be from the local authority rates department, and told them that they could obtain a rebate of £155 on payment immediately of £50 in cash; in one case a larger sum was stolen. Accepting that the appellant's seventy offences were 'the meanest type of deception practised upon those who were least able to defend themselves', the Court considered that sentences totalling nine and a half years were 'too long . . . even for this long series of offences', and substituted sentences totalling six and a half years. In another case[6] two men defrauded two old ladies by pretending that their houses were infested by woodworm and that they were experts in the treatment of woodworm and dry rot. The instigator of the 'fraudulent business' received three years' imprison-

---

[1] *Darlington* 28.11.74, 885/B/74.
[2] *Garrib* 27.7.73, 1871/B/73.
[3] *Southee* 29.6.73, 2484/A/73.
[4] 20.3.75, 3881/B/74; see also *King* 26.9.73, 896/C/73 (large numbers of people defrauded of small amounts aggregating over £2,300 by persistent 'con man' with numerous previous convictions; seven years upheld).
[5] 4.3.75, 2796/C/74.
[6] *Ryan and Blake* 24.6.75, 5148/C/74.

ment, which was upheld. On a different level, two men who attempted to obtain small sums of money from passers-by by pretending to be touts for indecent shows received nine months' and eighteen months' imprisonment respectively; the Court upheld these sentences with the observation that, considered as deterrent sentences, they were not excessive.[1]

HANDLING STOLEN PROPERTY

Sentences for handling stolen property rarely exceed seven years,[2] and those in the range of five to seven years are usually reserved for handlers who have received the proceeds of a major theft or have been party to an extensive conspiracy to steal and dispose of valuable property. In *Owens*[3] the appellants were convicted of receiving goods worth about £30,000 taken from a stolen lorry, the goods having been found in a warehouse which they controlled. The Court considered that the existence of the warehouse had made the original theft possible, and sentences of seven years' imprisonment were upheld. In *Marks*[4] a Post Office worker of previous good character admitted handling stolen National Insurance stamps, part of the proceeds of the theft of stamps with a face value in excess of half a million pounds; he had sold stamps worth £100,000. The sentence of six years was not considered excessive.

Regular handlers of the proceeds of less ambitious burglaries or thefts are likely to receive sentences between three and five years' imprisonment. In *Joyner*[5] a man with two previous convictions for handling was convicted on six counts of receiving a substantial quantity of stolen cigarettes and disposing of them through various outlets. The Court observed that the evidence justified the inference that the appellant was 'the central receiver to whom others came to deal with any stolen goods', and upheld the sentence of three years. In *Fallon*[6] a sentence of five years was imposed on a man who admitted

[1] *Haire and Spencer* 2.10.75, 3016/B/75.

[2] For an exceptional case, see *Turner* 9.2.73, 6306/B/71 (conspiracy to handle property stolen in long series of hijackings; thirteen years upheld).

[3] 24.1.74, 3362/A/73; see also *Granville* 21.3.75, 3108/B/74 (receiving whisky worth £30,000 stolen from lorry at dock; five years upheld); *French* 8.2.73, 4074/B/72 (handling lorry-load of Oxo cubes worth £17,000 stolen from docks; five years 'by no means excessive').

[4] 16.12.75, 4540/C1/74.

[5] 2.10.73, 5043/A/72; see also *Nearn* 8.4.74, 5538/B/73 (receiving proceeds of three burglaries of houses, property found shortly after burglary, justifying inference that 'the burglars must have known where they would be able to dispose of goods before they actually stole them'; thirty months upheld).

[6] 20.5.75, 738/C/75; see also *Mackey* 20.2.73, 2102/C/72 (receiving proceeds of substantial burglary 'very shortly after it had been stolen'; five years reduced to three, partly in view of mitigation).

conspiring to handle stamps and postal orders stolen in a number of burglaries at post offices; the sentence was reduced to four years, partly because a mistake made by the sentencer in pronouncing sentence might have left the appellant with a justified grievance. In *Murphy*[1] the appellant admitted two counts of handling 'a very large quantity of clothing and soft goods' which were found in his garage. Although the appellant had 'a perfectly clear record' the Court stated that as there was evidence which justified the view that 'this was not just one lapse from grace but . . . a continuous procedure of handling stolen goods', the sentence of three years 'cannot be criticized.'

The level of sentence appropriate to the casual or opportunist handler who receives property on an isolated occasion will vary with the value and quantity of the property and the circumstances of the theft; the sentence may well also reflect substantial mitigation. In *Brown*[2] 'a man whose life had been a credit to him . . . up to the moment when he was tempted' agreed to buy a large quantity of tinned meat which had originally been stolen from a lorry; the appellant's dealings were with earlier receivers rather than the original thieves. The Court considered that despite the 'powerful mitigation', a substantial custodial sentence was inevitable in the case of 'a man of good character deciding for greed . . . to embark on a criminal enterprise', and upheld the sentence of two years' imprisonment. In *Gray*[3] the appellant was convicted of receiving a substantial number of records stolen from a lorry. The Court stated that although there was no evidence of any other incidents and the appellant had no previous convictions, 'persons who behave in this way . . . can only expect to go to prison for a substantial period of time', and that the only grounds for reducing the sentence of three years' imprisonment imposed for the offence were mitigating factors of an unusual kind.

The casual handler who receives a single item or small quantity for his personal use will receive a shorter sentence or be fined. In one example[4] nineteen people were convicted of offences resulting from the theft of forty-six washing machines and other domestic appliances by an employee of the distributor. The original thief received four years' imprisonment, which was upheld; two men who either

---

[1] 22.6.73, 497/C/73; see also *Shannon* 21.12.73, 2027/A/73 (handling goods stolen from factory by employees, appellant and accomplice 'plainly the main handlers', large quantities involved; three years upheld despite previous good character).

[2] 28.11.74, 3450/A/74, [1975] Crim. L. R. 177; see also *Street* 24.4.75, 1017/C/75 (man of good character receiving one hundred cases of stolen whisky, admitting desire to 'earn some easy money quickly', no suggestion of other incidents, but 'having been tempted, he has to be punished'; eighteen months upheld).

[3] 1.4.74, 3810/B/73.

[4] *Mills and others* 20.6.75, 859/B/75.

bought a number of appliances from the thief for resale or acted as a contact between him and the ultimate purchasers were sentenced to eighteen months and two years respectively, while those who received single items for their own use received sentences of nine months' imprisonment suspended and were fined varying amounts. The Court held that these sentences were all appropriate and observed that 'the best that . . . receivers in these sort of circumstances can hope for is that their good characters . . . and their family circumstances . . . may be such that the court will be willing to suspend the sentence'.[1] In a case where a man with a 'very bad record' but no recent offence of dishonesty received a stolen cash register worth about £600 at the time of the theft, the Court considered two years' imprisonment 'excessive' and reduced the sentence to fifteen months (both immediate).[2] A man of good character who received in the course of his business a single stolen colour television set was sentenced to six months' imprisonment. The Court observed that for an isolated act of receiving the appropriate sentence would normally be a substantial fine, and varied the sentence, which was not 'right in principle', to a conditional discharge (in view of the period spent in custody prior to the appeal).[3] On the other hand, a sentence of twenty-eight days' imprisonment imposed on a dock worker for handling six tins of corned beef worth £3, stolen from a cargo in transit, was upheld despite his age (58) and good character, as a deterrent in view of the prevalence of the offence in the locality.[4] While there are clearly difficulties in reconciling these cases, it may be that they support the proposition that while the usual sentence for an isolated act of handling will in practice be a fine, a sentence of imprisonment will not be inappropriate either where the offender has no mitigation to offer or where there are other reasons for disregarding the mitigation.

Section 5: Other Offences

CRIMINAL DAMAGE

Arson

Offences of arson are frequently connected with mental disturbance. The Court has recommended that a person convicted of arson should

---

[1] In two cases the Court suspended immediate sentences which had been imposed on appellants who had bought several items for their own use or had resold a very small number of items.

[2] *Tierney* 13.12.76, 3602/C/76.

[3] *Harris* 20.12.76, 5897/A/76; but compare *Coles* 16.12.74, 4099/A/74 (van driver; minor convictions in distant past, receiving television set stolen from employer, nine months upheld).

[4] *Bogle* 3.6.75, 2334/R/75, [1975] Crim. L. R. 726.

not normally be sentenced without psychiatric investigation.[1] Where there is a sufficient basis of evidence, the appropriate sentence may be a hospital order[2] or sentence of life imprisonment,[3] subject to the principles discussed in chapter 7. Such sentences are generally preferable to long fixed-term sentences if the offender is likely to represent a continuing danger in the future.[4] Probation orders, with or without a requirement of submission to psychiatric treatment, have been used in appropriate cases.[5]

Where there is no psychiatric explanation for the offence, arson normally attracts a sentence of imprisonment. While sentences of seven years and over have been upheld in a few cases involving immediate danger to life[6] or extensive property damage,[7] the more usual bracket is from three to five years' imprisonment. Sentences of five years have been upheld for deliberate acts of arson not related to emotional disturbance. Examples include *Cutler*,[8] where the appellant, as a 'deliberate calculated act of revenge', set fire to a restaurant from which he had earlier been ejected, and *Reynolds*,[9] where the appellant threw petrol bombs through the window of a house where a party was taking place. In *Frost*[10] a security officer deliberately set fire to his employers' premises, causing £75,000 worth of damage for no apparent reason. As there was no medical explanation for his behaviour, the sentence of four years was upheld. A shopkeeper who set fire to his shop with intent to defraud his insurers was sentenced to

[1] *McLoughlin* 19.12.75, 5301/A/75, [1976] Crim. L. R. 144; *Calladine* 25.11.75, 4204/B/75.
[2] See, for example, *Maddison* 3.6.75, 4988/A/74.
[3] See, for example, *Lishman* 8.7.71, 543/B/71, [1971] Crim. L. R. 548; *Thornton* 11.10.74, 2404/C/74, [1975] Crim. L. R. 51.
[4] See *Bowman* 9.10.73, 1868/B/73 (ten years for setting fire to house 'not too severe', life 'might have been appropriate' in view of psychiatric evidence).
[5] See, for example, *McLoughlin* 19.12.75, 5301/A/75, [1976] Crim. L. R. 144; *Appleby* 3.12.74, 3050/C/74 (setting fire to curtains in course of argument with ex-husband, history of matrimonial conflict and depressive illness; eighteen months 'appropriate' but varied to probation in view of 'exceptional' circumstances).
[6] See, for example, *Dawes* 21.6.74, 64/C/74 (setting fire to one of a pair of semi-detached houses, other occupied at time); *Power and others* 21.11.72, 6297/C/71 (petrol bombs thrown at shop in order to put proprietor out of business; eight years upheld).
[7] See, for example, *Biggs* 27.6.74, 969/C/74 (setting fire to mill, damage in excess of £225,000); see also *Tether* 21.1.71, 5071/A/70 (setting fire to school with prepared device, minor damage caused, previous history of arson; five years upheld); *Northfield* 2.7.71, 5718/B/70 (burglar setting fire to premises 'to cause confusion'; twenty cases of arson admitted, no mental disorder; ten years aggregate reduced to seven).
[8] 26.1.71, 1735/A/70.
[9] 29.7.71, 2878/B/71.
[10] 17.11.75, 1148/A/75; see also *Stedman* 12.7.71, 213/A/71 (setting fire at factory during night shift, offence attributed to boredom, no previous convictions, no mental disorder; three years appropriate for youth of 22, 'a substantially heavier sentence' appropriate for older man); *Jowett* 13.7.71, 429/A/71 (setting fire to employer's factory as a result of grievance over holiday pay, £10,000 worth of damage; 'grave offence meriting severe punishment', but four years reduced to thirty months in view of 'exceptionally tragic personal circumstances').

three years' imprisonment, which the Court considered 'appropriate to the offence'.[1] In *Kirkland*[2] a 'level-headed young man' set fire to an unoccupied house belonging to his former employer who had recently discharged him on the grounds of redundancy. The fire caused modest damage and no danger to the neighbours. Accepting that the appellant had acted 'on the spur of the moment without proper appreciation of what he was doing', as a result of heavy drinking, the Court upheld the sentence of three years' imprisonment as 'the minimum for this class of offence' in the absence of 'mental imbalance'. As this statement indicates, reductions below the level of three years' imprisonment are usually attributable to mitigating factors.[3] In *Smithson*[4] a 'reliable . . . honest and conscientious worker' set fire to the terrace house where he lived after a violent argument with his wife, who had taken the children to a neighbour's house for the night. The fire apparently caused no major damage to the structure of the house and there was 'no sign of any mental illness'. The Court said that 'the penalty should be a custodial one' and that the sentence of eighteen months actually imposed 'was too short'.

Causing explosions

The principles to be adopted in sentencing persons guilty of causing explosions and related offences were considered in *Byrne*.[5] The Court

[1] *Dyson* 14.1.72, 1670/A/71.

[2] 25.11.75, 4026/C/75; see also *Ambler* 30.10.73, 3167/B/73 (youth, 18, two offences of arson totalling £100,000 worth of damage, no mental illness, no previous convictions; four and a half years upheld).

[3] See e.g. *Coughlan* 14.3.74, 5082/C/73 (three years for setting fire to neighbour's house following dispute 'cannot possibly be criticized'; reduced to eighteen months in view of 'difficulties in . . . domestic background'); *Taylor* 21.11.75, 3278/A/75 (setting fire in flat after sending children out, appellant in 'very confused and abnormal . . . state of mind' at time of offence, voluntary social worker in depressed area of city; 'there must be a custodial term for this class of offence', but five years reduced to two); *Foley* 26.7.72, 2506/B/73 (young man, ineffective attempt to set fire to armchair in parent's house following conflict with mother; two years 'in no way wrong', but reduced to equivalent of six months as mother reconciled and hopes for more stable future).

[4] 23.11.73, 3460/B/73. Compare *Gordon* 26.1.71, 3107/A/70 (husband setting fire during night to house occupied by wife and daughter, history of depressive illness but no treatment possible, minor damage only but wife and child endangered; three years upheld); *Nairn* 14.10.74, 3042/C/74 (man, 34, setting fire to wife's clothing, causing damage to house: conditional discharge; subsequent bomb hoax: three years for arson upheld).

[5] (1975) 62 Cr. App. R. 159. Earlier decisions include *Greenfield and others* (1973) 57 Cr. App. R. 849 (conspiracy to cause explosions over period of three and a half years, no serious injuries caused; ten years upheld); *Prescott* 20.6.73, 5769/C/71 (fifteen years reduced to ten to avoid disparity with previous case); *Fell* 20.6.74, 4918/R/73, [1974] Crim. L. R. 673 (conspiracy to damage buildings, no verdict on charge of conspiracy to cause explosions; twelve years upheld); *Williams* 1.2.71, 1870/A/70, (possession of explosives with intent to destroy aircraft; ten years upheld).

indicated that a distinction should be drawn between explosions intended to endanger life and explosions intended to cause damage to property, and that there should be 'an appreciable gap' between the two types of cases. For offenders in the latter category a sentence of fourteen years might be appropriate. Much shorter sentences have been considered suitable for causing small explosions not intended to cause injury or damage property. In *Travers*[1] the appellant constructed a small bomb as an experiment and left it in his car; the bomb exploded when handled by a police officer, causing injuries which were serious but not permanent. The Court accepted that the appellant had no political motives and 'no animosity towards anybody'; the offence was 'some kind of practical joke'. Although 'the ordinary minimum sentence is about seven years', the sentence could be reduced to four years 'as an act of mercy'. Similarly in *Ladd and Tristam*[2] the appellants were convicted of placing two small incendiary devices and one smoke bomb in various public buildings; no serious damage was done and no injuries were caused. The Court stated that while offences connected with explosions were 'grave matters indeed' it was necessary to keep the facts of the case 'in their proper perspective'; the offences did not constitute 'a major menacing attack upon the community or its safety'. The sentences were reduced from seven years to five in the case of one defendant and six years to four in the case of the other.

Bomb hoaxes and threats The Court has indicated that the perpetrator of a bomb hoax should normally receive a custodial sentence. Sentences as high as seven years have been upheld where the hoax has been part of a blackmail attempt,[3] although the more usual bracket for such cases appears to be three to five years' imprisonment.[4] Where aggravating features are not present, the appropriate sentence will rarely exceed two years and may be less. In *Farrell*[5] the appellant left home and after drinking 'too much whisky', got into a taxi and told the taxi driver that a holdall he was carrying contained a bomb which was about to explode. The taxi driver drove him to a

[1] 16.12.74, 1824/C/74.

[2] 14.10.74, 1260/C/74, [1975] Crim. L. R. 50; see also *Howells and Prior* 23.6.70, 7501/B/69, [1970] Crim. L. R. 540 (attempt to blow up office; five years upheld).

[3] See *King* 4.11.75, 1803/B/75, [1976] Crim. L. R. 200 (bank manager threatened with imitation bomb, £730 stolen; seven years upheld).

[4] See, for example, *Willey* 1.12.76, 1173/B/76, [1977] Crim. L. R. 302 (£25,000 demanded under threat to set explosive devices in shops; five years upheld); *Parsons* 21.12.76, 4295/C/76, [1977] Crim. L. R. 302 (£20,000 demanded from department store; four years upheld); *Kiss* 1.5.73, [1973] Crim. L. R. 55 (£5,000 demanded from railway booking office; three years upheld); *Scott-Robinson* 25.4.77, 5502/A/76 (money demanded from department store; three years properly reflected mitigating factors, otherwise sentence would 'exceed by a considerable amount' this figure; upheld).

[5] 15.12.75, 1410/A/75, [1976] Crim. L. R. 318.

police station. Traffic was diverted and business premises were closed while a bomb disposal squad was called, but the bag was found to contain only clothing. The appellant, a man of good character, was sentenced to two years' imprisonment. The Court stated that while 'people who commit bomb hoaxes must expect to go to prison', the sentence was 'too much' in view of his background; a sentence of twelve months was substituted. In *Weeder*[1] one of three youths who planted an imitation bomb in a museum, causing the museum to be evacuated, appealed against his sentence of five years' imprisonment; the sentence was considered 'excessive' and reduced to eighteen months.

Other criminal damage

Sentences of imprisonment have been upheld in cases of criminal damage inflicted deliberately and with no significant mitigation, but sentences in excess of two years appear to be considered unusual in the absence of abnormal features.[2] In one case six young men made an expedition in several cars to premises occupied by a rival group and smashed windows, doors and internal equipment. Sentences of two years were upheld against three of them who had previous convictions and reduced to twelve months in the other cases.[3] In a second example a man of 23 with an 'unblemished record' walked around a town centre smashing windows with dustbins, bricks, stones and iron piping, doing damage worth over £2,000, apparently 'for no rhyme or reason'. The Court stated that 'others who might be minded to commit comparable acts of vandalism must be reminded that they will be treated severely . . . if they do so', but considered that twelve months would have been 'adequate' in place of the two years actually imposed. The sentence was accordingly reduced.[4]

PERJURY

With rare exceptions[5] the Court upholds sentences of imprisonment in perjury cases, irrespective of the nature of the proceedings in which

[1] 24.2.77, 4345/A1/76, [1977] Crim. L. R. 487.

[2] See *Allen and Ling* (1975) 62 Cr. App. R. 148 (throwing stones at moving vehicles from other car or from road side, causing grave injuries in some cases; sentences of five years upheld, concurrent with eight years for causing grievous bodily harm); *Neal* 22.1.76, 4356/C2/76 (deliberately causing gas explosion in house, four houses demolished or seriously damaged, several people endangered; nine years upheld).

[3] *Kavanagh and others* 18.5.73, 24/B/73.

[4] *Atkins* 17.12.74, 3952/C/74; see also *Farley* 5.10.71, 3390/A/71 (applying paint stripper to car belonging to landlady of premises from which appellant was banned, no relevant previous conviction; nine months upheld).

[5] See, for example, *Lye* 12.2.73, 380/B/73 (youth, 17, false explanation of reason for late arrival in magistrates' court hearing on question of estreatment of bail; three months' detention varied to conditional discharge).

the perjured evidence is given and its effect on their outcome. In *Davies*[1] the appellant gave evidence in mitigation of sentence in favour of his two sons, who had pleaded guilty in the magistrate's court to various offences of dishonesty. His evidence that they were employed was not believed, and his subsequent sentence of twelve months' imprisonment was upheld with the comment that 'perjury and imprisonment are synonymous in most cases'. In *Wright*[2] the appellant gave false evidence during his own trial for driving a car which was not insured or taxed. The Court varied the sentence from eighteen months' imprisonment to six, stating that it did not intend 'to minimize . . . the seriousness of perjury or the principle that a prison sentence . . . must . . . in nearly all cases follow a conviction for perjury'.[3] The principle extends to perjury by prosecution witnesses and witnesses in civil proceedings.[4]

The range of sentences for perjury is difficult to identify, as most of the cases dealt with on appeal relate to perjury in minor criminal proceedings or civil cases where modest amounts are in issue; it is not clear whether the Court would uphold longer sentences for perjury in the course of major criminal cases. In the kind of cases most frequently heard on appeal, the Court is unlikely to uphold a sentence much in excess of two years. In *Jesson*[5] four members of a family gave false evidence at the trial of one of them for driving while disqualified; two were sentenced to five years' imprisonment. Despite the facts that 'this was a very bad instance' of perjury and that both appellants had substantial records, the Court considered the sentences 'very severe' and reduced them to two years in each case.

CONSPIRACY TO PERVERT THE COURSE OF JUSTICE

A similar policy is evident in cases of conspiracy to pervert the course of justice and analogous offences. A sentence of imprisonment will

[1] (1974) 59 Cr. App. R. 311.

[2] 6.4.73, 459/C/73; see also *Jowett* 23.9.74, 1046/A/74 (false evidence of drink consumed between accident and administration of breath test; eighteen months 'within the tariff for this kind of offence', but reduced because of mitigating factors to equivalent of ten months).

[3] See *Gordon* 29.3.71, 5282/A/70 (false statements against person accused of theft in trial on indictment, directed acquittal of accused on relevant counts of theft; sentences totalling eighteen months for perjury by appellant 'by no means excessive').

[4] See *Yarney and Cullen* 14.6.74, 296/B/74 (false evidence in proceedings to determine ownership of car seized to satisfy judgement debt, supported by forged receipt; two years upheld on instigator, reduced to twelve months on co-defendant); *Lal* 17.10.77, 3796/C/77, [1978] Crim. L. R. 52 (perjury in county court action to recover £214; nine months upheld).

[5] 25.11.71, 3248/A/71; see also *Murphy* 12.12.75, 3848/A/75 (false evidence in Crown Court trial for driving with excess blood alcohol level, two other witnesses suborned; offence 'serious' but 'does not require such long sentences as were . . . imposed'— three and a half years reduced to fifteen months).

usually be upheld, varying in length according to the nature of the conspiracy and, in particular, the extent to which the appellant persisted in it. In *Lee and others*[1] the wife of a man suspected of robbery gave the police a false statement about her husband's whereabouts at the time of the offence and persuaded two friends to support her. All three retracted their statements under police questioning. The Court held that although there was no suggestion that the false alibi had been arranged before the offence was committed, 'a custodial sentence . . . is necessary to mark the gravity of the offence'. As the attempt had been abandoned at an early stage and there were personal mitigating factors, the sentences were reduced from six months' imprisonment to three. Rather longer sentences are likely to be upheld where the attempt takes the form of an offer of a bribe to a police officer to refrain from reporting the appellant or otherwise abandon the proceedings against him. In *Pett*[2] the appellant, who had been arrested for a number of offences of violence, offered the officers concerned several hundred pounds not 'to make too much of this'. He was sentenced to twelve months' imprisonment for the attempt to bribe, consecutive to his sentences for the other offences; the Court varied the sentences under the totality principle to run concurrently, observing that the sentence was 'not in anyway too much' for the offence. In *Andrews*[3] a witness to an accident solicited a bribe from one of the drivers involved, in return for a promise to give false evidence in his favour in any proceedings that followed. The Court upheld the sentence of eighteen months' imprisonment. A sentence of two years was considered appropriate for threatening a witness who had been wounded in a public house fight.[4]

Longer sentences again have been upheld where false allegations have been made against a person, either for revenge or blackmail. In

[1] 29.4.75, 1652/C/75, [1975] Crim. L. R. 589; see also *Devito and Devito* 14.11.74, 4063/A/74, [1975] Crim. L. R. 175 (substitution of licence of one driver for another, first driver unlicensed to drive vehicle concerned, second driver admitting speeding and incurring disqualification; imprisonment 'right', but reduced from six months to three); *Mehmet and Ahmet* 18.4.75, 1383/B/75 (passenger claiming to have been driver of vehicle at time of accident, no conspiracy; nine months reduced to four); *Roy* 14.5.73, 6181/A/72 (police officer claiming to have been driver at time of accident; fifteen months upheld).

[2] 6.9.72, 1352/C/72; see also *Shamel* 7.7.75, 1822/B/75 (offer of £1,000 to officer not to oppose bail and to 'go easy' on person accused of serious drug offence; offence justified imprisonment, but two years reduced to twelve months in view of appellant's good character); *Witcomb* 30.10.73, 3119/B/73 (offer of £10 to officer to refrain from administering breath test; two years' imprisonment probably reflected appellant's record—reduced to six months).

[3] (1972) 57 Cr. App. R. 254; see also *Panayiotou* 14.5.73, 2230/C/71 (approach to complainant in rape case with apparent offer of money to withdraw complaint; three years reduced to twelve months).

[4] *Dallas* 18.10.71, 1079/C/71.

Singh[1] four men who had made false allegations of assault against four others were sentenced to varying terms between two years and thirty-two months; reducing the sentences in view of exceptional mitigating circumstances, the Court indicated that sentences of about three years would be appropriate in normal circumstances.

IMPEDING THE APPREHENSION OR PROSECUTION OF A PERSON GUILTY OF AN ARRESTABLE OFFENCE

The Court has upheld sentences of between three and five years on offenders convicted of assisting persons wanted for murder to evade arrest. In one instance a man of good character harboured for about a month a man wanted for the murder of a police officer; his sentence of five years' imprisonment was upheld.[2] The same sentence was upheld on a man who assisted in the disposal of the body of a murder victim.[3] The statutory scheme of penalties for the offence implies that the gravity of the impeding varies according to the gravity of the principal offence; the few decisions which have been found do not indicate how far this principle is applied in judicial practice.[4]

CORRUPTION

The pattern of sentences in cases of corruption is affected by the curious structure of maximum penalties for the offences concerned. Generally the maximum sentence is two years' imprisonment, but a sentence of seven years is permissible where government contracts or public works are involved.

The Court appears to expect a sentence of immediate imprisonment in any case of corruption. Sentences of four years have been approved in cases involving corruption on a substantial scale, in each instance the Court indicating that the sentence made allowance for mitigating circumstances.[5] In cases subject to the two-year maximum, the Court has upheld sentences of between six months and two years for acts of corruption in relation to duties owed to both public

[1] 12.2.71, 3043/A/70.

[2] *Kerrigan and Panayiotou* (1972) 57 Cr. App. R. 269; see also *Morgan* (1971) 56 Cr. App. R. 181.

[3] *Harvey and Ryan* 16.7.71, 753/A/71, [1971] Crim. L. R. 664; see also *Raymond* 5.10.71, 156/A/71 (assisting murderers by harbouring and loan of car; three years 'by no means excessive'); *Sultana* 6.10.77, 3513/B/76 (assisting in arrangement to bribe principal witness in murder inquiry to leave country; five years 'out of line' with sentences in comparable cases; reduced to three).

[4] See *Love* 8.11.71, [1972] Crim. L. R. 119 (four years upheld for arranging accommodation for man wanted for major bank robbery involving £125,000).

[5] See *Sporle* (1971) 56 Cr. App. R. 31; *Pottinger* 10.7.74, 876/R/74, [1974] Crim. L. R. 675; *Cunningham* 11.7.74, 2009/R/74.

and private employers. A sentence of twelve months' imprisonment imposed on a local council member who accepted £600 to ensure that a particular tender was accepted,[1] and a sentence of nine months on an official who accepted bribes totalling about £125 for issuing certificates of completion which entitled a builder to claim a higher rate of grant,[2] were each upheld. The maximum sentence was upheld for bribing a prison officer to bring whisky, brandy and hack-saw blades into prison.[3] A similar approach is seen in cases arising out of private employment. A manager who received a commission for placing a haulage contract with a particular contractor was sentenced to six months' imprisonment, which the Court considered adequately reflected his age (70) and previous good character; his younger co-defendant's sentence of twelve months was upheld.[4] Sentences aggregating five years were considered too severe for a works superintendent who used his position to extract payments from immigrant workmen, as a reward either for offering a job or for allowing the job to continue. Sentences totalling thirty months were substituted.[5]

TAX FRAUD

With rare exceptions[6] the Court upholds sentences of imprisonment imposed for fraudulent evasion of tax and analogous offences. In *Kennedy*[7] the appellant admitted falsely claiming allowances for dependent relatives over a period of three years, causing a loss to the Revenue of £176. The Court upheld the sentence of six months' imprisonment with the comment that 'these offences were . . . deliberate and calculated'. In *Brice*[8] the proprietor of a family

---

[1] *Herron* 26.11.75, 3322/R/75.

[2] *Littler* 1.9.75, 2822/C/75.

[3] *Ambler* 24.11.75, 3625/C/74, [1976] Crim. L. R. 266.

[4] *Bowdler and Sutton* 24.4.75, 1135/A/75, [1975] Crim. L. R. 590.

[5] *Walsh* 17.6.71, 3429/A/70.

[6] See, for example, *Curtis* 23.2.73, 410/B/73, [1973] Crim. L. R. 379 (insurance agent claiming excessive expenses, £113 lost to Revenue; nine months' imprisonment varied to £225 fine, in view of 'exemplary existence' of appellant); *Taylor* 30.3.73, 6495/C/72 (understatement of company profits, £29,000 lost to Revenue, instigator evaded jurisdiction, full repayment likely; twelve months varied to fine of £5,000 as an 'unusual course').

[7] 2.9.75, 3354/B/75; see also *Aslam* 21.6.71, 1498/C/71, [1971] Crim. L. R. 659 (falsely claiming allowances for non-existent wife and children over three years, £350 lost to Revenue; nine months 'a minimum sentence . . . for offences of this nature'); *Bishop* 11.7.74, 1631/A/74 (failure to declare part of income over period of six years, £3,400 lost to Revenue; fifteen months not 'wrong in principle', but reduced to six as 'an act of mercy', in view of age and other mitigation); *Parkash* 13.4.72, 351/A/72, [1972] Crim. L. R. 648 (false claims in respect of non-existent dependents over five years; twelve months upheld, imprisonment generally appropriate sentence).

[8] 12.3.73, 5700/A/72; see also *Deffley* 8.11.71, 2603/C/71, [1972] Crim. L. R. 123 (failure to declare profits of company, 'very large' loss to Revenue; three years'

business understated the profits of the business over a period of fifteen years, causing a Revenue loss of £11,000. The Court stated that the sentence of two years' imprisonment was 'fully and completely justified', but in view of the appellant's age and deteriorating medical condition the sentence was reduced to twelve months.

The upper limit of the relevant sentencing bracket is not clearly identified in the Court's decisions. In *King*[1] the appellant was sentenced to three years' imprisonment for his part in a scheme to defraud the Revenue by using false documents to obtain exemption from P.A.Y.E. deductions; the Court stated that although there were 'no mitigating circumstances at all', the sentence was 'not in line with the normal kind of sentence . . . for deliberate frauds on the Inland Revenue'. The sentence was reduced to eighteen months. Sentences totalling five years were upheld in *Hayes*[2] where the appellant admitted evading value added tax and defrauding the Inland Revenue (the total sentence consisted of consecutive terms of three and two years' imprisonment). The total tax losses amounted to over £70,000 and the offence was considered to have been aggravated by the purchase of companies for the purpose of carrying out the fraud. These cases may indicate that a sentence in excess of three years for a single offence (or series of related offences) will rarely be upheld.[3]

FORGERY OF TREASURY NOTES AND COINAGE OFFENCES

A small number of cases indicate the main distinctions to be drawn in cases of forgery of banknotes and related offences. Sentences of ten years' imprisonment (extended) and seven years' were upheld on two men convicted of conspiracy to forge banknotes, with the comment that 'anyone who commits this kind of offence can expect this kind of sentence'.[4] A man of good character convicted of uttering four forged banknotes and processing over one hundred others received a

---

imprisonment 'entirely appropriate', but reduced to nine months in view of deteriorating eyesight and other mitigation); *Brice* 3.11.77, 4450/B/76 (bookmaker making false returns over six years, £12,000 loss repaid; two years reduced to twelve months).

[1] 27.6.75, 1350/C/75, [1975] Crim. L. R. 596; see also *Hoyland and others* 17.10.75, 3718/C/75 ('lump' frauds; sentences up to eighteen months upheld); *Robinson* 24.3.77, 4643/A/76 ('lump' fraud over about two years, £2,800 lost to Revenue; three years reduced to two).

[2] (1976) 63 Cr. App. R. 292; see also *Flood and Lampert* 5.11.76, 1840/C/76 (evasion of purchase tax, £51,000 lost; five years reduced to three).

[3] In *Kane* 4.7.77, 1869/B/76 a sentence of seven years imposed for a variety of offences, including fraudulently obtaining a refund of £19,000 V.A.T., was reduced to five years.

[4] *Jackson and Phelan* 6.7.73, 2142/C/73.

sentence of four years' imprisonment, which was upheld.[1] In a third case the Court reduced to eighteen months' imprisonment a sentence of three years imposed for possession of five banknotes, where it was accepted that there had been no attempt to utter them.[2]

EVADING IMMIGRATION CONTROL

While the individual alien who enters the country unlawfully, or remains after the expiration of his permitted period of residence, will not normally attract a custodial sentence in the absence of aggravating features (such as possession of forged documents[3] or defiance of an earlier deportation order[4]), the Court will normally uphold substantial sentences on persons convicted of facilitating the illegal entry of immigrants on a large scale. Sentences of between five and seven years have been upheld in cases of 'immigrant smuggling' involving careful preparation and exploitation of the immigrants concerned. In *Badwal*[5] the appellant was convicted of conspiring to enable forty immigrants to enter the country illegally, using a fishing boat and a cattle-truck to transport them; 'a good deal of money was . . . being extracted from those who were illegally seeking their entry'. The Court upheld a sentence of seven years on the basis that the appellant was 'high up in the hierarchy of those responsible'. Sentences of four and five years have been upheld on men of good character convicted of similar offences on a smaller scale.[6] In *Nash*[7] a lorry driver accepted £6,000 to attempt to bring twenty-seven illegal

[1] *Young* 16.3.73, 2509/C/72, [1973] Crim. L. R. 585; see also *Marsh-Broughton* 23.1.73, 4627/A/72 (uttering eight banknotes; three years 'by no means excessive', but reduced and suspended in view of 'dramatic change in this man's attitude towards life').

[2] *Deathe* 27.3.73, 4181/A/72; see also *Lewington* 23.1.73, 2672/A/72 (possession and uttering of single banknote; consecutive sentences of twelve months ordered to run concurrently).

[3] See, for example, *Oddin* 27.7.71, 1666/A/71 (obtaining entry by means of forged passport; eighteen months suspended upheld).

[4] *Bissett* 9.8.72, 2515/C/72, [1973] Crim. L. R. 132.

[5] 21.3.72, 6582/C/70; see also *Dhaliwal and Sandhu* (1971) 55 Cr. App. R. 417 (five illegal immigrants concealed in caravan; seven years upheld on appellant involved in earlier offence, reduced to five where appellant not proved to be involved in earlier episode).

[6] See, for example, *Desai* 13.10.72, 105/A/71 (conspiracy to forge and utter passports and immigrant documents; five years upheld); *Ali and Johal* 23.3.72, 5956/B/70 (conspiracy to secure entry of two men, no inhumane treatment; six years reduced to four); *Tarsem Singh* 7.12.76, 530/B/76 (five years for organiser of attempt to smuggle immigrants by fishing boat within the right range).

[7] 10.10.74, 1546/C/74; see also *Tuart* 9.10.73, 2833/B/73 (assisting in importing immigrants in container lorry, over £2,000 received; four years reduced to three, appellant apparently not prime mover); *Marwaha* 8.5.72, 5471/C/71 (minor part in smuggling immigrants by sea; three years reduced to eighteen months, partly in view of sentences of four years imposed on prime mover); *Harding* 26.2.74, 5468/A/73, p. 324 below.

immigrants into the country in a compartment (not specially prepared for the purpose) in his lorry. The Court stated that his sentence of four years was 'the length of sentence that one must expect for this type of offence', but that as it was an isolated act so far as the appellant was concerned, and he had been fined a substantial sum in France as a result of the same incident, the sentence could be reduced to three years.

OBSCENE PUBLICATIONS AND EXHIBITIONS

Sentences of imprisonment have been upheld in a number of cases involving the sale or importation of obscene publications, usually where there has been a deliberate attempt to make a substantial profit from material which, to the offender's knowledge, clearly contravened the law. The manager of a bookshop with two previous convictions for exposing an indecent exhibition was sentenced to twelve months' imprisonment for possessing a number of typescript obscene books with a view to publication for gain.[1] A sentence of nine months was imposed on the proprietor of a bookshop with two previous convictions for possessing obscene material, who restocked the shop with 'very bad pornography including . . . violence and perversion' after a series of seizures of material.[2] Both sentences were upheld. An appellant operating 'on a very large scale', who smuggled seventy thousand indecent magazines into the country on a lorry carrying bacon, was sentenced to a total of three years' imprisonment; although 'this was a most flagrant breach of the law' the fact that the material was described in the indictment as indecent rather than obscene meant that sentences were reduced to a total of eighteen months' imprisonment.[3]

Sentences of imprisonment in cases of exhibitions have been upheld where, in addition to a high degree of intrinsic obscenity in the performance, there has been an element of corruption of young people, either as performers or as members of the audience. Sentences of fifteen months' imprisonment were upheld on the producers of a play considered 'grossly obscene by any standard', in which a number of young girls were persuaded to take part. The Court observed that the appellants 'deliberately set out to make money out of as filthy a

---

[1] *Sanghui* 7.8.73, 3068/A/73, [1974] Crim. L. R. 133; see also *Whelan* 23.9.74, 1603/A/74 (selling books after police raid, appellant knew material was obscene; twelve months upheld); *Wrate* 2.3.73, 5022/C/72 (sending various publications by post, advertised as 'high quality pornography'; nine months upheld); *Emmerson* (1977) 65 Cr. App. R. 154 (conspiracy to print and distribute pornography 'on a very large scale'; twelve months upheld).
[2] *Pitblado* 10.2.75, 3921/C/74, [1975] Crim. L. R. 471.
[3] *Waterfield* 17.2.75, 2787/C/74.

performance as they dared put on'.[1] In another case where the appellants organized striptease performances involving a measure of audience participation but there was no suggestion that either the performers or the audience were being corrupted and the show 'was not so crude and distasteful . . . that there was an outrage to public decency', sentences of imprisonment were varied to fines.[2]

OFFENCES CONNECTED WITH DRUGS

Most of the statutory law relating to drug abuse was re-enacted in the Misuse of Drugs Act 1971, which took effect in 1973. This statute introduced new distinctions between offences and created a new structure of maximum penalties. While the new scheme did not lead directly to major changes in judicial sentencing policy, cases decided under the new legislation provide a better indication of current sentencing practice than those decided earlier.

The drug addict

Sentencing offenders addicted to heroin or similar drugs can present particular difficulty. Neither drug addiction nor habitual use of drugs is a condition within the definition of 'mental disorder' for the purposes of the Mental Health Act 1959,[3] and a hospital order may not be made on that ground alone. A probation order requiring submission to psychiatric treatment may be made, if the circumstances are otherwise favourable.[4] Where the sentencer has no practicable alternative to a sentence of imprisonment, he may not impose a disproportionate sentence to ensure that the offender will remain in custody for a period long enough for treatment to take place,[5] although he may ignore mitigating factors. In *Grimes*[6] the appellant was sentenced to three years' imprisonment with the comment that 'it is necessary to detain you in custody for a sufficient period for the authorities to take some action in relation to your drug

---

[1] *Brownson and others* 29.6.71, 2649/A/71, [1971] Crim. L. R. 551; see also *Goldstein* 21.1.71, 4153/B/70, [1971] Crim. L. R. 300 (obscene stage performances, including 'recondite variations on most sexual themes', no evidence of corruption of audience or performers; nine months upheld for 'outrage to public decency').

[2] *Griffin and Farmer* (1973) 58 Cr. App. R. 229.

[3] See *Winter* 14.3.74, 165/A/74 (cannabis use); *Molyneaux* (1968) 52 Cr. App. R. 233.

[4] See, for example, *Whelan* 26.7.74, 559/B/74 (possession of heroin, previous suspended sentences; imprisonment justified but varied to probation in view of favourable psychiatric and social inquiry reports); *O'Sullivan* 19.12.74, 3817/B/74 (possession of morphine; borstal training varied to probation as appellant had 'severed her connections . . . with drugs').

[5] See the cases discussed at p. 44 above.

[6] 14.11.74, 2420/C/74.

addiction'. The Court stated that the sentencer had not sentenced the appellant 'by reference to what the proper sentence was for the offences as such' and added that 'if his drug addiction can be treated in prison so much the better, but it is not right to pass a longer sentence . . . merely because a shorter sentence might not produce that result'. The sentence was reduced to eighteen months.

The scale of sentence

The legislative framework contained in the Misuse of Drugs Act 1971 reflects distinctions which have been recognized in sentencing practice for many years. For the purpose of assessing culpability, offenders are divided into categories according to whether they are users or suppliers, and according to the nature of the substance involved. Each category may be divided into further subcategories. In deciding into which category a particular offender falls, the sentencer is bound by the general principles governing the determination of a factual basis for sentence[1] and must not impose a sentence on the assumption that the offender is guilty of a more serious offence than has been proved or admitted. In particular, the sentencer may not sentence the offender as a pusher or supplier if he has been convicted only of possession of the substance concerned, as opposed to possession with intent to supply, or supplying the substance. In *Fleming*[2] the appellant was convicted of possession of morphine but acquitted of possession with intent to supply. Observations made by the sentencer indicated that 'he was plainly dealing with this man upon the basis that he was concerned in drug trafficking'. The Court stated that the sentencer 'was wrong to do that'; as the appellant had neither admitted nor been convicted of such an offence 'he was entitled to be dealt with upon the basis that all that had been proved against him was the unlawful possession of certain prohibited drugs'. The sentence was varied to borstal training.

The application of this principle where the offender is convicted under the Customs and Excise Act 1952 of fraudulently evading the prohibition on the importation of controlled substances was considered in *Ribas*.[3] The Court held that fraudulent importation was 'a category of offence . . . separate and distinct from the categories of possessing a drug once it has got into this country' and the sentencer was entitled to draw such inferences as the evidence justified, even

[1] See below, p. 366.
[2] 9.5.75, 4225/C/74; see also *Prince* 25.10.73, 2262/A/73 (three years for simple possession reduced to two: 'to sentence them as pushers was to sentence them for an offence with which they were not charged').
[3] (1976) 63 Cr. App. R. 147. For a discussion of the same problem where the offence charged is cultivating cannabis, see *Anderson* 2.6.77, 210/A/77, [1977] Crim. L. R. 757.

though there was no charge of possession with intent to supply. The decision suggests that it is not open to the prosecution in such a case to call evidence on its own initiative after conviction tending to establish a commercial purpose, but that the issue of the offender's intention can be examined in the light of evidence called by both sides for the purpose of 'testing the validity of the alleged mitigation' that the drug was intended for personal use only.

Cannabis The ranges of sentences imposed for offences connected with cannabis are related to the chain of distribution, from importers to ultimate consumers. Sentences upheld for importation of cannabis are usually within the bracket of three to five years. In *Khan*[1] the appellant imported about 15 kilogrammes of cannabis by air, after passing through the airport on an earlier occasion to test the system of inspection. The Court upheld a sentence of five years' imprisonment for 'a deliberate offence . . . planned and carried out with a great deal of care'. In *Lynch*[2] the appellant arranged to receive cannabis sent by post from abroad, and eventually received two parcels containing a total of 1.3 kilogrammes of cannabis. His sentence of four years was 'within the bracket for offences of this kind'. In *Griffin*[3] a man of good character was sentenced to four years' imprisonment for importing a substantial quantity of cannabis resin, estimated to be worth £15,000 at retail. The Court upheld this sentence with the observation that 'sentences for evading the prohibition on the importation of controlled drugs on a large scale . . . range between . . . three to five years' imprisonment unless there are wholly exceptional features', which could not include good character.

Within the range of three to five years' imprisonment, sentences vary in relation to the quantity of cannabis imported, the extent to which the offence reflects careful planning and organization and the role of the offender in relation to others concerned in the transaction. In *Ward*[4] a man of good character attempted to smuggle 25 kilogrammes of cannabis through London Airport. The Court considered his sentence of five years' imprisonment 'too much' for a

[1] 23.10.73, 2784/A/74; see also *Cummings* 30.7.74, 3530/C/73 (importation of 17.4 kilogrammes by air; five years upheld).
[2] 20.12.74, 3865/B/74; see also *Ridgway* 3.2.75, 4923/A/74 (importing cannabis by post; three and a half years upheld).
[3] 1.7.75, 1140/A/75.
[4] 15.10.73, 3832/C/73; see also *Winter* 18.7.72, 5616/B/71, [1973] Crim. L. R. 63; *Henry* 4.6.74, 1114/B/74 (importation of 200 kilogrammes; five years, 'the top end of the scale for this type of offence', reduced to three years, in view of good character and minor role in operation); *Shadmi* 24.7.75, 1006/C/75 (youth, 21, importing 13 kilogrammes of cannabis; 'calculated and deliberate offence', but five years reduced to four); *Noor* 7.2.77, 4850/76 (importing 7 kilogrammes of cannabis concealed in hollowed pumpkin, 'unsophisticated' offence; five years reduced to three).

man who was 'not shown to have been the ringleader of an organized conspiracy', and reduced it to three. The fact that the offender acted under some degree of coercion may justify a sentence at or below the lower limit of the range. In *Taonis*[1] the appellant agreed to act as a carrier of cannabis after being beaten in a 'truly terrifying' manner; although the circumstances did not amount to a strict defence of duress, the sentence for importing 47 kilogrammes of cannabis resin was reduced from four years' imprisonment to two. Even where there is substantial mitigation, the Court is reluctant to reduce a sentence below the level of three years. In *Begum*[2] a mother of six children admitted smuggling 6 kilogrammes of cannabis and was sentenced to three years' imprisonment. The Court declined to reduce the sentence, observing that such persons as the appellant were deliberately selected by international traffickers to act as couriers and there was no other means of stopping the practice.

Sentences above the level of five years have been upheld in a few cases involving extremely large amounts of cannabis and careful planning,[3] or a series of offences,[4] but are rarely considered appropriate in unexceptional cases. In *Ainjad*[5] the appellant admitted importing about 30 kilogrammes of cannabis by post in a sophisticated manner, and living on the proceeds. The Court considered that although 'a substantial sentence was necessarily imposed', seven years was 'outside that bracket and excessive'. A sentence of five years was substituted.

The fact that the cannabis was intended for re-export to another country rather than for distribution in the United Kingdom is not a significant factor in sentencing. In *Dhingra*[6] a man of 24 admitted attempting to smuggle 7 kilogrammes of cannabis through London Airport in his coat pockets; the Court refused to reduce the sentence of thirty months, saying that 'it is not an answer . . . that the drug was not going to be sold here but . . . in the United States', and that the sentence already reflected mitigating factors. Where the offence is charged as fraudulently exporting, or conspiring to avoid the prohibition on the export of cannabis, the sentencer is limited by the

[1] (1974) 59 Cr. App. R. 160.
[2] 8.11.73, 3816/C/73; see also *Fetters* 18.12.75, 4818/R/75, p. 14 above; *Palmer* 25.3.74, 5400/A/73, [1974] Crim. L. R. 375.
[3] See, for example, *South and others* 2.4.73, 303/C/72 (importing 200 kilogrammes in specially constructed boxes concealed in lorry; six years upheld); *Borro* 22.5.73, 5856/C/71 (importing 160 kilogrammes of cannabis; seven years, 'at the top of the range', upheld).
[4] *Amankwah* 17.10.75, 5221/A/74 (two separate importations of a total of 70 kilogrammes sentences totalling ten years reduced to seven).
[5] 6.12.73, 3926/A/73; see also *Shuck* 23.4.74, 2689/C/73 (conspiracy to obtain cannabis, participation in scheme but not principal organizer; seven years reduced to five).
[6] 12.2.73, 3184/B/72.

maximum sentence of two years' imprisonment (as opposed to fourteen years for importation) and must adjust the sentence accordingly.[1]

Below the importer in the scale of sentences comes the offender who may be considered a wholesale distributor, dealing in substantial quantities of cannabis. Sentences in this kind of case, in the absence of exceptional circumstances[2] are likely to fall within the bracket of three to four years' imprisonment. In *Walsh*[3] the appellant admitted possession with intent to supply of 5 kilogrammes of cannabis which he had just bought for £1,600. Apparently rejecting the appellant's claim to have acted merely as a carrier for someone else, the Court upheld his sentence of three years' imprisonment, with the observation that 'there was . . . trafficking on a large scale'. In *Donovan*[4] a man of 27 admitted participating in transactions involving 20 kilogrammes of cannabis, and was sentenced to five years' imprisonment. The Court reduced this sentence to three and a half years, partly to avoid a disparity between the appellant and his accomplice.

A lower bracket of sentences, between one and three years, is usually considered appropriate for the retail distributor dealing in smaller quantities of cannabis and selling the substance in relatively small packages to individual consumers. The level of sentence within the bracket will depend on the amount of cannabis involved and on whether the offender's dealings in cannabis can be considered regular or isolated occurrences. In *Moylan*[5] the appellant was convicted of supplying cannabis following the discovery of 91 grammes of cannabis in small packets in his car; he admitted buying quantities of the cannabis and packaging them for resale on three previous occasions. Although the appellant was 'supplying cannabis on a fairly extensive scale' he was not dealing in 'a major or highly organized manner'. His sentence of five years' imprisonment was therefore 'plainly too much' and a sentence of three years was substituted. In *Mulqueen*[6] the appellant pleaded guilty to possessing 650 grammes of cannabis with intent to supply. He admitted buying the drug for £185 and hoped to sell it in small packets at £9 each. The Court observed that the appellant was a distributor and 'hoped to have a profit even though the profit may have been small'; his sentence of three years was upheld.

[1] See *Devaney and others* 25.9.73, 2431/A/73; *Hayward* 7.10.75, 2819/C/75.
[2] See *Taylor* 5.7.77, 5298/A/77 (conspiracy to supply cannabis over period of five years, 'operations . . . on a very large scale,' seven years upheld).
[3] 24.10.74, 2678/B/74; see also *Wool-Lewis* 19.2.74, 3590/C/73 (dealing in cannabis worth £3,000; three and a half years upheld).
[4] 28.4.75, 3626/C/74.
[5] 1.3.73, 277/A/73.
[6] 15.3.74, 5494/A/73.

A shorter sentence will be appropriate where smaller quantities are involved. In *Sallah*[1] the appellant was arrested in possession of 15.3 grammes of cannabis and pleaded guilty to counts charging supply and possession with intent to supply. The Court accepted that 'his dealing was at a minor level' and considered that 'having regard to the size of the dealing and the nature of what he was doing, the sentence was excessive'. A sentence of eighteen months was substituted. In *Fursey*[2] the appellant admitted possessing cannabis with intent to sell it in small quantities, but claimed that some of the 2 kilogrammes of cannabis found in her flat did not belong to her. The Court stated that while 'all supplying cases can be treated more seriously than simple possession cases' the present case was 'not by any means one of the worst which the Court has to deal with' and two years' imprisonment was more appropriate than the original sentence of four years. The sentence was accordingly reduced and (in view of unusual mitigating circumstances) suspended. Sentences in cases where an intent to supply is established will rarely fall below twelve months. In *Francis*[3] the appellant was found in possession of 100 grammes of cannabis, divided into small packets marked with various prices. Observing that the appellant was 'plainly trafficking—buying from a wholesaler in London and selling' in the town where he was arrested—the Court upheld the sentence of twelve months' imprisonment. At this level the absence of a commercial motive is of limited importance.[4]

The distinction between the distributor and the consumer is well established in sentencing practice and reflected in the substantive law. While a person convicted of simple possession only may not be sentenced as a distributor, however much cannabis he has in his possession,[5] the Court has upheld sentences of imprisonment on consumers in possession of substantial quantities of cannabis (by comparison with the more common user). In *Andrews*[6] the appellant was sentenced to twelve months' imprisonment for simple possession of over 200 grammes of cannabis; upholding the sentence the Court stated that 'treating this man as not being a supplier, which in loyalty to his plea we must do, the quantity of cannabis found in his house

[1] 20.10.77, 2534/C/77.

[2] 25.3.74, 295/B/74; see also *Singer* 20.12.73, 1905/B/73 (supplier 'on a very small scale'; three years reduced to twenty-one months).

[3] 21.1.73, 5691/A/72, [1973] Crim. L. R. 319; see also *Duce* 2.12.74, 2487/C/74 (possession of 800 grammes, 'the appellant . . . was a pusher, although not in respect of a large quantity . . .'; twelve months upheld); *Bowers* 13.5.76, 893/B/76 (supplying 'comparatively small quantity', no profit; twelve months upheld).

[4] See *Powrie* 14.6.73, 875/C/73, [1973] Crim. L. R. 708 (student growing cannabis to share with friends; imprisonment appropriate, fifteen months reduced to allow immediate release in view of mitigation.)

[5] See *Murray* 19.6.75, 1139/A/75 (simple possession of 3 kilogrammes of cannabis; thirty months reduced to nine, appellant not to be sentenced as supplier).

[6] 16.5.74, 774/A/74.

entirely justified the sentence'. A similar sentence was upheld in *Cox*[1] on 'a user on a substantial personal scale' for possession of about 80 grammes of cannabis resin. In *Greaves*[2] the appellant admitted possession of 500 grammes of cannabis resin, which he had bought as a supply to last for four months. The Court stated that while 'we cannot regard this as a trivial offence', the sentence could be reduced from eighteen months' imprisonment to nine.

In the more usual case of possession, where the quantities involved are measured in milligrammes, a custodial sentence will rarely be upheld; while in some cases the Court has suspended a sentence of imprisonment,[3] the more usual sentence is a fine. In *Marsh*[4] the appellant was convicted of possessing a small quantity of cannabis— one cigarette and some traces in the bowl of a pipe. The Court stated that 'having regard to the minimal nature of the offences within the spectrum of offences of this character, a fine of £25 would have been appropriate'; the sentence was varied accordingly.

Heroin The distinctions made in cases involving cannabis are also seen in cases concerning heroin and other Class A controlled substances, although the corresponding brackets are considerably higher. Importers of heroin or cocaine in any quantity are likely to attract sentences in excess of seven years, despite the presence of mitigating factors. In *Wingfield*[5] a young man of good character imported 3.2 kilogrammes of cocaine from South America; the Court upheld a sentence of seven years' imprisonment, with the comment that 'deterrent sentences are . . . essential'. In *Po*[6] a man of 46 with no previous convictions attempted to import 167 grammes of heroin; the Court upheld a sentence of six years' imprisonment with the observation that 'seven years was the proper sentence for this serious offence'.[7] A sentence of nine years was upheld on a man of 54 of previous good character who attempted to carry about seven kilogrammes of heroin through London Airport.[8]

The bracket of sentences for the supplier of heroin appears to extend from five to seven years. The Court has stated that 'we are

[1] 23.8.74, 2012/B/74.
[2] 23.7.74, 1510/B/74.
[3] See, for example, *Roberts* 17.6.74, 1985/A/74 (possession of 48 milligrammes, previous conviction; nine months' imprisonment varied to nine months suspended.)
[4] 29.7.75, 2051/A/75.
[5] 11.10.74, 1715/B/74.
[6] 11.6.74, 1076/A/74, [1974] Crim. L. R. 557. In *Blamey* 22.2.77, 4561/C/77, the Court reduced a sentence for importing 133 grammes from seven years to four, on the basis that the importation was 'for personal use' and 'not a commercial importation'.
[7] A fine of £5,000, with twelve months' imprisonment in default, was quashed.
[8] *Li* (1973) 57 Cr. App. R. 704; see also *Coray* 9.10.75, 647/B/75 (importation of 1.11 kilogrammes of cocaine; seven years, 'an appropriate sentence for such an offence', reduced to four, in view of unusual mitigating circumstances).

not . . . persuaded . . . that . . . the . . . sentence of five years even upon a social pusher as distinct from a commercial pusher is wrong in principle or excessive'[1] and sentences at this level have been upheld in cases involving supplying on a relatively small scale. In *Owen*[2] a young woman, herself a registered addict, was convicted of possession of 8.5 grammes of heroin which was found packaged for sale in small quantities,[3] and of supplying heroin. Her sentence of five years' imprisonment was 'not so severe as to warrant any interference'. In *Langham*[4] the appellant sold a single 'shot' of heroin to a plain-clothes police officer in a public house in a provincial city, together with other substances. The Court reduced the sentence on the count charging supply of heroin from six years' imprisonment to four, leaving the appellant subject to a total of five years in respect of the whole transaction.

Distributors higher in the chain of supply between the importer and the retailer will receive a longer sentence. In one such case the Court reduced a sentence from ten years' imprisonment to eight, partly because ten years was at that time the maximum sentence,[5] and a similar sentence was upheld in a more recent decision[6].

Few cases of simple possession of heroin leading to a sentence of imprisonment have been found, but the Court considered a sentence of two years' imprisonment appropriate for an appellant convicted of attempting to possess a small quantity of heroin found under a carpet outside his door, specifically disregarding any suggestion of an intent to supply.[7]

Amphetamine Decisions in relation to suppliers of amphetamine suggest that the bracket of sentences is comparable to the equivalent bracket in cannabis cases. The Court considered six years' imprisonment for attempting to supply 144 grammes of amphetamine sulphate, estimated to be worth over £13,000 at retail, to leave insufficient room for worse examples, and substituted four years' imprisonment;[8] sentences at this level have been upheld in several

---

1 *Baird* 12.6.75, 4028/A/74.

2 3.4.73, 5657/C/72, [1973] Crim. L. R. 455; see also *Blampied* 18.3.75, 915/C/74 (girl, 22, registered addict, supplying heroin to other addicts; five years upheld); *Ogunmokum* 16.1.75, 976/C/74 (supplying in small quantities; five years upheld).

3 The case was decided before the Misuse of Drugs Act 1971 came into force.

4 13.3.73, 4675/A/72; see also *Stancer* 27.1.76, 4341/C/75 (supplying small quantities by post; five years upheld).

5 *Fu* 1.4.74, 2518/B/73.

6 *Dhalai* 14.10.77, 330/B/77, [1978] Crim. L. R. 176.

7 *Foo* 15.1.76, 3400/C1/75, [1976] Crim. L. R. 456; see also *Shearer* 7.7.77, 1324/C/77 (eighteen months for simple possession of heroin 'appropriate', upheld concurrently with similar sentences for other offences).

8 *Tucker* 31.7.75, 43/B/75.

comparable cases.[1] Shorter sentences will be approved for suppliers on a smaller scale.[2]

LSD The small number of cases suggest that the ranges of sentences applicable in cases involving LSD are comparable to those seen in relation to cannabis. Sentences of three years' imprisonment have been upheld for retail dealing in moderate quantities.[3]

DRIVING OFFENCES

The majority of motoring offences result in a fine, often accompanied by a period of disqualification from driving. The principles governing these sentences are discussed in chapters 9 and 10 respectively. Imprisonment is usually reserved for particularly serious examples of certain offences—causing death by reckless driving (above 87), dangerous driving, driving with an excess blood alcohol level, driving while disqualified and taking a conveyance.

Reckless driving

The use of imprisonment in cases of reckless driving reflects its use in cases of causing death by reckless driving—the sentence may be appropriate where the offender has endangered other road users by taking a deliberate risk. In *Swain*[4] the appellant drove a heavy lorry down a steep hill. The lorry's brakes were inefficient as a result of poor maintenance and the load of eight tons of sheet steel was inadequately secured; another car was struck by flying sheets of metal when the lorry went out of control. The Court observed that 'this was dangerous driving which resulted from deliberately taking a risk' and upheld the sentence of twelve months' imprisonment. In *Lewis*[5] the appellant was alleged to have driven at his estranged wife as she walked along a road, although it was accepted that he stopped before getting close. The Court held that a sentence of twelve months' imprisonment was 'appropriate' but had properly been suspended in view of other circumstances. By contrast in *Ryder*[6] a man of 30 rode a

[1] See, for example, *Davies* 14.11.74, 1270/C/74 (man, 23, one previous drug conviction, selling amphetamine tablets in clubs, significant quantities; four years not 'too much', but reduced to thirty months because of mitigation); *Withers* 11.6.74, 668/C/74 (woman, 28, possession of 4,400 tablets; four years upheld).

[2] See, for example, *Emson* 16.12.74, 4220/C/74 (supplying small quantities in individual portions; four years reduced to two).

[3] See, for example, *Blum and Vickery* 25.9.75, 1060/C/75 (youth, 19, 200 tablets; three years upheld); *Wilkinson and Walton* 29.3.76, 4886/B/75 (300 tablets; four years upheld).

[4] 16.7.73, 2783/A/73.
[5] 4.6.74, 975/C/74.
[6] 16.1.76, 5405/B/75.

motor cycle through a built-up area at a high speed, carrying a young pillion passenger, and passed a traffic signal at red. The Court stated that 'although it was a disgraceful piece of driving' the appropriate sentence was 'a substantial financial penalty and a substantial period of disqualification'. The sentence of three months' imprisonment was varied to a fine of £50.

Blood alcohol offences

Although this offence is no longer triable on indictment, the decisions of the Court may be helpful to magistrates dealing with cases of driving with a blood alcohol level above the permitted limit. A considerable number of cases support the proposition that a sentence of imprisonment is appropriate if the offender has previous convictions for similar offences and the blood alcohol level on the present occasion exceeded the permitted level by a substantial amount. In *Peverill*[1] the appellant was found driving with a blood alcohol level of 230 milligrammes per 100 millilitres only a few weeks after being arrested for driving with a similar blood alcohol level; he had been convicted of a similar offence two years previously. The Court upheld the sentence of twelve months' imprisonment, with the comment that 'those . . . convicted for the third time for a breathalyser offence cannot complain if they find themselves given a custodial sentence'. Many similar cases can be found.[2] In *Baptista*[3] the appellant had three previous convictions for driving while unfit through drink, although the last had taken place nine years before his present offence of attempting to drive with a blood alchool level of 372 milligrammes per 100 millilitres of blood. His sentence of eight months' imprisonment was upheld.

A second category of case in which a sentence of imprisonment is likely to be upheld is that where a high blood alcohol level is combined with dangerous driving. In *Pashley*[4] the appellant was convicted of driving with a blood alcohol level of 154 milligrammes per 100 millilitres of blood and dangerous driving. He had driven dangerously in an apparent attempt to evade a following police car, and was arrested only after two collisions. The Court upheld the

[1] 4.12.75, 4023/C/75.
[2] For example, *Gardiner* 11.1.73, 2309/A/72 (many previous convictions, 205mg per 100ml; nine months upheld); *McCarthy* 8.11.74, 3964/C/74 (237mg per 100ml, two similar convictions in distant past; nine months upheld); *Davitt* 7.10.74, 2375/B/74, [1974] Crim. L. R. 719 (204mg per 100ml, two recent similar convictions, other motoring offences in past; nine months aggregate upheld; *Calhoun* 11.2.74, 4888/A/73, [1974] Crim. L. R. 436 (272mg per 100ml, 'dismal record' including two similar offences; two years upheld).
[3] 2.5.75, 944/B/75.
[4] 12.11.73, 3741/B/73, (1973) 5 R.T.R. 149; see also *Nokes* (1977) 66 Cr. App. R. 3.

sentence of twelve months' imprisonment, 'looking at the offence alone and without regard to the record of the offender'. In *Jenkins*[1] the appellant caused an accident by overtaking on a dangerous bend; his blood alcohol level, as measured five hours later, was 91 milligrammes per 100 millilitres of blood, indicating that at the time of the accident the level must have been substantially higher. The sentence of six months' imprisonment was upheld.

A third group of cases suggests that where the offender has no record of similar offences and his driving on the occasion in question is not unusually dangerous, a sentence of imprisonment is not likely to be upheld, despite a high blood alcohol level. In *Thomas*[2] the appellant had no previous conviction of a similar nature and his driving at the time of the offence was erratic but did not apparently endanger anyone. Despite an alcohol level of 272 milligrammes per 100 millilitres of urine, the Court considered a sentence of imprisonment unjustified and substituted a fine of £100. In *Newman*[3] the appellant drove his car into the rear of a parked car, and was subsequently found to have a blood alcohol level of 270 milligrammes per 100 millilitres. He had no previous convictions for offences involving alcohol, although he had never possessed a driving licence. The Court stated that 'this is not a case in which it was necessary to impose a sentence of imprisonment' and varied the sentence of three months to a fine of £50. These two decisions appear to conflict with statements made in *Tupa*[4] that a custodial sentence would be 'entirely proper . . . in many cases of this kind' where the blood alcohol level is approximately three times the permitted limit of 80 milligrammes per 100 millilitres, but it appears that a sentence of imprisonment is unlikely to be upheld unless a high blood alcohol level is combined with either a record of similar offences in the past, or especially dangerous driving, or both.

Driving while disqualified

Sentences of imprisonment are commonly upheld for driving while disqualified. In *Cowley*[5] the appellant was convicted of driving after two years of a three-year disqualification for driving with an excess blood alcohol level. The Court rejected his claim that he believed that his licence had been restored and upheld the sentence of six months' imprisonment for 'a deliberate flouting of the law'. In *Gambell*[6] the

1 1.9.75, 2921/A/75, [1976] Crim. L. R. 264.
2 (1973) 57 Cr. App. R. 496.
3 14.11.75, 4996/B/75, [1976] Crim. L. R. 265.
4 (1973) 58 Cr. App. R. 234.
5 25.2.75, 577/A2/75.
6 7.11.74, 2505/A2/75.

appellant admitted obtaining a driving licence while disqualified and two offences of driving while disqualified. Observing that he had 'consistently flouted the motoring laws' over a period of years the Court upheld sentences totalling eighteen months' imprisonment.

The imposition of a sentence of imprisonment is not automatic and the sentence may in appropriate circumstances be suspended. In *Smithers*[1] a man in his twenties, who had earlier shown 'a complete lack of responsibility' in relation to motoring, was convicted of driving a tractor while disqualified. The appellant was employed as a tractor driver and could lawfully drive on farm lands, but had to drive about one hundred and eighty yards on a public road to get from one part of the farm to another. Despite the appellant's 'record of irresponsible law-breaking' the Court considered that the circumstances of the offence justified the 'merciful course' of suspending the sentence.

Taking vehicles without authority Most of the cases in which sentences of imprisonment are upheld for offences of taking a vehicle without the consent of the owner involve relatively young men with substantial records of similar behaviour. In *Barker*[2] a youth of 20, whose record extended over almost eleven years, was sentenced to eighteen months' imprisonment for taking a car and incidental offences. Observing that he had previously 'been dealt with in almost every manner . . . known to the law' the Court upheld the sentence. In *Dawtrey*[3] a sentence of eighteen months imposed on a youth of 20 for taking a car from one city to another was upheld, the Court referring to his 'long and depressing record of convictions', and observing that he had been 'given a chance' in the form of a probation order on his last appearance a few months before the present offence. Probation orders will often be made in such cases when there is any reason to hope they may be effective.[4]

[1] 11.10.74, 3554/B/74.
[2] 4.11.74, 2709/C/74.
[3] 16.12.75, 3655/B/75.
[4] See, for example, *Halcro* 9.12.74, 3714/A/74 (several offences related to alcoholism, appellant undergoing treatment, prognosis hopeful; twelve months' imprisonment varied to probation).

4

Mitigation

It has been argued that the process of calculating the length of a tariff sentence involves three stages—defining a scale of sentences in relation to the most typical instances within the general category of the offence concerned, fixing by reference to that scale the level of sentence which would be appropriate to the facts of the particular offence committed by the offender and, finally, making such allowance for mitigating factors as may be just by reducing the sentence below that level. The third stage of the process is the subject of this chapter. The term 'mitigating factors' is used to refer to such matters as the character and history of the offender, the pressures which led to the commission of the offence and the consequences of the conviction and sentence for him, rather than variations in the immediate circumstances of the offence, such as the value of the property stolen or the relationship between the offender and the victim.

As has been shown, allowance for mitigation is not considered to be an entitlement of the offender. The sentencer may withhold a reduction which might normally be expected if some recognized penal objective, such as general deterrence or the preventive confinement of a dangerous offender, requires the imposition of the whole of the permissible sentence. Apart from this, the value of a particular factor varies considerably from one category of offence to another; a factor which has a critical impact on the sentence in one kind of case will often have no more than a marginal effect in another. Additionally, mitigating factors seldom occur singly, and the weight of a combination of mitigating factors will usually be greater than the sum of their individual values considered separately, as the presence of one factor will enhance the significance of another. For these reasons it is not possible to construct a 'negative tariff' of mitigating factors showing that a particular factor will normally justify a reduction of a specified proportion of the notional level of sentence fixed by reference to the facts of the offence. It is possible, however, to examine the more common mitigating factors and to identify the circumstances under which they are most likely to be effective.

The Age and History of the Offender

AGE

Youth is one of the most effective mitigating factors. As has been shown, the Court strongly favours the use of individualized measures for offenders under 21, a policy which has long been endorsed by statute.[1] Where an offender in this age group is sentenced to imprisonment, the sentence will normally be considerably shorter than would be awarded to a man of mature years for the same offence. In *Ireland*[2] a youth of 19, previously convicted for unlawful wounding, was sentenced to five years' imprisonment for maliciously inflicting grievous bodily harm on a man whom he had kicked in the face in the course of a fight, causing him to lose the sight of one eye. Reducing the sentence to three years, the Court stated that the appellant's behaviour was 'inexcusable' and 'the sentence should be a heavy one', but five years was 'too much . . . where the accused is only 19 . . . an older man might have merited such a sentence; a younger man does not'. In *Street and Gray*[3] two youths of 17 and 19 respectively were sentenced to four years' imprisonment for robberies involving threats with a knife. The Court stated that 'this offence is all too common and it is necessary to bring home to offenders the gravity of their conduct' but 'having regard to their youth' the sentence could be reduced to three years. Recognition of the mitigating effect of youth does not mean that long sentences are necessarily wrong when imposed on offenders below the age of 21; in a case where a youth of 19 was sentenced to six years' imprisonment for robbery, burglary and wounding with intent, having stabbed a taxi driver in the arm and neck, the Court upheld the sentence with the comment that the offences 'merited a severe penalty despite this young man's age'.[4]

Youth continues to have some value as a mitigating factor throughout the early twenties,[5] and the age of the offender may be mentioned as a matter of concern as late as 30,[6] although its effect declines progressively. In the case of a man in his middle or late twenties, age is likely to be considered only in relation to relatively long sentences, and is more likely to mitigate a cumulative sentence

[1] Powers of Criminal Courts Act 1973 s. 19(2), originally enacted as Criminal Justice Act 1948 s. 17(2).

[2] 19.10.73, 3665/C/73.

[3] 3.10.74, 2844/A/74.

[4] *Sparrow* 5.6.75, 964/B/75.

[5] See, for example, *Allen* 24.4.75, 6/B/75 (thirty months for theft too long for man of 22 going to prison for first time; reduced to two years).

[6] See, for example, *McNamara* 15.1.75, 2548/C/72 (six years and nine months 'a very long sentence for a man of this age'; reduced to five years on this and other grounds).

consisting of a series of consecutive terms, in accordance with the totality principle, than a long single term imposed for a grave crime. In *Fogarty*[1] a man of 24 with 'a perfectly shocking record' was sentenced to six and a quarter years' imprisonment for taking a bus, driving it so dangerously as to merit the maximum sentence for that offence, and robbery at a service station on a different occasion. The Court took the view that despite the gravity of the individual offences the sentence was 'too long . . . for a young man of 24' and reduced it to five years.

Age begins to be a relevant consideration again once the offender has passed 60, although at this end of the spectrum it is most effective as a mitigating factor when combined with another, such as good character. In *Wilkinson*[2] a man of 60 appealed against sentences totalling five years for offences of indecency committed over a period of several years with his young grandnieces. The Court observed that while 'a substantial custodial sentence' was inevitable, the appellant had a 'perfectly good' record and the offences began when he became a 'desperately lonely' widower. Stating that 'no court willingly sentences a man of 60 to spend a large part of the remainder of his life in prison', the Court reduced the sentence to thirty months. In *Bishop*[3] the Court reduced a sentence of fifteen months for an 'extremely serious' tax fraud on a man of 61 with 'the highest personal reputation', not because the sentence was 'in any way wrong in principle but simply as an act of mercy to this man at this stage of his life'.

Recognition of age as a mitigating factor does not mean that imprisonment should never be imposed on elderly offenders, and the Court has upheld sentences of imprisonment on men in their seventies.[4] It is however a long-established principle that a sentence should normally be shortened so as to avoid the possibility that the offender will not live to be released. In *Brice*[5] a man of 69 was sentenced to two years' imprisonment for a substantial fraud on the

[1] 5.5.75, 4953/B/74.

[2] 14.11.74, 3025/C/74; see also *Greenlees* 11.2.75, 4456/B/74 (ten years for man, 62, indecency with boys and girls, offences arising from 'emotional stress combined with a sense of loneliness'; reduced to three: custodial sentence 'absolutely necessary', but 'was it necessary that this man should be sent to prison at the age of 62 for ten years?'); *Nicholls* 27.6.75, 1233/B/75 (ten years for buggery and gross indecency by man, 62, no previous convictions, justified on facts, but sentencer 'did not pay sufficient attention to the factor of age'; reduced to seven years).

[3] 11.7.74, 1631/A/74.

[4] For example, *Waterfall* 24.11.75, 4321/C/75, [1976] Crim. L. R. 203 (two years upheld for forgery of will by man, 70, previous good character); *Bowdler* 24.4.75, 1107/A/75, [1975] Crim. L. R. 590 (six months for man, 70, good record, corruptly receiving commission, upheld; sentence made adequate allowance for mitigating factors).

[5] 12.3.73, 5700/A/72.

Inland Revenue. The Court considered that the sentence was 'fully and completely justified' for the offences and would not have been varied if it had been imposed on 'a younger man or . . . a man in a better state of health', but in the light of a medical report which indicated that the appellant was seriously ill and had a limited expectation of life, the sentence was reduced to twelve months 'as an act of mercy'.

THE OFFENDER'S RECORD

It has been argued that the maximum length of a tariff sentence is governed by the nature of the offence for which it is imposed. The fact that an offender has a substantial record of previous convictions does not justify the imposition of a sentence above the level appropriate to the kind of offence he has committed, although an offender with no previous convictions, or only a few, may expect his sentence to be reduced below that level to reflect his good, or relatively good, character. The differential which will normally be observed when offenders with different records are sentenced for similar offences is not the result of a progressive aggravation of the sentence beyond the level fixed by reference to the gravity of the offence. The imposition of longer sentences as a criminal record is extended reflects a progressive loss of credit until the offender has exhausted all the mitigating effect of good character and arrived at the point where he is exposed to the full length of the sentence appropriate to his offence.

Formulating the principle in this way has three consequences. First, it means that the process of gradually increasing the severity of the sentence imposed on an offender as his career develops is a finite one. Once the offender has reached the stage where all credit for good character has been expended, his sentences will become stable at the level which fully reflects the gravity of his offences, assuming that the nature of his offences does not significantly change. In *Craig*[1] a man in his fifties with 'an enormous list of previous convictions' was sentenced to ten years' imprisonment for a number of burglaries in schools; he had served varying terms for similar offences, the most recent being a sentence of seven years. The Court considered the sentence of ten years excessive for the offences, which involved no element of violence or causing alarm to householders, and reduced it to five years with the comment that 'the sentence . . . does not necessarily involve a steady progression up the scale . . . regard must be had to the nature of the offences'. In *Sherlock*[2] a man of 32 with a 'shocking record' received four years' imprisonment for a series of

[1] 19.11.74, 2079/B/74.
[2] 14.1.74, 2731/A/73.

thefts; his three main co-defendants each received three years. The Court stated that if the sentencer had 'increased the sentence which he passed upon this particular appellant by reason of his past record', there would have been grounds for appeal, but the sentencer had not done so. He had first decided that 'the proper sentence . . . was one of four years', but for the other three defendants 'he was able to make that basic sentence of four years one of three years because of their relatively good previous character'. As it was 'not a question of increasing from three to four years' but 'reducing a basic four years to one of three years', the appellant had no grounds for complaint.

The second effect of the principle is that while it is normally necessary to make a distinction in the sentences imposed on offenders with significantly different records, such a distinction is not necessary where both offenders have passed the point where all the mitigating effect of good character has been exhausted, even though one has been convicted in the past on more occasions, or for offences of greater gravity, than the other. In one case[1] three men were convicted of handling a substantial amount of stolen property. The first appellant, who apparently had a substantial record, was sentenced to five years imprisonment, while the second, whose record was 'longer and worse', received seven years. The Court stated that this was the wrong approach: 'Men are not sentenced on their records. They are sentenced for their offences. If they have got bad records then nothing can be taken off by way of mitigation, while if they have not got bad records a great deal can be taken off.' The sentences on the two defendants should therefore have been the same, and the seven-year sentence was reduced accordingly. (A differentiation in favour of the third defendant was justified on other grounds.)

Finally, the principle that previous convictions do not aggravate the sentence beyond the level warranted by the facts of the offence means that in those cases where an emphasis on general deterrence justifies the sentencer in ignoring mitigating factors, there will be no basis for a distinction between the experienced offender and the man of good character. In *Inwood*[2] a man with no previous convictions admitted fifty offences of fraud, involving over £15,000, committed over a period of five years. The Court stated that 'the gravity of the whole string of offences . . . is such that a custodial sentence was imperative to mark public disapproval' and that 'in the balance that the Court has to make between the mitigating factors and society's interest in marking its disapproval for this kind of conduct . . . we must not yield to the mitigating factors'. As the sentence of four years' imprisonment was 'correct in principle when measured against

[1] *Bowman, Murphy and Bromwell* 29.6.73, 1543/B/72.
[2] (1974) 60 Cr. App. R. 70.

the gravity of the offences', it was upheld.

While it is possible to illustrate the mitigating effect of some aspects of a criminal record, it is not possible to construct a detailed scale showing the weight to be attached to varying kinds of history or indicating the precise point at which the mitigating effect of good character is considered to be exhausted. It appears that in making these assessments, the Court is as much influenced by quality as by quantity, and a record which contains a relatively small number of offences in the first order of gravity will be considered at least equal to one consisting of a large number of less serious offences.[1] In evaluating the record of the offender and its relevance to sentence, it will be recalled that at different stages in his progress the offender may qualify for individualized treatment as an 'intermediate' or 'inadequate recidivist', and that where the statutory conditions of eligibility are satisfied, an extended term of imprisonment, not restricted by the inherent gravity of his offence, may be imposed.

The man of good character

Many cases illustrate the mitigating effect of good character. In *Markus*[2] the appellant was sentenced to seven years' imprisonment— the maximum under the relevant statutory provision[3]—for 'a vast fraud'. The Court did not consider the sentence excessive but was 'impressed by the fact that it is unusual to give a man of previous good character the maximum sentence' and reduced the sentence to five years. In *Sheldon*[4] the appellant was sentenced to five years for a series of 'very grave burglaries' in which 'very large amounts of property' were stolen. The Court considered that as he had no previous convictions, the sentence was excessive despite the gravity of the offences, and reduced it to three years. In *Bredbury*[5] the appellant received twelve months' imprisonment for stealing about £1,000 from his employer. The Court stated that an offence involving deliberate breach of trust over a period of months 'normally warrants an

[1] See, for example, *Lewis* 20.11.72, 2660/A/72 (appellant sentenced to three and a half years for series of burglaries, co-defendant equally involved sentenced to eighteen months; co-defendant had three convictions but all for relatively minor offences leading to fines, while appellant had seven convictions with five custodial sentences; 'very different record' justified 'a sentence substantially different and more severe than had been passed on the co-defendant'); *Smith* 3.5.76, 4430/A/75 (appellant and co-defendant had long depressing lists of previous convictions', but appellant's record 'had nothing on it which was comparably as serious' as one particular conviction on co-defendant's antecedents; this and other factors justified discrimination in favour of appellant).

[2] [1974] 3 W. L. R. 645.
[3] Prevention of Fraud (Investments) Act 1958 s. 13(1)(b).
[4] 12.3.74, 5073/C/74.
[5] 7.10.74, 2339/B/74.

immediate custodial sentence, even though the offender is a man of previous good character . . . but the length of the sentence is another matter'. Having regard to his 'hitherto blameless character' the sentence was reduced to allow his immediate release.

The concept of good character is not limited to an absence of previous convictions. An offender may show that he has behaved in a commendable way in relation to matters wholly unrelated to the offence, and receive credit for this conduct—sometimes described as 'positive good character'. In *Cook*[1] a carpark attendant admitted stealing a substantial amount from his employers over a period of years by issuing false tickets; the Court stated that eighteen months' imprisonment was not wrong in principle but, having regard to various factors including 'most distinguished, adventurous and courageous service through the war', his sentence could be reduced. In *Ducasse*[2] the appellant was sentenced to six months' imprisonment for conspiring to pervert the course of justice by falsely claiming to have been the driver of a vehicle involved in an accident. The Court considered the offence to be 'a grave one' which 'merits a custodial sentence', but the case had 'special features'—the appellant had some time previously started a youth club to provide constructive leisure occupation for young people; in view of his 'good public service', the sentence was suspended. In *Keightley*[3] (cited above, p. 68) a 'lenient' sentence for fraud was reduced to reflect the appellant's heroism in rescuing a drowning child.

Consideration of mitigating factors of this kind is not limited to offenders of previous good character. In *Playfair*[4] a man previously convicted of a similar offence received eighteen months' imprisonment for stealing from a telephone box, an offence which the Court considered to warrant a sentence of such length. The Court heard that some years before the present offence was committed the appellant had gone to the assistance of a gravely injured police officer and helped to save his life. The sentence was reduced to nine months with the comment that the only reason for the reduction was that 'he is on this occasion, entitled to credit for his earlier action'.

The effect of a gap in the offender's record

The fact that an offender who has a criminal record has made an effort to 'go straight' since his last conviction or release from prison normally carries considerable weight as a mitigating factor if he

---

[1] 16.1.76, 4316/C1/76.
[2] 5.4.74, 1045/A/74.
[3] 20.12.71, 4080/C/71, [1972] Crim. L. R. 272.
[4] 10.3.72, 4457/B/71, [1972] Crim. L. R. 387.

subsequently commits an offence. Isolated convictions in the long distant past are normally disregarded and the offender is treated as a person of good character.[1] A significant period free from conviction will normally justify substantial mitigation of the sentence, even though the offender had committed a considerable number of offences before the recent period of law-abiding behaviour began. In one case[2] the appellant had acquired a 'formidable' record, including several custodial sentences, but had no convictions during the seven years preceeding the offences of handling for which he was sentenced to eighteen months' imprisonment. In view of his 'stout efforts to rehabilitate himself' the sentence was reduced to the equivalent of six months. In *Mead*[3] a sentence of three years' imprisonment for indecently assaulting a boy was reduced to allow the immediate release of a man with five previous convictions, the Court observing that although the offences were serious the sentencer 'did not pay sufficient attention . . . to the excellent fight this man put up for twelve years to control his sexual impulses'.

Even where the gap is relatively short, some credit will be given if there is evidence of an attempt to adopt a stable pattern of life on release from the last sentence. In *Canham*[4] a man of 34 with twenty-three previous convictions was released from prison, found a job, was made redundant, found another job and did not commit the offence of burglary for which he received eighteen months' imprisonment until he lost the second job. The Court was 'impressed with the fact that during the fifteen months the appellant did try to pull himself together' and although 'it was not a very long period' his efforts 'must stand in his favour'. His sentence was reduced to nine months. Similarly in *Vinyard*[5] a man with 'a very bad criminal record' over a period of seventeen years received three years' imprisonment for handling stolen cars. Stating that 'ringing' cars was an 'extremely serious' matter and that 'a severe sentence must be imposed to deter people from indulging in this offence', the Court concluded that the

[1] See, for example, *Kingsman* 13.6.74, 905/C/74 (eighteen months for handling stolen car reduced to twelve and suspended; conviction in 1945 'rightly disregarded' and appellant 'treated as of good character'); *Eustice* 21.1.75, 4554/C/74 (six months for indecent assault on male, suspended, partly as appellant had 'kept out of trouble' since conviction for similar offence in 1950).

[2] *Stone-Barrett* 18.8.75, 1529/B/75.

[3] 15.10.74, 2507/A/74; see also *Hobbs* 17.1.75, 4715/B/74 (nine months for handling stolen painting worth £1,000, no conviction since release from borstal fourteen years previously; sentence reduced and suspended, Court 'influenced entirely by the long period of honest life which appears in this man's record', sentence would have been unchallengeable if 'committed within a year or so' after last previous conviction).

[4] 13.5.75, 4939/A/74.

[5] 1.3.74, 5499/A/73; see also *McGarrity* 22.5.75, 902/B/75 (seven years for burglary by man, 30, with 'appalling record' too high as appellant 'has made a real effort to go straight' over period of nearly two years and should have received credit; reduced to three years).

sentence 'does not give effect to the fact that he had gone straight for three years and partly lived down his record'.

As was shown in chapter 1, the existence of a gap in a substantial record may have an effect beyond mitigation. Evidence that an offender has made an attempt to change the pattern of his behaviour after a history of successive convictions may lead the Court to the conclusion that the circumstances justify an experiment with probation or such other non-custodial measures as may appear promising.

In many cases where the Court makes allowance for the fact that the appellant has not committed offences during a period of time since his last release and has tried to live a stable life, the subsequent offence is related to some extent to external pressures, such as a crisis in a recently established relationship, or the loss of newly acquired employment by redundancy or as a result of his history becoming known. In these cases the most recent offence can be seen as a lapse from a course of conduct directed towards a settled pattern of law-abiding behaviour. Where the subsequent offence has the appearance of the determined resumption of a criminal career, the period without conviction is less likely to have mitigating effect. In *Sheldon*[1] a man of 51 who had established a 'very bad record' in his early life but had committed no offences during the last ten years was convicted of aggravated burglary and wounding with intent. Together with another man he had planned a burglary at a house whose occupier was believed to keep large sums of cash at home, and when disturbed he attacked the occupier with a cosh, causing serious injuries. The Court stated that 'when men with bad records make a real attempt to put the past behind them and to lead an honest life, that is a factor which must always be looked at and weighed', but the present offence was a planned burglary in which the appellant went prepared to use violence, and 'the offences were so grave that the fact that they had avoided convictions . . . for some years was not in itself sufficient to justify any reduction' in the sentence of eight years' imprisonment.

The offence out of character with the offender's record

Where the offender has a criminal record, but his most recent offence is of a kind quite different from those he has committed in the past, his remaining credit for good character may be enhanced. He may expect a greater degree of mitigation than if he had committed a further offence similar to those for which he has previously been convicted. In *Gibbs*[2] the appellant was sentenced to four years' imprisonment

[1] 2.12.75, 1608/C/75.
[2] 2.5.75, 4208/C/74.

for living on the earnings of prostitution. He had several previous convictions for burglary and related offences, for which he had served terms of imprisonment up to four years, but the Court stated that 'these matters have no real bearing upon the appropriate sentence in relation to the present offence', and reduced the sentence to two years, in view of various circumstances. In *Rackley*[1] a man of 34 with a 'large number of previous convictions but none for offences of violence', received seven years' imprisonment for wounding with intent a man who had spent the night with the appellant's common law wife during his absence from the house. The Court considered that the sentence did not reflect 'his previous good character and the provocation' and reduced it to four years.

While it is usual to ignore certain kinds of previous convictions altogether when they are wholly unrelated to the circumstances of the present offence,[2] the fact that the most recent offence is different from earlier offences does not necessarily mean that the offender will be treated as if he had no previous convictions at all. In *Farley*[3] a man of 29 with eleven previous convictions for offences of dishonesty was sentenced to nine months' imprisonment suspended for possession of a small quantity of cannabis. Refusing to vary the sentence, the Court stated that 'it was not improper for the sentencing court to take into account as a factor the appellant's previous criminal record, though they were also right to take into account . . . that this was a first offence in connection with drugs'.

The existence of a difference between the immediate offence and those recorded against the offender in the past is most significant where the latest offence is committed as a result of pressures or provocations which might affect a man of good character, or can be seen, despite the earlier offences, as an isolated departure from normal patterns of behaviour.[4] Where the offence seems to be a deliberate excursion into a previously unexplored area of criminal behaviour, the difference between the present and previous offences

---

[1] 26.3.74, 5267/B/73.

[2] Thus previous convictions for motoring offences will usually be ignored where the offender is to be sentenced for violence or dishonesty (see, for example, *Smith* 8.5.75, 1275/B/75) and previous convictions for 'criminal' offences are often disregarded when the present offence is a motoring offence (see, for example, *Dudley* 4.2.75, 214/A/75).

[3] 9.5.74, 599/B/74.

[4] See, for example, *Miller* 28.1.75, 5105/C/74 (indecent assault by young man on eve of his wedding; previous convictions for motoring offences but 'nothing . . . in the past indicative that he was likely to behave in this way'; nine months reduced and suspended, although offence 'a very serious one . . . that did merit a custodial sentence', partly as appellant 'starting out on his married life'); see also *Smith* 8.5.75, 1275/B/75 (twelve months for maliciously inflicting grievous bodily harm following provocation; suspended on appeal, previous convictions for non-violent offences ignored, appellant treated as of 'substantial good character').

will carry less weight. In *McDonald*[1] the appellant was sentenced to four years' imprisonment for various offences concerned with controlled drugs, including two of supplying cannabis and LSD respectively. None of his sixteen previous convictions was for offences involving drugs, but the Court, upholding the sentence, commented that he 'could not rely on good character for the purpose of mitigating the offences'.

The 'jump effect'

It has been argued that progressive increases in the lengths of sentences imposed on a particular offender reflect his gradual loss of credit for good character as the number of his previous convictions expands, rather than an aggravation of the basic penalty for the offence. It follows that until all mitigation for good character is exhausted, his sentences should increase in length by gradual stages rather than by sudden large jumps. For this reason the Court will frequently reduce a sentence not considered excessive in relation to the offence for which it is imposed, if the difference between the present sentence and the longest sentence previously received by the appellant is too great to be justified by changing circumstances. In *Berridge*[2] a man of 26 received sentences totalling seven years for his part in a series of burglaries. He had fourteen previous convictions and had served several previous terms of imprisonment for burglary and similar offences, the longest being a sentence of thirty months. The Court came to the conclusion that seven years was too long a sentence, partly because it represented 'too big a leap from the longest sentence to which he had previously been subjected'. The sentence was reduced to five years. In *White*[3] the appellant was sentenced to a total of thirty months' imprisonment for offences of theft and assault; his longest previous sentence was nine months. The Court was told that the imposition of the longer sentence had had 'a shattering effect on this man', and decided to reduce the sentence to eighteen months. In *Davis*[4] a man of 24 whose longest previous sentence was twelve months received consecutive sentences of five years for robbery and two years for theft; the Court considered that seven years was 'excessive in the case of a young man who has not previously received longer sentences than twelve months and whose record does not show him . . . to be a hopeless case'. The sentences were made concurrent.

[1] 3.7.75, 1260/B/75.
[2] 28.1.75, 2402/B/74.
[3] 20.5.71, 5293/A/70; see also *Silver* 11.7.72, 4933/B/72 (five years for obtaining diamond ring by deception, long record of convictions; 'to advance from two years to five on this occasion . . . is too great an increase'—reduced to four years extended).
[4] 15.10.73, 1659/C/73.

The same considerations apply where an offender is sentenced to imprisonment for the first time, possibly after experiencing other kinds of custodial sentence. The fact that the offender has not previously undergone imprisonment may justify some reduction in the length of his sentence. In *Cresswell*[1] a youth of 18 who had previously committed over one hundred offences was sentenced to seven years' imprisonment for robbing a young woman at knife-point in her home. He had previously experienced various custodial measures, including borstal training, and the Court came to the conclusion that 'to jump . . . from a sentence of borstal training to a sentence of seven year's imprisonment, even for an offence of this gravity' was too much. The sentence was reduced to five years. Similarly in *Cavey*[2] a man of 59 appealed against a sentence of twelve months for indecently assaulting a boy of eleven. The Court commented that on the facts 'it was not a particularly serious example of its kind' and, as he had been fined on his two previous appearances for similar offences (both a long time previously), 'the jump from a relatively small fine to twelve months' imprisonment is too great'. The sentence was reduced to six months.

As these cases suggest, the existence of a substantial difference between the present and the longest previous sentence is most likely to be an effective mitigating factor when the offender has generally committed offences of a similar kind. Where he changes the pattern of his behaviour and commits for the first time offences of a much more serious character than he has been accustomed to commit in the past, he is not entitled to complain that he has now received a much more severe sentence than he expected. In *Sharp*[3] the appellant had a record of comparatively minor offences of dishonesty and his most severe sentence was a suspended term of six months. He appealed against sentences of six years for various offences, including handling goods 'stolen in the course of what is sometimes called a "first division" crime'. The Court accepted that there was a substantial jump between his present and previous sentences but upheld the sentence with the comment that 'the answer . . . is that there is also a very great jump in the gravity of the crime'.

[1] 25.2.74, 4643/A/73; see also *Rudden* 6.12.74, 3810/B/74 (sentences totalling seven years for drug offences reduced to five; 'to be sent to prison on the first occasion for a total period of seven years can only be justified in the gravest sort of case').

[2] 24.6.75, 2473/B/75.

[3] 27.10.72, 541/C/72; see also *McGuinness* 25.10.71, 249/C/71 (six years for robbery upheld; longest previous sentence six months but previous convictions all for offences of considerably lesser degree of gravity).

The Circumstances Leading to the Commission of the Offence

The commission of an offence is frequently not the result of a considered decision but an uncharacteristic reaction to a situation of stress of one kind or another. A violent crime is often the result of provocation or domestic tension, and an offence of dishonesty may be committed in desperation in a financial crisis. Drink is a significant causative element in the commission of many offences. The extent to which these factors, which may well occur simultaneously, mitigate sentence can be illustrated by reference to a number of decisions.

PROVOCATION

Illustrations of the mitigating effect of provocation were given in the previous chapter in relation to offences of violence. Clearly, provocation has substantial mitigating effect. In *Morris*[1] a young man of 'blameless character' admitted striking a man on the head with a knife, causing a serious wound; the incident followed provocation by taunting and physical assault. The Court stated that 'the use of a knife . . . as an offensive weapon . . . must inevitably result in sentences of some severity', but the sentence of eighteen months could be reduced to six 'on the ground that it reflected insufficiently the measure of provocation which the appellant received'. The mitigating effect of provocation is not limited to offences of violence. In *Wright*[2] the appellant was convicted of blackmailing a man who had had an affair with his wife by threatening to damage his house; the Court endorsed the sentencer's statement that blackmail is 'always . . . an exceedingly serious offence', but in view of various circumstances, including the fact that the appellant 'had suffered real damage at the hands of the victim so far as his domestic and married life was concerned', the sentence of twelve months was reduced to six and suspended. Similarly in *Harris*[3] a man of 23 of previous good character was sentenced to four years' imprisonment for setting fire to a bed in a house where his former girlfriend was now living with another man (the house being empty at the time). The Court accepted that the offence was 'a symbolic gesture' committed in a state of 'emotional disturbance' and reduced the sentence to the equivalent of twenty-one months.

[1] 5.8.74, 2382/B/74.
[2] 22.1.74, 5262/B/73.
[3] 18.8.75, 1581/B/75.

DOMESTIC OR EMOTIONAL STRESS

A frequent explanation of uncharacteristic offences is that they result from acute emotional stress. The most common example is the offence of violence committed against wife or husband, or a third party who has become involved with one of them, as a result of a deteriorating marriage. In such cases the circumstances which precipitate the violent act are usually treated as significant mitigating factors.[1] Similar circumstances may mitigate other offences. In *Law*[2] a man of 'positive good character' received three years' imprisonment for setting fire to the house he occupied, in a period of depression during the final stages of the breakdown of his marriage. The Court stated that the sentence was appropriate to the facts of what was 'a very serious offence' but, in view of the circumstances which had given rise to the offence, 'the risk of his re-offending is absolutely minimal', and other factors—particularly the risk that he would lose contact with his children—justified the Court in reducing the sentence and suspending it. In another case[3] two parents were each sentenced to two years' imprisonment for wilfully neglecting their younger child over a period of three years, at the end of which he died. The Court heard that the couple's elder child was autistic and that the younger child suffered from a complaint which impeded his physical development. While the sentence could not be considered too long for the offence, the Court considered that the sentencer had given insufficient weight 'to the appalling burden which this couple had to bear in having two children retarded . . . in different ways', and reduced the sentence to eighteen months in each case.

FINANCIAL DIFFICULTIES

Offences, usually of dishonesty, are frequently attributed to the fact that the offender found himself in a financial crisis to which misappropriation appeared to be the only solution. Where the offender's financial embarrassment is the result primarily of events beyond his own control rather than extravagance or gambling, these circumstances may have some mitigating effect. In *Oakes*[4] a car salesman was sentenced to two years' imprisonment for stealing the proceeds of the sale of several cars. The Court heard that the appellant had undertaken substantial financial commitments to

[1] See the cases discussed at pp. 76 and 101 above.
[2] 24.4.75, 38/B/75.
[3] *Piazzani and Piazzani* 19.7.74, 1872/C/74.
[4] 4.11.74, 2497/C/74.

improve his house in the hope of saving his marriage, but that his income had fallen off sharply when the general economic recession led to a decline in the sales of cars, and hence of his commission, and he had been unable to meet his obligations. He had subsequently found another position and worked long hours in the hope of clearing his debts. The Court stated that although the offences constituted 'a serious breach of trust' the circumstances justified suspension of the sentence. In *Owens*[1] a former coal miner was convicted of robbery at a sub-post office involving a 'callous and brutal attack' on an elderly couple. The Court was told that the appellant, while employed as a miner, bought a house on a large mortgage and undertook other commitments which became too heavy when he was forced to change his work following an injury to his leg, and found employment as a commission-only sales representative. Accepting that the appellant was in 'a desperate situation financially' at the time of the offence and 'had fallen into a state of depression', the Court stated that his sentence of six years' imprisonment was not wrong in principle for 'a grave offence' but the various mitigating circumstances distinguished the appellant from the more usual 'professional criminal who had carried out a robbery of this kind . . . after considerable planning' and justified a reduction to four years.

A different kind of situation in which financial pressures lead to the commission of offences, often of a substantial nature, is that in which the offender resorts to dishonesty in the hope of saving a failing business from disaster, often with the intention of making good the depredations when more favourable conditions return. In such a case the circumstances leading to the offence may have mitigating effect, if the sentencer is satisfied that the business was begun honestly and not as a cover for deliberately planned fraud. An example is *Crotty*[2] where a village storekeeper and sub-postmaster admitted stealing almost £3,000 from the post office. He had undertaken substantial commitments in order to extend his premises, and became insolvent as a result of rising costs and interest rates at a time when his marriage was in difficulty. The Court took the view that the nature of the offence was such that a deterrent sentence was necessary, but the sentence could be reduced from two years to eighteen months to reflect the mitigating circumstances. A strong example is *Liddle*[3] where a man of 50, who had become managing director of a company 'through many years of endeavour and effort, conducted with absolute integrity', admitted a large number of offences of obtaining for the company by deception a government subsidy amounting to

[1] 14.4.75, 4250/C/74.
[2] 17.12.74, 4127/B/74.
[3] 17.5.73, 6513/C/72.

£132,000 to which it was not entitled. The Court stated that his sentence of three years' imprisonment was not 'over-severe for a . . . fraud from the Government, involving public money in sums of such magnitude', and could not have been criticized if the appellant had committed the offence 'to enrich either the company or himself'. The Court was satisfied that the appellant had not personally profited from the frauds, and his main motive was to keep the company alive during a period of 'special difficulties in this particular industry' not arising from mismanagement of the company's affairs, in order to maintain the employment of the company's work force. In these circumstances the Court decided that 'justice will not be stretched too far' by reducing the sentence to two years and suspending it.

DRINK

While intoxication is associated with a wide variety of offences, it is rarely recognized as a substantial mitigating factor when standing alone. In *Kirkland*[1] a man of 21 with no previous convictions was sentenced to three years' imprisonment for setting fire to the home of his former employer. The Court accepted that the appellant was 'normally a level-headed young man' and that 'this offence came to be committed because the appellant had had far too much to drink'; however, the offence was such that three years was the lowest term which would adequately reflect its gravity, and 'the courts do not normally take drunkenness into account as a mitigating factor'. The sentence was upheld. In *Kirk*[2] the appellant was sentenced to four years for stabbing a man in a fight, following his ejection from a club. The Court accepted that 'the appellant had too much to drink' but upheld the sentence with the comment that 'whatever the situation, there was no justification for drawing a knife'. In *Drever*[3] a man of previous good character broke into a house in the early hours of the morning and raped the occupant, a single woman in her late fifties. Despite evidence that the appellant had been drinking heavily during the evening before the offence, the Court refused to vary his sentence of seven years' imprisonment.

Drunkenness, while having little or no independent mitigating effect, may add some marginal weight to other more substantial mitigating factors. In *Winter*[4] the appellant had broken into a public house to steal some drink to take to a party. He had made six previous

[1] 25.11.75, 4026/C/75.
[2] 18.4.72, 36/A/72.
[3] 25.4.72, 5587/A/71.
[4] 9.3.73, 420/B/73.

court appearances and experienced various custodial sentences including borstal training, but had committed no offence for over three years since his last previous conviction. He was now married with one child and another expected, and had obtained the tenancy of a flat; the Court was advised that 'there are hopeful signs that he has now settled down'. The Court considered that 'it would be unfortunate if we had to allow that sudden deviation to mar the prospects of his leading an honest and industrious life', particularly as the offence 'was in effect, a drunken frolic', and suspended the sentence. In another case[1] the appellant was sentenced to two years' imprisonment for encouraging the commission of unlawful sexual intercourse and indecent assault on his two daughters during the course of a party at which 'a good deal of drink was consumed'. Hearing that the events of the evening concerned had jeopardized the appellant's distinguished career and endangered his marriage, the Court came to the conclusion that he 'has already been punished very severely for his folly . . . at a time when no doubt he was drunk' and suspended the sentence.

The refusal of the Court to accept drunkenness as a mitigating factor in its own right must be distinguished from a more sympathetic attitude normally displayed toward offenders who have become alcoholics. The victim of alcoholism will normally be considered a candidate for individualized treatment, if there are any reasonable prospects of success. In *Halcro*[2] a man of 21 had acquired habits of heavy drinking while apprenticed to a boat builder; having left home for London he found company only in public houses and for about two years 'was in and out of trouble largely because of his drinking habits'. He was eventually sentenced to a total of twenty-one months' imprisonment for taking vehicles and related offences, a sentence which the Court considered could not be criticized. As 'his criminal behaviour is almost certainly the result of his alcoholism' and there was 'an excellent chance' that this could be cured, the sentence was varied to probation with appropriate conditions. In *Wilkes*[3] a man of 27 admitted burglary and other offences and received three years' imprisonment. The appellant had a series of previous convictions and the Court was advised that 'this man's main problem is drink'. The sentence 'was not excessive . . . for the offence', but the Court had to consider whether it was entitled 'to take . . . a constructive attitude and see if something cannot be done to cure him of this addiction'. As the appellant had indicated his willingness to make an effort, a probation order was substituted for the sentence of imprisonment.

[1] *Young* 5.4.73, 542/C/73.
[2] 9.12.74, 3714/A/74.
[3] 23.3.73, 6337/B/72.

This course will rarely be taken when the offender has previously failed to co-operate with other treatment programmes.[1]

The Indirect Effect of the Conviction or Sentence

A third group of mitigating factors are those which relate to the indirect effect on the offender of the conviction or sentence. A sentence of imprisonment may cause suffering to the offender's wife and children, or the loss of a career and valuable pension rights. For some offenders a sentence of imprisonment may mean additional hardship as a result of ill health or physical disability, or because their status or offence will expose them to hostility on the part of their fellow prisoners.

THE EFFECT OF THE SENTENCE ON THE OFFENDER'S FAMILY

The Court has stated on many occasions that the hardship caused to the offender's wife and children is not normally a circumstance which the sentencer may take into account. In *Lewis*[2] the Court refused to reduce sentences of imprisonment totalling three and a half years imposed for burglary, stating that it had been urged 'to take into consideration the unhappiness and the distress that his misdeeds have brought upon his dependants. That alas is something which is an inevitable consequence of crime, and it is something which the Court cannot regard as a mitigating circumstance'. In another case[3] a sentence of four years and three months was upheld on a man of 32 whose wife had just given birth to a baby, after losing a child some time previously, with the comment that 'this Court is very sensitive . . . to the distress and hardship which sentences of this nature must necessarily bring upon the family, friends and relations of convicted persons; but this is one of the penalties which . . . convicted persons must pay'. In *Ingham*[4] the appellant was sentenced to a total of twenty-one months' imprisonment for driving while disqualified; the Court was told that his wife was in an advanced state of pregnancy and her husband's imprisonment had caused severe depression. The Court refused to interfere, saying that 'imprisonment of the father inevitably causes hardship to the rest of the

---

[1] See, for example, *Grimwood* 25.1.73, 4035/B/72 (history of alcoholism explanation for criminal record of man, 38, sentenced to six years extended for fraud; various treatments tried but none 'seems to have been of any permanent or lasting success'; sentence upheld).

[2] 20.11.72, 2660/A/72.

[3] *Sherlock* 14.1.74, 2731/A/73.

[4] 3.10.74, 3120/A/74.

family . . . part of the price to pay when committing a crime is that imprisonment does involve hardship on the wife and family, and it cannot be one of the factors which can affect what would otherwise be the right sentence'.

This policy appears to be subject to three recognizable exceptions, although none is automatically applied. Family hardship may be a ground for mitigation of the sentence where the particular circumstances of the family are such that the degree of hardship is exceptional, and considerably more severe than the deprivation suffered by a family in normal circumstances as a result of the imprisonment. In one such case the offender's wife and child suffered serious injuries in a traffic accident shortly after he was sentenced, and his wife, on discharge from the hospital, was suffering from serious physical disabilities which were expected to cause difficulty over a long period of time[1]; in another the appellant's wife was a permanent cripple who could not cope with domestic matters without her husband's assistance.[2] In a third case the Court considered that the appellant's sentence of twenty-one months for handling the proceeds of a substantial burglary was 'in no way excessive' despite his previous good character, but suspended the sentence as an act of mercy on hearing that the appellant's wife suffered a serious progressive disabling disease, which was likely to be aggravated by the stress and anxiety resulting from their daughter's emotional problems, which in turn were related to the sudden death of their son some years previously.[3]

A second exception to the principle that family considerations do not have mitigating effect is the case of an offender who is the mother of young children. While such circumstances by no means guarantee reduction or suspension of a sentence of imprisonment imposed for a grave offence,[4] they may have some effect in relation to less serious offences. In *Charles*[5] a young woman was convicted of unlawfully

---

[1] *Crompton* 22.7.74, 356/C/74; see also *Winig* 10.3.72, 6217/C/71 (death of child during sentence aggravating emotional and physical problems of wife and surviving child resulting from earlier traffic accident).

[2] *Anderson* 14.11.74, 2571/A/74; see also *Ringwood* 18.2.77, 207/A/77 (twelve months for receiving substantial amount of stolen property, young son seriously ill and in need of medication which only father could administer; sentence varied to conditional discharge 'in mercy'); *Renker* 29.6.76, 2266/A/76 ('perfectly fair and proper sentence' for burglary reduced to enable appellant to spend time with son dying of leukaemia).

[3] *Vuolo* 17.3.72, 4825/B/71.

[4] See, for example, *Ayoub* 6.3.72, 4705/A/71, [1972] Crim. L. R. 446 (six years upheld for woman with six children, some very young, for fraudulently importing large quantity of cannabis).

[5] 10.7.75, 1942/C/75; see also *Parkinson* 4.11.76, 4719/B/76 (sentences totalling nine months for young woman for uttering forged banknote 'properly imposed'; reduced because of effect of sentence on her two young children).

wounding another woman by stabbing her with a pair of scissors; the Court suspended her sentence of nine months' imprisonment, partly because 'she is the mother of a number of small children'. In *Arnold*[1] the appellant received sentences totalling three years for bankruptcy offences which had caused losses amounting to several thousand pounds. The Court said that there was 'absolutely nothing wrong' with such sentences for deliberate offences committed over a period of two years, but in view of the uncertain future of the appellant's children, from whose father she had been divorced some years earlier, the Court reduced the sentence to eighteen months as 'some contribution towards keeping this family together as a unit'.

The third situation in which family hardship may mitigate a sentence is where both parents are imprisoned simultaneously, or other family circumstances mean that the imprisonment of one parent effectively deprives the children of parental care.[2] In *Moore*[3] a husband and wife were both involved in a fight in a club and each received sentences of imprisonment, of nine months and six months respectively. Although the sentence 'correctly marked the gravity of this type of offence' it 'did not reflect the special circumstances' that the imprisonment of both parents would result in their children being left without parental care. The wife's sentence was accordingly suspended. By the same reasoning, the needs of the children may be taken into account where the offender is the head of a single-parent family. In *Fels*[4] a woman with no previous convictions, whose marriage had collapsed some years previously, received five years' imprisonment for fraudulently importing a substantial quantity of cannabis. The Court heard that the appellant's 5-year-old son was suffering in her absence, and although the 'real gravity' of her offence precluded suspension of the sentence, the term was reduced to three years. In another case[5] the appellant pleaded guilty to the manslaughter of his wife under 'very grave provocation' and was sentenced to thirty months' imprisonment. Hearing that the sudden separation from both parents might have unpredictable long-term effects on the children, and accepting that the appellant 'is never likely to offend in this way again', the Court reduced the sentence to twelve months' imprisonment, observing that an immediate custodial sentence was necessary in such cases, 'no matter how great the provocation has been, unless the circumstances were wholly exceptional'.

[1] 5.7.74, 1366/A/74.
[2] See *Sykes* 11.3.75, 3736/A/74 (parents of family of eight children, varying ages, both imprisoned for handling stolen mail; sentences upheld, as 'the family are coping well in the circumstances').
[3] 16.1.76, 5705/B/75.
[4] 25.7.72, 5421/C/71.
[5] *Liddell* 4.12.75; 3129/C/75.

LOSS OF CAREER AND OTHER INDIRECT HARDSHIPS

It appears to be generally accepted that losses and hardships suffered by an offender over and above the sentence imposed by the Court may be taken into account as mitigating factors, although they will probably carry more weight when the offence is unconnected with the career or position that is jeopardized than when it is committed in the course of the offender's work. In *Hart*[1] a naval rating with no previous convictions was sentenced to twenty-one months' imprisonment for attacking a taxi driver, causing him a broken jaw. In view of the appellant's 'positively good character' and the fact that he had been discharged from the Royal Navy as a result of the sentence, the Court reduced the sentence to twelve months. In *Williams*[2] a police officer convicted of stealing clothing while off duty was sentenced to twelve months' imprisonment. The Court considered that for the appellant 'the conviction involves punishment other than that imposed by the sentence', in the loss of his career and pension rights accumulated over twenty years, and 'this was a matter to be given weight'. His sentence was reduced. In *Godfrey*[3] the licensee of a public house admitted handling foodstuffs stolen from a wholesale grocer and was sentenced to twelve months' imprisonment; in addition, the conviction meant that he would probably lose his licence and the tenancy of the public house, with the result that his wife and other relatives who worked in the public house would also lose their livelihoods. Although the Court did not consider the sentence excessive, it was reduced to six months 'as an act of mercy . . . related to the personal circumstances'.

In cases which involve a grave abuse of the offender's position, the loss of career and other hardships will clearly have less weight as mitigating factors,[4] but even in cases where the offence is committed in the course of the offender's employment the additional losses may have some mitigating effect. In *Fell*[5] a male nurse received nine months' imprisonment for assault occasioning actual bodily harm to a patient in the mental hospital where he was employed. Although the Court took the view that 'an assault by a nurse on a refractory patient must be regarded with repugnance', the sentence was reduced, partly to reflect the fact that the appellant 'has lost a profession of which he

---

[1] 20.3.72, 5467/A/71; see also *Gentile* 3.5.74, 1684/A/74 (member of United States Air Force sentenced to six months for possessing cannabis; varied to fine in view of good character and possibility of dishonourable discharge if sentence stands).

[2] 6.12.71, 3849/A/71.

[3] 9.7.73, 2618/C/73.

[4] See, for example, *Cairns* 9.7.74, 1351/A/74, [1974] Crim. L. R. 674 (prison officer conspiring to effect escape of prisoner serving life sentence).

[5] 17.2.75, 4921/A/74, [1975] Crim. L. R. 349.

was obviously fond'. In *Grieve*[1] a police officer was sentenced to four and a half years' imprisonment for offences of theft and burglary committed while on duty. The Court stated that in view of his position the offences were of a 'special gravity', but as the appellant had suffered the loss of his career and other consequences the sentence was reduced to three years.

In other cases the Court has extended the principle to other kinds of hardship flowing from the offence, such as serious injuries received by the offender in the course of its commission. In *Barbery*[2] the appellant took part in an affray, in the course of which his hand was severed by a blow from a scythe. The Court reduced his sentence in view of the 'most terrible injury' he had received, in order that he might practise the use of his artificial limb in normal conditions.

ADDITIONAL HARDSHIPS IN PRISON

For some offenders, the experience of being imprisoned may present problems not encountered by the majority of persons sentenced to imprisonment. Certain groups of offenders may experience hostility from their fellow prisoners, either because they have previously held positions as police officers or prison officers or have given information or assistance to the police or prison authorities, or because the nature of their offences, typically sexual or violent offences against children, makes them particularly unpopular and exposed to assault. These factors have been allowed some weight in a small number of cases, but their general effect is uncertain. In *Fletcher*[3] a man in his thirties with a 'substantial previous record' received two years' imprisonment for over forty offences involving the fraudulent use of cheques and credit cards. The Court heard that while serving a previous sentence the appellant had assisted prison officers to prevent an escape, and as a consequence was serving his present term, for his own protection, in solitary confinement. Recognizing that 'imprisonment in those circumstances bears substantially more heavily upon those subjected to it than imprisonment in . . . more ordinary circumstances', the Court reduced the sentence 'as an act of clemency'. Similarly in *Geraghty*[4] the appellant was sentenced to three years' imprisonment for inflicting grievous bodily harm on his 4-year-old daughter by leaving her in a cold bath for half an hour. The Court received evidence that the condition of the child on her arrival at the hospital

[1] 5.5.75, 4898/C/74.
[2] (1975) 62 Cr. App. R. 248; see also *Rimmer* 13.8.75, 1486/A/75 (six months' imprisonment for causing death by dangerous driving suspended, as appellant, having spent six months in hospital following accident, 'has suffered enough').
[3] 17.1.74, 5320/C/73.
[4] 19.12.74, 3346/C/74.

might have been partly caused by her consuming tablets prescribed for her mother; for that reason, but 'to some extent . . . influenced by the fact that . . . this appellant has been having an unpleasant time in prison from fellow inmates', the sentence was reduced to twelve months.

The additional hardship suffered by a prisoner as a result of bad health or physical disability may also be treated as a ground for mitigation. In *Deffley*[1] the appellant was sentenced to three years' imprisonment for substantial frauds on the Inland Revenue; while the Court considered that 'no possible criticism' could be made of the sentence, the appellant's eyesight had deteriorated to the point where he was eligible for registration as a blind person, and it was accepted that 'prison in those circumstances must be a far more grievous penalty'. The sentence was accordingly reduced. In another case[2] the appellant received two years' imprisonment for causing grievous bodily harm with intent; although the sentence was not considered excessive in relation to the facts, the Court reduced and suspended it on receiving evidence that the appellant had suffered two previous heart attacks and would risk further, possible fatal, attacks if he did not avoid all physical exertion. In less extreme cases, where imprisonment will not necessarily aggravate the offender's condition and adequate medical treatment is likely to be available during the sentence, the Court is less likely to treat the condition as a ground of mitigation.[3]

Ill health will have greater effect in mitigation where it can be shown to be related to the commission of the offence as a causative factor. In *Murfin*[4] a sub-postmaster was sentenced to two years' imprisonment for stealing from the post office. The Court considered that the sentence was 'not manifestly excessive', but reduced it to twelve months on hearing that at the time of the offences the appellant had been suffering a cerebral tumour which might have affected his insight and judgement. In a similar case where the amounts involved were much smaller, the Court suspended a sentence of nine months' imprisonment, which 'in a normal case . . . would have been on the lenient side', in the light of medical evidence relating to cerebral haemorrhage, which might have been a cause of the offender's behaviour.[5]

---

[1] 8.11.71, 2603/C/71, [1972] Crim. L. R. 123.

[2] *Herasymenko* 12.2.75, 2073/A/75.

[3] See, for example, *Minashi* 7.11.74, 3606/C/74 (appellant suffering from long-term ailment requiring medication and possibly surgery; while Court 'sympathetic to the submission that for a person suffering from this condition life in prison might be . . . more of a hardship than that imposed upon an ordinary prisoner not suffering in this way', adequate medical care available and 'grave offence' justified twelve months).

[4] 30.7.74, 184/A/74.   [5] *Thompson* 9.12.74, 3793/A/74.

The Behaviour of the Offender since the Commission of the Offence

The behaviour of the offender since the commission of the offence may be a significant mitigating factor. The offender who shows remorse by surrendering to the police, pleading guilty or giving information relating to other participants in the offence may expect some reduction in his sentence, and the voluntary payment of compensation may also be a relevant consideration.

REMORSE

It has already been shown that a plea of guilty, sometimes described as the best evidence of remorse, justifies the sentencer in reducing a sentence below the level appropriate to the facts of the offence, although the offender who contests the case against him may not be sentenced to a term longer than is warranted by the gravity of his offence.[1] In other cases evidence of remorse goes further than the usual plea of guilty and statements of contrition made by the offender or on his behalf. In *Norman*[2] the appellant was sentenced to fifteen months' imprisonment for stealing television sets from his employers. The offences came to light when the appellant made a statement to the police on his own initiative before the offences were even suspected; this put the case 'in a category quite apart from the case . . . of a person acting dishonestly . . . who says after he is found out "I am sorry I did it" '. In view of this and other factors the sentence was reduced and suspended. In *Stewart*[3] a man of 40 with many previous convictions was sentenced to five years' imprisonment for stealing wage packets from his employer's safe; he had given himself up to the police and returned the remaining portion of the stolen money. The Court stated that the sentence was 'quite justifiable' in relation to the offence and his record but did not 'recognize, as always should be recognized, the fact that this man did give himself up and pleaded guilty'. The sentence was reduced to four years.

[1] See above, p. 50.
[2] 16.5.75, 607/B/75.
[3] 19.12.74, 4012/A/74.

ASSISTANCE TO THE POLICE

The offender who provides information which leads to the apprehension of other persons involved in the offence, or gives evidence at their trial, may expect to receive some consideration for these actions in the assessment of his own sentence. In *Wright*[1] a sentence of three years' imprisonment was imposed on 'a regular handler of stolen property on quite a large scale'. It was argued on his behalf that the sentencer was unaware that at the time of his trial he had given information to the police, and that subsequently he gave evidence against other persons involved in the enterprise. The Court was invited to treat his co-operation with the police as evidence 'that this appellant has had a change of heart and does really regret becoming involved', and on that basis reduced the sentence to two years. Similarly in *Fels*[2] a sentence of five years' imprisonment for fraudulently importing cannabis was reduced to three years, partly because the appellant had given information relating to other persons concerned in dealing in controlled drugs in several countries.

PAYMENT OF COMPENSATION

The relevance of the payment of compensation to the assessment of an appropriate sentence has been complicated by the enactment of legislation empowering a sentencer to order the offender to pay compensation for any personal injury, loss or damage which has resulted from his offence (these provisions are discussed in detail in chapter 9), and by an incidental reference to the payment of compensation in Powers of Criminal Courts Act 1973 s. 1. This section, discussed in detail in chapter 12, empowers a sentencer to defer passing sentence for a period not exceeding six months 'for the purpose of enabling the court to have regard, in determining his sentence, to his conduct after conviction (including, *where appropriate*, the making by him of reparation for his offence)'. It appears that neither of these provisions has altered the previously established principle that compensation paid voluntarily by the offender, or intended to be paid, may be taken into account as a mitigating factor but does not entitle the offender to a specific discount from his sentence.

The making of a compensation order has no direct relevance to the process of determining the nature or length of the sentence imposed

[1] 18.10.74, 355/C/74.
[2] 25.7.72, 5421/C/71.

on the offender: 'Compensation orders were not introduced into our law to enable the convicted to buy themselves out of the penalties for crime. Compensation orders were introduced . . . as a convenient and rapid means of avoiding the expense of . . . civil litigation when the criminal clearly has means which would enable the compensation to be paid'.[1] The proper procedure appears to require the sentencer first to determine the sentence on the basis of all relevant considerations, before passing to the question of compensation orders, applying the principles described in chapter 9. As no compensation has been paid at this stage, and if it is paid under the coercion of a compensation order will not be paid voluntarily, it appears that the possibility of a compensation order should have no effect on the decision whether to impose a sentence of imprisonment or the calculation of its length. Compensation paid under the order of the court can rarely be regarded as evidence of remorse, which is the basis for treating payment of compensation as a mitigating factor.

The same reasoning applies to the ambiguous reference to 'making . . . reparation for his offence' in Powers of Criminal Courts Act 1973, s. 1, which states that the sentencer may have regard to the making of reparation *where appropriate*. This qualification indicates that the section is not intended to alter the underlying principle that payment of compensation may be treated as a mitigating factor where it can be seen as evidence of remorse. It appears to be wrong in principle to defer sentence in order to put pressure on an offender to pay compensation and then adjust his sentence according to whether or not he has managed to fulfil the sentencer's expectations.[2] In *Crosby and Hayes*[3] two men of previous good character admitted participating in a variety of frauds involving several thousand pounds. At the conclusion of the trial the judge deferred sentence in response to representations that the offenders might be able to recompense the victim for his losses. During the period of deferment one defendant was able to raise £3,600, which was paid over; the second defendant found employment and saved a substantial portion of his net salary, but the amount, £800, was far less than his co-defendant had made available. The first defendant was sentenced to twelve months' imprisonment suspended for two years, and the second defendant received an immediate sentence of eighteen months. Suspending this sentence also, the Court stated that the fact that one defendant had a source of finance while the other did not

---

[1] *Inwood* (1974) 60 Cr. App. R. 70; see also *Stapleton and Lawrie* 4.2.77, [1977] Crim. L. R. 366.
[2] *Mortimer* 15.3.77, 2204/A/76, [1977] Crim. L. R. 624 may be seen to support the contrary position.
[3] (1974) 60 Cr. App. R. 234.

'does not seem to us to be a firm foundation for the administration of justice'. The disparity in the sentences was therefore unjustified.

This case appears to support the wider principle that the payment of compensation under pressure is not a mitigating factor which should affect the sentence imposed for the offence. The proper approach to the treatment of compensation as a mitigating factor is illustrated by *Cockburn*,[1] where a man of previous good character admitted stealing a total of about £6,000 from his employer; the money was apparently used to meet debts arising from a business venture which had failed. There was evidence before the sentencer, who imposed three years' imprisonment, that the appellant was anxious to repay the stolen money and had taken some steps towards doing so; the Court was invited to suspend his sentence so that the appellant's chances of making good the loss would be improved. This the Court declined to do, as 'this matter cannot be looked at simply from the point of view . . . of people from whom money has been stolen. These were thefts on a large scale and over a substantial period and . . . it is necessary to impose a substantial punishment in order to deter others'. However, there was room for some mitigation in view of 'this man's character' and 'his genuine, and we hope continuous, desire to pay'. His sentence was reduced to eighteen months.

GRIEVANCES ARISING IN THE COURSE OF THE PROCEEDINGS

A final group of cases illustrate the practice of mitigating a sentence to alleviate a legitimate grievance which the offender suffers as a result of the way the case against him has been conducted, or to remove the appearance of injustice which has arisen as a result of an incident in the course of the proceedings. The reduction of an otherwise appropriate sentence in cases of unjustified disparity (discussed above, p. 71) is the most common example. Other aspects of the conduct of proceedings which may justify some mitigation of a sentence include long delays between the discovery of the offence and the commencement of the prosecution, with the result that the offender suffers a prolonged period of suspense and anxiety;[2] the fact

[1] 22.7.74, 1788/B/74; see also *Gernat* 23.11.73, 3104/B/73 (solicitor misappropriating client's funds, restitution out of own assets made after striking off but before beginning of police investigations; 'appropriate sentence' of four years reduced to two, as delay of three years occurred before trial commenced and 'this man parted with everything he had in order to make restitution').

[2] See, for example, *Lavender* (1971) 56 Cr. App. R. 355 (fraudulent conversion of cheques worth £22,000 and fraudulent trading; three years reduced to eighteen months, partly because 'of the long delay in bringing the matter to trial, which led the

that the offender has spent time in custody in connection with proceedings for the offence in circumstances in which the time does not count as part of the sentence;[1] or the provision to the sentencer of inaccurate information about the offender's current offences[2] or his antecendents.[3] Confusion arising from deferment of sentence has led to grievances which the Court has recognized by reducing sentences on appeal.[4] In other cases sentences have been reduced as a result of unguarded or inappropriate comments made by the sentencer when passing sentence,[5] apparent failure to listen to counsel's speech in

appellant to have this hanging over his head for something like four years'); *Rohan* 23.8.72, 1000/A/72 (three years for drug offences reduced and suspended, as appellant had 'completely transformed himself' during the 'appalling delay' in the case's coming to trial); *Doyle* 12.10.71, 2202/C/71 (eighteen months for assault and other offences reduced to twelve, as 'through no fault of the appellant, the matter has been kept hanging over his head for a very long time').

[1] See, for example, *Bennett* 4.2.75, 3837/B/74, [1975] Crim. L. R. 654 (period spent in custody in Canada prior to rendition subtracted from appropriate sentence); *Deering* 10.2.76, 3218/A/75, [1976] Crim. L. R. 638 (period spent in custody prior to passing of suspended sentence).

[2] For instance, *White* 3.5.73, 751/B/73 (four years for wounding with intent reduced to three, sentencer having passed sentence on basis that offence was committed shortly after being fined for other offences of violence, when fines were in fact imposed subsequent to the wounding for offences committed earlier); *Dodd* 25.11.75, 3642/B/75 (thirty months for taking vehicles reduced to two years, as sentencer originally thought third charge of driving without insurance related to taking conveyance on separate occasion; appellant 'may be suffering from a sense of grievance' even though error corrected at time).

[3] See, for example, *Stokes* 22.4.75, 4959/A2/74 (four years for burglaries reduced to three; sentencer having been misinformed about appellant's longest previous sentence, appellant 'was left at the end labouring under some feeling of injustice' although error corrected at the time); *Mulligan* 8.10.71, 1051/C/71 (two years for burglary reduced to twelve months as misleading details in antecedents statement were 'substantial ground for a sence of grievance'); *Jordan* 11.2.74, 5173/A/73 (incorrect information about date of appellant's most recent previous conviction created 'legitimate grievance' as it was considered relevant by sentencer; eighteen months for burglary and theft reduced to twelve).

[4] See, for example, *Marchant* 18.3.75, 4845/C/74 (sentence deferred with suggestion that offender's behaviour during deferment would affect decision, borstal training imposed despite 'wholly favourable report' of behaviour during this period; sentence would have been appropriate if passed in first instance but 'quite wrong' to pass it after deferment varied to probation); *Gurney* 5.4.74, 2/C/74 (nine months for systematic thefts from employers 'absolutely right in principle' but reduced to allow release as sentence previously deferred with suggestion that repayment might result in non-custodial sentence, with resulting 'sense of injustice').

[5] See, for example, *Evans* 23.10.72, 1296/B/72 (twenty-one months for frauds involving about £300 reduced to fifteen, partly because sentencer in describing frauds as 'vast' used 'the language of exaggeration rather than of accuracy'); *Woods* 14.10.74, 2890/A/74 (nine months for indecent assault on boy reduced to allow immediate release; sentencer's adverse comments on appellant's failure to plead guilty 'wholly inappropriate' as appellant acquitted on three of four counts in indictment, and 'must have conveyed . . . a sense of injustice'); *Stocker and Cain* 25.7.74, 5156/A/73 (fourteen years for armed robbery reduced to twelve as observations of sentencer might have been understood to imply that sentencer was imposing sentence on basis that appellant was really guilty of charges on which he was acquitted, even though Court satisfied that this was not the case and sentences not wrong in principle).

mitigation[1] or other departures from proper standards of judicial behaviour.[2]

[1] See, for example, *Watson* 13.2.73, 4946/A/72 (three and a half years for various offences reduced to three years as sentencer's apparent failure to listen to speech in mitigation 'calculated to leave a sense of grievance').

[2] See, for example, *Young* 13.7.72, 2494/C/72 (sentencer's comment that he never made psychiatric probation orders or passed suspended sentences 'inconsistent with a proper exercise of the judicial function; appellant's 'sense of grievance' one ground for suspending sentence); *Bird* 6.12.77, 2567/C/77, [1978] Crim. L. R. 237 (immediate sentence imposed following conviction by jury, after indication that sentence would be suspended in the event of plea of guilty, sentence not inappropriate to offence but varied to suspended sentence in view of 'irregular' circumstances).

Part III

INDIVIDUALIZED MEASURES AND OTHER SENTENCES

As the last three chapters have argued, the process of determining the length of a tariff sentence follows reasonably well established paths. Where the primary decision is in favour of individualization, a different kind of secondary process takes place. The sentencer must search among the various individualized measures available for the one most suited to the particular offender; sometimes the court will come to the conclusion that there is no suitable individualized measure and find itself forced back to the tariff. The choice of individualized measure is made empirically in each case, on the basis of an assessment of the individual offender's needs. For this reason, the principles found in this area of sentencing differ in kind from those considered earlier. There are no clear policies governing the choice of particular measures, indicating for instance which offenders should be put on probation, which sentenced to borstal training and which committed to hospital. The principles developed by the Court in this context centre on the scope and limitations of the forms of sentence themselves, elaborating the basic statutory criteria of eligibility, and thus refining the area of choice of the sentencing court seeking an appropriate measure in a particular case.

This difference in the nature of the principles to be described necessitates a different presentation. In the next six chapters, groups of sentences which can broadly be considered individualized measures are considered. In relation to each of them a detailed account of the statutory framework is given, followed by a discussion of the further policy considerations developed by the Court. For convenience, a discussion of law and practice governing a number of sentences which are not properly classed as individualized measures is also included in this part.

5

Non-custodial Measures

The non-custodial measures discussed in this chapter are discharges, bind-overs, probation orders, community service orders, suspended sentences and sentences partially held in suspense. Psychiatric probation orders are examined in chapter 7 and the power to defer sentence in chapter 12.

Discharge

Powers of Criminal Courts Act 1973 s. 7 empowers a court before which a person is convicted of an offence (other than an offence for which the sentence is fixed by law) to grant an absolute discharge or a conditional discharge, if it is 'of the opinion, having regard to the circumstances including the nature of the offence and the character of the offender, that it is inexpedient to inflict punishment and that a probation order is not appropriate'.

An absolute discharge terminates the proceedings in relation to the offence in respect of which it is granted. A conditional discharge is a discharge subject to the condition that the offender commits no offence during the period of the conditional discharge, which may be for up to three years.[1] Before making an order for conditional discharge, the sentencer must explain to the offender 'in ordinary language' that if he commits an offence during the period of the conditional discharge he will be liable to be sentenced for the original offence[2] (the consent of the offender is not required).

If the offender is convicted and dealt with for an offence[3] committed during the period of the conditional discharge, he may be sentenced by the appropriate court[4] in respect of the offence for

[1] Powers of Criminal Courts Act 1973 s. 7(1).
[2] *Ibid.*, s. 7(3). The Court has held that the sentencer may delegate the duty of explaining the effect of the order, so long as he is satisfied that the explanation has been given and understood; see *Wehner* (1977) 65 Cr. App. R. 1.
[3] Not necessarily an offence punishable with imprisonment: contrast s. 23.
[4] See ss. 8(2), 8(8), discussed below, p. 232. The Crown Court may deal with an offender for an offence in respect of which he was granted a conditional discharge by either the Crown Court or a magistrates' court, but where the conditional discharge was granted by the magistrates' court, the Crown Court may impose only a sentence which would be within the powers of the magistrates' court, even if the offence is triable on indictment.

which the conditional discharge was granted 'in any manner in which it could deal with him if he had just been convicted by or before that court of that offence'.[1] Where the offender is sentenced for the original offence, the conditional discharge ceases to have effect.[2] If no such sentence is passed, the conviction in respect of which the discharge was granted 'shall be deemed not to be a conviction for any purpose other than the purpose of the proceedings in which the order is made and of any subsequent proceedings which may be taken against the offender' in relation to breach of probation or discharge.

A conditional discharge takes the place of any sentence for the offence and may not be combined with a fine.[3] It may be combined with a disqualification from driving,[4] a compensation order[5] or an order to pay a sum towards the costs of the prosecution. Where the offender is convicted of more than one offence, there is no barrier to the imposition of a conditional discharge on one count and some other form of sentence on another.

POLICY IN THE USE OF ABSOLUTE AND CONDITIONAL DISCHARGES

Absolute discharges are rarely granted in the Court of Appeal, but the few cases where they occur suggest that the use of power may be appropriate, even in relation to offences tried on indictment, for offences committed in circumstances of minimal culpability and substantial mitigation. In *O'Toole*[6] an ambulance driver was convicted of dangerous driving on evidence that he was driving at a high but lawful speed along a straight road, with warning lights flashing and siren sounding, when he collided with a car which was driven into his path by an elderly lady whose driving on the occasion was described as 'careless' and 'disastrous'. The Court considered that as 'it was difficult . . . to say that there was any moral blame', the fine of £50 and disqualification for twelve months should be quashed and an absolute discharge substituted. In another case[7] a man of 'impeccable character' admitted minor violations of the Firearms Act 1968 (possessing a non-working firearm not covered by the firearms

---

[1] *Ibid.*, s. 8(7).
[2] Powers of Criminal Court Act 1973 s. 13(1), discussed below, p. 236.
[3] See *McClelland* (1951) 35 Cr. App. R. 22.
[4] Road Traffic Act 1972 s. 102(1).
[5] Powers of Criminal Courts Act 1973 ss. 13(1) and 35(1); the offence is treated as a conviction for the purpose of the proceedings in which the order is made (s. 13(1)), and a compensation order may be made 'in addition to dealing with him in any other way' (s. 35(1)).
[6] (1971) 55 Cr. App. R. 206.
[7] *Kavanagh*, 16.5.72, 4680/A/71.

certificate he held, and failing to disclose a minor previous conviction when applying for a certificate, in the belief that disclosure was not required). As there was no 'question of illegal trading in firearms or deliberate criminal means adopted to gain possession of firearms' and the conviction had led to substantial financial losses, the Court quashed the suspended sentence imposed by the trial court and substituted an absolute discharge.

Cases in which conditional discharges are used appear to fall into several distinct classes. The first category may involve an offence of some degree of seriousness committed by an offender whose circumstances are such that a non-custodial individualized measure is appropriate, but for whom the supervision of a probation officer is either unnecessary or unsuitable. In one such case[1] the appellant was put on probation and ordered to pay compensation for several minor thefts committed in the course of a confused business relationship; in the light of the probation officer's comment that the appellant was 'not in need of the . . . casework relationship usually associated with probation', the Court substituted a conditional discharge.[2]

An alternative use of the conditional discharge is as a tariff sentence in cases of minimal gravity, where the facts of the offence would not justify a sentence of imprisonment (whether or not suspended) and a fine is inappropriate as the offender has no means. In *Wilson*[3] the appellant was convicted of stealing materials worth about £3 from a building site and sentenced to nine months' imprisonment suspended for two years. The Court held this sentence to be 'wrong in principle', as the offence would not justify a sentence of immediate imprisonment; the alternative was a fine, but as the appellant was disabled and his family was living on social security, the only kind of fine that could be imposed would make the offence appear 'of no consequence at all'. Accordingly, the only appropriate disposal was a conditional discharge. Similarly in *McGowan*[4] a man of 22 was sentenced to twelve months' imprisonment suspended for two years for picking up three crabs which had just been dropped by a friend who had stolen them a few minutes earlier. The Court held that the sentence 'erred in principle in a number of ways', despite the sentencer's intention to deal with the offender leniently. Although the offender had several convictions for dishonesty, the sentencer's duty was 'to arrive at an appropriate sentence for this particular offence'. A sentence of immediate imprisonment for the offence would have

---

[1] *Harrison-Jones*, 19.2.73, 2878/B/72.
[2] The question of the Court's jurisdiction was not discussed.
[3] 13.11.73, 3834/C/73.
[4] 1.11.74, 932/C/74, [1975] Crim. L. R. 113; see also *Wood* 4.11.74, 2450/C/74 (nine months suspended for handling £2 'wrong in principle and manifestly excessive', no means to pay a fine; conditional discharge substituted).

been 'quite inappropriate and wrong' and accordingly a suspended sentence was 'wrong in principle'. The suspended sentence was not justified by the fact that the offender was not in a financial position to pay a fine: 'if a person cannot pay a fine it does not mean to say that imprisonment is the proper punishment'. In these circumstances the 'only . . . realistic way of dealing with the situation' was a conditional discharge.

A conditional discharge may be preferred to a fine in cases of modest gravity to reflect the presence of general mitigating factors, where the offence considered in the abstract might have justified a custodial sentence. In *McLaughlin*[1] the appellant admitted breaking into his father's house to recover property belonging to himself, and stealing property belonging to his father when he discovered that his own property was missing. The Court described the offence as 'outside . . . the normal run of offences of burglary' and as the appellant had made an effort to 'put behind him . . . the adolescent lapses' which had led to an earlier sentence of borstal training, varied his sentence of nine months' imprisonment to a conditional discharge.

Binding Over

The term 'binding over' describes two procedures which are essentially different, although they may share a common origin. A person who appears before a court may be bound over in a stated sum to keep the peace and be of good behaviour; failure to do so may lead to the forfeiture of the amount of the recognizance. Alternatively, the Crown Court may bind over a person who has been convicted of an offence to come up for judgment if called upon to do so; if the offender is called upon, he may subsequently be sentenced for the original offence. Binding over to keep the peace is analogous to the imposition of a suspended fine, while binding over to come up for judgment might be compared to the procedure for deferment of sentence.

BINDING OVER TO KEEP THE PEACE

The power of judges of the Crown Court to bind over a person before the court to keep the peace and be of good behaviour is recognized by statute.[2] The power does not depend on a conviction; it may be exercised against a witness or a person who has been acquitted.[3]

---

[1] 16.7.73, 2115/A/73.
[2] Justice of the Peace Act 1968 s. 1(7).
[3] *Gilbert* 4.4.74, 4400/C/73.

Where the sentencer contemplates using the power against a person who has not been convicted, he should give him an opportunity to show cause why he should not be bound over.[1] A person who has been convicted of an offence may be bound over to keep the peace in addition to and in lieu of any other sentence.[2]

Where it is alleged that a person who has been bound to keep the peace has broken the term of his recognizance, the matters alleged to constitute the breach must be formally proved against the person bound, who may give or call evidence to the contrary.[3] If the breach is established, the recognizance may be estreated, but no further sentence may be passed in respect of the original offence.[4] In ordering the recognizance to be estreated, the sentencer should fix a term of imprisonment to be served in default and make such other incidental orders as may be appropriate as in the case of the imposition of a fine.[5]

BINDING OVER TO COME UP FOR JUDGMENT WHEN CALLED

The procedure of binding over a person who has been convicted of an offence to come up for judgment when called is essentially a power to postpone sentence on specified conditions. It may not be employed, as in the case of binding over to keep the peace, where the offender is sentenced for the offence,[6] and its use precludes the exercise of any other power to deal with the offender arising out of his conviction.

Where the offender fails to comply with the conditions specified in the recognizance, he may be brought back before the court[7] which, on proof of the breach of the condition,[8] may sentence him for the original offence. Complications may arise where the offender has

[1] *Sheldon v. Bromfield JJ.* [1964] 2 Q. B. 573; *R. v. Woking JJ. ex p. Gossage* [1973] 2 All E. R. 621; *R. v. Hendon JJ. ex p. Gorchein* [1971] 1 All E. R. 168.

[2] *Quaere*, whether the circumstances of the offence must disclose a tendency to break the peace.

[3] See *McGarry* (1945) 30 Cr. App. 187 (decided on binding over to come up for judgment).

[4] *Gilbert* 4.4.74, 4400/C/73 ('when a person has been bound over to keep the peace and is in breach of the terms of the recognizance, the court has got power to estreat the recognizance but has no power, save within the statutory provisions which govern this matter, to sentence the person to imprisonment for a breach of the recognizance'—the statutory provisions mentioned are those relating to fixing a term of imprisonment to be served in default). This point was apparently overlooked in *Coker* 21.12.71, 2942/C/71, where the Court upheld a sentence apparently passed for breach of a recognizance to keep the peace.

[5] Powers of Criminal Courts Act 1973 s. 31, discussed in chapter 9 below.

[6] See *Ayu* (1958) 43 Cr. App. R. 31.

[7] The law provides no specific mechanism for initiating the proceedings or securing his appearance.

[8] See *McGarry* (1945) 30 Cr. App. R. 187; *Philbert* 9.10.72, 3096/A/72, [1973] Crim. L. R. 129.

passed from one legally significant age-group to another between the date of his conviction and the day on which he comes up for judgment.[1]

The growth of a wide range of statutory powers to suspend or defer sentence, or to subject the offender to probation or conditional discharge, has led to a decline in the use of the power to bind over to come up for judgment, and it is submitted that it is inappropriate to use the power where a statutory power to the same effect is available, or to use the power in order to exceed the limitations imposed by statute on the exercise of the particular power (such as to defer sentence for a period in excess of six months or to subject the offender to requirements which might be included in a probation order, but for a period longer than three years).[2]

Probation

CONDITIONS OF ELIGIBILITY

Where a person of or over 17 years of age is convicted of an offence for which the sentence is not fixed by law, the court may make a probation order if it is 'of the opinion that having regard to the circumstances, including the nature of the offence and the character of the offender, it is expedient to do so'.[3] A probation order requires the offender to be under the supervision of a probation officer for the period specified, which may be not less than six months[4] nor more than three years, and to comply with such other requirements 'as the court, having regard to the circumstances of the case, considers necessary for securing the good conduct of the offender or for preventing a repetition by him of the same offence or the commission of other offences'.[5] The additional requirements of the order may include conditions relating to the residence of the offender (before making any such requirement the court 'shall consider the home surroundings of the offender')[6] but may not include requirements

---

[1] It appears that if the sentence is to be imprisonment, his age on the date of the sentence determines the powers of the sentencer (see Powers of Criminal Courts Act 1973 s. 19); if he is to be sentenced to borstal training, his relevant age is his age on the date of conviction (see Criminal Justice Act 1948 s. 20(1)).

[2] One case which does not support this proposition is *Farnborough*, 13.3.70, 6735/69, where a sentence of six years' imprisonment for indecent assault on a number of boys was varied to a bind-over for five years, on condition the appellant submitted to psychiatric treatment for this period.

[3] Powers of Criminal Courts Act 1973 s. 2.

[4] See Probation Orders (Variation of Statutory Limits) Order 1978.

[5] Powers of Criminal Courts Act 1973.

[6] *Ibid.*, s. 2(5); the order may not require residence in an approved probation hostel for more than twelve months (2(5) (b)).

relating to the payment of compensation or damages.[1] A requirement that the offender submit to treatment for his mental condition may be made only if the conditions specified in Powers of Criminal Courts Act 1973 s. 3 are satisfied.

Where the court has been notified that a day training centre exists for persons of the offender's class or description who reside in the petty sessional area where he resides, and is satisfied that arrangements can be made for his attendance at that centre, the order may require the offender to attend the centre on not more than sixty days and comply with the instructions of the person in charge of the centre.[2]

Before making a probation order the court 'shall explain to the offender in ordinary language the effect of the order' and the consequences of failure to comply with it or of the commission of another offence.[3] The order may not be made 'unless he expresses his willingness to comply with its requirements'.[4] The consent must be genuine. Where an offender unwillingly consented to the making of a probation order on the understanding that the only other measure which could be considered was a custodial sentence, when on the facts of the offence this was 'an exceedingly remote alternative', the Court held that the consent was invalid and the probation order was accordingly void.[5]

A probation order is made 'instead of sentencing the offender'.[6] Accordingly the sentencer may not impose a fine for the same offence,[7] but the offender may be disqualified from driving,[8] ordered to pay compensation[9] or ordered to pay a sum towards the costs of the prosecution.[10] Where the offender receives a suspended sentence for one offence, the court which imposes the suspended sentence may not make a probation order in respect of another offence for which he is dealt with by the court.[11] The Court has held that a probation order should not be made to run concurrently with a custodial sentence,[12]

---

[1] Powers of Criminal Courts Act 1973 s. 2 (4); a compensation order may be made under s. 35 in conjunction with a probation order.

[2] *Ibid.*, s. 4. For a general discussion of the use of this power, where it is available, see *Cardwell* (1973) 58 Cr. App. R. 241.   [3] *Ibid.*, s. 2(6).

[4] *Ibid.*, s. 2 (6).

[5] *Marquis* (1974) 59 Cr. App. R. 228.

[6] Powers of Criminal Courts Act 1973 s. 2(1).

[7] *Ibid.*, s. 30(1).

[8] Road Traffic Act 1972 s. 102(1).

[9] Powers of Criminal Courts Act 1973 s. 35(1).

[10] Costs in Criminal Cases Act 1973.

[11] Powers of Criminal Courts Act 1973 s. 22(3). The restriction applies even though the offences are charged in different indictments (*Wright* 30.6.75, 1204/B/75, [1975] Crim. L. R. 728). It is submitted that the section should be read as if it contained the words 'on the same occasion'.

[12] See *Evans* (1959) 43 Cr. App. R. 66; *Emmett* (1968) 53 Cr. App. R. 203; *Barnes* 19.2.73, 5551/C/72.

and a probation order may not be made to commence on a day other than the day on which it is made.[1] Where the offender is subject to more than one probation order at the same time, each is effective in the case of a further conviction or breach of a requirement of the order for the purpose of sentencing him for the offence for which it was imposed but only the most recent is effective for the purpose of supervision.[2]

DISCHARGE OF A PROBATION ORDER

A probation order made by the Crown Court following a conviction on indictment, or by the Court of Appeal (Criminal Division), may be discharged by the supervising court[3] on the application of either the probation officer or the probationer, unless the order contains a direction that the power to discharge be reserved to the Crown Court. In this case only the Crown Court may exercise the power to discharge the order.[4] Where the probation order is made on a committal for sentence, the power to discharge may be exercised only by the Crown Court.[5] A court having the power to discharge a probation order may, if it considers that 'the order is no longer appropriate in the case of the probationer', substitute a conditional discharge for the probation order.[6] The effect of such a substitution is that the offender is treated 'in all respects' as if the original order had been a conditional discharge made for the same period as the original probation order.[7] A probation order ceases to have effect if the offender is subsequently sentenced for the original offence, either following the commission of a further offence or on a breach of one of the requirements of the order.[8]

BREACH OF THE REQUIREMENTS OF THE ORDER

Where a probationer fails to comply with the requirements of a probation order made by the Crown Court, the supervising court may issue process against him and, if the failure is proved to its

[1] See *Evans* (1959) 43 Cr. App. R. 66.
[2] *Keeley* (1960) 44 Cr. App. R. 176.
[3] The magistrates' court for the petty sessional area in which the probationer resides: see Powers of Criminal Courts Act 1973 s. 2(2).
[4] Powers of Criminal Courts Act 1973 s. 5(1) and sch. 1 para. 1.
[5] *Ibid.*, para. 1(4).
[6] *Ibid.*, s. 11(1).
[7] *Ibid.*, s. 11(2). It appears to be clear that the offender may be dealt with in respect of an offence committed before the substitution, for which he is convicted after the substitution, as a breach of the condition of his discharge under s. 8.
[8] *Ibid.*, s. 5(2).

satisfaction, may impose a fine not exceeding £50, or (if the appropriate conditions are satisfied) make a community service order[1] or attendance order[2] against the probationer. Alternatively, the supervising court may commit the probationer, in custody or on bail, to the Crown Court.[3] If the failure to comply with the requirements of the order is proved to the satisfaction of the Crown Court,[4] the Crown Court may impose a fine not exceeding £50, make a community service order against the probationer (provided the normal conditions for making a community service order are satisfied) or 'deal with him for the offence in respect of which the probation order was made in any manner in which it could deal with him if he had just been convicted before the Crown Court of that offence'[5] (this power includes the power to make a fresh probation order, even though the effect is a total period of probation exceeding three years for the original offence).[6]

This procedure may not be used when the only matter alleged against the probationer is the commission of a further offence.[7]

COMMISSION OF A FURTHER OFFENCE DURING THE CURRENCY OF THE PROBATION ORDER

Where a person subject to a probation order made by the Crown Court[8] is convicted by any court in Great Britain of an offence committed during the probation period, the Crown Court or the supervising court may issue process to secure his appearance;[9] if such a person is convicted by a magistrates' court, the magistrates' court may commit him to the Crown Court in custody or on bail.[10] If it is then proved to the satisfaction of the Crown Court that the probationer has been convicted of an offence committed during the relevant period, the court may 'deal with him, for the offence for which the order was made, in any manner in which it could deal with him if he had just been convicted by or before that court of that offence'.[11]

[1] Powers of Criminal Courts Act 1973 s. 14; see s. 6(10).
[2] Criminal Justice Act 1948 s. 19.
[3] Ibid., s. 6(4).
[4] The Crown Court must hear the relevant evidence itself; the certificate of the finding of the failure by the magistrates' court is admissible but not conclusive evidence; see Holmes (1965) 50 Cr. App. R. 86.
[5] Powers of Criminal Courts Act 1973.
[6] See R. v. Havant JJ. ex p. Jacobs (1957) 41 Cr. App. R. 62.
[7] Powers of Criminal Courts Act 1973 s. 6(7).
[8] Or the Court of Appeal (Criminal Division); see Powers of Criminal Courts Act 1973 s. 12(2).
[9] Powers of Criminal Courts Act 1973 s. 8(1).
[10] Ibid., s. 8(6).
[11] Ibid., s. 8(7).

Where a person subject to a probation order made by a magistrates' court is convicted before the Crown Court of an offence committed during the relevant period, or dealt with by the Crown Court for any such offence following a committal for sentence, the Crown Court may deal with the offender for the offence for which the order was made 'in any manner in which the magistrates' court could deal with him if it had just convicted him of that offence'.[1] In exercising this power the Crown Court is limited to the maximum sentence available for the offence on summary conviction, even though the offence is triable on indictment, and must observe any other limitations applicable to magistrates' courts.[2] If the necessary information is available to the Crown Court, this power should generally be exercised.[3] (The consent of the magistrates' court which made the order is not necessary.)

In all these cases the power to deal further with the offender arises where he is convicted of an offence committed during the probation period. It does not arise where there is a conviction during the probation period of an offence committed before the probation order was made, but it does arise where the conviction occurs after the probation period has expired but relates to an offence committed during the probation period. There must however be a conviction; the power does not arise where the relevant offence is taken into consideration in dealing with the offender for offences committed outside the probation period. The Court has held that where the offender is subjected to a further probation order or a conditional discharge in respect of the latest offence, the conviction for the latest offence is effective as a conviction for the purpose of dealing with the offender for the original offence, notwithstanding Powers of Criminal Courts Act 1973 s. 13(1).[4]

The Court has frequently stressed the importance of observing strict procedural standards in dealing with an offender for an offence for which he has been subject to a probation order. The offender should be asked to admit the original conviction and the terms of the order, and the subsequent conviction and adjudication. If he does not admit them, they should be proved by the evidence of a person who was in court when the original order was made and formal evidence of the subsequent conviction.[5]

[1] *Ibid.*, s. 8(8).
[2] For example, the Crown Court may not disqualify from driving under Powers of Criminal Courts Act 1973 s. 44, and must observe financial limits relating to fines and compensation orders.   [3] See *Calvert* (1962) 47 Cr. App. R. 26.
[4] *Wilcox* 21.11.64, 2275/64, decided on the same words in Criminal Justice Act 1948 s. 12(1). The Court held that the reference in the sub-section to 'any subsequent proceedings which may be taken against the offender under the foregoing provisions of this Act' was not limited to such proceedings in respect of the same offence.
[5] See generally *Devine* (1956) 40 Cr. App. R. 45; *Holmes* (1965) 50 Cr. App. R. 86;

In dealing with an offender who has committed an offence during the currency of a probation order, the sentencer has the choice between imposing a punitive sentence such as a fine or imprisonment, which will terminate the order, imposing a further probation order or other individualized measure, or ignoring the offence and allowing the order to continue unaffected. In *Crowley*[1] a young man with a long history of institutional life was convicted for the second time of offences committed during the currency of a probation order made for a number of burglaries (the first offences resulted in a fresh probation order). The sentencer was advised that despite the latest offences the offender had for the first time gone for a year without committing an offence, but felt bound to impose a sentence of imprisonment. The Court indicated that this approach was not necessarily correct. While 'every court should be slow to make another probation order when one has been breached, and even slower still if there have been more than one breaches of that order . . . all cases must be viewed in the light of their particular facts'. In view of the 'dramatic improvement' in the appellant's behaviour, and the fact that the latest offences were the result of a spontaneous outburst of temper, the Court decided to give the appellant 'a final chance'. A further probation order was substituted. Similarly in *Hyland*[2] the appellant was put on probation for assisting an offender to avoid apprehension; having complied with the conditions of the order for about eighteen months, he was convicted of possessing an offensive weapon (two pieces of broken glass) and sentenced by a magistrates' court to three months' imprisonment suspended for two years. He had picked up the glass after being threatened by a fellow lodger with a history of disturbed behaviour, and was arrested by police officers to whom he reported the threats. Following this conviction he was brought before the Crown Court which had made the original probation order and sentenced to nine months' imprisonment for the original offence. The Court held that this sentence was 'not justified', in view of the appellant's positive response to the probation order and the facts of the subsequent offence. A further probation order was made. Many similar cases can be found.

Where the probationer who commits a further offence during the currency of the probation order is sentenced to imprisonment for the subsequent offence, he should normally be sentenced also for the offence in respect of which the probation order was made. This

---

see also *Philbert* 9.10.72, 3096/A/72, [1973] Crim. L. R. 129.
[1] 19.11.71, 3759/A/71.
[2] 19.10.73, 4175/C/73.

sentence will terminate the probation order, prevent the operation of Powers of Criminal Courts Act 1973 s.13(1) and affect the application of the Rehabilitation of Offenders Act 1974.[1] The Court has stated that such a sentence should normally be consecutive to the sentence for the later offence.[2] An offence in respect of which a probation order has been made should never be taken into consideration on sentencing the probationer for a subsequent offence,[3] and a sentence passed for the original offence should properly reflect its gravity (subject to the totality principle).

Where the offender is sentenced for the subsequent offence to a sentence such as borstal training or detention in a detention centre, where a consecutive sentence of imprisonment would be inappropriate, the proper course is to pass a concurrent similar sentence in respect of the original offence, or, if the original order was made by a magistrates' court, a concurrent nominal sentence of imprisonment[4] (which must be for not less than five days).[5]

POLICY IN THE USE OF PROBATION

The probation order is clearly the most important individualized measure available to the sentencer. It is not limited to any one group of offenders; as the discussion in chapter one illustrates, probation is used to deal with recidivists of mature years as well as the young and those of good character. The essential feature of probation is the supervision of the probation officer; where the offender does not require or is unlikely to respond to such supervision, or where supervision will be impractical because of the offender's occupation, a different measure will usually be appropriate.[6]

Community Service

CONDITIONS OF ELIGIBILITY

A community service order may be made against an offender who has attained the age of 17 and is convicted of an offence punishable in the case of an adult with imprisonment.[7] The effect of the order is to

[1] See Rehabilitation of Offenders Act 1974 s. 6(3).

[2] See *Webb* (1953) 2 Q. B. 390 ('it is important that offenders should be made to realize that discharge, whether on probation or conditionally, is not a mere formality, and that a subsequent offence committed during the operative period of the order will involve punishment of the crime for which the offender was originally given the benefit of this lenient treatment').

[3] See *Fry* (1955) 38 Cr. App. R. 157.

[4] See *Stuart* (1964) 49 Cr. App. R. 17.

[5] This is the shortest term of imprisonment that a magistrates' court may impose; see Magistrates' Courts Act 1952 s. 107(1).

[6] See, for example, *Harrison-Jones* 19.2.73, 2878/B/72, p. 227 above.

[7] Powers of Criminal Courts Act 1973 s. 14(1).

require the offender to perform unpaid work under the direction of a probation officer [1] for the number of hours (not less than 40 nor more than 240) specified in the order. The nature of the work to be performed, and the precise distribution of the hours of work over the permitted period of twelve months, are the responsibility of the probation officer. [2]

A community service order may be made only if the court has been notified that arrangements exist for the performance of work under such orders by persons who reside in the petty sessions area in which the offender resides or will reside, and that provision can be made for the particular offender. The sentencer must also be satisfied, 'after considering a report by a probation officer about the offender and his circumstances', that the offender is a suitable person to be subject to a community service order. [3] Where community service orders are made in respect of more than one offence, the court may direct that the hours of work specified in the orders be performed concurrently or separately, but the total number of hours of work ordered to be performed must not exceed 240. [4] Where an offender already subject to a community service order is made the subject of a further order, the court making the later order may order it to take effect consecutively to the existing order. [5]

A community service order takes the place of any other sentence for the offence in respect of which it is imposed, but the court may order the offender to pay the costs of the prosecution, pay compensation or make restitution under the relevant statutory provisions. The offender may also be disqualified from driving, an order for confiscation of property may be made against him [6] or he may be made subject to a criminal bankruptcy order. [7] There is no statutory prohibition against combining a community service order in respect of one offence with any other form of sentence for an offence for which the offender is convicted at the same time. It is submitted that it is inappropriate to impose either an immediate custodial sentence or a suspended sentence of imprisonment at the same time as a community service order.

Before making a community service order the sentencer must explain to the offender 'in ordinary language' the purpose and effect

[1] *Ibid.*, s. 14(4). A person other than a probation officer may be appointed to direct the work.

[2] *Ibid.*, s. 15.

[3] Powers of Criminal Courts Act 1973 s. 14(2).

[4] *Ibid.*, s. 14(3). The statutory limit of 240 hours appears to apply only to orders made on the same occasion.

[5] *Evans* (1976) 64 Cr. App. R. 127.

[6] Under Powers of Criminal Courts Act 1973 s. 43; the application of Misuse of Drugs Act 1971 s. 27 and Firearms Act 1968 s. 52 are not clear.

[7] Powers of Criminal Courts Act 1973 s. 14(8).

of the order, the consequences of failure to comply with the order and the existence of the court's power to review the order.[1] The offender must consent to the making of the order.[2]

FAILURE TO COMPLY WITH THE REQUIREMENTS OF A COMMUNITY SERVICE ORDER

Where an offender subject to a community service order made by the Crown Court fails to comply with the requirement of the order, he may be brought before the magistrates' court for the petty sessions area specified in the order; if the court is satisfied that he has 'failed without reasonable excuse to comply' with the statutory requirements attaching to an order, the court may impose a fine not exceeding £50 and allow the order to continue, or commit him (in custody or on bail) to the Crown Court. If it is proved[3] to the satisfaction of the Crown Court that the offender has failed to comply with the statutory requirements, the court may impose a fine not exceeding £50[4] and allow the order to continue, or revoke the order and deal with the offender for the offence in respect of which the order was made 'in any manner in which he could have been dealt with for that offence by the court which made the order if the order had not been made'.[5]

AMENDMENT OF THE ORDER

Either the probation officer responsible for the administration of the order or the offender may apply to the appropriate magistrates' court for amendment or revocation of a community service order made in the Crown Court. The magistrates' court may extend the period of twelve months within which the requirements of the order must be fulfilled, if 'it appears . . . that it would be in the interests of justice to do so having regard to circumstances which have arisen since the order was made'.[6] Where the application to revoke the order is made,

[1] *Ibid.*, s. 14(5).

[2] *Ibid.*, s. 14(2).

[3] The certificate of the magistrates' court is admissible but not conclusive evidence (Powers of Criminal Courts Act 1973 s. 16(4)). The issue is determined by the court without a jury (*ibid.*, s. 16(7)).

[4] The fine is deemed to be adjudged to be paid by a conviction (*ibid.*, s. 16(8)) and the usual ancillary orders should be made as in the case of a fine imposed on conviction (see p. 317).

[5] *Ibid.*, s. 16(5); contrast s. 6(6)(c) dealing with the equivalent situation in respect of a probation order where the court is empowered to deal with the offender 'as if he had just been convicted . . . of that offence'. These provisions create different effects where the offender reaches the age of 21 between the making of the original order, whether probation or community service, and the subsequent appearance.

[6] Powers of Criminal Courts Act 1973 s. 17(1).

the magistrates' court may commit the offender to the Crown Court,[1] where the order may be revoked if it appears to the Crown Court to be in the interests of justice to do so, having regard to circumstances which have arisen since the order was made. If the order is revoked the court may deal with the offender for the original offence as if the order had not been made, but is not bound to do so.[2]

CONVICTION OF AN OFFENCE DURING THE CURRENCY OF THE ORDER

Where an offender subject to a community service order is convicted before the Crown Court of an offence, or committed for sentence to the Crown Court following a conviction in the magistrates' court, the Crown Court may revoke the order and deal with the offender for the original offence as if the order had not been made.[3] It is not necessary that the offence should have been committed during the currency of the community service order. A conviction after the completion of the work required by the order, for an offence committed while the order was current, does not give the sentencer power to deal with the offender for the offence in respect of which the community service order was made (the converse of the rule applicable to probation orders and suspended sentences).

POLICY IN THE USE OF THE COMMUNITY SERVICE ORDER

The small number of cases where the Court has substituted a community service order for a sentence of some other kind do not provide a basis for generalization.

Suspended Sentences of Imprisonment

A court which passes a sentence of imprisonment for an offence[4] for a term of not more than two years may order that the sentence shall not take effect unless the offender commits another offence punishable with imprisonment during the period specified in the order (the 'operational period'). The operational period must be at least twelve months and may not exceed two years.[5]

The fact that a sentence is to be suspended does not release the

---

[1] *Ibid.*, s. 17(2).
[2] *Ibid.*, s. 17(3).
[3] *Ibid.*, s. 17(3) as amended.
[4] A sentence imposed on an 'incorrigible rogue' under Vagrancy Act 1824 s. 10 may not be suspended (*Theophile* 23.6.75, 2179/B/75, [1975] Crim. L. R. 644).
[5] Powers of Criminal Courts Act 1973 s. 22(1).

sentencer from any of the restrictions surrounding the imposition of sentences of imprisonment on particular categories of offenders. The sentence must comply with the requirements of Criminal Justice Act 1961 s. 3[1] and Powers of Criminal Courts Act 1973 s. 19(2),[2] s. 20(1)[3] and s. 21(1),[4] where those provisions apply.[5]

The Court has stated many times that a sentencer contemplating a suspended sentence should first consider whether the offence would justify a sentence of imprisonment in the absence of a power to suspend.[6] If the offence would justify an immediate sentence of imprisonment, the proper length of the sentence should be determined, having regard to the gravity of the offence and the mitigation. If the length of the sentence so determined is not more than two years, the sentencer may consider suspension. The making of an order for suspension does not justify the imposition of a sentence of imprisonment where an immediate sentence of imprisonment would be wrong in principle. In *Bubber*[7] the appellant was sentenced to six months' imprisonment suspended for causing death by dangerous driving. The Court stated that on the facts of the offence 'the present case does not begin to come within the category which merits an immediate sentence of imprisonment . . . by parity of reasoning it certainly does not merit a suspended sentence'. The sentence was quashed. In *O'Leary*[8] a man of good character was convicted of handling a stolen ring; in view of the statutory injunction against imposing a sentence of imprisonment on such an offender unless 'no other means of dealing with him is appropriate'[9] the Court held that the sentence was incorrect: 'before one can pass a suspended sentence one has to be certain that the offence calls for imprisonment . . . on general principles'. The sentence was quashed.

Equally, an order for suspension does not justify the imposition of a sentence of any greater length than would be appropriate as an immediate sentence. In *Cochrane*[10] the Court held that the 'right approach . . . was to determine the period of imprisonment

[1] Lengths of sentence which may be imposed on young adult offenders (see below p. 276).
[2] General restriction on imposition of imprisonment on young adult offenders (see below p. 275).
[3] General restriction on imposition of imprisonment on adult offenders who have not previously served a term of imprisonment (see below, p. 376).
[4] Restriction on imposition of imprisonment on unrepresented offender in certain circumstances (see below, p. 378).
[5] See *Reynolds* 27.7.71, 77/C/71 (decided on Criminal Justice Act 1948 s. 17(2)).
[6] This principle has been given legislative effect; see Powers of Criminal Courts Act 1973 s. 22(2).
[7] 11.7.74, 551/B/74.
[8] 2.12.74, 1236/C/74, see also *Green* 20.2.76, 4520/B/75.
[9] Powers of Criminal Courts Act 1973 s. 20(1).
[10] 14.1.74, 4683/A/73. For a similar statement, see *Willis* 23.11.76, 4262/C/76.

. . . appropriate to the case and then, after deciding what that period was, to decide whether it should be suspended or not'. As a co-defendant, whose responsibility for the offence (handling stolen goods) was considered by the sentencer to be equal to the appellant's, had received six months' immediate imprisonment, 'there was an error in principle' in imposing two years' imprisonment suspended on the appellant. The sentence was reduced to six months suspended. In *Crichton*[1] a sentence of two years' imprisonment suspended was imposed on a young man for burglary of a wine shop in the course of a 'drunken escapade'. The Court observed that the sentencer's object in passing the sentence was 'to get this young man on the right lines', but he had made the 'very common error' of 'forgetting the elementary principle that the sentence must be appropriate to the offence'. The sentence was reduced to twelve months suspended. In *Trowbridge*[2] a man of essentially good character was sentenced to two years' imprisonment suspended for his part in a burglary; his co-defendants, both with substantial records, received immediate sentences of twelve months and six months imprisonment respectively. The Court assumed that the sentencer had 'imposed a longer sentence on the appellant, because he suspended the sentence, whereas the sentences imposed on the other two were immediate'. This was 'a wrong reason' for such discrimination; the length of sentence should be determined before considering the question of suspension, and 'the sentences passed must be related to the nature of the offence, the antecedents and all other relevant considerations, whether the trial judge decides to suspend that sentence or not'. The sentence was reduced to six months suspended.[3]

CONSECUTIVE AND CONCURRENT TERMS

Where the offender is sentenced on the same occasion for two or more offences, the power to suspend arises only where the aggregate of the sentences imposed does not exceed two years.[4] Where a sentencer imposes a series of sentences consecutive to each other, each individually not more than two years but amounting in aggregate to a term in excess of that period, he may not suspend the aggregate.[5] Where a sentence in excess of two years, whether an aggregate of

[1] 9.12.74, 2897/A/74.

[2] 23.9.74, 1210/C/74, [1975] Crim. L. R. 295.

[3] The decision of the Court in *Jacobson* 31.1.77, 1696/A/76, [1977] Crim. L. R. 368 appears to be inconsistent with the cases cited in the text.

[4] Powers of Criminal Courts Act 1973 s. 57(2); see *Coleman* (1969) 53 Cr. App. R. 445.

[5] See *Wallace* 21.4.70, 2407/69 (three terms each of two years, all consecutive, suspended; sentence invalid; reduced to two years on each count concurrent, all suspended).

individual terms or a single term, is ordered to be suspended, the sentence of imprisonment is valid but the order for suspension is ineffective, with the result that the offender is liable to serve the sentence immediately.[1]

Where a sentencer is dealing with the offender on the same occasion in respect of two or more offences and intends to suspend the sentence he imposes, he must decide whether they will take effect, if enforced, consecutively or concurrently; this is necessary, in particular, to determine whether there is power to suspend.[2] If he orders them to take effect, if enforced, as consecutive terms, a court enforcing the sentence on a conviction for a subsequent offence should treat them as if they were a single term;[3] the court dealing with the offender on the subsequent occasion has no power to order the earlier terms to take effect in a manner contrary to the original order.[4] Different principles apply where an offender already subject to a suspended sentence comes before a court for a different offence and receives a second suspended sentence. In this event the court imposing the second suspended sentence has no power to order the sentences to take effect in a particular manner if they come to be enforced on a subsequent occasion. This decision is the responsibility of the court which eventually enforces the sentence.[5]

SUSPENDED SENTENCES COMBINED WITH OTHER SENTENCES

As a general principle, it is undesirable that an offender should be subject at the same time to a custodial sentence and a suspended sentence. A sentencer should not impose on the same occasion a suspended sentence and a custodial sentence, whether in the form of an immediate sentence of imprisonment[6] or borstal training.[7] An offender who is already serving a custodial sentence should not be

---

[1] *Arkle* (1972) 56 Cr. App. R. 722. A sentencer dealing with an offender who has been unlawfully at large under such a sentence has no power to order the sentence to be served in the event of a conviction for a subsequent offence, and may not cure the defect by ordering the sentence to be served with a reduced term under Powers of Criminal Courts Act 1973 s. 23(1)(b) (*Dainton* 21.4.70, 7851/A/69). The Court of Appeal on appeal from such a sentence may substitute a term which is capable of suspension (*Roberts* 11.4.73, 758/A/73). As this variation amounts to the substitution of a suspended term for a term which was effectively an immediate term, an offence committed after the purported suspension in the Crown Court, but before the suspension on appeal, is not grounds for enforcing the sentence.

[2] *Wilkinson* (1970) 54 Cr. App. R. 437.

[3] See *Gall* 17.2.70, 6273/69, [1970] Crim. L. R. 297.

[4] The court enforcing the sentence may order it to take effect with a reduced term; see Powers of Criminal Courts Act 1973 s. 23(1)(b).

[5] *Blakeway* (1969) 53 Cr. App. R. 498; *Packer* 8.2.74, 4833/A/73.

[6] *Sapiano* (1968) 52 Cr. App. R. 674.

[7] *Baker* (1971) 55 Cr. App. R. 182.

subjected to a suspended sentence so that part of the operational period will run while he is in custody and the sentence will be hanging over him on his release.[1] A similar principle applies where an offender already subject to a suspended sentence receives an immediate sentence of imprisonment for a subsequent offence. The sentencer should normally activate the suspended sentence, to avoid 'a mixing-up of immediate and suspended sentences'.[2] In some cases (where the later offence was committed before the suspended sentence was imposed) this course will not be possible. In such cases the fact that the offender has just received a suspended sentence in respect of one offence should not necessarily inhibit a sentencer, dealing with him on a different occasion for other offences of a more serious nature, from imposing an immediate sentence of imprisonment in respect of those offences where that sentence is clearly required and 'mixing-up' cannot be avoided.[3]

Powers of Criminal Courts Act 1973 s. 22(3) prohibits a court which passes a suspended sentence on an offender from making a probation order in his case in respect of other offences.[4] The restriction applies whether the offences are charged as different counts of the same indictment or in different indictments.[5] (It is submitted that the section should be read as if it contained the words 'on the same occasion', otherwise its effect would be to prevent the Crown Court from making a probation order in any case where the offender was subject to a suspended sentence made in the Crown Court, whether by the same or a different judge of the Crown Court.)[6] Where a suspended sentence and a probation order are imposed in such a way as to infringe the section, the suspended sentence is valid and the probation order is void.[7]

A suspended sentence may be combined with a fine.[8] The sentencer must approach the case by determining that imprisonment is appropriate in principle, fixing the term and then deciding to suspend; the fine is imposed as a supplementary penalty.[9] A suspended sentence will not be upheld where the sentencer decides that the case is one which can properly be dealt with by means of a fine, and adds a suspended sentence, either as a penalty supplementary to the fine or because the offender has no means to pay

---

[1] See *Fitzgerald* (1971) 55 Cr. App. R. 515; *Dick* 20.9.71, 2249/C/71, [1972] Crim. L. R. 58; *McDonnell* 14.9.76, 1633/A/76.
[2] *Goodlad* (1973) 57 Cr. App. R. 586.
[3] See *Sorrell* (1971) 55 Cr. App. R. 573; *Goodlad, ibid.*
[4] The restriction does not apply to conditional discharges.
[5] See *Wright* 30.6.75, 1204/B/75, [1975] Crim. L. R. 728.
[6] See Courts Act 1971 s. 4.
[7] *Wright, ibid.*; *Watler* 6.4.76, 5160/B/75.
[8] *Leigh* (1969) 54 Cr. App. R. 169; and see the discussion at p. 324 below.
[9] See *Genese* (1976) 63 Cr. App. R. 152.

it.[1] In *Hewkin*[2] a woman of good character was convicted of two offences of shoplifting and sentenced to a total of twelve months' imprisonment suspended and a fine of £100. The Court took the view that 'this was a case where the applicant could appropriately be dealt with by a susbstantial financial penalty', and while the fine was 'entirely appropriate' the sentence of imprisonment, although suspended, was wrong in principle; it was accordingly quashed.

PROCEDURE

A court passing a suspended sentence must explain to the offender 'in ordinary language' his liability to serve the sentence if he is subsequently convicted of an offence committed during the operational period of the sentence.[3] The consent of the offender is not required.

Where the offender has spent a substantial period of time in custody pending trial for the offence in respect of which the suspended sentence is imposed, the sentencer imposing the suspended sentence should allow in the length of the suspended term for the fact that this time will not be deducted from the length of the sentence if it is subsequently enforced.[4]

POLICY IN THE USE OF SUSPENDED SENTENCES

The suspended sentence does not fit easily into the general body of sentencing principles which was evolved by the Court before the legislative creation of the suspended sentence in 1967. The correct approach to the use of the power to suspend a sentence, as has been illustrated, requires the sentencer to consider and reject the use of individualized measures such as probation before concluding that imprisonment is the appropriate sentence. The proper length of the sentence must then be determined, having regard to the gravity of the offence and the mitigation. When this process has been completed, the sentencer may turn his attention to the question of suspension. The difficulty that arises at this point is that if the first two stages have been followed correctly, all factors which are relevant to the sentence should have been taken into account already. The sentencer must either give double weight to some factors for which he has previously made allowance in calculating the length of the sentence, or search for some new factors which will justify suspension although they are not

[1] See the cases discussed at p. 325 above.
[2] 16.2.76, 2426/B/75.
[3] Powers of Criminal Courts Act 1973 s. 22(4).
[4] *Deering* 10.2.76, 3218/A/75, [1976] Crim. L. R. 638.

relevant to the other issues which the sentencer has already considered. The process is not made easier by the existence of statutes prohibiting the imposition of imprisonment on certain categories of offenders unless 'no other means of dealing with him is appropriate'.[1]

A clear illustration of this problem is provided by *Fisk*.[2] A farmer was sentenced to thirty months' imprisonment for possessing a firearm with intent to endanger life. It was alleged that he had loaded a rifle when police officers came to his house in connection with a driving offence, but he had not threatened them. The Court stated that 'the questions which the sentencing court has to ask are, first, whether or not a custodial sentence is required; secondly . . . if it is required, how long a custodial sentence, and thirdly, are there any special circumstances . . . which indicate that a sentence of that particular length should be suspended'. Two matters were urged as grounds for suspension—the fact that the appellant's intent was short-lived and did not extend to the making of threats, and the effect of his imprisonment on the farm. The Court held that the first of these matters was relevant to the length of the term rather than the question of suspension, and justified a reduction in the length of the sentence to twelve months. As that factor was then 'taken . . . out of the question which one has to consider when looking at . . . suspension', the only factor which could justify suspension of the sentence as reduced was the effect of the appellant's imprisonment on the future of the farm; in the particular circumstances this was not a 'substantial reason for suspending the sentence for an offence as serious as this'.

In practice the suspended sentence has become associated with certain categories of cases, although it is not limited to them. The most typical use of the suspended sentence, so far as the Court of Appeal is concerned, is in the case of an offender of previous good character who has committed an offence of a relatively serious nature (but not in the first order of gravity) under circumstances of substantial mitigation. In *Law*[3] a farm worker of 'positive good character' set fire to the semi-detached cottage where he lived, while depressed as a result of matrimonial problems. It was accepted that the appellant had no intent to cause injury or endanger life, and that he had lost many of his own possessions in the fire; the risk of repetition was 'absolutely minimal'. The Court considered that the sentence of three years' imprisonment imposed by the trial judge was neither wrong in principle nor manifestly excessive, but the possibility of a complete breakdown of the marriage, and the favourable

---

[1] See Powers of Criminal Courts Act 1973 s. 19 (young adult offenders); also s. 20(1) (adult offender who has not served a previous sentence of imprisonment).

[2] 6.9.73, 2174/A/73.

[3] 24.4.75, 38/B/75.

attitude of his employer who owned the cottage, justified the Court in reducing the sentence to eighteen months and suspending it for two years. In *Parker*[1] a man of 'positively excellent character' threw at his wife the contents of a bottle of a solution of acid which had been obtained for normal domestic use; no significant injury was caused. The Court held that 'the gravity of this offence demanded that a sentence of imprisonment should be passed', but that the sentence of two years imposed by the trial judge did not make sufficient allowance for the appellant's record; a term of twelve months would have been sufficient. In addition, the fact that the offence was 'an isolated incident arising as a result of an unhappy marriage', and was 'quite out of character', enabled the Court to suspend the sentence for two years. In a third case[2] two university students admitted possessing a substantial quantity of cannabis and were each sentenced to twelve months' imprisonment. The Court held that in view of the quantity of cannabis involved the sentence could not be faulted, but as the appellants had both left the university and were determined to give up using cannabis, the Court could find 'special circumstances which enable it to be merciful whilst at the same time making it clear that imprisonment for this type of offence may well follow the finding of these quantities of cannabis'. The sentence was suspended.

The use of the suspended sentence is not limited to first offenders; in particular it may be used in the case of an offender with a substantial record who has succeeded in avoiding conflict with the law over a recent period of time. In *Murdoch*[3] a man of 36 with three previous convictions for breaking offences was sentenced to twelve months' immediate imprisonment for handling a quantity of stolen brass. The Court stated that 'a sentence of imprisonment is the right one for this kind of offence', but the fact that the appellant had had no convictions during the last six years, and had 'conscientiously supported the family' (a total of eleven children), made it 'possible to suspend the sentence'. In *Glenister*[4] a man with 'a very long and bad record' was sentenced to eighteen months' immediate imprisonment for stealing a quantity of building materials worth about £50 from his employer. The Court held that an eighteen months was 'far too long . . . for the type of theft' and that the fact that 'he did manage to

[1] 15.4.75, 5280/A/74.

[2] *Molins and Robson* 26.10.72, 4011/A/72, [1973] Crim. L. R. 62; see also *Weller* 20.12.74, 3928/C/74 (forgery of wife's signature on transfer of house held on joint tenancy, wife not deprived of share of proceeds of sale, offender 'a person of good character under strain'; "a sentence of imprisonment was right in principle, but on the facts there were special reasons which would have justified the suspension of that sentence'—eighteen months immediate varied to twelve months suspended).

[3] 30.7.73, 2962/C/73.

[4] 25.7.72, 2655/A/72.

keep out of trouble for more than a year' enabled the Court to 'give him a chance'. The sentence was varied to six months' imprisonment, suspended for two years.

Apart from these categories of cases, the suspended sentence may be used where unusual circumstances justify a departure from the normal sentence. The Court does not appear to favour the use of a suspended sentence as part of a progression from probation towards immediate imprisonment, and has warned against the dangers of allowing multiple combinations of suspended sentences and in-dividualized measures to mount up against an individual offender, which may result in his facing a long sentence of imprisonment if the various sentences are eventually enforced.[1]

SUSPENDED-SENTENCE SUPERVISION ORDERS

Provision is made for a court which imposes[2] a suspended sentence of more than six months to make a suspended-sentence supervision order placing the offender under the supervision of a probation officer for a specified period, not exceeding the operational period of the suspended sentence.[3] The order, which does not need the consent of the offender, requires him to 'keep in touch with the supervising officer' and to notify the officer of any change of address.[4] No additional requirements may be inserted. The order ceases to have effect if the offender is subsequently ordered to serve the sentence,[5] or the order is discharged by the appropriate court.[6] If the offender fails to comply with the requirements of a supervision order, he may be brought before the appropriate magistrates' court and fined an amount not exceeding £50. There is no power to order him to serve the sentence.

A suspended-sentence supervision order is not an alternative to probation. It should be used only where the other requirements of the suspended sentence are satisfied.

ENFORCEMENT OF A SUSPENDED SENTENCE

An offender subject to a suspended sentence imposed by the Crown

---

[1] *Smith* 26.11.71, 1895/C/71, [1972] Crim. L. R. 124 (above, p. 60); see also *Thompson* 4.12.73, 3829/C/73 ('the moral of this case might be . . . do not pass a series of suspended sentences one after another . . . because . . . when the time comes. . . to activate . . . the result may . . . produce an aggregate sentence which is very much too high').

[2] The power may also be exercised when a court extends the operational period of an existing suspended sentence of more than six months (Powers of Criminal Courts Act 1973 s. 26(10)).

[3] Powers of Criminal Courts Act 1973 s. 26(1).   [5] *Ibid.*, s. 26(8).

[4] *Ibid.*, s. 26(4).   [6] *Ibid.*, s. 26(9).

Court, who is subsequently convicted in the Crown Court of an offence punishable with imprisonment committed during the operational period of the suspended sentence, must be dealt with by the Crown Court in respect of the suspended sentence.[1] The Crown Court must also deal with an offender convicted before the Crown Court of an offence committed during the operational period of a suspended sentence imposed by a magistrates' court.[2] Where an offender subject to a suspended sentence imposed by the Crown Court is convicted of an offence in the magistrates' court, the magistrates' court may commit the offender to the Crown Court to be dealt with in respect of the suspended sentence;[3] alternatively the Crown Court may issue process to bring the offender before it.[4]

The power to deal with the offender in respect of a suspended sentence arises where he is 'convicted of an offence punishable with imprisonment committed during the operational period of a suspended sentence'.[5] Where the offender is convicted during the operational period of an offence committed before the imposition of the suspended sentence, there is no power to enforce sentence,[6] but the sentence may be enforced where the offender is convicted after the expiration of the operational period of an offence committed during the operational period.[7]

The suspended sentence may be enforced only if there is a conviction for the subsequent offence. If the offender is granted a conditional discharge or made subject to a probation order for the subsequent offence there is no conviction and accordingly no power to enforce the sentence, unless the offender is subsequently sentenced for the offence in respect of which the discharge or probation order was made.[8] Where the court dealing with the offender for the later offence defers sentence under Powers of Criminal Courts Act 1973 s. 1, there is no power to enforce the suspended sentence until the offender is eventually sentenced.[9] By the same reasoning, an offence which is taken into consideration cannot provide a basis for enforcing a suspended sentence.

Where an offender subject to a suspended sentence is subsequently sentenced to borstal training, whether or not the offence for which he is sentenced to borstal training was committed during the operational

---

[1] *Ibid.*, s. 24(1).
[2] Powers of Criminal Courts Act 1973 s. 24(1).
[3] *Ibid.*, s. 24(2). If it fails to commit, the magistrates' court must notify the Crown Court of the conviction.
[4] *Ibid.*, s. 25.
[5] *Ibid.*, s. 23(1).
[6] *Daurge* 13.11.72, 2443/A/72.
[7] See *Taylor* 18.4.75, 709/C/75.
[8] See Powers of Criminal Courts Act 1973 s. 13(1); *Tarry* (1970) 54 Cr. App. R. 322.
[9] See *Salmon* (1973) 57 Cr. App. R. 953.

period of the suspended sentence, the offender ceases to be liable to the suspended sentence.[1] The sentence may accordingly not be enforced either on the same occasion as the sentence of borstal training is imposed,[2] or in the event of a further conviction,[3] even though the further conviction is for an offence committed before the sentence of borstal training was imposed. Liability in respect of the suspended sentence revives if the sentence of borstal training is subsequently quashed.[4]

A court which has power to deal with an offender in respect of a suspended sentence must 'consider his case and deal with him' in one of four ways: the court may order the sentence to take effect with the original term unaltered; it may order the sentence to take effect with the substitution of a lesser term for the original term; it may vary the original order by substituting a further period of suspension expiring not later than two years from the date of the variation; or it may make no order with respect to the suspended sentence.[5] The sentencer must order the sentence to take effect with the original term unaltered unless the court is 'of opinion that it would be unjust to do so in view of all the circumstances which have arisen since the suspended sentence was passed', and where it is of that opinion 'the court shall state its reasons'.[6]

An offender subject to a suspended sentence who is convicted of a further offence may be 'dealt with' only once in respect of each subsequent conviction. If a judge of the Crown Court having power to deal with the offender makes no order under Powers of Criminal Courts Act 1973 s. 23(1)(d), the offender cannot be brought before another judge of the Crown Court to be dealt with in respect of the same subsequent conviction.[7] Where a judge of the Crown Court has power to deal with an offender in respect of a suspended sentence, but fails to exercise the power, the offender may be brought before the Crown Court on a subsequent occasion and dealt with.[8] For this reason the sentencer should ensure that his intention to deal with the offender by making no order under s. 23(1)(d) is understood and recorded.

Although the court enforcing the suspended sentence may order it to take effect with a reduced term, it may not vary the nature of the sentence by substituting a different form of custodial sentence. Where

[1] Powers of Criminal Courts Act 1973 s. 22(5).
[2] See *Talbot* 14.5.70, 2264/70. The sentencer should not deal with the suspended sentence in this situation.
[3] See *Courtney* 3.3.70, 8593/B/69.
[4] Powers of Criminal Courts Act 1973 s. 22(5).
[5] *Ibid.*, s. 23(1).
[6] Powers of Criminal Courts Act 1973 s. 23(1).
[7] See *Barrett* 30.7.70, 485/A/70.
[8] See Powers of Criminal Courts Act 1973 s. 25(1).

the offender could have been sentenced to detention in a detention centre on the occasion of the original order, if he had been convicted by the court enforcing the sentence, and the sentence is ordered to take effect with a term not exceeding six months, the court may direct that the sentence be served in a detention centre,[1] but it remains a sentence of imprisonment.

The Court has stated that in dealing with an offender who is subject to a suspended sentence the first duty of the sentencer is to decide what sentence is appropriate to the latest offence, before passing to consider the question whether the suspended sentence should be enforced.[2] If the sentencer imposes an immediate sentence of imprisonment for the latest offence and decides to enforce the suspended sentence,[3] the suspended sentence should normally be ordered to take effect consecutively to the immediate sentence.[4] A different principle applies where the latest sentence is an extended sentence; in this case the suspended sentence should be enforced concurrently.[5] There is no power to certify the suspended sentence as an extended term on the occasion of enforcement.[6] As the length of an extended sentence is not necessarily limited by the gravity of the offence for which it is imposed, the sentencer may reflect in the length of the extended sentence the fact that the suspended sentence is to be enforced concurrently rather than consecutively,[7] but as the main function of an extended sentence is preventive rather than punitive, 'a judge passing sentence should bear in mind that that sentence already exceeds the period strictly required for the instant offence and should not be ready . . . to extend it still further on account of some other offence'.[8]

The enforcement of a suspended sentence does not constitute the imposition of a sentence of imprisonment for the purpose of Criminal Justice Act 1961 s. 3,[9] and a sentencer dealing with a young adult offender who is subject to an existing suspended sentence must disregard the effect of enforcing that sentence in observing the requirements of the section. The sentence may be enforced even

---

[1] *Ibid.*, s. 23(3). Such a direction may be included where the enforced term is less than three months, if the offender is then liable to be detained in a detention centre in respect of another offence, whether or not he could have been sentenced to detention at the time of the original conviction (s. 23(4)).

[2] *Ithell* (1969) 53 Cr. App. R. 210; *Miller* 23.7.74, 2481/C/74.

[3] Where an immediate sentence is passed for the later offence, the suspended sentence should normally be enforced; see *Goodlad* (1973) 57 Cr. App. R. 586.

[4] *Ithell* (1969) 53 Cr. App. R. 210.

[5] See generally, *Wilkinson* (1969) 53 Cr. App. R. 560; *Moran* 7.5.70, 6921/69; *Roberts* (1971) 55 Cr. App. R. 329.

[6] *Barrett* (1969) 53 Cr. App. R. 531.

[7] *Wilkinson, Ibid.*

[8] *McCutcheon* 27.4.71, 6437/C/70.

[9] *Lamb* (1968) 52 Cr. App. R. 667.

though the cumulative length of the enforced suspended sentence and the sentence imposed for the latest offence is within the prohibited range.[1] Conversely the enforcement of a suspended sentence consecutive to an immediate sentence which is within the prohibited range will not justify that sentence, even though if imposed as a single term the aggregate sentence would be lawful.[2] A sentencer may enforce a suspended sentence with a reduced term even though the original sentence would not have been lawful if passed with that term.[3]

An offender who is ordered to serve a suspended sentence does not receive credit for any time spent in custody in connection with the proceedings which led to the original sentence.[4] Where an offender has spent a substantial period in custody before the imposition of the suspended sentence, the sentencer should reflect that period in the length of the suspended sentence;[5] it is not a matter which can properly be considered as a ground for enforcing the sentence with a reduced term, as it is not a circumstance which has arisen since the suspended sentence was passed.[6]

A court considering whether to enforce a suspended sentence following a subsequent conviction is not concerned with the propriety of the sentence in relation to the offence for which it was originally imposed[7] and may not enforce the sentence with a reduced term because it considers the original term excessive. A sentencer may shorten either the immediate sentence for the later offence or the term of the enforced suspended sentence, if the aggregate of the two sentences is excessive under the totality principle, and for this reason should ensure that he has information about the circumstances of the original offence.[8] Where a sentencer is dealing with an offender in respect of a suspended sentence following a later conviction by another court (for example, where a suspended sentence passed in the Crown Court is followed by a conviction in the magistrates' court), the sentencer should have full details of the later offence so that he can

---

[1] *Pike* (1971) 55 Cr. App. R. 455.
[2] *Halse* (1971) 55 Cr. App. R. 47.
[3] *Pike* (1971) 55 Cr. App. R. 455.
[4] Criminal Justice Act 1967 s. 67(1).
[5] See *Pollitt* 13.4.70, 6661/69. The loss of credit may be compensated by reducing the notional sentence by two-thirds of the period spent in custody, as the period spent in custody is subtracted from the nominal length of the sentence, rather than the portion that must be served before remission. Questions of parole eligibility do not arise, as the same minimum period of twelve months must be served in all cases where the sentence is long enough to allow the offender to qualify for parole, but short enough to be capable of supervision.
[6] Powers of Criminal Courts Act 1973 s. 23(1); see *Deering* 10.2.76, 3218/A/75, [1976] Crim. L. R. 638; *contra, Singh* 14.11.74, 2483/A/74.
[7] See *Metcalf* 17.11.70, 8706/R/69, [1971] Crim. L. R. 112.
[8] See *Munday* (1971) 56 Cr. App. R. 220.

decide whether the circumstances justify any course other than activation.[1] Where the offender is subject to more than one suspended sentence, the sentencer should not activate more than an aggregate of two years (not including the sentence for the latest offence).[2]

POLICY IN THE ENFORCEMENT OF SUSPENDED SENTENCES

Powers of Criminal Courts Act 1973 s. 23(1) requires a court which has power to deal with an offender in respect of a suspended sentence to enforce the sentence in full 'unless the court is of opinion that it would be unjust to do so in view of all the circumstances which have arisen since the suspended sentence was passed'. The court must state its reasons for being of this opinion. A number of principles relating to the exercise of this power have been established.

The Court has held that the fact that the subsequent offence is of a different kind from the original offence is not in itself a ground for not enforcing the sentence. In *Saunders*[3] the appellant was sentenced to six months' imprisonment suspended for stealing a tape recorder. Eleven months later he pleaded guilty to dangerous driving and driving while disqualified, for which he was sentenced to twelve months' imprisonment, with the suspended sentence enforced consecutively. The Court upheld these sentences with the observation that 'the mere fact that the current offence is of a different character from the offence for which the suspended sentence was given is no ground whatever for not bringing the suspended sentence into force'. This principle has generally been followed.[4] In *Barton*[5] the appellant was sentenced to twelve months' imprisonment suspended for driving while disqualified and was subsequently convicted of conspiring to handle stolen goods, on evidence that he had lent a car log-book to a friend to facilitate the disposal of a stolen car. The Court upheld the activation of the suspended sentence with the observation that it was not necessary to show that 'the second offence bears some relation to

[1] See *Mordecai* 29.5.70, 2138/70.
[2] *Brown* 1.4.77, 4782/B/76.
[3] (1970) 54 Cr. App. R. 247.
[4] See, for example, *Vanston* 19.10.71, 2120/B/71, [1972] Crim. L. R. 57 (two years suspended for burglary activated on subsequent conviction for driving while disqualified: 'the difference in nature between the offences is a matter which he cannot properly rely on today'); *Smith* 26.6.72, 198/B/72 (six months suspended for burglary activated on conviction for taking conveyance and refusing specimen); *Garrett* 11.2.74, 5399/C/73 (nine months suspended for burglary activated on conviction for dangerous driving and driving with excess blood alcohol level); *Wootton* 28.10.74, 3580/B/74 (eighteen months suspended for burglary activated on conviction for assault occasioning actual bodily harm to mother-in-law).
[5] 11.6.74, 936/C/74, [1974] Crim. L. R. 555.

the earlier offence for which the suspended sentence was passed'.

The cases generally support the view that the relative triviality of the subsequent offence is a factor which the sentencer may consider in deciding whether it would be unjust to enforce the suspended sentence.[1] In *Wilson*[2] a man of 29 with a substantial record was convicted by a magistrates' court of stealing food worth 70p from a supermarket; he was subsequently brought before the Crown Court, where a suspended sentence of two years previously imposed for burglary was activated. The Court received evidence that the appellant had recently married and there was hope for more stable behaviour in the future. Observing that 'when the new offence is comparatively trivial and . . . appears to fall into a different category from that of the offence for which the suspended sentence was passed', there might be grounds for not activating the suspended sentence, the Court came to the conclusion that the new information about the appellant and 'the disparity between that offence and the two-year sentence which was ordered to take effect' had resulted in 'an injust consequence'. The order activating the suspended sentence was quashed. In *Bonehill*[3] the appellant was subject to a suspended sentence of two years for burglary when he broke into a park pavilion to find shelter for himself and the woman with whom he was living. They subsequently consumed some biscuits, thereby completing the offence of burglary for which the appellant was eventually sentenced to three months' imprisonment, with the suspended sentence enforced consecutively. The Court quashed the order enforcing the sentence in view of the nature of the latest offence and evidence that the appellant (who had 'been through the gamut of sentences') had made 'a genuine effort . . . to change his course of life': 'it was wrong to have ordered the activation of so long a suspended sentence as a term of two years . . . when the instant offence which triggered off the possibility . . . was as trivial as that here involved'.

As these cases suggest, the inherent triviality of the subsequent offence is not necessarily a sufficient ground in itself for avoiding activation; the sentencer should consider other factors, such as the behaviour of the offender during the period of suspension, the circumstances preceding the later offence and the length of the suspended sentence. In *Gray*[4] the appellant was convicted of attempting to steal lead from the roof of a building while subject to a

[1] Powers of Criminal Courts Act 1973 s. 23(1) specifically includes 'the facts of the subsequent offence' among the circumstances which may be considered.

[2] 26.10.73, 2989/C/73.

[3] 14.5.76, 1341/A/76; see also *Arnett* 22.6.73, 1536/B/73 (eighteen months suspended sentence for assault and causing grievous bodily harm, subsequent offence of damaging glass covering of bus timetable while drunk; activation quashed).

[4] 14.12.71, 3530/B/71.

suspended sentence of twelve months for burglary, which was enforced consecutively to the twelve months imposed for the new offence. The Court stated that although stealing lead from buildings 'has to be treated seriously', the present offence 'can be regarded as a minor one . . . as that class of offence goes'. The sentence for the later offence was reduced to six months, but partly in view of an unfavourable social inquiry report, the order activating the suspended sentence in full was not varied. In *Brown*[1] a man with a substantial record who was subject to two years' imprisonment suspended for two burglaries, was convicted of stealing nine pairs of ladies' tights in a supermarket. He was sentenced to twelve months' imprisonment for the latest offence, with the suspended sentence activated in full. The Court considered that although the latest offence could be considered 'trivial' and justified no more than six months' imprisonment, there was no ground for avoiding activation of the suspended sentence. The first sentence was reduced but the order enforcing the sentence was upheld.

Although the later offence must be 'punishable with imprisonment' before the suspended sentence may be enforced, it is not necessary that the sentencer should impose a sentence of imprisonment for the later offence in order to enforce the suspended sentence. The Court has upheld the activation of suspended sentences in appropriate circumstances where the later offence was dealt with by means of a fine. In *Murphy*[2] a man of 23 with eighteen previous appearances for 'a wide variety . . . of offences' was sentenced to twelve months' imprisonment suspended for theft of a watch from a jeweller's shop. He had previously served a sentence which had originally been suspended. He subsequently committed two offences of driving while disqualified and without insurance, for which he was fined a total of £30 by the magistrates' court. The Crown Court enforced the suspended sentence, a course the Court endorsed with the comment that although the later offences were both different in character and relatively trivial, they were part of a pattern of persistent law-breaking. In *Raeburn*[3] the appellant was fined a total of £32 for driving while disqualified and stealing a pair of handcuffs from a police station. The Crown Court subsequently enforced a sentence of six months for obtaining by deception which had earlier been suspended as a 'last chance'. As the Crown Court in suspending the sentence had given the appellant credit for a previous interval of five years without conviction, the Court upheld the decision to activate.

The fact that a substantial proportion of the operational period has

1 1.3.71, 4533/B/70.
2 21.10.71, 3839/A/71.
3 3.6.75, 1645/C/75.

elapsed before the commission of the subsequent offence is not a ground for refraining from activation of the sentence,[1] but it is usually held to require some recognition. Most frequently this takes the form of a reduction in the term of the suspended sentence. In *Rafferty*[2] a man of 26 was sentenced to eighteen months' imprisonment for stealing metal worth £6 from a car; a suspended sentence of eighteen months imposed nearly two years earlier for receiving scrap metal was enforced consecutively. The Court held that the sentence of eighteen months for the later offence was excessive and reduced it to six months. Additionally, although the activation of the suspended sentence was justified, the fact that the appellant had almost survived the operational period without committing an offence and had made 'considerable efforts' during that time justified 'a discount' off the suspended sentence, which was reduced to twelve months. In *Broshan*[3] the appellant was sentenced to three months' imprisonment for an offence of obtaining by deception, committed one month before the expiration of the operational period of a suspended sentence of eighteen months imposed for robbery. As he had 'stayed out of trouble for seventeen of the eighteen months . . . for which the sentence was operative', and behaved creditably during the interval, the suspended sentence was activated, but with the term reduced to nine months. In some cases, where the operational period had almost expired before the commission of the later offence, the Court has departed from the normal policy of activating the suspended sentence consecutively to a sentence imposed for the later offence, and ordered it to run concurrently.[4]

As in all cases where sentences are ordered to run consecutively, the final duty of the sentencer is to review the totality of the sentences and reduce it if the aggregate is unjust or excessive, even though the individual component parts are correctly calculated. The detailed application of this principle is discussed in chapter 2; it has been held to apply to the enforcement of suspended sentences as much as to any other context.[5]

[1] See *Evans* 12.10.70, 3026/C/70.

[2] 23.11.71, 2800/B/71.

[3] 21.9.71, 2800/B/71; see also *Smith* 7.5.73, 1001/A/73 (criminal damage committed after twenty-eight months of operational period of suspended sentence imposed under earlier legislation; suspended sentence implemented with term reduced by half).

[4] See, for example, *Toppar* 24.7.75, 1472/A/75 (wounding and assault on police committed twenty-three months after imposition of suspended sentence for burglary and assault with intent to resist arrest; three years upheld but suspended sentence to take effect concurrently); *Doyle* 12.10.71, 2202/C/71 (common assault committed within five weeks of expiration of operational period of suspended sentence for malicious wounding; sentences ordered to run concurrently for this and other reasons, case 'not to be taken as a precedent').

[5] See *Bocskei* (1970) 54 Cr. App. R. 519; see also *Munday* (1972) 56 Cr. App. R. 220.

Sentences held partly in suspense

Criminal Law Act 1977 s. 47 empowers a sentencer who passes on a person of or over the age of 21 a sentence of imprisonment for a term of not less than six months and not more than two years, to order that after part of the sentence has been served the remainder shall be 'held in suspense'. The part ordered to be held in suspense must be not less than one-quarter and not more than three-quarters of the nominal term of the sentence. On making such an order, the sentencer must explain the effect of the order to the offender, 'using ordinary language and stating the substantial effect' of the section. Where such an order is made, the sentencer must not make a probation order against the offender, even though he is convicted of another offence.[1]

Where an offender subject to a sentence held partly in suspense is convicted of an offence punishable with imprisonment committed during any part of the nominal period of the sentence (including presumably the part actually served in prison), a court with authority to do so[2] may restore the part of the sentence held in suspense and order the offender to serve it, unless 'in view of all the circumstances, including the facts of the subsequent offence' it would be 'unjust' to do so.[3] In this event the court may restore a lesser part of the sentence[4] or 'declare, with reasons given, its decision to make no order under the sub-section'. Where an offender is ordered to serve the restored part of a sentence partly held in suspense, the sentencer may order the restored part to be served either immediately or consecutively to another term of imprisonment.[5]

The purpose of this provision, and the criteria which should govern its use, remain to be seen.[6] Presumably the sentencer should not consider the question of partial suspension until he has gone through the normal process of deciding that imprisonment is necessary and determining the proper length of the sentence of imprisonment, and must observe the relevant statutory restrictions on the use of imprisonment in respect of the nominal length of sentence.

[1] Criminal Law Act 1977 sch. 9, para. 1.
[2] The Crown Court may deal with an offender wherever the original order was made; a magistrates' court may deal with an offender subject to an order made by a magistrates' court, and may commit an offender who is subject to an order made in the Crown Court (ibid., para. 2).
[3] Powers of Criminal Courts Act 1973 s. 47(3) and (4).
[4] Presumably in this event the balance of the part of the sentence originally ordered to be held in suspense remains held in suspense and liable to be enforced in the event of any further conviction in respect of an offence committed during the relevant period.
[5] Powers of Criminal Courts Act 1973 s. 47(2). The order for restoration is a 'sentence' for the purpose of rights of appeal (sch. 9, para. 6).
[6] At the time of going to press, the section is not in force.

Sentences for the Young Offender

Offenders under the age of 21 are divided into three groups for the purposes of sentencing legislation:—those aged 17 and under 21 (young adults),[1] those aged 14 and under 17 (young persons),[2] and those under 14 (children).[3] Although the availability of particular sentencing powers does not always coincide with these divisions (the minimum age for borstal training is 15), they provide a useful framework for an examination of the powers of sentencers and the principles on which they should be exercised.

The Young Adult Offender

For offenders aged 17 and under 21 the law provides two special custodial sentences—detention in a detention centre and borstal training—and restricts the use of imprisonment in certain ways. All other forms of sentence available for adults are available to this age group, with the single exception of the extended sentence. For this reason only detention, borstal training and the restrictions on imprisonment are discussed in this section.

DETENTION IN A DETENTION CENTRE

Conditions of eligibility

Detention in a detention centre may be ordered in the case of a young adult offender in any case where the court has power or would have power in the case of an adult to pass a sentence of imprisonment.[4] Where the maximum term of imprisonment for the offence exceeds three months, the sentence of detention must be for not less than three and not more than six months; in any other case it must be three months.[5]

---

[1] This term has no statutory basis, but was used by the Advisory Council on the Penal System to describe offenders in this age group; see their Report *Young Adult Offenders* (1974).
[2] Children and Young Persons Act 1933 s. 107(1).
[3] *Ibid.*
[4] Criminal Justice Act 1961 s. 4(1).   [5] *Ibid.*, s. 4(2).

A sentence of detention may be ordered to run consecutively to another sentence of detention,[1] and a sentence ordered to run consecutively to another sentence of detention may be for a period of less than six months.[2] The aggregate period for which a person may be ordered to be detained on any one occasion by the same court must not exceed six months,[3] and the total term for which a person may be continuously detained in a detention centre under orders made on different occasions or by different courts may not exceed nine months.[4]

A court may not make an order for detention in a detention centre against an offender unless there is a detention centre available for reception from that court of persons of his class or description.[5] A person who is serving or has served a sentence of borstal training or a sentence of imprisonment of six months or more may not be sentenced to detention 'unless it appears to the court that there are special circumstances (whether relating to the offence or the offender)' which warrant making the order in the particular case.[6]

A person who has not previously served a sentence of detention in a detention centre may not be sentenced to detention if he is not legally represented for the purpose of sentence, unless his application for legal aid has been refused on the ground that it did not appear that his means were such that he required assistance or, having been informed of his right to apply for legal aid, he has refused or failed to take the opportunity to do so.[7]

A person aged 17 or over may be committed to a detention centre in default only where he is already detained in a detention centre under a previous order; in this event the committal may be for any term not exceeding six months and it is not necessary that an appropriate detention centre should be available to the court making the committal.[8]

Policy in the use of detention in a detention centre

The primary use of the sentence of detention in a detention centre is as

[1] Ibid., s. 7(1).   [2] Ibid., s. 7(3).   [3] Ibid., s. 7(4).

[4] Ibid., s. 7(5). This section does not restrict the power of the court to order consecutive periods of detention, but the authority of the prison department to detain the offender under such orders. Consecutive orders made on different occasions and totalling twelve months are thus lawful, and allowing for normal remission, would be fully carried out.

[5] Ibid., s. 4(3). This restriction applies even though the offender is already serving a term of detention imposed by another court.

[6] Ibid., s. 4(4). The court must consider any report made in respect of him by the Prison Department, and a magistrates' court which has not received such a report must adjourn until such a report is available.

[7] Powers of Criminal Courts Act 1973 s. 21(1).

[8] Criminal Justice Act 1961 s. 6.

a short-term custodial sentence for offenders who have not manifested a need for training or supervision over a longer period of time (in which case borstal training or probation would be the appropriate measure) but whose offences are such that a custodial sentence is necessary to mark their gravity. In this capacity the sentence forms part of the tariff and is governed by tariff principles (such as those prohibiting unjustified disparity between co-defendants).[1] Many examples can be found. In *Jolley*[2] a student with no previous convictions was convicted of unlawful possession of a quantity of cannabis, and admitted supplying small quantities to his friends. A sentence of six months' detention was upheld, with the comment that the appellant had been concerned in 'a purposeful and deliberate breaking of the law' which was not to be 'disregarded and broken with impunity'. In *Fitzpatrick*[3] the appellant played a minor part in interfering with a witness; the Court stated that the offence 'in the ordinary way would fully justify a short sharp shock of a three-month detention sentence on a first offender', but in view of various factors, including the sentencer's failure to distinguish between the appellant and those more deeply involved in the offence, the Court reduced the sentence to allow his release. In *Jackson*[4] a youth of 19, with previous convictions for which he had been discharged or fined, was convicted of assault with intent to rob and sentenced to three years' imprisonment. The Court, affected by 'very favourable' social inquiry reports and the fact that the offence was 'an unpremeditated incident undoubtedly influenced by drink', decided that six months' detention was sufficient 'to mark the gravity of the offence', and varied the sentence accordingly.

A secondary use of the sentence is to provide a short custodial sentence for an offender who does not appear to require a substantial period of training or supervision, but whose persistence in relatively minor crimes, after appropriate warnings in the form of conditional discharge or fines, indicates a growing disregard for the law. In *Taylor*[5] the appellant was convicted of taking a conveyance and driving while disqualified; he had previously been fined and disqual-

---

[1] See, for example, *O'Callaghan* 27.5.71, 2082/A/71 (six months' detention for involvement in 'perfectly disgraceful episode' of violence; sentence not excessive but other defendants equally culpable, sentenced to three months' detention: 'no real justification for dealing with this man . . . twice as severely as any of the others'—reduced to three months).

[2] (1971) 56 Cr. App. R. 217. See also *Cordaroy and Pring* (1977) 65 Cr. App. R. 158 (six months' detention upheld for youths, 19 and 20, for burglary; 'there is a public interest to be served by making it clear that crime of this sort does receive condign punishment').

[3] 5.12.72, 5351/A/72.

[4] 6.5.75, 1090/C/75.

[5] 12.10.72, 4697/A/72.

ified on two occasions. Upholding the sentence of three months' detention the Court stated that 'a short custodial sentence on a young man who is demonstrating that he is going to go on offending with motor cars cannot be criticized'. In *Rowlands*[1] a youth of 17 received three months' detention for a common assault arising out of an incident with a street vendor. A few weeks before the incident he had been bound over to keep the peace on a conviction for threatening behaviour, and shortly after that offence assaulted a police officer, for which he was fined. Upholding the sentence the Court commented that no 'other or lesser punishment could meet this offence . . . in all the circumstances'.

A few specific principles have emerged from the cases. It is generally preferable to impose three months' detention rather than six months unless there are particular circumstances justifying the longer period,[2] and consecutive terms in excess of six months appear to be extremely rare in practice. An offender who has previously served a term of detention should not normally be sentenced to detention a second time,[3] particularly where the later sentence is imposed for an offence committed before the earlier sentence was imposed.[4]

BORSTAL TRAINING

Conditions of eligibility

A sentence of borstal training may be passed on an offender convicted of an offence punishable with imprisonment and aged under 21 on the day of his conviction,[5] if the court is 'of opinion, having regard to the circumstances of the offence, and after taking into account the offender's character and previous conduct, that it is expedient that he should be detained for training for not less than six months'.[6] Before passing a sentence of borstal training the court must consider any report made in respect of the offender by the

---

[1] 16.11.71, 4672/A/71.

[2] See, for example, *Hayes* 2.6.72, 1554/B/72 (six months for youth, 17, no previous convictions, for malicious wounding; 'no reason why a sentence of six months' detention was imposed as against . . . the more normal period of three months'—reduced accordingly); *Anders* 13.4.76, 767/A/76 (six months' detention for 'link man' between supplier and purchaser of controlled drug; 'sentence of a custodial character . . . was correct in principle', but 'the appropriate sentence . . . would have been not six months . . . but the more usual period of three').

[3] See *DiBenedetto* 13.3.70, 1273/B/69.

[4] See *Strickland* 18.7.72, 2945/C/72.

[5] Criminal Justice Act 1948 s. 20(1) (as amended). The minimum age for borstal training is 15 (see below, p. 282).

[6] Criminal Justice Act 1961 s. 1(2).

Prison Department,[1] but there is no obligation to obtain such a report.[2]

A person who has not previously been sentenced to borstal training may not be sentenced to borstal training if he is not legally represented for the purpose of sentence, unless his application for legal aid has been refused on the ground that it did not appear that his means were such that he required assistance or, having been informed of his right to apply for legal aid, he has refused or failed to take the opportunity to do so.[3].

A person sentenced to borstal training may be detained for any period between six months and two years[4] (unless the Secretary of State directs him to be released earlier) and remains under licence for one year from the date of his release. If during that period he fails to comply with any of the conditions of his licence he may be recalled to a borstal institution, where he may be detained until the expiration of two years from the date of the original sentence, or six months from being taken into custody under the order for recall, whichever is the later.[5] Where a person subject to a sentence of borstal training, whether on licence or unlawfully at large, is convicted of an offence punishable in the case of an adult with imprisonment, the court may order him to be returned to a borstal institution instead of dealing with him in any other manner.[6] A person ordered to be returned in these circumstances is in the same position as one who has been recalled by the Prison Department.[7] Before making such an order the court must consider any report made by the Prison Department on the offender's response to training.[8]

A person eligible for borstal training who is convicted by a magistrates' court of an offence punishable with imprisonment may be committed for sentence to the Crown Court.[9] The powers of the

[1] *Ibid.*, s. 1(3). A copy of the report must be given to the offender or his solicitor or counsel (*Ibid.*, s. 37).

[2] *Lowe* (1964) 48 Cr. App. R. 165.

[3] Powers of Criminal Courts Act s. 21.

[4] The sentencer should not recommend that any particular period be served before release on license; *Purdon* 4.10.74, 2350/B/74; *Brown* 28.2.74, 5234/B/73, [1975] Crim. L. R. 293.

[5] Prison Act 1952 s. 45.

[6] Criminal Justice Act 1961 s. 12(1). The sentencer should ensure that his intention to order recall, rather than impose a fresh sentence of borstal training, is clearly understood and recorded.

[7] *Ibid.*, s. 12(2).

[8] *Ibid.*, s. 12(3). A copy must be given to the offender or his solicitor or counsel. (*Ibid.*, s. 37). A magistrates' court dealing with an offender subject to a borstal licence (unless he has already been recalled by the Prison Department) must adjourn until such a report is made; this obligation applies whether or not the court contemplates ordering his return to borstal.

[9] Magistrates' Court Act 1952 s. 28 (magistrates may order the return to a borstal institution of an offender already serving a sentence of borstal training, but may not impose a sentence of borstal training).

Crown Court in relation to sentencing the offender to borstal training in such a case are the same as in the case of a person convicted on indictment.[1] If a person committed for sentence with a view to borstal training is not sentenced to borstal training, the Crown Court may pass only such sentence as the magistrates' court would have had power to pass at the time of his committal.[2]

Policy in the use of borstal training

The sentence of borstal training was originally intended to provide the courts with a training measure for offenders in their late adolescence who were developing persistently delinquent tendencies. It was accordingly seen as an individualized measure to be used as an alternative to imprisonment, which was the appropriate sentence where the sentencer's object was deterrence. The Criminal Justice Act 1961 led to a major change in the judicial approach to the use of borstal training. By restricting the powers of the sentencer to impose sentences of imprisonment on offenders under 21, the Act made borstal training effectively the only intermediate-length custodial sentence available for the majority of young adult offenders; as a result the sentence of borstal training was no longer seen exclusively as a training measure and came to be approved in cases where a deterrent sentence was considered necessary, but the offence did not justify a sentence of three years' imprisonment. As has already been shown, the sentence of borstal training has consequently assumed a dual function, as a training measure and as a tariff sentence equivalent to a sentence of imprisonment between the limits within which imprisonment is prohibited for young adult offenders. As different principles apply in each context the propriety of the sentence in a particular case depends on the object with which it is imposed.

Borstal training as a rehabilitative measure

Examples were given in an earlier chapter of the use of borstal training to provide the offender with the social, vocational or educational training he requires. Where this is the sentencer's object, 'the real problem . . . is not . . . a question of punishment . . . it is a question of the court's assessment . . . on the information before it of what is going to be best for this young man himself'.[3] The choice of borstal training in preference to other possible measures (usually

[1] Criminal Justice Act 1961 s. 1(4).
[2] Criminal Justice Act 1948 s. 20(5). This restriction applies to indictable offences but does not apply where the offender is committed for an indictable offence under Magistrates' Courts Act 1952 s. 29. See generally ch. 12, (below, p. 386).
[3] *Beattie* 11.10.73, 3245/C/73.

probation) is based on a prediction of the likely effect of the experience on the offender's future behaviour, and does not reflect the application of detailed general principles. A number of general issues affecting the use of borstal training as a rehabilitative measure have arisen in the cases, and these require discussion.

The principle of proportionality between offence and sentence It has long been established that the principle requiring proportionality between offence and sentence has no application to the sentence of borstal training, where that sentence is imposed as a training measure in the offender's best interests. The Court has held that a sentence of borstal training may be imposed even though the maximum term of imprisonment for the offence concerned is less than the minimum period of detention under a sentence of borstal training,[1] and many examples can be found of the Court upholding a sentence of borstal training where a sentence of six months' imprisonment would probably have been considered too severe. In *Plaw*[2] a youth of 20 with a substantial record of court appearances and custodial sentences admitted stealing a scarf from a parked car and was sentenced to borstal training. The Court stated that 'with a record of that kind . . . the court cannot simply ask itself what is the appropriate sentence for stealing a scarf. It is necessary to look into the young man's background and see what is the best course for him'. In the light of the available reports the Court upheld the sentence. In another case[3] two youths of 17, each with several previous appearances, admitted damaging a street light to the value of £19. Stating that 'whilst it is true that the particular offence . . . is not the most serious of offences, the Court has to look not only at the offence but at the offender', the Court upheld the sentences. In a third case[4] a young woman with several convictions for similar offences received a sentence of borstal training for attempting to steal a purse. The Court rejected the argument that the sentence was too severe, 'bearing in mind the whole history of the case', and upheld the sentence.

These cases reflect the usual view of the Court, but in *Preston*[5] the

---

[1] *Amos* (1961) 45 Cr. App. R. 42, overruling *James* [1960] 2 All. E. R. 863, [1960] 1 W.L.R. 812 and *Longstreeth* [1960] 2 All. E. R. 864 n. The subsequent inconsistent decision in *Power and Power* 29.1.68, 4552/67 may, it is submitted, be treated as *per incuriam*. For a more recent application of the principle, see *Graham* 17.6.75, 927/B/75 (soliciting for prostitution).

[2] 29.9.70, 2881/B/70.

[3] *Happe and Goodwin* 19.3.73, 299/A/73; see also *Tyler* 17.2.77, 5859/A/76 (handling ten stolen bars of chocolate; borstal training upheld in view of record).

[4] *Reddish* 2.10.75, 1965/C/75; see also *Gibbs* 9.11.76, 4626/A/76 (youth of 15, long history of 'erratic and violent' behaviour; borstal training for causing minor damage to car upheld; 'borstal is a training (measure) . . . to say it was in any sense excessive . . . here we think is entirely wrong').

[5] 14.4.76, 1856/R/76.

Court quashed a sentence of borstal training imposed on a young woman for causing criminal damage to the extent of £4 in the course of a quarrel with her boyfriend. The Court accepted that 'on the facts of her history . . . the applicant required consistent control and consistent support', but 'as a matter of principle the Court is loath to pass a sentence of a custodial nature . . . where . . . the criminal offence is a trivial one'. Following *Clarke*[1] and *Eaton*[2] the Court varied the sentence to probation. In a subsequent decision (in which *Preston* was not cited) the Court took the view that the principle in *Clarke* applied only to sentences of imprisonment and did not extend to borstal training. In *Coleman*[3] a youth of 15 broke a small window in the course of a visit to an assessment centre, causing damage costing about £5. The Court heard that the appellant had a long history of institutional life, with instances of absconding and violence to others and to himself; a particular borstal institution was recommended as providing the best hope for his future. The appellant argued that the sentence offended the principle in *Clarke*,[4] but the Court, upholding the sentence, observed that 'a distinction has to be drawn . . . between a prison sentence' and a sentence of borstal training imposed on 'somebody of the youth of this particular appellant', adding that 'there are times when although an offence is slight an apparently disproportionate sentence is correct'. Although it is possible to read the judgment in *Coleman* as applicable only to young persons as opposed to young adult offenders, it is submitted that consistently with the earlier authorities, the decision applies generally to borstal training where it is imposed as an individualized measure as opposed to a penal sanction, and that the principle in *Clarke* applies only to sentences of imprisonment.

To argue that the principle of proportionality between offence and sentence has no application where borstal training is imposed as an individualized measure does not mean that the inherent gravity of the offence is not one of the considerations which the sentencer should take into account when assessing whether the particular offender would benefit from borstal training. In *Adams*[5] a youth of 18 was sentenced to borstal training for obtaining a pecuniary advantage in the amount of £2.87 by deception, by ordering and consuming a meal in a restaurant without having the means to pay for it. The Court observed that although the offence was 'comparatively trivial' the sentence of borstal training was 'not surprising' as 'everybody recommended that borstal training should be the sentence to be

[1] (1975) 61 Cr. App. R. 320 (above, p. 39).
[2] 31.7.75, 3182/R/75, [1975] Crim. L. R. 390.
[3] (1976) 64 Cr. App. R. 124.
[4] (1975) 61 Cr. App. R. 320.
[5] 4.5.73, 1089/B/73.

passed'. In the light of a further assessment of the appellant's capabilities and attitudes the Court concluded that he could be given 'one more chance . . . on probation', but added that if he broke the terms of the order 'there can be little doubt that he will then have to serve the sentence of borstal training[1] for the offence of obtaining this meal by deception'. As this case indicates, the gravity of the latest offence is one matter which the sentencer should consider in deciding whether to impose a sentence of borstal training with a view to the offender's benefit; but the triviality of the instant offence does not prevent the imposition of a sentence of borstal training where a strong case for that disposition can be made on other grounds.

The first offender Although borstal training was originally conceived as a sentence for young offenders who had displayed delinquent tendencies over a period of time, there is no principle restricting the use of the sentence as a training measure to deal with offenders with no previous convictions. The Court has upheld sentences of borstal training on first offenders where the available evidence indicated that borstal training was the most promising course available. In *Beattie*[2] a youth of 18 with no previous convictions received a sentence of borstal training following his conviction for possessing various drugs and prohibited substances. The Court received reports from a variety of sources and concluded that while there was 'more than one legitimate view . . . the best answer in the interests of this young man . . . is that the borstal training should continue'. In many other cases the absence of a previous conviction is one factor which enables the sentencer to choose probation in preference to borstal training. In *Williams*[3] a young woman of 20 admitted a number of offences of burglary committed in company with 'a professional burglar in a substantial way' who received an extended sentence of eight years. The Court stated that although there could be 'no criticism' of the sentence of borstal training when imposed, the appellant had 'a clean record' and her 'difficulties in the past' with her family had largely been resolved; for these reasons it was possible to vary the sentence to a probation order with appropriate requirements. In another case,[4] where two young people with no previous convictions admitted a number of offences, including the theft of a substantial sum from the parents of one of them, the Court, having considered a variety of reports, varied the sentences from borstal training to probation in each case 'in view of the antecedents of these young people and all the opinions expressed'.

[1] Strictly, the sentence would be a new sentence of borstal training.
[2] 11.10.73, 3245/C/73.
[3] 2.9.75, 2931/A/75.   [4] *Anderson and Newman* 4.10.74, 3284/B/74.

The offender with previous experience of detention in a detention centre There is no general principle restricting the use of borstal training as an individualized measure in cases where the offender has previously served a sentence of detention in a detention centre, although the offender's behaviour during and after such a sentence is a relevant factor to be considered. The Court has frequently upheld sentences of borstal training on offenders with previous experience of detention centres: in one example[1] a youth was sentenced to borstal training for the theft of a vehicle excise licence. The Court received a report on his behaviour while under the sentence of detention which was 'as adverse a report as any young man is likely to earn'; a preliminary report from the borstal institution where he was detained was more promising. Observing that the reports indicated that 'this young man ought to profit from his stay in borstal', the Court upheld the sentence.

Some difficulties have arisen as a result of a statement made in 1955, eight years before the current legislative provisions governing the sentencing of young adult offenders took effect, in the case of *Gooding*.[2] In that case the appellant was placed on probation, and during the currency of the probation order committed a further offence for which he was sentenced to three months' detention; having served that sentence he was brought back to the court which made the probation order and sentenced to borstal training. This sentence was varied on appeal with the comment that 'this Court cannot consider that it is right unless in a most exceptional case . . . that a sentence of borstal training should be passed on a young offender who has just come out of a detention centre, if the offence for which he is being sent to borstal was committed before the offence for which he was sent to the detention centre'. This statement has been considered in many subsequent cases where a similar problem has arisen, either as a result of a breach of probation or as a consequence of one charge being dealt with more expeditiously than another. The trend of the more recent cases is clearly to the effect that *Gooding* does not lay down any general or binding principle, and that the fact that the offender has recently experienced detention in a detention centre for an offence committed later than the offence for which he is being sentenced is only one factor for the sentencer's consideration in deciding whether or not to impose borstal training.[3]

[1] *Richardson* 5.9.73, 3179/B/73.

[2] (1955) 39 Cr. App. R. 187.

[3] See, for example, *Ward* 17.2.70, 8016/69, [1970] Crim. L. R. 294 ('exceptions to that principle are not as rare as . . . at the time of *Gooding's* case was considered'); *Kingshott* 15.5.70, 1767/A/70 ('it really is no longer of much value . . . to go back to the judgment . . . of *Gooding* . . . this is a matter which should be approached . . . by looking at the circumstances of the individual'); *Smith* 16.11.70, 3079/A/70, [1971]

After a review of some of the decisions subsequent to *Gooding*, the position was stated in these terms: 'these cases indicate that there is no actual rule as such which a reading of *Gooding* may at first indicate. All these cases have to be looked at in the light of their special circumstances, although it is right that care should be taken . . . before ordering a period of borstal training shortly after a period of detention centre for an offence which had been committed before the detention centre period began'.[1]

The proper approach is illustrated by a number of decisions. In *Ward*[2] a youth of 18 with four previous court appearances was sentenced to borstal training for burglary; he had just completed a sentence of three months' detention imposed by a magistrates' court for an offence of driving without insurance, committed shortly after the burglary. The Court was told that the sentence of detention had been 'manifestly a shock' which had had 'a very salutary effect on him' and in the light of this factor, as well as the fact that the burglary was the earlier of the offences, varied the sentence to a probation order. Similarly in *Granados*[3] a youth of 18 was sentenced to borstal training for being in possession of a flick-knife in a public place; between his arrest for that offence and completion of the proceedings he served a sentence of three months' detention for an offence of theft committed shortly before the offensive weapon offence. A report to the Court stated that following the sentence of detention the appellant 'had matured considerably and was trying to behave in a more responsible fashion'; in the light of the report the Court considered that he 'ought . . . to be given a chance to show that he is prepared to continue to . . . abide by the law', and varied the sentence to a conditional discharge. By contrast, in *White*[4] a sentence of borstal training was upheld on a youth, originally convicted of

---

Crim. L. R. 113; *Henshaw* (1972) 56 Cr. App. R. 387 (*Kingshott* followed); *Poole* 11.5.72, 173/B/72 ('it is . . . not a strict rule that there should be no sentence of borstal training immediately on top of a sentence of detention; it must be dependent upon the circumstances in every case'); *Horler* 22.11.74, 3572/B/74, [1974] Crim. L. R. 175; *White* 20.2.76, 4997/C/75 (principle in *Gooding* 'not . . . of necessarily universal application'); *Shaw* 9.8.76, 2554/A/76 (general proposition 'quite sound', but not applied in particular facts); *Binns and others* (1976) 64 Cr. App. R. 292 ('the Court has departed from [the principle in *Gooding*] time and again for a variety of reasons'); *Simpson* (1977) 65 Cr. App. R. 308; *Edwards* 11.3.77, 233/A/77 (*Binns* followed). In *McWilliams* 25.5.71, 854/B/71 the Court referred to *Gooding* with the observation that 'for many years it has been accepted that one ought not, if one can possibly avoid it, to follow a detention centre sentence with an immediate sentence of borstal training, particularly where the report from the detention centre was a favourable one'.

[1] *Murphy and Rider* 9.12.75, 4385/C/75.
[2] 17.2.70, 8016/69, [1970] Crim. L. R. 294.
[3] 23.8.76, 2726/C/76.
[4] 20.2.76, 4997/C/75.

burglary and placed on probation, who had received a term of
detention for subsequent offences connected with taking a vehicle.
The sentencer received a report from the detention centre which
indicated that 'training has left no . . . lasting impression' and on
appeal there was available 'one of the worst reports that we have
seen . . . from borstal'. The sentence was upheld.

The offender with previous experience of borstal training Where the
offender has previously served a sentence of borstal training, the
sentencer has a wider range of choices than in other cases. He may
sentence him to a further term of borstal training, impose a sentence
of imprisonment of up to six months or eighteen months or more[1] (as
opposed to the normal minimum of three years) or, if he is still subject
to licence, order his return to a borstal institution.[2] The choice
between these alternatives is not determined by general principles
(although imprisonment must not be imposed 'unless the court is of
opinion that no other method of dealing with him is appropriate').[3]
The approach suggested by the cases appears to be that the sentencer
should first consider whether any purpose would be served by
subjecting the offender to a further period of borstal training; if it is
clear that no such purpose would be served, the appropriate course
may be a term of imprisonment (which must be for not more than six
and not less than eighteen months).[4] In *Chapman*[5] a youth of 18 was
sentenced to eighteen months' imprisonment for taking a vehicle
without authority. He had eight previous court appearances, and had
been sentenced to a second term of borstal training shortly before the
present sentence was imposed; he had absconded during his first term
and been returned to borstal following a further conviction. Upholding the sentence, the Court observed that 'at the age of 18 an accused
person is looked at by the Court with particular reference to his
individual problems', but as 'borstal training has failed to provide a
solution in the past, and he has offended again and again despite the
order of borstal training', the appropriate choice was imprisonment.
Many similar examples can be found. Where the evidence suggests
that further borstal training may be useful, the sentencer must choose
between a fresh sentence of borstal training and an order for recall to
borstal (assuming the offender is still under licence).The practical
difference between these alternatives depends primarily on the time

[1] Criminal Justice Act 1961 s. 3(3). This power is available where the offender has
been released on licence, even though subsequently recalled; it does not apply to
offences committed by absconders (below, p. 278).

[2] Criminal Justice Act 1961 s. 12 (above, p. 261).

[3] Powers of Criminal Courts Act 1973 s. 19(2).

[4] Criminal Justice Act 1961 s. 3(3).

[5] 21.3.74, 129/A/74.

that has elapsed since the original sentence was passed. A person returned to a borstal institution is liable to be detained until the expiration of two years from the date of the original sentence, or for six months (whichever is the later), and if subsequently released on licence, remains on licence until the end of one year from the date of his original release on licence.[1] Where the offender has been on licence for a relatively short period, after a relatively short period of training, the appropriate order may well be a return to borstal rather than a fresh sentence of borstal training. In *Sanders*[2] a youth of 19 with several previous appearances was sentenced to a second term of borstal training two months after his release on licence from a sentence imposed about twelve months previously. Although the reports before the Court did 'not really encourage a great deal of optimism for the future', the sentence was varied to an order for return to borstal. Where the relevant periods are close to expiry, or the evidence suggests that a more extended period of training may be required, a fresh sentence may be the appropriate course. In *Churchill*[3] a youth of 19 who had previously completed a sentence of borstal training was sentenced to eighteen months' imprisonment for burglary. The Court considered 'whether imprisonment really is the only method for dealing with this young man', and decided in the light of favourable reports that 'although on the previous occasions . . . it did not seem to have achieved the result desired . . . it is worth giving borstal a second chance'. On the choice between recall and a fresh sentence the Court decided that a fresh sentence was the better course, 'so as to give a wider discretion to the authorities at borstal as to how long he is to stay there in view of the response to the further training which he receives'. A fresh sentence of borstal training was accordingly substituted.

The Court has stated that although there is no firm principle on the matter, it is seldom appropriate to impose a third sentence of borstal training on an offender. Where an offender commits further offences after being released from a second sentence, or after absconding, 'there should be a reassessment of his needs and those of the public'. If imprisonment is not the appropriate course at this stage, 'an order for return to borstal normally would seem appropriate, rather than yet another sentence of borstal training'.[4]

The offender with previous experience of imprisonment Statutory restrictions on the imposition of imprisonment on young adult

[1] Prison Act 1952 s. 45(4). as applied by Criminal Justice Act 1961 s. 12(2).
[2] 26.9.75, 2944/A/75.
[3] 30.4.76, 1445/B/76.
[4] *Elliott* 16.12.74, 3012/C/74, [1975] Crim. L. R. 174, commenting on *Noseda* (1958) 42 Cr. App. R. 221; see also *Teskowski* 24.9.76, 3547/B/76.

offenders mean that relatively few offenders considered as possible subjects for borstal training will have experienced imprisonment, and those who have will have received terms of less than six months. The cases indicate that the fact that an offender has previously served such a term is no bar to a sentence of borstal training. In *Dennis*[1] a youth of 19 with several previous convictions, one of which had led to three months' imprisonment, was sentenced to borstal training for assault occasioning actual bodily harm committed in company with a friend. Upholding the sentence, the Court commented that 'that kind of behaviour plainly shows that these two young men required a long period of training, and that view is fortified by their records of convictions for violence'.

The offender in need of psychiatric treatment Young adult offenders who satisfy the conditions of eligibility described in chapter 7 below may be made the subject of psychiatric probation orders or hospital orders in the same manner as adults, and where appropriate arrangements can be made a young adult offender in need of psychiatric treatment will usually be dealt with under the general provisions for dealing with mentally disordered offenders.[2] In cases where the diagnosis is not such as to allow or require these powers to be exercised, and the sentencer is satisfied that the offender's condition does not justify a longer period of detention than a sentence of borstal training provides, borstal training may well be the most appropriate sentence. In one case[3] a youth of 19 was sentenced to three years and four months' imprisonment for arson and theft, having set fires at two garages. The Court commented that 'these sentences were well merited' for 'grave offences of arson', but in view of evidence that they were committed while the appellant was suffering from reactive depression and that he now 'appears to want to see that his problems are sorted out', the sentence was varied to borstal training, on the understanding that appropriate therapy would be available. In another example[4] a youth of 18, who had previously been subject to two hospital orders, was sentenced to borstal training despite medical evidence that he was of sub-normal intelligence, unlikely to benefit from training and probably at a serious disadvantage in company with others. In the event, later reports indicated that 'borstal training is . . . exactly what he

[1] 8.10.74, 3219/B/74.

[2] For example, *Donaldson* 2.3.73, 6604/C/72 (youth, 20, no previous convictions for violence; borstal training for unlawful wounding varied to psychiatric probation order following evidence of mental illness); *Rampling* 10.6.74, 1765/B/74 (girl, 17, minor acts of violence while under influence of drink; borstal training varied to probation).

[3] *Calladine* 25.11.75, 4204/B/75.

[4] *Webb* 9.7.71, 1786/B/71.

requires' and the Court upheld the sentence with the comment that 'the decision made in the court below, albeit on somewhat flimsy grounds, has turned out to be the right one'.

Borstal training as a tariff sentence

It has already been shown that the restrictions on the use of imprisonment imposed by the Criminal Justice Act 1961 meant that borstal training, previously seen entirely as a rehabilitative measure, came to be used also as a tariff sentence in cases where the appropriate sentence of imprisonment would have fallen within the restricted range of more than six months and less than three years. In the leading case[1] the Court held that where the sentencer wishes to pass a custodial sentence to mark the gravity of the offence but is prevented from imposing the appropriate term of imprisonment by the statutory restrictions, it is not permissible to pass a disproportionate sentence of imprisonment in order to avoid those limitations. In such a case the proper sentence is borstal training. This decision has been followed many times.[2] In *Ward*[3] a youth for whom borstal training was considered inappropriate on personal grounds received a sentence of three years' imprisonment for one burglary and a series of attempts, committed by trying doors to see if they were unlocked. The Court stated that the proper approach was 'to ask ourselves this question: what was the appropriate term of imprisonment, for certainly a custodial sentence was necessary . . . ? Is it a period of less than six months? The answer to that is clearly no. Is it a period of imprisonment that falls somewhere between six months and three years? . . . The answer to that question is yes . . . it therefore follows that in compliance with the provisions of section 3 of the 1961 Act . . . the answer inevitably must be borstal training'.

The Court has frequently indicated that in such circumstances the fact that the offender himself will probably not derive any benefit from the sentence is not a reason for not imposing it. In *Broadhurst*[4] a youth of 19 was sentenced to three years' imprisonment for the rape

[1] *Lowe* (1964) 48 Cr. App. R. 165.
[2] See, for example, *Farr and Brown* 26.6.70, 3105/R/70, [1970] Crim. L. R. 658; (students conspiring to set fire to building in course of demonstration; borstal training 'the appropriate deterrent sentence for this type of offence'); *Caird and others* (1970) 54 Cr. App. R. 499; *Driscoll* 23.11.72, 3549/B/72, [1972] Crim. L. R. 190; *Crossland* 8.6.73, 1047/B/72 ('where the right sentence would have been something between six months and three years, the court really is driven to a sentence of borstal training by reason of the Act'); *Bishop* 4.10.74, 3193/A/74 ('Post Office officials who steal in the course of their work can expect custodial sentences. Those who are over 21 can expect to go to prison, and those who cannot be sent to prison because of the provisions of the Criminal Justice Act can expect to go to borstal training').
[3] 20.5.76, 1032/A/76.
[4] 28.2.75, 4533/C/74.

of a girl of 18 who had previously given him some encouragement. Varying the sentence, the Court stated that three years' imprisonment was too long in the circumstances, and although 'there is no particular reason for thinking that borstal is the most appropriate treatment for this young man', it was in practice the only alternative sentence. In *Shackleton*[1] a youth of good character who admitted importing a quantity of cannabis was sentenced to three years' imprisonment. The Court stated that 'it seems to have been in the mind of the Crown Court that since this is a young man who plainly does not need training in the ordinary borstal sense, therefore borstal was inappropriate. That is not a correct view'. As the mitigating factors justified a reduction in the sentence below the level of three years' imprisonment, a sentence of borstal training was substituted. In a third example[2] the appellant had been sentenced to three years' imprisonment for robbery, the sentencer commenting that the case was not suitable for borstal training as the offender had no previous convictions, was in steady employment, and the offence was wholly out of character. Varying the sentence to borstal training the Court observed that 'a sentence of borstal training nowadays is not one that merely has regard to the training aspect. It is a standard form of sentence of medium length for a person in this particular age group . . . when a custodial sentence is necessary'. Although occasional inconsistent statements can be found,[3] these decisions represent the balance of the authorities.

Borstal training in cases such as these forms part of the tariff, and is accordingly governed by the principles which apply generally to fixed terms of imprisonment. The most important of these is the principle of proportionality between offence and sentence. Although this principle does not apply where the sentence is used as an individualized training measure, it is relevant where the sentence is imposed for punitive or deterrent purposes. In such cases the sentence will not be upheld if it is disproportionate to the gravity of the offence for which it is imposed. The Court in *Bikram*[4] endorsed the proposition founded on *English*[5] that 'a sentence of borstal training passed

---

[1] 16.10.73, 2473/A/73.

[2] *Bryan* 12.4.76, 5757/B/75; see also *McDonnell* 23.11.76, 3972/C/76 ('this young man of previous good character is unlikely to benefit directly from a sentence of training in a borstal; nevertheless these were serious offences . . . a sentence longer than six months but shorter than three years would have been appropriate'; three years reduced to borstal training).

[3] For example, *Stickels* 6.3.73, 282/A/73, [1973] Crim. L. R. 378 (two years' imprisonment for causing grievous bodily harm to child unlawful: 'no indication . . . that borstal training will do this young man the slightest good . . . to correct a sentence which was beyond the law by imposing a sentence which is within the law but . . . wholly inappropriate is no way of administering criminal justice'; six months substituted).

[4] 16.7.73, 1704/C/73, [1974] Crim. L. R. 55.   [5] (1967) 52 Cr. App. R. 119.

primarily as a deterrent will be upheld only if on ordinary tariff principles and making full allowance in mitigation for the appellant's youth, a sentence of more than six months' imprisonment would be considered appropriate apart from the restrictions imposed by the 1961 Act'. A youth of 18 convicted of fraudulently abstracting electricity by making a false report that a bomb had been planted at a police station was sentenced to borstal training 'by way of punishment and punishment only'. The Court stated that 'such a sentence is perfectly proper . . . but should only be imposed where the appropriate sentence for a person of full age would be of the order of two years, certainly somewhere between the minimum of six months and the maximum of three years provided under the statute'. Although the case was 'very near the borderline' the Court concluded that 'the sentence of borstal training was perhaps somewhat too severe', and substituted six months' detention in a detention centre.

Section 67(1) of the Criminal Justice Act 1967, which requires any period of time spent in custody on remand prior to sentence to be deducted from the length of a sentence of imprisonment, does not apply to a person sentenced to borstal training. Where an offender has spent a substantial period in custody pending the determination of his case and receives a sentence of borstal training imposed as a punitive sentence, he may well be at a disadvantage in comparison with an older offender in similar circumstances sentenced to an equivalent term of imprisonment. It appears to be appropriate for the sentencer to take this factor into account in deciding whether the offence justifies a sentence of borstal training under the principle in *English* and *Bikram*; if a sentence of borstal training is still necessary, it is permissible for the sentencer to invite the attention of the appropriate authority to the matter for the purpose of excercising the power under Prison Act 1952 s. 45(2).[1]

Combination of borstal training with other forms of sentence

A sentence of borstal training should not normally be combined with any other form of custodial sentence, either concurrently or consecutively,[2] and it is inappropriate to subject the offender simultaneously to a combination of borstal training and a suspended sentence[3] or borstal training and probation.[4] It is not usually appropriate to make a recommendation for deportation in a case where borstal training is imposed, but this course may be permissible

[1] See *Shields* 6.11.70, 4001/A/70 (six months in custody prior to sentence; Secretary of State invited to consider exercise of power under s. 45(2)).
[2] See p. 63 above.
[3] See p. 64 above.
[4] *Barnes* 19.2.73, 5551/C/72, following *Evans* (1958) 43 Cr. App. R. 66.

in exceptional circumstances.[1] A person sentenced to borstal training may be disqualified from driving at the same time if he is convicted of an offence for which that penalty is available, but it is generally inadvisable to impose long periods of disqualification on young adolescent offenders,[2] particularly if there is good reason to hope that the experience of borstal training will encourage them to behave more responsibly on discharge.[3]

Although an offender sentenced to borstal training may lawfully be subject in addition to a fine[4] or compensation order[5] (unless he has been committed for sentence under Magistrates Courts Act 1952 s. 28),[6] it will rarely be appropriate to exercise either of these powers in conjunction with a sentence of borstal training. In *Jarrard*[7] the appellant was sentenced to borstal training on one count and ordered to pay fines totalling £140 within eighteen months on five others. Quashing the fines, the Court stated that 'it is wrong in principle that a young person who is sent to borstal training should be faced with the necessity to pay fines, particularly substantial fines, after his release . . . at a time when one hopes he is going to be able to take advantage of the training he has received'.

Similar statements have been made in respect of compensation orders,[8] although more frequently the compensation order is quashed or reduced on the ground that the sentencer has failed to have regard to the offender's means, as the statute requires. In *Bradburn*[9] the appellant was sentenced to borstal training for doing criminal damage to the extent of £3,100 and ordered to pay £400 compensation by instalments beginning one month after his release

[1] See *Castelli* 16.12.75, 4180/A3/75, [1976] Crim. L. R. 387 ('where a sentence of borstal training is passed . . . it is not usual to make a recommendation for deportation . . . because the object of borstal training is to train young offenders to lead thereafter useful and honest lives . . . this approach . . . is always subject to the exceptional case'). Presumably this combination is less likely to be objectionable where borstal training is imposed as a tariff sentence.

[2] See *Dawtrey* 24.9.74, 2509/A/74 (six years' disqualification 'counterproductive'; reduced to three).

[3] See *Wells* 2.7.73, 2415/A/73 (eighteen months' disqualification 'fully justified' but reduced to end on date of release from borstal, in view of appellant's 'professed intentions . . . of settling down').

[4] Powers of Criminal Courts Act 1973 ss. 30, 42.

[5] *Ibid.*, ss. 35(1) 42.

[6] See Criminal Justice Act 1948 s. 20(5) (a).

[7] 10.3.72, 5366/C/71, [1972] Crim. L. R. 449; see also *Gear* 24.7.75, 2319/A/75 (it is wrong in principle when sending a young person . . . to borstal to impose upon him in addition fines, even though they may not be a great amount in total, because . . . when comes out of that institution he should not be encumbered in putting into effect all the resolves that it is hoped a young man in borstal does make'; fines of £40 reduced to 20p).

[8] See, for example, *Adamson* 12.11.74, 3318/C/74 ('it is only in very exceptional cases, where a borstal sentence is passed, that a young man . . . should have to face a substantial bill recoverable civilly after serving his penal sentence').

[9] (1973) 57 Cr. App. R. 948.

from borstal. The Court held that it was 'not right to restrict compensation orders to cases where the defendant can easily pay', but that an order which would require four years to discharge was wrong in principle. The order was reduced to £100, payable in weekly instalments of £2, beginning one month after his release on licence. Similarly in *Williamson*[1] the appellant was sentenced to borstal training and ordered to pay £797 compensation for stealing a cheque in the amount of £822 (his co-defendant was ordered to pay the balance). The Court stated that in considering the means of the offender 'one is not restricted to his circumstances on the day he is sentenced', but as the order could only be paid over a long period of time and would be 'hanging over him . . . upon release', it was 'entirely inappropriate and excessive'. The order was reduced to the amount of £22, representing the balance of the proceeds of the theft still in the appellant's hands.

IMPRISONMENT

Statutory restrictions

The imposition of sentences of imprisonment on young adult offenders is subject to a number of statutory limitations. No court may impose imprisonment on an offender under twenty-one unless it is 'of opinion that no other method of dealing with him is appropriate',[2] and for the purpose of determining whether any other method of dealing with him is appropriate, 'the court shall obtain and consider information about the circumstances, and shall take into account any information before the court which is relevant to his character and his physical and mental condition'.[3] This provision does not require the sentencer as a matter of law to obtain a social inquiry report if one is not available,[4] although it will rarely be appropriate to proceed without one. A sentence of imprisonment must not be passed on an offender of any age who has not previously been sentenced to imprisonment [5] if he is not legally represented for the purpose of sentence, unless his application for legal aid has been refused on the ground that his means were such that he did not require assistance or he has refused the opportunity to apply for legal aid.[6]

---

[1] 28.1.75, 4188/B/74.
[2] Powers of Criminal Courts Act 1973 s. 19(2). A magistrates' court must give its reasons for so deciding (*ibid.*, s. 19(3)).
[3] *Ibid.*
[4] See *Ampleford* (1975) 61 Cr. App. R. 325, decided on the identical terms of s. 20(1).
[5] A sentence which has been suspended and has not taken effect must be disregarded for this purpose (Powers of Criminal Courts Act 1973 s. 21(3)(a)).
[6] *Ibid.*, s. 21(1).

Specific limitations on the use of imprisonment in the case of young adult offenders are provided by Criminal Justice Act 1961 s. 3. This section provides that a sentence of imprisonment shall not be passed on a person under the age of 21 on the day of his conviction, [1] except for a term not exceeding six months or (where the court otherwise has power to pass such a sentence) for a term of not less than three years. [2] There are three exceptions to these provisions. An offender who has served a sentence of borstal training or a sentence of imprisonment of not less than six months may be sentenced to a term of eighteen months' imprisonment or more (or up to six months). [3] An offender who is already serving a term of imprisonment of any length at the time when sentence is passed may be sentenced to a term of imprisonment of any length. [4]

For the purpose of these provisions, consecutive terms and terms which are wholly or partly concurrent are treated as a single term. [5] It follows that a cumulative sentence consisting of a series of consecutive sentences, each individually within the prohibited range but exceeding in aggregate the relevant limitations (three years or eighteen months as the case may be), is lawful, while a cumulative sentence consisting of two or more sentences, each less than six months but aggregating more than six months and less than the appropriate minimum, is unlawful. [6] For this purpose however it is necessary to disregard a suspended sentence which is enforced consecutively to the instant sentence, so that an otherwise lawful sentence is not made unlawful by the addition of an activated suspended sentence producing an overall aggregate within the prohibited range, [7] and an unlawful sentence is not made lawful by the addition of an activated suspended sentence making up a total period in excess of the relevant minimum. [8] The reason for this rule is that the activation of an existing suspended sentence is not the same as the imposition of a sentence of imprisonment; [9] accordingly the rule does not apply where a sentence of imprisonment is imposed consecutively to the instant sentence in respect of an earlier offence for which the

[1] Criminal Justice Act 1961 s. 3(1), applying Criminal Justice Act 1948 s. 20(1). The age of any person 'shall be deemed to be or have been that which appears to the court . . . after considering any available evidence, to be or to have been his age at that time' (Criminal Justice Act 1961, s. 39(3)). This section validates a sentence passed on the assumption that the offender is 21, even though subsequent inquiry establishes that he is not; see *Farndale* (1973) 58 Cr. App. R. 135.
[2] Criminal Justice Act 1961 s. 3(3).
[3] *Ibid.*, s. 3(3).
[4] *Ibid.*, s. 3(2).
[5] *Ibid.*, s. 38(4).
[6] See *Scully* (1966) 50 Cr. App. R. 258.
[7] *Pike* (1971) 55 Cr. App. R. 455; *Slade* 4.2.72, 3677/C/71.
[8] *Halse* (1971) 56 Cr. App. R. 47.
[9] *Lamb* (1968) 52 Cr. App. R. 667.

offender was placed on probation or conditionally discharged.[1] All of these points are illustrated in *Fenton*.[2] A youth of 20 who had previously served a sentence of borstal training was subject to both a conditional discharge and a suspended sentence of three months' imprisonment imposed on different occasions. On being convicted of two further offences of assault and criminal damage, he was sentenced to six months for the assault, six months for the criminal damage and three months in respect of the offence for which he had been discharged. The suspended sentence was activated consecutively, making a total of eighteen months' imprisonment. Although this would have been lawful as a single sentence in view of the appellant's previous sentence of borstal training, for the purposes of section 3(1) the activated suspended sentence could not be counted, leaving a total of fifteen months, which fell within the prohibited range. The Court decided not to exercise its powers to vary the internal composition of the sentences to make up a lawful sentence of eighteen months,[3] taking the view that the total sentence was in any event excessive. The sentences for the two instant offences and the offence in respect of which a conditional discharge had been imposed were all made concurrent, making a total of six months' imprisonment, and the suspended sentence of three months was activated consecutively, leaving an aggregate sentence of nine months' imprisonment, which was lawful although within the prohibited range.

The fact that a sentence is suspended does not affect the application of either the general restrictions imposed by the Powers of Criminal Courts Act 1973[4] or the specific limitations imposed by the Criminal Justice Act 1961. A sentence falling within the prohibited range applicable to the particular offender is not saved by being suspended.[5] However, where an existing suspended sentence is enforced with the substitution of a lesser term for the original term under Powers of Criminal Courts Act 1971 s. 23(1)(b), the sentencer may reduce the length of the activated sentence to a term falling within the prohibited range. This course was allowed without argument in *Pike*,[6] where the Court upheld the sentencer's decision to impose three months' imprisonment for the instant offence and activate twelve months of a suspended sentence of eighteen months con-

---

[1] *Taylor* (1974) 60 Cr. App. R. 143 (eighteen months with eighteen months consecutive for earlier offence dealt with by probation order, constituting lawful sentence of three years).

[2] 17.11.75, 3808/A/75.

[3] See *Halse* (1971) 56 Cr. App. R. 47.

[4] See *Reynolds* 27.7.71, 77/C/71.

[5] *Halloran* 20.7.70, 1582/C/70; *Peach* 20.5.71, 1228/A/71, [1971] Crim. L. R. 494; *Garnett* 14.1.72, 5973/A/71.

[6] (1971) 55 Cr. App. R. 455.

secutively. The Court's reasoning in that case, that 'the order putting a suspended sentence into effect is not the passing of a sentence', would support the view that an activation under section 23(1)(b) is not restricted by Criminal Justice Act 1961 s. 3(1).

Although Criminal Justice Act 1961 s. 38(4) provides that 'terms which are wholly or partly concurrent are treated as a single term', the Court generally requires that a sentence imposed for a lesser offence concurrently with a longer sentence of three years or more should comply with the restrictions imposed by section 3. In *Crout*[1] a youth of 17 was sentenced to life imprisonment for wounding with intent and twelve months concurrent for another offence. Upholding the life sentence in view of the medical evidence, the Court varied the sentence of twelve months to six months, 'in view of the provisions of section 3'. It is not clear whether the decision should be treated as a ruling on the interpretation of the relevant sections.

Section 3(2) provides that no restriction applies 'in the case of a person who is serving a sentence of imprisonment at the time when the Court passes sentence'. Although the statute does not define the point at which a person begins to serve a sentence, other legislation indicates that the day on which the sentence is passed is the first day of the sentence. It could be argued that an offender who is sentenced on several counts of an indictment begins to serve the sentence on the first count as soon as it is pronounced, and accordingly the sentencer is free from any restriction in respect of the sentence on the second or subsequent counts. This interpretation is inconsistent with the object of the Act, and it is submitted that section 3(2) should be read as if it included the words 'passed on a different occasion' after 'sentence of imprisonment'. The section clearly contemplates that a person who has been released from prison on licence is not serving the sentence while on licence, although he is treated as serving the sentence if he has been recalled or returned to prison. The application of the section to the case where the sentencer exercises his power under Criminal Justice Act 1967 s. 62(2) to revoke the licence before passing sentence for the instant offence is uncertain.

Where the offender has previously served a sentence of borstal training, the three-year minimum is reduced to eighteen months. To qualify for this exception the offender must have been released on licence;[3] an offender who commits an offence within the institution while on home leave[5] or after absconding[6] is not eligible and the

---

[1] 5.11.73, 3170/B/73.
[2] Courts Act 1971 s. 11(1).
[3] Criminal Justice Act 1961 s. 3(3).
[4] See *Harrison* 10.2.76, 5908/A/75; *Barclay and Hughes* (1968) 52 Cr. App. R. 214.
[5] See *Mattocks* 22.10.71, 3658/C/71.
[6] See *Harrison* 10.2.76, 5908/A/75.

normal three-year minimum applies. An offender who has been transferred from borstal to hospital under the Mental Health Act 1959 and released under the provisions of that Act is also ineligible. [1]

As has already been shown, the Court has held consistently that it is improper for a sentencer to seek to avoid the statutory limitations by imposing a disproportionate sentence of three years' imprisonment, whether as a single sentence [2] or as a series of consecutive sentences. [3] A sentencer confronted with the 'inflexibility' of the restrictions must be 'meticulously careful not to impose a sentence greater than the offence warrants'. [4] Following the leading case of *Lowe*, [5] the Court has stated many times that 'if a judge . . . has concluded a custodial sentence having immediate effect is necessary in the case, and finds that the sentence which he feels appropriate by way of imprisonment . . . cannot be passed by virtue of section 3, then the course . . . for him to follow, unless there are other circumstances which render this impracticable, is to sentence the person to borstal training'. [6] Other decisions cited earlier indicate that 'other circumstances' do not include the offender's unsuitability for borstal training; the reference was probably to the case where the offender has already spent a substantial period in custody prior to being sentenced.

This firmly established principle does not mean that the fact that the sentencer has originally imposed (or expressed the intention of imposing) a sentence within the prohibited range, and subsequently corrected the error by imposing a longer sentence in compliance with the statute, is necessarily a ground for varying the sentence on appeal. The same applies where the sentencer, on imposing a sentence of three years' imprisonment, has indicated his view that a shorter sentence would have been appropriate if the statute had permitted one. In either case the question on appeal is whether or not the sentence can be objectively justified, having regard to the facts of the offence and all relevant mitigation, rather than whether the sentencer himself considered it excessive or would have imposed a less severe sentence if he had been able to do so. In *Gillespie* [7] the appellant was sentenced to twenty-one months' imprisonment for a burglary committed while on three days' special leave from a sentence of borstal training. When the sentencer was reminded that in these

[1] *Leonard* 4.5.64, 317/65, [1964] Crim. L. R. 551.
[2] See, for example, *Ryall* 15.6.75, 2007/A/75.
[3] See, for example, *Cripps* 19.12.75, 4579/B/75; *Pare* 7.10.74, 1571/C/74, [1974] Crim. L. R. 720.
[4] *Melvin, Timms and Saville* 22.4.77, 5735/C/76.
[5] (1964) 48 Cr. App. R. 165.
[6] *Pare* 7.10.74, 1571/C/74, [1974] Crim. L. R. 720.
[7] (1973) 58 Cr. App. R. 124.

circumstances the appellant did not qualify under the exception to the general rule permitting a sentence of eighteen months or more in the case of a person who had previously served a sentence of borstal training, the appellant was brought back before him and a sentence of three years was imposed. The Court, considering the earlier cases, stated that in such circumstances 'it is for this Court to consider whether in all the circumstances the second thoughts of the sentencing judge were appropriate for the offence, having regard to the circumstances, age and previous character of the particular appellant'. In the present case the eventual sentence was 'entirely proper' and was upheld. Similarly in *Quinn*[1] a sentence of three years' imprisonment was passed on a youth of 20, with the comment that 'I would have liked to have given less than three years, but I cannot do it . . . as the law now stands'. The Court stated that if a substantial sentence of imprisonment was appropriate, the court could not be considered to 'err in principle if it passes a sentence of three years, unless it can be demonstrated from the facts of the case that a sentence of three years is itself either excessive or wrong in principle . . . what matters is not the opinion of the sentencing judge but what he did'. The sentence was upheld. These decisions have generally been followed,[2] although on occasion the Court has reduced a sentence of three years' imprisonment passed in such circumstances on the ground that the manner of its passing gave rise to a justified sense of grievance.[3]

The same principles apply where the statutory minimum is eighteen months' imprisonment as opposed to three years. In *Lyons*[4] a youth of 20 who had previously served a sentence of three years' imprisonment was sentenced to a total of twenty months' imprisonment for five thefts which 'arose out of a single shoplifting expedition . . . during the same afternoon'. The Court found itself in 'the usual difficulty with a young man of this age', but being 'satisfied that the total sentence of twenty months' imprisonment was too much', reduced it to six months.

[1] (1975) 60 Cr. App. R. 314.
[2] See, for example, *Burn and Moran* 1.9.75, 1322/C/75; *Harris* 15.1.76, 4311/C1/75; *Judd* 28.10.76, 2235/A/76.
[3] See, for example, *Johnson* 12.5.75, 3878/B/74, [1975] Crim. L. R. 470 (three years for wounding with intent and affray 'in every way justified and not a day too long', but as sentencer had imposed two years on first count and 'added one year consecutive in order to overcome the statutory difficulty', sentence varied to borstal training, 'lest there should be any sense of grievance'); see also *Smith* 26.5.77, 794/C/77 (eighteen months 'appropriate', but reduced to six months to avoid 'sense of grievance' arising from sentencer's expressed view that twelve months would have been appropriate). See, generally, p. 220 above).
[4] 10.11.75, 2774/B/75. See also *Smith* 26.5.77, 794/C/77 (above n. 3).

Policy in the use of imprisonment

The statutory requirement that no court should impose imprisonment on an offender under 21 unless it is 'of opinion that no other method of dealing with him is appropriate' has never been held to prohibit the use of imprisonment as a deterrent or punitive sentence justified by the inherent gravity of the offence without regard to the needs and potentialities of the offender as an individual. In *Bramley*[1] a youth of 17 took part in two bank robberies in which sawn-off shotguns were used and was sentenced to five years' imprisonment. The Court heard that he came from an 'excellent home' and had no previous convictions, but having considered the statutory caution,[2] came to the conclusion that 'in spite of his age, having regard to the nature of these offences, there is no other method of dealing with this young man except a prison sentence'. (The sentence was reduced to three years). Many similar examples can be found. As has been shown, a sentence of imprisonment may be justified for a less serious offence where the offender has demonstrated that the available means of dealing with him as an individual are unlikely to prove effective. In *Shaw*[3] a youth of 20 who pleaded guilty to ten offences of theft, taking a conveyance, driving while disqualified and going equipped for theft received sentences totalling three years' imprisonment. The Court heard that he had eight previous appearances and had experienced probation, detention in a detention centre, conditional discharge, fines and binding over, although he had never undergone borstal training. Upholding the sentence the Court observed that 'having regard to that record and . . . to the great number of offences which were being dealt with . . . this was a case where a prison sentence was wholly appropriate . . . we do not take the view that there was any departure from the spirit of the Act.'

Subject to these qualifications, sentences of imprisonment imposed on young adult offenders are governed by the principles which apply to sentences of imprisonment generally. Youth, as has been shown, is a substantial mitigating factor, and the young adult offender may expect a significant discount on account of his age, particularly where the sentence is an aggregation of consecutive terms; but where offences of sufficient gravity are committed in circumstances allowing limited scope for mitigation, a substantial sentence of imprisonment may be appropriate. In *Fry*[4] a youth of 18 admitted a series of offences including robbery and burglary, involving two violent

[1] 5.4.71, 6160/C/70.
[2] Then contained in Criminal Justice Act 1948 s. 17(2).
[3] 29.11.74, 3670/B/74.
[4] 13.3.73, 6579/C/72.

attacks on women in the street, one of whom was struck on the head with a 'very substantial' piece of stone. The Court heard that the appellant's mental condition was not wholly normal, although there was apparently no basis for making a hospital order. Stating that 'no court lightly contemplates sending a boy of 17 to prison for five years . . . but this Court cannot feel that the learned judge had any practical alternative', the Court upheld the sentence with the comment that 'if these were offences committed by a young man of normal . . . mental stability, even though he were only 17 . . . a very long sentence of imprisonment would . . . be called for'. Sentences as long as ten years' imprisonment[1] have been upheld on young adult offenders in recent years, although clearly these were cases of exceptional gravity.

The principles governing the use of the sentence of life imprisonment are discussed in chapter 7. Where the conditions for the use of the sentence are satisfied, the youth of the offender does not necessarily prevent its imposition. Sentences of life imprisonment imposed on young adult offenders have been upheld in appropriate cases,[2] and when such sentences have been varied, the grounds have usually been the failure of the case to satisfy the general criteria rather than the youth of the offender.[3]

Young Persons

Offenders between the ages of 14 and 17 may not be sentenced to imprisonment[4] or made the subject of a probation order[5] or community service order.[6] They may be sentenced to detention in a detention centre,[7] and an offender between 15 and 17 may be sentenced to borstal training if the court is 'of opinion that no other method of dealing with him is appropriate'.[8] Powers available only in respect of young persons and children enable courts to make care orders[9] or supervision orders,[10] or order detention for a period to be

---

[1] See, for example, *Sweeting* 7.7.75, 4718/B/74, [1976] Crim. L. R. 81 (youth, 20, substantial record, series of robberies involving violence, tying and gagging of householders; ten years upheld); *Aslam* 26.7.73, 1182/B/72 (youth, 19, manslaughter by deliberately setting fire to house, four people killed, second house attacked; 'the enormity of the crime was such that the sentence was fully justified').

[2] See, for example, *Ashdown* 1.11.73, 3001/C/72, [1974] Crim. L. R. 130; *Thompson* 23.3.71, 6537/C/70 (youth, 18, two offences of arson, 'immature and disturbed'); *Crout* 5.11.73, 3170/B/73.

[3] See, for example, *Picker* (1970) 54 Cr. App. R. 330; *Wheat* 7.10.74, 2781/C/74; *Williams* 11.2.74, 3833/C/73, [1974] Crim. L. R. 376; *Atkinson* 5.4.73, 5761/A/72.

[4] Powers of Criminal Courts Act 1973 s. 19(1).

[5] *Ibid.*, s. 2(1).

[6] *Ibid.*, s. 14(1).

[7] Criminal Justice Act 1961 s. 4.

[8] *Ibid.*, s. 1(2), proviso.

[9] Children and Young Persons Act 1969 s. 7(7)(a).   [10] *Ibid.*, s. 7(7)(b).

determined by the Secretary of State.[1] Young persons are liable to fines[2] and compensation orders[3] in the same way as adults, and may be subjected to hospital orders in appropriate circumstances.[4]

Any court before which a child or young person is found guilty of an offence may remit the offender to a juvenile court to be dealt with in respect of the offence; the court must exercise this power unless it is satisfied that it would be undesirable to do so.[5] Every court in dealing with a child or young person who is brought before it 'shall have regard to the welfare of the child or young person and shall in a proper case take steps for removing him from undesirable surroundings, and for seeing that proper provision is made for his education and training'.[6]

DETENTION IN A DETENTION CENTRE

The powers of the sentencer to impose detention in a detention centre on a young person are similar to those which apply in the case of a young adult offender, except that the young person may not be committed to a detention centre in default.[7]

The use of detention in a detention centre in relation to young persons reflects its use in relation to young adult offenders. The sentence appears to be considered appropriate primarily where the offender's background and history do not suggest the need for training or supervision over a long period, but the gravity of the offence is such that a short custodial sentence is necessary to mark the court's disapprobation. In *Campbell*[8] a youth of 14 was convicted of participating with other youths in an attempt to steal a woman's handbag at an Underground station, and received a sentence of six months' detention. Stating that 'this kind of activity at the present time requires deterrent sentences', the Court approved the choice of detention in a detention centre, but reduced the length of the sentence to three months. In *Moon*[9] a youth of 15 was involved with three

---

[1] Children and Young Persons Act 1933 s. 53(2).

[2] Powers of Criminal Courts Act 1973 s. 30. Difficulty arises where the Crown Court imposes a fine on a young person, as Powers of Criminal Courts Act 1973 s. 31(2) requires the Crown Court on imposing a fine to 'make an order fixing a term of imprisonment which that person is to undergo if any sum . . . is not duly paid', while s. 19(1) states that 'neither the Crown Court nor the magistrates' court shall impose imprisonment on a person under 17 years of age'.

[3] *Ibid.*, s. 35.

[4] Mental Health Act 1959 s. 60.

[5] Children and Young Persons Act 1933 s. 56 (as amended).

[6] *Ibid.*, s. 44(1).

[7] A magistrates' court may not impose detention on a young person for more than three months for a single offence (Criminal Justice Act 1961 s. 4(2)(b)).

[8] 9.4.76, 1542/C/76, [1976] Crim. L. R. 519.

[9] 15.2.73, 6012/C/72.

older boys in an 'exceedingly bad case of indecent assault' on a girl. His sentence of three months' detention was approved.

BORSTAL TRAINING

A sentence of borstal training may be imposed on a young person who has attained the age of 15 years on the day of his conviction,[1] if the court is 'of opinion that no other method of dealing with him is appropriate'.[2] As in the case of the young adult offender, the sentence may be used as an individualized training sentence or as a punitive sentence of intermediate length. Used as an individualized measure, borstal training will typically be considered appropriate for the offender with a substantial record of offences and experience of a variety of other dispositions. In *Lumb*[3] a youth of 16 with two previous court appearances admitted several offences, including burglary and assault occasioning actual bodily harm, committed while subject to a care order under which he had been allowed to live at home. The sentencer had been advised to consider a sentence of detention in a detention centre but imposed borstal training, a sentence which the Court upheld with the observation that 'a short term in a detention centre would not have been enough to cope with the rather deep-seated troubles of this young man'. The use of borstal training as an individualized measure to deal with young persons is not limited to those with substantial records; the sentence has been upheld in appropriate circumstances on first offenders.[4] Similarly, the fact that the offender has a significant record does not necessarily mean that a sentence of borstal training is inevitable. In *Brooks*[5] a youth of 15 with 'quite a serious . . . record . . . for a boy of his age' (including two periods of three months' detention) was sentenced to borstal training for burglary. The probation officer recommended non-custodial treatment, while reports of his behaviour at the detention centre indicated that 'in the surroundings of a detention centre or borstal institution he is able to work and to live a fairly settled life'. Faced with this evidence, the Court referred to the

[1] Criminal Justice Act 1961 s. 1(1).
[2] *Ibid.*, s. 1(2) proviso.
[3] 17.7.72, 2451/C/72; see also *Fuller* 26.10.72, 3888/A/72 (youth, 15, eight findings of guilt, twice on probation, three conditional discharges, non-custodial treatment recommended; borstal training upheld).
[4] See, for example, *Huntley* 4.11.75, 4015/C/75 (youth, 15, no previous appearances, five burglaries admitted, long-standing behavioural problems at school, 'if ever there was a case in which borstal sentence was required in the youth's own interests . . . this was it'; upheld).
[5] 6.12.74, 3839/B/74; see also *Holland* 20.12.73, 4197/C/73 (youth, 16, previously conditionally discharged, on probation, sentenced to detention; borstal training for burglary varied to three years' supervision in view of optimistic report and changed family circumstances).

statutory requirement that it should be satisfied that no other method of dealing with the offender was appropriate, and observed that 'in this particular case it would . . . be difficult . . . to come to that conclusion'. The sentence was varied to a supervision order for two years. These cases, and others, suggest a greater reluctance to uphold borstal training on an offender who is only just old enough to receive the sentence than on a person who is approaching 17.

As in the case of the equivalent provision restricting the imprisonment of young adult offenders, the statutory caution against the use of borstal training to deal with young persons does not prevent the imposition of the sentence as a deterrent or punitive measure in appropriate circumstances. The Court has upheld sentences of borstal training as a deterrent on young persons guilty of offences of particular gravity, despite the absence of any indication of a need for training. In *Norton*[1] a youth of 15 with no previous record was convicted of participating in a robbery in company with four other boys, in the course of which a man was attacked with a piece of wood while crossing a common late at night. Observing that 'although this was his first effort in crime, he has made a rather ugly entrance into it', the Court upheld the sentence with the comment that 'it would be wrong to weaken the effect of any deterrent sentence' in such a case.

LONG-TERM DETENTION

Children and Young Persons Act 1933 s. 53(2) provides for a court to order a child or young person 'to be detained in such place and on such conditions as the Secretary of State may direct'. This power may be exercised only where the offender is convicted of an offence punishable in the case of an adult with fourteen years' imprisonment or more and the court is satisfied that 'none of the other methods in which the case may legally be dealt with is suitable'.[2] An offender sentenced under this provision may be detained in whatever institution the Secretary of State may consider appropriate and may be released on licence on the recommendation of the Parole Board at any time.[3] The period of detention must not exceed the maximum

[1] 28.11.75, 2821/C/75; see also *Horton* 21.12.72, 5676/A/72 (youth, 16, no record, 'good home', good educational record; robbery of man walking street late at night, causing unconsciousness, fractured jaw, lacerations to face; borstal training not 'too harsh'); *Devlin* 20.10.70, 4005/C/70 (youth, 16, participating in attacks on people crossing common, 'essential that severe deterrent sentences should be passed'; borstal training upheld).

[2] Although this formula is similar to that applicable to the use of borstal training for those under 17, it is clear that the power under s. 53(2) should be used only after consideration of borstal training (where that sentence is available); see *Bosomworth* (1973) 57 Cr. App. R. 708.

[3] Criminal Justice Act 1967 s. 61 (1).

term of imprisonment which could be awarded in the case of an adult convicted of the same offence, but a sentence of detention for life may lawfully be passed where the offence is punishable with imprisonment for life in the case of an adult.[1] The power may be exercised in respect of common law offences for which no maximum sentence is fixed[2] and its use is not subject to the restrictions imposed by Criminal Justice Act 1961 s. 3 on the lengths of imprisonment which may be passed on young adult offenders.[3] In making an order under this section the sentencer should not make any recommendation relating to the minimum period which should elapse before the offender is released on licence.[4] The Court has stated on several occasions that an order under this section is not a sentence of imprisonment.[5]

The power to order detention under section 53(2) is used in three distinct kinds of case. The first is that of the dangerous offender—a youth who has committed an offence of considerable gravity, often involving serious violence or risk to life, and who appears to be likely to commit further similar acts in the future. The use of the power in this case is analogous to the use of life imprisonment in the case of adults, but there are two significant differences: the sentencer may (and where possible should) fix an upper limit to the period for which the offender is liable to be detained, and it appears that the power may be exercised where the evidence on which the assessment of dangerousness is based would be insufficient to justify the use of life imprisonment in the case of an adult.

The principles governing the use of the power to order detention of dangerous young persons were considered in *Storey*,[6] where a youth of 16 was ordered to be detained for a period of twenty years after admitting the attempted murder and robbery of a man who was repeatedly struck on the head with a brick while lying unconscious. There was no evidence of mental illness and no rational motive for the degree of violence used. The Court stated that there was an apparent danger of repetition and 'the safety of the public' was the most important consideration; the power under section 53(2) was therefore the most appropriate form of sentence. The length of the period specified by the sentencer was to be based not on the length of imprisonment which would be appropriate as a tariff sentence in the case of an adult, but on 'the possible period during which public danger may arise from the activities of the prisoner before him'. In cases where there was doubt about the length of this period, the

---

[1] *Flemming* (1973) 57 Cr. App. R. 524.
[2] *Bosomworth* (1973) 57 Cr. App. R. 708.
[3] *Bosomworth, ibid.*
[4] *Flemming, ibid.*
[5] *Bosomworth, ibid.*
[6] (1973) 57 Cr. App. R. 840; see also *Jones* 7.6.74 [1974] Crim. L. R. 614.

period should be longer rather than shorter: 'if he fixes too short a period the prisoner may be released necessarily whilst an element of danger still remains . . . if he chooses too long a period . . . it matters less because whatever the length of the period chosen, the Home Secretary can act to release on licence before that period has expired'. In the present case it was conceivable that the appellant would remain dangerous until he was 'fully matured' in his early thirties, and a period of twenty years' detention was accordingly appropriate, although frequently a significantly shorter period would be sufficient.

An order for detention for life is lawful (if the offence of which the young person is convicted is punishable with imprisonment for life in the case of an adult), and may properly be imposed where it is impossible to predict the future development of the offender with any degree of confidence.[1] Where there are reasonable grounds for believing that a young person will cease to be dangerous within a definable period, a sentence of detention for life is inappropriate. In *Tunney*[2] an 'emotionally disturbed' girl of 16 with experience of a variety of institutions set fire to her bed at a treatment centre 'as an exhibition of despair', and was sentenced to detention for life. The Court stated that 'it is wrong in a case where the offender is not inherently a dangerous criminal to say that . . . we must exclude all possible risk that there might be a relapse'; the responsibility of the court was to 'decide itself what the measure of risk is and fix . . . the term which is the maximum period for which she will have to be in custody'. The sentence was varied to detention for three years. More typically the period of detention will be fixed between six and ten years, leaving sufficient time for the offender to pass through adolescence.[3]

The second class of case in which the power to order detention under section 53(2) is used is that of a young person who is not necessarily considered to be dangerous for the future, but who has

[1] See, for example, *Bryson* (1973) 58 Cr. App. R. 464 (boy, 14, arson of dormitory, psychiatric evidence that appellant 'potentially dangerous . . . prognosis . . . extremely poor', 'when one asks oneself whether it is feasible here to impose a detention for a definite number of years . . . we ask ourselves what that period of years would be and none of the experts give us an answer'; detention for life upheld); see also *Flemming* (1973) 57 Cr. App. R. 524 (youth, 16, manslaughter in course of robbery, detention for life: 'he is a dangerous young man . . . nobody can say with any degree of certainty what the future holds . . . the Court cannot afford to take a risk'; sentence upheld).

[2] 11.11.75, 1905/C/75.

[3] See, for example, *Szulimowski* 18.6.71, 3984/70 (boy, 14, burglary with intent to rape; six years' detention upheld); *McCauliffe* 23.7.70, 2037/B/70 (youth, 16, blackmail of young woman, accompanied by threats against children and demand for sexual intercourse; detention for fourteen years reduced to six); *Fuat, Duignan* (1973) 57 Cr. App. R. 840 (participation in attempted murder and robbery; ten years' detention upheld).

committed an offence of such seriousness that a custodial sentence must be passed for deterrent or punitive purposes and the alternative of borstal training is inadequate to reflect the gravity of the offence. In *Ford*[1] a youth of 16 was sentenced to five years' detention for his part in two robberies; his co-defendants, all a few years older, were sentenced to five years' imprisonment. The robberies consisted of snatching women's handbags in the street and were accompanied by violence in some cases. Having referred to the term of sections 53(2) and 44(1) of the Act, the Court held that 'the language of section 53(2) is wide enough to enable the court in a proper case to pass on a child or young person a sentence of general deterrence', but that 'the court will not decide in favour of a deterrent sentence . . . until it has explored every other way of dealing with the case and . . . weighed most carefully in the balance deterrence on one side against individual treatment for . . . the young offender on the other'. The sentence was upheld with the observation that it was not 'a sentence which will lead to a lack of care . . . for the welfare of the young man'. A number of similar cases can be found.[2]

In cases such as these the governing principles are those of the tariff. The sentencer should reflect in the length of the period of detention the presence of mitigating factors[3] (including the offender's extreme youth) and the varying degree of culpability of co-defendants. In one case[4] four youths aged between 15 and 17, all of previous good character, were concerned together in setting fire to rolls of printing paper stacked near a printing works; the incident led to a serious fire causing damage to the extent of £37,000. One of the offenders primarily responsible for the incident, who was over 17, was sentenced to three years' imprisonment; the other, under 17, received

---

[1] (1976) 62 Cr. App. R. 303.

[2] *Bryce* 2.10.70, 3373/A/70 (boy, 16, manslaughter by stabbing, apparently by reason of provocation; five years' detention appropriate for 'a very grave case'); *Bosomworth* (1973) 57 Cr. App. R. 708 (affray leading to death; thirty months' detention upheld); *Shah* 26.7.73, 1152/B/72 (manslaughter of four people by deliberately setting fire to house; eight years' detention upheld); *Swannell* 13.1.75, 1433/C/74 (assault with intent to rob, gratuitous violence against semi-conscious man, 'truly appalling record for a man of his age'; five years' detention upheld); *Lee* 26.1.76, 3786/B/75 (youth, 16, robbery of woman at her home; three years' detention upheld, other co-defendants sentenced to terms of seven and ten years' imprisonment); *Cawford* 22.6.76, 798/A/76 (assault with intent to rob, householder punched and kicked; four years detention upheld, partly in view of history of disturbed behaviour in past); *Shales* 25.6.76, 5647/A/75 (youth, 15, wounding with intent, struck victim on head with glass mug after encounter in street; three years' detention upheld, reports on appellant 'left very little option'); *West* 12.7.76, 1228/C/76 (youth, 16, robbery of elderly man in own home, some violence; four years' detention upheld, partly on assessment of appellant's own needs); *Llewellyn and others* 14.9.77, [1977] Crim. L. R. 105 (bag snatching with violence; deterrent sentence necessary; three years and four years detention appropriate).

[3] See, for example, *Jones* (1975) 62 Cr. App. R. 291 at 295 (above p. 9).

[4] *Manley and others* 5.2.73, 4183/C/73.

four years' detention. The Court considered that the younger defendant who received four years' detention 'has a real grievance', because his sentence exceeded the sentence of imprisonment imposed on the older offender. His sentence was accordingly reduced to two years' detention. As this case illustrates, where sentences are based on deterrence the Court will normally endeavour to apply the principle of proportionality despite statutory complexities. Similarly in *Fothergill*[1] a youth of 16 was sentenced to four years' detention for an assault with intent to rob in which a night watchman was violently attacked. His co-defendant, aged 15, was sentenced to borstal training. Although the appellant's previous behaviour was such that 'this is not simply a case of a very grave offence', the Court considered that 'there may be a sense of injustice having regard to the disparity between the two sentences'. As the appellant was 'clearly the more serious offender of the two' and some differential was necessary, his sentence was reduced to three years' detention.

The third, and least common, use of the power under section 53(2) is as an improvised sentence of borstal training for offenders who are just below the minimum age limit for that sentence and would otherwise probably have received it. In *Houlihan*[2] a boy of 14 was sentenced to twelve months' detention for burglary with the observation that he was not yet old enough for borstal training, a sentence which would offer 'one last hope . . .'. The Court was advised that the appellant was 'mature beyond his years' and had apparently 'entered on a wildly delinquent period'. His sentence was upheld.

CARE ORDERS

A young person found guilty of an offence punishable in the case of an adult with imprisonment may be made the subject of a care order.[3] The effect of a care order is to confer on the relevant local authority[4] the powers and duties of a parent and to empower the authority to 'restrict his liberty to such extent as the authority consider appro-

---

[1] 3.2.72, 5323/C/71; see also *Meadowcraft* 28.2.72, 3015/A/71 (youth, 16, robbery in company with others aged 17 and 24, accomplices sentenced to five years' imprisonment; four years' detention for appellant reduced to two in view of lesser role in offence).

[2] 7.3.75, 448/C/75; see also *Gill* 21.9.71, 1082/C/71, [1971] Crim. L. R. 721 (eighteen months' detention on boy one month too young for borstal training 'an appropriate order', but varied to care order to provide for possibility of longer period at residential school and statutory aftercare over longer period). In *Kissack* 8.4.74, 384/C/74 a youth of 14 with 'a clean record' was ordered to be detained for two years on conviction for wounding with intent. The Court indicated that the case was 'a bad case of its kind' and borstal training would not have been appropriate. The decision must therefore be seen as an extreme application of the principle in *Ford*.

[3] Children and Young Persons Act 1969 s. 7 (7) (a).

[4] *Ibid.*, s. 24 (2).

priate'. A care order remains in effect until the person concerned reaches the age of 18, unless he is 16 or over when the order is made, in which case it continues until he is 19.[1]

The effect of a supervision order is to place the offender concerned under the supervision either of a local authority or of a probation officer,[2] and the order may include requirements relating to residence and compliance with directions given by the supervisor.[3] The duty of the supervisor is to 'advise, assist and befriend' the supervised person.[4] An order made following a finding of guilt expires at the end of three years from the day on which it is made, or of such shorter period as may be specified in the order.[5]

Children

Children under 14 rarely come before the Crown Court. The powers of the court in relation to children are to order detention under section 53 (2), to make care orders and supervision orders,[6] to impose a fine,[7] to make a hospital order or to grant an absolute or conditional discharge.

[1] *Ibid.*, s. 20 (3).
[2] *Ibid.*, s. 11.
[3] *Ibid.*, s. 12.
[4] *Ibid.*, s. 14.
[5] *Ibid.*, s. 17.
[6] A supervision order in respect of a child may place the child under the supervision of a probation officer only if the local authority so request and the probation officer is already performing duties in respect of the family (ibid. s. 13 (2)).
[7] Subject to the difficulty mentioned in n. 2, p. 283 above.

Sentences for the Mentally Disordered Offender

In sentencing mentally disordered offenders the Court generally favours individualized treatment in preference to the tariff. Where an offender is shown to be in need of psychiatric help, and the necessary help is available in a suitable setting, the sentencer should normally use the power to make either a psychiatric probation order or a hospital order. Where an offender's condition is such that he is likely to commit grave offences in the future and no specific treatment can be proposed, the indefinite sentence of life imprisonment may be appropriate. Often the limited scope of the statutory provisions or the lack of secure hospital accommodation leaves the sentencer with no alternative to a fixed term of imprisonment. Although some psychiatric facilities are available within the prison system, the sentencer has no means of ensuring that an offender will be allocated to an institution where a particular form of treatment is available.

Probation with a Requirement that the Probationer Submit to Psychiatric Treatment

CONDITIONS OF ELIGIBILITY

The statutory framework for a psychiatric probation order is provided by Powers of Criminal Courts Act 1973 s. 3. The section provides that if a court makes a probation order it may include in the order a requirement that the offender shall submit, during the whole of the probation period or for such part of the period as may be specified, to treatment by, or under the direction of, a duly qualified medical practitioner, with a view to the improvement of the offender's mental condition. Such a requirement may be included if the court is satisfied on the evidence of an approved medical practitioner[1] that the mental condition of the offender 'is such as requires and may be susceptible to treatment but is not such as to

[1] See Mental Health Act 1959 s. 28.

warrant his detention in pursuance of a hospital order'. The order may specify treatment as a resident patient in a mental hospital (other than a special hospital) or nursing home, treatment as a non-resident patient at a specified institution, or treatment under the direction of a specified practitioner. The clinical nature of the treatment should not be specified. The court must not make a psychiatric probation order unless it is satisfied that arrangements for the intended treatment have been made. The order may not be made without the consent of the offender to the requirement of treatment and to the general requirements of the order.[1]

Where the order requires the probationer to submit to treatment as a resident patient, he is not in the custody of the hospital or institution concerned,[2] although leaving the hospital in contravention of the requirement constitutes a breach of the order for which he may be brought before the court in the normal way.[3] A probationer who refuses to undergo surgical, electrical or other treatment in pursuance of a requirement included in a probation order is not to be treated as in breach of the order on that ground only, if the court before which he is brought considers that 'his refusal was reasonable, having regard to all the circumstances'.[4]

POLICY IN THE USE OF PSYCHIATRIC PROBATION ORDERS

The psychiatric probation order offers the sentencer the advantage that the offender need not be shown to be suffering from 'mental disorder' within the meaning of Mental Health Act 1959 s. 4, and is accordingly available as a means of dealing with some offenders (particularly those addicted to drugs) who are not eligible for hospital orders. Its limitations are that the duration of treatment under the sanction of the order cannot extend beyond the maximum period of the order (three years), and the probationer cannot effectively be detained against his will under the requirements of the order. The power is therefore appropriate only where there is a reasonable chance that the necessary treatment can be completed successfully within three years, and the offender will not represent a substantial risk to the community if at large. In *Binns*[5] a man who set fire to some

[1] Powers of Criminal Courts Act 1973 s. 2(6).
[2] For changes in the location of treatment, see s. 3(5).
[3] *Ibid.*, s. 6.
[4] *Ibid.*, s. 6(7).
[5] 7.5.74, 278/B/74; see also *Lowry* 15.11.74, 756/A/74 (man, 51, good character, threatening neighbour with shot-gun after 'trivial incident', evidence of 'a psychiatric condition . . . susceptible to treatment, not under a hospital order'; four years' imprisonment imposed, as sentencer 'felt . . . that the degree of security which would be offered to the public . . . was not really sufficient' under probation order—upheld).

furniture in his house was put on probation with a condition that he submitted to psychiatric treatment for depression and emotional stress; shortly after the probation order was made he committed a further similar offence for which he was sentenced to a total of five years' imprisonment. The Court declined to vary this sentence to a further probation order with the comment that 'for the protection of the public a prison sentence is the only appropriate way of dealing with this man'. However, as the sentence was too long, a sentence of thirty months' was substituted. In *West*[1] the appellant received two years' imprisonment for stealing almost £7,000 from his employer. Invited to vary the sentence to a psychiatric probation order so that the appellant could receive treatment for chronic alcoholism, the Court stated that 'if we felt that . . . this man's hope of salvation lay in the making of a section 3 order, this Court might be prepared to consider making such an order'. As the failure of previous attempts to treat the appellant meant that the chance of success was not such 'as to justify our ignoring the other considerations which the Court has to take into account', the sentence was upheld.

Where the making of a psychiatric probation order appears to offer a reasonable chance of solving the offender's problems without serious danger to public, an order will usually be made, even though the offence concerned is one of substantial gravity. Psychiatric probation orders have been made in cases of manslaughter,[2] wounding with intent,[3] blackmail,[4] arson[5] and indecent assault,[6] as well as many offences of a less serious nature. The Court is likely to

[1] 30.7.75, 982/B/75; see also *Winter* 14.3.74, 165/A/74 (nine months for drug offences, previous probation order with condition requiring residential treatment ineffective; 'he has had his chances and he has not availed himself of those chances'—sentence upheld).

[2] See, for example, *Miles* 6.5.76, 528/B/76 (manslaughter of wife while suffering from acute depressive illness, appellant substantially recovered by time of trial); *Clemence* 25.7.75, 1051/C/75 (manslaughter by gross neglect of new-born child, immature girl: 'it was not a case which called so much for punishment as assistance'; four years' imprisonment varied to psychiatric probation order).

[3] See, for example, *Smith* 17.6.71, 448/A/71 (wife stabbing husband, 'long history of mental trouble' arising out of matrimonial problems; three years varied to probation); *Hayes* 29.1.74, 3658/A/73 (husband stabbing wife as culmination of period of depression'; three years varied to probation order requiring treatment as outpatient).

[4] *Bond* 27.2.75, 4770/B/74 (see above, p. 24).

[5] See, for example, *McLoughlin* 19.12.75, 5301/A/75 (woman, 41, setting fire to furniture in house 'in a state of mental turmoil' as a result of long periods of matrimonial stress, evidence of a 'pathological state of depression'; two years varied to probation with condition requiring treatment); *Long* 28.5.76, 231/B/76 (youth, 18, setting fire to school, damage costing £30,000, 'severely maladjusted'; three years varied to probation with requirement of treatment).

[6] See, for example, *Watkins* 17.1.72, 4357/A/71 (man, 41, previous good character, indecency with girls aged 5 and 10; two years varied to probation); *Fletton* 6.9.71, 3101/B/71 (indecent assault on two girls, history of similar offences, previous psychiatric treatment ineffective, but Court prepared 'to give him one last chance'; three years varied to probation with condition requiring out-patient treatment).

uphold a sentence of imprisonment in deference to the claims of the tariff only where the offence is of the utmost inherent gravity and the need for treatment minimal.[1]

Hospital Orders

CONDITIONS OF ELIGIBILITY

The statutory provisions governing hospital orders are contained in Part Five of the Mental Health Act 1959. The Act allows the Crown Court to make a hospital order in respect of a person convicted of any offence[2] (other than one with a sentence fixed by law) if it is satisfied on the evidence of two medical practitioners that the offender is suffering from mental illness, psychopathic disorder, subnormality or severe subnormality, that the disorder is of a nature or degree which warrants the detention of the patient in a hospital for medical treatment and that the most suitable method of dealing with the case is a hospital order.[3] The order must specify the form of mental disorder from which the offender is found to be suffering, and no order may be made unless two practitioners describe the offender as suffering from the same form of disorder, 'whether or not he is also described by either of them as suffering from another of those forms'.[4] The order must specify the hospital to which the offender will be admitted,[5] and no order may be made unless the court is satisfied that arrangements have been made for the admission of the offender to that hospital within twenty-eight days of the making of the order.[6] Where a hospital order is made the court must not impose any sentence involving detention, a fine or a probation order in respect of the offence, but 'may make any other order which the Court has power to make'[7] (such as a compensation order or an order disqualifying the offender from driving).

A hospital order is authority for the removal of the offender to the hospital specified in the order and his detention by the managers of the hospital for a period of twelve months in the first instance. The

---

[1] See, for example, *Tenconi* 9.3.72, 601/A/71 (manslaughter of woman by strangulation while suffering 'mild degree of depressive illness'; treatment available but three years' imprisonment upheld in view of 'the measure of deliberation'). Compare *Lagden* (1970) 54 Cr. App. R. 499 at 511.

[2] Where the conviction is by a magistrates' court, the offence must be punishable by imprisonment (Mental Health Act 1959 s. 60(1)).

[3] Mental Health Act 1956 s. 60(1).

[4] *Ibid.*, s. 60(5).

[5] *Ibid.*, s. 60(1).

[6] *Ibid.*, s. 60(3).

[7] *Ibid.*, s. 60(6).

period of detention may be extended for two years at a time if the managers receive a report from the responsible medical officer that it is necessary, in the interests of the patient's health or safety or for the protection of other persons, that the offender should continue to be liable to be detained.[1] The offender may be discharged at any time by the responsible medical officer or the managers of the hospital,[2] or by the Mental Health Review Tribunal on the application of the offender following the renewal of authority for his detention.[3] The liability of the offender to be detained expires automatically if he is absent without leave from the hospital and is not taken into custody within twenty-eight days or (if he is over 21 and subject to an order as a psychopathic or sub-normal patient) six months.[4]

Where the Crown Court makes a hospital order, it may add to the hospital order an order restricting the discharge of the offender, if it considers that it is necessary for the protection of the public to do so, having regard to the nature of the offence, the antecedents of the offender and the risk of his committing further offences if set at large.[5] The restriction order may be for a specified period or for an indefinite period. The effect of a restriction order is to exclude the offender from the general provisions relating to the expiration and renewal of authority for his detention,[6] and to subject the power to discharge, transfer or grant leave of absence to the offender to the consent of the Secretary of State.[7] The Secretary of State may direct that the restriction order shall cease to have effect, in which case the offender remains subject to the hospital order and the provisions of the Act applicable to hospital orders without restriction orders.[8] Alternatively the Secretary of State may discharge the offender from hospital, either absolutely or on conditions;[9] a patient who has been conditionally discharged may be recalled at any time during the currency of the original order.[10]

Neither the hospital order nor the restriction order necessarily means that the offender will be detained in conditions of physical security. Where the offender may abscond from a local mental hospital and commit further grave offences, the sentencer should specify as the hospital where he is to be detained one of the special hospitals offering secure facilities under Part Seven of the Act. This

[1] Mental Health Act 1959 s. 63, applying s. 43.
[2] *Ibid.*, s. 47(2).
[3] *Ibid.*, s. 43(6).
[4] *Ibid.*, s. 40(3).
[5] *Ibid.*, s. 65(1).
[6] *Ibid.*, s. 65(3) (a).
[7] *Ibid.*, s. 65(3) (1).
[8] *Ibid.*, ss. 66(1), 65(5).
[9] *Ibid.*, s. 66(2).
[10] *Ibid.*, s. 66(3).

may not be done unless the hospital is able to receive the offender, and pressure on the limited accommodation available often means that a particular offender cannot be accepted.[1] In such a case the sentencer may have no alternative to a sentence of imprisonment. Where an order is made for the detention of an offender in a special hospital, it is usual for a restriction order to be made so that the Secretary of State may control the discharge of the offender or his transfer to another hospital; but such an order is not necessary as a matter of law.

POLICY IN THE USE OF HOSPITAL ORDERS AND RESTRICTION ORDERS

Where an offender satisfies the statutory conditions for a hospital order the Court will usually require a hospital order to be made, even though the offence would normally attract a substantial sentence of imprisonment on the grounds of general deterrence. The most common reasons for failing to make a hospital order where the offender's mental condition is not normal relate to the limitations of the statutory provisions and the facilities available for their implementation. The reasons are: the failure to establish the presence of 'mental disorder' in the manner required by the Act, the failure to establish that the appellant will benefit from medical treatment under a hospital order, and the lack of secure accommodation for a potentially dangerous patient.

Mental disorder

As has been shown, a hospital order may be made only if the sentencer is satisfied that the offender is suffering from 'mental disorder' as that term is defined in the Act[2] and two medical witnesses agree on the diagnosis.[3] This requirement excludes those offenders whose condition cannot be diagnosed with confidence, those who are the subject of a disagreement between the medical witnesses (although it is sufficient if any two medical witnesses agree on the presence of one statutory disorder, even though other medical witnesses disagree with their assessment), and those whose condition

[1] For a discussion of the administrative problems, see *Parker, Griffiths and Rainbird* 21.3.75, 248/R/75; *McFarlane* (1975) 60 Cr. App. R. 320.

[2] Mental Health Act 1959 s. 4.

[3] See *Smith* 30.7.74, 5558/B/74. It is not necessary that the disorder should be causally connected with the offence for which the hospital order is imposed: see *McBride* 13.1.72, 3959/B/71 ('even if there were no causal connection between the state of depression and the offences, it would not necessarily follow that an order ought not to be made under section 60').

does not amount to 'disorder' within the definition of that term in the Act. Unless in such cases a psychiatric probation order (which does not require proof of mental disorder) can be made, often the only alternative is a sentence of imprisonment, either for life or for a fixed term. In *Robinson*[1] the appellant kidnapped a police officer at gun-term. and ordered him to drive him away from the scene of a burglary; he subsequently repeated the offence with two other people. In view of his history, which included a previous hospital order, he was sentenced to life imprisonment. The Court heard that he was an 'unstable and impulsive person in respect of whom no specific recommendation can be made'. Concluding that 'he is an abnormal person, although he does not fall into any of the four categories of section 60 of the Mental Health Act', the Court upheld the sentence. Similarly in *Bland*[2] a life sentence for arson was upheld on the basis of medical evidence that although the appellant had been described as a psychopathic personality, his condition did not amount to psychopathic disorder within the meaning of the Act.

Treatability

Before a hospital order may be made the sentencer must be satisfied that the nature of the offender's disorder is such as to warrant his detention for medical treatment; medical treatment is defined to include nursing or care and training under medical supervision.[3] The Court may approve a sentence of imprisonment in preference to a hospital order where the offender's condition, although amounting to mental disorder within the meaning of the Act, is not likely to improve as a result of therapy. In *Bringins*[4] a man in his early twenties was sentenced to life imprisonment for buggery of a small boy. The medical evidence was that the appellant 'could be classified as mentally subnormal' but no treatment likely to prevent him repeating the offence was available. The sentence was upheld. In *Ashdown*[5] the appellant was sentenced to life imprisonment for a variety of offences. The consensus of the medical evidence was that although he was suffering from psychopathic disorder, his condition was not amenable to psychotherapy. His sentence was upheld.

Although it is not made explicit in the cases, the main reason for this policy appears to be a desire to reserve hospital places, particularly in special hospitals, for offenders likely to benefit from

[1] 13.6.75, 4384/A/74.
[2] 21.9.71, 1018/C/71.
[3] Mental Health Act 1959 s. 147(1).
[4] 5.5.75, 421/C/75.
[5] 1.11.73, 3001/C/72, [1974] Crim. L. R. 130.

treatment. Where the only function of the hospital would be containment, and the offender can be maintained as effectively in prison as in hospital, a sentence of imprisonment may be the more appropirate choice. The possibility of improvement in response to treatment is not a statutory condition for the making of a hospital order, which may be the appropriate choice where the condition of the offender, although unlikely to change, requires nursing care of a kind unlikely to be available in prison. A hospital order may also be preferred where the offender can safely be detained in a local mental hospital as opposed to a special hospital. In *Smith*[1] a woman who had spent most of her life in hospitals for the mentally subnormal was sentenced to imprisonment for stealing a small amount of money. The Court was told that a place in a local hospital was available for her, and varied the sentence to a hospital order on the basis of a diagnosis of subnormality with the comment that 'the future is not going to be plain sailing'.

Security

The majority of mental hospitals do not provide a high degree of physical security. Where the sentencer is concerned to ensure that the offender will not be able to abscond from a hospital to which he is committed under a hospital order, he should specify as the hospital where the offender is to be detained one of the special hospitals. The decision to accept an offender as a patient in a special hospital is within the responsibility of the Department of National Health and Social Security,[2] and cases may arise where although the sentencer considers that a hospital order can be made only if the offender is accepted at a special hospital, the Department decides that the offender is not a suitable candidate for accommodation at such a hospital. In these cases the sentencer has 'no option . . . but to impose a prison sentence',[3] and it is inappropriate to 'adjourn . . . in the pious hope that something may transpire in the future'.[4]

The use of hospital orders

Where the offender satisfies the conditions of eligibility for a hospital order and the problems mentioned above do not arise, the sentencer

[1] 13.1.76, 5919/B/75.
[2] See National Health Service Reorganization Act 1973 s. 40.
[3] *Parker, Griffiths and Rainbird* 21.3.75, 248/R/75, where the statutory provisions are examined.
[4] *Howard* 24.7.75, 1351/C/75. It is inappropriate to give leave to appeal in such cases merely to draw attention to the problem; see *Jones* 19.11.76, 4420/B/76, [1977] Crim. L. R. 158.

will normally be expected to make a hospital order. It is rarely appropriate to impose a sentence of imprisonment relying on the power of the Secretary of State to transfer the offender to hospital,[1] if a hospital order can be made immediately, as any restriction order made in conjuction with such a transfer lapses at the expiration of the sentence of imprisonment,[2] and if the offender recovers from his disorder before the date on which he would be released from imprisonment, he is liable to be returned to prison to serve the balance of his sentence.[3] Although hospital orders are frequently made in cases involving grave offences of violence, the gravity of the offences is not an important consideration in making a hospital order (except in so far as it indicates a need for detention in secure conditions). Hospital orders have been upheld or imposed on appeal on offenders whose offences would not have justified a substantial term of imprisonment. In *Allison*[4] the appellant was made the subject of a hospital order authorizing his detention in a special hospital, with an indefinite restriction order, on his conviction for the 'very minor offence' of stealing £4.80 from his sister. Upholding the sentence, the Court stated that the order was justified on the 'overwhelming body of evidence . . . that in the interests of both the appellant and the public it was necessary for him to receive treatment for a prolonged period in a secure hospital', and 'the fact that the offence itself was of a minor character is neither here nor there'.

THE RESTRICTION ORDER

The main effect of a restriction order is to subject to the consent of the Secretary of State all decisions in respect of the offender relating to discharge, transfer or grant of leave. The restriction order also prevents the offender from taking advantage of the provisions under which authority for detention lapses when the patient is absent without leave for a specified period of time.[5] The restriction order does not mean that the offender will not be discharged before the period of restriction expires, or that he will not be detained after that time.

The general policy of the Court is to make a restriction order in any

[1] Mental Health Act 1959 s. 72.
[2] See Mental Health Act 1959 ss. 74, 75(2); *Rose* 15.5.70, 550/A/70.
[3] Mental Health Act 1959 s. 75(1).
[4] 31.1.77, 119/A/76; see also *Eaton* 31.7.75, 3182/R/75, [1975] Crim. L. R. 390 (woman with long history of disturbed behaviour; sentence of imprisonment for breaking two panes of glass in telephone kiosk varied to hospital order with indefinite restriction order); *Smith* 13.1.76, 5919/R/75 (subnormal offender convicted of stealing 36p; twelve months' imprisonment varied to hospital order with indefinite restriction order).
[5] Mental Health Act 1959 s. 40(3) (p. 295 above).

case where there is a possible threat to the public from the premature discharge of the offender,[1] even though the offence for which the order is made is neither violent nor particularly serious.[2] Any restriction order which is made should normally be 'without limit of time'[3] unless 'the doctors are able to assert confidently that recovery will take place within a fixed period'.[4] In *Toland*[5] a youth who had been transferred from borstal to a hospital committed a number of burglaries after twice absconding from the hospital. He was made subject to a hospital order and an unlimited restriction order. Upholding the restriction order, the Court observed that although there was no history of violence 'the public is entitled to be protected because when he is put in open hospitals he absconds and . . . unless a restriction order is made he may through absconding obtain ultimate freedom'. These decisions do not mean that a restriction order should necessarily be made in every case.[6]

GUARDIANSHIP ORDERS

As an alternative to a hospital order, the sentencer may make a guardianship order placing the offender under the guardianship of a local health authority or of such other person (approved by the local health authority) as may be specified.[7] The conditions relating to proof of mental disorder must be satisfied, as in the case of a hospital order, and the sentencer must be satisfied that the authority or approved person concerned is willing to receive the offender into guardianship.[8] A guardianship order confers on the guardian 'all such powers as would be exercisable by them or him in relation to the patient, if they or he were the father of the patient and the patient were under the age of 14 years'.[9]

Life Imprisonment

The sentence of life imprisonment was not created legislatively as a special measure for dangerous offenders. It emerged as the maximum sentence for a considerable number of offences as a result of

---

[1] See generally *Gardiner* (1967) 51 Cr. App. R. 187.
[2] See, for example, *Eaton* 31.7.75, 3182/R/75, [1976] Crim. L. R. 390 (n. 1, p. 40 above); *Smith* 30.7.74, 5558/B/73 (series of minor frauds, diagnosis of paranoid schizophrenia; hospital order with indefinite restriction order upheld).
[3] Mental Health Act 1959 s. 65(1).
[4] *Gardiner*, (1967) 51 Cr. App. R. 187, followed in *Toland* (1973) 58 Cr. App. R. 453.
[5] (1973) 58 Cr. App. R. 453; see also *Blackwood* (1974) 59 Cr. App. R. 170.
[6] *Gardiner* (1967) 51 Cr. App. R. 187 at 192.
[7] Mental Health Act 1959 s. 60(1).
[8] *Ibid.*, s. 60(4).
[9] Mental Health Act 1959 s. 34(1).

amendments, consolidations and partial codifications of the criminal law at various times.[1] Its distinctive use as an indefinite preventive sentence began as a result of judicial initiative after the enactment of provisions enabling a person subject to a sentence of life imprisonment to be released by the Home Secretary subject to conditions and recalled at any time. The current provisions[2] empower the Home Secretary to release on licence a person sentenced to life imprisonment if recommended to do so by the Parole Board and after consultation with the Lord Chief Justice and the trial judge (if the trial judge is available). The licence may be subject to conditions and the offender may be recalled by the Home Secretary on the recommendation of the Parole Board, or by the Home Secretary without such recommendation, if he considers it 'expedient in the public interest to recall that person before such consultation is practicable'.[3] The licence may also be revoked by the Crown Court if the offender is convicted on indictment or committed for sentence. Whether or not the offender is released on licence, the sentence continues in effect until the end of his natural life, and he remains (if released) permanently subject to such conditions as may have been imposed at the time of his release and to the possibility of recall to prison.

The proper use of the sentence of life imprisonment has been considered in a large number of cases. Their general effect is that the sentence is reserved for persons who have committed offences of substantial gravity and who appear to be suffering from some disorder of personality or instability of character which makes them likely to commit grave offences in the future if left at large or released from a fixed term of imprisonment. The sentence is not normally used as a tariff sentence to deal with offenders of normal mentality who have committed offences of great gravity.

THE DANGEROUSNESS OF THE OFFENDER

The Court has said that the sentence of life imprisonment should be used only where the mental condition of the offender is such that he will probably commit grave offences in the future. In *Picker*[4] it was stated that 'where the nature of the offence and the make-up of the offender are of such a nature that the public require protection for a considerable time unless there is a change in his condition . . . it is

[1] For the history of maximum sentences, see D. A. Thomas, *The Penal Equation*, Institute of Criminology, Cambridge, (1978).

[2] Criminal Justice Act 1967 s. 61.

[3] Criminal Justice Act 1967 s. 62(1) and (4). For the right of persons recalled in this way to have their cases reconsidered by the Parole Board, see s. 62(4) and (5).

[4] (1970) 54 Cr. App. R. 330.

right for the judge to impose a life sentence. This will enable some other authority to ascertain from time to time whether the condition has changed and it is safe for the offender to be released . . . but where no such conditions exist, it is quite clear . . . that a judge should not pass the difficult matter of sentencing and the length of detention to others'. This principle has been applied many times.[1]

The nature of the mental condition required to justify a sentence of life imprisonment eludes precise definition. In some cases the offender suffers from a mental disorder within the meaning of the Mental Health Act 1959 but cannot be dealt with by means of a hospital order for one or more of the reasons given earlier;[2] in other cases the offender is subject to a condition which is clinically recognizable but is not within the statutory definition.[3] Life sentences have been upheld on the basis of evidence that the offender is emotionally immature,[4] subject to abnormal sexual drives or fantasies[5] or impulsive and unstable.[6] What is important is not whether the offender's condition can be accurately described by a recognized psychiatric term, but whether it can be predicted with a sufficient degree of confidence that the offender will, unless restrained, commit further grave offences in the future, and that his propensity to do so will not decline within a forseeable period. In *Stanford*[7] a man with a long record of violence was sentenced to life imprisonment for causing grievous bodily harm to a sixteen-month-old-girl. The evidence was that the appellant had a 'defective personality' and had previously been classified as psychopathic, although no psychiatric treatment was possible. The present offence was thought to be related to a hostility towards small girls which resulted from an accident

[1] See, for example, *Blythin* 15.6.70, 9288/69 (arson); *Waterman* 5.10.70, 1370/B/70 (rape); *Beever* 3.5.71, 144/A/71, [1971] Crim. L. R. 492 (attempted murder); *Ditta* 23.7.70, 1941/B/70 (manslaughter); *Atkinson* 5.4.73, 5761/A/72 (manslaughter), *Johannsen* (1977) 65 Cr. App. R. 101 (buggery).

[2] See, for example, *Bringins* 5.5.75, 421/C/75 (p. 297 above); *Gallagher* 2.2.70, 5284/69 (robbery and causing grievous bodily harm with intent, appellant 'very psychopathic and dangerous'); *McInerney* 27.7.70, 774/B/70 (manslaughter);

[3] See, for example, *Robinson* 13.6.75, 4384/A/74 (p. 297 above); *Williamson* 5.3.70, 6846/A/69 (appellant 21, several offences of arson, 'mild personality disorder', treatment 'not likely to alter his dangerous proclivities'); *Wilkins* 18.3.74, 3917/A/73 (manslaughter, personality disorder falling short of psychopathic disorder).

[4] *Buchanan* 16.6.75, 4783/B/74 (attempting to wound with intent); *Chaplin* 4.12.75, 3985/B/75, [1976] Crim. L. R. 320 (wounding with intent); *Thompson* 23.7.71, 6537/C/70 (arson).

[5] See, for example, *Skelding* (1973) 58 Cr. App. R. 313; *O'Rourke* 27.11.72, 3920/A/72, (rape).

[6] *Chaplin* 4.12.75, 3985/B/75, [1976] Crim. L. R. 320.

[7] 3.7.72, 708/A/72; see also *Watson* 25.3.76, 2267/C/75, [1976] Crim. L. R. 698 (man of mature years, previous convictions for indecent assault and buggery of young boys, 'a responsible, highly intelligent, law-abiding individual . . . apart from these activities . . . not a psychiatric problem'; life imprisonment upheld for four offences of buggery).

suffered by the appellant's father shortly before his death; further acts of violence to children were 'a clear possibility'. The sentence was upheld.

It seems clear from the cases that a sentence of life imprisonment should not be passed without a full psychiatric investigation of the offender. The fact that the offender can be characterized as abnormal in some respect will not justify a sentence of life imprisonment if a sentence proportionate to the gravity of the offence will provide adequate protection for the public.[1] The sentencer's responsibility is to assess the dangerousness of the offender on the basis of the available evidence, and impose life imprisonment only if a fixed-term sentence would be insufficient for this purpose. In *Lewis*[2] the appellant was sentenced to life imprisonment for the violent rape of the 14-year-old daughter of the woman with whom he was living. Conflicting medical evidence was presented. One witness considered that the appellant represented 'a real risk to the community' as a result of brain damage which had impaired his capacity for self-control, and that he required treatment in conditions of maximum security; the second witness, while agreeing with the diagnosis, described the risk as 'minimal' in view of the absence of other incidents of violent behaviour, and considered that 'he is no special danger to the public'. In the event the Court preferred the latter evidence and varied the sentence to five years' imprisonment. In *Adams*[3] the appellant was convicted of manslaughter by reason of diminished responsibility following the death of the young son of the woman with whom her husband was living. The evidence was that the appellant had committed the offence in a temporary state of severe depression and anxiety, but was subject to a 'weakness in her personality' in that she could not deal with stress or emotional conflict; although she was not suffering from mental disorder, there was a 'serious risk' of further violence if similar circumstances were to arise in the future. The sentence of life imprisonment was upheld with the comment that it was not imposed 'because this appellant required punishment', and would be 'kept constantly under review'. In

---

[1] See, for example, *Dearden* 11.2.74, 3414/B/73 (man, 55, buggery of boy, long history of similar behaviour; life imprisonment would be appropriate for 'a young man with many years of sexual activity before him', but reduced to ten years, as appellant's 'urges to commit offences of this kind are likely to be on the wane in a few years').

[2] 14.1.74, 2845/B/73; see also *Poyntoon* 16.3.76, 5174/B/75 ('utterly incompetent' attempt to rob post office, no violence or weapon, appellant suffering from 'personality disorder' but not 'an aggressive psychopath'; life imprisonment varied to seven years).

[3] 11.4.75, 3291/B/74. Compare *Kightley* 9.11.73, 5684/C/72 (five offences of arson, no likelihood of change in appellant's condition or prospect of treatment, offences 'not so serious and the likelihood of repetition . . . not so great as to make it a prospect that one can contemplate that this appellant should . . . be detained in prison for the rest of his life'; life imprisonment varied to five years); *Riley* 1.3.74, 5474/A/73 (wounding with intent, treatment possible within limited time; life imprisonment varied to three years).

Rankin[1] the appellant set two small fires in a house after a quarrel with the woman with whom he lived, causing modest damage. The Court received evidence that although his state of mind was still 'disturbed' there were hopes of stability in the future, and commented that 'the problem . . . is whether . . . the danger to be public of this man being at large, and the difficulty in assessing when he will be safe to be at large, is so great that life imprisonment is really the only practical course . . . a fixed term is clearly proper if . . . the risk of this man being at liberty at the end of the fixed term is one which the public ought . . . to bear'. The sentence of life imprisonment was varied to three years' imprisonment.[2]

While these examples indicate that the continuation of a state of dangerousness for an unpredictable period of time is a characteristic of many cases in which life imprisonment is upheld, the possibility of some improvement in the appellant's mental state is not a necessary condition for the imposition of the sentence. A life sentence may be imposed where the prospect is one of continuing detention. In *Chaplin*[3] a man of 22 with previous convictions for wounding and violence was sentenced to life imprisonment for wounding with intent a man whose face was severely lacerated by a broken bottle which the appellant pushed into his face and twisted around. The appellant was described as 'emotionally immature' and likely to become involved in 'impulsive' acts of violence; there was 'no forecast of immediate maturity supervening' and 'every prospect that he will commit some extremely violent and dangerous crimes' if released. The sentence was upheld.

It is not necessary that the future offences which the sentence is intended to prevent be of the same kind as those for which the sentence is imposed. In *Hildersley*[4] the appellant was involved in a robbery in which a couple were attacked in their home and a quantity of property stolen. The appellant had a number of previous convictions and was currently unlawfully at large from a hospital order with restriction made two years previously. The medical evidence was that he had a 'long-standing personality disorder characterized by an abnormal sexual instinct with a fixation on small boys'. The Court upheld a sentence of life imprisonment with the

[1] 24.5.73, 846/C/73; see also *Ford* 22.11.76, 5026/A/75 (youth, 19, arson leading to destruction of factory, damage estimated at £250,000, evidence of 'real prospect' of maturity within five years; life imprisonment reduced to six years).

[2] On 3.7.73.

[3] 4.12.75, 3985/B/75, [1976] Crim. L. R. 320. It is submitted that *Douglas* 13.10.75, 2495/B/75 is inconsistent with the general body of cases in so far as it indicates that 'some prospect of treatment' or other grounds for expecting improvement in the offender's condition are necessary before a life sentence can be imposed.

[4] 7.12.73, 1205/C/73, [1974] Crim. L. R. 197.

comment that the appellant was 'a menace to householders and small boys'.

THE GRAVITY OF THE IMMEDIATE OFFENCE

As a general principle, the maximum sentence provided by the law for a particular offence is reserved for the worst example of that offence likely to be encountered in practice. This principle clearly does not apply to the sentence of life imprisonment imposed as a preventive measure on dangerous offenders, but the Court has stated on occasion that the sentence should be used only in cases of 'serious crimes'. In *Williams*[1] a youth was sentenced to life imprisonment for assault with intent to rob on two occasions. While on probation for attempted rape he had attacked a woman and stolen her purse; on the second occasion he threatened a woman in her home with a toy pistol and obtained 50p from her. The sentence was passed on the basis of evidence that the appellant was 'severely disabled as a personality' and required psychological treatment under secure conditions. The Court stated that 'this is an approach which in cases of serious crimes this Court has endorsed' but the two offences 'would not support a sentence of life imprisonment'; a sentence of five years' imprisonment was substituted. Similarly in *Scott*[2] a man with an 'appalling record' was sentenced to life imprisonment for aggravated burglary and seven years (the maximum) for attempted rape. He had obtained access to a house by fraud, threatened an *au pair* girl with a knife and attempted to rape her. The Court recognized that life imprisonment could properly be imposed where 'a man . . . has committed a really serious offence and . . . as a result of some mental condition or defect in personality it might be dangerous for him to be released after a determinate sentence', but this approach was appropriate 'only . . . in the case . . . of really serious offences'. The aggravated burglary—'getting into premises by false pretences and consuming a bottle of port'—was not sufficient to justify the sentence, which was varied to an extended term of seven years.

By contrast with these decisions, the Court in *Ashdown*[3] upheld a sentence of life imprisonment for a robbery consisting of the theft of £2 from a man accosted in the street and threatened with an air pistol. The sentence was based on medical evidence that the appellant was subject to an 'abnormally high sexual drive which . . . pursues a deviant course', with limited ability to control his impulses. No treatment offered a permanent and guaranteed improvement in the

[1] 11.2.74, 3833/C/73, [1974] Crim. L. R. 376.
[2] 15.5.70, 8885/69.
[3] 1.11.73, 3001/C/72, [1974] Crim. L. R. 130.

appellant's condition, and there was a real probability of violent sexual offences if the appellant was released. Although the Court considered that if the case had been dealt with by means of a determinate sentence, a sentence of five years' imprisonment would have been sufficient, the sentence of life imprisonment was upheld.

The question of how serious the immediate offence must be before a sentence of life imprisonment can be imposed was examined in two further decisions, which indicate that the dangerousness of the offender and the gravity of the immediate offence may properly be considered in relation to each other. In *Wheal*[1] a youth of 19 was sentenced to life imprisonment for raping a woman of 63 under threat. The evidence was that the appellant was a person of high sexual drive and grossly immature, but there was not 'a very grave risk of repetition of this type of offence'. The Court stated that 'life imprisonment may be justified in a case where, although the facts of the offence themselves were not of the gravest, nevertheless the likelihood of repetition of the offence was strong . . . where the risk of repetition is very remote, then life imprisonment would only be justified if, on a balancing exercise, the gravity of the offence was of the greatest'. Applying this principle, the sentence was reduced to six years. In *Thornton*[2] the appellant set fire to some curtains in a hospital, causing minor damage. The medical evidence was that the appellant was suffering from psychopathic disorder leading to persistent and abnormal aggression; he was not suitable for treatment in a local hospital and if committed to a special hospital, the 'hospital role would . . . be custodial rather than therapeutic'. The Court accepted that on the facts the offences committed by the appellant were 'at the lower end of the scale' for arson, but applying the principle that 'when considering the appropriateness of a life sentence, the gravity of the offence need not be so serious in a case where the likelihood of repetition is high as it must be in a case when the likelihood of repetition is remote', the sentence was upheld. The implication of these decisions appears to be that there is no minimum level of gravity which the immediate offence must reach before the sentence of life imprisonment may be imposed, provided the evidence of dangerousness is sufficiently compelling.

THE AVAILABILITY OF ALTERNATIVE SENTENCES

As the cases cited illustrate, life imprisonment is a sentence of last resort and will not normally be upheld where the offender can

[1] 7.10.74, 2781/C/74.
[2] 11.10.74, 2404/C/74, [1975] Crim. L. R. 51.

properly be dealt with by means of a psychiatric probation order,[1] hospital order[2] or fixed term of imprisonment.[3] One decision which appears to be inconsistent with this approach is *Harvey*,[4] where the appellant was sentenced to life imprisonment for manslaughter by reason of diminished responsibility, following evidence that she was suffering from psychopathic disorder and her condition might be ameliorated by treatment in hospital. The sentencer declined to make a hospital order on the ground that the appellant might be discharged prematurely and to the danger of the public if the responsible medical authority took the view that no further treatment was possible, and the sentence was upheld on that ground. The decision appears to ignore the possibility of a restriction order, which would prevent premature discharge without the consent of the Home Secretary, and it is submitted that the decision must be treated as *per incuriam*.

Life imprisonment is not normally seen by the Court as a deterrent sentence[5] and is frequently described as a more merciful alternative than a long fixed term. At least one decision suggests that it may be appropriate to impose a fixed-term sentence in preference to an indefinite sentence where there is a compelling demand for a deterrent sentence, even though the offender would otherwise qualify for a life sentence. In *Beagle*[6] a man said to be subject to 'a personality disorder of the psychopathic type with aggressive and paranoid features' admitted kidnapping a man and his fiancée and demanding money for their release. Stating that 'when cases of kidnapping come before the Courts it is imperative that the sentence passed should be genuinely deterrent', but that life imprisonment was not appropriate for this purpose, the Court varied the sentence to eighteen years' imprisonment. The Court did not appear to consider whether the sentence of life imprisonment could have been upheld on the principles discussed above, although the evidence suggests that it could have been approved on those grounds, and it is not clear how far this decision is a basis for generalization.

---

[1] See, for example, *McBride* 9.11.73, 3573/C/73 (p. 11 above); *Griffith* 1.5.75, 3537/C/74 (p. 11 above).

[2] See, for example, *Horan* 23.4.74, 3023/A/73, [1974] Crim. L. R. 438 (appellant suffering from chronic schizophrenia, arson while subject to hospital order specifying local hospital, life imprisonment imposed as no place available in special hospital, special hospital place subsequently made available; life imprisonment varied to hospital order: 'we have . . . the three alternatives before us—a life sentence, a non-secure hospital or Broadmoor . . . the proper thing to do . . . is to give the appellant . . . the opportunity of being treated').

[3] See, for example, *Rankin* 24.5.73, 846/C/73 (p. 304 above).

[4] 16.7.71, 753/A/71, [1971] Crim. L. R. 664.

[5] For an exception, see *Trusty* 8.3.77, 5469/R/75 (robbery and attempted murder).

[6] (1975) 62 Cr. App. R. 151.

Fixed-term Sentences

Cases arise where the offender, although not wholly normal, does not qualify for psychiatric treatment under a probation order or hospital order, and does not satisfy the criteria for a sentence of life imprisonment. A typical example is the offender suffering from some degree of subnormality and personality disorder who persistently commits offences of modest gravity.[1] In such cases there is often no practical alternative to a fixed term of imprisonment. If such a sentence is imposed, the normal principles of the tariff apply, and the sentence must not be disproportionate to the gravity of the immediate offence unless passed as an extended sentence.[2] The sentencer is entitled to mitigate the sentence if he considers that the mental disorder affected the offender's responsibility,[3] or if there are prospects that treatment available within the prison system may enable him to be discharged at an earlier date than would be possible if the full proportionate sentence were imposed.[4]

[1] See, for example, *Gwilliam* 5.5.72, 272/C/72, [1972] Crim. L. R. 514.

[2] See the discussion of the authorities, including those inconsistent with this proposition, at pp. 44–46 above.

[3] See, for example, *Macauley* 8.5.75, 4570/B/74 (man of good character, handling substantial quantity of stolen property; eighteen months reduced to allow immediate discharge on evidence that at time of offence appellant was suffering from disturbance of brain function, now corrected).

[4] See p. 49 above.

8

Extended Sentences

Under the heading 'Powers Relating to Persistent Offenders', Powers of Criminal Courts Act 1973 s. 28 provides for the imposition of an extended term of imprisonment on offenders who satisfy the statutory conditions of eligibility. Before an extended sentence may be imposed six conditions must be fulfilled. These are that:

(1) the offender is convicted on indictment[1] of an offence punishable with imprisonment for two years or more;

(2) the offence was committed before the expiration of three years either from a previous conviction[2] of an offence punishable with imprisonment for a term of two years or more, or from his final release[3] from prison after serving a sentence of imprisonment passed on such a conviction;[4]

(3) the offender has been convicted on indictment[5] on at least three previous occasions since he attained the age of 21 of offences punishable on indictment with imprisonment for two years or more (a conviction followed by a probation order or conditional discharge does not count for this purpose unless the offender was eventually sentenced for the offence);[6]

(4) the offender was sentenced on those occasions to a total period of not less than five years' imprisonment[7] (including terms which were suspended);[8]

[1] This condition is satisfied where the offender is committed for sentence under Magistrates' Courts Act 1952 s. 29; see Powers of Criminal Courts Act 1973 s. 42.

[2] Apparently including a summary conviction for an indictable offence.

[3] Including release on licence; see Powers of Criminal Courts Act 1973 s. 29(5).

[4] The cases are in conflict on the application of this condition where the immediate offence is committed while the offender is serving a sentence in respect of a conviction which occurred more than three years before the immediate offence, and has not been released from that sentence. In *Clark* 3.7.70, 700/B/70 and *Gillingham* 24.7.70, 4351/C/70 the Court held that the condition was not satisfied in these circumstances (the offender committing an offence while on pre-release leave towards the end of a long sentence); a contrary view was taken in *Johnson* (1976) 62 Cr. App. R. 300.

[5] A conviction in a magistrates' court followed by a sentence of imprisonment, corrective training or preventive detention in the Crown Court or Quarter Sessions, satisfies this condition; see Powers of Criminal Courts Act 1973 s. 29(3).

[6] *Ibid.*, s. 13(1); see *Spearpoint* 31.10.72, 3538/B/71.

[7] Or preventive detention or corrective training.

[8] See Powers of Criminal Courts Act 1973 s. 22(6)(a).

(5) either the offender was sentenced on one of those occasions to preventive detention, on at least two of those occasions a sentence of imprisonment (other than a suspended sentence which did not take effect) or of corrective training was passed, and one sentence of imprisonment was for three years or more or two sentences of imprisonment were for two years or more in respect of one offence; [1]

(6) the court is 'satisfied, by reason of his previous conduct and the likelihood of his committing further offences, that it is expedient to protect the public from him for a substantial time'.

An extended sentence imposed under these provisions may exceed the maximum term authorized for the offence, but must not exceed:

(1) in the case of an offence punishable normally with a maximum of less than five years imprisonment, five years;

(2) in the case of an offence punishable normally with a maximum of five years or more, but less than ten years' imprisonment, ten years.

In the case of an offence punishable with ten years' imprisonment or more, the normal maximum sentence may not be exceeded. [2] An extended sentence may be passed for a term which is below the maximum sentence authorized for the offence in normal circumstances. [3]

PROCEDURE

In determining whether the qualifying conditions relating to previous convictions and sentences are satisfied, the sentencer may rely only on those convictions and sentences set out in a notice served on the offender at least three days before the extended sentence is passed, informing the offender that it is intended to prove the convictions and sentences. [4] Where the existence of a previous sentence or conviction is disputed by the offender, it should be formally proved. [5] A certificate signed by the governor of the prison concerned is evidence that the prisoner was finally released from a specified sentence, or had not been so released, on a specified date. [6]

---

[1] The term 'sentence of imprisonment' in s. 28(3)(c)(ii) does not include a sentence of corrective training (*Newton* (1973) 57 Cr. app. R. 346), and the requirements of this sub section in relation to length of sentences can be met only reference to sentences of imprisonment.

[2] Powers of Criminal Courts Act 1973 s. 28(2).

[3] *D.P.P. v. Ottewell* (1968) 52 Cr. App. R. 679.

[4] Powers of Criminal Courts Act 1973 s. 29(3). Where the notice is not served in sufficient time, the proper course is to adjourn to allow the required period to elapse (*Connolly* 19.10.73, 3993/A/73).

[5] See Criminal Justice Act 1948 s. 39(1).

[6] Powers of Criminal Courts Act 1973 s. 29(1).

FORM OF SENTENCE

Where an extended sentence is imposed, the sentencer must issue an 'extended sentence certificate', stating that the term was so imposed.[1] Where the offender is sentenced on the same occasion in respect of a number of different offences, it is incorrect to issue a single certificate in respect of an aggregate term consisting of two or more shorter terms;[2] the correct practice is to impose concurrent sentences of sufficient length, certifying each as an extended term.[3]

CONSECUTIVE SENTENCES

The practice relating to consecutive terms of imprisonment and extended sentences is discussed at p. 62 above.

EFFECT OF AN EXTENDED SENTENCE

An extended sentence takes effect as if it were a normal sentence of imprisonment of equivalent length, except in respect of release on licence. The extended-term prisoner becomes eligible for release on licence at the same time as a prisoner serving a normal sentence (after one-third of his sentence or twelve months) but if he is released on licence, the extended-sentence prisoner remains subject to the licence for the full nominal length of the sentence, rather than the length of the sentence less remission.[4] Additionally, the extended-sentence prisoner may be detained beyond the date on which he would otherwise have been released on the remission of the final third of his sentence, and released on licence at any time after that date, if the Home Secretary so directs.[5] If he is not released on licence during the middle third of his sentence, and no direction is made by the Home Secretary, he is released absolutely after two-thirds of his sentence (assuming he has not lost remission for misconduct).

POLICY IN THE USE OF EXTENDED SENTENCES

The sentence of preventive detention[6] replaced by the extended sentence was used to deal with persistent offenders who repeatedly committed offences of modest (although not minimal) gravity which

[1] *Ibid.*, s. 28(4).
[2] See *McKenna* (1973) 58 Cr. App. R. 237.
[3] See *Blythin* 5.3.74, 3794/B/73.
[4] Criminal Justice Act 1967 s. 60(6)(a).
[5] *Ibid.*, s. 60(3)(a).
[6] See Criminal Justice Act 1948 s. 21 (repealed).

would not individually justify sentences of imprisonment of substantial length.[1] A sentence of seven years' preventive detention
would be upheld on a suitable offender whose immediate offence
would not have justified more than eighteen months on tariff
principles.[2] The extended sentence has been used in this way,
although there is an increasing reluctance to uphold long sentences
on persistent petty offenders. A second use of the extended sentence is
as a means of ensuring that the offender will be subject to a licence,
and therefore to some degree of supervision, whenever he is released
from his sentence, and that his licence will run until the expiration of
the full nominal period of his sentence. Where the sentence is used in
this way it may be relatively short, and need not be longer than would
be appropriate if the sentence were passed as an ordinary term of
imprisonment. In *Houldsworth*[3] a man of 47 with nineteen previous
convictions was sentenced to an ordinary term of four years for a
burglary committed while on licence from an earlier sentence of six
years' imprisonment. In view of the appellant's 'real effort to go
straight' while subject to parole licence, the Court reduced his
sentence to thirty months but certified it as an extended sentence, with
the comment that 'an extended sentence has a dual purpose. It is
designed to protect the public in two different ways: one, where
necessary, by keeping a man in prison for a longer period than would
otherwise be required; the other by providing for compulsory
aftercare where this is desirable for a longer period than would
otherwise be the case'.

EXTENDED SENTENCES PASSED TO AUTHORIZE PREVENTIVE CUSTODY

Where an extended sentence is passed to provide for a long period of
preventive custody, the term of the sentence may be greater than
would be appropriate if the sentence were not certified as extended. In
Seaman[4] a man of 48 with twenty-two previous convictions received
'what would otherwise be a very heavy sentence for a single act of
burglary'. In view of his extensive record and failure on probation in
the recent past the Court upheld an extended sentence of seven years

---

[1] See *Preventive Detention*, Report of the Advisory Council on the Treatment of
Offenders, 1963, para. 59.

[2] See, for example, *Caine* 19.6.62, 879/62, [1963] Crim. L. R. 63.

[3] 17.1.72, 4191/A/71; see also *Hulme* 29.10.71, 4766/A/70 (five years extended varied
to three years extended: 'it is not necessary that the sentence should be a very long
one').

[4] 15.11.73, 364/A/73; see also *Howland* 17.7.75, 1198/A/75, (six years extended for
man with twenty-one previous convictions not excessive for two minor burglaries while
on probation; no objectionable disparity between six years extended and two years
ordinary imprisonment imposed on co-defendant).

with the comment that 'if the public is to be protected . . . a sentence of seven years . . . cannot be said to be too long'. A sentence of this kind will be upheld only where there is no possible hope for a change in the offender's pattern of behaviour. In *Bowen*[1] a man who had served two previous sentences of preventive detention received eight years extended for two burglaries committed while subject to a probation order for other burglaries. The Court stated that the sentencer had 'had a choice of three alternatives: to continue the experiment begun . . . when the appellant was put on probation . . . to pass the kind of sentence which was appropriate for the two offences of burglary considered in themselves, or to pass an extended sentence for the protection of the public against this persistent recidivist'. Taking the view that to uphold the extended sentence would be 'to write this man off as hopeless', and in the circumstances 'this would be too pessimistic a view', the Court varied the sentence to four years, not extended. In other cases the Court has varied an extended sentence to probation, where this course has held out some hope. In *Jones*[2] a man of 57 with an 'appalling' record was sentenced to an extended term of seven years for burglary. Observing that 'resort should only be had to these very long sentences if there is no other course open', and that a hostel place was available, the Court varied the sentence to probation.

An extended sentence passed on preventive grounds will rarely be upheld where there has been a significant attempt to conform to the law since the offender's last release from custody[3] or where there is a reasonable prospect that a change in his circumstances may lead to a new pattern of conduct.[4] An extended sentence of substantial length will be inappropriate where the offender has not previously served a substantial term of ordinary imprisonment.[5]

Although an extended sentence may be disproportionate to the offence for which it is imposed, the concept of proportionality is not wholly excluded. An inordinate degree of disproportionality may

[1] 6.7.72, 773/B/72.
[2] 12.3.73, 3911/A/72; see also *Ford* 6.8.74, 5573/B/73 (man, 54, 'quite appalling' record, six years extended for minor theft and dishonesty: 'is one to say that he is to go away for a long period of time in order to protect society, or is one justified in taking a chance . . . ?'; probation substituted).
[3] See, for example, *Wright* 14.6.73, 5994/A/71 (eight years extended for conspiracy to defraud, 'fairly extensive period of sustained effort to mend his ways' since last release; extended sentence 'not appropriate').
[4] See, for example, *Featherstone* 14.12.71, 2871/C/71 (seven years extended for possession of forged banknote, appellant's history 'the story of a wasted life' but 'he may be in the process of changing', prospect of marriage; three years' imprisonment substituted).
[5] See, for example, *Melville* 4.5.71, 5268/A/70 (ten years extended for burglaries while householders attending funerals; extended sentence correct but too long in view of longest previous sentence of four years—reduced to six years extended).

lead to the reduction of an extended term. Extended sentences for relatively undistinguished burglaries will rarely be allowed to exceed seven years,[1] and a minor offence of theft is unlikely to justify an extended sentence of more than about five years.[2] In *Price*[3] a man of 39 with 'an appalling criminal record' was sentenced to extended terms of seven years for stealing a cigarette lighter and obtaining £11.50 by deception while unlawfully at large from an extended sentence of four years for burglary. The Court agreed that 'manifestly the sentences were out of proportion to the offences . . . even with his appalling record' and substituted a sentence of twelve months extended consecutive to the term for burglary.

EXTENDED SENTENCES IMPOSED FOR THE SAKE OF THE SPECIAL LICENCE PROVISIONS

Where the sentencer's purpose in imposing an extended sentence is to subject the offender to a longer period of licence on his release than would be possible in the event of an ordinary sentence of imprisonment, the length of the term need not exceed the length of the permissible sentence of imprisonment for the offence. Used in this way, ' "extended sentence" is perhaps a misnomer . . . its use is that it enables the Home Secretary to control somebody who is let out on licence when he would otherwise come out having earned his full remission'.[4] While the principle is not entirely clear, it appears to be accepted that where an extended sentence is imposed for this purpose and the term is not significantly longer than would have been imposed in the form of an ordinary sentence of imprisonment, the restrictive principles applied to the use of the extended sentence as a means of providing long-term preventive custody do not apply. (The statutory conditions, including the court's satisfaction that 'it is expedient to protect the public from him for a substantial time'[5] must be fulfilled).

---

[1] See, for example, *Munro* 18.12.70, 4369/C/70 (ten years extended for series of burglaries of houses, extensive record; extended sentence 'absolutely right' but ten years 'too heavy'—reduced to seven); see also *Connolly* 19.10.73, 3993/A/73 (twelve years for burglary by man, 57, extensive record; 'substantial sentence required' but twelve years too long'—reduced to seven years extended).

[2] See, for example, *Jack* 23.7.70, 1355/B/70 (theft of wallet containing £17, numerous convictions, recent suspended sentence; five years extended upheld); *Ives* 11.12.70, 4821/A/70 (man, 43, theft of lead worth £5 from demolition site, extensive record; 'it was a case for an extended sentence but . . . six years is too long'—reduced to four years extended).

[3] 21.3.72, 5817/C/71.

[4] *John* 13.2.75, 4183/B/74. As this consequence is not automatic (it will follow only where the offender is released on licence before he would be released on the completion of his sentence less remission, *or* where the Home Secretary makes an order under Criminal Justice Act 1967 s. 60(6)(a)), the sentencer should make his intentions explicit.

[5] Powers of Criminal Courts Act 1973 s. 28(1).

Relatively short extended terms have been upheld on men in their twenties who would probably not be considered old enough for an extended sentence on preventive grounds.[1] In *Long*[2] a man of 29, with an extensive record of imprisonment and other institutional confinement, received an extended term of eight years for a series of burglaries committed while subject to an earlier sentence from which he had absconded while on pre-release leave. The Court accepted that 'looking at it simply from the point of view of the public . . . it might be said that the longer he is in prison, the better', but for a man of his age the sentence 'may destroy forever any hope that . . . he might . . . be able to take a useful place in society'. While it was 'an appropriate case for an extended sentence', the term was too long; a sentence of four years was accordingly substituted.

[1] For example, *Stewart* 16.3.71, 5771/B/70 (man, 26, substantial record; two years extended for going equipped for burglary upheld); *Winter* 18.5.73, 913/A/73 (man, 29, 'bad record for violence'; five years extended for two incidents of malicious wounding and assault occasioning actual bodily harm, involving use of weapon and severe injury respectively, upheld).
[2] 10.4.70, 6577/A/69.

9

Fines and Financial Orders

The financial orders discussed in this chapter are compensation orders, restitution orders (which may relate to goods), confiscation orders, criminal bankruptcy orders and orders to pay the costs of the prosecution. While these orders are governed by differing statutory provisions and, to some extent, by varying principles, they are generally (with the exception of restitution orders) subject to the principle that in imposing them the sentencer should have regard to the means of the offender, in respect of both the individual orders, and their total effect where two or more are combined. The Court does not appear to have stated which form of order should have priority where more than one is possibly appropriate but the means of the offender are limited; it is submitted that the order of priority is first the fine, second the compensation order and third the order to pay the prosecution costs. The reason for giving priority to the fine over the compensation order is that an offender should not be allowed to 'buy himself out' of the penal consequences of his action by the payment of compensation under compulsion. This principle has been stated emphatically in relation to imprisonment and should logically apply also to fines.

Fines

A fine may be imposed on conviction on indictment for any offence in addition to or in lieu of any other sentence, except where the sentence for the offence is fixed by law or the court exercises a power which precludes it from sentencing the offender (such as the power to make a probation order or grant a discharge).[1] The amount of the fine is not subject to statutory limitation.[2]

On imposing a fine 'on any person'[3] the Crown Court must make an order fixing a term of imprisonment not exceeding twelve months,

---

[1] Powers of Criminal Courts Act 1973 s. 30(1).
[2] Criminal Law Act 1977 s. 32(1).
[3] Including, presumably, a young person: see above, p. 283. A young person may not actually be committed to prison under such an order (Powers of Criminal Courts Act 1973 ss. 19(1), 19(4)).

to be served in default of payment.[1] This term may be ordered to run consecutively to any other term of imprisonment to which the offender is subject.[2] Where the fine is imposed on a committal for sentence in circumstances in which the powers of the Crown Court are limited to those of the magistrates' court,[3] the Crown Court must impose the term to be served in default, notwithstanding the restrictions which would prevent a magistrates' court from fixing a term in the first instance,[4] but the length of the term fixed by the Crown Court in such a case must not exceed the length of the term which a magistrates' court could have fixed eventually.[5]

A person may not be committed to prison in default of payment of a fine on the occasion when the fine is imposed, unless one of four conditions is satisfied. These are that: (in the case of an offence punishable with imprisonment) he appears to the court to have sufficient means to pay the sum forthwith; it appears to the court that he is unlikely to remain long enough at a place of abode in the United Kingdom to enable payment of the sum to be enforced by other methods; he is sentenced at the same time to immediate imprisonment or detention in a detention centre; or he is already serving such a sentence.[6] On imposing a fine, the sentencer may make an order allowing time for payment of the amount of the fine, or directing that the fine be paid by instalments of such amounts and on such dates as may be specified.[7]

Where a fine is imposed on a child or young person, the sentencer may order the fine to be paid by the offender's parent or guardian, unless the parent or guardian cannot be found or the court is satisfied that 'he has not conduced to the commission of the offence by neglecting to exercise due care of the child or young person'.[8] Such an order is to be enforced 'in the like manner as if the order had been made on the conviction of the parent',[9] and it is submitted that where such an order is made in the Crown Court, the sentencer should fix the term to be served by the parent in the event of default.[10]

The collection, enforcement and remission of fines imposed by the

[1] Powers of Criminal Courts Act 1973 s. 31(2).
[2] Ibid., s. 31(4).
[3] In particular, where there is a committal under Magistrates' Courts Act 1952 s. 28, Mental Health Act 1959 s. 67, or Criminal Justice Act 1967 s. 56.
[4] Powers of Criminal Courts Act 1973 s. 31(6).
[5] Ibid., s. 31(7).
[6] Ibid., s. 31(3).
[7] Ibid., s. 31(1). Where the fine is to be paid out of current income, it is usual to specify instalments.
[8] Children and Young Persons Act 1933 s. 55(1).
[9] Ibid., s. 55(4).
[10] This argument assumes that an order against a parent under Children and Young Persons Act 1933 s. 55(1) amounts to the imposition of a fine on the parent for the purposes of Powers of Criminal Courts Act 1973 s. 31(2).

Crown Court is the responsibility of the magistrates' court by which the offender was committed for trial, or by a magistrates' court specified in an order made by the trial court.[1] A magistrates' court may not remit in whole or in part a fine imposed by the Crown Court without the consent of the Crown Court,[2] and if it commits the offender to prison in default of payment, it must do so for the period specified by the Crown Court, less any reduction on account of part payment.[3]

PRINCIPLES GOVERNING THE USE OF FINES

Fines are governed to a significant extent by principles analogous to those applicable to fixed-term sentences of imprisonment. They constitute the lower reaches of the scale of tariff sentences (discharges, absolute or conditional, may be regarded as the lowest point) and are generally used in cases where a deterrent or punitive sentence is necessary, but either the inherent gravity of the offence is insufficient to justify a sentence of imprisonment, or the presence of mitigating factors justifies the sentencer in avoiding a sentence of imprisonment.

The first consideration for a sentencer contemplating the imposition of a fine is whether the offence and surrounding circumstances require the imposition of a custodial sentence. It is wrong in principle to impose a heavy fine on a wealthy man in a case where a person of less substantial means would normally be sentenced to imprisonment. The Court has indicated in earlier decisions that the power to impose fines should not be used to 'give persons of means an opportunity of buying themselves out of being sent to prison',[4] and this approach is reflected in more recent decisions. In *Pennell*[5] the manager of a butchery department admitted receiving a quantity of meat stolen by fellow employees from their mutual employer, which he sold in the employer's shop, keeping the proceeds. The Court stated that 'the appropriate sentence for the offences here disclosed would have been an immediate effective sentence of imprisonment', but as there was no power to substitute on appeal a sentence more severe than that imposed by the sentencer in the court below, the propriety of fines of £2,100 would have to be considered without

---

[1] Criminal Justice Act 1967 s. 47(3). Such an order should always be made where the offender has been tried on a voluntary bill of indictment, as otherwise there will be no means of enforcing the fine.

[2] See Criminal Justice Act 1967 s. 47(8), as amended by Courts act 1971.

[3] Criminal Justice Act 1967 s. 47(6).

[4] *Markwick* (1953) 37 Cr. App. R. 125; see also *Lewis* 30.11.64, 667/64, [1965] Crim. L. R. 121.

[5] 7.5.74, 4921/B/73.

reference to this possibility. As they would take almost eight years for the appellant to pay off, they were 'wrong in principle' and the Court reduced them to £850. Similarly in *Thompson*[1] the appellant was convicted of destroying property in the course of a violent incident in a public house, as a result of which a co-defendant was sentenced to imprisonment for wounding with intent. The Court stated that 'offences of this sort . . . are properly to be dealt with, in the absence of abnormal mitigating circumstances, with a custodial penalty' and that in imposing a fine of £250 'too great a degree of leniency was extended'. As there was no power on appeal to substitute a custodial sentence, and the appellant's financial resources were such that he could not pay the fine within a reasonable time, the amount was reduced to £100.

Given that the offence is not one which requires the imposition of a custodial sentence, the second step for the sentencer is to determine the level of fine appropriate to the offence in question. The principles and to some extent the terminology are similar to those applicable to sentences of imprisonment,[2] although it is not possible to identify a detailed 'tariff' of fines related to particular examples of offences. In determining the level of fine appropriate to the gravity of the offence, the sentencer may have regard to the appropriate level of penalties in comparable cases of greater and lesser gravity. In *Donovan*[3] the appellant pleaded guilty to damaging a window pane in the door of a warehouse where he was later found asleep (a plea of not guilty to burglary was accepted). He had caused damage by vomiting and other means to furniture inside the premises, to the total extent of £11. The Court described the fine of £200 as 'excessively heavy' and commented that the sentencer 'left himself no margin for dealing with what might be a serious case of criminal damage'. The fine was reduced to £25. Similarly, in *Lea*[4] a fine of £50 for possession of 'a small quantity of cannabis' contained in one cigarette was excessive, 'having regard to the minimal nature of the offences in the spectrum of offences of this character'. A fine of £25 was substituted.

Although specific recent authority has not been found, the cases do not appear to support the view that the amount of the fine may be increased where the offender is unusually affluent, although the amount of the fine may reflect the extent to which the offender has

[1] 7.10.74, 2331/B/74, [1974] Crim. L. R. 720.
[2] See, for example, *Tate* 29.1.76, 3099/B2/75 (£50 fine 'within the normal bracket of financial penalty imposed for such an offence as this').
[3] 21.6.73, 1438/B/73.
[4] 29.7.75, 2051/A/75; see also *Owen* 20.2.73, 2103/C/72 (fine of £200 on count for possessing one mandrax tablet disproportionate when compared with identical fine on count for possessing substantial quantity of cannabis; reduced to £20); *Beynon* (1972) 57 Cr. App. R. 259 (£250 fine for possession of twenty-two pills containing pemoline 'goes far beyond what was appropriate for this particular offence'; reduced to £25).

made a profit from his offences. In *Royle*[1] the appellant admitted dishonestly handling property worth about £6,500, and was fined a total of £6,000. The Court heard that a co-defendant had received a substantial share in the proceeds of the offence, amounting to about £2,000, and reduced the fines on the appellant to a total of £5,000. The value of the property involved in the offence is only one factor in determining the amount of the appropriate fine, and a fine may in suitable circumstances exceed the value of the property involved. In *Verrall*[2] a supervisor was convicted of stealing from his employers a small quantity of meat, valued at £1, and was fined £50; the sentence was upheld. By contrast in *Jamieson*[3] a man with an 'absolutely blameless record' was fined £300 for stealing half a bottle of whisky worth £1.55 from a shop. Observing that 'this particular act of shoplifting can fairly be ascribed to a momentary aberration by a man . . . suffering from a degree of depression' and that 'one must maintain a certain balance in these matters', the Court varied the sentence to a conditional discharge.

THE OFFENDER'S MEANS

When the sentencer has determined that the offence does not require a custodial sentence, and the facts of the offence considered in the abstract would justify a fine of a given amount, the next question is whether the proposed fine can be paid by the offender within a reasonable time. Although the principle is not expressed in statute so far as the Crown Court is concerned,[4] a fine should not normally be imposed without an investigation of the offender's means,[5] and the amount appropriate to the offence considered in the abstract should be reduced, where necessary, to an amount which the offender can realistically be expected to pay. The Court has stated that 'it is axiomatic that where it is decided not to impose a custodial sentence, the court should be careful in imposing a fine not to fix that fine at such a high level that it is inevitable that that which the court has decided not to impose, namely a custodial sentence, will almost certainly follow'.[6] In *Wilson*[7] nine youths admitted causing damage

[1] 3.7.75, 1080/C/75.
[2] 8.2.74, 2461/A/73.
[3] (1975) 60 Cr. App. R. 318.
[4] For magistrates' courts, see Magistrates' Courts Act 1952 s. 31.
[5] See, for example, *Deaga* 10.10.75, 3231/A/75 ('the financial penalty must be related to the evidence of means'); *Palmer* 30.4.70, 9108/69 (appellant 'may consider himself lucky' that sentencer imposed fine for 'a serious assault', but as 'no inquiry was made whatsoever about the appellant's means', the fine imposed was 'higher than is fair'; fine reduced from £100 to £30).
[6] *Stevens* 5.4.76, 5408/B/75, (systematic handling of stolen goods, custodial sentence more appropriate, but fines totalling £2,500 'completely wrong'; varied to £250). For

to a disused barn; each was fined £100 and ordered to pay compensation of £25. All the other defendants were in full-time employment, but the appellant was earning £9 weekly for part-time work. Stating that 'we see a reason for treating this young man differently because of his personal circumstances, which . . . the court must take into consideration when fixing a fine', the Court reduced the fine to £50 payable at the rate of £1 per week. In *Paley*[8] a student living on a grant of £90 per year was fined £75 for possession of two cigarette ends containing cannabis. Stating that 'although a fine was right in principle, the sum imposed was out of proportion to her financial position', the Court reduced the fine to £25. In a third example[9] two young men were each fined £300 (together with a suspended sentence) for burglary of a shop. One appellant was earning £30 weekly as a builder's labourer, the other was unemployed but expected to be engaged in a similar capacity in the near future. Stating that 'any fine has to be fixed at a sum which is well within the means of the defendant to pay', the Court reduced the fine to £150 in each case.

In assessing the means of the offender the Court may have regard to his expected income over the likely period of payment,[10] but the period of payment should not be allowed to extend over an excessive duration. While no precise limit has been recognized (although the Court has stated that a period of eight years is excessive)[11] it appears to be unusual to allow the period of payment to exceed twelve months. The sentencer may also take into account any capital assets which the offender possesses, but must bear in mind any charges against those assets. In one case[12] a professional man was fined a total of £10,000 for being concerned in the importation of cannabis. It was accepted that the appellant had allowed his address to be used for the delivery of cannabis by post from abroad and had not taken any active part in the enterprise. The Court stated that 'if a sentence of imprisonment taking immediate effect had been passed . . . he ought not to have been surprised', but any fine imposed should be reasonable having regard to the means of the offender. In the present case the appellant had just realized £15,000 by the sale of his house

---

the application of the principle where the offender is sentenced to immediate imprisonment at the same time, see p. 322 below.

[7] 1.11.73, 3324/A/73.   [8] 25.6.74, 1675/A/74.

[9] *Nagle and Deieham* 8.4.75, 3950/C/74.

[10] See, for example, *Little* 14.4.76, 1221/C/76 (fine of £400, with other orders amounting to £200, for handling stolen car, appellant temporarily out of work but expecting to be re-employed within few days; fine reduced to £150, payable by weekly instalments of £5).

[11] *Pennell* 7.5.74, 4921/B/73.

[12] *Neville-O'Brien*, 16.2.76, 4910/C/75.

but 'he had to live somewhere' and that was 'a relevant factor in deciding whether the whole or a substantial part of the fluid capital should be made available for a fine'. His annual gross income was about £7,000, out of which the substantial expenses of his practice had to be found. In these circumstances the fine was 'out of proportion to the means of this appellant' and fines totalling £3,000 were substituted, to be paid within eight months of the original sentence.

It is wrong in principle to assess a fine on the assumption that someone other than the offender will provide the means to pay it. In *Baxter*[1] an undischarged bankrupt was fined £100 and subjected to a suspended sentence for bankruptcy offences, on the assumption that his wife would pay the fine. The Court stated that this approach was 'wrong . . . in principle' and quashed the fine. In *Deaga*[2] a young man with no previous convictions was fined £4,000 for attempting to smuggle cannabis through London Airport to a destination abroad. Stating that 'it is wrong . . . to impose very large fines for offences of this kind with the idea . . . that someone else will pay the fine', the Court reduced the fine to £500, which the appellant had available.

Although the sentencer is under an obligation to ensure that the fine is reasonably related to the offender's income and resources, he is entitled (although not bound) to rely on information provided by the offender. Where the offender provides information which leads the sentencer to overestimate his resources, he cannot complain that the fine or other financial order is excessive. In *Wright*[3] the appellant simply provided the Court with a figure for his earnings, without explaining his outgoings; upholding a combination of financial orders the Court stated that although 'it is . . . a fundamental principle of sentencing that financial obligations must be matched to the ability to pay . . . that does not mean that the Court has to set out on an inquisitorial function and dig out all the information that exists about the appellant's means. The appellant knows what his means are and he is perfectly capable of putting them before the court'.

COMBINING A FINE WITH A CUSTODIAL SENTENCE

The Crown Court has power to impose a fine in addition to any other

[1] 28.6.74, 1242/C/74, [1974] Crim. L. R. 611.

[2] 10.10.75, 3231/A/75; see also *Po* 11.6.74, 1076/A/74, [1974] Crim. L. R. 557 (six years' imprisonment and fine of £5,000 for importing heroin, fine imposed on assumption that 'the organization' would pay; quashed, following *Lewis* [1965] Crim. L. R. 121); *Griffin* 1.7.75, 1140/A/75 (four years' imprisonment and fine of £7,500 for importing cannabis, fine imposed to 'see if the fine is paid either by you or those responsible for putting you in the position you are in'; fine 'departed entirely from accepted sentencing principle—quashed).

[3] 12.11.76, 5022/A/75, [1977] Crim. L. R. 236.

sentence it imposes (but not in addition to measures which are 'in lieu' of any other sentence, such as a probation order). [1] A fine may be imposed in addition to a sentence of imprisonment or other custodial sentence. The usual reason for imposing a fine where the offender is sentenced to custody is to ensure that he does not enjoy any profit from the offence. In *Waterfield* [2] the appellant was sentenced to imprisonment and fined £9,000 for importing a substantial quantity of indecent films and magazines with a view to gain. Stating that the appellant 'broke the law on a vast scale' in order to make 'vast profits', the Court upheld the sentence with the comment that 'the first thing the law should do is . . . ensure that those who break it in the sort of way this appellant has broken it should not make any money out of their wrong doing'.

Fines imposed in circumstances such as these are subject to the general principle that there must be a reasonable possibility that the offender will be in a position to pay the fine. In *Millington* [3] the appellant was sentenced to four years' imprisonment and fined £1,000 with £500 costs for conspiring to import cannabis. Although the prison sentence was 'in no way excessive', the fine was inappropriate as the appellant was bankrupt and its effect was to make him 'liable to serve an additional twelve months' imprisonment to the four years, which is quite enough already'. It is no less wrong to impose a fine to be paid by instalments over a long period of time, so that the offender will remain liable to make payments on his release from prison. In *McCormack* [4] a man with no previous convictions was sentenced to twelve months' imprisonment and fined £100 for supplying cannabis; the fine was to be paid by instalments of £2 per week commencing one month after his release from the sentence of imprisonment. The Court upheld the sentence of imprisonment as 'entirely proper' but quashed the fine as 'it is sufficient punishment to serve his term of imprisonment without this further millstone round his neck, which could hamper him when he seeks to get employment and rehabilitate himself'.

Some cases support the existence of an exception to the principle that the offender should not be fined unless he has a realistic chance of avoiding default. If the offender is sentenced to a term of imprison-

---

[1] Powers of Criminal Courts Act 1973 s. 30.

[2] 17.2.75, 2787/C/74.

[3] 3.7.75, 1282/B/75; see also *Shadmi* 18.11.71, 3058/A/71 (thirty months' imprisonment and fines totalling £2,000,with terms totalling two years in default, for smuggling watches and coins; fines reduced to £1,000 with six months in default, as original order 'could result in a further two-year imprisonment over and above the two and a half years directly ordered').

[4] 16.1.76, 4827/B/75. For similar statements made in relation to persons sentenced to borstal training, see *Jarrard* 10.3.72, 5366/C/71, [1972] Crim. L. R. 449, and *Gear* 24.7.75, 2319/A/75, p. 274 above.

ment as the primary sentence, and the sentencer discounts what would be the appropriate sentence by a period equal to or greater than the term fixed in default of payment, a fine may be upheld even if the chances that the offender will be able to pay are slender. The justification for this exception appears to be that if the offender is committed to prison in default, he will not serve a longer total sentence than would have been passed without the fine. In *Harding*[1] an undischarged bankrupt was sentenced to two years' imprisonment and fined £1,000, with twelve months in default, for assisting in the entry of illegal immigrants. It was argued that the fine was 'far beyond this man's capacity to pay', but the Court stated that it was justifiable to pass 'a global sentence, partly imprisonment and partly fine, with the clear intention that if the fine . . . was not paid, there would be an extra consecutive term of imprisonment . . . so that the maximum sentence . . . would be three years', as the term of three years was well within the permissible range of sentences for the offence in question. Although an earlier case supports this proposition,[2] it is submitted that it is inconsistent with the broader principle that a fine should not be imposed where imprisonment is the appropriate sentence, and amounts in effect to allowing the offender to buy his way out of part of his proper sentence.

COMBINING A FINE WITH A SUSPENDED SENTENCE

There is no general objection, either in law[3] or as a matter of sentencing principle,[4] to the combination of a fine with a suspended sentence of imprisonment. A fine may be imposed in conjunction with a suspended sentence, in the same way as it may be combined with an immediate sentence, as a means of depriving the offender of any profit from the offence. Alternatively the fine may be imposed as a supplementary penalty in a case where 'the scales were very nicely balanced as to whether the deterrent sentence ought not to be a sentence of immediate imprisonment'.[5] The proper approach to the use of the fine in this way was explained in *Genese*.[6] 'If the court decides there is no other appropriate method of dealing with the offender than imprisonment, and imposes a prison sentence, the court can then, in the appropriate case, go on to consider that the sentence should be suspended . . . if the court does go on to consider

---

[1] 26.2.74, 5468/A/73.
[2] *Savundranayagan* (1968) 52 Cr. App. R. 637.
[3] See *Leigh* (1969) 54 Cr. App. R. 169; *Ffoulkes* 16.1.76, 4032/C1/75, [1976] Crim. L. R. 458.
[4] See *Genese* (1976) 63 Cr. App. R. 152.
[5] See *Leigh* (1969) 54 Cr. App. R. 169; *Matthews* 26.10.71, 2500/B/71.
[6] (1976) 63 Cr. App. R. 152.

that the sentence should be suspended . . . the court can also consider whether an additional penalty by way of a fine is justified'. (Although this decision was concerned with an offender under 21, the principle appears to apply generally.) It is incorrect to approach the issues in the reverse order, deciding that the appropriate sentence is a fine and adding a suspended sentence as a supplementary penalty. 'A sentence of imprisonment is to be regarded as the primary punishment and the decision that a sentence of imprisonment is appropriate must be made before the question of whether a supplemental penalty by way of fines is to be imposed [is decided]'.[1] In *Hewkin*[2] a woman of good character was convicted of two thefts of property worth a total of £35 from the same store. She was sentenced to two consecutive terms of six months' imprisonment suspended and fined a total of £100. The Court held that in view of her good character and the small amount of property involved 'this . . . was a case where the applicant could be appropriately dealt with by a substantial financial penalty'. The fines were accordingly upheld, but the suspended sentences, 'wrong in principle', were quashed.

The Court has not yet clarified the principles which govern the determination of the amount of a fine imposed in conjunction with a suspended sentence under the principle in *Genese*.[3] The suspended sentence, as the primary sentence, will be calculated to reflect the gravity of the offence and other relevant considerations; as the fine is a secondary and additional penalty it should presumably be less than would be appropriate if the fine stood alone. In *Hadjizade*[4] the appellant was fined £1,000 and sentenced to twelve months' imprisonment suspended for receiving a number of valuable antiques. The fine was reduced to £250, 'bearing in mind . . . that a prison sentence suspended is an important sentence to pass on a man of good character'. In *Dale*[5] the appellant was sentenced to eighteen months' imprisonment suspended and fined £2,000 for conspiring to forge permits relating to international road transport. Apart from questions relating to the appellant's means, the Court stated that 'taking into account the fact that a sentence of imprisonment even though suspended remains a sentence of imprisonment', the fines were 'too high' in relation to the circumstances of the offence. Fines totalling £500 were substituted. On the other hand, if the fine is seen as the price of suspending a sentence which would otherwise have been

[1] *Foster and others* 10.2.76, 4061/C/75; see also *Ankers* (1975) 61 Cr. App. R. 170 (Sentencer 'having decided . . . to deal with the appellant by the imposition of fines was wrong in deciding to impose, in addition, sentences of imprisonment').
[2] 16.2.76, 2426/B/75.
[3] (1976) 63 Cr. App. R. 152, above.
[4] 19.3.73, 2764/C/72.
[5] 10.11.75, 1367/C/75.

ordered to take immediate effect, there is a danger of infringing the fundamental principle that a fine must not be used to enable an affluent offender to buy his way out of going to prison (see above, p. 318).

Whatever other principles govern the calculation of the amount of a fine imposed as a supplementary penalty in conjunction with a suspended sentence of imprisonment, there is no doubt that the general principle that the fine must be reasonably related to the appellant's means applies as strongly in this context as in others. In *King*[1] the Court pointed out that where a fine was imposed in conjunction with a suspended sentence, 'special care should be taken . . . to see that it is well within the man's means', as the enforcement of a term of imprisonment in default of payment of the fine might mean that 'a man might in the end serve two sentences of imprisonment on two separate occasions for the same offence'.

Compensation Orders

STATUTORY CONDITIONS

A court before which a person is convicted of an offence may, in addition to dealing with him in any other way, make a compensation order requiring him to pay compensation for 'any personal injury, loss or damage resulting from that offence or any other offence which is taken into consideration by the court in determining sentence'.[2] No compensation order may be made 'in respect of loss suffered by the dependents of a person in consequence of his death', or in respect of any loss, damage or injury 'arising out of the presence of a motor vehicle on a road', except damage resulting from an offence under the Theft Act 1968.[3] Where property which has been the subject of an offence under the Theft Act 1968 is recovered, any damage to the property while it was out of the owner's possession is to be treated as resulting from the offence, 'however and by whomsoever the damage was caused'.[4] In determining whether to make a compensation order against an offender, and the amount to be paid under such an order, 'the Court shall have regard to his means so far as they appear or are known to the Court'.

A compensation order may not be made unless a specific loss is established (it is not necessary to show that the offender has made a

---

[1] (1970) 54 Cr. App. R. 362.
[2] Powers of Criminal Courts Act 1973 s. 35(1).
[3] Theft Act 1968 s. 35(3). For the interpretation of this provision, see *Quigley v. Stokes* (1976) 64 Cr. App. R. 198 (Div. Ct.).
[4] *Ibid.*, s. 35(2).

profit).[1] In *Sharkey*[2] the appellant was ordered to pay compensation in respect of some clothing which he had received, knowing it to have been stolen. As there was no evidence that the articles had suffered any damage as a result of the theft, or that they were of any less value to the owners once recovered, the Court quashed the order. The order must be related to specific charges or particular offences taken into consideration; a general order covering the offences as a whole, or failing to specify the person who has suffered the loss, is invalid.[3] In *Wood*[4] the appellant admitted fifty offences of obtaining various sums of money from small business concerns by criminal deception, amounting in all to £12,000. The Court held that a single compensation order was inappropriate: 'where there is a large number of offences, there ought to be not one compensation order, but a separate compensation order for each sum of money in respect of each offence', and the sentencer must be 'very clear as to the relationship between the compensation order, the offence and the victim to whom it relates'. The amount of the order must be based on evidence rather than on speculation or estimates.[5] In deciding whether loss or damage can be attributed to a particular offence, the sentencer must ask himself 'whether the loss or damage can fairly be said to have resulted . . . from the offence.' It is not necessary to apply 'the concepts of causation which apply to the assessment of damages under the law of contract and tort.'[6]

Compensation orders are enforced by magistrates' courts,[7] and it is inappropriate for the sentencer making a compensation order to fix a term of imprisonment in default unless he wishes to fix a term longer than the magistrates' court may impose.[8] The Crown Court may allow time for payment of the sum due under the order, and direct

---

[1] *Ford* 22.6.76, 1058/A/76.

[2] 15.1.76, 3608/B/75, [1976] Crim. L. R. 388; see also *Hier* (1976) 62 Cr. App. R. 233 (handling stolen goods, goods recovered intact, no loss suffered by owner; compensation order quashed). These decisions do not mean that a compensation order is never appropriate in cases of handling stolen property (see *Sharkey*). See also *Green* 20.2.76, 4520/B/75 (furnishing false information to cover deficiency in funds held on account of club, no evidence of theft; compensation order quashed).

[3] *Oddy* (1974) 59 Cr. App. R. 66; *Lappin* 23.9.74, 2381/B/74.

[4] (1974) 60 Cr. App. R. 70. A single order in respect of a series of thefts from the same victim was upheld in *Warton* 24.11.75, 3735/C/75, [1976] Crim. L. R. 520.

[5] See, for example, *Spencer* 11.3.76, 6006/B/75 (thefts of food from hotel over period of time, various estimates of value, no evidence; compensation order quashed); see also *McConnell and Leveridge* 22.1.76, 2681/A/75 (dispute over amount of money stolen, court to decide correct amount on evidence; order quashed for want of means).

[6] *Thomson Holidays Ltd.* [1974] 1 All E. R. 823 at 829.

[7] See Administration of Justice Act 1970 ss. 41 and 9.

[8] See *Amin* 2.7.73, 516/C/73; see also *Bunce* (1977) 66 Cr. App. R. 109. The longest term which the magistrates' court may impose, where the amount of the order exceeds £5,000, is twelve months. (See Magistrates' Courts Act 1952 s. 64 and sch. 3 as amended by Criminal Law Act 1977 s. 59). Shorter maximum terms are prescribed where the amount of the order is less than £5,000.

payment to be made by instalments of specific amounts on specific dates.[1] A single compensation order made jointly and severally against more than one offender is not necessarily unlawful,[2] but 'ought only to be made sparingly and in exceptional circumstances, and if substantial justice could not be achieved by several orders against the respective defendants concerned'.[3]

POLICY IN MAKING COMPENSATION ORDERS

The general principles governing the exercise of the power to order payment of compensation have been considered on a number of occasions. They are summarized in a passage from the judgment in *Inwood*:[4] 'compensation orders were introduced . . . as a convenient and rapid means of avoiding the expense of . . . civil litigation when the criminal clearly has the means which would enable the compensation to be paid . . . Compensation orders should certainly not be used when there is any doubt as to the liability to compensate, nor should they be used when there is a real doubt as to whether the convicted man can find the compensation'. The compensation order is in addition to, and not in substitution for, the primary sentence for the offence.[5]

The cases indicate that in considering whether to make a compensation order, the first responsibility of the sentencer is to ascertain what loss has occurred and whether it is attributable to the offence for which the offender is to be sentenced or which is being considered. Alleged loss arising from an offence of which the offender is acquitted,[6] or in respect of which guilt is not established,[7] must be disregarded. Where there is a dispute over liability for the loss, the extent of the damage or the amount of property for which the offender is accountable, the sentencer may hear evidence to determine the question, but should 'hesitate to embark on any complicated investigation . . . even at the suit of an applicant making a positive application'; in cases where there is a dispute of fact

[1] Powers of Criminal Courts Act 1973 s. 34.
[2] *Grundy* [1974] 1 W. L. R. 139, [1974] 1 All. E. R. 292.
[3] *Whitehead* 28.11.74, 4600/A/74.
[4] (1974) 60 Cr. App. R. 70.
[5] 'Compensation orders were not introduced into our law to enable the convicted to buy themselves out of the penalties for crime' (*Inwood* (1974) 60 Cr. App. R. 70).
[6] See, for example, *Murray* 27.6.75, 582/A/75 (appellant indicted for assault and causing damage to clothes and spectacles of victim, acquitted of charges of causing damage; compensation orders in respect of damage to clothing quashed).
[7] See, for example, *Davies* 27.1.76, 4660/C/75 (indictment charging separate obtainings of £70 and £10 from same person, evidence of single obtaining of £80, no verdict on count charging obtaining £10; compensation order for £80 in respect of count charging obtaining £70 reduced to £70).

and no such application is made the sentencer should leave the victim with his civil remedy.[1]

Where loss is satisfactorily established and related to a particular offence, the sentencer must consider the financial resources of the offender. The statute imposes an obligation to 'have regard to his means as far as they appear or are known to the court',[2] and an order made without a basis in evidence for believing that the offender can discharge the liability within a reasonable time will not normally be upheld.[3] In *Broadhead*[4] the appellant was convicted of damaging the plate-glass window of a jeweller's shop and stealing a ring worth £80, which was recovered immediately on his arrest. A compensation order for £620 in respect of the damaged window was made on the application of the owner, the sentencer observing that the order was made 'for what it is worth . . . the prospects of getting that are rather thin'. The Court stated that this was 'not . . . the correct approach' and quashed the order.

While it is not necessary to show that the offender has the means to pay the order immediately or can pay over a period of time without inconvenience,[5] the sentencer must be satisfied that the offender will have a reasonable chance to meet the obligations imposed by the order within a reasonable time. In *Smith*[6] a petrol-pump attendant, who admitted stealing over £2,800 from her employers in daily amounts of £2 or £3 over a period of about two years, was ordered to pay compensation of £2,852 to her employers at the rate of £1 per week. Her usual earnings were £16 per week, from which she supported a child. The Court stated that 'compensation orders must be realistic and there must be a reasonable prospect of the person ordered to pay the compensation being able to do so out of their resources'; the order was quashed with the comment that an order which will 'hang over a person for many years' should not be made.

---

[1] *Kneeshaw* (1974) 58 Cr. App. R. 439.

[2] Powers of Criminal Courts Act 1973 s. 35(4).

[3] See, for example, *Kelly* 17.12.73, 4315/B/73 (theft of copper worth £1,850, compensation order in same amount, no inquiry into means; compensation order quashed); *Teasdale* 30.6.75, 1105/A/75 (thefts from employers totalling £288, compensation order in same amount; 'no evidence . . . that he had any immediate means to pay or the likelihood of the means to pay'—order quashed); *Aldon-Barnes* 11.6.74, 5310/C/73 (obtaining pecuniary advantage by deception, order for £315, offender living on social security; order quashed).

[4] 23.4.74, 617/C/74; see also *Billet* 17.6.75, 952/B/75 (compensation orders in excess of £2,000; comment by sentencer that order will not be any use 'a confession of error in principle'—orders quashed).

[5] See *Bradburn* (1973) 57 Cr. App. R. 948 ('it is not right to restrict compensation orders to cases where the defendant can easily pay; there are good moral reasons for making compensation orders which will in a measure hurt the defendant's pocket and act to remind him of what he has done').

[6] 23.1.76, 3933/B/75.

Many similar decisions can be found.[1] In *LeGros*[2] the appellant was put on probabtion for arson and ordered to pay compensation of over £5,000 at the rate of £7 per week. Observing that the order would take nearly fifteen years to discharge, the Court stated that 'it was wholly unreasonable to impose . . . so great a burden' and quashed the order.

The same principles apply where the primary sentence is custodial. The fact that the offender is sentenced to imprisonment or borstal training does not mean that a compensation order is necessarily inappropriate, so long as it is in a relatively modest amount and there is a reasonable expectation that the offender will be able to discharge it within a short period of his release. In *McKinley*[3] the appellant received two years' imprisonment for two burglaries and six other offences and was ordered to pay compensation amounting to £150. The Court was informed that the appellant had generally been able to secure regular employment at a reasonable wage and was expected to be able to do so after his release. As the amount of the order was not large and could probably be repaid within a reasonable period of his release, it was not inappropriate and the Court upheld it. Where the offender's prospects of future employment are uncertain and the amount of compensation substantial, an order should be avoided. In *Hancox*[4] a man with a substantial record was ordered to pay £399 compensation for various frauds on banks and sentenced to two years' imprisonment. The Court stated that 'the concept of this inadequate man ever having jobs which will enable him to save £399 is unrealistic', in view of his history of unemployment. The order was quashed with the comment that 'when this man comes out of prison he is going to have a difficult enough task in rehabilitating himself if

[1] For example, *Bradburn* (1973) 57 Cr. App. R. 948 (order requiring payment over four years is 'being stretched out too long'); *Daly* (1973) 58 Cr. App. R. 333 (compensation order for £1,200, payable at £3.50 per week over six years, inappropriate); *Miller* 2.4.76, 5159/B/75, [1976] Crim. L. R. 694 (order for payment of £6,000, appellant able to pay £5 per week; order quashed).
[2] 23.1.76, 2678/A/75.
[3] 6.12.74, 3811/B/74, [1975] Crim. L. R. 294; see also *Darby* 1.11.73, 3412/B/73 (credit card frauds, fifteen months' imprisonment and compensation order for £41 at £2 weekly, reasonable prospects of adequately paid employment; order upheld).
[4] 17.5.76, 582/B/76; see also *Jones* 7.7.75, 4161/B/74 (credit card frauds, compensation order for £1,200, offender sentenced to two years' imprisonment, previously unemployed for several years following industrial injury; 'no basis for making a compensation order'—order quashed); *Keep* 15.1.74, 4855/A/73 (eighteen months' imprisonment and compensation order for £470 in respect of thefts, appellant unemployed for two years prior to offence; 'no means, nor was there any evidence that he was likely to earn money when he came out of prison', order 'not . . . realistic'—quashed); *Litten* 4.10.74, 1227/C/74 (two years' imprisonment and compensation orders amounting to £422, no immediate means; 'it is particularly important not to saddle him with compensation orders which he will have to meet when he comes out of prison, and the effect of which may very well take him back to crime again'—orders quashed).

he tries so to do'. Similar statements have been made in respect of young adult offenders sentenced to borstal training.[1]

Where the offender's means are such that he is able to pay some compensation for the loss or damage that has resulted from the offence but it is unrealistic to expect him to pay the full amount, the sentencer may properly make an order for an amount which is within the means of the offender, even though it is for less than the full amount of the loss or damage. In *Murfin*[2] a sub-postmaster was ordered to pay compensation to the Post Office in the amount of £1,228 for theft. The appellant's business had collapsed and his expected earnings on his release from prison would be about £17 per week, from which he was considered to be able to pay £2 per week. The compensation order was reduced to £300. Where the difference between the amount of the loss or damage and the amount which the offender can be expected to pay is so great that a compensation order would be derisory, the better course may be to refrain from making an order. In a case where the appellant had done £5,400 worth of damage by arson and would probably not have been able to pay more than £100 over a period of eighteen months, the Court considered that such an order would represent 'the worst of both worlds', in that 'the offender is put under an obligation which he may find difficult to fulfil, and the man who has suffered the loss gets really only a nominal compensation towards it'.[3]

Orders for Restitution

Theft Act 1968 s. 28 authorizes a sentencer to make four types of restitution order. The power to make a restitution order arises where goods[4] have been stolen[5] and a person is convicted of any offence 'with reference to the theft (whether or not the stealing is the gist of the offence)'.[6] The power is available also where a person is convicted of an offence not related to the theft, but asks for an offence related to the theft to be considered when he is sentenced.[7] A restitution order may not be made 'unless . . . the relevant facts sufficiently appear

[1] See p. 274 above; see also *Unwin* 10.4.75, 349/B/75 (borstal training and compensation order for £400, appellant unemployed at time of arrest, history of intermittent unskilled employment; order 'a burden he should not be asked to carry once he is released from borstal'—quashed).

[2] 30.7.74, 184/A/74.

[3] *LeGros* 23.1.76, 2678/A/75, p. 330 above; see also *Copson* 22.3.77, 6172/A/76 (arson causing damage of £3,000, appellant unable to meet order for payment of £1,000; order quashed: 'it is not desirable that the order should be in respect of part of the loss . . . because that . . . gives a false impression to members of the public').

[4] Including money and 'every other description of property except land' (Theft Act 1968 s. 34(2).

[5] In the broad sense of that term; see Theft Act 1968 s. 24(1) and (4).

[6] Theft Act 1968 s. 28(1).   [7] Criminal Law Act 1972 s. 6(3).

from evidence given at the trial or the available documents,[1] together
with admissions made by or on behalf of any person in connection
with any proposed exercise of the powers'.[2] A restitution order may
be made even though the passing of sentence is otherwise deferred.[3]

RESTORATION OF THE STOLEN GOODS

Where the conditions for the exercise of the power are satisfied, the
sentencer may order 'anyone having possession or control of the
goods' to restore them to 'any person entitled to recover them from
him'.[4] An order of this kind may be made against a person who is not a
party to the proceedings, such as an innocent purchaser of the goods,
so long as the original owner can still establish a right to recover them
from him. Where the existence of this right is not clear from the
evidence before the court, the power to order restitution should not
be exercised.[5]

DELIVERY OF THE PROCEEDS OF THE STOLEN GOODS

Where the person convicted has parted with possession of the stolen
goods, the sentencer may order him to deliver or transfer to the owner
of the stolen goods any other goods (including money) 'directly or
indirectly representing the stolen goods as being the proceeds or
realization of the whole or part of them or of goods so representing
them'. This power may be exercised only on the application of a
person entitled to recover and against a person convicted (or
admitting for consideration) the relevant offence, as opposed to an
innocent third party. The sentencer may order the offender to deliver
to the original owner any assets, including cash or credit balances,
which represent the proceeds of the relevant offence in his hands. The
connection between the goods stolen in the relevant offence and the
assets which it is proposed to order the offender to transfer must be
established on the evidence given in the trial or prepared for the
purposes of the trial, supplemented by admissions made by or on
behalf the offender or any other person.[6] Where it is shown that the
offender is in possession of substantial assets but the connection
between those assets and the stolen goods does not appear from the

---

[1] 'Available documents' means written statements which would have been admissible as evidence at the trial, or depositions or statements used in the committal
proceedings (Theft Act 1968 s. 28(4)).
[2] *Ibid.*, s. 28(4).
[3] Criminal Law Act 1977 sch. 12, amending Theft Act 1968 s. 28 (1).
[4] *Ibid.*, s. 28(1) (9).
[5] See, generally, *Stamp* v.*United Dominions Trust Ltd.* [1967] 1 All. E. R. 251
(decided under Larceny Act 916).
[6] Theft Act s. 28(4).

evidence prepared for the trial and any admission made by the accused, the court has no power to receive any further evidence tending to establish the existence of a connection unless that evidence constitutes an admission, and no evidence may be tendered once the offender has been sentenced.[1] Where the goods have been returned to the owner by a third party, an order for restitution out of their proceeds in the hands of the defendant should not be made.[2]

RESTITUTION OUT OF MONEY TAKEN FROM THE OFFENDER ON HIS APPREHENSION

Where money belonging to the offender was taken out of his possession at the time of his apprehension, the sentencer may order that a sum not exceeding the value of the stolen goods be paid to the owner out of that money. This power may be exercised only in relation to money taken from the offender at the time of his arrest. It is not necessary to show that the money was stolen in the relevant offence or was the proceeds of the relevant offence[3] so long as the money belongs to the offender.[4] Where the offender whose money has been seized has received only a part of the stolen goods, the sentencer may order payment out of his seized money in respect of all the goods stolen, at least if he was a party to an offence in respect of all the goods.[5] The power may not be exercised where the goods have been recovered.[6]

Where the person convicted is no longer in possession of the stolen goods, but is in possession of some assets representing them, and money belonging to him has been seized at the time of his arrest, the sentencer may combine his powers and make an order for the delivery of assets representing the stolen goods and payment out of money seized at the time of arrest, so long as the applicant does not recover more than the value of the goods.[7]

RESTITUTION IN FAVOUR OF AN INNOCENT THIRD PARTY

Where the Court makes a restitution order requiring a third party to return the stolen goods to the owner, and is satisfied that the person convicted sold or pledged the goods to the third party, who received

---

[1] *Church* (1970) 55 Cr. App. R. 65.
[2] *Parsons and Haley* 14.10.76, 434/C/75.
[3] *Ferguson* (1970) 54 Cr. App. R. 410.
[4] *Lewis* 31.1.75, 1365/A/74, [1975] Crim. L. R. 353.
[5] *Lewis, ibid.*
[6] See *Lucas* 9.10.70, 4935/A/70; *Parker* (1970) 54 Cr. App. R. 339.
[7] Theft Act 1968 s. 28 (2).

them in good faith, the sentencer may, without application by the third party, make an order in favour of the third party for payment of a sum not exceeding the sum paid or lent for the goods, out of money belonging to the offender and taken from him at the time of his arrest. The sentencer is not empowered to make such an order in respect of other assets in the possession of the offender, even if they represent the proceeds of the stolen goods obtained from the third party.

POLICY IN RELATION TO RESTITUTION ORDERS

The statutory provisions authorizing restitution orders are intended to provide a simple procedure for clear cases.[1] The sentencer is not permitted to embark on detailed investigations of the rights and liabilities of the parties where the facts are in dispute, although there appears to be no reason why he should not hear legal argument where the facts sufficiently appear from the available evidence. The restitution order, although much narrower in scope than the compensation order, does not require any investigation or consideration of the offender's means, and it follows that a restitution order will often be permissible where a compensation order is not, so long as the strict statutory conditions are fulfilled. In *Marks*[2] the appellant was sentenced to six years' imprisonment for a series of offences related to the theft from the Post Office of national insurance stamps to a face value in the region of £100,000. The Court upheld restitution orders in respect of insurance stamps found in his possession, and other assets including bank balances, premium bonds and a postage stamp collection, all of which were admitted to be the proceeds of the thefts. The total amount involved in the restitution orders was in excess of £17,000. The sentencer made in addition a compensation order for £10,000, which the Court quashed on being satisfied that the appellant had no means other than those to which the restitution orders related.

As the statutory conditions and the relevant principles differ in each case, the sentencer should ensure that his intention to make a restitution order, as opposed to a compensation order, is clearly understood. Where a restitution order is made, there are no powers to fix periods of time for the satisfaction of the order, authorize instalments or fix periods of imprisonment to be served in default of compliance.[3]

[1] See *Ferguson* (1970) 54 Cr. Ap. R. 410.
[2] 16.12.75, 4540/C1/74; see also *Lewis* 31.1.75, 1365/A/74, [1975] Crim. L. R. 353 (robbery; restitution order for £5,445 from money seized from offender although his share of proceeds only £2,000, upheld; compensation order for £1,000 quashed, as 'there is . . . no sufficient evidence of this appellant's means, apart from the £5,445').
[3] A restitution order under Theft Act 1968 s. 28(1)(b) is not included among those

Forfeiture of Property Used for the Purposes of an Offence

Where a person is convicted of an offence punishable with two years' imprisonment or more, the court may make an order depriving the offender of any rights in respect to any item of property, if the court is satisfied that the property was 'in his possession or under his control at the time of his apprehension'[1] and has been, or was intended to be, used for 'the purpose of committing or facilitating the commission of any offence'.[2] It is not apparently necessary that the property was used or intended to be used in connection with the offence for which the offender is convicted, and the expression 'facilitating the commission of an offence' includes taking steps after it had been committed to dispose of property involved in the offence or to avoid apprehension or detection.[3] The power is not available where the proceedings which led to the conviction began by summons.

Relatively few cases have been decided in relation to this provision, but the outline of the relevant principles are beginning to emerge. The connection between the offence and the property concerned must be clearly established by evidence that the offender used the property in order to commit the offence and presumably could not have committed the offence without it or similar equipment. In *Lucas*[4] the appellant was convicted of indecently assaulting a girl who had accepted a lift in his car, consented (according to the verdict) to sexual intercourse but objected subsequently to other conduct. The Court held that as there was no evidence that the offence was intended when the girl entered the car, the car was not used for the purpose of committing or facilitating the offence, and a confiscation order in respect of the car was accordingly quashed. By contrast in *Brown*[5] the appellant was deprived of his rights in respect of a van in which he admitted transporting stolen carpets worth £28,000, and was thereby

---

orders of the Crown Court mentioned in Administration of Justice Act 1970 sch. 9 as enforcible by magistrates' courts. Failure to comply with the order is a contempt.

[1] Property which has been lawfully seized by police officers acting under common law or statutory powers prior to the arrest is not in the possession of the offender at the time of his apprehension and accordingly not subject to confiscation under this provision (*Hinde* 25.2.77, 3766/A/76, [1977] Crim. L. R. 488). The same principle would presumably apply to property seized prior to arrest under a search warrant.

[2] Powers of Criminal Courts Act 1973 s. 43(1). For the disposal of the property, see ibid., s. 43(4) and (5).

[3] *Ibid.*, s, 43(2).

[4] 4.7.75, 167/C/75, [1976] Crim. L. R. 79.

[5] 28.2.74, 5234/B/73, [1975] Crim. L. R. 293.

guilty of handling by assisting in their disposal on behalf of another. The order was upheld as 'perfectly appropriate'.

Where the power to order confiscation arises, the sentencer should consider the order in relation to the whole of the sentence and as a part of the sentence. In *Miele*[1] the appellant was concerned in a robbery at a shop in which an assistant was threatened with a shotgun. He was sentenced to two years' imprisonment and ordered to forfeit his car, in which he left the scene of the robbery. Accepting that the offence was committed 'on the spur of the moment', the Court quashed the order relating to the car as 'not . . . correct in principle', with the comment that 'to impose the burden of forfeiture upon him is . . . like a £1,600 punishment additional to the sentence of imprisonment' (an order relating to the shotgun was apparently upheld). The distinction which this case may suggest between property which is owned or acquired specifically as an instrument of crime and property which is owned for general use and employed incidentally for the purpose of crime is supported by *Attarde*,[2] where the appellant was sentenced to imprisonment and ordered to forfeit his car for stealing petrol from other cars. The evidence was that the car had been specially equipped with an additional petrol pump and tubing so that petrol could be pumped from other vehicles into petrol cans in the car. The confiscation order was upheld. These cases may justify the view that where the property is specifically adapted for the commission of the offence, or has no other use to the offender, it may be confiscated without regard to the totality of the other sentence or sentences imposed; but where the property is used for a wide variety of purposes and used incidentally in connection with the offence, a confiscation order should be treated as analogous to a fine.

Where the sentencer considers that a confiscation order may be appropriate, he should raise the issue so that the offender may mitigate in relation to it.[3] The sentencer should consider any special hardship which the offender may suffer as a result of the forfeiture of the property concerned.[4]

---

[1] 17.1.75, 4916/A/74; see also *Lidster* 24.10.75, 2762/B/75, [1976] Crim. L. R. 80 (deprivation of car 'an additional penalty' but justified in circumstances); see also *Thompson* 9.5.77, 6046/C/76 (fine of £5,000 with forfeiture of car worth £8,000 resulted in aggregate financial penalty 'out of proportion' to offence).

[2] 18.2.75 4680/A/74, [1975] Crim. L. R. 729.

[3] See *Lucas* 4.7.75, 167/C/75, [1976] Crim. L. R. 79 (above), which appears to imply that this procedure is required.

[4] See, for example, *Tavernor* 4.4.74, 4189/C/73 (handling stolen drugs, order to forfeit car in which drugs conveyed from scene, car required by offender as mobility affected by injury; order quashed); see also *Buchholz* 10.5.74, 657/C/74 (appellant conveying drugs by motor cycle, specially adapted in view of disability; confiscation order quashed).

POWERS TO ORDER FORFEITURE OF PROPERTY IN PARTICULAR CASES

Powers to order forfeiture of property on conviction for specific offences are given by the Misuse of Drugs Act 1971, the Firearms Act 1968, and the Immigration Act 1971.

By Misuse of Drugs Act 1971 s. 27 a court before which a person is convicted of an offence may order 'anything shown to the satisfaction of the court to relate to the offence'[1] to be forfeited and either destroyed or dealt with in such other manner as the court may order. If a person claiming to be the owner of the property concerned, or otherwise interested in it, applies to the court, the sentencer may not make an order for forfeiture 'unless an opportunity has been given to him to show cause why the order should not be made'. The section does not appear to prevent the court making an order for the forfeiture of property belonging to a person who has not been convicted of the offence in question.[2] The power is broader than the power under Powers of Criminal Courts Act 1973 s. 43, as the property concerned need not have been in the possession of the offender at the time of his apprehension, as that section requires. It may, accordingly, be exercised in respect of material seized by virtue of a search warrant, and in cases where the offender has been summoned rather than arrested.

Firearms Act 1968 s. 52 allows a court to order the forfeiture and disposal of any firearm or ammunition found in the possession of a person convicted of an offence under the Firearms Act 1968,[3] or any other offence for which he is sentenced to imprisonment,[4] borstal training or detention in a detention centre. The power may be exercised where the offender is bound over to keep the peace or placed on probation subject to a condition not to possess, carry or use a firearm. It may not be used where the offender is subjected to a hospital order or ordered to be detained under Children and Young Persons Act 1933 s. 53(2), except where the offence concerned is an offence against the Firearms Act 1968.

The power may be exercised even though the firearm or ammunition was not used in connection with the offence for which the offender is sentenced, and it is not necessary to show that it was in his possession at the time of his apprehension.

---

[1] The property must relate to the offence for which the offender has been convicted and not merely to similar offences intended in the future; see *Morgan* 28.2.77, 3226/B1/76, [1977] Crim. L. R. 488.

[2] Such a person would have no right of appeal against an order made in the Crown Court, as he is not a person convicted of an offence: see *Ioannu* 26.6.75, 4905/B/74, [1976] Crim. L. R. 319.

[3] Except an offence under s. 22(3) or an offence relating specifically to airguns.

[4] Presumably including a suspended sentence.

In addition or as an alternative to ordering forfeiture of the firearm and ammunition, the court may cancel any firearm certificate which the offender may hold.

Immigration Act 1971 s. 25(6) provides for the forfeiture of a ship, aircraft, or vehicle in which more than twenty illegal entrants are brought into the United Kingdom at one time, subject to certain conditions relating to the weight and ownership of the ship, aircraft or vehicle concerned.

Orders to Pay the Costs of the Prosecution

By Costs in Criminal Cases Act 1973 s. 4(1) the Crown Court may order a person convicted on indictment to pay the whole or any part of the costs of the prosecution, including the costs of committal proceedings.[1] The sentencer should specify the precise amount to be paid or the maximum limit of the offender's liability; the usual order is to 'pay the costs of the prosecution, not exceeding [a specified amount]'.[2] An order to pay the costs of the prosecution generally or a proportion of the costs of the prosecution, without reference to a specific amount, is inappropriate.[3]

On making an order to pay the costs of the prosecution, the sentencer may allow time for payment and direct that payment be made by instalments on specified dates.[4] A term of imprisonment in default need not be fixed, but the sentencer may fix a term (not exceeding twelve months) where the term which the magistrates' court could impose in default is inadequate.[5]

The Court has stated many times that an order to pay the costs of the prosecution should not be made unless the offender has the means to pay; where the offender's means are limited, the amount of costs ordered to be paid should be reduced to a figure which the appellant can reasonably be expected to find, or no order should be made. In *Elsdon*[6] the appellant was fined £25 and ordered to pay prosecution costs amounting to £900; the Court held that although an order to pay some part of the costs was justifiable, the amount was 'clearly way out of his reach' in view in his 'very limited income'. An order to pay £50 was substituted. In *Hall*[7] a man sentenced to eighteen

---

[1] The power applies where an offender is committed for sentence under Magistrates Courts Act 1952 s. 29 or Criminal Justice Act 1967 s. 62 (revocation of parole licence) but not where the committal is under other provisions; see Powers of Criminal Courts Act 1973 s. 42.

[2] See *Stephenson* 15.3.76, 22/C/76; *Hier* (1976) 62 Cr. App. R. 233.

[3] See *Welford* 14.4.75, 230/A/75; *McKenzie* 3.7.70, 311/B/70.

[4] Powers of Criminal Courts Act 1973 s. 34.

[5] Administration of Justice Act 1970 s. 41(8). For the periods which the magistrates' court may impose, see Magistrates' Courts Act 1952 sch. 3, as substituted by Criminal Law Act 1977 s. 57.   [6] 3.7.75, 2030/A/75.

[7] 10.12.71, 3272/C/71; see also *Judd* (1970) 55 Cr. App. R. 14; *Gaston* (1970) 55 Cr. App. R. 88.

months' imprisonment for conspiracy to steal was ordered to pay £500 towards the costs of the prosecution. In view of his family responsibilities and low earning potential, the Court considered that on his release the appellant 'is extremely unlikely to be in a position at any reasonable time in the future' to comply with the order, which was accordingly quashed. The fact that the offender receives an immediate custodial sentence does not mean that an order to pay a sum towards the costs of the prosecution is necessarily inappropriate, if the offender has means available to discharge it. In Nicolls[1] the appellant was imprisoned for a period of four years and a quarter and ordered to pay £1,000 towards the costs of the prosecution; the Court held that although no specific evidence of means was available, the appellant 'did make money out of this scheme' and the order was not inappropriate. As a general rule, it is inappropriate to order payment of prosecution costs where the offender is sentenced to an immediate custodial sentence and has no resources other than his future earnings from which to make payments.[2]

The decisions of the Court generally suggest that an order to pay part of the costs of the prosecution will be appropriate where the offender has contested a case without any real hope of acquittal, or has unnecessarily prolonged the trial of a relatively simple case. In Yoxall[3] the appellant was convicted of driving with a blood alcohol level of 236 milligrammes per 100 millilitres of blood. Upholding an order to pay £40 towards the costs of the prosecution, the Court stated that 'a court is entitled to take all the circumstances into account, including the strength of the case against the accused and his knowledge of the strength of the case at the time he pleaded not guilty. He has . . . a right to plead not guilty . . . and to take his chance with a jury . . . but if he fights and loses a case in which the evidence against him was very strong, he cannot reasonably complain that he is ordered to pay a part of the costs within his means'. It will rarely be appropriate to order payment of prosecution costs on a plea of guilty,[4] or where the offender's contesting the case is justified by a partial acquittal. In Dealey[5] the appellant was acquitted on two

[1] 15.7.74, 5439/A/73; see also Houry 15.12.72, 2353/B/72 (six years' imprisonment for fraud on bank, order to pay prosecution costs not exceeding £15,000).
[2] See Leaman 21.1.71, 3469/B/70; Navarro 28.6.75, 591/A/75 ('orders for costs ought only to be made after investigation of a defendant's means and when the Court is satisfied that, even though there is to be a sentence of imprisonment taking immediate effect, there are assets out of which costs can be paid').
[3] (1972) 57 Cr. App. R. 263.
[4] See, for example, Butler 21.10.74, 1394/A/74 (plea of guilty, committed for trial on refusal of consent to summary trial by co-defendant; order to pay costs of prosecution quashed).
[5] 25.6.71, 5755/B/70; see also Thatcher 17.7.72, 5310/B/71 (convicted of seven counts, ordered to pay £300 towards prosecution costs; convictions on five counts quashed on appeal, order to pay costs quashed); Bate 11.4.73, 5768/A/72 (appellant

of the five counts in the indictment; the Court quashed an order to pay the costs of the prosecution with the comment that 'the . . . order should not have been made . . . the appellant was justified by the acquittal on two counts . . . in contesting the case'. An order to pay the costs of the prosecution should not be made on the sole ground that the offender has exercised his right to be tried on indictment for an offence which might otherwise have suitably been tried in the magistrates' court,[1] but an 'extravagant or unreasonable' election may be a ground for ordering a payment towards the costs of the prosecution.[2] The Court has not elaborated on the meaning of 'extravagant or unreasonable' in this context, but the expression may apply to cases where there is no real intention to contest the case and the election is made for collateral reasons (such as securing a delay in the imposition of a driving disqualification). Where the election itself is not 'extravagant or unreasonable', so that the mere fact of election does not justify the making of an order, an order should not be made unless the case is one in which an order would otherwise be appropriate; but if an order is made, the amount of the order may properly reflect the higher level of costs in the Crown Court.[3]

The amount of the order is not necessarily limited by the gravity of the offence, and may in appropriate circumstances exceed the amount of the fine imposed for the offence. In *Sethi*[4] the appellant elected to be tried in the Crown Court on a charge of damaging the window of a railway booking office, and 'put up a defence which was manifestly untrue'. He was fined £100 and ordered to pay £150 towards the costs of the prosecution; the Court reduced the fine to £20, but upheld the order to pay £150 costs. The sentencer should however have regard to the totality of the financial burden suffered by the offender as a result of the offence; where the combined total of any fine, contribution to the costs of the defence[5] and order to make a payment towards the costs of the prosecution constitutes a penalty which is totally out of proportion to the offence, it may be appropriate to scale down the amount of the order to pay prosecution costs. In *Glenister*[6] the

convicted on only six out of twenty-nine counts; order to pay costs reduced in amount from £750 to £200); *Smith* 4.5.76, 202/B/76 (conviction on one count of nine-count indictment; order to pay costs up to £100 quashed).

[1] *Hayden* (1975) 60 Cr. App. R. 304.

[2] *Dawood* 23.11.73, 3318/A/73, [1974] Crim. L. R. 486.

[3] *Hayden* (1975) 60 Cr. App. R. 304.

[4] 29.6.76, 5181/B/75; see also *Bailey* 2.4.76, 559/C/75 (five shoplifting offences, fines totalling £25; order to pay £150 towards prosecution costs upheld).

[5] An order to pay a contribution to the costs of the defence is not a 'sentence' (see *Hayden* (1975) 60 Cr. App. R. 304) and is accordingly not subject to appeal.

[6] 28.11.75, 1662/C/75; see also *King* 4.3.77, 4030/A/76 (possession of controlled drug, fine of £25, costs not exceeding £180; sentencer 'fell into two errors: firstly, he did not have regard to the appellant's means . . . secondly he made an order wholly out of proportion to the fine imposed' — costs reduced to £25).

appellant, convicted on indictment of possessing a small quantity of cannabis, was fined £50 and ordered to pay £100 towards the costs of the prosecution and the whole of his defence costs, which were estimated at about £350. The Court held that while an order to pay the costs of the prosecution was not unjustified in principle, the total burden of £500 amounted to a penalty which is 'really out of scale to the gravity of the offence which he committed'. While these cases are not entirely reconcilable, they appear to reflect the existence of a principle relating to financial orders analogous to the totality principle applicable to consecutive terms of imprisonment.[1]

Criminal Bankruptcy Orders

A criminal bankruptcy order may be made where a person is convicted in the Crown Court and the sentencer is satisfied that loss or damage (not attributable to personal injury) in an amount exceeding £15,000 has been suffered by one or more persons as a result of the offences for which the offender is convicted or which the sentencer takes into consideration.[2] The order must specify the total amount of the damage or loss resulting from the offences in respect of which it is made, the persons who have suffered the loss or damage and the amount which each has suffered respectively, and the date which appears to be the earliest date on which the offence, or the earliest of the offences, was committed. A criminal bankruptcy order may be made against two or more offenders in respect of the same loss or damage, but may not be made where a compensation order is made against the offender.

No appeal lies against the making of a criminal bankruptcy order[3] and accordingly no cases have been decided on the principles governing its use.

---

[1] See above, p. 56.
[2] Powers of Criminal Courts Act 1973 s. 39(1).
[3] *Ibid.*, s. 40(1). An appeal lies where it is claimed that the order is a nullity (*Anderson* (1977) 66 Cr. App. R. 134).

10

Disqualification from Driving

An offender may be disqualified from driving in four categories of cases, three involving motoring offences and the other the commission of an offence in which a motor vehicle is used.

Discretionary Disqualification for Motoring Offences

Road Traffic Act 1972 provides that on conviction for one of a number of offences, the sentencer may disqualify the offender from driving or holding a driving licence for such period as the court thinks fit.[1] The sentencer has unfettered discretion whether or not to disqualify, and in the choice of the period of disqualification.

Mandatory Disqualification on Conviction for Specified Offences

An offender convicted of one of a number of specified offences must be disqualified for a period of not less than twelve months, unless for 'special reasons' the sentencer decides to disqualify him for a shorter period or not to disqualify him at all. There is no limit on the maximum period of such a disqualification.[2]

THE OBLIGATION TO DISQUALIFY: 'SPECIAL REASONS'

The term 'special reasons' has been used in road traffic legislation for many years and has been subject to interpretation on a number of

[1] Road Traffic Act 1972 s. 93(2). The offences involving discretionary disqualification which are triable on indictment are: reckless driving (where disqualification is not mandatory); being in charge of a vehicle while unfit to drive (s. 5(2)); being in charge of a vehicle with a blood alcohol level in excess of the permitted level (s. 6(2)); failing to supply a specimen of blood or urine where the offender was not driving or attempting to drive (s. 9(3)); stealing a car (Theft Act 1968 s. 7); taking a conveyance without authority (*ibid.*, s. 12).
[2] Road Traffic Act 1972 s. 93(1). The offences concerned are: causing death by reckless driving (s. 1); reckless driving within three years of a conviction for the same offence (s. 2); driving while unfit (s. 5(1)); driving with an excess blood alcohol level (s. 6(1)); failing to supply a specimen of blood or urine, where the offender was driving or attempting to drive at the relevant time (s. 9(3)).

occasions both in the Court of Appeal, Criminal Division, and the Divisional Court of the Queen's Bench Division. It has long been established that 'special reasons' means reasons relating to the facts of the offence rather than the circumstances of the offender;[1] mitigating circumstances (as that term is used in this book) cannot constitute special reasons for not disqualifying where disqualification is obligatory. Thus the severe impact of disqualification on the offender's professional[2] or personal life,[3] or the loss of his services by his employer,[4] cannot constitute 'special reasons'.

A number of specific issues have been decided in relation to the meaning of 'special reasons' in connection with driving with an excess blood alcohol level. The small amount of the excess over the permitted level cannot constitute a special reason,[5] nor can the fact that the offender's ability to drive was not affected,[6] or that no other person was put at risk by the offender's driving.[7] When the offender's blood alcohol has been affected by circumstances outside his control or knowledge, such as exposure to alcoholic fumes in the course of an industrial process[8] or the 'lacing' of his drink by someone else,[9] the sentencer may find a special reason, if there has been no negligence and the amount by which the offender's blood alcohol exceeds the permissible limit is attributable to the alcohol taken in ignorance.[10] The effect of the offender's metabolism on his blood alcohol level cannot constitute a special reason,[11] but the effect of an unknown disease may do so.[12]

The fact the offender drove only a very short distance has been held to constitute a special reason,[13] but later decisions suggest that this will be so only in the most extreme cases.[14] Where the offender has consumed alcohol on the assumption that he will not be driving in the near future, but is then confronted with a medical or domestic

---

[1] *Whittall v. Kirkby* [1947] 1 K.B. 194; *Steel* (1968) 52 Cr. App. R. 510; *Brown v. Dyerson* (1968) 52 Cr. App. R. 63; *James v. Hall* [1968] Crim. L. R. 507; *McClean v. Cork* [1968] Crim. L. R. 507.

[2] See *Holroyd v. Berry* (1973) 4 R. T. R. 145; *Mullarkey v. Prescott* (1970) 1 R. T. R. 296.

[3] *See Reynolds v. Roche* (1972) 3 R. T. R. 282.

[4] *See Gordon v. Smith* (1971) 2 R. T. R. 52.

[5] *Delaroy-Hall v. Tadman* (1968)53 Cr. App. R. 143.

[6] *Taylor v. Austin* [1969] 1 W. L. R. 264.

[7] *Milliner v. Thorner* (1972) 1 R. T. R. 279; see also *Kerr v. Armstrong* (1974) 4 R. T. R. 139.

[8] See *Brewer v. Metropolitan Police Commissioner* (1968) 53 Cr. App. R. 157.

[9] See *Messom* (1972) 57 Cr. App. R. 481, reviewing earlier decisions; *Newton* 15.2.74, 4737/C/73, [1974] Crim. L. R. 321.

[10] *Pugsley v. Hunter* [1973] 2 All. E. R. 10; see also *Alexander v. Latter* (1972) 3 R. T. R. 441.

[11] *Knight v. Baxter* (1971) 2 R. T. R. 270.

[12] *Jackson* [1969] 2 All. E. R. 453.

[13] *James v. Hall* [1972] 2 All. E. R. 59.

[14] See *Coombs v. Kehoe* [1972] 2 All. E. R. 55.

emergency which necessitates his driving, the sentencer may find a special reason for not disqualifying,[1] providing that the circumstances required urgent action and no alternative means of transportation were available.[2]

The existence of circumstances capable of amounting to special reasons does not determine the question of disqualification. Where special reasons for not disqualifying are established, the sentencer is released from the obligation to disqualify but retains a discretion to do so. The Court has stressed that the sentencer should exercise that discretion: 'The proof of facts amounting to special reasons is not an end to the matter . . . The final question of whether the driver merits the avoidance of disqualification must be decided having regard to all the circumstances in the case . . . in particular, to the driver's own conduct'.[3] Where special reasons are found, they must be stated in open court.[4]

THE PERIOD OF DISQUALIFICATION

Where disqualification is mandatory on conviction for a specific offence, the period of disqualification must be at least twelve months, unless there are special reasons for imposing a shorter period.[5] The term 'special reasons' clearly has the same meaning in this context as in the context of the decision whether or not to disqualify.[6] In the case of a person convicted of an offence involving an excessive blood alcohol level within ten years of a conviction for any such offence, the minimum period of disqualification is three years, unless special reasons for a shorter term are present. In neither case is the period of disqualification subject to any maximum period.

Mandatory Disqualification on a Third Conviction for an Endorsible Offence: 'Totting Up'

Where a person is convicted of an offence for which disqualification is either obligatory or discretionary, and has within the three years preceding the offence been convicted on not less than two occasions of any such offence, and the court has on those occasions ordered particulars of the convictions to be endorsed on his licence, the sentencer must impose a disqualification for at least six months, in

---

1 *Taylor v. Rajan* [1974] 1 All. E. R. 1087.
2 See *Baines* (1970) 54 Cr. App. R. 481.
3 *Newton* 15.2.74, 4737/C/73, [1974] Crim. L. R. 321.
4 Road Traffic Act 1972 s. 105.
5 *Ibid.*, s. 93(1).
6 See *Cherlin* 30.10.73, 880/C/73.

addition to any other period of disqualification which he has power or is obliged to order, unless 'the court is satisfied, having regard to all the circumstances, that there are grounds for mitigating the normal consequence of the conviction'.[1] If the court is satisfied of this, it may refrain from disqualification or order disqualification for a period shorter than six months.

The three-year period begins with the conviction for the first of the three offences and ends on the commission of the last, even though conviction for the last of the offences does not take place until after the end of the period. The convictions must have taken place on separate occasions; two convictions on the same occasion in respect of different offences committed on separate occasions do not satisfy the requirements of the section. A previous conviction does not count if the court has exercised its power not to order endorsement of the offender's licence with particulars of the conviction,[2] but a conviction remains a qualifying conviction for this purpose, despite the fact that the court has imposed a conditional discharge or probation order in respect of it.[3]

THE OBLIGATION TO DISQUALIFY: 'MITIGATING GROUNDS'

Where the statutory conditions are satisfied, the offender must be disqualified for at least six months (in addition to any other disqualification imposed for the offence), unless 'there are grounds for mitigating the normal consequences of the conviction'. 'Grounds for mitigating' is a broader term than 'special reasons' and extends to such matters as the relative triviality of the previous offence[4] and the effect of disqualification on the offender.[5]

The fact that the offender has been disqualified under the 'totting-up' provisions in respect of the earlier conviction does not prevent that conviction or any earlier conviction from counting as a qualifying conviction in relation to the present offence: the disqualification does not 'wipe the slate clean'.[6] Where on the third occasion the offender is convicted of more than one offence requiring disqualification under the 'totting-up' provisions, a separate consecutive period of disqualification must be imposed in respect of each

[1] Road Traffic Act 1972 s. 93(3), (4).
[2] *Ibid.*, s. 101(2).
[3] *Ibid.*, s. 102(2).
[4] *Lambie v. Woodage* (1972) 3 R. T. R. 396.
[5] *Baker v. Cole* [1971] 3 All. E. R. 680.
[6] *Fearon v. Sydney* [1966] 1 W. L. R. 1003, [1966] 2 All. E. R. 694.

offence unless there are 'grounds for mitigating'.[1] Where mitigating grounds are established they must be stated in open court.[2]

PERIOD OF DISQUALIFICATION

The period of disqualification must be at least six months unless there are mitigating grounds which justify a shorter period of disqualification. There is no maximum period of disqualification. The sentencer has discretion to disqualify for such period as he thinks fit. Whatever period of disqualification is imposed under the 'totting-up' provisions must be in addition to any other period of disqualification to which the offender is already subject or which is imposed on him at the same time.

Disqualification where a Motor Vehicle is Used for the Purposes of an Offence

Where a person is dealt with[3] by the Crown Court for an offence punishable with imprisonment for two years or more, and the court is satisfied that a motor vehicle was used (either by the person convicted or by anybody else) for the purpose of committing or facilitating the commission of the offence,[4] the court may disqualify the offender from driving for such period as it thinks fit.[5] It is sufficient if the vehicle is used incidentally to the commission of the offence. In *Mathews*[6] the appellant cashed stolen cheques, using a stolen cheque card, at a series of banks; he was driven from bank to bank by an accomplice. The Court held that the sentencer had jurisdiction to disqualify. As the use of the car had enabled the appellant to visit a larger number of banks within a short space of time, the facts were 'plainly within the words of the section'. The few cases that have been decided on the use of this power suggest that it should be used sparingly,[7] and that an offender sentenced to imprisonment for the offence should not be disqualified for a period likely to extend beyond

---

[1] See *R. v. Sixsmith ex p. Morris* [1966] 3 W. L. R. 1200, [1966] 3 All. E. R. 473.
[2] Road Traffic Act 1972 s. 105(1).
[3] On conviction on indictment or on a committal under Magistrates' Courts Act 1952 s. 29.
[4] This expression includes taking any steps after the offence has been committed for the purpose of disposing of any property involved in the offence or avoiding apprehension or detection; see Powers of Criminal Courts Act 1973 s. 43(2) as applied by s. 44(2).
[5] Powers of Criminal Courts Act 1973 s. 44.
[6] 29.7.74, 2283/A/74, [1974] Crim. L. R. 612.
[7] See, for example, *Thomas* 23.4.74, 5362/C/73, [1975] Crim. L. R. 296; *Hall* 1.2.74, 4831/A/73.

the term of his imprisonment, if the disqualification is likely to hinder his efforts to find employment on his release.[1]

General Provisions Governing Disqualification

CONSECUTIVE TERMS OF DISQUALIFICATION

The Court has held many times that there is no power to impose a period of disqualification to begin on a day other than the day on which it is imposed, except in the case of a disqualification under the 'totting-up' procedure, which must be consecutive to any other period of disqualification to which the offender is already subject or which is then imposed.[2] Where the offender is convicted on the same occasion of two offences subject to obligatory disqualification under section 93(1) the sentencer must impose at least twelve months' disqualification for each offence, running concurrently; if either (or both) offences qualify under section 93(3) the sentencer must impose a further period of six months' disqualification consecutive to the twelve months under section 93(1) in respect of each qualifying offence.

EFFECTS OF DISQUALIFICATION

A person disqualified by a court may not obtain or hold a driving licence during the period of disqualification, or drive a motor vehicle on a road.[3] Any licence which the offender holds is automatically suspended for the period of disqualification, and any licence which he obtains is void.[4] Where a person is disqualified until he has passed a driving test and is not subject to any other disqualifications, he may obtain a provisional driving licence and drive in accordance with the restrictions applicable to the holders of provisional licences.

REMOVAL OF DISQUALIFICATION

A person who has been disqualified may apply to the court which

---

[1] See, for example, *Cohen* 17.11.75, 3573/A/75 (seven years' imprisonment for two hundred thefts and burglaries involving £24,000, committed shortly after release from prison; disqualification for fifteen years reduced to five years to enable appellant to find employment on release); see also *Reed* 14.2.75, 371/R/75, [1975] Crim. L. R. 729 (disqualification for two years, six months' imprisonment for burglary of car showroom; disqualification reduced to twelve months to allow resumption of employment within a few months of release from prison); *Mathews* 29.7.74, 2283/A/74, [1974] Crim. L. R. 612 (above, p. 346).

[2] *Sibthorpe* (1973) 57 Cr. App. R. 447; *Meese* (1973) 57 Cr. App. R. 568; *Townsley* 3.7.75, 1146/A/75.

[3] Road Traffic Act 1972 ss. 98, 99.

[4] *Ibid.*, s. 98.

disqualified him to remove the disqualification. On such an application the court may remove the disqualification from a specified date if it 'thinks proper, having regard to the character of the person disqualified and his conduct subsequent to the order, the nature of the offence, and any other circumstances'.[1] No application may be made until two years from the imposition of the disqualification if the disqualification is for less than four years; one half of the period of disqualification if it is for four years and up to ten years, or five years in any other case. Where an application for removal is refused, no further application may be made for three months.[2]

The Court has stated that in determining the proper length of a period of disqualification in any case, the sentencer should disregard these provisions. 'It is quite wrong for a judge in imposing a period of disqualification to . . . advert to the statutory provision which enables an accused person . . . to seek a reduction in the disqualification. If the proper disqualification is two years, then it is two years.'[3]

DISQUALIFICATION UNTIL THE OFFENDER HAS PASSED THE DRIVING TEST

Where a person is convicted of an offence for which disqualification is possible, the court may order him to be disqualified until he has passed the driving test, whether or not he has already passed the test and whether or not the court disqualifies him for a specified period.[4] Where the offender is also disqualified for a specific period, the order is that he be disqualified for the specified period and remain disqualified thereafter until he has passed the driving test. The effect of such an order is to prohibit the offender from driving during the specified period; when that period has elapsed the offender may obtain a provisional licence and drive subject to its restrictions.

The Court has held that the power to require an offender to take a driving test is not to be used punitively.[5] It should be used where there is reason to question the offender's general competence to drive—where the offender's driving record and conduct on the occasion of the offence raise doubts about his capability as a driver,[6] or the

[1] Road Traffic Act 1972 s. 95(1).
[2] *Ibid.*, s. 95(3).
[3] *Lobley* (1974) 59 Cr. App. R. 373.
[4] Road Traffic Act 1972 s. 95(7).
[5] *Donnelly* (1975) 60 Cr. App. R. 250 ('section 93(7) is not a punitive section'); see also *Mallender* 10.2.75, 5733/C/74, [1975] Crim. L. R. 725.
[6] See, for example, *O'Donovan* 21.3.75, 204/A1/75 (extensive record of driving offences, driving on occasion of present offence shows that 'he has no regard whatsoever for traffic law or the lives and safety of other road users').

nature of the offence suggests that the offender's powers are failing.[1] A requirement to take the driving test may also be appropriate where the offender is disqualified for a substantial period of time, so that he may have become unfamiliar with changing traffic conditions by the time his disqualification has expired.[2]

ENDORSEMENT OF LICENCE

Where a person is convicted of an offence for which he must or may be disqualified, the court must order his licence to be endorsed with particulars of the conviction, unless it refrains from disqualifying and for 'special reasons' thinks fit not to endorse the licence.[3] The principal effect of endorsement is to make the conviction concerned a qualifying conviction for the purpose of the 'totting-up' procedure: failure to endorse means that the conviction concerned does not count towards disqualification.

INTERIM DISQUALIFICATION ON COMMITTAL FOR SENTENCE

Where an offender is committed for sentence under Criminal Justice Act 1967 s. 56(1), 'or any enactment to which that section applies', the magistrates' court may order him to be disqualified until the court to which he is committed has dealt with him in respect of the offence.[4] Any such period of disqualification is deducted from the period of disqualification imposed by the Crown Court[5] if he is not at the same time disqualified under some other provision.

DISQUALIFICATION AND THE PRINCIPAL SENTENCE

A court may order disqualification or endorsement notwithstanding that it makes a probation order or grants a conditional discharge for the same offence[6] or makes a community service order.[7] The Crown Court may impose disqualification in conjunction with a sentence of borstal training passed following a committal under Magistrates' Court Act 1952 s. 28,[8] except where the only power to disqualify

---

[1] See, for example, *Rowe* 23.1.75, 4785/B/74, [1975] Crim. L. R.245 ('aberration' by man, 64, with excellent record until recent years; 'perhaps his powers of concentrated attention . . . are not quite as great . . . as during his younger years').
[2] See *Guilfoyle* (1973) 57 Cr. App. R. 549.
[3] Road Traffic Act 1972 s. 101.
[4] *Ibid.*, s. 103(1).
[5] *Ibid.*, s. 103(5).
[6] Road Traffic Act 1972 s. 102.
[7] Powers of Criminal Courts Act 1973 s. 14(8).
[8] See Criminal Justice Act 1967 s. 56(5), (6).

would arise under Powers of Criminal Courts Act 1973 s. 44 (disqualification where vehicle is used to commit or facilitate offence). [1] This power may be exercised where a sentence of borstal training is imposed on conviction on indictment or on a committal under Magistrates' Court Act 1952 s. 29.

Policy in the Use of Disqualification Generally

Disqualification from driving may be used in two distinct ways—as a preventive measure designed to restrain a persistently dangerous driver from driving, or as a punitive measure intended to add a further element to the primary sentence for the offence.

DISQUALIFICATION AS A PREVENTIVE MEASURE

The Power to disqualify is not subject to any maximum limit, and wherever there is power to disqualify the court may impose disqualification for any period up to life. [2] The Court has been prepared to endorse the use of disqualification as a preventive measure in the case of drivers with unusually bad driving records, but is generally opposed to extremely long periods of disqualification; a period in excess of ten years' disqualification is unlikely to be upheld, even in cases where a preventive disqualification is justified. In *Baptista*[3] a man of 43, whose 'very many previous convictions indicated a scant regard for the law' and included three previous convictions for driving or attempting to drive while affected by drink, was disqualified for twenty years on conviction for attempting to drive with blood alcohol level of 372 milligrammes per 100 millilitres of blood. The Court accepted that the appellant represented a danger 'for as long as he goes on drinking excessively and while in drink tries to drive motor cars', but this had to be balanced against 'the frustration which he is found to feel in connection with possible future employment'. The period of disqualification was reduced to ten years. In *Artley*[4] a man of 23, described as 'an absolute menace on the road', was disqualified for fifteen years on two convictions of failing to provide a specimen. The Court stated that 'very long orders

[1] S. 44(1) applies only where there is a conviction on indictment or committal under Magistrates' Court Act 1952 s. 29.

[2] *Tunde-Olarinde* (1967) 51 Cr. App. R. 249.

[3] 2.5.75, 944/B/75; see also *Humphries* 6.3.73, 6352/B/72 (refusal to supply specimen, various previous convictions, including two for driving or attempting to drive with excess blood alcohol level; 'right to impose long period of disqualification' but twenty years unnecessarily long—reduced to ten); *Chenery* 6.9.75, 2067/C/73 (man, 32, 'considerable number' of previous convictions, history of alcoholism; ten years' disqualification 'abundantly right').

[4] 29.4.75, 388/B/75.

of disqualification . . . tend to defeat their object, to lead to further crime and to discourage young men . . . from leading honest working lives which may require the use of a motor car'. The disqualification was reduced to ten years.

The same policy is evident in cases of younger offenders who persistently commit offences of taking a conveyance and related offences. The Court is generally opposed to periods of disqualification which are likely to last beyond the offender's early twenties. In *Dawtrey*[1] a youth of 18 was disqualified for six years for a series of offences relating to motor vehicles. The Court accepted that although the appellant 'has been a thorough nuisance and danger to the public', the imposition of a lengthy period of disqualification was 'counter-productive', in that it had created 'a deep sense of grievance, which has made him even more determined to break the law'. The disqualification was reduced to three years. In *Smith*[2] a youth of 19 was sentenced to borstal training and disqualified for thirty months for taking a conveyance and driving while disqualified. The Court observed that 'as far as motor cars are concerned' the appellant appeared to consider himself a law unto himself; but that a reduction in the period of disqualification 'may encourage him to toe the line'. A period of twelve months' disqualification was substituted.

DISQUALIFICATION AS A PUNITIVE MEASURE

Where disqualification from driving is imposed as a punitive measure, the length of the period of disqualification is determined by a process analogous to that followed in relation to sentences of imprisonment—a period is selected which reflects the gravity of the instant offence, which may then be reduced in view of mitigating factors. In many cases the statutorily prescribed minimum period will be considered sufficient, but the offences of causing death by reckless driving and driving with an excessive blood alcohol level are often held to justify a term in excess of the minimum.

Causing death by reckless driving

In *Guilfoyle*[3] the Court indicated that where the case did not fall into the category for which a preventive disqualification was necessary 'to relieve the public of a potential danger for a very long time indeed', the sentencer should distinguish between offenders who have committed the offence through 'momentary inattention or misjudgement'

---

1 24.9.74, 2509/A/74.
2 3.10.74, 2448/C/74.
3 (1973) 57 Cr. App. R. 549.

and those who have 'driven recklessly' or shown 'a careless disregard for the safety of other road users'. In the former case, the minimum period of disqualification would be appropriate if the offender's driving record was good; if the record was indifferent the period should be longer, within the bracket of five to ten years. In the latter case a long period of disqualification would be appropriate (apparently irrespective of record), and a very long period where reckless driving was combined with a bad driving record.

Although in subsequent decisions the Court has warned that this statement should not be treated as if it were a statute,[1] it does appear to reflect the general policy of the Court. Where there is a combination of a good record and a minor lapse of driving standards leading to fatal consequences, a disqualification in excess of twelve months is unlikely to be upheld, as in *Carlin*[2] where a man of 'hitherto unblemished record' caused the death of a woman who was using a pedestrian crossing one evening. The Court accepted that there was no evidence of excessive speed or recklessness and reduced the disqualification from five years to twelve months. By contrast in another case where a man of 50 with 'a very good driving record' caused the death of the driver of another car by driving 'very dangerously', the Court considered a four-year disqualification appropriate.[3]

Driving with an excessive blood alcohol level

The cases suggest that a period of disqualification for driving with an excessive blood alcohol level, or one of the related offences, should not normally exceed the relevant statutory minimum of twelve months or three years (where there is a previous conviction for a similar offence within the last ten years), unless the offence is aggravated by an unusually high blood alcohol level or particularly bad driving.[4] In some such cases the sentencer may mitigate the disqualification in view of the more substantial primary sentence. In *Pashley*[5] the appellant was sentenced to twelve months' imprison-

---

[1] See *Lobley* (1974) 59 Cr. App. R. 373; *Hetta* 15.3.74, 517/B/74.
[2] 17.11.75, 3903/B/75.
[3] *Hetta* 15.3.74, 517/B/74; see also *Foster* 17.1.72, 5464/A/71 (man, 48, no previous convictions, overtaking at pedestrian crossing, excess blood alcohol level; ten years' disqualification reduced to five); *Tyrer* 25.10.71, 925/B/71, [1972] Crim. L. R. 55 (driver deliberately taking calculated risk which 'any reasonable driver would recognize as unsafe', no previous conviction; ten years' disqualification 'out of scale'—reduced to seven).
[4] See, for example, *Myers* 8.10.74, 1504/C/74 (driving with blood alcohol level 'minimally' above the prescribed level, no previous convictions; 'Nothing in this case to distinguish it from any other case in which a man for the first time is convicted of this . . . offence'—two years' disqualification reduced to twelve months).
[5] (1974) 5 R. T. R. 149.

ment and disqualified for three years for dangerous driving and driving with a blood alcohol level of 154 milligrammes per 100 millilitres of blood. The Court held that the term of imprisonment was 'an ample deterrent' and reduced the disqualification to twelve months. Similarly in *Wicks*[1] the appellant was fined £100 and disqualified for three years for driving with a blood alcohol level of 261 milligrammes per 100 millilitres of blood. The Court said that as the appellant had no previous convictions, the only reason for the longer period of disqualification was the higher level of blood alcohol; but as this factor was already reflected in the amount of the fine, it was not necessary to reflect it also in the disqualification, which was reduced to twelve months. Where this consideration does not apply and there is no question of long-term preventive disqualification, periods of disqualification in excess of three years are rarely upheld. In *French*[2] the appellant was disqualified for three years (including six months under the 'totting-up' provisions) for driving with a blood alcohol level of 254 milligrammes per 100 millilitres of blood. Although the high level of blood alcohol made it 'inevitable that a substantial period of disqualification must be imposed', the appellant's previous good record, which included only two minor motoring offences, and the interference with his employment as a professional driver, justified a reduction to two years. In *Yoxall*[3] the Court considered that a three-year disqualification imposed on a driver of 24 with no previous convictions, who was convicted of driving with a blood alcohol level of 236 milligrammes per 100 millilitres of blood, was 'not excessive for this bad offence'. In *Pegg*[4] the appellant was disqualified for five years for driving with a blood alcohol content of 270 milligrammes per 100 millilitres; the period was chosen so that he could be disqualified for three years following his likely release from a sentence of imprisonment for an unrelated offence. The Court considered that this disqualification would be 'too severe' and reduced it to three years.

MITIGATION

The length of a disqualification (other than an obligatory disqualification for the statutory minimum period under Road Traffic Act 1972 s. 93(1)) may be reduced to reflect the presence of mitigating factors, by analogy with the process followed in relation to sentences of imprisonment. One mitigating factor which is parti-

[1] 3.7.75, 1768/A/75.
[2] 6.7.72, 329/A/72.
[3] (1972) 57 Cr. App. R. 263.
[4] 3.10.72, 2206/A/72.

cularly significant in relation to disqualification is the effect of disqualification on the offender's employment, especially where he is sentenced to imprisonment and may expect difficulty in finding employment on his release. In *Aspden*[1] a man with 'a very poor driving record' was disqualified for a total of three years (including six months under the 'totting-up' provisions) for driving with a blood alcohol level of 115 milligrammes per 100 millilitres of blood. The Court stated that as the appellant 'requires the use of a car to follow the only trade that he really knows', the term was excessive; the minimum applicable term of eighteen months was substituted. In *Reid*[2] a man of 43 with several convictions for minor motoring offences was disqualified for five years for causing death by dangerous driving; the Court reduced this period to two years, 'having regard to the fact that the appellant's livelihood depends to a very large extent upon his driving'.

[1] 22.4.75, 1483 B 74.
[2] 10.5.73, 641/A/73.

11

Recommendation for Deportation

The Immigration Act 1971 distinguishes between persons who have the right of abode in the United Kingdom (patrials) and those who do not.[1] A person who is not a patrial who is convicted of an offence punishable with imprisonment in the case of an adult[2] may be recommended for deportation by the Court which sentences him for the offence.[3] Where a recommendation is made, the Secretary of State may, at his discretion, make an order for the deportation of the offender.[4]

A recommendation may not be made if the offender has not attained the age of 17 years on the day of his conviction.[5] If the offender is a Commonwealth citizen[6] who is ordinarily resident in the United Kingdom on the date of his conviction, a recommendation may not be made if he has been ordinarily resident for a continuous period of five years immediately prior to that date.[7] In determining whether the offender has been ordinarily resident in the United Kingdom for a period of five years, the sentencer must disregard any period of time during which he was undergoing imprisonment or detention by virtue of a sentence passed for an offence on a conviction in the United Kingdom and Islands, if the period for which he was in fact imprisoned or detained by virtue of the sentence amounted to six months or more.[8] The question whether the continuity of a period of

---

[1] For the details of the definition, see Immigration Act 1971 s. 2.
[2] *Ibid.*, ss. 3(6), 6(3).
[3] *Ibid.* s. 6(1).
[4] *Ibid.* s. 3(6).
[5] *Ibid.* s. 3(5). He may be deemed to be 17 if he appears to the court, on consideration of the available evidence, to have attained that age (*ibid.* s. 6 (3)).
[6] See British Nationality Act 1948 s. 1.
[7] Immigration Act 1971 s. 7.
[8] *Ibid.* s. 7(3). For this purpose, the offender is deemed to be detained by virtue of a sentence at any time when he is liable to be so detained, but is unlawfully at large (*ibid.* s. 7(4)(c)(i). The application of the statute to time spent in custody prior to trial, which subsequently goes to reduce the sentence passed, is uncertain; see s. 7(4)(c)(ii). This paragraph appears to require such time to be treated as time spent in custody under a sentence, but subject to the exception 'unless the sentence is passed after the material time'. The exception appears to exclude all cases within the rule except time spent in

ordinary residence has been broken by a substantial spell of time spent out of the United Kingdom is one of fact for the sentencer to decide.[1] A holiday abroad does not break the continuity of the period of ordinary residence.[2]

PROCEDURE

A court may not make a recommendation unless the offender has received a written notice at least seven days before the recommendation is made, setting out the effect of the relevant provisions of the Immigration Act 1971.[3] The court may adjourn after conviction to allow the notice to be served, or to allow the period of the notice to expire.[4] The burden of proof of the question whether the offender is or is not a patrial, or is otherwise entitled to any exemption from the power to recommend deportation, lies on the offender.[5] The offender should be given the opportunity to mitigate with specific reference to deportation before any recommendation is made.[6]

An offender may be recommended for deportation even though he is also sentenced to imprisonment for life.[7] A recommendation is treated as a "sentence" for the purposes of appeal.[8]

CITIZENS OF MEMBER STATES OF THE EUROPEAN ECONOMIC COMMUNITY

The E.E.C. Treaty requires member states to secure freedom of movement for workers within the Community, subject to limitations 'justified on grounds of public policy, public security or public health'.[9] In pursuance of this object the Commission has issued a directive which provides that 'measures taken on grounds of public policy or of public security shall be based exclusively on the personal conduct of the individual concerned' and that 'previous convictions

---

custody in proceedings concerned with the enforcement of a suspended sentence. Time spent in custody on remand in proceedings which terminate in an acquittal or non-custodial sentence counts as part of the period of continuous residence.

[1] See, for example, *Hussain* (1971) 56 Cr. App. R. 165, decided on Commonwealth Immigrants Act 1972 (offender spending twenty months in country of origin, leaving wives, children and plot of land there, not ordinarily resident in United Kingdom during that period.)

[2] *Hussain* (1971) 56 Cr. App. R. 165 ('the mere breaking of any residence to take a holiday abroad . . . does not render the person no longer a resident').

[3] Immigration Act 1971 s. 6(2).

[4] *Ibid.*

[5] *Ibid.* s. 3(8).

[6] *Philogene* 5.4.71, 4839/A/70; *Antypas* (1972) 57 Cr. App. R. 207 at 212.

[7] *Ibid.* s. 6(4).

[8] Criminal Appeal Act 1968 s. 50(1).

[9] E.E.C. Treaty, art. 48.

shall not in themselves constitute grounds for the taking of such measures'.[1] The Court of Justice of the European Economic Community has held that the restrictions contained in the Treaty and the Directive apply to recommendations for deportation made under the Immigration Act 1971, even though the recommendation is not binding on the Home Secretary.[2] Interpreting the Directive, the Court of Justice held that the concept of public policy 'presupposes the existence, in addition to the perturbation of the social order which any infringement of the law involves, of a genuine and sufficiently serious threat to the requirements of public policy affecting one of the fundamental interests of society' although 'the particular circumstances justifying recourse to the concept of public policy may vary from one country to another'.[3] The Court of Justice added that the reference in the Directive to previous convictions meant that 'a previous criminal conviction can . . . only be taken into account in so far as the circumstances which gave rise to that conviction are evidence of personal conduct constituting a present threat to the requirements of public policy'.[4]

The implications of this decision appear to be that a court contemplating a recommendation against a person protected by the Treaty[5] must be satisfied that, whether by reason of previous convictions or otherwise, the continued presence of the offender in the United Kingdom constitutes a serious threat to 'the fundamental interests of society'. A recommendation may not be made punitively, or on the grounds that the offender can be considered a nuisance.

POLICY IN MAKING RECOMMENDATIONS FOR DEPORTATION

In earlier cases decided under legislation replaced by the Immigration Act 1971, the Court emphasized that the sentencer should impose the sentence appropriate to the offence in all the relevant circumstances, before considering the question of a recommendation for deportation.[6] It was incorrect to impose an unduly lenient sentence in conjunction with a recommendation, on the basis that the offender should be deported as soon as possible without the expense of his imprisonment falling on public funds in this country. A major reason

[1] Directive 64/221.
[2] *Bouchereau* (1978) 66 Cr. App. R. 202.
[3] *Ibid.*
[4] *Ibid.*
[5] The Treaty applies only to workers, their spouses and certain dependents; see Reg. 1612/68 Art. 10.
[6] *Edgehill* (1963) 47 Cr. App. R. 41 ('courts should deal with the offence on its merits and sentence the prisoner to the penalty or sentence which he deserves, and having done that, should deal with the recommendation quite separately').

for this policy was the uncertainty that a recommendation for deportation would be acted on in any particular case. This principle appears to be still in effect. The making of a recommendation for deportation should be treated as an ancillary issue, to be decided once the primary sentence has been imposed. In *Kamara*[1] the appellant was sentenced to four years' imprisonment and recommended for deportation on his conviction for a number of offences of dishonesty. The Court was invited to approach the case in terms of the question: 'how long should this man remain in prison in this country . . . at the expense of the taxpayer before he is sent packing to his home country?', but stated that 'this Court . . . has to look at the case in the ordinary way in the light of the personal circumstances of the offender and . . . the gravity of the offence'. (In view of a series of mitigating factors the sentence was reduced from four years to two, but the recommendation was upheld.)

The fact that a recommendation is not a final determination is probably the reason why relatively few clear principles have emerged to govern its use.[2] It is clear that there is no presumption in favour of a recommendation and the sentencer must exercise his discretion in relation to the particular case.[3]

The cases suggest that recommendations are likely to be considered appropriate in a number of different kinds of case, although the categories clearly cannot be considered exhaustive.

Serious crime

A recommendation will usually be upheld, in conjunction with a substantial sentence, where the offender is convicted of a serious crime involving some degree of deliberation. The most common example is fraudulently evading the prohibition on the importation of cannabis, at least where substantial quantities and a commercial motive are involved. Frequently the offender in such cases is not resident in the United Kingdom and does not resist the recom-

---

[1] 16.1.76, 2979/A/75.

[2] See, for example, *Ashraf and Mahfooz* 11.5.71, 5883/A/70 (sentencer's comments that 'there are enough native-born criminals without importing them' might be 'rather strong language', in view of previous good character, but 'we do not have to decide whether or not these men are to be deported. That, happily, is the function of the executive and not the judiciary'; recommendation not incorrect having regard to the gravity of the offence).

[3] See, for example, *Kent and Byrd* 20.10.75, 4097/C/75 (recommendations quashed, as 'there is no material before this Court that the judge considered himself . . . to be exercising any discretion in the matter'); see also *Idriss* 25.8.77, 1367/C/77 (recommendation on man of good character, convicted of wounding after provocation, quashed as there was no evidence of potential detriment to this country from the appellant staying here).

mendation,[1] but the Court has upheld recommendations where the offender wished to remain. In *Sethi*[2] the appellant, who had lived in the United Kingdom intermittently over a period of years, was sentenced to four years' imprisonment and recommended for deportation, despite his previous good character, for attempting to smuggle a substantial quantity of cannabis. The sentence and recommendation were upheld with the comment that importing drugs would attract 'very severe punishment'. In another case two youths with no previous convictions were sentenced to three years' imprisonment and recommended for deportation for the premeditated robbery of another youth who had just received his pay packet. The Court upheld the recommendation.[3]

The persistent offender

The second identifiable category of case where a recommendation is likely to be considered appropriate is that of the offender who has accumulated a record of convictions in the United Kingdom, even for less serious offences, and whose behaviour in other respects leaves limited scope for mitigation. In *Manghan*[4] a man of 26, with thirteen previous convictions in the United Kingdom and several more in Eire, was sentenced to four years' imprisonment and recommended for deportation for robbing a man of £1.15. The sentence and recommendation were upheld. In *Letizia*[5] the Court upheld a recommendation made on the conviction for burglary of a man whose previous recommendation for deportation had been quashed on appeal. Although the appellant's wife and family were living in the United Kingdom, the Court commented that he had engaged in 'very serious offences' despite the 'clear warning' provided on the earlier occasion.

The offender with no ties

A recommendation is likely to be upheld in the case of an offender, particularly a relatively young offender, who has no family ties or

[1] See, for example, *Winter* 18.7.72, 5616/R/71, [1973] Crim. L. R. 63; *Lakhousky* 6.4.71, 6380/A/70.
[2] 5.11.71, 2666/A/71; see also *Lee* 19.12.75, 5042/A/75 (robbery of elderly petrol-pump attendant by youth, 22, acting in company with two others, two minor convictions; recommendation upheld, twelve months' imprisonment criticized as 'inadequate').
[3] *Ashraf and Mahfooz* 11.5.71, 5883/A/70.
[4] 27.7.72, 2333/B/72.
[5] 8.6.76, 1010/A/76; see also *Alman* 8.11.71, 2719/A/71 (man, 37, convictions in United Kingdom over period of ten years, previously recommended for deportation six times; recommendation upheld).

other connections in the United Kingdom. The Court upheld a recommendation against a youth of 20, whose family were still living in his country of origin, for sexual offences against the son of the uncle with whom he was living, commenting that as he could no longer live with his uncle, he would have no home in the United Kingdom 'where he is likely to be looked after'.[1]

Immigration offences

Although a recommendation for deportation should not be made automatically where there is a conviction for an offence under the Immigration Act 1971 itself,[2] the Court has indicated that a recommendation may be appropriate where there is evidence of a deliberate attempt to evade restrictions on immigration. In *Uddin*[3] the appellant admitted entering the United Kingdom with a forged passport; since his arrival he had proved 'an excellent, conscientious worker' and 'his record in this country has been admirable in every way'. The Court stated however that his record could not condone his illegal entry, and upheld the recommendation with the comment that 'those who come here by fraudulent means must expect to be deported'.

The relevance of the circumstances prevailing in the offender's country of origin

The Court has indicated that difficulties which will face the offender on his return to his country of origin are not relevant to the decision whether or not to recommend deportation, although they may be considered by the Home Secretary in deciding whether to make an order on the basis of the recommendation.[4] In *Baruwa*[5] a young woman was recommended for deportation on conviction for importing a substantial quantity of cannabis. The Court was told that in her country of origin she would have limited opportunity to follow the occupation for which she was trained, her family would reject her because of her illegitimate child and she would be unable to maintain herself and the child, although she was able to do so in the United Kingdom. The Court held that while these grounds might be 'solid

[1] *Rayasat* 24.6.71, 53/C/71.
[2] See, for example, *Akan* 22.6.72, 306/C/72 (decided under Aliens Order 1953 art. 20).
[3] 27.7.72, 1666/A/71.
[4] See *Caird and others* (1970) 54 Cr. App. R. 499 at 510; *Thesis* 4.10.71, 3519/B/71; see also *Antypas* (1972) 57 Cr. App. R. 207. A different view was taken in *Walters* 10.8.77, 507/A/77, [1978] Crim. L. R. 175, where the Court indicated that circumstances of a purely personal nature might be considered 'at least to some extent'.
[5] 6.12.74, 3869/B/74.

material' to put before the Home Secretary, they did not justify the Court in quashing the recommendations.

COMBINING A RECOMMENDATION WITH OTHER SENTENCES

The recommendation for deportation is an ancillary measure which is made in addition to the sentence imposed for the offence. Most commonly, the principal sentence will be a term of immediate imprisonment, but the Court has held that a recommendation may be made in conjunction with a conditional discharge,[1] although the circumstances in which such a combination will be appropriate are presumably rare. A recommendation should not normally be combined with a sentence of borstal training, at least where that sentence is imposed as a training measure, but there may be exceptions where borstal training is imposed as a tariff sentence as a result of Criminal Justice Act 1961 s. 3. In *Castelli*[2] a youth of 18 with two previous convictions was sentenced to borstal training and recommended for deportation for living on the earnings of prostitution. The Court stated that the combination was 'not usual, because the object of borstal training is to train young offenders to lead thereafter useful and honest lives', but 'this approach . . . is always subject to exceptional cases'. The sentence and recommendation were upheld.

[1] *Akan* 22.6.72, 306/C/72 (considering the combined effects of Aliens Order 1953 art. 20 and Criminal Justice Act 1948 s. 12(1); a similar result would presumably follow from current legislation (Immigration Act 1971 s. 6 and Powers of Criminal Courts Act 1973 s. 13(1)).
[2] 16.12.75, 4180/A3/75, [1976] Crim. L. R. 387.

Part IV

THE PROCEDURE OF SENTENCING

12

The Procedure of Sentencing

The first section of this chapter describes procedural aspects of sentencing in the Crown Court, dealing first with sentencing following conviction on indictment and then with sentencing following committal for sentence. The second section is concerned with appeals to the Court of Appeal (Criminal Division).

Section 1 : Sentencing in the Crown Court

CONVICTION ON INDICTMENT

Pre-arraignment conferences

The Court has established firm limitations on the practice of consulting the sentencer about his sentencing intentions before a plea is entered to the indictment. In *Turner*[1] the Court indicated that while 'there must be complete freedom of access between counsel and judge', any discussion which takes place must be in the presence of counsel for the defence and for the prosecution, and the defence solicitor if he wishes to be present. Such discussions should be regarded as extraordinary: 'so far as possible justice must be administered in open court'. The Court emphasized that private discussions between the judge and counsel should not be regarded as a normal practice, either by judge or by counsel:[2] 'in a very limited class of cases the exercise of that privilege is in the interests of the administration of justice . . . it should only be sparingly used . . . it should only be used if an unusual incident has happened or there is a difficulty which is outside counsel's experience. It should not be used for the purpose of helping counsel to make decisions which are their own professional responsibility'.[3]

Where such a discussion takes place, the judge 'should . . . never indicate the sentence which he is minded to impose', with the

[1] (1970) 54 Cr. App. R. 352.
[2] See *Plimmer* (1975) 61 Cr. App. R. 265.
[3] *Mainwood* 13.6.75, 4674/A/74.

exception of the case where the judge is able to say that 'whether the accused pleads guilty or not guilty the sentence will or will not take a particular form'. This exception does not allow the sentencer to indicate in detail the nature of the sentence he has in mind. He should not disclose the length of the sentence of imprisonment he intends to pass, or the amount of a fine.[1]

The sentencer must not indicate, expressly or by implication, that his intention to choose a particular form of sentence depends on the accused person's willingness to plead guilty: 'a statement that on a plea of guilty he would impose one sentence but that on a conviction following a plea of not guilty he would impose a severer sentence . . . should never be made'. Similarly, the sentencer must not indicate that a particular form of sentence will be passed in the event of a plea of guilty, with no reference to the likely outcome in the event of a conviction by the jury.[2]

Where a judge of the Crown Court is sitting with lay magistrates, the decision on matters of sentence is a decision of the court as a whole, and the lay magistrates may outvote the judge.[3] If in such a case any indication of the intended sentence is to be given, it should be given with the concurrence of the lay magistrates, who should (it is submitted) be parties to any discussion which takes place.[4]

If a discussion on the possible sentence has taken place between counsel and the judge, counsel must inform the accused of the fact.[5]

The limitations on the extent to which the sentencer may disclose his intentions to counsel does not prevent counsel, on his own responsibility, from advising the accused 'that a plea of guilty, showing an element of remorse, is a mitigating factor which may well enable the court to give a lesser sentence than would otherwise be the case'; but the accused must have 'complete freedom of choice whether to plead guilty or not guilty'.[6]

Establishing a factual basis for the sentence

The formal determination of guilt, whether by plea or by verdict, does not necessarily establish a sufficiently precise factual basis for the sentencer to assess the culpability of the offender. The responsibility of the sentencer to make his own assessment of the facts for this purpose is subject to an evolving body of principle designed to ensure that the version of the facts adopted for the purpose of sentence is

[1] See *Quartey* 23.5.75, 4936/A/74, [1975] Crim. L. R. 592.
[2] *Turner* (1970) 54 Cr. App. R. 352.
[3] See Courts Act 1971 s. 5(8).
[4] See *Deary* 8.6.76, 554/B/76, [1977] Crim. L. R. 47.
[5] *Turner* (1970) 54 Cr. App. R. 352.
[6] *Ibid.*

supported by evidence and reached according to appropriate procedural standards.

The first principle is that the version of the facts on which the sentence is premised must be consistent with the formal determination of guilt. If the offender has been acquitted of a graver charge and convicted of a lesser offence, the sentencer must accept that determination as the starting point for his consideration of the appropriate sentence, even though his own view is that the offender was guilty of the graver offence and has been fortunate in his jury. In *Thomas*[1] the appellant was convicted of maliciously inflicting grievous bodily harm on an indictment which charged him with attempted murder and causing grievous bodily harm with intent. The evidence was that he had attacked a man with a spade and boiling water. The Court observed that 'the judge seems to have taken the view that the jury had reached a verdict which was merciful' and imposed a sentence which would have been appropriate on a conviction for causing grievous bodily harm with intent. This was incorrect: 'the judge, despite his own views as to what the jury should have done, was . . . in law bound to sentence this man on the basis that he was not proved to have intended to do any of the harm which was in fact done'. Many similar cases can be found.[2]

The principle requires the sentencer to reflect not only differences in the formal definition of the two offences, but also any incidental findings of fact which the jury must have made in arriving at its verdict on the evidence in the particular case. In *Aliperti*[3] the appellant was indicted for possessing a firearm with intent to endanger life, on evidence that he had fired a shot from an air rifle in the direction of an off-duty police officer; the jury acquitted him of this charge but convicted him of common assault. The Court interpreted this verdict to mean that the jury had found that although the gun was pointed at the officer, no shot was fired. In passing a sentence of borstal training the sentencer observed that 'anyone who fires a weapon at another must pay the consequences'. The Court stated that the sentencer had 'approached . . . the question of

[1] 14.3.74, 5141/A/73.
[2] *Beard* 11.6.71, 1012/C/71 (ten years' imprisonment for manslaughter on grounds of provation 'did not sufficiently reflect the jury's verdict', although appellant may have been 'fortunate in his verdict'; reduced to seven); *Worstolf* 29.4.75, 3974/C/74 (appellant convicted of burglary and acquitted of assaulting police; sentencer's reference to violent resistance to arrest in passing sentence 'probably conveyed . . . that he was being punished for offence which he had been found not guilty'—sentence reduced from five years' imprisonment to three); *Prosser* 11.2.77, 5596/A/76 (alternative charges of theft of company property by making unauthorized sale, and theft of proceeds of sale on basis that sale was authorized; plea to latter charge accepted—wrong for sentencer to assume long standing dishonest intention).
[3] 12.3.73, 6126/A/72.

sentence on an entirely wrong basis' and varied the sentence to a probation order.

Analogous principles apply where the accused pleads guilty to the lesser offence and a verdict of not guilty is entered in respect of the graver charge, or the count is ordered to lie on the file. The sentencer must proceed on the basis of the facts which have been determined, expressively or by implication, by the plea and formal acquittal. In one case[1] the appellants were indicted for damaging property, 'being reckless as to whether the life of another would be thereby endangered'; they pleaded guilty to a lesser offence, not including the element of recklessness towards endangering life. The Court stated that 'those pleas . . . were accepted and therefore in passing sentence the court had to put out of its mind any question of recklessness in relation to loss of life or the possibility of loss of life'. As the sentencer had used words in passing sentence which suggested that he had not done so, the sentences were reduced. In another example[2] the appellant pleaded guilty to indecently assaulting his daughter on an indictment charging him with incest. The Court stated that 'we must be careful . . . not to sentence or appear to sentence for incest when in fact the offence with which we are dealing is the lesser one of indecent assault'. The sentence was reduced from eighteen months' imprisonment to nine. The Court has on several occasions referred to 'the mischief that can result when a plea is accepted in the face of strong . . . evidence that . . . a more serious offence has been committed than that which is involved in the plea which is accepted',[3] but has indicated that where this is done the sentencer must proceed on the 'narrow basis of the pleas' however artificial that approach may seem.[4]

The principle that the sentencer must adopt a view of the facts consistent with the verdict or plea is extended to cases where there are conflicting accounts of the number of occasions on which an offence was repeated, when the defence dispute the prosecution claim that the offender was engaged in a systematic course of conduct. While it is permissible to confine an indictment to representative counts, the sentencer must not proceed on the basis that there was a series of offences other than those charged in the indictment unless the offender admits that this was so. Where the accused denies any incidents other than those in respect of which he has been convicted or has pleaded guilty, the sentencer must determine the sentence strictly by reference to the offences proved or admitted, leaving the

[1] *Willder and Willder* 18.10.73, 2398/C/73.
[2] *Rogina* (1975) 64 Cr. App. R. 79.
[3] *Smith* 6.5.76, 1459/B/76.
[4] *Burns* 4.5.76, 1021/A/76.

prosecution to proceed separately in respect of the other allegations.[1] In *Corby and Corby*[2] the appellants were convicted respectively of stealing and handling property belonging to the employers of one of them. A greater quantity of stock was apparently missing than was mentioned in the counts to which the pleas were entered, and the sentencer proceeded on the basis that the employers 'had been cheated of their goods by a . . . systematic process of fraud'. The Court accepted that it was a 'well established and . . . very important . . . principle' that the appellants could only be sentenced 'on the basis that they had either pleaded guilty to or been found guilty of a particular charge and that no other offences by them could properly be considered, since such offences were not the subject of any charge and had not been admitted'. The sentences were reduced.

These principles do not mean that the sentencer is necessarily bound to accept the whole of the defendant's version of the offence. He may exercise his own judgment on the evidence, so long as he does not assume the existence of a fact that has been negated, expressly or by implication, by the formal finding of guilt. In *Whittle*[3] the appellant was convicted of manslaughter on an indictment for murder, on evidence that he had pushed a glass into the throat of a man who had provoked him. The appellant claimed that he had struck out without realizing that he had a glass in his hand, but the judge sentenced him on the basis that he was aware of the glass although he did not intend to inflict serious injury. The Court observed that the judge in sentencing was not bound to assume that the jury had convicted 'on the basis of the most favourable view of the facts which would justify the conviction. A judge at the stage of sentencing can make his own findings of the facts consistent with the verdict of the jury'. The sentence was upheld. The sentencer's finding of fact must be supported by the general body of the evidence. Where a judge passing sentence for wounding with intent observed that the appellant had struck his wife with a carving knife 'not once but several times', when the evidence was more consistent with a single blow with the carving knife and several fist blows, the Court reduced the sentence from three years' imprisonment to two.[4] If a fact relevant to sentence but not affecting conviction is in dispute between different witnesses, the sentencer is entitled to reach his own

---

[1] See *Huchison* (1972) 56 Cr. App. R. 307 ('this man was, in effect, deprived of trial by a jury in regard to these additional offences'). It is submitted that the statement to the contrary in *Goss* 16.7.70, 1236/A/70 is incorrect.

[2] 9.12.74, 3787/A/74.

[3] 30.4.74, 5274/B/73, [1974] Crim. L. R. 487.

[4] *McElroy* 22.4.75, 4318/A1/74; see also *Clark* 4.12.75, 4248/B/75 (receiving two specific items, no evidence of other incidents or of 'professionalism', sentence passed on basis that appellant was professional handler; sentence reduced).

conclusion on the credibility of the witnesses concerned and base his sentence on that conclusion. [1] The Court has not considered the question how far a sentencer making such a determination is bound by general principles relating to the burden and quantum of proof, but where the issue is in serious doubt the benefit should be given to the offender. [2]

The same principle applies where there is a plea of guilty. The judge must not assume the existence of facts inconsistent with the plea, but he is not bound to accept the whole of the defendant's version of the offence. In *Newell* [3] the appellant pleaded guilty to shortening the barrel of a shotgun, with the explanation that he had done so in order to make the gun easier to carry on pigeon-shooting expeditions. The sentencer indicated that he did not accept this 'utter rubbish', and sentenced the appellant to three years' imprisonment. The Court held that he was entitled to come to the conclusion that the gun was not shortened for an innocent purpose and upheld the sentence.

An important principle, whose precise scope is not yet clear, was recognized in *Lester*. [4] The appellant was convicted of a variety of offences under the Trades Descriptions Act 1968 concerned with the sale of cars with false mileometer readings. The appellant claimed that he had not personally altered the readings, but the sentencer imposed a sentence of imprisonment on the basis that the appellant knew that the readings had been falsified. The Court held that while that inference might have been consistent with the evidence, the sentencer should have mentioned the matter and given counsel the opportunity to mitigate directly on the question: 'The appropriate course . . . would have been to indicate to counsel . . . what was provisionally in his mind, to point out the basis of the suggested inference, and . . . to offer counsel the opportunity . . . to call his

[1] See *Quirk* 8.12.75, 4117/A/75 (conflicting evidence on circumstances leading up to wounding; 'the learned judge made up his mind on seeing and hearing the witnesses and it was upon that he based his sentence . . . on the view which the learned judge formed, as he was entitled to form it', sentence was not wrong in principle or excessive); see also *Leslie* 14.10.74, 2858/A/74 ('there are indications in the evidence, which it was open to the sentencing judge to accept, that this man was . . . a professional receiver . . . this Court does not feel that it should interfere with the assessment . . . made by the sentencing judge').

[2] See *Sandler* 22.11.73, 1804/R/73 (appellant claimed offence was incited by police informer; if claim established 'it would be a mitigating factor', evidence inconclusive but Court 'unable to rid itself of suspicion', in those circumstances 'his punishment must take into account the benefit of the doubt which this Court believes should in these circumstances be accorded to him'—sentence reduced from three years to two); *Brassell* 11.2.77, 3817/B/76 (sentencer to exercise discretion 'against the background of legal principles which state that persons facing charges . . . should have the benefit of any reasonable doubt that there may be). For a review of Australian decisions on this question, see Fox and O'Brien, *Fact Finding for Sentencers* (1975) 10 Melbourne University Law Review 163 at 181.

[3] 20.6.72, 207/B/72.

[4] (1975) 63 Cr. App. R. 144.

client to give evidence about this matter'. It is submitted that this principle is not limited to offences of strict liability, but applies to any case where the judge is inclined to form a view on an issue relevant to sentence which has not already been canvassed, either in the course of the trial (if the plea was not guilty) or in counsel's address in mitigation.

Evidence after conviction

Where there is a trial on a plea of not guilty, the sentencer is entitled to base his view of the facts on the evidence given in the course of the trial. On a plea of guilty it is the responsibility of counsel for the prosecution to give a full account of the circumstances of the offence, on the basis of the evidence that would have been called. In a case where the circumstances of the offence had been described in a few sentences, the Court deprecated 'the very cursory way in which the facts of the matter were put by prosecuting counsel before the judge . . . Justice requires that a court should be fully informed as to the matters constituting the offence'.[1]

Whether the finding of guilt is by plea or the verdict of the jury, either the prosecution or the defence may call evidence after conviction on factual issues relevant to sentence. If the prosecution wish to call evidence on matters not in issue in the trial but relevant to sentence, notice must be served on the defence in sufficient time to allow the offender to meet the evidence, and the evidence itself must be particularized and given by a witness who can speak from first-hand knowledge without reliance on hearsay or records.[2] General allegations incapable of substantiation or refutation should not be made.[3]

It follows from the principles discussed earlier that the prosecution may not call evidence after conviction for the purposes of sentence, if that evidence shows that the offender is guilty of other offences than those which have been established, whether they are graver, more numerous or different in character. In this position the prosecution must charge the additional matters or ignore them.

The defence may call evidence after conviction to establish relevant facts, whether relating to the immediate circumstances of the offence

---

[1] *Mychajluk* 23.11.72, 3494/B/73.

[2] *Robinson* (1969) 53 Cr. App. R. 314; see also *Noble* 22.7.71, 6423/B/70.

[3] See *Dovey* 12.10.73, 5883/B/72 (statement by antecedents officer that appellant 'the main pusher (of drugs) in and around the area', and after appellant's arrest 'the drug situation . . . did ease quite considerably'; view that appellant a pusher supported by other evidence, but sentence reduced in view of grievance arising from 'prejudicial picture'); *Wilkins* (1977) 66 Cr. App. R. 49 (document setting out appellant's history over several years 'highly prejudicial evidence'; rules in *Robinson* not observed—sentence reduced from three years to two).

or unrelated mitigating factors. In a case where the appellant, who admitted an assault occasioning actual bodily harm, wished to establish that he was not responsible for starting the fight but had overreacted in self-defence, the Court stated that 'when a person does plead guilty on the basis of facts which substantially differ from the facts alleged by the prosecution, it is important, in order that the court should be able to do justice, that evidence should be called to support the factual account upon which the accused relies. In that way, the court can then decide the facts and sentence the accused upon the proper basis'.[1] The offender may give evidence himself at this stage.[2]

If neither party calls evidence to clarify a factual issue relevant to sentence, the sentencer may call the necessary evidence himself.[3] The sentencer may not rely on evidence given in other proceedings against the offender's accomplices,[4] nor may he base his sentence on one offender on statements made by a co-defendant, either in the course of a trial to which the offender is not a party (having pleaded guilty)[5] or in mitigation of his own sentence,[6] unless the co-defendant is called as a witness, before or after conviction, against the offender.

In some cases the sentencer may require information about matters only indirectly related to the immediate offence, such as the prevalence of offences of a particular kind in the area concerned. While information of this kind does not appear to be objectionable, it is submitted that it should be admitted only subject to the rules established in *Robinson*.[7] To allow the prosecution to tender, or the sentencer to elicit, vague statements of a general nature based on personal impressions, would be inconsistent with the requirements which relate to evidence on other issues relevant to sentence.

Antecedents statement

It is the usual practice for a police officer to prepare a statement of the offender's previous convictions (if any), family circumstances, edu-

---

[1] *Evans* 19.12.74, 4771/B/74.

[2] See *Cross* 1.7.75, 1192/A/75, [1975] Crim. L. R. 591.

[3] See *Clark* 18.3.75, 5071/B/74 (indecent assault and malicious wounding, conflict in accounts of offence by victim and accused respectively, plea of guilty, victim called by judge, appellant given opportunity to give his account; judge 'took . . . clearly the right course'); see also *Hinds* 1.12.75, 2758/B/75 (plea of guilty, prosecution witness called by judge to be cross-examined on behalf of offender to establish version of facts favourable to him; judge entitled to draw appropriate conclusions from evidence).

[4] See *Cripps* 19.12.75, 4579/B/75 (assault occasioning actual bodily harm to child by man, mother of child previously tried before same judge; judge relied on evidence given in trial of woman as basis of sentence on man—sentence 'wrong in principle').

[5] See *Bremner and Rawlings* 4.3.74, 3433/B/73.

[6] See *Lee* 28.1.72, 4946/C/71, [1972] Crim. L. R. 319.

[7] (1969) 53 Cr. App. R. 314.

cation and employment record.[1] Counsel for the prosecution, who calls the officer, must decide how much of the statement the officer will give in evidence.[2] The judge may put such questions as he sees fit to the officer, who may also be cross-examined by the defence.[3] No reference should be made in the statement or in the evidence given by the officer to occasions when the offender has been acquitted.[4] If any conviction is disputed, it should be formally proved,[5] and any other issue on which the assertions in the statement are not accepted by the defence should be resolved by calling direct admissible evidence.[6] The statement should not contain general observations about the behaviour of the offender.[7]

When a person has reached the age of 21, evidence of findings of guilt before the age of 14 cease to be admissible in any criminal proceedings.[8] No reference to such findings of guilt should be included in the antecedents statement or made in the course of giving evidence. Under the Rehabilitation of Offenders Act 1974 certain convictions become spent after the lapse of varying periods of time. The Act does not apply to criminal proceedings. Spent convictions should be included in the antecedents statement prepared for the court, but so far as is practicable should be marked as such. No reference to a spent conviction should be made in open court without the authority of the judge, which should not be given 'unless the interests of justice so require', and the sentencer when passing sentence should make no reference to a spent conviction unless it is

[1] See *Practice Direction* (1966) 50 Cr. App. R. 271. The statement should include particulars of the prisoner's age, education and employment, the date of arrest, whether the prisoner has been on bail, and a summary of any previous convictions or findings of guilt. It should also set out the date of last discharge from prison or other custody, and may contain a concise statement as to the prisoner's domestic circumstances.

[2] See *Van Pelz* [1943] K. B. 157.

[3] A copy of the statement must be given to counsel for the defendant, who should inform the prosecution of any matter which is disputed; see *Sargeant* (1974) 60 Cr. App. R. 74.

[4] See *Haigherty* 12.4.65, 125/65.

[5] See Criminal Justice Act 1948 s. 39.

[6] See *Sargeant* (1974) 60 Cr. App. R. 74 (dispute on circumstances in which accused left his last employment, evidence of police officer based on conversation with employer inadmissible; 'on finding that this allegation was disputed, admissible evidence should have been called'); see also *Young* (1976) 63 Cr. App. R. 33 at 39.

[7] See *Van Pelz* (1943) K. B. 157, affirmed in *Sargeant* (1974) 60 Cr. App. R. 74; *Oliver and Turnage* 8.7.74, 4997/B/73. The Court considered in *Curley* 27.6.74, 906/C/74 that to ask the officer which one of two defendants was the more blameworthy did not conflict with these decisions, at least where the sentencer had already formed a provisional view on the matter and could be considered to be giving an opportunity to the officer to correct him and to the defence to challenge the assessment. In so far as statements made in *Crabtree* (1952) 36 Cr. App. R. 161 are inconsistent with the general rule, they should be disregarded; see *Wilkins* (1977) 66 Cr. App. R. 109.

[8] Children and Young Persons' Act 1963 s. 16(2).

necessary to do so for the purpose of explaining the sentence to be passed.[1]

Taking offences into consideration

The practice of taking offences into consideration is 'a convention under which, if a court is informed that there are outstanding charges against a prisoner who is before it for a particular offence, the court can, if the prisoner admits the offences and asks that they should be taken into account . . . give a longer sentence than it would if it were dealing with him only on the charge mentioned in the indictment'.[2] Taking an offence into consideration does not create a conviction in respect of that offence, and the offender may not enter a plea of *autrefois convict* if he is subsequently charged with the offence,[3] although it is contrary to normal practice to institute subsequent proceedings in relation to offences taken into consideration unless the conviction for the principal offence is quashed on appeal.[4] If a sentencer finds himself dealing with an offender for an offence which was taken into consideration on an earlier occasion, he should 'see to it without any doubt whatsoever that no additional punishment is imposed on the prisoner on account of those offences'.[5]

Taking an offence into consideration does not enlarge the statutory powers of the sentencer, except in relation to compensation orders[6] or criminal bankruptcy orders.[7] The sentencer must not impose a term of imprisonment in excess of statutory maximum for the offences charged in the indictment.[8] The sentencer is not obliged to take any offence into consideration and should in appropriate cases consider whether the public interest requires a separate investigation and prosecution.[9] The sentencer should not take into consideration an offence which he would have no jurisdiction to try,[10] and (it is submitted) a judge of the Crown Court should not take into consideration an offence which would normally be dealt with by a more senior judge under the Practice Direction relating to the distribution of Crown Court business.[11] A sentencer should not take

---

1 See *Practice Direction* (1975) 61 Cr. App. R. 260.
2 *Batchelor* (1952) 36 Cr. App. R. 67.
3 *North* 9.7.71, 2114/B/71.
4 See *Neal* [1949] 2 K. B. 590 at 600.
5 *North* 9.7.71, 2114/B/71.
6 Powers of Criminal Courts Act 1973 s. 35(1) (p. 326 above).
7 *Ibid.*, s. 39(2) (p. 341 above).
8 *Hobson* (1942) 29 Cr. App. R. 30.
9 *McClean* [1911] 1 K. B. 333.
10 See *Simons* (1953) 37 Cr. App. R. 120. Civil offences committed by members of the armed forces may be considered; see *Anderson* (1958) 42 Cr. App. R. 91.
11 (1971) 56 Cr. App. R. 52.

into consideration an offence in respect of which a probation order or conditional discharge has been made,[1] or which gives rise to a mandatory disqualification from driving.[2]

The procedure for ascertaining the offences which the offender wishes to have taken into consideration has been considered on a number of occasions and the Court has emphasized the need for 'meticulous care' at all stages of the process.[3] The police should prepare a list of offences in sufficient time for the accused to study it before he appears for sentence. If the accused is prepared to admit the offences described, he should sign a copy of the list to acknowledge service. The responsibility for ensuring that the accused has considered the list and understands its contents rests with the sentencer; if there is any doubt the court should adjourn. Before proceeding to sentence, 'the court must be clear not only that he understands the document that he has received and has had time to study it, but that he accepts that the listed offences are offences which he has committed and that he desires them to be taken into consideration'.[4] Where there is any doubt about the number or the identity of the offences which the offender wishes to admit and have taken into consideration, the doubt must be resolved in open court by putting the offences to the offender one by one.[5] The court should not put any pressure on an offender to admit an offence and have it taken into consideration.[6] The offender must admit the offences personally and not through counsel.[7]

Social inquiry reports

Although it is almost invariable practice for a sentencer in the Crown Court to receive a social inquiry report on an offender before deciding on sentence[8] he is not under a statutory obligation to do so[9] unless he

[1] See *Webb* [1953] 2 Q. B. 391; *Fry* (1955) 38 Cr. App. R. 157.
[2] See *Simons* (1953) 37 Cr. App. R. 120.
[3] *Walsh* 8.3.73, 4083/B/72; see also *D. P. P. v. Anderson* [1978] 2 All E. R. 512 (H.L.).
[4] *Walsh* 8.3.73, 40833/B/72.
[5] *Urbas* 24.6.63, 543/63, [1964] Crim. L. R. 37.
[6] See *Nelson* (1967) 51 Cr. App. R. 98.
[7] See *Mortimer* 10.3.70, 6922/A/69.
[8] The administrative arrangements for the preparation of social inquiry reports are described in Home Office Circular 59/1971. Reports are normally prepared before trial on accused persons under 31 at the date of committal, those over 31 who have not received a custodial sentence since the age of 17, any accused person who has recently been in contact with the probation service, or is subject to a medical or psychiatric report, and any woman defendant, subject in all cases to the consent of the defendant. Courts may ask for pre-trial inquiries in other categories, and may adjourn after conviction for a social inquiry report in any case.
[9] A power to make rules requiring a court to consider a social inquiry report before passing sentence in specified categories of cases is conferred on the Home Secretary by

wishes to make a community service order.[1] Statutory provisions requiring courts to 'obtain and consider information about the circumstances and . . . take into account any information before the court which is relevant to his character and his physical and mental condition' before imposing imprisonment on an offender under 21,[2] or on one over 21 who has not previously served a sentence of imprisonment,[3] have been held not to impose a mandatory obligation on the court to obtain a social inquiry report before imposing imprisonment in the cases to which the section refers.[4] The Court has however emphasized that sentencers should not normally proceed in the absence of a social inquiry report, even where there is no alternative to a substantial sentence of imprisonment. In *Bell*[5] a man with eleven previous court appearances was sentenced to nine years' imprisonment for robbery at a bank while in possession of a imitation firearm. The Court considered that although the offence was 'very serious', it was 'amateurish' and 'when measured against the gravity of other bank robberies' the sentence was out of scale; in addition, the sentencer 'did not have the benefit of a social inquiry report', which was 'unfortunate' as it might have assisted in the consideration of possible mitigating factors. The sentence was reduced to six years.

The precise form and content of a social inquiry report is not regulated by statute[6] but it is generally accepted that 'probation officers should be free . . . to express opinions on the likely response of accused persons to probation; and that, subject to the wishes of the court, and if their knowledge and experience enable them to do so, probation officers should be free to give their assessment of the likely response of the offender to any other form of treatment'.[7] It is not the responsibility of the probation officer to advise the sentencer whether or not the public interest requires or permits a particular course to be taken, but the recommendation is subject to the sentencer's decision that the public interest allows him to take the course suggested.[8] The

---

Powers of Criminal Courts Act 1973 s. 45(1), but the section has not been brought into force.

[1] Powers of Criminal Courts Act 1973 s. 14(2)(b)(i).

[2] *Ibid.*, s. 19(2).   [3] *Ibid.*, s. 20(1)

[4] *Ampleford* (1975) 61 Cr. App. R. 325. The Court had added that the section means that 'generally speaking it is desirable to have a social inquiry report' (*Excelby* 23.1.75, 4697/C/75).

[5] 13.1.75, 3801/B/74; see also *Wopling* 10.4.73, 5580/C/72 (man, 29, nine previous convictions for relatively minor offences, burglary of house with theft of property worth £2,000; 'remarkable and regrettable' that no social inquiry report obtained).

[6] Powers of Criminal Courts Act 1973 s. 45(1) refers to a social inquiry report as 'a report about him and his circumstances'. A more detailed indication of the appropriate contents is given in Home Office Circular 59/1971 at para. 24.

[7] Home Office Circular 59/1971 at para. 25.

[8] See *Mulcahy* 29.3.77, 4881/C/76 ('the probation officer's duty is to recommend what he or she thinks is most appropriate for the individual, without having regard necessarily to the public consequences').

sentencer is not bound by the recommendation in any way.[1]

Where a social inquiry report is made to the court, a copy must be given by the court to the offender or his counsel,[2] and counsel should not be called on to mitigate before the report has been received.[3] The probation officer presenting the report may be cross-examined on behalf of the defendant, but the report should not normally be read aloud in an open court.[4]

Prison reports

Reports are normally prepared by the governor of the appropriate institution on offenders eligible for borstal training who have previously served, or are currently serving, a sentence of imprisonment, borstal training or detention in a detention centre. In other cases the court may adjourn after conviction in order to obtain a prison report; if it does so, it should state 'explicity . . . what subjects should receive special attention' and from which officers the court requires a report.[5]

Where a prison report is made to the court, a copy must be given to the accused or his legal representatives.[6]

Medical reports

Medical reports dealing with the accused person's mental or physical health may result from a decision by the magistrates' court committing the offender for trial to order such a report,[7] or from the initiative of the medical officer of the prison to which the accused has been committed pending trial. A probation officer making inquiries for a social inquiry report may suggest that a medical report be obtained, or the accused's representatives may obtain and present to the court such medical evidence as they see fit. The court responsible for imposing sentence may on its own initiative adjourn after conviction to obtain a medical report.

If a report is tendered in evidence, otherwise than by or on behalf of

---

[1] See, for example, *Rawden* 19.12.74, 2093/B/74 (Crown Court 'fully entitled' to impose suspended sentences despite strong recommendations for probation with conditions for residence in probation hostel).

[2] Powers of Criminal Courts Act 1973 s. 46(1). Where the defendant is under 17 and not represented, the copy should be given to his parent or guardian (*ibid.*, s. 46(2)). There is no statutory obligation to give a copy to the prosecution.

[3] *Kirkham* 9.2.68, 671/68, [1968] Crim. L. R. 210.

[4] *Smith* 23.10.67, 3349/67, [1968] Crim. L. R. 33.

[5] See Home Office Circular 59/1971, para. 19.

[6] Criminal Justice Act 1961 s. 37 (which applies only where there is a statutory obligation on the court to consider the report).

See Magistrates' Courts Act 1952 s. 26.

the accused, with a view to the making of a hospital order,[1] a copy must be given to the accused's representatives or (if he is not represented) the substance of the report must be disclosed to the accused, who may require the practitioner who has made the report to give oral evidence, and may call evidence in rebuttal.[2]

Legal representation

Where a person appears before the Crown Court, whether for trial or on a committal for sentence, the court may make a legal aid order in his favour, if such an order has not already been made by the magistrates' court by which he was committed.[3] A legal aid order made by the Crown Court may, in cases of urgency, be for representation by counsel only.[4] The court must make a legal aid order where it appears to the court to be desirable to do so in the interests of justice, unless the accused person's means are such that he does not require assistance in meeting the costs of representation.[5]

Powers of Criminal Courts Act 1973 s. 21 prohibits the imposition of certain sentences on certain categories of offenders unless they are legally represented. The section provides that the court must not impose a sentence of imprisonment (including a suspended sentence), borstal training or detention in a detention centre on an offender who has not been previously sentenced to that punishment[6] by a court in the United Kingdom, unless the offender is legally represented before the court after conviction and before sentence. The section is not restricted to offenders of any particular age group, but does not apply where the offender's application for legal aid has been refused on the grounds that his means were such that he did not appear to require assistance, or where he has refused or failed to apply for legal aid, having been informed of his right and given the opportunity to do so. The section is clearly mandatory and a sentence passed in contravention of the section is (it is submitted) unlawful.[7]

Apart from the statutory provisions, the Court has frequently

---

[1] Mental Health Act 1959 s. 60; p. 294 above.
[2] Mental Health Act 1959 s. 62(3).
[3] See, generally, Legal Aid Act 1974, part 2.
[4] Legal Aid Act 1974 s. 30(3).
[5] Legal Aid Act 1974 s. 29(1).
[6] A previous suspended sentence must be disregarded for this purpose: see s. 21(3)(a).
[7] See *McGinlay and Ballantyne* (1975) 62 Cr. App. R. 156, which leaves the precise effect of the section uncertain. It is submitted that where a sentencer has imposed a sentence in contravention of the section, the position is that no effective sentence has been passed, and the Court of Appeal under Criminal Appeal Act 1968 s. 11 (3) may impose such sentence as it considers appropriate, provided that the sentence is not more severe than the sentence intended to be imposed by the sentencer (see below, p. 399).

emphasized the importance of ensuring that defendants are legally represented for the purpose of sentence.[1] Legal aid should be granted on the same principles when the offender appears to be dealt with in respect of suspended sentences, or to be sentenced for offences for which probation orders or conditional discharges were originally granted.[2]

The principal function of counsel appearing for the offender in connection with sentence is to address the court in mitigation of sentence, drawing the attention of the court to any factors which may weigh in his favour. The sentencer should not decline to listen to counsel's address in mitigation on the ground that he has already decided what sentence to pass, whether the sentence he intends to impose is lenient[3] or severe,[4] but should draw counsel's attention to any question on which he may require specific argument, particularly where he is considering the exercise of a sentencing power which counsel may not have anticipated.

Whether or not he is represented, the offender may be allowed to address the court in person. An unrepresented defendant may submit his mitigation in writing if he wishes.[5]

Adjournments after conviction and before sentence

The Crown Court has power at common law to adjourn after conviction before passing sentence, or to delay the imposition of part of a sentence.[6] This power, which is not limited to any specific period of time, should be exercised only for the purposes of obtaining social inquiry reports or other reports which are not available at the time of conviction, to await the outcome of the trial of an accomplice, or 'in circumstances of a very special nature'.[7] It should not be used to see whether the offender's expressed intention to pay compensation is genuine.[8] Where the court adjourns under its common law powers for a substantial period of time, it should make clear that it is exercising those powers rather than its statutory powers to defer sentence (see below).[9]

---

[1] See, for example, *Williams* 19.8.70, 3661/C/70 ('this Court has frequently stressed how important it is that legal aid should be granted . . .').

[2] See, for example, *Granger* 11.10.71, 802/A/71, [1971] Crim. L. R. 720 ('where the man was at risk in respect of a two years' suspended sentence, we think it is at best desirable that . . . the man concerned should have the benefit of representation').

[3] See *Williams* 15.4.69, 6550/69.

[4] See *Marchesi and Wakeford* 22.5.75, 22/B/75.

[5] See *Gout* 29.7.66, 679/66.

[6] *Annesley* (1975) 62 Cr. App. R. 113.

[7] See *Spittle* 22.3.76, 4486/A/75, [1976] Crim. L. R. 698.

[8] *Spittle, ibid.*

[9] See *Fairhead* (1975) 61 Cr. App. R. 102.

Deferment of sentence

A statutory power to defer sentence is contained in Powers of Criminal Courts Act 1973 s. 1. The section empowers the court to defer passing sentence on an offender 'for the purpose of enabling the court to have regard, in determining his sentence, to his conduct after conviction (including, where appropriate, the making by him of reparation for his offence)[1] or to any change in his circumstances'. The power to defer sentence may be exercised only with the consent of the defendant and if the court is 'satisfied, having regard to the nature of the offence and the character and circumstances of the offender, that it would be in the interests of justice to exercise the power'.[2] The period of deferment may not exceed six months (from the date of deferment) and sentence may not be deferred more than once.[3]

The use of the power to defer sentence has given rise to many difficulties and the Court has emphasized the need for sentencers to be 'meticulously careful' when exercising it.[4] A court which decides to delay the imposition of sentence should indicate clearly whether it is proceeding under its common law power to postpone sentence (see above, p. 379) or the statutory power to defer,[5] and if the latter, should ensure that the consent of the offender to deferment is obtained, normally from the offender in person rather than through counsel.[6] The Court has not resolved the problem which confronts a court which purports to defer sentence without obtaining the consent of the offender, except to indicate that it may not sentence him at the expiration of the period of deferment.[7] The statute does not make clear whether the power to defer sentence may be exercised in relation to individual counts of an indictment or separate indictments with which the court is dealing on the same occasions, and the Court has not ruled on this question. It is submitted that whether or not it is lawful to sentence on one count and defer sentence on another, it is generally inadvisable to do so; the same reasoning would apply where there are separate indictments.

A sentencer who defers sentence may not exercise any power arising from the conviction except that of making a restitution order.[8] He may not bind the offender to come up for judgment,[9]

---

[1] See the discussion of the relevance of the payment of compensation to mitigation at p. 218 above.
[2] Powers of Criminal Courts Act 1973 s. 1(3).
[3] *Ibid.*, s. 1(2).
[4] *McQuaide* (1974) 60 Cr. App. R. 239.
[5] *Fairhead* (1975) 61 Cr. App. R. 102.
[6] *Fairhead, ibid.*
[7] *McQuaide* (1974) 60 Cr. App. R. 239.
[8] Theft Act 1968 s. 28, as amended by Criminal Law Act 1977 sch. 12.
[9] *Dwyer* (1974) 60 Cr. App. R. 39.

disqualify him from driving,[1] or make any similar order.[2] A conviction in respect of which the sentencer has deferred sentence does not count as a conviction for the purposes of activation of an existing suspended sentence, whether by the court deferring sentence or by another court, until sentence is eventually imposed.[3] While the same principle may not apply where the offender is subject to an existing probation order or conditional discharge, it clearly does apply where the offender is already subject to a deferment in respect of another offence.[4]

The power to defer passing sentence is not analogous to a non-custodial measure. The Court has emphasized that the power should be exercised only for the statutory reasons[5] and 'is not to be regarded as another soft option . . . available to judges who find it difficult to bring themselves to pass a specific sentence'.[6] Where the information available to the court at the normal time of sentence is such that the sentencer can pass sentence and there is no reason to except a profound change in the relevant circumstances, the sentence should not be deferred. In *Burgess*[7] the appellant admitted five offences of burglary involving property worth over £2,000; in view of evidence that he had 'changed the pattern of his life', the sentencer deferred sentence for six months, subsequently imposing a sentence of thirty months' imprisonment when the appellant was convicted of a further offence. The Court stated that the sentence should not have been deferred; if the judge accepted the evidence of the offender's change in attitude he should have imposed a suspended sentence.

[1] *Fairhead* (1975) 61 Cr. App. R. 102.
[2] Orders relating to the payment of defence costs, which are not sentences (see *Hayden* (1974) 60 Cr. App. R. 304) may presumably be made. It is submitted that deferment of sentence does not preclude binding over the offender to keep the peace, as the power to do so does not depend on the conviction and it is not a 'sentence' for other purposes (p. 391 below).
[3] See *Salmon* (1973) 57 Cr. App. R. 953.
[4] *Salmon* (see n. 3, p. 381 above) rests on the rule that a conviction resulting in a probation order or conditional discharge is not a conviction for any purpose other than the proceedings in which it was made, or proceedings relating to the imposition of sentence for offences which have originally been dealt with by probation or conditional discharge (Powers of Criminal Courts Act 1973 s. 13(1). Such a conviction is therefore not a conviction for the purposes of Powers of Criminal Courts Act 1973 s. 23(1) (see *Tarry* (1970) 54 Cr. App. R. 322, p. 248 above). Accordingly, while there is a possibility of a probation order or conditional discharge being made, there is no effective conviction. The Court has however held that s. 13(1) allows a sentencer to deal with an offender for an offence for which a probation order has been made, on the basis of a subsequent conviction which has itself led to a probation order or conditional discharge (*Wilcox* 21.11.64, 2275/64), and the reasoning in *Salmon* will not apply to that case. The old common law rule that 'a conviction is not complete until perfected by judgement' may, however, lead to the same result; see *S. v. Recorder of Manchester* [1971] A. C. 481.
[5] See *Gilby* (1975) 61 Cr. App. R. 112; *Greenaway* 19.5.75, 1963/A/75.
[6] *Burgess* 18.7.74, 1679/A/74.
[7] 18.7.74, 1679/A/74.

The statutory purpose of the deferment of sentence on an offender is to 'enable the court to have regard . . . to his conduct after conviction (including, where appropriate, the making by him of reparation for his offence) or to any change in his circumstances'. If it is clear that whatever changes may occur in the offender's conduct or circumstances after conviction, a substantial custodial sentence is probable, the power should not be exercised.[1] Although the statute refers to the making of reparation by the offender, this reference is qualified by the words 'where appropriate', and it is rarely appropriate to allow mitigating effect to reparations made under compulsion.[2] It is submitted that it is inconsistent with principle to defer passing sentence on the basis that the offender's efforts to pay compensation will entitle him to a more favourable sentence; the proper course is to impose sentence and make a compensation order.[3]

An order deferring sentence may be varied within twenty-eight days of being made,[4] but otherwise there is no power to deal with the offender before the date to which sentence has been deferred,[5] unless he is convicted of an offence during the period of deferment.[6] Although the power to defer sentence may not be exercised more than once in respect of the same matter,[7] a court dealing with an offender at the expiration of a period of deferment may postpone sentence under its common law powers, but should not do so unless there are 'strong reasons'.[8] If the court cannot deal with the offender on the precise date specified in the original order, it may deal with him on a later date.[9]

If an offender subject to a deferment of sentence is convicted of any offence during the period of the deferment, (whether or not the offence was committed before the deferment), he may be sentenced before the expiration of the period of deferment.[10] An offender who is

---

[1] See *Crosby and Hayes* (1974) 60 Cr. App. R. 234; *Gilby* (1975) 61 Cr. App. R. 112. This principle does not inhibit a sentencer dealing with the offender during the period of deferment for offences committed earlier, from imposing a custodial sentence for those offences (*Harling* 9.5.77, 784/C/77).

[2] See *Crosby and Hayes* (1974) 60 Cr. App. R. 234, and the discussion at p. 218 above. The decision in *Mortimer* 15.3.77, 2204/A/77, [1977] Crim. L. R. 624 is in some respects inconsistent with this view.

[3] The course taken in *Morris* 22.3.73, 1066/B/73, [1973] Crim. L. R. 451, where the Court deferred sentence while upholding a compensation order, is (it is submitted) contrary to both law and principle.

[4] Courts Act 1971 s. 11(2); see *McQuaide* (1974) 60 Cr. App. R. 239.

[5] *Ingle* (1974) 59 Cr. App. R. 306.

[6] Powers of Criminal Courts Act 1973 s. 1(4). The offence need not have been committed during the period of deferment.

[7] *Ibid.*, s. 1(2).

[8] *Ingle* (1974) 59 Cr. App. R. 306.

[9] *Ingle* (1974) 59 Cr. App. R. 306.

[10] Powers of Criminal Courts Act 1973 s. 1(4).

convicted by a magistrates' court during the period of deferment should normally be committed to the location of the Crown Court where the sentence was deferred, although this is a matter of administration rather than jurisdiction, and the Crown Court sitting elsewhere may lawfully deal with him.[1] If he is convicted in the Crown Court, the Crown Court may deal with him in respect of the deferment wherever the order for deferment was made.[2]

At the expiration of the period of deferment, the offender should be brought, if possible, before the court similarly constituted as on the occasion of the deferment; if the court is not similarly constituted, it should be fully informed of the circumstances of the case and, in particular, of 'the reasoning of the court which deferred the sentence'.[3] Counsel who appears for the accused on the occasion of the deferment should consider himself bound to appear for him when he returns to the court for sentence to be passed.[4] The sentencer dealing with the offender at the end of the period of deferment should inquire into the behaviour of the offender during the period of the deferment, in relation to the reasons given for deferment. If the defendant has made an effort to comply with the expectations of the sentencer who deferred sentence, it will rarely be proper to impose a substantial custodial sentence,[5] even though such a sentence would have been appropriate if imposed at the time of conviction. In *Jacobs*[6] the appellant pleaded guilty to driving while disqualified and the court deferred sentence for six months with a warning to the defendant that the deferment did not mean that 'you will automatically find yourself free' at the end of this period. He was subsequently sentenced to twelve months' immediate imprisonment, although there was no evidence of misbehaviour during the period of the deferment. The Court quashed this sentence with the comment that although such a sentence might have been appropriate in the first instance, the circumstances in which it was passed left a 'justifiable sense of injustice'. A suspended sentence was substituted. Several similar cases have occurred.[7]

[1] *Street* 18.2.74, 4640/B/73.

[2] See Powers of Criminal Courts Act 1973 s. 1(4)(a).

[3] *Gurney* 5.4.74, 2/C/74. A judge deferring sentence should record his reasons for doing so; see *Jacobs* 24.11.75, 4606/C/75, [1976] Crim. L. R. 201.

[4] *Ryan* 9.3.76, 6094/B/75.

[5] *Gilby* (1975) 60 Cr. App. R. 112; see also *Smith* (1976) 64 Cr. App. R. 116.

[6] 24.11.75, 4606/C/75, [1976] Crim. L. R. 201.

[7] See, for example, *Marchant* 18.3.75, 4845/C/74 (borstal training imposed following five months' deferment, despite favourable report on offender's conduct during interval; 'although the sentence passed would have been amply merited if passed in the first instance, it was quite wrong to pass it after the . . . deferment'—varied to probation); *Gurney* 5.4.74, 2/C/74 (nine months' imprisonment for series of thefts from employer 'absolutely right in principle', but reduced to allow immediate release, as appellant has endeavoured to comply with suggestions of judge deferring sentence, with resulting 'sense of injustice').

Imposition of sentence

The sentence is pronounced orally by the presiding judge and recorded on the indictment by the clerk of the court. The sentencer must personally allocate the sentence to the specific counts of the indictment and indicate clearly whether sentences are to be served concurrently or consecutively.[1] There is no general statutory obligation to give reasons for the sentence, although such an obligation exists in certain cases.[2]

Alteration of sentence

Under Courts Act 1971 s. 11(2) a sentence imposed by the Crown Court may be varied or rescinded by the judge of the Crown Court who passed it[3] within twenty-eight days of the day on which it was passed. Where two or more persons are tried jointly on an indictment, the sentence on any one of them may be varied within either twenty-eight days of the conclusion of the joint trial or fifty-six days of the date on which the particular sentence was imposed, whichever is the shorter period. Any variation in sentence should be made in the presence of the accused, who should be represented and given the opportunity to mitigate in relation to the proposed variation.[4] There is no restriction in law on the kind of variation which may be made,[5] but the provision was included 'in order that slips made by the judge can be corrected'; in a case where a suspended sentence was varied so as to take effect immediately, the Court stated that it was 'quite wrong' to use the provision to give effect to 'a fundamental change of mind',[6] but this may be permitted in exceptional cases.[7]

Commencement of sentence

A sentence imposed by the Crown Court takes effect from the beginning of the day on which it is imposed, unless the court

---

[1] See *Practice Direction* (1962) 46 Cr. App. R. 119. Where a sentence is passed generally on an indictment containing more than one count, it will be held to have been imposed concurrently on all counts; see *Re Hastings* (1958) 42 Cr. App. R. 132.

[2] See Powers of Criminal Courts Act 1973 s. 23(1) (failure to activate a suspended sentence with original term unaltered); Road Traffic Act 1972 s. 105(1) (failure to disqualify or endorse in certain cases); Criminal Law Act 1977 s. 47(4) (failure to order restoration of part of sentence of imprisonment). A magistrates' court must give reasons for imposing a sentence of imprisonment on an offender under the age of 21 (Powers of Criminal Courts Act 1973 s. 20(2)).

[3] See s. 11(4). It is not necessary for justices who were sitting when the sentence was passed to sit when it is varied.

[4] See *Rowe* 10.5.74, 5524/B/73.

[5] See *Tuart* 9.10.73, 2833/B/73 (period of imprisonment fixed in default of payment of fine to run consecutively with sentence of imprisonment imposed at same time, instead of concurrently).

[6] *Grice* (1977) 66 Cr. App. R. 167.   [7] See *Sodhi* [1978] Crim. L. R. 565.

otherwise directs. [1] The sentencer has no power to order a sentence to begin on a day earlier than the day on which it was imposed, [2] but may order it to begin at the conclusion of a sentence which is imposed at the same time or which the offender is already serving. If the sentence is to begin at the expiration of an existing sentence, the sentencer should use the formula that the sentence will be 'consecutive to the total period of imprisonment to which you are already subject', unless it is intended that the sentence should run consecutively to one sentence which the offender is already serving, but concurrently with another which is itself consecutive to the first sentence. [3]

Sentencing on a retrial

Where an offender is convicted after a retrial ordered by the Court of Appeal under Criminal Appeal Act 1968 s. 7, the sentencer must not pass a sentence 'of greater severity' than was passed on the original conviction. [4] The sentencer may impose a sentence (such as borstal training) for which the offender is no longer eligible because of his age, if that sentence was imposed at the first trial. [5]

This provision does not apply where the Court has ordered a *venire de novo*. [6]

COMMITTAL FOR SENTENCE

The procedure of committal for sentence allows a person who has been convicted in the magistrates' court to be sent to the Crown Court for sentence. There are nine different forms of committal, and the relevant legislation is scattered through the statute book. Failure to observe the detailed variations in the forms of committal is the most common cause of unlawful sentences. The nine forms of committal fall into two groups: committal following the original conviction, and committal for further proceedings in respect of an earlier offence for which the offender has already been dealt with in the Crown Court.

Incorrigible rogues

A person convicted by a magistrates' court for the second time of an offence enabling him to be dealt with as a rogue and a vagabond, [7] or

---

[1] Courts Act 1971 s. 11(1).
[2] *Gilbert* (1974) 60 Cr. App. R. 220.
[3] See *Practice Direction* (1959) 43 Cr. App. R. 154. For the formula to be used where the offender is already subject to an extended sentence, see p. 62 above.
[4] Criminal Appeal Act 1968 sch. 2, para. 2(1).
[5] *Ibid.*, sch. 2, para. 2(2).
[6] See *Turner* (1971) 55 Cr. App. R. 336 at 341.
[7] See Vagrancy Act 1824 ss. 3, 4.

of certain other offences, may be committed to the Crown Court to be sentenced as an incorrigible rogue.[1] The Crown Court may impose a sentence not exceeding twelve months' imprisonment (however many offences have been committed)[2] or make a hospital order without a restriction order.[3] No other form of sentence may be imposed[4] and the sentence of imprisonment may not be suspended.[5] The Crown Court is not bound to make any order at all.[6] The Court has observed that this 'antiquated law' is 'out of touch with modern developments in the administration of criminal law', and expressed the hope that pending legislative revision magistrates' courts will so far as possible avoid its use.[7]

Committal under the Magistrates' Court Act 1959 s. 29

Magistrates' Courts Act 1952 s. 29 empowers a magistrates' court which has convicted a person not less than 17 years old of an offence triable either way to commit him for sentence to the Crown Court if after conviction, 'on obtaining information about his character and antecedents, the court is of the opinion that they are such that greater punishment should be inflicted for the offence than the court has power to inflict'. The expression 'character and antecedents' has been considered on a number of occasions and includes such matters as the relationship of the offender to the victim[8] and the admission of other offences,[9] but does not include the facts of the immediate offence![10]

Where the offender committed under section 29 appears before the Crown Court, the court 'shall inquire into the circumstances of the case and shall have power to deal with the offender in any manner in which it could deal with him if he had just been convicted of the offence on indictment before the court'.[11] The age of the offender for the purposes of sentencing under this provision is his age on the day he appears before the Crown Court; if he attains the age of 21 between committal and his appearance in the Crown Court, he may not be sentenced to borstal training but he may be sentenced to imprisonment without regard to Criminal Justice Act 1961 s. 3 (see above, p. 275).

---

1 Vagrancy Act 1824 s. 10.
2 *Walters* [1969] 1 Q. B. 255.
3 Mental Health 1969 s. 67(5).
4 *Jackson* (1974) 59 Cr. App. R. 23.
5 *Graves* 7.4.76, 521/B/76; *Theophile* 23.6.75, 2179/B/75, [1975] Crim. L. R. 644.
6 *Jackson* (1974) 59 Cr. App. R. 23.
7 *Jackson* (1974) 59 Cr. App. R. 23.
8 See *Vallett* (1950) 34 Cr. App. R. 251.
9 See *R. v. Kings Lynn JJ. exp. Carter* (1968) 53 Cr. App. R. 42.
10 See *R. v. Tower Bridge Magistrates ex p. Osman* (1971) 55 Cr. App. R. 436.
11 Powers of Criminal Courts Act 1973 s. 42.

The Court has frequently stated that magistrates' courts should use this form of committal, where it is available, in preference to other forms of committal, in particular under Magistrates' Court Act 1952 s. 28.[1]

Committal under the Magistates' Courts Act 1952 s. 28

Magistrates' Courts Act 1952 s. 28 authorizes a magistrates' court which has convicted a person between the ages of 15 and 21 of an offence punishable with imprisonment to commit him to the Crown Court, if it is 'of opinion, having regard to the circumstances of the offence and after taking into account the offender's character and previous conduct, that it is expedient that he should be detained for training for not less than six months'.[2] The power may be exercised even though the offence is triable only summarily, and in the case of an offence triable either way it is the only available power where the offender is under 17. Although it may be used where an offender aged 17 has been convicted of an offence triable either way, the committal under section 29 should be used in such cases in normal circumstances.[3]

Where an offender committed under section 28 appears before the Crown Court, the court must 'inquire into the circumstances of the case' and may either sentence him to borstal training or deal with him in any manner in which the magistrates' court might have dealt with him if it had not committed him for sentence.[4] The relevant age of the offender is his age on the date of his conviction by the magistrates' court.[5]

If the Crown Court decides not to impose borstal training, it is limited to sentences which the magistrates' court might have imposed at the time of conviction and may not make use of a sentence for which the offender has become eligible since being committed for sentence.[6] In particular, the Crown Court must observe the maximum sentence of imprisonment applicable on summary conviction, whether the offence is triable either way or triable only summarily.

Committal under Mental Health Act 1959 s. 67

Under this section a magistrates' court may commit to the Crown Court an offender aged 14 or over who has been convicted of an

[1] See *Rees* 24.10.74, 2255/A/74; *Hannigan* 9.3.71, 458/A/71, [1971] Crim. L. R. 302.
[2] Criminal Justice Act 1961 s. 1(2), (4).
[3] See above, p. 386. s. 29 will not be applicable where there is no relevant evidence falling within the definition of 'character and antecedents'.
[4] Criminal Justice Act 1948 s. 20(5).
[5] *Baxter* (1969) 54 Cr. App. R. 9.
[6] See *Hammond* [1963] 2 Q. B. 450.

offence punishable with imprisonment, if the conditions for making a hospital order under Mental Health Act 1959 s. 60 (above) are satisfied and the court considers that, 'having regard to the nature of the offence, the antecedents of the offender and the risk of his committing further offences if set at large', a restriction order should be made in conjunction with a hospital order. The Crown Court dealing with an offender committed under this procedure may either make a hospital order, with or without restriction, or 'deal with the offender in any other manner in which the magistrates' court might have dealt with him'. As in the case of a committal under Magistrates' Courts Act 1952 s. 28, the Crown Court must observe all restrictions applicable to magistrates' courts if it imposes imprisonment, even though the offence is triable either way.[1]

Committal in respect of subsidiary offences

Where a magistrates' court commits a person for sentence for an offence triable either way, it may at the same time commit him for sentence in respect of any other offence for which the magistrates' court has power to deal with him.[2] Where there is a committal for sentence for a summary offence, the magistrates' court may at the same time commit the offender to be dealt with in respect of any other offence of which it has convicted the offender, if that offence is punishable with imprisonment or disqualification from driving,[3] or any suspended sentence for which the magistrates' court has power to deal with the offender.

The Crown Court dealing with an offender under this provision should first sentence him for the principal offence, for which he will have been committed under another provision, and then impose sentence for the subsidiary offences for which the offender has been committed under this provision. In passing sentence for the subsidiary offences, the Crown Court must observe the limits applicable to magistrates' courts, even though the offences are triable either way. In particular, a sentence of borstal training may not be imposed for an offence for which the offender has been committed under this procedure,[4] and the Crown Court must observe the maxima

[1] See *Lyne-Ley* 9.6.72, 6213/C/71.
[2] Criminal Justice Act 1967 s. 56(1), as substituted by Criminal Law Act 1977 s. 46.
[3] *Ibid.*, s. 56(b)(i).
[4] See *Francis* 15.7.74, 2116/C/74. Where an offender committed under Magistrates' Courts Act 1952 s. 28 and Criminal Justice Act 1967 s. 56 is sentenced to borstal training for the principal offence, the correct sentence for the offence in respect of which he is committed under s. 56 is five days' imprisonment or one day's detention (see Magistrates' Courts Act 1952 s. 107(1); *Weller* 20.12.73, 4803/A/73).

governing terms of imprisonment on summary conviction, in relation to both individual offences[1] and aggregate terms.[2]

Committal for further proceedings in respect of prior offences

An offender subject to a conditional discharge,[3] probation order[4] or suspended sentence[5] imposed by the Crown Court, or to a parole licence,[6] who is convicted by a magistrates' court, may be committed to the Crown Court for further proceedings in connection with the original order. The nature of the qualifying conviction may vary in each case. A conviction for any offence is sufficient if the offender is subject to a probation order or conditional discharge, while if he is subject to a suspended sentence, the offence must be punishable with imprisonment. In the case of an offender subject to a parole licence, the offence must be punishable with imprisonment on indictment. A magistrates' court which commits an offender under one of these procedures may sentence the offender in respect of the latter offence for which it has convicted him, but it is usually preferable to commit the offender for sentence for the later offence under Magistrates' Courts Act 1952 s. 29 or Criminal Justice Act 1967 s. 56.

In dealing with an offender committed under one of these provisions, the Crown Court must establish the details of the earlier conviction, the precise terms of the order made in respect of that conviction and the circumstances of the subsequent conviction. If the offender does not admit any part of the relevant history, it must be proved by evidence.[7]

Similar procedures apply where an offender fails to comply with the requirements of a probation order[8] or community service order made in the Crown Court.[9]. In either case the Crown Court must satisfy itself of the facts alleged to constitute a breach of the order, either by admission or proof, before exercising its powers to deal with the offender for the original offence.[10]

---

[1] See, for example, *O'Dea* 10.12.71, 4664/A/71. (The maximum term of imprisonment on summary conviction for a single offence is six months, and in many cases less; see Criminal Law Act 1977 ss. 27, 28.)

[2] See, for example, *Smith* 7.11.72, 5008/B/72 (committal in respect of suspended sentence imposed by Quarter Sessions, and committal under s. 56 in respect of two other offences, one summary, one hybrid; sentences aggregating more than six months unlawful under Magistrates' Courts Act 1952 s. 108).

[3] Powers of Criminal Courts Act 1973 s. 8(6).

[4] *Ibid.*

[5] *Ibid.*, s. 24(2).

[6] Criminal Justice Act 1967 s. 62(7).

[7] See *Devine* (1956) 40 Cr. App. R. 45.

[8] Powers of Criminal Courts Act 1973 s. 6(4).

[9] *Ibid.*, s. 16(3)(b).

[10] See *Chapman* (1960) 44 Cr. App. R. 115; *Tucker* (1967) 51 Cr. App. R. 410.

Procedure on committal for sentence

An offender may be committed for sentence in custody or on bail[1] in all cases except that of a committal order under Mental Health Act 1959 s. 67; in this case the offender may be committed either in custody or under a temporary hospital order.[2] A committal for sentence is not itself a sentence, and no appeal lies against an order committing an offender for sentence.[3] Where a committal is invalid and the Crown Court declines to sentence the offender, the magistrates' court may sentence him, using any necessary process to bring him before them.[4] The Crown Court dealing with an appeal against a conviction or sentence in the magistrates' court may not commit the offender to itself for sentence at the conclusion of the appeal, in order to have wider powers of sentence available.[5] A magistrates' court which has deferred sentence under Powers of Criminal Courts Act 1973 s. 1 may not thereafter commit the offender for sentence.[6]

When the offender appears in the Crown Court, counsel for the prosecution should inform the sentencer of the provision under which the offender has been committed for sentence in respect of each offence,[7] and identify the maximum permissible sentences, particularly where the powers of the Crown Court are limited to those of the magistrates' court.[8] All the practices which apply to the provision of information to the sentencer for the purposes of sentence following conviction or indictment (see above, p. 365) apply where the sentence is to be passed following a committal for sentence.

Where an offender is committed for sentence to the Crown Court, the exercise of all powers incidental to sentence is the responsibility of the Crown Court.[9] A temporary disqualification from driving may be imposed by the magistrates' court.[10]

Section 2: Appeal against Sentence

SENTENCE

The term 'sentence' is defined by Criminal Appeal Act 1968 s. 50(1) to include 'any order made by a court when dealing with an offender'

[1] Criminal Justice Act 1967 s. 20.
[2] Mental Health Act 1959 s. 68.
[3] See *Birtles* (1975) 61 Cr. App. R. 267.
[4] *R. v. Norfolk J.J. ex. p. D.P.P.* [1950] 2 Q. B. 558.
[5] *Bullock* [1964] 1 Q. B. 481.
[6] *Gilby* (1975) 61 Cr. App. R. 112; see also Powers of Criminal Courts Act 1973 s. 1(8) (as substituted by Criminal Law Act 1977), dealing with the case where the offender is sentenced under s. 1(4)(9).   [7] *Heathcote* 22.2.72, 4613/C/71.
[8] See *Clarke* (1974) 59 Cr. App. R. 298; *Morrell* 16.2.71, 3852/B/70.
[9] See Criminal Justice Act 1967 s. 56(5); *Brogan* (1975) 60 Cr. App. R. 279.
[10] Road Traffic Act 1972 s. 103(1); p. 349 above.

and specifically includes hospital orders with or without restriction orders and recommendations for deportation.[1] The definition includes sentences of imprisonment, whether immediate or suspended, borstal training and detention in a detention centre, orders for the detention of children and young persons, orders for the activation of suspended sentences, the revocation of parole licences, or the restoration of parts of sentences held in suspense and care orders. Fines, compensation orders, orders to pay a sum towards the costs of the prosecution, restitution orders and orders for the forfeiture of property are covered, as are disqualifications from driving or holding a driving licence and other disqualifications.[2]

The definition of a sentence excludes recommendations made under Murder (Abolition of Death Penalty) Act 1965 s. 1[3] and orders to enter recognizances to keep the peace.[4] (The Court has not decided whether an order to enter a recognizance to come up for judgment is a 'sentence'; it is submitted that as the power to make such an order depends on the existence of a conviction, it is within the definition.) An order for the estreatment of a recognizance of bail and the fixing of a term of imprisonment in default is not a sentence,[5] and the Court has no power to deal with orders made against persons in breach of a recognizance to keep the peace, even where the recognizances were entered subsequent to a conviction of indictment.[6] A legal aid contribution order is not a sentence.[7]

The Court has held that although a probation order is a 'sentence' for the purposes of the Criminal Appeal Act 1968, the effect of Powers of Criminal Courts Act 1973 s. 13(1) is to prevent an appeal against the order,[8] unless the order was made without the consent of the offender or in other circumstances which render it invalid.[9] The same rules apply to a conditional discharge,[10] but not to a community service order.

Where a court in sentencing an offender makes an order which affects the interests of a person who has not been convicted of the offence in respect of which the order is made, the order is not a sentence against that person,[11] although it may be a sentence against

---

[1] Criminal Appeal Act 1968 s. 50(1).

[2] For example, from acting as a company director (Companies Act 1948 s. 188).

[3] See *Aitken* (1966) 50 Cr. App. R. 204; *Sewell* 5.12.72, 1686/C/72.

[4] See *R. v. London Sessions Appeal Committee ex. p. Beaumont* [1951] 1 Q. B. 557; this case appears to be supported by the reasoning in *Hayden* (1975) 60 Cr. App. R. 304.

[5] *Harman* (1959) 43 Cr. App. R. 161; *Thayne* (1969) 53 Cr. App. R. 582.

[6] *Gilbert* 4.4.74, 4400/C/73; *contra, Finch* (1962) 47 Cr. App. R. 58.

[7] *Hayden* (1975) 60 Cr. App. R. 304.   [8] *Tucker* (1974) 59 Cr. App. R. 71.

[9] *Marquis* (1974) 59 Cr. App. R. 228.

[10] See *Wehner* (1977) 65 Cr. App. R. 1.

[11] See *Ioannu* 26.6.75, 4905/B/74, [1976] Crim. L. R. 319 (disqualification of premises under Licensing Act 1964 s. 100).

the person convicted.[1] Specific provision is made for a parent who is ordered to pay a fine imposed on his child to appeal against that order.[2] A criminal bankruptcy order, although an 'order made by a court when dealing with an offender', is specifically excluded from appeal by Powers of Criminal Courts Act 1973 s. 40(1).

SENTENCES FROM WHICH AN APPEAL LIES

A person convicted on indictment may appeal against any sentence passed on him for the offence of which he was convicted, whether passed on his conviction or in subsequent proceedings, unless the sentence is fixed by law[3] or the right to appeal is expressly excluded.[4] A person sentenced in the Crown Court following a committal for sentence, or dealt with in the Crown Court in respect of a probation order, conditional discharge[5] or suspended sentence[6] imposed in a magistrates' court, may appeal against the sentence concerned only if one of five conditions is satisfied.[7] These are that the Crown Court sentences him on the same occasion[8] to six months' imprisonment[9] or more or to a sentence which the court convicting him had no power to pass, recommends him for deportation, disqualifies him from driving; or makes an order in relation to an existing suspended sentence. Where the Crown Court imposes a disqualification from driving or makes a recommendation for deportation in conjunction with another sentence, the offender may appeal against the whole of his sentence (including those parts which do not independently satisfy the conditions) but, apart from this, he may not appeal against other sentences passed in respect of different offences at the same time as an appealable sentence, unless those sentences also fall within one of the specified categories.[10]

The Court has held that the validity of a committal for sentence cannot be questioned on an appeal against the sentence imposed on the committal. If the committal was invalid, the remedy is by way of prerogative order; on an appeal against sentence following an invalid

---

[1] *Ioannu* (see above, p. 337).

[2] Children and Young Persons Act 1933 s. 55(5)(b).

[3] Criminal Appeal Act 1968 s. 9.

[4] But see *Anderson* (1977) 66 Cr. App. R. 134.

[5] Powers of Criminal Courts Act 1973 s. 8(8).

[6] *Ibid.*, s. 24(1).

[7] Criminal Appeal Act 1968 s. 10(3).

[8] See Criminal Appeal Act 1968 s. 10(4). The fact that one sentence is consecutive to another does not necessarily make them 'substantially one sentence' for the purposes of s. 10(4)(b), where the second sentence is passed a long time after the first: see *McCullough* 21.3.75, 3660/C/74, [1975] Crim. L. R. 456.

[9] A sentence of six months' detention does not satisfy this condition; see *Moore* (1968) 52 Cr. App. R. 180; *Keelan* (1975) 61 Cr. App. R. 212.

[10] See *Moore* (1968) 52 Cr. App. R. 180.

committal, the Court will assume that the Crown Court had jurisdiction and deal with the sentence on its merits.[1]

The fact that a sentence has already been served does not prevent the offender from appealing against it.[2]

LEAVE TO APPEAL

Leave to appeal against sentence is required in all cases, whether or not a point of law is involved.[3] The sentencer has no power to grant a certificate that the sentence is fit for appeal (as he has in relation to a conviction)[4] but his expressed views that the sentence raises a question suitable for the Court's consideration is usually considered a ground for giving leave.

An application for leave to appeal must be notified to the Court within twenty-eight days of the sentence,[5] but the Court has power to extend the time limit[6] and will frequently do so where the application appears to have some chance of success. The power of the Court to extend the time limit is not subject to any restriction, and substantial extensions have been granted in unusual cases.[7]

The application for leave to appeal against sentence must be supported by grounds of appeal,[8] and a bare application which fails to state grounds of appeal is ineffective.[9] Where grounds of appeal are prepared by counsel they should be signed; counsel should not draft vague grounds of appeal[10] or grounds which cannot be supported.[11]

Applications for leave to appeal against sentence only are normally considered first by a single judge of the Court in private,[12] but an applicant whose application is refused by a single judge is entitled to have the application determined by the full Court.[13] The Registrar is required to notify the applicant of the decision of the single judge and

[1] *Birtles* (1975) 61 Cr. App. R. 267, following *Warren* (1954) 38 Cr. App. R. 44 and *Jones* (1969) 53 Cr. App. R. 87, not following *Gilby* (1975) 61 Cr. App. R. 112 on this point.

[2] See *Herring* (1972) 56 Cr. App. R. 422.

[3] Criminal Appeal Act 1968 s. 11(1).

[4] *Ibid.*, s. 1(2).

[5] Criminal Appeal Act 1968 s. 18(1).

[6] *Ibid.*, s. 18(3).

[7] The longest extension in recent times was probably the sixteen years granted in *Poster* 4.7.72, 5738/B/71, which the Court emphasized was 'not . . . to be taken as a precedent'.

[8] Criminal Appeal Rules 1968, rule 2(2)(a).

[9] See *Statham* 31.7.72, 5642/B/71.

[10] See *Howitt* (1975) 61 Cr. App. R. 327.

[11] *Practice Direction* (1966) 50 Cr. App. R. 290.

[12] Criminal Appeal Act 1968 s. 31(1).

[13] *Ibid.*, s. 31(3). The Court for this purpose may consist of two judges only; see Administration of Justice Act 1970, s. 9(2).

advise him of his right to renew his application to the full Court.[1] Where the application goes to the full Court, either in the first instance by direction of the Registrar or on the renewal of the application following a refusal by the single judge, it is determined in open court. A reasoned judgment is delivered orally.

An application which has been refused by the single judge may be renewed to the full court within the prescribed period.[2] A judge of the Court may extend the time for renewing an application,[3] but such extensions are granted 'only in exceptional circumstances'.[4]

It is a common practice of the Court in straightforward cases to treat an application for leave to appeal as the appeal itself and make an immediate reduction or variation in the sentence. Where the applicant is present or represented by counsel, the Court normally obtains his consent to taking this course. If the applicant is neither present nor represented, the Court takes steps to inform the appellant that he may pursue the matter further in the hope of a greater reduction, but normally indicates that it does not encourage him to do so. It is rare for the Court to make a further reduction in a sentence which has already been reduced on the hearing of the application.[5]

LEGAL AID

A legal aid order made by the magistrates' court or Crown Court under the Legal Aid Act 1974 extends to cover advice on the question whether there appear to be reasonable grounds of appeal and assistance in making a provisional application while the question whether to appeal is being considered.[6] Legal aid for representation at the appeal itself must be sought from the Court of Appeal;[7] the Court may grant a limited legal aid order authorizing in the first instance advice on the question whether there appear to be reasonable grounds of appeal and assistance in preparing the application for leave to appeal, or a full legal aid order for representation at the appeal and any preliminary or incidental proceedings. The order may be for representation by counsel only or, in the case of a limited legal aid order, assistance by a solicitor only.

The general practice of the Court is for the application for legal aid to be considered at the same time as the application for leave to appeal, and it is rare for an application for legal aid to be dealt with

---

[1] Criminal Appeal Rules 1968, rule 15(1).
[2] See Criminal Appeal Rules 1968, rule 12.
[3] *Ward* 6.7.71, 6020/B/70.
[4] *Hatfield* 29.9.71, 104/C/71; *Sullivan* (1972) 56 Cr. App. R. 541.
[5] For an exceptional example, see *Rankin* 3.7.73, 846/C/73.
[6] Legal Aid Act 1974 s. 30(3).
[7] *Ibid.*, s. 28(8).

separately.[1] Where leave to appeal is granted, legal aid is normally ordered as a matter of course; in the case of sentence appeals it is usual for the order to be limited to representation by counsel only. Where the appellant is represented privately on an application for leave to appeal which is treated as the hearing for the appeal, the Court may order legal aid with retrospective effect.[2]

BAIL PENDING APPEAL AGAINST SENTENCE

An applicant or appellant can be admitted to bail only by the Court of Appeal or a judge of the Court.[3] The Court has generally adopted the view that appellants should not be released on bail unless the sentence is extremely short and there is a strong chance that the appeal will be successful: 'once bail is granted pending an appeal, judges who later hear it are presented with an additional heavy problem. Bail inevitably raises hopes, and to wreck them by ordering a return to custody is a painful duty . . . there are times when such a duty is unavoidable'.[4] The Court has frequently stated that the grant of bail pending an appeal is not material to the determination of the appeal: 'the Court cannot accept the granting of bail as . . . a reason why . . . this Court should reduce a perfectly proper sentence'.[5]

HEARING OF THE APPEAL

The appellant has the right to be present at the hearing of his appeal, unless he is in custody and the appeal is on a ground involving a question of law alone.[6] There is no right to be present at the hearing of an application for leave to appeal, or other incidental or preliminary proceedings, unless the Court gives leave. The Court may pass sentence in the absence of the appellant.[7]

POWERS OF THE COURT

The powers of the Court to deal with a sentence which is subject to appeal are broadly defined. Criminal Appeal Act 1968 s. 11(3)

---

[1] See *Smith* 7.11.72, 5008/B/72.

[2] Legal Aid Act 1974 s. 30(9).

[3] Criminal Appeal Act 1968 s. 19.

[4] *Gruffyd* (1972) 56 Cr. App. R. 585; see also *Shah* 13.8.76, 3321/C/76 (judges dealing with applications for leave to appeal against short sentences 'rather than grant bail . . . should take steps to see that the case is expedited').

[5] *Loudon* 30.11.72, 4090/B/72; see also *McElhinney* 29.2.72, 6371/A/70 (appellant on bail eleven months pending determination of appeal against sentence of twelve months' imprisonment; sentences not excessive: 'this Court . . . is not prepared to allow the fact that he has been out on bail as a factor affecting the sentence'—appeal dismissed).

[6] Criminal Appeal Act 1968 s. 22.   [7] *Ibid.*, s. 22(3).

provides that 'if they consider that the appellant should be sentenced differently for an offence for which he was dealt with by the court below', the Court may quash the sentence and pass 'such sentence . . . as they think appropriate for the case'. The power is subject to two statutory restrictions: the substituted sentence must be one which would have been within the power of the Crown Court when dealing with the offender, and the outcome of the appeal must be such that 'the appellant is not more severely dealt with on appeal than he was dealt with by the court below'.

From the earliest days of the Court of Criminal Appeal, the powers to vary sentences on appeal have been exercised with restraint. Cases in which sentences are varied may be classified into five broad categories, although these are not necessarily exhaustive. A sentence of imprisonment may be varied if the Court considers that an individualized measure or non-custodial sentence is preferable in the particular circumstances of the case, even though the sentence imposed cannot be criticized as wrong in principle or excessive in relation to the offence. In *Singh*[1] the appellant was sentenced to eighteen months' imprisonment for fraudulently claiming tax allowances to which he was not entitled. The Court stated that the sentencer's decision was 'perfectly sound and . . . not open to criticism on any ground of law or practice. He did his duty . . . rationally and moderately. It does not follow that this Court may not, in the exercise of its duty to take a wide view of all that is involved and to have regard to public interests . . . take a different view for other reasons . . .'. The sentence was varied to a fine. Many other examples of the variation of sentences which were not open to criticism are given in chapter 1. A second ground for variation in a sentence of imprisonment is the failure of the sentencer to apply the correct principles in reaching his decision on sentence. In this case the sentence will be considered 'wrong in principle', and a variation will be made to correct the error even if the effect of the variation on the position of the offender is marginal. In *Crouch*[2] the appellant was sentenced to fifteen months' imprisonment for possessing a quantity of cannabis, the sentencer observing that 'I am increasing your sentence . . . because of the course you saw fit to adopt in your defence'. The Court held that although the sentence was 'thoroughly justified' on the facts of the case, it was necessary for the sentence to be reduced 'on account of the reasons given for its imposition', 'as it is well established that it is not permissible to increase a sentence for reasons of that kind'. The sentence was reduced to twelve months. A third ground for varying a sentence of imprisonment is the failure of

[1] 30.1.70, 6025/B/69.
[2] 21.12.71, 4762/A/71.

the sentencer to give weight to a mitigating factor which should have had some effect; again a very small reduction in sentence may be made in such cases to ensure that the offender is not left with a sense of grievance. Examples of variations of this kind are given in chapter 4.

Where the sentence is challenged on the ground that it is disproportionate to the offence, the Court has consistently adopted the view that the relevant criterion is not the sentence which members of the Court would have passed if they had dealt with the case in the Crown Court, but whether the sentence falls within the appropriate 'range' or 'bracket' of sentences.[1] Minor variations in sentence are not normally made on the ground that the sentence is excessive (as opposed to being wrong in principle or failing to reflect mitigating factors); the Court is reluctant to 'tinker' with sentences. The precise limits of the concept of 'tinkering' are difficult to identify, but it is unusual for the Court to reduce a sentence on the ground of simple disproportionality by less than one-fifth.[2]

Where the appeal is against an individualized measure such as borstal training or a hospital order, the Court is less likely to be restrained in the exercise of its powers than in other cases. The Court will normally review the sentence in the light of all available information, including information not available to the Crown Court, and vary the sentence if an alternative measure appears to promise more favourable results, even though the original sentence is not necessarily wrong in principle or inappropriate. Examples of such variations were given in chapter 1.

Criminal Appeal Act 1968 s. 11 imposes two statutory restrictions on the power of the Court to vary sentences. The first is that the sentence substituted must be a sentence which would have been within the power of the Crown Court to impose when it was dealing with the offender. This restriction is important where the Crown Court was dealing with the offender on a committal for sentence on which its powers are limited,[3] or where the offender has passed from one relevant age group to another between the imposition of the sentence and the hearing of the appeal.

The second and more important restriction is that the Court 'shall so exercise their powers . . . that taking the case as a whole, the appellant is not more severely dealt with on appeal than he was dealt with by the court below'. The application of this provision becomes increasingly complex as the variety of measures available to sen-

---

[1] See the cases discussed at p. 33.
[2] The Court stated in *Herbert* 7.2.75, 4393/A/74 that a reduction from twenty-four months to fifteen was not 'tinkering with the sentence which has been imposed'.
[3] In particular, Magistrates' Courts Act 1952 s. 28, Criminal Justice Act 1967 s. 56.

tencers expands and the Court is faced with new questions concerning the relative severity of different forms of sentence, particularly where sentences are imposed in combination.

The first principle to be observed in applying the section is that the relative severity of the sentences imposed in the Crown Court and those to be substituted on appeal must be considered as a whole; a variation in one component in the sentence may be balanced by a variation in another.[1] The Court may increase individual components within an aggregate sentence, so long as the aggregate is not increased.[2] In *Rice*[3] the appellant was sentenced to two years' imprisonment for corruptly accepting a reward and two years consecutive for handling stolen property. The Court took the view that the total of four years' imprisonment was appropriate in the circumstances, but that as the two offences were part of the same transaction the sentences should not have been consecutive. The sentences were varied to two years and four years imprisonment respectively, to run concurrently.

A number of specific variations have been considered. It is well established that a fixed term of imprisonment may not be varied to a sentence of life imprisonment,[4] even though the effect of that sentence might be to shorten the period of custody, but that a hospital order with an indefinite restriction order may be substituted on appeal, even though its effect will probably be to subject the appellant to a longer period of confinement than under his original sentence.[5] A sentence of imprisonment may not be certified on appeal as an extended sentence[6] unless there is a balancing reduction in the length of the sentence.[7] The precise relationship of borstal training to imprisonment is uncertain; the Court has held that eighteen months' imprisonment is more severe than borstal training,[8] but the maximum sentence of imprisonment which may be substituted for borstal training has not been established. (In practice the longest alternative

---

[1] See, for example, *Kruger* 21.11.72, 470/B/72, [1973] Crim. L. R. 133 (two years' imprisonment varied to twenty-one months with recommendation for deportation; 'the reduction in . . . sentence . . . balances the recommendation for deportation and prevents the . . . disposal of the case . . . from being a more severe sentence than that passed below').

[2] See, for example, *Halse* (1971) 56 Cr. App. R. 47; *Rice* 28.4.75, 382/B/75.

[3] 10.12.73, 3700/B/73.

[4] See, for example, *Rose* 20.12.73, 2281/B/73, [1974] Crim. L. R. 266, p. 10 above.

[5] *Bennett* (1968) 52 Cr. App. R. 514.

[6] See *Wallace* 16.1.70, 4893/69.

[7] See *Jones* 19.1.70, 5670/69, [1970] Crim. L. R. 356 (eight years reduced to five years and four months extended); *Dolan* 21.1.71, 5087/A/70, [1971] Crim. L. R. 297; *Marshall* 22.7.71, 2012/A/71 (eight years varied to five years extended).

[8] See *Roderick* (1967) 51 Cr. App. R. 70; *Bernard* 24.7.69, 2197/69, [1969] Crim. L. R. 550.

sentence of imprisonment will usually be six months, which may be substituted.)[1]

The relationship between custodial and financial penalties does not lend itself to generalization. The Court has reduced a sentence of eighteen months to twelve months with the addition of a fine of £1,000,[2] and suspended a sentence of eighteen months (reduced from two years to reflect the period already served), with the addition of a fine of £5,000.[3] On a different level, the Court considered itself precluded from varying a fine of £10 to a sentence of one day's imprisonment.[4]

Particular difficulties have arisen where the Crown Court has failed to take a procedural step necessary to the imposition of sentence, by deferring sentence without the consent of the offender or by imposing a sentence without complying with the requirements of Powers of Criminal Courts Act 1973 s. 21. The Court has taken the view that although the sentence imposed in such cases is technically a nullity, to impose a lawful sentence does not amount to dealing with the offender more severely on appeal, so long as the lawful sentence is not more severe than the invalid sentence would have been if it had been effective.[5] A similar position has been reached where the sentence imposed is inherently unlawful; the Court may substitute a lawful sentence so long as it is not more severe than the unlawful sentence would have been.[6]

SENTENCES NOT THE SUBJECT OF APPEAL

In a number of situations the Court may interfere with a sentence which is not expressly made the subject of the appeal by the appellant. The first is where the appellant has received in the same proceeding two or more sentences, and appeals against one of them. In this case the appeal or application is treated as being in respect of all of the sentences.[7] This provision does not extend to sentences from which an appeal would not lie (as in the case of a sentence of less than six months' imprisonment passed by the Crown Court on a committal),[8] or orders which are not 'sentences'. Sentences are treated as passed in

---

[1] See, for example, *Morris* (1975) 62 Cr. App. R. 41. The observation in *Squire* 7.5.76, 1103/B/76, that a sentence of borstal training can be varied to imprisonment only if the sentence which is suspended appears to be inconsistent with the general body of authority.

[2] *Kirkby* 8.3.74, 72/C/74.

[3] *Collins* 27.6.75, 1421/A/75.

[4] *Gear* 24.7.75, 2314/A/75.

[5] See *McQuaide* (1974) 60 Cr. App. R. 239; *McGinlay* (1971) 56 Cr. App. R. 47.

[6] See *Halse* (1971) 56 Cr. App. R. 47.

[7] Criminal Appeal Act 1968 s. 11(2).

[8] *Moore* (1968) 52 Cr. App. R. 180; *Keelan* (1975) 61 Cr. App. R. 212.

the same proceedings if they are passed in the same day, or are passed on different days but the court in passing any one of them 'states that it is treating that one together with the other or others as substantially one sentence'.[1]

The other cases all arise where the appeal is an appeal against conviction. Where the appeal is confined to the conviction, the Court does not have power to interfere with the sentence unless it interferes with the conviction. If the conviction is quashed in its entirety, the sentence is quashed in consequence, but where the conviction is quashed in part only, the Court has power to adjust the sentence accordingly. Where convictions on one or more counts of an indictment are quashed, but convictions on other counts remain, the Court may either affirm the sentence passed in respect of those counts or 'pass such sentence in substitution . . . as they think proper' within the statutory maximum.[2] In exercising this power the Court must not pass a sentence 'such that the appellant's sentence on the indictment as a whole will in consequence of the appeal, be of greater severity than the sentence (taken as whole) which was passed at the trial for all the offences of which he was convicted on the indictment'.[3] This section allows the Court to increase a sentence passed on the surviving count up to the level of the total sentence originally passed at the trial.[4] Similarly, when the Court in quashing a conviction substitutes a conviction for a lesser offence, the Court may impose a sentence in respect of this conviction which is 'not . . . a sentence of greater severity' than the original sentence.[5]

Finally, provision is made for the case where an appellant against sentence was liable to be dealt with by Crown Court in respect of a suspended sentence, but that court exercised its power under Power of Criminal Courts Act 1973 s. 24 to make no order in respect of the suspended sentence.[6] The Court may activate the suspended sentence, subject to the general provision that the appellant is not more severely dealt with on appeal than in the court below, taking the case as a whole.[7] The same applies where the Crown Court imposed a sentence of borstal training which is quashed on appeal, and for that reason did not deal with the appellant in respect of the suspended sentence. If the Court quashes the sentence of borstal training, it may deal with the appellant in respect of the suspended sentence, again subject to the 'greater severity' limitation.[8]

---

[1] Criminal Appeal Act 1968 s. 10(4).   [2] Criminal Appeal Act 1968 s. 4(2).
[3] Criminal Appeal Act 1968 s. 4(3).
[4] See *Craig* (1967) 51 Cr. App. R. 8.
[5] Criminal Appeal Act 1968 s. 3.
[6] The Court may not exercise this power where the Crown Court did not purport to deal with the offender at all; see *Gordon* (1969) 53 Cr. App. R. 307.
[7] Criminal Appeal Act 1968, s. 11(4).   [8] *Ibid.*, s. 11(4).

LOSS OF TIME PENDING APPEAL

The time which the appellant spends in custody pending the determination of his appeal counts as part of his sentence unless the Court directs that all or part of the time shall not count.[1] The Court may not give a direction that time shall not count if leave to appeal has been granted or if the case has been referred to the Court by the Home Secretary under Criminal Appeal Act 1968 s. 17. If the Court gives a direction, 'they shall state their reasons for doing so'.[2]

The majority of applications in which time is ordered not to count towards the sentence are cases where the applicant renews his application to the full court, having been refused leave by the single judge; but the Court has exercised the power in cases where the application has gone directly before the full court[3] and the single judge may order time not to count on the initial application in an appropriate case.[4] The fact that the application is made or renewed on legal advice is a factor the Court (or the single judge) will consider in deciding whether to give a direction,[5] but does not necessarily guarantee that no direction will be given.[6]

Orders that time will not count towards the sentence are usually reserved for cases where the application can be considered 'hopeless' or 'impudent'—where in effect the applicant has received a sentence which is already more lenient than might have been expected. Orders are not normally made where the applicant has received a long sentence.[7]

APPEAL TO THE HOUSE OF LORDS

Either the appellant or the prosecutor may appeal to the House of Lords, with leave of either court and a certificate from the Court of Appeal that the case involves 'a point of law of general public importance'.[8] A few appeals involving the interpretation of statutory provisions or the extent of the sentencer's powers in relation to

[1] Criminal Appeal Act 1968 s. 29(1).
[2] *Ibid.*, s. 29(2).
[3] See *Penfold* 18.1.73, 4477/B/72, [1973] Crim. L. R. 249.
[4] See *Howitt* (1975) 61 Cr. App. R. 327.
[5] See *Blower* 30.10.75, 2011/A/75.
[6] See *Walker and Curry* 22.4.71, 1685/A/70 ('counsel should be very careful to consider where their duty does lie in this matter and cannot . . . advise their clients to count on this Court not forfeiting extra time simply because counsel has advised that an application should be pursued').
[7] See *Hughson* 24.1.71, 3817/B/70 (ten years' imprisonment for manslaughter; order to lose one hundred days 'really idle'—application refused but direction quashed).
[8] Criminal Appeal Act 1968 s. 33.

common law offences have proceeded to the House of Lords,[1] but the Court has declined to certify an issue of sentencing principle not raising a question of law in the strictest sense as 'a point of law of general public importance'.[2] Where the point of law certified by the Court of Appeal relates to conviction, the House of Lords will not hear argument relating to sentence.[3]

[1] See *Verrier v. D. P. P.* [1967] A. C. 195; *D. P. P. v. Ottwell* (1968) 52 Cr. App. R. 679.
[2] *Ashdown* (1973) 58 Cr. App. R. 339.
[3] *Jones v. D. P. P.* [1962] A. C. 635.

Index